Social Problems
Continuity and Change
Version 2.0

Steven E. Barkan

978-1-4533-9215-7

Social Problems: Continuity and Change
Version 2.0

Steven E. Barkan

Published by:

FlatWorld
175 Portland Street
Boston, MA 02114

Gen: 202008171509

Brief Contents

Contents

About the Author

Steven E. Barkan

Steven E. Barkan is professor of sociology at the University of Maine and a former president of both the Society for the Study of Social Problems and the Textbook and Academic Authors Association. He is the author of two other FlatWorld texts: *Sociology: Understanding and Changing the Social World*, which won a Textbook Excellence Award from the Text and Academic Authors Association, and *Fundamentals of Criminal Justice*. He is also the author of several other textbooks, including *Criminology: A Sociological Understanding*, 7e (Pearson); *Health, Illness, and Society: An Introduction to Medical Sociology*, 2e (Rowman & Littlefield); *Race, Crime, and Justice: The Continuing American Dilemma* (Oxford); and *Law and Society: An Introduction* (Routledge). He has also authored more than thirty journal articles and book chapters in venues such as the *American Sociological Review*; *Journal for the Scientific Study of Religion*; *Journal of Research in Crime and Delinquency*; *Justice Quarterly*; *Mobilization*; *Review of Religious Research*; *Public Opinion Quarterly*; *Social Forces*; *Social Problems*; *Social Science Quarterly*; and *Sociological Forum*.

Professor Barkan serves on the Advisory Panel of the American Sociological Association's Honors Program and has also served on the Council of Alpha Kappa Delta, the sociology honor society. He has spent more than twenty years (fortunately, not all consecutive) as chair of his department, and he received the Outstanding Faculty Award from his university's College of Liberal Arts and Sciences. A native of Philadelphia, Pennsylvania, Professor Barkan has lived in Maine since he began his academic career. He received his PhD in sociology from the State University of New York at Stony Brook and his BA in sociology from Trinity College (Hartford, Connecticut), where he began to learn how to think like a sociologist and also to appreciate the value of a sociological perspective for understanding and changing society. He sincerely hopes that instructors and students enjoy reading this book in the format of their choice and welcomes their comments at barkan@maine.edu.

Acknowledgments

As always in my books, I express my personal and professional debt to two sociologists, Norman Miller and Forrest Dill. Norman Miller was my first sociology professor in college and led me in his special way into a discipline and profession that became my life's calling. Forrest Dill was my adviser in graduate school and helped me in ways too numerous to mention. Both men are long gone, but I will be forever grateful for everything they taught me and for everything with which they helped me.

My professional life since graduate school has been at the University of Maine, where my colleagues over the years have nurtured my career and provided a wonderful working environment. I trust they will see their concern for social problems reflected in the pages that follow. Thanks to them all for being who they are.

I also thank everyone at FlatWorld for helping bring this text to fruition and for helping today's students afford high-quality, peer-reviewed textbooks at a time when college costs keep rising while the economy keeps faltering. Special thanks go to Sean Wakely for his continuing interest in my textbook efforts and especially to Lindsey Kaetzel for all the work she did in helping to bring this second edition to fruition. My efforts also benefited greatly from the many sociologists who reviewed some or all of the text. These reviewers were tough but fair, and I hope they are pleased with the result. As every author should say, any faults that remain are not the reviewers' responsibility. I am grateful to include their names here:

- Celesta Albonetti, University of Iowa
- Anne Barrett, Florida State University
- Sarah Becker, Louisiana State University
- Laurian Bowles, Western Illinois University
- Joyce Clapp, Guilford College
- Mary Fischer, University of Connecticut
- Otis Grant, Indiana University–South Bend
- Art Houser, Fort Scott Community College
- Michael Kimmel, SUNY at Stony Brook
- Matthew Lee, University of Akron
- William Lockhart, McLennan Community College
- Brea Perry, University of Kentucky
- Nancy Reeves, Rowan University
- Daniel Roddick, Rio Hondo College
- Debra Welkley, California State University–Sacramento

In addition to these reviewers, I would also like to thank Joel Barkan for his valuable comments that improved Chapter 15's discussion of environmental problems involving oceans and ocean life.

Authors usually save the best for last in their acknowledgments, and that is the family members to whom they owe so much. So I extent my profound thanks, as usual, to Barbara Tennent and our grown sons David and Joel, for always sharing with me the joy and effort of writing a textbook.

I have saved two family members for the very last, and they are my late parents, Morry and Sylvia Barkan. They have been gone many years, but whatever I have achieved in my personal and professional life, I owe to them.

Preface

The founders of American sociology a century or more ago in cities like Atlanta and Chicago wanted to reduce social inequality, to improve the lives of people of color, and more generally to find solutions to the most vexing social problems of their times. A former president of the Society for the Study of Social Problems, A. Javier Treviño, has used the term *service sociology* to characterize their vision of their new discipline. The second edition of this book continues to be grounded in this vision by offering a sociological understanding of today's social problems and of possible solutions to these problems.

As this book's subtitle, *Continuity and Change*, implies, social problems are persistent, but they have also improved in the past and can be improved in the present and future, provided that our nation has the wisdom and will to address them. It is easy to read a social problems textbook and come away feeling frustrated by the enormity of the many social problems facing us today. This book certainly does not minimize the persistence of social problems, but neither does it overlook the possibilities for change offered by social research and by the activities of everyday citizens working to make a difference. Readers of this book will find many examples of how social problems have been improved and of strategies that hold great potential for solving them today and in the future.

This book was in the final stages of production when the coronavirus pandemic involving COVID-19 shut down the United States in March 2020. Students everywhere in our vast country suddenly had to go home and take their classes via remote learning for the rest of the term. By mid-May 2020, nearly 1.5 million Americans had been infected with the coronavirus, and nearly 90,000 Americans had died from it. The United States was obviously not unique in this regard. COVID-19 killed hundreds or thousands of people in nations around the world and shut down their societies as well.

As infections and deaths mounted, it soon became all too clear the pandemic was not just a medical crisis, but also a social crisis that amplified virtually every social problem faced by society. Accordingly, the publisher and author delayed production of this book to allow for initial information about the pandemic to be incorporated throughout the text before it was published in summer 2020. Of course, the true impact of the pandemic on our health and social lives may not be known for years to come. Therefore, the decision to include early information about the pandemic had two goals: (1) to help readers better understand how the coronavirus was both illustrating and aggravating current social problems, and (2) to encourage readers to develop a sociological perspective that will help them better interpret the far-reaching impacts of the pandemic as they become clearer. Although the pandemic's trajectory will certainly take unpredictable directions, a firm understanding of why social problems exist and how the lives of people everywhere can be improved will help us all better navigate the unfamiliar waters ahead.

Readers should know in advance that several of the photos in the text do not observe social distancing and that several of the "Using What You Know" chapter-ending scenarios depict inappropriate situations during the pandemic. These features were chosen long before the pandemic began and were retained not only to enable the book to be published sooner, but also in the spirit of cautious optimism that the world will soon become normal enough that these features will again be perfectly suitable.

Several pedagogical features help to convey the "continuity and change" theme of this text and the service sociology vision in which it is grounded:

- Each chapter begins with a "Social Problems in the News" story related to the social problem discussed in that chapter. These stories provide an interesting starting point for the chapter's discussion and show its relevance for real-life issues.

- Three types of boxes in each chapter provide examples of how social problems have been changed and can be changed. In no particular order, a first box, "Applying Social Research," discusses how the findings from sociological and other social science research either have contributed to public policy related to the chapter's social problem or have the potential of doing so. A second box, "Lessons from Other Societies," discusses how another nation or nations have successfully addressed the social problem of that chapter. A third box, "People Making a Difference," discusses efforts by individuals, nonprofit organizations or social change groups, or social movements relating to the chapter's social problem. Students will see many examples in this box of how ordinary people can indeed make a difference.

- A fourth box in each chapter, "Children and Our Future," examines how the social problem discussed in that chapter particularly affects children, and it outlines the problem's repercussions for their later lives as adolescents and adults. This box reinforces for students the impact of social problems on children and the importance of addressing these problems for their well-being as well as for the nation's well-being.

- Each chapter ends with a "Using What You Know" feature that presents students with a scenario involving the social problem from the chapter and that puts them in a decision-making role. This feature helps connect the chapter's theoretical discussion with potential real-life situations.

- Each chapter also ends with a "What You Can Do" feature that suggests several activities, strategies, or other efforts that students might undertake to learn more about and/or to address the social problem examined in the chapter. Like other aspects of the book, this feature helps counter "doom and gloom" feelings that little can be done about social problems.

- Other pedagogical features in each chapter include Learning Objectives at the beginning of a major section that highlight key topics to be learned; Key Takeaways at the end of a major section that highlight important points that were discussed in the section; For Your Review questions, also at the end of a major section, that have students think critically about that section's discussion; and a Summary that reviews the major points made in the chapter.

What's New in Version 2.0

This second edition represents a thorough revision and includes many changes since the publication of the first edition several years ago, including the use of dozens of new and up-to-date references, updated data, and new examples throughout. Chapter-specific changes include:

- Chapter 1: new Social Problems in the News story; new example of Donald Trump's allegations of immigrant violence to illustrate an aspect of social constructionism; new example of California health care legislation for certain undocumented immigrants to illustrate social change stemming from the actions of policymakers

- Chapter 2: new Social Problems in the News story; updated U.S. poverty data; new discussion of why one-fourth of SNAP recipients do not work; new People Making a Difference account; updated global poverty data

- Chapter 3: new Social Problems in the News story; new material on antebellum slavery; new discussion of increased stress levels and health problems associated with Donald Trump's presidency; new Using What You Know feature

- Chapter 4: new Social Problems in the News story; updated domestic and international gender inequality data; new People Making a Difference account; new material on sexual violence perpetration by male college students

- Chapter 5: new Social Problems in the News story; updated data on public opinion about LGBTQ status and on discrimination against LGBTQ people; new material on discrimination against LGBTQ people in health care settings
- Chapter 6: new Social Problems in the News story; updated data throughout chapter; new discussion of food insecurity among older Americans; new People Making a Difference account
- Chapter 7: new Social Problems in the News story; updated data throughout chapter
- Chapter 8: new Social Problems in the News story; updated crime and criminal justice data; new material on hiding of evidence of motor vehicle defects; new material on racial differences in police brutality victimization; new Applying Social Research account on immigration and crime
- Chapter 9: new Social Problems in the News story; updated sexual behavior data throughout chapter
- Chapter 10: new Social Problems in the News story; updated family data throughout chapter; updated research on cohabitation
- Chapter 11: new Social Problems in the News story; updated education data throughout chapter
- Chapter 12: new Social Problems in the News story; updated work and labor data throughout chapter
- Chapter 13: new Social Problems in the News story; updated health and health care data throughout chapter
- Chapter 14: new Social Problems in the News story; updated urban and rural data throughout chapter
- Chapter 15: new Social Problems in the News Story; updated population data; revised discussion of contemporary immigration in the United States; updated Lessons from Other Societies discussion; updated data on environmental problems; new discussion of contamination of water supply in Flint, Michigan
- Chapter 16: updated data on military losses in Afghanistan and Iraq; updated data on sexual assaults in the military; updated data on military spending

In addition to the changes just listed, this edition includes COVID-19 material in every chapter to show the mutual relevance of the pandemic and every social problem discussed in the text. The most notable such material includes discussions of the following topics:

- Chapter 1: discussion of how the perception of the coronavirus as a social and medical problem illustrates the social constructionist view, how the high unemployment rate from the pandemic illustrates the sociological imagination's emphasis on public issues and how the decline in shaking hands in greeting during the pandemic illustrates symbolic interactionism; inclusion in research methods discussion of national survey data on views of the pandemic that can be generalized to the entire adult population
- Chapter 2: evidence that low-income Americans were suffering higher rates of COVID-19 infection and death; discussion of the especially harsh impact of the pandemic on low-income nations
- Chapter 3: new opening news story on structural racism and the pandemic; discussion of how and why the pandemic illustrates a structural explanation of racial and ethnic inequality
- Chapter 4: discussion of how and why low-income women in poor nations suffer because of the pandemic; new section on "Gender Inequality in the COVID-19 Pandemic" that focuses on the United States
- Chapter 5: new section on "Gay Men and Blood Donations during the COVID-19 Pandemic" to further illustrate discrimination against the LGBTQ community
- Chapter 6: new data on the higher COVID-19 death rate for older Americans; discussion of the pandemic's impact on nursing homes to further illustrate their generally substandard conditions

- Chapter 7: included content on concerns over how the pandemic would affect recovering alcoholics
- Chapter 8: discussion of urban density as a contributing factor to both higher crime rates and to higher COVID-19 rates during the early pandemic; discussion of the risk to police for contracting COVID-19; examination of the high rates of COVID-19 in prisons and jails to further highlight prison and jail crowding and other substandard living conditions
- Chapter 9: discussion of efforts to restrict abortion access that accelerated after the pandemic began
- Chapter 10: consideration of a possible decline in marriages because of the pandemic; the pandemic's lessons about parenting and working parents, and concerns about an increase in both domestic violence and child abuse in the wake of the pandemic
- Chapter 11: discussion of how and why low-income students in secondary schools and higher education experienced special difficulties trying to learn remotely during the pandemic
- Chapter 12: new section on "American Workers amid the COVID-19 Pandemic"
- Chapter 13: several examples of how the pandemic both manifested and aggravated the many problems of health and health care discussed in the chapter; consideration of how and why the poor diets of many Americans contributed to the spread and severity of the coronavirus across the nation; discussion of concerns over financial costs that were deterring many Americans from seeking health care for COVID-19 symptoms
- Chapter 14: examination of how the pandemic threw into sharp relief certain features of both urban and rural life that contribute to health problems and other social problems
- Chapter 15: discussion of air pollution as a risk factor for contracting and dying from COVID-19
- Chapter 16: discussion of concerns that the pandemic could heighten military conflict in the Middle East and elsewhere and interfere with efforts of international organizations to prevent or resolve armed conflict

PART 1
Social Problems in Sociological Perspective

Source: Ben Harding/Shutterstock.com

CHAPTER 1
Understanding Social Problems

As we move into the third decade of the twenty-first century, the United States and the rest of the world face many social problems: poverty and hunger, racism and sexism, drug use and violence, and climate change, to name just a few. Looming over all these problems as this book went to press is the COVID-19 pandemic. Why do these problems exist? What are their effects? What can be done about them? How does the pandemic both exhibit and aggravate them? This affordable textbook from a student-friendly publisher, FlatWorld, attempts to answer these questions with the latest theory and research from sociology and other social sciences.

The discipline of sociology began in Western Europe during the late 1800s and soon made its way to the United States. Many of the new American sociologists focused on the various social problems facing the United States at the time. This was perhaps especially true at two institutions: Atlanta University (now known as Clark Atlanta University) and the University of Chicago. Befitting their urban locations, sociologists at both universities were very interested in studying poverty and racial/ethnic inequality, and they sought to use sociological theory and research to address these problems and, more generally, to improve society (Calhoun, 2007; Morris, 2015).[1]

A. Javier Treviño (2011:1),[2] former president of the Society for the Study of Social Problems, refers to the vision and goals of these early American sociologists as *service sociology*, and he emphasizes that "early American sociology was primarily a reformist endeavor." Trevino adds, "Service sociology is a sociology of social problems intended to ameliorate conditions of life for those in need of assistance, and to insure and promote the welfare of the community. Motivated by care and compassion, a service-oriented sociology is aimed at helping people meet their pressing social needs. As such, service sociology involves the application of sociological knowledge combined with the expression of humanitarian sentiment."

In the spirit of early American sociology and service sociology, this book brings sociological insights to bear on the important problems of our time. Using the latest social science evidence, it discusses the dimensions and effects of various kinds of social problems, the reasons for them, and possible solutions to them.

This first chapter begins our journey into the world of social problems by examining how sociology understands social problems and gathers research about them.

1.1 What Is a Social Problem?

Learning Objectives

1. Define "social problem."
2. Explain the objective and subjective components of the definition of a social problem.

3. Understand the social constructionist view of social problems.
4. List the stages of the natural history of social problems.

social problem

Any condition or behavior that has negative consequences for large numbers of people and that is generally recognized as a condition or behavior needs to be addressed.

Sometimes disputes occur over whether a particular condition or behavior has negative consequences and is thus a social problem. A current example is climate change: Although almost all climate scientists think climate change is real, serious, and the result of human activity, many Americans believe that the effects of climate change have not already started and that human activity does not cause climate change.

Source: © Thinkstock

social constructionist view

The belief that negative social conditions or behaviors do not become social problems unless citizens, policymakers, and other parties call attention to the condition or behavior and define it as a social problem.

A **social problem** is any condition or behavior that has negative consequences for large numbers of people and is generally recognized as a condition or behavior that needs to be addressed. This definition has both an *objective* component and a *subjective* component.

The *objective* component is this: For any condition or behavior to be considered a social problem, it must have negative consequences for large numbers of people, as each chapter of this book discusses. Ordinarily a body of evidence accumulates—from work by academic researchers, government agencies, news media, activist groups, and other sources—that strongly points to these consequences. A current example is *climate change*, as the overwhelming majority of climate scientists say that climate change (changes in the earth's climate due to the buildup of greenhouse gases in the atmosphere) is real, serious, and the result of human activity.

Even so, only 59% of Americans in a 2019 Gallup poll believed that the effects of climate change have already started, and only 66% believed that human activity causes climate change (Saad 2019).[3] This gap between scientific evidence and public opinion underscores the *subjective* component of the definition of social problems: There must be a perception that a condition or behavior needs to be addressed for it to be considered a social problem. This component lies at the heart of the **social constructionist view** of social problems (Loseke and Best 2017).[4] In this view, many types of negative conditions and behaviors exist. Many of these are considered negative enough to be considered social problems; some do not receive this consideration and thus do not become a social problem; and some become considered a social problem only if citizens, policymakers, or other parties call attention to the condition or behavior.

The history of attention given to rape and sexual assault in the United States before and after the 1970s provides an example of the aforementioned situation. These acts of sexual violence have probably occurred from the beginning of humanity and certainly were very common in the United States before the 1970s. Although men were sometimes arrested and prosecuted for rape and sexual assault, sexual violence was otherwise ignored by legal policymakers, it received little attention in college textbooks and the news media, and many people thought that rape and sexual assault were just something that happened (Allison and Wrightsman 1993).[5] Thus, although sexual violence existed, it was not considered a social problem. When the contemporary women's movement began in the late 1970s, it soon focused on rape and sexual assault as serious crimes and as manifestations of women's inequality. Thanks to this focus, rape and sexual assault eventually entered the public consciousness, views of these crimes began to change, and legal policymakers began to give them more attention. In short, sexual violence against women became a social problem.

The social constructionist view raises an interesting question: when is a social problem a social problem? According to some sociologists who adopt this view, negative conditions and behaviors are *not* a social problem unless they are recognized as such by policymakers, large numbers of lay citizens, or other segments of our society; these sociologists would thus say that rape and sexual assault before the 1970s were not a social problem because our society as a whole paid them little attention. Other sociologists say that negative conditions and behaviors *should be* considered a social problem even if they receive little or no attention; these sociologists would thus say that rape and sexual assault before the 1970s were a social problem.

This debate recalls the age-old question: if a tree falls in a forest and no one is there to hear it, does it make a sound? As such, the debate is difficult to resolve, but it does reinforce one of the key beliefs of the social constructionist view: perception matters at least as much as reality, and sometimes more so. In line with this belief, social constructionism emphasizes that citizens, interest groups, policymakers, and other parties often compete to influence popular perceptions of many types of conditions and behaviors. All these parties try to influence news media coverage and popular views of the nature and extent of any negative consequences that may be occurring, the reasons underlying the condition or behavior in question, and possible solutions to the problem.

Before the 1970s, rape and sexual assault certainly existed and were very common, but they were generally ignored and not considered a social problem. When the contemporary women's movement arose during the 1970s, it focused on sexual violence against women and turned this behavior into a social problem.

Source: Image courtesy of Women's eNews, http://www.flickr.com/photos/wenews/5167303294/.

The coronavirus illustrates the importance of perception as emphasized by the social constructionist view. As early as January 2020, there was clear evidence that the coronavirus would soon overwhelm the United States unless appropriate preventive measures were taken (Harris et al. 2020).[6] On an objective level, then, the coronavirus was not only an incredibly serious health problem, but also an incredibly serious social problem. Yet many people and agencies in the federal, state, and local governments, as well as much of the news media, ignored or played down the threat posed by the coronavirus (Lipton et al. 2020).[7] On a subjective level, then, the coronavirus was not a social problem until it became recognized as such by March 2020, when American society shut down.

Sometimes a condition or behavior becomes a social problem even if there is little or no basis for this perception. A historical example involves women in college. During the late 1800s, medical authorities and other experts warned women not to go to college for two reasons: they feared that the stress of college would disrupt women's menstrual cycles, and they thought that women would not do well on exams while they were menstruating.

Source: © Thinkstock

The emphasis on perception within social constructionism has a provocative implication: Just as a condition or behavior may not be considered a social problem even if there is a strong basis for this perception, so may a condition or behavior be considered a social problem even if there is little or no basis for this perception. The "issue" of women in college provides a historical example of this latter possibility. In the late 1800s, leading physicians and medical researchers in the United States wrote journal articles, textbooks, and newspaper columns in which they warned women not to go to college. The reason? They feared that the stress of college would disrupt women's menstrual cycles, and they also feared that women would not do well on exams during "that time of the month" (Ehrenreich and English 2005; Koren 2019)![8] We now know better, of course, but the sexist beliefs of these writers turned the idea of women going to college into a social problem and helped to reinforce restrictions by colleges and universities on the admission of women.

In a related dynamic, various parties can distort certain aspects of a social problem that does exist: politicians can give speeches, the news media can use scary headlines and heavy coverage to capture readers' or viewers' interest, and businesses can use advertising and influence news coverage. During his 2016 presidential campaign and presidency, for example, Donald Trump often depicted immigrants as dangerous violent criminals, even though much research shows this is false (Ousey and Kubrin 2018).[9] News media coverage of violent crime provides another example of this dynamic (Robinson, 2018).[10] The news media overdramatize violent crime, which is far less common than property crime like burglary and larceny, by featuring many stories about it. This coverage contributes to public fear of crime. Media stories about violent crime also tend to be more common when the accused offender is black and the victim is white and when the offender is a juvenile. This type of coverage is thought to heighten the public's prejudice toward African Americans and to contribute to negative views about teenagers.

The Natural History of a Social Problem

We have just discussed some of the difficulties in defining a social problem and the fact that various parties often try to influence public perceptions of social problems. These issues aside, most social problems go through a *natural history* consisting of several stages of their development (Spector and Kitsuse 2001).[11]

Stage 1: Emergence and Claims Making

claims-making process

The use of arguments to try to influence public perceptions of a social problem, the reasons for it, and possible solutions to it.

A social problem emerges when a social entity (such as a social change group, the news media, or influential politicians) begins to call attention to a condition or behavior that it perceives to be in need of a remedy. As part of this process, it tries to influence public perceptions of the problem, the reasons for it, and possible solutions to it. Because the social entity is making claims about all these matters, this aspect of Stage 1 is termed the **claims-making process**. Not all efforts to turn a condition or behavior into a social problem succeed; if they do not succeed, a social problem does not emerge. Because of the resources they have or do not have, some social entities are more likely than others to succeed at this stage. A few ordinary individuals have little influence in the public sphere, but masses of individuals who engage in protest or other political activity have greater ability to help a social problem emerge. Because politicians have the ear of the news media and other types of influence, their views about social problems are often very influential. Most studies of this stage of a social problem focus on the efforts of social change groups and the larger social movement to which they may belong, as most social problems begin with bottom-up efforts from such groups.

A social problem emerges when a social change group successfully calls attention to a condition or behavior that it considers serious. Protests like the one depicted here have raised the environmental consciousness of Americans and helped put pressure on businesses to be environmentally responsible.

Source: Image courtesy of ItzaFineDay, http://www.flickr.com/photos/itzafineday/3085307050/.

Stage 2: Legitimacy

Once a social group succeeds in turning a condition or behavior into a social problem, it usually tries to persuade the government (local, state, and/or federal) to take some action—spending and policymaking—to address the problem. As part of this effort, it tries to convince the government that its claims about the problem are legitimate—that they make sense and are supported by *empirical* (research-based) evidence. To the extent that the group succeeds in convincing the government of the legitimacy of its claims, government action is that much more likely to occur.

Stage 3: Renewed Claims Making

Even if government action does occur, social change groups often conclude that the action is too limited in goals or scope to be able to successfully address the social problem. If they reach this conclusion, they often decide to press their demands anew. They do so by reasserting their claims and by criticizing the official response they have received from the government or other established interests, such as big businesses. This stage may involve a fair amount of tension between the social change groups and these targets of their claims.

Stage 4: Development of Alternative Strategies

Despite the renewed claims making, social change groups often conclude that the government and established interests are not responding adequately to their claims. Although the groups may continue to press their claims, they nonetheless realize that these claims may fail to win an adequate response from established interests. This realization leads them to develop their own strategies for addressing the social problem.

1.2 Sociological Perspectives on Social Problems

The sociological understanding of social problems rests heavily on the concept of the *sociological imagination*. We will discuss this concept in some detail before turning to various theoretical perspectives that provide a further context for understanding social problems.

The Sociological Imagination

Many individuals experience one or more social problems personally. For example, many people are poor and unemployed, many are in poor health, and many have family problems, drink too much alcohol, or commit crime. When we hear about these individuals, it is easy to think that their problems are theirs alone, and that they and other individuals with the same problems are entirely to blame for their difficulties.

Sociology takes a different approach, as it stresses that individual problems are often rooted in problems stemming from aspects of society itself. This key insight informed C. Wright Mills's (1959)[12] classic distinction between **personal troubles** and **public issues**. *Personal troubles* refer to problems affecting individuals that the affected individual, as well as other members of society, typically blame on the individual's own personal and moral failings. Examples include such different problems as eating disorders, divorce, and unemployment. *Public issues*, whose source lies in the social structure and culture of a society, refer to social problems affecting many individuals. Thus, problems in society help account for problems that individuals experience. Mills felt that many problems ordinarily considered private troubles are best understood as public issues, and he coined the term **sociological imagination** to refer to the ability to appreciate the structural basis for individual problems.

To illustrate Mills's viewpoint, let's use our sociological imaginations to understand some contemporary social problems. We will start with unemployment, which Mills himself discussed. If only a few people were unemployed, Mills wrote, we could reasonably explain their unemployment by saying they were lazy, lacked good work habits, and so forth. If so, their unemployment would be their own personal trouble. But when millions of people are out of work, unemployment is best understood as a public issue because, as Mills (1959:9)[13] put it, "the very structure of opportunities has collapsed. Both the correct statement of the problem and the range of possible solutions require us to consider the economic and political institutions of the society, and not merely the personal situation and character of a scatter of individuals."

The high U.S. unemployment rate stemming from the coronavirus pandemic that began in March 2020 provides a telling example of the point Mills was making. Millions of people suddenly lost their jobs through no fault of their own. While some individuals are undoubtedly unemployed because they may lack motivation or good work habits, a more structural explanation focusing on the shutdown of the economy is needed to explain why so many people were out of work. If so, unemployment is best understood as a public issue, rather than a personal trouble.

If only a few people are out of work, it might be fair to say that their unemployment is their personal trouble. However, when millions of people are out of work, as was true after the coronavirus pandemic began in March 2020, this massive unemployment is more accurately viewed as a public issue. As such, its causes lie not in the unemployed individuals but rather in our society's economic and social systems and, in the case of the pandemic, the need to shut down the economy for the sake of public health.

Source: Mongkolchon Akesin/Shutterstock.com

personal troubles

C. Wright Mills's term for the personal problems that many individuals experience.

public issues

C. Wright Mills's term for problems in society that underlie personal troubles.

sociological imagination

From C. Wright Mills, the realization that personal troubles are rooted in public issues.

Unemployment During the Great Recession

The Great Recession that began in 2008 put millions of Americans out of work. C. Wright Mills viewed unemployment as a public issue that stems from problems in a society's economic and political systems rather than from laziness or other faults among the people who are unemployed.

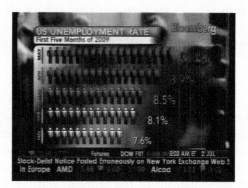

View the video online at: http://www.youtube.com/embed/Chtl7UQyR9M?rel=0

Another social problem is eating disorders. We usually consider a person's eating disorder to be a personal trouble that stems from a lack of control, low self-esteem, or another personal problem. Although such personal problems do matter for eating disorders, this type of explanation does not address why so many people have the personal problems that lead to eating disorders. It also neglects the larger social and cultural forces that help explain such disorders. For example, most Americans with eating disorders are women, not men. This gender difference forces us to ask what it is about being a woman in American society that makes eating disorders so much more common. To begin to answer this question, we need to look to the standard of beauty for women that emphasizes a slender body (Chou 2018).[14] If this cultural standard did not exist, far fewer American women would suffer from eating disorders than do now. Because it does exist, even if every girl and woman with an eating disorder were cured, others would take their places unless we could somehow change this standard. Viewed in this way, eating disorders are best understood as a public issue, not just as a personal trouble.

blaming the victim

The belief that people experiencing difficulties are to blame for these problems.

Picking up on Mills's insights, William Ryan (1976)[15] pointed out that Americans typically think that social problems such as poverty and unemployment stem from personal failings of the people experiencing these problems, not from structural problems in the larger society. Using Mills's terms, Americans tend to think of social problems as personal troubles rather than public issues. As Ryan put it, they tend to believe in **blaming the victim** rather than **blaming the system**.

blaming the system

The belief that personal difficulties stem from problems in society.

To help us understand a blaming-the-victim ideology, let's consider why poor children in urban areas often learn very little in their schools. According to Ryan, a blaming-the-victim approach would say the children's parents do not care about their learning, fail to teach them good study habits, and do not encourage them to take school seriously. This type of explanation, he wrote, may apply to some parents, but it ignores a much more important reason: the sad shape of America's urban schools, which, he said, are overcrowded, decrepit structures housing old textbooks and out-of-date equipment. To improve the schooling of children in urban areas, he wrote, we must improve the schools themselves and not just try to "improve" the parents.

As this example suggests, a blaming-the-victim approach points to solutions to social problems such as poverty and illiteracy that are very different from those suggested by a more structural approach that blames the system. If we blame the victim, we would spend our limited dollars to address the personal failings of individuals who suffer from poverty, illiteracy, poor health, eating disorders, and other difficulties. If instead we blame the system, we would focus our attention on the various social conditions (decrepit schools, cultural standards of female beauty, and the like) that account for these difficulties. A sociological understanding suggests that the latter approach is ultimately needed to help us deal successfully with the social problems facing us today.

Theoretical Perspectives

Three theoretical perspectives guide sociological thinking on social problems: *functionalist* theory, *conflict* theory, and *symbolic interactionist* theory. These perspectives look at the same social problems, but they do so in different ways. Their views taken together offer a fuller understanding of social problems than any of the views can offer alone. Table 1.1 summarizes the three perspectives.

TABLE 1.1 Theory Snapshot

Theoretical perspective	Major assumptions	Views of social problems
Functionalism	Social stability is necessary for a strong society, and adequate socialization and social integration are necessary for social stability. Society's social institutions perform important functions to help ensure social stability. Slow social change is desirable, but rapid social change threatens social order.	Social problems weaken a society's stability but do not reflect fundamental faults in how the society is structured. Solutions to social problems should take the form of gradual social reform rather than sudden and far-reaching change. Despite their negative effects, social problems often also serve important functions for society.
Conflict theory	Society is characterized by pervasive inequality based on social class, race, gender, and other factors. Far-reaching social change is needed to reduce or eliminate social inequality and to create an egalitarian society.	Social problems arise from fundamental faults in the structure of a society and both reflect and reinforce inequalities based on social class, race, gender, and other dimensions. Successful solutions to social problems must involve far-reaching change in the structure of society.
Symbolic interactionism	People construct their roles as they interact; they do not merely learn the roles that society has set out for them. As this interaction occurs, individuals negotiate their definitions of the situations in which they find themselves and socially construct the reality of these situations. In so doing, they rely heavily on symbols such as words and gestures to reach a shared understanding of their interaction.	Social problems arise from the interaction of individuals. People who engage in socially problematic behaviors often learn these behaviors from other people. Individuals also learn their perceptions of social problems from other people.

Functionalism

Functionalism, also known as the functionalist theory or perspective, arose out of two great revolutions of the eighteenth and nineteenth centuries. The first was the French Revolution of 1789, whose intense violence and bloody terror shook Europe to its core. The aristocracy throughout Europe feared that revolution would spread to their own lands, and intellectuals feared that social order was crumbling.

    The Industrial Revolution of the nineteenth century reinforced these concerns. Starting first in Europe and then in the United States, the Industrial Revolution led to many changes, including the rise and growth of cities as people left their farms to live near factories. As cities grew, people

functionalism

The view that social institutions are important for their contributions to social stability.

lived in increasingly poor, crowded, and decrepit conditions, and crime was rampant. Here was additional evidence, if European intellectuals needed it, of the breakdown of social order.

In response, the intellectuals began to write that a strong society, as exemplified by strong social bonds and rules and effective socialization, was needed to prevent social order from disintegrating. Without a strong society and effective socialization, they warned, social order breaks down, and violence and other signs of social disorder result.

This general framework reached fruition in the writings of Émile Durkheim (1858–1917), a French scholar largely responsible for the sociological perspective as we now know it. Adopting the conservative intellectuals' view of the need for a strong society, Durkheim felt that human beings have desires that result in chaos unless society limits them (Durkheim, 1897/1952:274).[16] It does so, he wrote, through two related social mechanisms: socialization and social integration. Socialization helps us learn society's rules and the need to cooperate, as people end up generally agreeing on important norms and values. Social integration, or our ties to other people and to social institutions such as religion and the family, helps socialize us and integrate us into society and reinforce our respect for its rules.

Today's functionalist perspective arises out of Durkheim's work and that of other conservative intellectuals of the nineteenth century. It uses the human body as a model for understanding society. In the human body, our various organs and other body parts serve important *functions* for the ongoing health and stability of our body. Our eyes help us see, our ears help us hear, our heart circulates our blood, and so forth. Just as we can understand the body by describing and understanding the functions that its parts serve for its health and stability, so can we understand society by describing and understanding the functions that its parts—or, more accurately, its social institutions—serve for the ongoing health and stability of society. Thus functionalism emphasizes the importance of social institutions such as the family, religion, and education for producing a stable society.

Similar to the view of the conservative intellectuals from which it grew, functionalism is skeptical of rapid social change and other major social upheaval. The analogy to the human body helps us understand this skepticism. In our bodies, any sudden, rapid change is a sign of danger to our health. If we break a bone in one of our legs, we have trouble walking; if we lose sight in both our eyes, we can no longer see. Slow changes, such as the growth of our hair and our nails, are fine and even normal, but sudden changes like those just described are obviously troublesome. By analogy, sudden and rapid changes in society and its social institutions are troublesome according to the functionalist perspective. If the human body evolved to its present form and functions because these made sense from an evolutionary perspective, so did society evolve to its present form and functions because these made sense. Any sudden change in society thus threatens its stability and future.

As these comments might suggest, functionalism views social problems as arising from society's natural evolution. When a social problem does occur, it might threaten a society's stability, but it does not mean that fundamental flaws in the society exist. Accordingly, gradual social reform should be all that is needed to address the social problem.

Functionalism even suggests that social problems must be functional in some ways for society, because otherwise these problems would not continue. This is certainly a controversial suggestion, but it is true that many social problems do serve important functions for our society. For example, crime is a major social problem, but it is also good for the economy because it creates hundreds of thousands of jobs in law enforcement, courts and corrections, home security, and other sectors of the economy whose major role is to deal with crime. If crime disappeared, many people would be out of work. Similarly, poverty is also a major social problem, but one function that poverty serves is that poor people do jobs that otherwise might not get done because other people would not want to do them (Gans 1972).[17] Like crime, poverty also provides employment for people across the nation, such as those who work in social service agencies that help poor people.

Émile Durkheim was a founder of sociology and is largely credited with developing the functionalist perspective.

Source: Marxists.org: https://www.marxists.org/glossary/people/d/pics/durkheim.jpg

Conflict Theory

In many ways, **conflict theory** is the opposite of functionalism but ironically also grew out of the Industrial Revolution, thanks largely to Karl Marx (1818–1883) and his collaborator, Friedrich Engels (1820–1895). Whereas conservative intellectuals feared the mass violence resulting from industrialization, Marx and Engels deplored the conditions they felt were responsible for the mass violence and the capitalist society they felt was responsible for these conditions. Instead of fearing the breakdown of social order that mass violence represented, they felt that revolutionary violence was needed to eliminate capitalism and the poverty and misery they saw as its inevitable results (Marx, 1867/1906; Marx and Engels, 1848/1962).[18]

According to Marx and Engels, every society is divided into two classes based on the ownership of the means of production (tools, factories, and the like). In a capitalist society, the *bourgeoisie*, or ruling class, owns the means of production, while the *proletariat*, or working class, is oppressed and exploited by the bourgeoisie. This difference creates a conflict of interest between the two groups. Simply put, the bourgeoisie is interested in maintaining its position at the top of society, while the proletariat's interest lies in overthrowing the bourgeoisie to create an egalitarian society.

In a capitalist society, Marx and Engels wrote, revolution is inevitable because of structural contradictions arising from the very nature of capitalism. Because profit is the main goal of capitalism, the bourgeoisie's interest lies in maximizing profit. To do so, capitalists try to keep wages as low as possible and to spend as little money as possible on working conditions. This central fact of capitalism, said Marx and Engels, eventually prompts the rise of **class consciousness**, or an awareness of the reasons for their oppression, among workers. Their class consciousness in turn leads them to revolt against the bourgeoisie to eliminate the oppression and exploitation they suffer.

Marx and Engels' view of conflict arising from unequal positions held by members of society lies at the heart of today's conflict theory. This theory emphasizes that different groups in society have different interests stemming from their different social positions. These different interests in turn lead to different views on important social issues. Some versions of the theory root conflict in divisions based on race and ethnicity, gender, and other such differences, while other versions follow Marx and Engels in seeing conflict arising out of different positions in the economic structure. In general, however, conflict theory emphasizes that the various parts of society contribute to ongoing inequality, whereas functionalist theory, as we have seen, stresses that they contribute to the ongoing stability of society. Thus while functionalist theory emphasizes the benefits of the various parts of society for ongoing social stability, conflict theory favors social change to reduce inequality.

Feminist theory has developed in sociology and other disciplines since the 1970s and for our purposes will be considered a specific application of conflict theory. In this case, the conflict concerns gender inequality rather than the class inequality emphasized by Marx and Engels. Although many variations of feminist theory exist, they all emphasize that society is filled with gender inequality such that women are the subordinate sex in many dimensions of social, political, and economic life (Collins and Andersen 2020).[19] Liberal feminists view gender inequality as arising out of gender differences in socialization, while Marxist feminists say that this inequality is a result of the rise of capitalism, which made women dependent on men for economic support. On the other hand, radical feminists view gender inequality as present in all societies, not just capitalist ones. Several chapters in this book emphasize the perspectives of feminist sociologists and other social scientists.

Conflict theory in its various forms views social problems as arising from society's inherent inequality. Depending on which version of conflict theory is being considered, the inequality contributing to social problems is based on social class, race and ethnicity, gender, or some other dimension of society's hierarchy. Because any of these inequalities represents a fundamental flaw in society, conflict theory assumes that fundamental social change is needed to address society's many social problems.

conflict theory

The view that society is composed of groups with different interests arising from their placement in the social structure.

Karl Marx and his collaborator Friedrich Engels were intense critics of capitalism. Their work inspired the later development of conflict theory in sociology.

Source: © Thinkstock

class consciousness

Awareness of one's placement in the social structure and the interests arising from this placement.

feminist theory

The view that society is filled with gender inequality characterized by women being the subordinate sex in the social, political, and economic dimensions of society.

Symbolic Interactionism

symbolic interactionism

A perspective in sociology that focuses on the meanings people gain from social interaction.

Symbolic interactionism focuses on the interaction of individuals and on how they interpret their interaction. Its roots lie in the work of early 1900s American sociologists, social psychologists, and philosophers who were interested in human consciousness and action. Herbert Blumer (1969),[20] a sociologist at the University of Chicago, built on their writings to develop symbolic interactionism, a term he coined. Drawing on Blumer's work, symbolic interactionists feel that people do not merely learn the roles that society has set out for them; instead they construct these roles as they interact. As they interact, they negotiate their definitions of the situations in which they find themselves and socially construct the reality of these situations. In doing so, they rely heavily on symbols such as words and gestures to reach a shared understanding of their interaction.

Symbolic interactionism focuses on individuals, such as the people conversing here. Sociologists favoring this approach examine how and why individuals interact and interpret the meanings of their interaction.

Source: © Thinkstock

An example is the familiar symbol of shaking hands. In the United States and many other societies before the coronavirus pandemic, shaking hands was a symbol of greeting and friendship. This simple act indicated that you were a nice, polite person with whom someone should feel comfortable. Before the pandemic, if someone had *refused* to shake hands, that action would have probably been both intended as either a sign of dislike or as an insult, and the other person would have interpreted it as such. But during the pandemic, shaking hands suddenly became regarded as a health risk, and no one felt disliked or insulted if someone declined to shake hands with them.

As the term *symbolic interactionism* implies, people's understanding of encounters like shaking hands arises from what they do when they interact and from interpretation of the various symbols involved in their interaction. According to symbolic interactionists, social order is possible because people learn what various symbols (such as shaking hands) mean and apply these meanings to different kinds of situations. If you visited a society where extending your right hand to greet someone was interpreted as a threatening gesture, you would quickly learn the value of common understandings of symbols. To return to the pandemic, extending your right hand to greet someone became interpreted as a stupid, inconsiderate, or risky gesture.

Symbolic interactionism views social problems as arising from the interaction of individuals. This interaction matters in two important respects. First, socially problematic behaviors such as crime and drug use are often learned from our interaction with people who engage in these behaviors; we adopt their attitudes that justify committing these behaviors, and we learn any special techniques that might be needed to commit these behaviors. Second, we also learn our perceptions of a social problem from our interaction with other people, whose perceptions and beliefs influence our own perceptions and beliefs.

Because symbolic interactionism emphasizes the perception of social problems, it is closely aligned with the social constructionist view discussed earlier. Both perspectives emphasize the subjective nature of social problems. By doing so, they remind us that perceptions often matter at least as much as objective reality in determining whether a given condition or behavior rises to the level of a social problem and in determining which possible solutions various parties might favor for a particular social problem.

Applying the Three Perspectives

To help you further understand the different views of these three theoretical perspectives, let's examine what they would probably say about *armed robbery*, a very serious form of crime, while recognizing that the three perspectives together provide a more comprehensive understanding of armed robbery than any one perspective provides by itself.

A functionalist approach might suggest that armed robbery actually serves positive functions for society, such as the job-creating function mentioned earlier for crime in general. It would still maintain that such efforts should be made to reduce armed robbery, but it would also assume that far-reaching changes in our society would be neither wise nor necessary as part of the effort to reduce crime.

Conflict theory would take a very different approach to understanding armed robbery. It might note that most street criminals are poor and thus emphasize that armed robbery is the result of the despair and frustration of living in poverty and facing a lack of jobs and other opportunities for economic and social success. The roots of street crime, from the perspective of conflict theory, thus lie in society at least as much as they lie in the individuals committing such crime. To reduce armed robbery and other street crime, conflict theory would advocate far-reaching changes in the economic structure of society.

To explain armed robbery, symbolic interactionists focus on how armed robbers decide when and where to rob a victim and on how their interactions with other criminals reinforce their own criminal tendencies.

Source: © Thinkstock

 ### Link Between Poverty and Violence

Conflict theory views armed robbery and other violent crime by the poor as the result of the despair and frustration of living in poverty.

View the video online at: http://www.youtube.com/embed/QXOb0fS2q18?rel=0

For its part, symbolic interactionism would focus on how armed robbers make such decisions as when and where to rob someone and on how their interactions with other criminals reinforce their own criminal tendencies. It would also investigate how victims of armed robbery behave when confronted by a robber. To reduce armed robbery, it would advocate programs that reduce the opportunities for interaction among potential criminal offenders, for example, after-school programs that keep at-risk youths busy in "conventional" activities so that they have less time to spend with youths who might help them get into trouble.

Key Takeaways

- According to C. Wright Mills, the sociological imagination involves the ability to recognize that private troubles are rooted in public issues and structural problems.
- Functionalism emphasizes the importance of social institutions for social stability and implies that far-reaching social change will be socially harmful.
- Conflict theory emphasizes social inequality and suggests that far-reaching social change is needed to achieve a just society.
- Symbolic interactionism emphasizes the social meanings and understandings that individuals derive from their social interaction.

1. Select an example of a "private trouble" and explain how and why it may reflect a structural problem in society.
2. At this point in your study of social problems, which one of the three sociological theoretical perspectives sounds most appealing to you? Why?

1.3 Continuity and Change in Social Problems

Learning Objectives

1. Explain what is meant by this book's subtitle, "Continuity and Change."
2. List the three sources of changes to social problems.
3. Describe how the United States compares to other democracies regarding the seriousness of social problems.

This book's subtitle, "Continuity and Change," conveys a theme that will guide every chapter's discussion. Social problems are, first of all, *persistent*. They have continued for decades and even centuries, and they show no sign of ending anytime soon. In view of social problems' long history, certainty of continuing for some time to come, and serious consequences, it is easy to feel overwhelmed when reading about them, to think that little can be done about them, and even to become a bit depressed. As a result, it is easy for students to come away from social problems courses with a rather pessimistic, "doom and gloom" outlook (Johnson 2005).[21]

That is why this book stresses the second part of the subtitle, *change*. Although social problems are indeed persistent, it is also true that certain problems are less serious now than in the past. Change is possible. As just one of many examples, consider the conditions that workers face in the United States. As Chapter 12 discusses, many workers today are unemployed, have low wages, or work in substandard and even dangerous workplaces. Yet they are immeasurably better off than a century ago, thanks to the U.S. labor movement that began during the 1870s. Workers now have the eight-hour day, the minimum wage (even if many people think it is too low), the right to strike, and workplaces that are much safer than when the labor movement began. In two more examples, people of color and women have made incredible advances since the 1960s, even if, as Chapter 3 and Chapter 4 discuss, they continue to experience racial and gender inequality, respectively. To repeat: change is possible.

How does change occur? One source of change in social problems is social science theory and research. Over the decades, theory and research in sociology and the other social sciences have pointed to the reasons for social problems, to potentially successful ways of addressing them, and to actual policies that succeeded in addressing some aspect of a social problem. Accordingly, each chapter of this book is based on sound social science theory and research, and each chapter presents examples of how the findings from sociological and other social science research have either contributed to public policy related to the chapter's social problem or have the potential of doing so.

The actions of individuals and groups may also make a difference. Many people have public-service jobs or volunteer in all sorts of activities involving a social problem: They assist at a food pantry, they help clean up a riverbank, and so forth. Others take on a more activist orientation by becoming involved in small social change groups or a larger social movement. Our nation is a better place today because of the labor movement, the Southern civil rights movement, the women's movement, the gay rights movement, the environmental movement, and other efforts too numerous to mention. According to Frances Fox Piven (2006),[22] a former president of the American Sociological Association, it is through such efforts that "ordinary people change America," as the subtitle of her book on this subject reads.

An important source of change in social problems is protest by a social change group or movement.

Source: © Thinkstock

 ### Women's March on Washington in January 2017

After Donald Trump was inaugurated as president in January 2017, hundreds of thousands of women and many men marched in Washington, DC, and in other cities across the nation and world to protest his election, his behavior and pronouncements, and his policies. Protests like these marches have often led to beneficial social change in the United States and other nations.

View the video online at: http://www.youtube.com/embed/v9B1bzg0TEA?rel=0

Sharing this view, anthropologist Margaret Mead once said, "Never doubt that a small group of thoughtful, committed citizens can change the world. Indeed, it is the only thing that ever has" (Lutkehaus 2008:261).[23] Change thus is not easy, but it can and does occur. Eleanor Roosevelt (1960, p. 168)[24] recognized this when she wrote, "Surely, in the light of history, it is more intelligent to hope rather than to fear, to try rather than not to try. For one thing we know beyond all doubt: nothing has ever been achieved by the person who says, 'It can't be done.'" In the optimistic spirit of these two famous women, we will see examples throughout this book of people making a difference in their jobs, volunteer activities, and involvement in social change efforts.

Many other democracies, including England, rank higher than the United States on poverty, health, and other social indicators. For this reason, the United States may have much to learn from their positive examples.

Source: © Thinkstock

Change also occurs in social problems because policymakers (elected or appointed officials and other individuals) pass laws or enact policies that successfully address a social problem. They often do so only because of the pressure of a social movement, but sometimes they have the vision to act without such pressure. It is also true that many officials fail to take action despite the pressure of a social movement, so those who do take action should be applauded. A recent example involves the governor of California, Gavin Newsom, who proposed legislation, passed by his state legislature, that made California the first state to provide health insurance for young-adult undocumented immigrants from low-income backgrounds (Axelrod 2019).[25]

A final source of change is the lessons learned from other nations' experiences with social problems. Sometimes these lessons for the United States are positive ones, as when another nation has tackled a social problem more successfully than the United States, and sometimes these lessons are negative ones, as when another nation has a more serious problem than the United States and/or has made mistakes in addressing this problem. The United States can thus learn from the good examples of some other nations, and it can also learn from the bad ones. For this reason, each chapter of this book discusses such examples. In this regard, the United States has much to learn from the experiences of other wealthy democracies like Canada, the nations of Western Europe, Australia, and New Zealand. Despite its great wealth, the United States ranks *below* most of its democratic peers on many social indicators, such as poverty, health, and so on (Russell 2018).[26] A major reason for this difference is that other democratic governments are far more proactive, in terms of attention and spending, than the U.S. federal and state governments in helping their citizens. Because the United States has much to learn from their positive example, this book's chapters all discuss policies that enable other democracies to address certain social problems far more successfully than the United States has addressed them.

Key Takeaways

- Social problems are persistent, but they have also changed over the years, and many social problems are less serious now than in the past.
- Three sources of change to social problems include social science research, the efforts of citizens acting alone or especially in social change groups, and the experiences of other nations.

For Your Review

1. Have you participated in any volunteering or other activity involving a social problem? If so, why did you do so? If not, why have you not participated in such an effort?
2. Do you share Eleanor Roosevelt's optimism that social change is possible? Why or why not?

1.4 Doing Research on Social Problems

Learning Objectives

1. List the major advantages and disadvantages of surveys, observational studies, and experiments.
2. Explain why scholars who study social problems often rely on existing data.

Sound research is an essential tool for understanding the sources, dynamics, and consequences of social problems and possible solutions to them. This section briefly describes the major ways in which sociologists gather information about social problems. Table 1.2 summarizes the advantages and disadvantages of each method.

TABLE 1.2 Major Sociological Research Methods

Method	Advantages	Disadvantages
Survey	Many people can be included. If given to a random sample of the population, a survey's results can be generalized to the population.	Large surveys are expensive and time consuming. Although much information is gathered, this information is relatively superficial.
Experiments	If random assignment is used, experiments provide fairly convincing data on cause and effect.	Because experiments do not involve random samples of the population and most often involve college students, their results cannot readily be generalized to the population.
Qualitative research	Observational studies and intensive interviewing may provide rich, detailed information about the people who are observed.	Because observation studies and intensive interviews do not involve random samples of the population, their results cannot readily be generalized to the population.
Existing data	Because existing data has already been gathered, the researcher does not have to spend the time and money to gather data.	The data set that is being analyzed may not contain data on all the variables in which a sociologist is interested or may contain data on variables that are not measured in ways the sociologist prefers.

Surveys

The *survey* is the most common method by which sociologists gather their data. The Gallup poll is perhaps the most well-known example of a survey and, like all surveys, gathers its data with the help of a questionnaire that is given to a group of **respondents**. The Gallup poll is an example of a survey conducted by a private organization, but sociologists do their own surveys, as does the government and many organizations in addition to Gallup. Many surveys are administered to respondents who are randomly chosen and thus constitute a **random sample**. In a random sample, everyone in the population (whether it be the whole U.S. population or just the population of a state or city, all the college students in a state or city or all the students at just one college, etc.) has the same chance of being included in the survey. The beauty of a random sample is that it allows us to generalize the results of the sample to the population from which the sample comes. This means that we can be fairly sure of the behavior and attitudes of the whole U.S. population by

respondents

People who answer a questionnaire.

random sample

A subset drawn from the larger population in which every unit in the population has the same chance of being included in the subset.

knowing the behavior and attitudes of just a few hundred or few thousand people randomly chosen from that population.

For example, in an April 2020 national survey of 4,917 American adults, 65 percent of respondents said that President Donald Trump was "too slow to take major steps to address the threat of the coronavirus outbreak to the U.S.," and 73 percent said "the worst is still to come" regarding "the problems the U.S. is facing from the outbreak" (Pew Research Center 2020).[27] Even though the sample of 4,917 adults was only a miniscule fraction of the more than 250 million adults in the U.S. population, we can be very sure that the findings of this survey applied to all adults, not just those in the sample.

Some surveys are *face-to-face* surveys, in which interviewers meet with respondents to ask them questions. This type of survey can yield much information, because interviewers typically will spend at least an hour asking their questions, and a high **response rate** (the percentage of all people in the sample who agree to be interviewed), which is important to be able to generalize the survey's results to the entire population. On the downside, this type of survey can be very expensive and time consuming to conduct.

Because of these drawbacks, sociologists and other researchers have turned to telephone and internet surveys. Most national polls are conducted via one of these methods. For telephone surveys, computers do random-digit dialing, which results in a random sample of all telephone numbers being selected. Although the response rate and the number of questions asked are both lower in telephone and internet surveys than in face-to-face surveys (with telephone surveys, people can just hang up the phone at the outset or let their answering machine take the call; with internet surveys, they can simply decide not to click a link), the ease and low expense of these surveys are making them increasingly popular.

Surveys are used in the study of social problems to gather information about the behavior and attitudes of people regarding one or more problems. For example, many surveys ask people about their use of alcohol, tobacco, and other drugs or about their experiences of being unemployed or in poor health. Many of the chapters in this book will present evidence gathered by surveys carried out by sociologists and other social scientists, various governmental agencies, and private research and public interest firms.

response rate

The percentage of a sample that agrees to be included in a study, usually a survey.

Surveys are very useful for gathering various kinds of information relevant to social problems. Advances in technology have made telephone surveys involving random-digit dialing perhaps a very popular way of conducting a survey.

Source: © Thinkstock

Experiments

Experiments are the primary form of research in the natural and physical sciences, but in the social sciences they are for the most part found only in psychology. Some sociologists still use experiments, however, and they are a powerful tool of social research.

The major advantage of experiments, whether they are done in the natural and physical sciences or in the social sciences, is that the researcher can be fairly sure of a cause-and-effect relationship because of the way the experiment is set up. Although many different experimental designs exist, the typical experiment consists of an **experimental group** and a **control group**, with subjects *randomly assigned* to either group. The researcher does something to the experimental group that is not done to the control group. If the two groups differ later in some variable, then it is safe to say that the condition to which the experimental group was subjected was responsible for the difference that resulted.

Most experiments take place in the laboratory, which for psychologists may be a room with a one-way mirror, but some experiments occur in the field, or in a natural setting (*field experiments*). In Minneapolis, Minnesota, in the early 1980s, sociologists were involved in a much-discussed field experiment sponsored by the federal government. The researchers wanted to see whether arresting men for domestic violence would deter them from committing such violence again. To test this hypothesis, the researchers had police do one of the following after arriving at the scene of a domestic dispute: they either arrested the suspect, separated him from his wife or partner for sev-

experimental group

In an experiment, the group that experiences the experimental condition.

control group

In an experiment, the group that does not experience the experimental condition.

eral hours, or warned him to stop but did not arrest or separate him. The researchers then determined the percentage of men in each group who committed repeated domestic violence during the next six months and found that those who were arrested had the lowest rate of recidivism, or repeat offending (Sherman and Berk 1984).[28] This finding led many jurisdictions across the United States to adopt a policy of mandatory arrest for domestic violence suspects. However, replications of the Minneapolis experiment in other cities found that arrest sometimes reduced recidivism for domestic violence but also sometimes increased it, depending on which city was being studied and on certain characteristics of the suspects, including whether they were employed at the time of their arrest (Sherman 1992).[29]

As the Minneapolis study suggests, perhaps the most important problem with experiments is that their results are not *generalizable* beyond the specific subjects studied. The subjects in most psychology experiments, for example, are college students, who certainly are not typical of average Americans: they are younger, more educated, and less likely to be from low-income families. Despite this problem, experiments in psychology and other social sciences have given us very valuable insights into the sources of attitudes and behaviors. Scholars of social problems are increasingly using field experiments to study the effectiveness of various policies and programs aimed at addressing social problems. We will examine the results of several such experiments in the chapters ahead.

Qualitative Research

Qualitative research takes two forms. The first type, observational research, also called *field research*, is a staple of sociology. Sociologists have long gone into the field to observe people and social settings, and the result has been many rich descriptions and analyses of behavior in juvenile gangs, bars, urban street corners, and even whole communities. The second type, intensive interviewing, also provides rich descriptions of the lives and viewpoints of the people interviewed.

Observational studies consist of both **participant observation** and **nonparticipant observation**. Their names describe how they differ. In participant observation, the researcher is part of the group that she or he is studying, spends time with the group, and might even live with people in the group. Several classic social problems studies of this type exist, many of them involving people in urban neighborhoods (Liebow, 1967; Liebow, 1993; Whyte, 1943).[30] In nonparticipant observation, the researcher observes a group of people but does not otherwise interact with them. If you went to your local shopping mall to observe, say, whether people walking with children looked happier than people without children, you would be engaging in nonparticipant observation.

Similar to experiments, observational studies and intensive interviews cannot automatically be generalized to other settings or members of the population. But in many ways they provide a richer account of people's lives than surveys do, and they are important methods of research on social problems.

participant observation

Field research in which the researcher is an active member of the group or setting being observed.

nonparticipant observation

Field research in which the researcher merely observes a group or setting.

Existing Data

Sometimes sociologists do not gather their own data but instead analyze *existing data* that someone else has gathered. The U.S. Census Bureau, for example, gathers data on all kinds of areas relevant to the lives of Americans, and many sociologists analyze census data on such social problems as poverty, unemployment, and illness. Sociologists interested in crime and the criminal justice system may analyze data from court records, while medical sociologists often analyze data from patient records at hospitals. Analysis of existing data such as these is called **secondary data**

secondary data analysis

The analysis of data from existing records.

analysis. Its advantage to sociologists is that someone else has already spent the time and money to gather the data. A disadvantage is that the data set being analyzed may not contain data on all the topics in which a sociologist may be interested or may contain data on topics that are not measured in ways the sociologist might prefer.

The Scientific Method and Objectivity

This section began by stressing the need for sound research in the study of social problems. But what are the elements of sound research? At a minimum, such research should follow the rules of the *scientific method*. As you probably learned in high school and/or college science classes, these rules—formulating hypotheses, gathering and testing data, drawing conclusions, and so forth—help guarantee that research yields the most accurate and reliable conclusions possible.

An overriding principle of the scientific method is that research should be conducted as *objectively* as possible. Researchers are often passionate about their work, but they must take care not to let the findings they expect and even hope to uncover affect how they do their research. This in turn means that they must not conduct their research in a manner that helps achieve the results they expect to find. Such bias can happen unconsciously, and the scientific method helps reduce the potential for this bias as much as possible.

This potential is arguably greater in the social sciences than in the natural and physical sciences. The political views of chemists and physicists typically do not affect how an experiment is performed and how the outcome of the experiment is interpreted. In contrast, researchers in the social sciences, and perhaps particularly in sociology, often have strong feelings about the topics they are studying. Their social and political beliefs may thus influence how they perform their research on these topics and how they interpret the results of this research. Following the scientific method helps reduce this possible influence.

Key Takeaways

- The major types of research on social problems include surveys, experiments, observational studies, and the use of existing data.
- Surveys are the most common method, and the results of surveys of random samples may be generalized to the populations from which the samples come.
- Observation studies and existing data are also common methods in social problems research. Observation studies enable the gathering of rich, detailed information, but their results cannot necessarily be generalized beyond the people studied.
- Research on social problems should follow the scientific method to yield the most accurate and objective conclusions possible.

For Your Review

1. Have you ever been a respondent or subject in any type of sociological or psychological research project? If so, how did it feel to be studied?
2. Which type of social problems research method sounds most interesting to you? Why?

1.5 End-of-Chapter Material

Summary

1. Some sociologists favor the social constructionist view that negative social conditions or behaviors are not social problems unless they are generally perceived as a social problem, but other sociologists say that these conditions and behaviors are still social problems even if they are not perceived as such. In this regard, the coronavirus pandemic was a major health and social problem for many weeks before it was finally perceived as such and American society shut down in March 2020.

2. According to C. Wright Mills, the sociological imagination involves the ability to realize that personal troubles are rooted in problems in the larger social structure. The sociological imagination thus supports a blaming-the-system view over a blaming-the-victim view.

3. Social problems have existed for decades or even centuries, but many of these have also lessened in their seriousness over time, and change in the future is indeed possible.

4. Several theoretical perspectives in sociology exist. Functionalism emphasizes the functions that social institutions serve to ensure the ongoing stability of society, while conflict theory focuses on the conflict among different racial, ethnic, social class, and other groups and emphasizes how social institutions help ensure inequality. Symbolic interactionism focuses on how individuals interpret the meanings of the situations in which they find themselves.

5. The major research methods to study social problems include surveys, experiments, qualitative research (observational studies and intensive interviewing), and the analysis of existing data. All these methods should follow the principles of the scientific method and be as objective as possible.

Endnotes

1. Calhoun, C. 2007. "Sociology in America: An introduction." In C. Calhoun (Ed.), *Sociology in America: A History* (pp. 1–38). Chicago, IL: University of Chicago Press; Morris, Aldon. 2015. The Scholar Denied: W. E. B. Du Bois and the Birth of Modern Sociology. Berkeley: University of California Press.

2. Treviño, A. Javier. (2011). Program theme: Service sociology. *Program of the 61st Annual Meeting of the Society for the Study of Social Problems*, 1. Retrieved from http://www.sssp1.org/file/2011AnnualMeeting/Final Program.pdf .

3. Saad, Lyida. 2019. "Americans as Concerned as Ever About Global Warming." *Gallup News* March 25:https://news.gallup.com/poll/248027/americans-concerned-ever-global-warming.aspx?g_source=link_NEWSV9&g_medium=TOPIC&g_campaign=item_&g_content=Americans as Concerned as Ever About Global Warming.

4. Rubington, E., & Weinberg, M. S. (2010). *The study of social problems: Seven perspectives* (7th ed.). New York, NY: Oxford University Press.

5. Allison, J. A., & Wrightsman, L. S. 1993. *Rape: The misunderstood crime.* Thousand Oaks, CA: Sage Publications.

6. Harris, Shane, Greg Miller, Josh Dawsey and Ellen Nakashima. 2020. "U.S. Intelligence Reports from January and February Warned About a Likely Pandemic." *The Washington Post* March 20:https://www.washingtonpost.com/national-security/us-intelligence-reports-from-january-and-february-warned-about-a-likely-pandemic/2020/03/20/299d8cda-6ad5-11ea-b5f1-a5a804158597_story.html.

7. Lipton, Eric, David E. Sanger, Maggie Haberman, Michael D. Shear, Mark Mazzetti and Julian E. Barnes. 2020. "He Could Have Seen What Was Coming: Behind Trump's Failure on the Virus." *The New York Times* April 11:https://www.nytimes.com/2020/04/11/us/politics/coronavirus-trump-response.html.

8. Ehrenreich, B., & English, D. 2005. *For Her Own Good: Two Centuries of the Experts' Advice to Women* (2nd ed.). New York, NY: Anchor Books; Koren, Marina. 2019. "The Pioneering Female Doctor Who Argued against Rest." *The Atlantic* July 6:https://www.theatlantic.com/science/archive/2019/07/menstruation-women-suffrage-voting-nineteenth-amendment/593260/.

9. Ousey, Graham C. and Chris E. Kubrin. 2018. "Immigration and Crime: Assessing a Contentious Issue." *Annual Review of Criminology* 1:63-84.

10. Robinson, Matthew. B. 2018. *Media Coverage of Crime and Criminal Justice.* Durham, NC: Carolina Academic Press, third edition.

11. Spector, Malcolm., and Kitsuse, John. I. 2001. *Constructing Social Problems.* New Brunswick, NJ: Transaction.

12. Mills, C. Wright. 1959. *The Sociological Imagination.* London, United Kingdom: Oxford University Press.

13. Mills, C. Wright. 1959. *The Sociological Imagination.* London, United Kingdom: Oxford University Press.

14. Chou, Chia-Chan. 2018. "Thinness = Beauty: Factors That Influence Women's Cognitive Bias toward Weight Loss." *Social Behavior and Personality: An International Journal* 46(6):905-24.

15. Ryan, William. 1976. *Blaming the victim* (Rev. ed.). New York, NY: Vintage Books.

16. Durkheim, Émile. 1952. *Suicide* (J. Spaulding & G. Simpson, Trans.). New York, NY: Free Press. (Original work published 1897)

17. Gans, Herbert J. 1972. "The Positive Functions of Poverty." *American Journal of Sociology.* 78:275–289.

18. Marx, Karl. 1906. *Capital.* New York, NY: Random House. (Original work published 1867); Marx, Karl, & Engels, Frederick. 1962. *The Communist Manifesto. In Marx and Engels: Selected Works* (Vol. 2, pp. 21–65). Moscow, Russia: Foreign Language Publishing House. (Original work published 1848).

19. Andersen, Margaret L. and Patricia Hill Collins, eds. 2020. *Race, Class, and Gender: An Anthology.* Belmont, CA: Cengage.

20. Blumer, Herbert. 1969. *Symbolic interactionism: Perspective and Method.* Englewood Cliffs, NJ: Prentice Hall.

21. Johnson, Brett. (2005). Overcoming "Doom and Gloom": Empowering Students in Courses on Social Problems, Injustice, and Inequality. *Teaching Sociology, 33:*44–58.

22. Piven, Frances Fox. (2006). *Challenging Authority: How Ordinary People Change America.* Lanham, MD: Rowman & Littlefield.

23. Lutkehaus, Nancy C. 2008. *Margaret Mead: The Making of an American Icon.* Princeton: Princeton University Press.

24. Roosevelt, E. (1960). *You learn by living: Eleven keys for a more fulfilling life*. New York, NY: Harper & Row.

25. Axelrod, Tal. 2019. "California Governor Signs Legislation Extending Health Care to Undocumented Immigrants." *The Hill* July 10:https://the-hill.com/homenews/state-watch/452395-california-governor-signs-legislation-extending-health-care-to.

26. Russell, James W. 2018. *Double Standard: Social Policy in Europe and the United States*. Lanham, MD: Rowman & Littlefield.

27. Pew Research Center. 2020. "Most Americans Say Trump Was Too Slow in Initial Response to Coronavirus Threat." *Pew Research Center*. Retrieved from https://www.people-press.org/2020/04/16/most-americans-say-trump-was-too-slow-in-initial-response-to-coronavirus-threat/.

28. Sherman, Lawrence W., & Berk, Richard A. 1984. The Specific Deterrent Effects of Arrest for Domestic Assault. *American Sociological Review, 49*, 261–272.

29. Sherman, Lawrence W. 1992. *Policing Domestic Violence: Experiments and Dilemmas*. New York, NY: Free Press.

30. Liebow, Elliot. 1967. *Tally's Corner*. Boston, MA: Little, Brown; Liebow, Elliot. 1993. *Tell Them Who I Am: The Lives of Homeless Women*. New York, NY: Free Press; Whyte, William F. (1943). *Street Corner Society: The Social Structure of an Italian Slum*. Chicago, IL: University of Chicago Press.

PART 2

Problems of Social Inequality

Source: Joseph Sohm/Shutterstock.com

CHAPTER 2
Poverty

Social Problems in the News

"Hunger Takes No Summer Break: When School's Out, the Challenge Is How to Feed More Kids," the headline said. In East Orange, New Jersey, where 70 percent of children are eligible for free or reduced-price lunches during the school year, many children were going hungry during the summer of 2019. One reason for this dismaying situation was that summer meal programs for low-income children are underfunded. Another reason is that it is logistically more difficult to provide meals to children in the summer than during the school year, when they are all in the same places—schools—at the same times, at least if they are of school age. These factors mean that six out of every seven children who qualify for meals during the summer are not receiving them and therefore may well be going hungry. The author of a report on this problem said, "There is a cost, but we have a choice in how we spend our money in this country. It's a sad commentary on the fact that we are not providing kids what they need in the summer." The mother of a child who was getting free meals in East Orange recalled her reaction when she discovered these meals were available. "That was amazing," she said, "I was like, 'Thank you so much. Do I have to pay something?' They said, 'No, it's for free.' I was 100 percent amazed." She added, "I'm so blessed we have this" (Ortiz 2019).[1]

The United States is one of the richest nations in the world. Many Americans live in luxury or at least are comfortably well-off. Yet, as this news story about childhood hunger reminds us, many Americans also live in poverty or near poverty, a situation that only worsened with the onset of the COVID-19 pandemic in spring 2020. This chapter explains why poverty exists and why the U.S. poverty rate is so high, and it discusses the devastating consequences of poverty for the millions of Americans who live in or near poverty. It also examines poverty in the poorest nations of the world and outlines efforts for reducing poverty in the United States and these nations.

Although this chapter will paint a disturbing picture of poverty, there is still cause for hope. As we shall see, the "war on poverty" that began in the United States during the 1960s dramatically reduced poverty. Inspired by books with titles like *The Other America: Poverty in the United States* (Harrington 1962)[2] and *In the Midst of Plenty: The Poor in America* (Bagdikian 1964)[3] that described the plight of the poor in heartbreaking detail, the federal government established various funding programs and other policies that greatly lowered the poverty rate in less than a decade (Lee et al. 2014).[4] Since the 1960s and 1970s, however, the United States has cut back on these programs, and the poor are no longer on the national agenda. Other wealthy democracies provide much more funding and many more services for their poor than does the United States, and their poverty rates are much lower than ours.

Still, the history of the war on poverty and the experience of these other nations both demonstrate that U.S. poverty can be reduced with appropriate policies and programs. If the United States were to go back to the future by remembering its earlier war on poverty and by learning from other Western democracies, it could again lower poverty and help millions of Americans lead better, healthier, and more productive lives. As the nation emerges from the pandemic, it would do well to keep the poor and near-poor foremost in its mind.

But why should we care about poverty in the first place? As this chapter discusses, many politicians and much of the public blame the poor for being poor, and they oppose increasing federal spending to help the poor and even want to reduce such spending. As poverty expert Mark R. Rank (2011:17)[5] summarized this way of thinking, "All too often we view poverty as someone else's problem." Rank said this unsympathetic view is shortsighted because, as he puts it, "poverty affects us all."[6] This is true, he explained, for at least two reasons.

First, the United States spends much more money than it needs to because of the consequences of poverty. Poor people experience worse health, family problems, higher crime rates, and many other issues, all of which our nation spends billions of dollars annually to address. In fact, childhood poverty is estimated to cost the U.S. economy an estimated $800 billion to $1.1 trillion annually because of the problems it leads to, including unemployment, low-paid employment, higher crime rates, and physical and mental health problems (Duncan and Le Menestrel 2019).[7] If the U.S. poverty rate were no higher than that of other democracies, hundreds of billions of tax dollars and other expenditures would be saved every year.

Second, the majority of Americans can actually expect to be poor or near poor at some point in their lives, with about 75 percent of Americans in the 20–75 age range living in poverty or near poverty for at least one year in their lives. As Rank (2011:18)[8] observed, most Americans "will find ourselves below the poverty line and using a social safety net program at some point." Because poverty costs the United States so much money and because so many people experience poverty, said Rank, everyone should want the United States to do everything possible to reduce poverty.

Sociologist John Iceland (2013)[9] adds two additional reasons for why everyone should care about poverty and want it reduced. First, a high rate of poverty impairs our nation's economic progress: When a large number of people cannot afford to purchase goods and services, economic growth is more difficult to achieve. Second, poverty produces crime and other social problems that affect people across the socioeconomic ladder. Reductions in poverty would help not only the poor but also people who are not poor.

We begin our examination of poverty by discussing how poverty is measured and how much poverty exists.

2.1 The Measurement and Extent of Poverty

Learning Objectives

1. Understand how official poverty in the United States is measured.
2. Describe problems in the measurement of official poverty.
3. Describe the extent of official poverty.

poverty line

The government's measure of official poverty, based on the cost of a minimal diet for a family that is then multiplied by three.

When U.S. officials became concerned about poverty during the 1960s, they quickly realized they needed to find out how much poverty we had. To do so, a measure of official poverty, or a **poverty line**, was needed. A government economist, Mollie Orshanky, first calculated this line in 1963 by multiplying the cost of a very minimal diet by three, as a 1955 government study had determined that the typical American family spent one-third of its income on food. Thus a family whose cash income is lower than three times the cost of a very minimal diet was considered officially poor.

This way of calculating the official poverty line has not changed since 1963. It is thus out of date for many reasons. For example, many expenses, such as heat and electricity, child care, transportation, and health care, now occupy a greater percentage of the typical family's budget than was true in 1963. In addition, this official measure ignores a family's noncash income from benefits such as food stamps and tax credits. As a national measure, the poverty line also fails to take into account regional differences in the cost of living. All these problems make the official measurement of poverty highly suspect. As one poverty expert observed, "The official measure no longer corresponds to reality. It doesn't get either side of the equation right—how much the poor have or how much they need. No one really trusts the data" (DeParle et al. 2011:A1).[10] In response to these issues, the federal government has developed a Supplemental Poverty Measure (SPM) that considers expenses for basic necessities (clothing, food, shelter, utilities), government aid, geographical housing costs, and certain expenses such as child care and out-of-pocket medical payments. The SPM shows that government aid programs are essential in keeping many people above the poverty level, even if these people still have trouble making ends meet and even though the poverty rate remains unacceptably high. Despite its advantages, the SPM measure has not yet become the nation's official poverty measure, and it is not used to determine eligibility for aid from various government programs. Poverty data presented in the remainder of this chapter thus rely on the official measure rather than the SPM.

The official poverty line is adjusted annually for inflation and takes into account the number of people in a family: The larger the family size, the higher the poverty line. In 2019, the poverty line for a nonfarm family of four with two children was $25,750. A four-person family earning even one more dollar than $25,750 in 2019 was *not* officially poor, even though its "extra" income hardly lifted it out of dire economic straits. Poverty experts have calculated a no-frills budget that enables a family to meet its basic needs in food, clothing, shelter, and so forth; this budget is about twice the poverty line. Families with incomes between the poverty line and twice the poverty line (or *twice poverty*) are barely making ends meet, but they are not considered officially poor. When we talk here about the poverty level, then, keep in mind that we are talking only about *official* poverty and that there are many families and individuals living in near poverty who have trouble meeting their basic needs, especially when they face unusually high medical expenses, motor vehicle expenses, or the like. For this reason, many analysts think families need incomes twice as high as the federal poverty level just to get by (Shierholz, 2014).[11] They thus use *twice-poverty* data (i.e., family incomes below twice the poverty line) to provide a more accurate understanding of how many Americans face serious financial difficulties, even if they are not living in official poverty.

The measure of official poverty began in 1963 and stipulates that a family whose income is lower than three times the cost of a minimal diet is considered officially poor. This measure has not changed since 1963 even though family expenses have risen greatly in many areas.

Source: © Thinkstock

 ## How Poverty Is Measured in the United States

The measurement of poverty in the United States is primarily based on the cost of a minimal diet for a family. Because this measurement is faulty for several reasons, many poverty experts say that families need incomes at least twice as high as the federal poverty level to make ends meet.

View the video online at: http://www.youtube.com/embed/M6QSI_Ze9hE?rel=0

The Extent of Poverty

With this caveat in mind, how many Americans are poor? The U.S. Census Bureau gives us some answers that use the official measure of poverty developed in 1963. In 2017, 12.3 percent of the U.S. population, or 39.7 million Americans, lived in official poverty (Fontenot et al. 2018).[12] This percentage represented a decline from the recession that began in 2008 but was higher than the 1977 rate (see Figure 2.1). If we were winning the war on poverty in the 1960s (notice the sharp drop from 1959 to 1971 in Figure 2.1), since then poverty has fought us to a standstill. Even worse, the massive unemployment caused by the pandemic in spring 2020 threatened to drive up the poverty rate dramatically to its highest levels since the 1960s (DeParle 2020).[13]

FIGURE 2.1 U.S. Poverty, 1959–2017

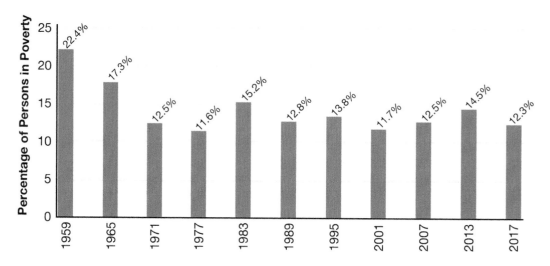

Source: Data from US Census Bureau. (2018). Historical poverty tables: People and Families-1959 to 2017. Retrieved from https://www.census.gov/data/tables/time-series/demo/income-poverty/historical-poverty-people.html.

episodic poverty

As defined by the Census Bureau, being poor for at least two consecutive months in some time period.

Another way of understanding the extent of poverty is to consider **episodic poverty**, defined by the Census Bureau as being poor for at least two consecutive months in some time period. About one-third of Americans live in episodic poverty at some point within a three-year period (Assari 2017).[14] As these figures indicate, people go into and out of poverty, but even those who go out of it do not usually move very far from it. And as we have seen, the majority of Americans can expect to experience poverty or near poverty at some point in their lives.

A final figure is worth noting. Recall that many poverty experts think that twice-poverty data—the percentage and number of people living in families with incomes below twice the official poverty level—are a better gauge than the official poverty level of the actual extent of poverty, broadly defined, in the United States. Using the twice-poverty threshold, nearly 30 percent of the U.S. population, or almost 96 million Americans, live in poverty or near poverty (Fontenot et al. 2018).[15] Those in near poverty are just one crisis—losing a job or sustaining a serious illness or injury—away from poverty. Twice-poverty data paint a very discouraging picture.

Key Takeaways

- The official poverty rate is based on the size of a family and a minimal food budget; this measure underestimates the true extent of poverty.

- The official poverty rate in 2017 was 12.3 percent, equal to nearly 40 million Americans.
- About one-third of the U.S. population, or more than 100 million Americans, have incomes no higher than twice the poverty line.

For Your Review

1. Write a short essay that summarizes the problems with how the official poverty rate is determined.
2. Sit down with some classmates and estimate what a family of four (two parents, two young children) in your area would have to pay annually for food, clothing, shelter, energy, and other necessities of life. What figure do you end up with? How does this sum of money compare with the official poverty line of $25,750 in 2019 for a family of four?

2.2 Who the Poor Are: Social Patterns of Poverty

Learning Objectives

1. Describe racial/ethnic differences in the poverty rate.
2. Discuss how family structure is related to the poverty rate.
3. Explain what poverty and labor force participation data imply about the belief that many poor people lack the motivation to work.

Who are the poor? Although the official poverty rate in 2017 was 12.3 percent, this rate differs by the important sociodemographic characteristics of race/ethnicity, gender, and age, and it also differs by region of the nation and by family structure. The poverty rate differences based on these variables are critical to understanding the nature and social patterning of poverty in the United States. We look at each of these variables in turn with 2017 census data (Fontenot et al. 2018).[16]

Race/Ethnicity

Here is a quick quiz; please circle the correct answer.

Most poor people in the United States are:

a. Asian

b. Black/African American

c. Latinx

d. Native American

e. White

What did you circle? If you are many people who answer a similar question in public opinion surveys, you would have circled "b. Black/African American." When Americans think about poor people, they tend to picture African Americans (Brown-Iannuzzi and Cooley 2019).[17] This popular image is thought to reduce the public's sympathy for poor people and to lead them to oppose increased government aid for the poor. The public's views on these matters are, in turn, thought to play a key role in government poverty policy. It is thus essential for the public to have an accurate understanding of the racial/ethnic patterning of poverty.

The most typical poor people in the United States are non-Latinx whites. These individuals comprise 42.8 percent of all poor Americans.

Source: De Visu/Shutterstock.com

Unfortunately, the public's racial image of poor people is mistaken, as census data reveal that *the most typical poor person is white (non-Latinx)*. To be more precise, 42.8 percent of poor people are white (non-Latinx), 27.2 percent are Latinx, 22.7 percent are black, and 4.9 percent are Asian (see Figure 2.2). As these figures show, non-Latinx whites certainly comprise the greatest number of the American poor. Turning these percentages into numbers, they account for 16.9 million of the 39.7 million poor Americans.

FIGURE 2.2 Racial and Ethnic Composition of the Poor, 2017 (Percentage of Poor Persons Who Belong to Each Group)

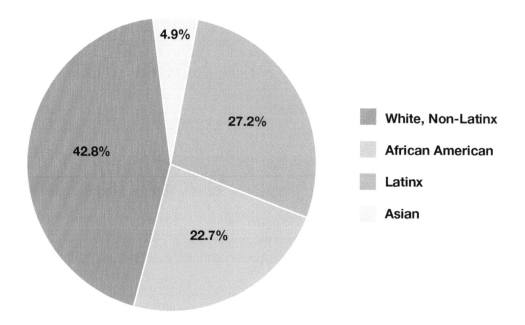

Source: Fontenot, Kayla, Jessica Semega and Melissa Kollar. 2018. *Income and Poverty in the United States: 2017*. Washington, DC: U.S. Census Bureau.

It is also true, though, that race and ethnicity affect the chances of being poor. While only 8.7 percent of non-Latinx whites are poor, 21.2 percent of African Americans, 10.0 percent of Asians, and 18.3 percent of Latinxs (who may be of any race) are poor (see Figure 2.3). Thus African Americans and Latinxs are more than twice as likely as non-Latinx whites to be poor. (Because there are so many non-Latinx whites in the United States, the greatest number of poor people are non-Latinx white, even if the percentage of whites who are poor is relatively low.) The higher poverty rates of people of color are so striking and important that they have been termed the "colors of poverty" (Lin and Harris, 2008).[18]

FIGURE 2.3 Race, Ethnicity, and Poverty, 2017 (Percentage of Each Group That Is Poor)

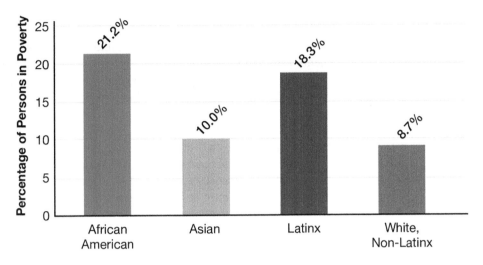

Source: Data from Fontenot, Kayla, Jessica Semega and Melissa Kollar. 2018. *Income and Poverty in the United States: 2017*. Washington, DC: U.S. Census Bureau.

 Poverty Rates Surge in American Suburbs

Contrary to popular belief, most poor people in the United States are white, rather than persons of color. However, a greater proportion of people of color are poor than of non-Latinx whites.

View the video online at: http://www.youtube.com/embed/9l7yjtKNOBk?rel=0

Gender

One thing that many women know all too well is that women are more likely than men to be poor. According to the census, 13.6 percent of all females live in poverty, compared to only 11.0 percent of all males. These figures translate to a large gender gap in the actual number of poor people, as 22.3 million women and girls live in poverty, compared to only 17.4 million men and boys, for a difference of 4.9 million people. The high rate of female poverty is called the *feminization of poverty* (Iceland 2013).[19] We will see additional evidence of this pattern when we look at the section on family structure that follows.

Age

Turning to age, 17.5 percent of children under age 18 (amounting to 12.8 million children) were poor in 2017, a figure that rises to 29 percent of African American children and 25 percent of Latinx children. More than one-third of all children live in poverty for at least one year before turning 18 (Ratcliffe 2015).[20] The *relative poverty rate* (living in households with incomes below 60 percent of a nation's median income) for U.S. children is the second-highest of all wealthy democracies and two to three times higher than several of these democracies (Brazier 2017).[21] As high as the U.S. childhood poverty rate is, twice-poverty data again paint an even more discouraging picture. Children living in families with incomes below twice the official poverty level are called *low-income children*, and their families are called *low-income families*. Almost 39 percent of American children, or some 28.4 million kids, lived in such families in 2017 (Fontenot et al. 2018).[22] In 2016, when 41 percent of all children lived in low-income families, 59 percent to 61 percent of African-American, Latinx, and Native American children lived in such families, compared to only 28 percent of non-Latinx white children (Koball and Jiang 2018).[23]

At the other end of the age distribution, 9.2 percent of people aged 65 or older were poor in 2017 (amounting to almost 4.7 million seniors). Turning around these age figures, 32 percent of all poor people in the United States are children, and 12 percent of the poor are 65 or older. Adding these figures, 44 percent of Americans living in poverty are children or the elderly.

The poverty rate for U.S. children is the highest in the Western world.

Source: © Thinkstock

Region

Poverty rates differ around the United States. Some states have higher poverty rates than other states, and some counties within a state are poorer than other counties within that state. A basic way of understanding geographical differences in poverty is to examine the poverty rates of the four major regions of the nation. When we do this, the South is the poorest region, with a poverty rate of 13.6 percent. The West is next at 11.8 percent, followed by both the Midwest and then Northeast at 11.4 percent. The South's historically higher poverty rate is thought to be an important reason for its high rate of illnesses and other health problems compared to the other regions (Maddock 2018).[24]

Family Structure

There are many types of family structures, including a married couple living with their children; an unmarried couple living with one or more children; a household with children headed by only one parent, usually a woman; a household with two adults and no children; and a household with only one adult living alone. Across the nation, poverty rates differ from one type of family structure to another.

Not surprisingly, poverty rates are higher in families with one adult than in those with two adults (because they often are bringing in two incomes), and, in one-adult families, they are higher in families headed by a woman than in those headed by a man (because women generally have lower incomes than men). Of all families headed by a woman only, 31.6 percent live in poverty, compared to only 15.8 percent of families headed by a man only. In contrast, only 6.2 percent of families headed by a married couple live in poverty (see Figure 2.4). The figure for female-headed families provides additional evidence for the feminization of poverty concept introduced earlier.

FIGURE 2.4 Family Structure and Poverty Rate, 2017 (Percentage of Each Type of Structure That Lives in Poverty)

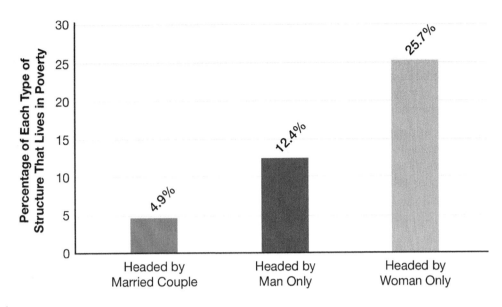

Source: Data from Fontenot, Kayla, Jessica Semega and Melissa Kollar. 2018. *Income and Poverty in the United States: 2017.* Washington, DC: U.S. Census Bureau.

We saw earlier that 22 percent of American children are poor. This figure varies according to the type of family structure in which the children live. Only 8.4 percent of children residing with married parents live in poverty, whereas 41 percent of those residing with only their mother live in poverty. This latter figure rises to 43 percent for African American children and 48 percent for Latinx children (Child Trends Databank 2019).[25]

Labor Force Status

As this chapter discusses later, many Americans think the poor are lazy and lack the motivation to work and, as is often said, "really could work if they wanted to." However, government data on the poor show that most poor people are, in fact, either working, unemployed but looking for work, or unable to work because of their age or health. Table 2.1 shows the relevant data. We discuss these numbers in some detail because of their importance, so please follow along carefully.

TABLE 2.1 Poverty and Labor Force Participation, 2017

Total number of poor people	39,698,000
Number of poor people under age 18	12,808,000
Number of poor people ages 65 and older	4,681,000
Number of poor people ages 18–64	22,209,000
Number of poor people ages 18–64 who were:	
Working full- or part-time	7,653,000
Unemployed but looking for work	1,440,000
Disabled	3,218,000
In the armed forces	33,000
Able-bodied but not in the labor force	9,866,000

Source: Data from US Census Bureau. 2018. Current population survey (CPS) table creator. Retrieved from http://www.census.gov/cps/data/cpstablecreator.html.

Let's examine this table to see the story it tells. Of the roughly 39.7 million poor people, almost 17.5 million were either under age 18 or at least 65. Because of their ages, we would not expect them to be working. Of the remaining 22.2 million poor adults ages 18–64, some 12.3 million, or more than 55 percent, fell into one of these categories: (a) they worked full-time or part-time, (b) they were unemployed but looking for work during a year of very high unemployment due to the nation's faltering economy, (c) they did not work because of a disability, or (d) they were in the armed forces. Subtracting all these adults leaves almost 9.9 million able-bodied people ages 18–64.

Doing some arithmetic, we thus see that almost 30 million of the 39.7 million poor people we started with, or three-fourths, were either working or unemployed but looking for work, too young or too old to work, disabled, or in the armed forces. It would thus be inaccurate to describe the vast majority of the poor as lazy and lacking the motivation to work.

What about the nearly 9.9 million able-bodied poor people who are ages 18–64 but not in the labor force, who compose only 25 percent of the poor to begin with? Like their non-poor counterparts, most of them were either taking care of small children or elderly parents or other relatives, retired for health reasons, or in school (Hipple 2015).[26] Others left the labor force out of frustration and did not look for work (and thus were not counted officially as unemployed). Taking all these numbers and categories into account, it turns out that the percentage of poor people who "really could work if they wanted to" is rather minuscule. A study of adults aged 18–59 who receive food stamps from the Supplemental Nutrition Assistance Program (SNAP) likewise found that three-fourths of them were either working at the time or soon after they receive SNAP help. Almost all of the remaining one-fourth were not working for one of the following reasons: (1) caring for family members; (2) chronic health problem; (3) can't find work; or (4) attending school (Keith-Jennings and Chaudhry 2018).[27] All this evidence strongly suggests that the common belief that the poor "really could work if they wanted to" is nothing more than a myth.

People Making a Difference

Building Bunk Beds for Kids Who Sleep on the Floor

Luke Mickelson, of Twin Falls, Idaho, was shocked to learn in 2012 that some children in his small city were so poor that they had to sleep on the floor. He built a bunk bed for one of these kids and later recalled, "This little girl had a nest of clothes, it looked like a little bird's nest. And that's what she slept on, that's what her bed was. When we delivered the bed, she hugged it and just couldn't let go." This experience led Mickelson to start a nonprofit effort, Sleep in Heavenly Peace, that builds beds for poor children. "I had no clue what the need was," he remembers. "There's kids next door whose parents are struggling just to put food on the table, clothes on their back, a roof over their head. A bed was just a luxury." Mickelson initially used his own money to buy wood and other items for the beds but then began receiving donations. His effort grew, and by late 2018 Sleep in Heavenly Peace had 65 chapters nationwide and had delivered more than 1,500 beds to poor kids across the nation. Along the way, Mickelson quit his job to work full-time on the beds, but ended up with another job for much less pay. "I found that the need I have isn't financial," he explained. "The need I have is seeing the joy on kids' faces, knowing that I can make a difference."

For more about Luke Mickelson's efforts, visit Sleep in Heavenly Peace at https://www.shpbeds.org/.[28]

Key Takeaways

- Although people of color have higher poverty rates than non-Latinx whites, the most typical poor person in the United States is non-Latinx white.

- The U.S. childhood poverty rate is the highest of all Western democracies.
- Labor force participation data indicate that the belief that poor people lack motivation to work is in fact a myth.

For Your Review

1. Why do you think the majority of Americans assume poor people lack the motivation to work?
2. Explain to a friend how labor force participation data indicate that it is inaccurate to think that poor people lack the motivation to work.

2.3 Explaining Poverty

Learning Objectives

1. Describe the assumptions of the functionalist and conflict views of stratification and poverty.
2. Explain the focus of symbolic interactionist work on poverty.
3. Understand the difference between the individualist and structural explanations of poverty.

Why does poverty exist, and why and how do poor people end up being poor? The sociological perspectives introduced in Chapter 1 provide some possible answers to these questions through their attempt to explain why American society is *stratified*—that is, why it has a range of wealth ranging from the extremely wealthy to the extremely poor. We review what these perspectives say generally about **social stratification** (rankings of people based on wealth and other resources a society values) before turning to explanations focusing specifically on poverty.

social stratification

Rankings of people based on wealth and other resources a society values.

In general, the functionalist perspective and conflict perspective both try to explain why social stratification exists and endures, while the symbolic interactionist perspective discusses the differences that stratification produces for everyday interaction. Table 2.2 summarizes these three approaches.

TABLE 2.2 Theory Snapshot

Theoretical perspective	Major assumptions
Functionalism	Stratification is necessary to induce people with special intelligence, knowledge, and skills to enter the most important occupations. For this reason, stratification is necessary and inevitable.
Conflict theory	Stratification results from lack of opportunity and from discrimination and prejudice against the poor, women, and people of color. It is neither necessary nor inevitable.
Symbolic interactionism	Stratification affects people's beliefs, lifestyles, daily interaction, and conceptions of themselves.

The Functionalist View

As discussed in Chapter 1, functionalist theory assumes that society's structures and processes exist because they serve important functions for society's stability and continuity. In line with this view, functionalist theorists in sociology assume that stratification exists because it also serves important functions for society. This explanation was developed more than sixty years ago by Kingsley Davis and Wilbert Moore (1945)[29] in the form of several logical assumptions that imply stratification is both necessary and inevitable. When applied to American society, their assumptions would be as follows:

1. *Some jobs are more important than other jobs.* For example, the job of a brain surgeon is more important than the job of shoe shining.

2. *Some jobs require more skills and knowledge than other jobs.* To stay with our example, it takes more skills and knowledge to perform brain surgery than to shine shoes.

3. *Relatively few people have the ability to acquire the skills and knowledge that are needed to do these important, highly skilled jobs.* Most of us would be able to do a decent job of shining shoes, but very few of us would be able to become brain surgeons.

4. *To encourage the people with the skills and knowledge to do the important, highly skilled jobs, society must promise them higher incomes or other rewards.* If this is true, some people automatically end up higher in society's ranking system than others, and stratification is thus necessary and inevitable.

To illustrate their assumptions, say we have a society where shining shoes and doing brain surgery both give us incomes of $300,000 per year. (This example is *very* hypothetical, but please keep reading.) If you decide to shine shoes, you can begin making this money at age 16, but if you decide to become a brain surgeon, you will not start making this same amount until about age 35, as you must first go to college and medical school and then acquire several more years of medical training. While you have spent nineteen additional years beyond age 16 getting this education and training and taking out tens of thousands of dollars in student loans, you could have spent those years shining shoes and making $300,000 a year, or $5.7 million overall. Which job would you choose?

Functional theory argues that the promise of very high incomes is necessary to encourage talented people to pursue important careers such as surgery. If physicians and shoe shiners made the same high income, would enough people decide to become physicians?

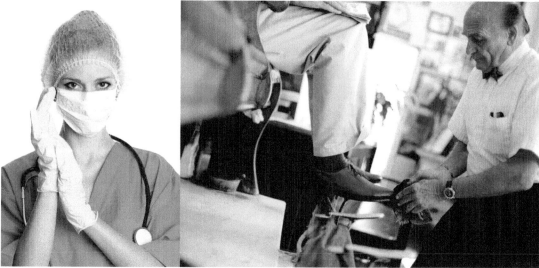

Source: © Thinkstock

As this example suggests, many people might not choose to become brain surgeons unless considerable financial and other rewards awaited them. By extension, we might not have enough people filling society's important jobs unless they know they will be similarly rewarded. If this is true, we must have stratification. And if we must have stratification, then that means some people will have much less money than other people. If stratification is inevitable, then poverty is also inevitable. The functionalist view further implies that if people are poor, it is because they do not have the ability to acquire the skills and knowledge necessary for the important, high-paying jobs.

The functionalist view sounds very logical, but a few years after Davis and Moore published their theory, other sociologists pointed out some serious problems in their argument (Tumin 1953; Wrong 1959).[30]

First, it is difficult to compare the importance of many types of jobs. For example, which job is more important, doing brain surgery or collecting trash? Although you might be tempted to answer "brain surgery," if no trash were ever collected, then our nation would be in considerable trouble. In another example, which job is more important, attorney or professor? (Be careful how you answer this one!)

Second, the functionalist explanation implies that the most important jobs have the highest incomes and the least important jobs the lowest incomes, but many examples, including the ones just mentioned, counter this view. Trash collectors make much less money than physicians, and professors, for better or worse, earn much less on the average than lawyers. A professional athlete making millions of dollars a year earns many times the income of the president of the United States, but who is more important to the nation? Elementary school teachers do a very important job in our society, but their salaries are much lower than those of sports agents, advertising executives, and many other people whose jobs are far less essential.

Third, the functionalist view assumes that people move up the economic ladder based on their abilities, skills, knowledge, and, more generally, their merit. This implies that if they do not move up the ladder, they lack the necessary merit. However, this view ignores the fact that much of our stratification stems from lack of equal opportunity. As later chapters in this book discuss, because of their race, ethnicity, gender, and class standing at birth, some people have less opportunity than others to acquire the skills and training they need to fill the types of jobs addressed by the functionalist approach.

Finally, the functionalist explanation might make sense up to a point, but it does not justify the extremes of wealth and poverty found in the United States. Even if we do have to promise higher incomes to get enough people to become physicians, does that mean we also need the amount of poverty we have? Do CEOs of corporations really need to make millions of dollars per year to get enough qualified people to become CEOs? Do people take on a position as CEO or other high-paying job at least partly because of the challenge, working conditions, and other positive aspects they offer? The functionalist view does not answer these questions adequately.

One other line of functionalist thinking focuses more directly on poverty than generally on stratification. This particular functionalist view provocatively argues that poverty exists because it serves certain positive functions for our society. These functions include the following: (1) poor people do the work that other people do not want to do; (2) the programs that help poor people provide a lot of jobs for the people employed by the programs; (3) the poor purchase goods, such as day-old bread and used clothing, that other people do not wish to purchase, and thus extend the economic value of these goods; and (4) the poor do housekeeping and other jobs (e.g., mowing lawns and gardening) for wealthy families and individuals, which frees up these parties' time for other activities (Gans 1972).[31] Because poverty serves all these functions and more, according to this argument, the middle and upper classes have a vested interested in neglecting poverty to help ensure its continued existence.

The Conflict View

Conflict theory's explanation of stratification draws on Karl Marx's view of class societies and incorporates the critique of the functionalist view just discussed. Many different explanations grounded in conflict theory exist, but they all assume that stratification stems from a fundamental conflict between the needs and interests of the powerful, or "haves," in society and those of the weak, or "have-nots" (Hurst et al. 2019).[32] The former take advantage of their position at the top of society to stay at the top, even if it means oppressing those at the bottom. At a minimum, they can heavily influence the law, the media, and other institutions in a way that maintains society's class structure.

In general, conflict theory attributes stratification and thus poverty to lack of opportunity from discrimination and prejudice against the poor, women, and people of color. In this regard, it reflects one of the early critiques of the functionalist view that the previous section outlined, and it counters the popular belief that the poor are to blame for their poverty. To reiterate an earlier point, several of the remaining chapters of this book discuss the various obstacles that make it difficult for the poor, women, and people of color in the United States to move up the socioeconomic ladder and to otherwise enjoy healthy and productive lives.

Because he was born in a log cabin and later became president, Abraham Lincoln's life epitomizes the American Dream, which is the belief that people born into poverty can become successful through hard work. The popularity of this belief leads many Americans to blame poor people for their poverty.

Source: U.S. Library of Congress, http://www.loc.gov/pictures/resource/cph.3a53289.

Symbolic Interactionism

Consistent with its micro orientation, symbolic interactionism tries to understand stratification and thus poverty by looking at people's interactions and understandings in their daily lives. Unlike the functionalist and conflict views, it does not try to explain why we have stratification in the first place. Rather, it examines the differences that stratification makes for people's lifestyles and their interaction with other people.

Many detailed, insightful sociological books on the lives of the urban and rural poor reflect the symbolic interactionist perspective (Desmond 2016; Liebow, 1993; Miller 2008; Rios 2011).[33] These books focus on different people in different places, but they all make very clear that the poor often lead lives of quiet desperation, that they must find ways of coping with being poor, and, especially if they are of color, that they must deal with policing in their daily lives. In these books, the consequences of poverty discussed later in this chapter acquire a human face, and readers learn in great detail what it is like to be poor everyday.

Some classic journalistic accounts by authors not trained in the social sciences also present eloquent descriptions of poor people's lives (Bagdikian 1964; Harrington 1962).[34] Writing in this tradition, a newspaper columnist who grew up in poverty has recalled, "I know the feel of thick calluses on the bottom of shoeless feet. I know the bite of the cold breeze that slithers through a drafty house. I know the weight of constant worry over not having enough to fill a belly or fight an illness... Poverty is brutal, consuming and unforgiving. It strikes at the soul" (Blow 2011:A19).[35]

Sociological accounts of the poor provide a vivid portrait of what it is like to live in poverty on a daily basis.

Source: © Thinkstock

Specific Explanations of Poverty

The functionalist and conflict views focus broadly on social stratification but only indirectly on poverty. When poverty finally attracted national attention during the 1960s, scholars began to try specifically to understand why poor people become poor and remain poor. Two competing explanations developed, with the basic debate turning on whether poverty arises from problems either within the poor themselves or in the society in which they live (Rank 2011).[36] The first type of explanation follows logically from the functional theory of stratification and may be considered an individualistic explanation. The second type of explanation follows from conflict theory and is a structural explanation that focuses on problems in American society that produce poverty. Table 2.3 summarizes these explanations.

TABLE 2.3 Explanations of Poverty

Explanation	Major assumptions
Individualistic	Poverty results from the fact that poor people lack the motivation to work and have certain beliefs and values that contribute to their poverty.
Structural	Poverty results from problems in society that lead to a lack of opportunity and a lack of jobs.

It is critical to determine which explanation makes more sense because, as sociologist Theresa C. Davidson (2009:136)[37] observed, "beliefs about the causes of poverty shape attitudes toward the poor." To be more precise, the particular explanation that people favor affects their view of government efforts to help the poor. Those who attribute poverty to problems in the larger society are much more likely than those who attribute it to deficiencies among the poor to believe that the government should do more to help the poor (Osborne and Weiner 2015).[38] The explanation for poverty we favor presumably affects the amount of sympathy we have for the poor, and our sympathy, or lack of sympathy, in turn affects our views about the government's role in helping the poor. With this backdrop in mind, what do the individualistic and structural explanations of poverty say?

Individualistic Explanation

According to the **individualistic explanation**, the poor have personal problems and deficiencies that are responsible for their poverty. In the past, the poor were thought to be biologically inferior, a wrongheaded view that has not entirely faded, but today the much more common belief is that they lack the ambition and motivation to work hard and to achieve success. According to survey evidence, one-fifth to more than one-third of Americans, depending on how the question is asked, hold this belief (Door et al. 2016).[39] A more sophisticated version of this type of explanation is called the *culture of poverty* theory (Banfield 1974; Lewis 1966; Murray 2012).[40] According to this theory, the poor generally have beliefs and values that differ from those of the nonpoor and that doom them to continued poverty. For example, they are said to be impulsive and to live for the present rather than the future.

individualistic explanation of poverty

The belief that poor people are poor because they lack the motivation to work and have other failings.

Regardless of which version one might hold, the individualistic explanation is a blaming-the-victim approach (see Chapter 1). Critics say this explanation ignores discrimination and other problems in American society and exaggerates the degree to which the poor and nonpoor do in fact hold different values (Assari 2017; Holland 2011).[41] Regarding the latter point, they note that poor employed adults often work more hours per week than wealthier adults and that poor parents interviewed in surveys value education for their children at least as much as wealthier parents. These and other similarities in values and beliefs lead critics of the individualistic explanation to conclude that poor people's poverty cannot reasonably be said to result from a culture of poverty.

Structural Explanation

structural explanation of poverty

The belief that poor people are poor because of various kinds of discrimination and lack of jobs and opportunity.

According to the **structural explanation**, which is a blaming-the-system approach, U.S. poverty stems from problems in American society that lead to a lack of equal opportunity and a lack of jobs. These problems include (a) racial, ethnic, gender, and age discrimination; (b) lack of good schooling and adequate health care; and (c) structural changes in the American economic system, such as the departure of manufacturing companies from American cities in the 1980s and 1990s, that led to the loss of thousands of jobs. These problems help create a vicious cycle of poverty in which children of the poor are often fated to end up in poverty or near poverty themselves as adults.

As Rank (2011:18)[42] summarized this view, "American poverty is largely the result of failings at the economic and political levels, rather than at the individual level... In contrast to [the individualistic] perspective, the basic problem lies in a shortage of viable opportunities for all Americans." Rank points out that the U.S. economy during the past few decades has created more low-paying and part-time jobs and jobs without benefits, meaning that Americans increasingly find themselves in jobs that barely lift them out of poverty, if at all. Sociologist Fred Block and colleagues share this critique of the individualistic perspective: "Most of our policies incorrectly assume that people can avoid or overcome poverty through hard work alone. Yet this assumption ignores the realities of our failing urban schools, increasing employment insecurities, and the lack of affordable housing, health care, and child care. It ignores the fact that the American Dream is rapidly becoming unattainable for an increasing number of Americans, whether employed or not" (Block et al.:17).[43]

Most sociologists favor the structural explanation. As later chapters in this book discuss, racial and ethnic discrimination, lack of adequate schooling and health care, and other problems make it difficult to rise out of poverty. On the other hand, some ethnographic research supports the individualistic explanation by showing that the poor do have certain values and follow certain practices that augment their plight (Small et al. 2010).[44] For example, the poor have higher rates of cigarette smoking (Centers for Disease Control and Prevention, 2019),[45] which leads them to have more serious health problems.

Adopting an integrated perspective, some researchers say these values and practices are ultimately the result of poverty itself (Small et al. 2010).[46] These scholars concede a culture of poverty does exist, but they also say it exists because it helps the poor cope daily with the structural effects of being poor. If these effects lead to a culture of poverty, they add, poverty then becomes self-perpetuating. If poverty is both cultural and structural in origin, these scholars say, efforts to improve the lives of people in the "other America" must involve increased structural opportunities for the poor and changes in some of their values and practices.

Key Takeaways

- According to the functionalist view, stratification is a necessary and inevitable consequence of the need to use the promise of financial reward to encourage talented people to pursue important jobs and careers.
- According to conflict theory, stratification results from lack of opportunity and discrimination against the poor and people of color.
- According to symbolic interactionism, social class affects how people interact in everyday life and how they view certain aspects of the social world.
- The individualistic view attributes poverty to individual failings of poor people themselves, while the structural view attributes poverty to problems in the larger society.

1. In explaining poverty in the United States, which view, individualist or structural, makes more sense to you? Why?
2. Suppose you could wave a magic wand and invent a society where everyone had about the same income no matter which job he or she performed. Do you think it would be difficult to persuade enough people to become physicians or to pursue other important careers? Explain your answer.

2.4 The Consequences of Poverty

1. Describe the family and housing problems associated with poverty.
2. Explain how poverty affects health and educational attainment.

Regardless of its causes, poverty has devastating consequences for the people who live in it. Much research conducted and/or analyzed by scholars, government agencies, and nonprofit organizations has documented the effects of poverty (and near poverty) on the lives of the poor (Duncan and Le Menestrel 2019; Duncan et al. 2017; Hinojosa et al. 2019; Murphy and Redd 2014; Ratcliffe, 2015).[47] Many of these studies focus on childhood poverty, which has lifelong consequences. In general, poor children are more likely to be poor as adults, more likely to drop out of high school, more likely to become a teenaged parent, and more likely to have employment problems. Although only 1 percent of children who are never poor end up being poor as young adults, 32 percent of poor children end up poor as young adults (Ratcliffe and McKernan 2010).[48]

A compelling study used government data to follow children born between 1968 and 1975 until they were ages 30 to 37 (Duncan and Magnuson, 2011).[49] The researchers compared individuals who lived in poverty in early childhood to those whose families had incomes at least twice the poverty line in early childhood. Compared to the latter group, adults who were poor in early childhood:

- had completed two fewer years of schooling on the average;
- had incomes that were less than half of those earned by adults who had wealthier childhoods;
- received $826 more annually in food stamps on the average;
- were almost three times more likely to report being in poor health;
- were twice as likely to have been arrested (males only); and
- were five times as likely to have borne a child (females only).

We expand on some of the major specific consequences of poverty here and will return to them in later chapters.

Poor children are more likely to have inadequate nutrition and to experience health, behavioral, and cognitive problems.

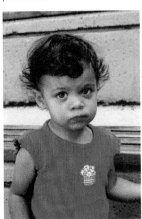

Source: © Thinkstock

Family Problems

The poor are at greater risk for family problems, including divorce and domestic violence. A major reason for these problems is stress. Even in families that are not poor, running a household can cause stress, children can cause stress, and paying the bills can cause stress. These ordinary stresses of family life become even more intense in poor families. Partly as a result, the various kinds of problems that families experience thus happen more commonly in poor families than in wealthier families. Compounding this situation, when these problems occur, poor families have fewer resources than wealthier families to deal with these problems.

Children and Our Future

Getting under Children's Skin: The Biological Effects of Childhood Poverty

As the text discusses, childhood poverty often has lifelong consequences. Poor children are more likely to be poor when they become adults, and they are at greater risk for antisocial behavior when young, and for unemployment, criminal behavior, and other problems when they reach adolescence and young adulthood.

According to growing evidence, one reason poverty has these consequences is that it has certain neural effects on poor children that impair their cognitive abilities and thus their behavior and learning potential. As Greg J. Duncan and Katherine Magnuson (2011:23)[50] observe, "Emerging research in neuroscience and developmental psychology suggests that poverty early in a child's life may be particularly harmful because the astonishingly rapid development of young children's brains leaves them sensitive (and vulnerable) to environmental conditions."

In short, poverty can change the way the brain develops in young children. The major reason for this effect is continuous high levels of stress, called *toxic stress*. Children growing up in poverty experience multiple stressful events: neighborhood crime and drug use; divorce, parental conflict, and other family problems, including abuse and neglect by their parents; parental financial problems and unemployment; physical and mental health problems of one or more family members; and so forth. These problems are called *adverse childhood experiences* (ACEs). The levels of toxic stress caused by ACEs in turn affect children's bodies in certain harmful ways. As two poverty scholars note, "These deep, enduring, and sometimes irreversible physiological changes are the very human price of running a high-poverty society" (Grusky and Wimer 2011:2).[51]

One way poverty gets "under children's skin" is as follows (Duncan and Le Menestrel 2019; Evans et al. 2011; Francis et al. 2018).[52] Poor children's high levels of stress produce unusually high levels of stress hormones such as cortisol and higher levels of blood pressure. Because these high levels impair their neural development, their memory and language development skills suffer, which in turn harms their behavior and learning potential. For other physiological reasons, high levels of stress also affect the immune system, so that poor children are more likely to develop various illnesses during childhood and to have high blood pressure and other health problems when they grow older. Other biological changes also occur that make poor children more likely to end up being obese and to have drug and alcohol problems.

The policy implications of the scientific research on childhood poverty are clear: Every effort should be made to reduce childhood poverty and to reduce its many effects on children's outcomes (Duncan and Le Menestrel 2019; Shonkoff 2011).[53] These efforts include: (1) promoting strong, stable relationships among all members of poor families; (2) improving the quality of the home and neighborhood physical environments in which poor children grow up; (3) improving the nutrition of poor children; and (4) providing free or heavily subsidized childcare and more generous income transfers to poor families with young children, as many Western Europe democracies already do. The scientific evidence on early childhood poverty underscores the importance of doing everything possible to reduce the harmful effects of poverty during the first few years of life.

Health, Illness, and Medical Care

The poor are also more likely to have many kinds of health problems, including infant mortality, earlier adulthood mortality, and mental illness, and they are also more likely to receive inadequate medical care. Poor children are more likely to have inadequate nutrition and, partly for this reason, to suffer health, behavioral, and cognitive problems. These problems in turn impair their ability to do well in school and land stable employment as adults, helping to ensure that poverty will persist across generations. Despite the passage of the 2010 Affordable Care Act, many poor people remain uninsured or underinsured. Regardless of insurance status, many poor families have no choice but to visit health clinics that are overcrowded and understaffed. All these problems mean that poverty may be a matter of life and death. According to some research, poverty is responsible for almost 150,000 deaths annually, a figure about equal to the number of deaths from lung cancer (Bakalar, 2011).[54]

 ## How Poverty Can Affect Health

Poor people tend to have higher rates of many health problems. Some research even finds that poverty contributes to almost 150,000 deaths of Americans every year.

View the video online at: http://www.youtube.com/embed/_kS1oy64EiM?rel=0

The situation of low-income Americans after the coronavirus pandemic hit the United States in early 2020 exposed the risk to health that poverty poses. To be more precise, there was alarming evidence that low-income Americans were contracting and dying from COVID-19 at higher rates than wealthier Americans. To poverty and health experts, this situation was not surprising. As a United Nations poverty expert explained, poor people "are more likely to work in jobs with a high risk of exposure, live in crowded and insecure housing, reside in neighbourhoods that are more vulnerable because of air pollution, and lack access to healthcare. . . . This is a moment to re-evaluate failing health, housing and social support systems that have made this crisis especially painful for the less well-off" (UN News 2020).[55]

It is unclear how much of poor people's worse health stems from their lack of money and lack of good health care versus their own behavior such as smoking and eating unhealthy diets (Barkan 2021).[56] Regardless of the exact reasons, however, the fact remains that poor health is a major consequence of poverty.

Education

Poor children typically go to rundown schools with inadequate facilities where they receive inadequate schooling. They are much less likely than wealthier children to graduate from high school or to go to college. Their lack of education in turn restricts them and their own children to poverty, once again helping to ensure a vicious cycle of continuing poverty across generations. Scholars debate whether the poor school performance of poor children stems more from the inadequacy of their schools and schooling versus their own poverty. Regardless of exactly why poor children are more likely to do poorly in school and to have low educational attainment, these educational problems are another major consequence of poverty.

Housing and Homelessness

The poor are, not surprisingly, more likely to be homeless than the nonpoor but also more likely to live in dilapidated housing and unable to buy their own homes. Many poor families spend more than half their income on rent, and they tend to live in poor neighborhoods that lack job opportunities, good schools, and other features of modern life that wealthier people take for granted; many of them face eviction for failure to pay rent or other reasons (Desmond 2016).[57] The lack of adequate housing for the poor remains a major national problem. Even worse is outright homelessness. Homelessness is notoriously difficult to measure, but at least 1.6 million people, including more than 300,000 children, are estimated to be homeless at least part of every year, with some estimates 2-3 times these numbers (Lee et al. 2010).[58]

Crime and Victimization

Poor (and near poor) people commit the bulk of our street crime (homicide, robbery, burglary, etc.), and they also account for the bulk of victims of street crime. Chapter 8 outlines several reasons for this dual connection between poverty and street crime, but they include the deep frustration and stress of living in poverty and the fact that many poor people live in high-crime neighborhoods. In such neighborhoods, children are more likely to grow up under the influence of older peers who are already in gangs or otherwise committing crime, and people of any age are more likely to become crime victims. Moreover, because poor and near-poor people are more likely to commit street crime, they also comprise most of the people arrested for street crimes, convicted of street crime, and imprisoned for street crime. Most of the almost 2 million people now in the nation's prisons and jails come from poor or near-poor backgrounds. Criminal behavior and criminal victimization, then, are other major consequences of poverty.

Lessons from Other Societies

Poverty and Poverty Policy in Other Western Democracies

To compare international poverty rates, scholars commonly use a measure of the percentage of households in a nation that receive less than 50 percent or 60 percent (depending on the study) of the nation's median household income after taxes and cash transfers from the government. In data from the 2015-2018, 17.8 percent of U.S. households lived in poverty as defined by this measure. By comparison, other Western democracies had the rates depicted in the figure that follows. The average poverty rate of the nations in the figure, excluding the United States, is 10.2 percent. The U.S. rate was thus 1.7 times higher than the average for all the other democracies.

Why is there so much more poverty in the United States than in its Western counterparts? Two major differences between the United States and the other nations stand out (Russell 2018).[59] First, other Western nations have higher minimum wages and stronger labor unions than the United States has, and these lead to incomes that help push people out of poverty. Second, these other nations spend a much greater proportion of their gross domestic product on social expenditures (income support and social services such as child-care subsidies and housing allowances) than does the United States.

The experience of the United Kingdom provides a striking contrast between the effectiveness of the expansive approach used in other wealthy democracies and the inadequacy of the American approach. In 1994, about 30 percent of British children lived in poverty; by 2009, that figure had fallen by more than half to 12 percent. Meanwhile, the U.S. 2009 child poverty rate, was almost 21 percent.

This graph illustrates the poverty rates in western democracies (i.e., the percentage of persons living with less than half of the median household income) as of 2015-2018.

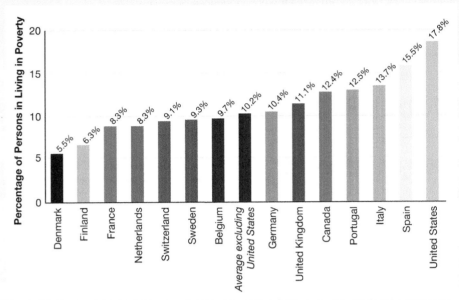

Source: Data from Organisation for Co-Operation and Economic Development (OECD). 2019. Income Distribution and Poverty. Retrieved July 13, 2019 from https://stats.oecd.org/Index.aspx?DataSetCode=IDD.

Britain used three strategies to reduce its child poverty rate and to help poor children and their families in other ways. First, it induced more poor parents to work through a series of new measures, including a national minimum wage higher than its U.S. counterpart and various tax savings for low-income workers. Because of these measures, the percentage of single parents who worked rose from 45 percent in 1997 to 57 percent in 2008. Second, Britain increased child welfare benefits regardless of whether a parent worked. Third, it increased paid maternity leave from four months to nine months, implemented two weeks of paid paternity leave, established universal preschool (which both helps children's cognitive abilities and makes it easier for parents to afford to work), increased child-care aid, and made it possible for parents of young children to adjust their working hours to their parental responsibilities (Waldfogel 2010).[60] While the British child poverty rate fell dramatically because of these strategies, the U.S. child poverty rate stagnated.

In short, the United States has so much more poverty than other democracies in part because it spends so much less than they do on helping the poor. The United States certainly has the wealth to follow their example, but it has chosen not to do so, and a high poverty rate is the unfortunate result.

Key Takeaways

- Poor people are more likely to have several kinds of family problems, including divorce and family conflict.
- Poor people are more likely to have several kinds of health problems, including higher rates of and deaths from COVID-19.
- Children growing up in poverty are less likely to graduate high school or go to college, and they are more likely to commit street crime.

For Your Review

1. Write a brief essay that summarizes the consequences of poverty.
2. Why do you think poor children are more likely to develop health problems?

2.5 Global Poverty

Learning Objectives

1. Describe where poor nations tend to be located.
2. Explain the difference between the modernization and dependency theories of poverty.
3. List some of the consequences of global poverty.

As serious as poverty is in the United States, poverty in much of the rest of the world is beyond comprehension to the average American. Many of the world's poor live in such desperate circumstances that they would envy the lives of poor Americans. Without at all meaning to minimize the plight of the American poor, this section provides a brief look at the world's poor and at the dimensions of global poverty.

Global Inequality

The world has a few very rich nations and many very poor nations, and there is an enormous gulf between these two extremes. If the world were one nation, its per-capita median annual income (at which half of the world's population is below this income and half is above it) would be only $2,791 (projections for 2015; Dikhanov 2005).[61] The richest 1 percent of the world's population would account for 47 percent of the world's household wealth, and an annual income of $32,400 (which is barely above the U.S. poverty line for a family of four) would rank someone in the top 1 percent of the world's population.[62]

In related numbers, the richest fifth of the world's population would have almost three-fourths of the world's entire income, while the poorest fifth of the world's population would have only 1.8 percent of the world's income, and the poorest two-fifths would have only 6 percent of the world's income (Dikhanov 2005).[63] According to the World Bank (2018),[64] 10 percent of the world's population, equivalent to 736 million people, live in extreme poverty, defined as per-capita income under $1.90 per day. The remaining 30 percent of the poorest two-fifths are not officially poor by this definition, but they are still very poor. As Figure 2.5 illustrates, the distribution of the world's income resembles a champagne glass.

FIGURE 2.5 Global Income Distribution, 2015 Projections (Percentage of World Income Held by Each Fifth of World Population)

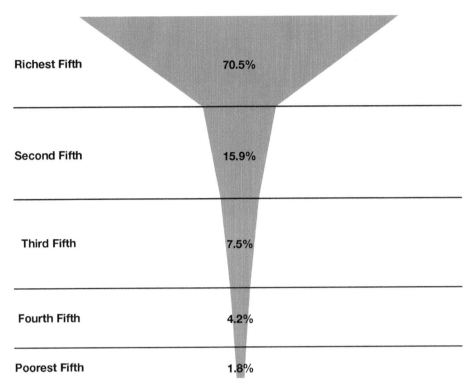

Richest Fifth	70.5%
Second Fifth	15.9%
Third Fifth	7.5%
Fourth Fifth	4.2%
Poorest Fifth	1.8%

Source: Data from Dikhanov, Yuri. 2005. Trends in Global Income Distribution, 1970–2000, and Scenarios for 2015. New York, NY: United Nations Development Programme.

To understand global inequality, it is helpful to classify nations into a small number of categories based on their degree of wealth or poverty, their level of industrialization and economic development, and related factors. Over the decades, scholars and international organizations such as the United Nations and the World Bank have used various classification systems, or typologies. A popular typology today simply ranks nations into groups called *wealthy*, or *high-income*, nations, *middle-income* nations, and *poor*, or *low-income*, nations. This ranking is based on measures such as **gross domestic product (GDP)** per capita, the total value of a nation's goods and services divided by its population. This typology has the advantage of emphasizing the most important variable in global stratification: how much wealth a nation has. At the risk of being somewhat simplistic, the other important differences among the world's nations all stem from their degree of wealth or poverty. Figure 2.6 depicts these three categories of nations (with the middle category divided into upper-middle and lower-middle). As should be clear, whether a nation is wealthy, middle income, or poor is heavily related to the continent on which it is found.

gross domestic product (GDP)

The total value of a nation's goods and services divided by its population.

FIGURE 2.6 Global Stratification Map (the World by Income)

The World Bank's income classifications split countries into one of four categories determined by the country's gross national income (GNI) per capita in US$. The GNI thresholds between income groups has changed through time based on World Bank definitions.

Source: Our World in Data. "World Bank's Income Groups, 2016." Retrieved from: https://ourworldindata.org/grapher/world-banks-income-groups?year=latest. Courtesy Our World in Data via Creative Commons Attribution 4.0 International (CC BY 4.0) license: https://creativecommons.org/licenses/by/4.0/deed.en_US.

Measuring Global Poverty

How do we know which nations are poor? A very common measure of global poverty was developed by the World Bank, an international institution funded by wealthy nations that provides loans, grants, and other aid to help poor and middle-income nations. Each year the World Bank publishes its World Development Report, which provides statistics and other information on the economic and social well-being of the globe's almost two hundred nations. As just noted, the World Bank puts the official global poverty line (which is considered a measure of extreme poverty) at income under $1.90 per person per day, which amounts to about $694 yearly per person or $2,774 for a family of four. Although "only" 10 percent of the world's population is officially poor by this definition, this level of poverty rises to 41 percent in sub-Saharan Africa (World Bank 2018).[65]

vulnerability to poverty

A significant probability that people who are not officially poor will become poor within the next year.

The World Bank (2016)[66] also emphasizes the concept of **vulnerability to poverty**, which refers to a significant probability that people who are not officially poor will become poor within the next year. Determining vulnerability to poverty is important because it enables antipoverty strategies to be aimed at those most at risk for sliding into poverty, with the hope of preventing them from doing so. Many of the people in the bottom two-fifths of the world's population are vulnerable in this way. This fact has led the World Bank (Haughton and Khandker 2009:246)[67] to observe, "As typically defined, vulnerability to poverty is more widespread than poverty itself. A wide swathe of society risks poverty at some point of time; put another way, in most societies, only a relatively modest portion of society may be considered as economically secure."

The World Bank has begun to emphasize vulnerability to poverty. Many people who are not officially poor have a good chance of becoming poor within a year. Strategies to prevent this from happening are a major focus of the World Bank.

Source: Yury Birukov/Shuttertstock.com

Explaining Global Poverty

Explanations of global poverty parallel those of U.S. poverty in their focus on individualistic versus structural problems. One type of explanation takes an individualistic approach by, in effect, blaming the people in the poorest nations for their own poverty, while a second explanation takes a structural approach in blaming the plight of poor nations on their treatment by the richest ones. Table 2.4 summarizes the two sets of explanations.

TABLE 2.4 Theory Snapshot

Theory	Major assumptions
Modernization theory	Wealthy nations became wealthy because early on they were able to develop the necessary beliefs, values, and practices for trade, industrialization, and rapid economic growth to occur. Poor nations remained poor because they failed to develop these beliefs, values, and practices; instead, they continued to follow traditional beliefs and practices that stymied industrial development and modernization.
Dependency theory	The poverty of poor nations stems from their colonization by European nations, which exploited the poor nations' resources and either enslaved their populations or used them as cheap labor. The colonized nations were thus unable to develop a professional and business class that would have enabled them to enter the industrial age and to otherwise develop their economies.

Modernization Theory

The individualistic explanation is called **modernization theory** (Rostow 1990).[68] According to this theory, rich nations became wealthy because early on they were able to develop the "correct" beliefs, values, and practices—in short, the correct culture—for trade, industrialization, and rapid economic growth to occur. These cultural traits include a willingness to work hard, to abandon tradition in favor of new ways of thinking and doing things, and to adopt a future orientation rather than one focused on maintaining present conditions. Thus Western European nations began to emerge several centuries ago as economic powers because their populations adopted the kinds of values and practices just listed. In contrast, nations in other parts of the world never became wealthy and remain poor today because they never developed the appropriate values and practices. Instead, they continued to follow traditional beliefs and practices that stymied industrial development and modernization.

According to modernization theory, poor nations are poor because their people never developed values such as an emphasis on hard work.

Source: © Thinkstock

Modernization theory has much in common with the culture of poverty theory discussed earlier. It attributes the poverty of poor nations to their failure to develop the "proper" beliefs, values, and practices necessary for economic success both at the beginning of industrialization during the nineteenth century and in the two centuries that have since transpired. Because modernization theory implies that people in poor nations do not have the talent and ability to improve their lot, it may be considered a functionalist explanation of global inequality.

Dependency Theory

The structural explanation for global stratification is called **dependency theory**, which may be considered a conflict explanation of global inequality. Not surprisingly, this theory's views sharply challenge modernization theory's assumptions (Packenham 1992).[69] Whereas modernization theory attributes global stratification to the "wrong" cultural values and practices in poor nations, dependency theory blames global stratification on the exploitation of these nations by wealthy nations. According to this view, poor nations never got the chance to pursue economic growth because early on they were conquered and colonized by European ones. The European nations stole the poor nations' resources and either enslaved their populations or used them as cheap labor. They installed their own governments and often prevented the local populace from getting a good education. As a result, the colonized nations were unable to develop a professional and business class that would have enabled them to enter the industrial age and to otherwise develop their economies. Along the way, wealthy nations sold their own goods to colonized nations and forced them to run up enormous debt that continues to amount today.

In today's world, huge multinational corporations continue to exploit the labor and resources of the poorest nations, say dependency theorists. These corporations run sweatshops in many nations, in which workers toil in inhumane conditions at extremely low wages (Williams 2020).[70] Often the corporations work hand-in-hand with corrupt officials in the poor nations to strengthen their economic stake in the countries.

Comparing the Theories

Which makes more sense, modernization theory or dependency theory? As with many theories, both make sense to some degree, but both have their faults. Modernization theory places too much blame on poor nations for their own poverty and ignores the long history of exploitation of poor nations by rich nations and multinational corporations alike. For its part, dependency theory cannot explain why some of the poorest countries are poor even though they were never European colonies; neither can it explain why some former colonies such as Hong Kong have been able to attain enough economic growth to leave the rank of the poorest nations. Together, both theories help us understand the reasons for global stratification, but most sociologists would probably favor dependency theory because of its emphasis on structural factors in the world's historic and current economy.

The Lives of the World's Poor

Poor nations are the least industrialized and most agricultural of all the world's countries. They consist primarily of nations in Africa and parts of Asia and constitute roughly half of the world's population. Many of these nations rely heavily on one or two crops, and if weather conditions render a crop unproductive in a particular season, the nations' hungry become even hungrier. By the same token, if economic conditions reduce the price of a crop or other natural resource, the income from exports of these commodities plummets, and these already poor nations become even poorer.

By any standard, the hundreds of millions of people in poor nations live a desperate existence in the most miserable conditions possible. They suffer from AIDS and other deadly diseases, live on the edge of starvation, and lack indoor plumbing, electricity, and other modern conveniences that most Americans take for granted. Most of us have seen unforgettable photos or video footage of African children with stick-thin limbs and distended stomachs, reflecting severe malnutrition.

People in poor nations live in the most miserable conditions possible.

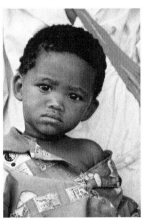

Source: © Thinkstock

It would be nice if these images were merely fiction, but unfortunately they are far too real. AIDS, malaria, starvation, and other deadly diseases are common. Many children die before reaching adolescence, and many adults die before reaching what in the richest nations would be considered middle age. Many people in the poorest nations are illiterate, and a college education remains as foreign to them as their way of life would be to us. The images of the world's poor that we see in television news reports or in film documentaries fade quickly from our minds. Meanwhile, millions of people on our planet die every year because they do not have enough to eat, because they lack access to clean water or adequate sanitation, or because they lack access to medicine that is found in every CVS and Walgreens in the United States. We now examine some specific dimensions and consequences of global poverty.

◉ East Africa's Tiny Children Starving to Death

This heartbreaking video reminds us that the extreme poverty rates found in many nations lead to severe health problems for hundreds of millions of children and adults worldwide.

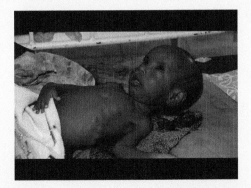

View the video online at: http://www.youtube.com/embed/2oijRiYMRXU?rel=0

Life Expectancy

When we look around the world, we see that global poverty is literally a matter of life and death. The clearest evidence of this fact comes from data on life expectancy, or the average number of years that a nation's citizens can be expected to live. Life expectancy certainly differs within each nation, with some people dying younger and others dying older, but poverty and related conditions affect a nation's overall life expectancy to a startling degree.

FIGURE 2.7 Average Life Expectancy across the Globe (Years)

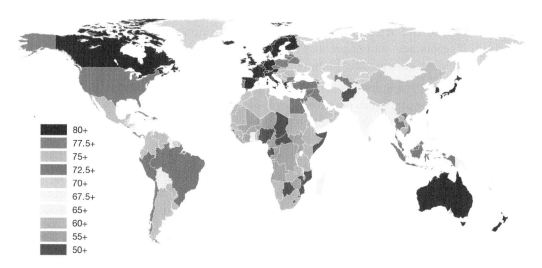

■	80+
■	77.5+
■	75+
■	72.5+
■	70+
■	67.5+
■	65+
■	60+
■	55+
■	50+

Source: Based on De728631. "Expectancy of life CIA2016.svg" at Wikipedia: https://en.wikipedia.org/wiki/File:Expectancy_of_life_CIA2016.svg (via Creative Commons Attribution 4.0 International license: https://creativecommons.org/licenses/by/4.0/deed.en). Also based on "Expectancy of life.svg" at Wikimedia: https://commons.wikimedia.org/wiki/File:Expectancy_of_life.svg (via Creative Commons Attribution-Share Alike International license: https://creativecommons.org/licenses/by-sa/4.0/deed.en).

A map of global life expectancy appears in Figure 2.7. Life expectancy is highest in North America, Western Europe, and certain other regions of the world and lowest in Africa, where life expectancy in many nations is at least 20 years shorter than in other regions. Another way of visualizing the relationship between global poverty and life expectancy appears in Figure 2.8, which depicts average life expectancy for high-income nations, upper-middle-income nations, lower-middle-income nations, and low-income nations. People in the wealthy nations can expect to live 81 years on average, compared to only 63 in poor nations. Life expectancy in poor nations is thus 18 years lower than in wealthy nations.

FIGURE 2.8 Global Income and Life Expectancy, 2017

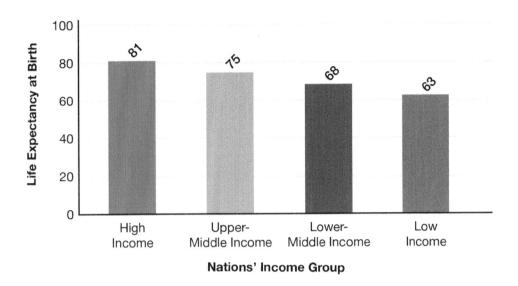

Source: Data from World Bank. 2017. World Development Indicators: Mortality. Washington, DC: World Bank. http://wdi.worldbank. org/table/2.18.

The global COVID-19 pandemic that began in early 2020 threatened to widen the life expectancy gap between low-income nations and high-income nations. In addition to horrid conditions that people in poor nations tend to live in, some one billion people also live in slums beset by serious overcrowding, dilapidated housing, unsafe water, and inadequate sanitation. All these conditions were ripe for the spread of COVID-19. Beyond these conditions, the fact that slum residents are often malnourished and suffer from respiratory disease and other chronic health conditions makes them very vulnerable to infectious diseases such as COVID-19. Recognizing this alarming situation when the COVID-19 pandemic began, public health experts warned that the world's slum residents were at especially high risk for contracting and dying from this new disease (Riley et al. 2020).[71]

People in poor nations were especially vulnerable to the COVID-19 pandemic when it swept across the world in early 2020.

Source: Sumit Saraswat/Shutterstock.com

Child Mortality

A key contributor to life expectancy, and also a significant consequence of global poverty in its own right, is child mortality: the number of children who die before age 5 per 1,000 children. More than 5 million children under age 5 die annually worldwide, with most of these deaths the result of poverty-related conditions (World Health Organization 2018).[72] As Figure 2.9 shows, the rate of child mortality in poor nations is 69 per 1,000 children, meaning that 6.9 percent of all children in these nations die before age 5. In a few African nations, child mortality exceeds 100 per 1,000. In contrast, the rate in wealthy nations is only 5 per 1,000. Children in poor nations are thus almost 14 times (69 ÷ 5) more likely to die before age 5 than children in wealthy nations.

FIGURE 2.9 Global Poverty and Child Mortality, 2017

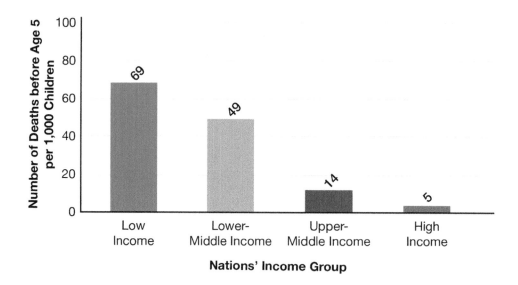

Source: Data from World Bank. 2017. World Development Report 2017. Washington, DC: World Bank. http://wdi.worldbank.org/table/2.18

Sanitation and Clean Water

Two other important indicators of a nation's health are access to adequate sanitation (disposal of human waste) and access to clean water. When people lack adequate sanitation and clean water, they are at much greater risk for life-threatening diarrhea, serious infectious diseases such as cholera and typhoid, and parasitic diseases such as schistosomiasis (World Health Organization 2019).[73] About 2 billion people around the world, almost all of them in poor and middle-income nations, lack adequate sanitation (toilets or latrines), and 423,000, most of them children, die annually from diarrhea because of inadequate sanitation. Millions of people worldwide, almost all of them again in poor and middle-income nations, suffer from a parasitic infections caused by intestinal worms.

Malnutrition

More than 500 million people around the world are malnourished.

Source: Robin Nieuwenkamp/
Shutterstock.com

Another health indicator is malnutrition. Although malnutrition includes those who are overweight and obese, our focus here will be on *undernutrition*: being *stunted* (low height for age) or *wasted* (low weight for height). This problem is caused by a lack of good food combined with infections and diseases such as diarrhea that sap the body of essential nutrients. Some 155 million children under age 5 are stunted worldwide, while 52 million are wasted (World Health Organization 2018).[74] Most of these children live in low-income or middle-income nations. Undernutrition is responsible for about 45 percent of all child deaths under age 5. Many adults worldwide are also malnourished, with more than 460 million adults underweight. Children who are malnourished are at much greater risk for fat and muscle loss, brain damage, blindness, and death; perhaps you have seen video footage of children in Africa or South Asia who are so starved that they look like skeletons.

Adult Literacy

Moving from the topic of health, another indicator of human development is adult literacy, the percentage of people 15 and older who can read and write a simple sentence. This rate is 100 percent in wealthy nations but much lower in poor (61 percent) and middle-income (86 percent) nations.[75] The high rate of illiteracy in poor nations not only reflects their poverty but also contributes to it, as people who cannot read and write are obviously at a huge disadvantage in the labor market.

Key Takeaways

- People in poor nations live in the worst conditions possible. Deadly diseases are common, and many children die before reaching adolescence.
- According to the modernization theory, rich nations became rich because their peoples possessed certain values, beliefs, and practices that helped them become wealthy. Conversely, poor nations remained poor because their peoples did not possess these values, beliefs, and practices.
- According to the dependency theory, poor nations have remained poor because they have been exploited by rich nations and by multinational corporations.

For Your Review

1. Considering all the ways in which poor nations fare much worse than wealthy nations, which one seems to you to be the most important problem that poor nations experience? Explain your answer.
2. Which theory of global poverty, modernization or dependency, makes more sense to you? Why?

2.6 Reducing Poverty

Learning Objectives

1. Explain why the United States neglects its poor.
2. List any three potentially promising strategies to reduce U.S. poverty.
3. Describe how to reduce global poverty from a sociological perspective.

As this chapter noted at the outset, the United States greatly reduced poverty during the 1960s through a series of programs and policies that composed the so-called war on poverty. You saw evidence of the success of the war on poverty in Figure 2.1, which showed that the poverty rate declined during the 1960s into the 1970s before rising and then fluctuating. Yet today, the poverty rate is no lower than it was in the late 1970s. The "Lessons from Other Societies" box showed that other democracies have much lower poverty rates than the United States because they have better funded and more extensive programs to help their poor.

The lessons from the 1960s war on poverty and the experience of other democracies are clear: It is very possible to reduce poverty if, and only if, a nation is willing to fund and implement appropriate programs and policies that address the causes of poverty and that help the poor deal with the immediate and ongoing difficulties they experience.

A major reason that the U.S. poverty rate reached its low in the 1970s before rising and then fluctuating is that the United States retreated from its war on poverty by cutting back on the programs and services it had provided during that good war (Soss et al. 2007).[76] Another major reason is that changes in the national economy during the past few decades have meant that well-paying manufacturing jobs have been replaced by low-paying service jobs with fewer benefits (Wilson 2010).[77] Yet this has also happened in other democracies, and their poverty rates remain lower than the U.S. rate because, unlike the United States, they have continued to try to help their poor rather than neglect them.

Why does the United States neglect its poor? Many scholars attribute this neglect to the fact that many citizens and politicians think the poor are poor because of their own failings. As summarized by sociologist Mark R. Rank (2011:18),[78] these failings include "not working hard enough, failure to acquire sufficient skills, or just making bad decisions." By thus blaming the poor for their fate, citizens and politicians think the poor do not deserve to have the U.S. government help them, and so the government does not help, or at least not nearly as much as other democracies do. We have seen that the facts do not support the myth that the poor lack motivation to work, but that does not lessen the blame given the poor for being poor.

To renew the U.S. effort to help the poor, it is essential that the actual facts about poverty become better known so that a fundamental shift in thinking about poverty and the poor can occur. Rank (2011:17)[79] says that one aspect of this shift must include the recognition, as noted at the beginning of this chapter, that "poverty affects us all" because it costs so many tax dollars to help the poor and because a majority of the public can expect to be poor or near poor at some point in their lives. A second aspect of this shift in thinking, adds Rank, is the recognition (following a blaming-the-system approach) that poverty stems much more from the lack of opportunity, lack of jobs, declining government help for the poor, and other structural failings of American society than from individual failings of the poor themselves. A third aspect of this shift in thinking, he concludes, is that poverty must become seen as a moral problem and severe injustice. As he forcefully argues, "Something is seriously wrong when we find that, in a country with the most abundant resources in the world, there are children without enough to eat, families who cannot afford health care, and people sleeping on the streets for lack of shelter" (p. 20).[80]

Joe Soss (2011:84)[81] argues that a change in thinking is not enough for a renewed antipoverty effort to occur. What is needed, he says, is political protest and other political activity by the poor and on behalf of the poor. Soss notes that "political conflict and mass mobilization played key roles" in providing the impetus for social-welfare programs in the 1930s and 1960s in the United States, and he adds that the lower poverty rates of Western European democracies "are products of labor movements, unions, and parties that mobilized workers to demand more adequate social supports." These twin histories lead Soss to conclude that the United States will not increase its antipoverty efforts unless a new wave of political activity by and on behalf of the poor arises. As he argues, "History suggests that major antipoverty victories can be achieved. But they won't be achieved by good will and smart ideas alone. They'll be won politically, when people—in poor communities, in advocacy groups, in government, in the academy, and elsewhere—mobilize to advance antipoverty agendas in ways that make politics as usual untenable."

Antipoverty Programs and Policies

If a renewed antipoverty effort does occur for whatever reason, what types of programs and policies show promise for effectively reducing poverty? Here, a sociological vision is essential. It is easy to understand why the hungry school-children described in the news story that began this chapter might be going without food during a very faltering national economy. Yet a sociological under-standing of poverty emphasizes its structural basis in bad times and good times alike. Poverty is rooted in social and economic problems of the larger society rather than in the supposed lack of willpower, laziness, or other moral failings of poor individuals themselves. Individuals born into poverty suffer from a lack of opportunity from their first months up through adulthood, and poverty becomes a self-perpetuating, vicious cycle. To the extent a culture of poverty might exist, it is best seen as a logical and perhaps even inevitable outcome of, and adaptation to, the problem of being poor and not the primary force driving poverty itself.

To help reduce poverty, it is essential to help poor parents pay for child care.

Source: © Thinkstock

This sort of understanding suggests that efforts to reduce poverty must address first and fore-most the structural basis for poverty. An extensive literature on poverty policy outlines many types of policies and programs that follow this dual approach (e.g. Iceland 2013; McKernon et al. 2019).[82] If these were fully adopted, funded, and implemented, as they are in many other democracies, they would offer great promise for reducing poverty. Although a full discussion of these policies is beyond the scope of this chapter, the following measures are commonly cited as holding strong potential for reducing poverty, and they are found in varying degrees in other Western democra-cies:

1. Adopt a national "full employment" policy for the poor, involving federally funded job training and public works programs, and increase the minimum wage so that individuals working full-time will earn enough to lift their families out of poverty.

2. Increase federal aid for the working poor, including higher earned income credits and child-care subsidies for those with children.

3. Establish well-funded early childhood intervention programs, including home visitations by trained professionals, for poor families.

4. Provide poor families with enough income to enable them to pay for food and housing.

5. Increase the supply of affordable housing.

6. Improve the schools that poor children attend and the schooling they receive and expand early childhood education programs for poor children.

7. Provide better nutrition and health services for poor families with young children.

8. Establish universal health insurance.

9. Increase Pell Grants and other financial aid for higher education.

Applying Social Research

The Consequences of Welfare Reform

Aid to Families with Dependent Children (AFDC) was a major government program to help the poor from the 1930s to the 1960s. Under this program, states allocated federal money to pro-vide cash payments to poor families with children. Although the program was heavily criticized for allegedly providing an incentive to poor mothers both to have more children and to not join the workforce, research studies found little or no basis for this criticism. Still, because many politi-cians and much of the public accepted the criticism as true, AFDC was replaced in 1997 by a new program, Temporary Assistance for Needy Families (TANF).

TANF is more restrictive in many respects than AFDC was. In particular, it limits the amount of time a poor family can receive federal funds to five years, and allows states to impose a shorter duration for such funding, which many have done. In addition, it requires single parents in families receiving TANF funds to work at least thirty hours a week (or twenty hours a week if they have a child under the age of 6) and two parents to work at least thirty-five hours per week combined. In most states, going to school to obtain a degree does not count as the equivalent of working and thus does not make a parent eligible for TANF payments.

Did welfare reform involving TANF work? Noting that many fewer families receive TANF payments than used to receive AFDC payments, many observers hail TANF as a success. However, sociologists and other scholars say that many poor families are being excluded from TANF funding because of its strict requirements, and they add that TANF cash benefits are simply too low to lift families out of poverty or to cover their housing costs or other needs. This situation demonstrates the failure of TANF, they say, not its success. As a sign of this failure, enrollment in TANF rose during the deep recession that began in 2008, but this increase lagged far beyond the steep rise in poverty that accompanied this recession.

Several problems explain why TANF has had these consequences. First, many families are poor for many more than five years, and the five-year time limit under TANF means that they receive financial help for only some of the years they live in poverty. Second, because the federal and state governments provide relatively little financial aid for child care, many parents simply cannot afford to work, and if they don't work, they lose their TANF payments. Third, jobs are certainly difficult to find, especially if, as is typical, a poor parent has relatively little education and few job skills; if parents cannot find a job, they again lose their TANF payments. Fourth, many parents cannot work because they have physical or mental health problems or because they are taking care of a family member or friend with a health problem; these parents, too, become ineligible for TANF payments.

Sociologist Lorna Rivera put a human face to these problems in a study of fifty poor women in Boston, Massachusetts. She lived among them, interviewed them individually, and conducted focus groups. She found that TANF worsened the situation of these women for the reasons just stated, and concluded that welfare reform left these and other poor women "uneducated, underemployed, underpaid, and unable to effectively move themselves and their families forward."

The research by social scientists on the effects of TANF reveals that the United States took a large step backward when it passed welfare reform in the 1990s. Far from reducing poverty, welfare reform only worsened it. This research underscores the need for the United States to develop better strategies for reducing poverty similar to those used by other Western democracies, as discussed in the "Lessons from Other Societies" box in this chapter.

Sources: Burnside and Floyd 2019; Center on Budget and Policy Priorities 2018; Parrott and Sherman 2008; Rivera 2008[83]

Global Poverty

Years of international aid to poor nations have helped them, but, as this chapter has shown, their situation remains dire. International aid experts acknowledge that efforts to achieve economic growth in poor nations have largely failed, but they disagree on why this is so and what alternative strategies may prove more successful. One promising trend has been a switch from macro efforts focusing on infrastructure problems and on social institutions, such as the schools, to micro efforts, such as providing cash payments or small loans directly to poor people in poor nations (a practice called *microfinancing*) and giving them bed nets to prevent mosquito bites (Karlan and Appel 2011).[84] However, much more to help the world's poor still needs to be done.

In this regard, sociology's structural approach is in line with dependency theory and suggests that global stratification results from the history of colonialism and from continuing exploitation today of poor nations' resources by wealthy nations and multinational corporations. To the extent such exploitation exists, global poverty will lessen if and only if this exploitation lessens. A sociological approach also emphasizes the role that class, gender, and ethnic inequality play in perpetuating global poverty. For global poverty to be reduced, gender and ethnic inequality must be reduced.

Writers Nicholas D. Kristof and Sheryl WuDunn (2010)[85] emphasize the need to focus efforts to reduce global poverty of women. We have already seen one reason this emphasis makes sense: women are much worse off than men in poor nations in many ways, so helping them is crucial for both economic and humanitarian reasons. An additional reason is especially illuminating: when women in poor nations acquire extra money, they typically spend it on food, clothing, and medicine, essentials for their families. However, when men in poor nations acquire extra money, they often spend it on alcohol, tobacco, and gambling. This gender difference might sound like a stereotype, but it does indicate that aid to women will help in many ways, while aid to men might be less effective and often even wasted.

Key Takeaways

- According to some sociologists, a change in thinking about poverty and the poor and political action by and on behalf of the poor are necessary for a renewed effort to help poor Americans.
- Potentially successful antipoverty programs and policies to help the U.S. poor include expanding their employment opportunities and providing them much greater amounts of financial and other aid.
- To help people in poor nations, gender and ethnic inequality must be addressed.

For Your Review

1. Write a brief essay summarizing the changes in thinking that some sociologists argue must occur before a renewed effort to reduce poverty can take place.
2. Write a brief essay summarizing any four policies or programs that could potentially lower U.S. poverty.

2.7 End-of-Chapter Material

Summary

1. Poverty statistics are misleading in at least two ways. First, the way that poverty is measured is inadequate for several reasons, and more accurate measures of poverty that have recently been developed suggest that poverty is higher than the official poverty measure indicates. Second, even if people live slightly above the poverty line, they are still living in very difficult circumstances and are having trouble making ends meet.
2. Children, people of color, the South, and single-parent families headed by women have especially high poverty rates. Despite what many Americans think, the most typical poor person is white, and most poor people who are able to work outside the home, in fact, do have jobs.
3. To explain social stratification and thus poverty, functionalist theory says that stratification is necessary and inevitable because of the need to encourage people with the necessary knowledge and skills to decide to pursue the careers that are most important to society.

Conflict theory says stratification exists because of discrimination against, and blocked opportunities for, the have-nots of society. Symbolic interactionist theory does not try to explain why stratification and poverty exist, but it does attempt to understand the experience of being poor.

4. The individualistic explanation attributes poverty to individual failings of poor people themselves, while the structuralist explanation attributes poverty to lack of jobs and lack of opportunity in the larger society.

5. Poverty has serious consequences in many respects. Among other problems, poor children are more likely to grow up to be poor, to have health problems, to commit street crime, and to have lower levels of formal education. Low-income people and families were also at higher risk for serious illness and death from COVID-19 when the pandemic overtook the United States in early 2020.

6. The nations of the world differ dramatically in wealth and other resources, with the poorest nations being found in Africa and parts of Asia.

7. Global poverty has a devastating impact on the lives of hundreds of millions of people throughout the world. Poor nations have much higher rates of mortality and disease and lower rates of literacy. In line with this sad reality, poor nations were also especially vulnerable to serious illness and death from COVID-19 when the pandemic overwhelmed the world in early 2020.

8. Modernization theory attributes global poverty to the failure of poor nations to develop the necessary beliefs, values, and practices to achieve economic growth. Dependency theory attributes global poverty to the colonization and exploitation by European nations of nations in other parts of the world.

9. A sociological perspective suggests that poverty reduction in the United States and around the world can occur if the structural causes of poverty are successfully addressed.

Using What You Know

It is December 20, and you have just finished final exams. In two days, you will go home for winter break and are looking forward to a couple weeks of eating, sleeping, and seeing your high school friends. Your smartphone signals that someone has texted you. When you read the message, you see that a friend is asking you to join her in serving a holiday supper on December 23 at a food pantry just a few miles from your campus. If you do that, you will not be able to get home until two days after you had been planning to arrive, and you will miss a big high school reunion party set for the night of the 23rd. What do you decide to do? Why?

What You Can Do

To help fight poverty and the effects of poverty, you may wish to do any of the following:

1. Contribute money to a local, state, or national organization that provides various kinds of aid to the poor.

2. Volunteer at a local food pantry or homeless shelter.

3. Start a canned food or used clothing drive on your campus.

4. Write letters or send e-mails to local, state, and federal officials that encourage them to expand antipoverty programs.

Endnotes

1. Ortiz, Erik. 2019. "Hunger Takes No Summer Break: When School's out, the Challenge Is to How to Feed More Kids." *NBCnews* July 10:https://www.nbcnews.com/news/us-news/hunger-takes-no-summer-break-when-school-s-out-challenge-n1025866.

2. Harrington, Michael. 1962. *The Other America: Poverty in the United States*. New York, NY: Macmillan.

3. Bagdikian, Ben H. 1964. *In the Midst of Plenty: The Poor in America*. Boston, MA: Beacon Press.

4. Lee, Jaeah, Lee Eichelberger and A.J. Vicens. 2014. "How We Won—and Lost—the War on Poverty, in 6 Charts." *Mother Jones* January 8:https://www.motherjones.com/politics/2014/01/charts-poverty-50-years-after-war-poverty/.

5. Rank, Mark R. 2011. Rethinking American Poverty. *Contexts, 10*(Spring):16–21.

6. Rank, M. R. (2011). Rethinking American poverty. *Contexts, 10*(Spring), 16–21.

7. Duncan, Greg and Suzanne Le Menestrel, eds. 2019. *A Roadmap to Reducing Child Poverty*. Washington, DC: The National Academies Press.

8. Rank, M. R. (2011). Rethinking American poverty. *Contexts, 10*(Spring), 16–21.

9. Iceland, John. 2013. *Poverty in America: A Handbook*, third edition. Berkeley: University of California Press.

10. DeParle, J., Geboloff, R., & Tavernise, S. 2011. *Bleak Portrait of Poverty is Off the Mark, Experts Say*. New York Times November 4:A1.

11. Shierholz, Heidi. 2014. *Low Wages and Few Benefits Mean Many Restaurant Workers Can't Make Ends Meet* Washington, DC: Economic Policy Institute.

12. Fontenot, Kayla, Jessica Semega and Melissa Kollar. 2018. *Income and Poverty in the United States: 2017*. Washington, DC: U.S. Census Bureau.

13. DeParle, Jason. 2020. "A Gloomy Prediction on How Much Poverty Could Rise." *The New York Times*. April 16. Retrieved from https://www.nytimes.com/2020/04/16/upshot/coronavirus-prediction-rise-poverty.html.

14. Assari, Shervin. 2017. "Why Poverty Is Not a Personal Choice, but a Reflection of Society." *The Conversation* June 30:https://theconversation.com/why-poverty-is-not-a-personal-choice-but-a-reflection-of-society-79552.

15. Fontenot, Kayla, Jessica Semega and Melissa Kollar. 2018. *Income and Poverty in the United States: 2017*. Washington, DC: U.S. Census Bureau.

16. Fontenot, Kayla, Jessica Semega and Melissa Kollar. 2018. *Income and Poverty in the United States: 2017*. Washington, DC: U.S. Census Bureau.

17. Brown-Iannuzzi, Jazmin L. and Erin Cooley. 2019. "Wealthy Whites and Poor Blacks: Implicit Associations between Racial Groups and Wealth Predict Opposition toward Helping the Poor." *Journal of Experimental Criminology* 82:26-34.

18. Lin, Ann Chih, and Harris, David R. (Eds.). 2008. *The Colors of Poverty: Why Racial and Ethnic Disparities Persist*. New York: Russell Sage Foundation.

19. Iceland, John (2013). *Poverty in America: A Handbook*, third edition. Berkeley, CA: University of California Press.

20. Ratcliffe, Caroline. 2015. *Child Poverty and Adult Success*. Washington, DC: Urban Institute.

21. Brazier, Chris. 2017. *Building the Future: Children and The Sustainable Development Goals in Rich Countries*. Florence, Italy: UNICEF Office of Research—Innocenti.

22. Addy, S., & Wright, V. R. (2012). *Basic facts about low-income children, 2010*. New York, NY: National Center for Children in Poverty.

23. Koball, Heather and Yang Jiang. 2018. "Basic Facts About Low-Income Children." *National Center for Children in Poverty*:http://www.nccp.org/publications/pub_1194.html.

24. Maddock, Jay. 2018. "5 Charts Show Why the South Is the Least Healthy Region in the Us." *The Conversation* February 5:https://theconversation.com/5-charts-show-why-the-south-is-the-least-healthy-region-in-the-us-89729.

25. Databank, Child Trends. 2019. "Children in Poverty."https://www.childtrends.org/?indicators=children-in-poverty.

26. Hipple, Steven F. 2015. "People Who Are Not in the Labor Force: Why Aren't They Working?". *Beyond the Numbers* (Bureau of Labor Statistics) 4(15):https://www.bls.gov/opub/btn/volume-4/people-who-are-not-in-the-labor-force-why-arent-they-working.htm.

27. Keith-Jennings, Brynne and Raheem Chaudhry. 2018. "Most Working-Age Snap Participants Work, but Often in Unstable Jobs." *Center on Budget and Policy Priorities*:https://www.cbpp.org/research/food-assistance/most-working-age-snap-participants-work-but-often-in-unstable-jobs.

28. Torgan, A. (2018, December 9) He quit his high-paying job to build beds for kids who sleep on the floor. *CNN*. Retrieved from: https://www.cnn.com/2018/06/28/us/cnnheroes-luke-mickelson-sleep-in-heavenly-peace/index.html

29. Davis, Kingsley., and Moore, Wilbert. 1945. "Some Principles of Stratification." *American Sociological Review* 10: 242–249.

30. Tumin, Melvin M. 1953. Some Principles of Stratification: A Critical Analysis. *American Sociological Review 18:* 387–393; Wrong, Dennis H. 1959. The Functional Theory of Stratification: Some Neglected Considerations. *American Sociological Review* 24:772–782.

31. Gans, Herbert. J. 1972. The Positive Functions of Poverty. *American Journal of Sociology* 78:275–289.

32. Hurst, Charles E., Heather M. Fitz Gibbon and Anne M Nurse. 2019. *Social Inequality: Forms, Causes, and Consequences*. New York: Routledge.

33. Desmond, Matthew. 2016. *Evicted: Poverty and Profit in the American City*. New York: Crown Publishers; Liebow, Elliot. 1993. *Tell Them Who I Am: The Lives of Homeless Women*. New York: Free Press; Miller, Jody. 2008. *Getting Played: African American Girls, Urban Inequality, and Gendered Violence* NYU Press: New York; Rios, Victor M. 2011. *Punished: Policing the Lives of Black and Latino Boys* New York: NYU Press.

34. Bagdikian, Ben H. (1964). *In the Midst of Plenty: The Poor in America*. Boston, MA: Beacon Press; Harrington, Michael. (1962). *The Other America: Poverty in the United States*. New York, NY: Macmillan.

35. Blow, Charles M. 2011. "Them That's Not Shall Lose." *The New York Times* June 25:A19.

36. Rank, Mark R. 2011. Rethinking American Poverty. *Contexts 10*(Spring):16–21.

37. Davidson, Theresa C. (2009). Attributions for Poverty among College Students: The Impact of Service-learning and Religiosity. *College Student Journal 43:*136–144.

38. Osborne, Danny and Bernard Weiner. 2015. "A Latent Profile Analysis of Attributions for Poverty: Identifying Response Patterns Underlying People's Willingness to Help the Poor." *Personality and Individual Differences* 85:149-54.

39. Doar, Robert, Karlyn Bowman and Eleanor O'Neil. 2016. "2016 Poverty Survey." *American Enterprise Institute*:http://www.aei.org/publication/2016-poverty-survey/.

40. Banfield, Edward. C. 1974. *The Unheavenly City Revisited*. Boston, MA: Little, Brown; Lewis, Oscar. 1966. "The Culture of Poverty." *Scientific American, 113:*19–25; Murray, Charles. 2012. *Coming Apart: The State of White America, 1960–2010*. New York, NY: Crown Forum.

41. Assari, Shervin. 2017. "Why Poverty Is Not a Personal Choice, but a Reflection of Society." *The Conversation* June 30:https://theconversation.com/why-poverty-is-not-a-personal-choice-but-a-reflection-of-society-79552; Holland, Joshua. 2011. "Debunking the Big Lie Right-Wingers Use to Justify Black Poverty and Unemployment ." *alternet.org* July 29:http://www.alternet.org/story/151830/debunking_the_big_lie_rightwingers_use_to_justify_black_poverty_and_unemployment_?page=entire.

42. Rank, Mark R. 2011. Rethinking American Poverty. *Contexts, 10*(Spring):6–21.

43. Block, F., Korteweg, A. C., & Woodward, K. (2006). The Compassion Gap in American Poverty Policy. *Contexts 5*(2):14–20.

44. Small, M. L., Harding, D. J., & Lamont, M. 2010. Reconsidering Culture and Poverty. *The Annals of the American Academy of Political and Social Science, 629*(May):6–27.

45. Centers for Disease Control and Prevention. 2019. "Current Cigarette Smoking among Adults in the United States."https://www.cdc.gov/tobacco/data_statistics/fact_sheets/adult_data/cig_smoking/index.htm.

46. Small, M. L., Harding, D. J., & Lamont, M. 2010. Reconsidering Culture and Poverty. *The Annals of the American Academy of Political and Social Science, 629*(May):6–27.

47. Duncan, Greg and Suzanne Le Menestrel, eds. 2019. *A Roadmap to Reducing Child Poverty*. Washington, DC: The National Academies Press; Duncan, Greg J., Katherine Magnuson and Elizabeth Votruba-Drzal. 2017. "Moving Beyond Correlations in Assessing the Consequences of Poverty." *Annual Review of Psychology* 68:413-34; Hinojosa, Melanie Sberna, Ramon Hinojosa, Melissa Bright and Jenny Nguyen. 2019. "Adverse Childhood Experiences and Grade Retention in a National Sample of Us Children." *Sociological Inquiry* 89(3):401-26; Murphy, David and Zakia Redd. 2014. "Five Ways Poverty Harms Children." *Child Trends*:https://www.childtrends.org/wp-content/uploads/2014/01/14-01CT5PovertyHarmsChildren1.pdf; Ratcliffe, Caroline. 2015. "Child Poverty and Adult Success." *Urban Institute*:https://www.urban.org/sites/default/files/publication/65766/2000369-Child-Poverty-and-Adult-Success.pdf.

48. Ratcliffe, Caroline, and McKernan, Signe-Mary. 2010. *Childhood Poverty Persistence: Facts and Consequences*. Washington, DC: Urban Institute Press.

49. Duncan, Greg. J., and Magnuson, Katherine. 2011. The Long Reach of Early Childhood Poverty. *Pathways: A Magazine on Poverty, Inequality, and Social Policy*. Winter 22–27.

50. Duncan, Greg J., & Magnuson, Katherine. 2011. The Long Reach of Early Childhood Poverty. *Pathways: A Magazine on Poverty, Inequality, and Social Policy* Winter:22–27.

51. Grusky, David, and Wimer, Christopher. (Eds.). 2011. Editors' Note. *Pathways: A Magazine on Poverty, Inequality, and Social Policy* Winter:2.

52. Duncan, Greg and Suzanne Le Menestrel, eds. 2019. *A Roadmap to Reducing Child Poverty*. Washington, DC: The National Academies Press; Evans, G. W., Brooks-Gunn, J., & Klebanov, P. K. .2011. Stressing Out the Poor: Chronic Physiological Stress and the Income-achievement Gap. *Pathways: A Magazine on Poverty, Inequality, and Social Policy*. Winter:16–21; Francis, Lucine, Kelli DePriest, Marcella Wilson and Deborah Gross. 2018. "Child Poverty, Toxic Stress, and Social Determinants of Health: Screening and Care Coordination." *Online Journal of Issues in Nursing* 23(3):1-11.

53. Shonkoff, Jack P. 2011. Building a Foundation for Prosperity on the Science of Early Childhood Development. *Pathways: A Magazine on Poverty, Inequality, and Social Policy* Winter:10–14; Duncan, Greg and Suzanne Le Menestrel, eds. 2019. *A Roadmap to Reducing Child Poverty*. Washington, DC: The National Academies Press.

54. Bakalar, Nocholas. 2011. "Researchers Link Deaths to Social Ills." *The New York Times* July D5.

55. UN News. 2020. "Us Must Improve Covid-19 Strategy to Keep Tens of Millions from Falling into Poverty, Urges Rights Expert." *UN News*. Retrieved from https://news.un.org/en/story/2020/04/1061982.

56. Barkan, Steven E. 2021. *Health, Illness, and Society: An Introduction to Medical Sociology*. Lanham, MD: Rowman & Littlefield.

57. Desmond, Matthew. 2016. *Evicted: Poverty and Profit in the American City*. New York: Crown Publishers.

58. Lee, B., Tyler, K. A., & Wright, J. D. 2010. The New Homelessness Revisited. *Annual Review of Sociology 36*:501–521.

59. Data from Organisation for Co-Operation and Economic Development (OECD). 2019. *Income Distribution and Poverty*. Retrieved July 13, 2019 from https://stats.oecd.org/Index.aspx?DataSetCode=IDD.

60. Waldfogel, Jane. 2010. *Britain's War on Poverty*. New York, NY: Russell Sage Foundation.

61. Dikhanov, Yuri. 2005. *Trends in Global Income Distribution, 1970–2000, and Scenarios for 2015*. New York, NY: United Nations Development Programme.

62. Kurt, Daniel. 2019. "Are You in the Top One Percent of the World?." *Investopedia* May 9:https://www.investopedia.com/articles/personal-finance/050615/are-you-top-one-percent-world.asp.

63. Dikhanov, Yuri. (2005). *Trends in Global Income Distribution, 1970–2000, and Scenarios for 2015*. New York, NY: United Nations Development Programme.

64. United Nations Development Programme. (2009). *Human development report 2009*. New York, NY: Author.Bank, World. 2018. *Poverty and Shared Prosperity 2018: Piecing Together the Poverty Puzzle*. Washington, DC: World Bank (License: Creative Commons Attribution CC BY 3.0 IGO).

65. Bank, World. 2018. *Poverty and Shared Prosperity 2018: Piecing Together the Poverty Puzzle*. Washington, DC: World Bank (License: Creative Commons Attribution CC BY 3.0 IGO).

66. World Bank. 2016. "Vulnerabile Groups."http://web.worldbank.org/WBSITE/EXTERNAL/TOPICS/EXTSOCIALPROTECTION/EXTSF/0,,content-MDK:20663797~menuPK:6344572~pagePK:148956~piPK:216618~theSitePK:396378,00.html.

67. Haughton, J., & Khandker, S. R. 2009. *Handbook on Poverty and Inequality*. Washington, DC: World Bank.

68. Rostow, Walt W. 1990. *The Stages of Economic Growth: A Non-Communist Manifesto* (3rd ed.). New York, NY: Cambridge University Press.

69. Packenham, Robert A. 1992. *The Dependency Movement: Scholarship and Politics in Development Studies*. Cambridge, MA: Harvard University Press.

70. Williams, Matthew S. 2020. *Strategizing against Sweatshops: The Global Economy, Student Activism, and Worker Empowerment* Philadelphia: Temple University Press.

71. Riley, Lee W., Eva Raphael and Robert Snyder. 2020. "Will People in Slums Survive?". *The New York Times* April 10:A27.

72. World Health Organization. 2018. "Children: Reducing Mortality."https://www.who.int/news-room/fact-sheets/detail/children-reducing-mortality.

73. World Health Organization. 2019. *Sanitation*. Retrieved from hhttps://www.who.int/en/news-room/fact-sheets/detail/sanitation.

74. World Health Organization. 2018. "Malnutrition."https://www.who.int/news-room/fact-sheets/detail/malnutrition.

75. The World Bank. 2017. "Literacy Rate, Adult Total."https://data.worldbank.org/indicator/se.adt.litr.zs.

76. Soss, J., Hacker, J. S., & Mettler, S. (Eds.). 2007. *Remaking America: Democracy and Public Policy in an Age of Inequality*. New York, NY: Russell Sage Foundation.

77. Wilson, William J. 2010. *More Than Just Race: Being Black and Poor in the Inner City*. New York, NY: W. W. Norton.

78. Rank, Mark R. (2011). Rethinking American Poverty. *Contexts* 10(Spring):16–21.

79. Rank, Mark R. 2011. Rethinking American Poverty. *Contexts,* 10(Spring):16–21.

80. Rank, Mark. R. 2011. Rethinking American Poverty. *Contexts* 10(Spring):16–21.

81. Soss, Joe. 2011. The Poverty Fight. *Contexts* 10(2):84.

82. Iceland, John. 2013. *Poverty in America: A Handbook*. Berkeley: University of California Press; McKernan, Signe-Mary, Caroline Ratcliffe and John Iceland. 2018. *Policy Efforts to Reduce Material Hardship for Low-Income Families*. Washington, DC: The Urban Institute.

83. Burnside, Ashley and Ife Floyd. 2019. *Policy Brief: Despite Recent Increases in Some States, Tanf Cash Benefits Are Still Too Low*. Washington, DC: Center on Budget and Policy Priorities; Center on Budget and Policy Priorities. 2018. "Policy Basics: An Introduction to Tanf."https://www.cbpp.org/research/policy-basics-an-introduction-to-tanf; Parrott, S., and Sherman, A. 2008. *TANF at 10: Program Results are More Mixed Than Often Understood*. Washington, DC: Center on Budget and Policy Priorities; Rivera, Lorna. 2008. *Laboring to Learn: Women's Literacy and Poverty in the Post-welfare ra*. Urbana, IL: University of Illinois Press.

84. Karlan, D., & Appel, J. 2011. *More Than Good Intentions: How a New Economics is Helping to Solve Global Poverty*. New York, NY: Dutton.

85. Kristoff, N. D., & WuDunn, S. (2010). *Half the Sky: Turning Oppression into Opportunity for Women Worldwide*. New York, NY: Vintage Books.

CHAPTER 3

Racial and Ethnic Inequality

Social Problems in the News

"Man Who Killed Heather Heyer at Charlottesville Sentenced to Life In Prison, Plus 419 Years," the headline said. In July 2019, a professed neo-Nazi was sentenced to life in prison for ramming his car into a group of people protesting a white nationalist rally in Charlottesville, Virginia, in 2017. His hate crime killed 32-year-old Heather Heyer and injured many more people. During the sentencing procedure, the judge told the defendant, "Today's verdict is based on what you did. It was not a spur of the moment action."[1]

"COVID-19 Racial Health Disparities Highlight Why We Need to Address Structural Racism," the headline said. In the wake of the pandemic that began in early 2020, there was troubling evidence that it was affecting African Americans, Latinx, and Native Americans at higher rates than other people. By mid-April 2020, for example, counties where the majority of residents were black had COVID-19 infection rates three times higher than counties where the majority of residents were white, and death rates almost six times higher (Kijakazi 2020). And in New Mexico, and Wyoming, where Native Americans comprise fewer than 10 percent of these states' populations, they nonetheless accounted for 57 percent, and 30 percent, respectively, of the states' COVID-19 cases (Artiga and Orgera 2020).[2][3]

During the Ku Klux Klan era between the 1880s and 1960s, white men dressed in white sheets and white hoods terrorized African Americans in the South and elsewhere. During this time period the KKK lynched over 3,000 black men and women. Thankfully, that era is long gone, but as this news story reminds us, racial issues continue to trouble the United States. Before and after he was elected president in November 2016, Donald Trump made many statements that were roundly denounced as racist (Blow 2019; Lopez 2019). These statements also remind us that racial issues have not gone away.

In the wake of the 1960s urban riots, the so-called Kerner Commission (1968:1)[4] appointed by President Lyndon Johnson to study the riots famously warned, "Our nation is moving toward two societies, one black, one white—separate and unequal." The commission blamed white racism for the riots and urged the government to provide jobs and housing for African Americans and to take steps to end racial segregation.

More than five decades later, racial inequality in the United States continues to exist and in many ways has worsened. Despite major advances by African Americans, Latinxs, and other people of color during the past few decades, they continue to lag behind non-Latinx whites in education, income, health, and other social indicators. As the second chapter-opening news story about COVID-19 reminds us, racial inequality can literally be a matter of life and death.

Why does racial and ethnic inequality exist? What forms does it take? What can be done about it? This chapter addresses all these questions. We shall see that, although racial and ethnic inequality has stained the United States since its beginnings, there is hope for the future as long as our nation understands the structural sources of this inequality and makes a concerted effort to reduce it. Later chapters in this book will continue to highlight various dimensions of racial and ethnic inequality. Immigration, a very relevant issue today for Latinxs and Asians and the source of much political controversy, receives special attention in the discussion of population problems in Chapter 15.

3.1 Racial and Ethnic Inequality: A Historical Prelude

Learning Objectives

1. Describe the targets of nineteenth-century mob violence in U.S. cities.
2. Discuss why the familiar saying "The more things change, the more they stay the same" applies to the history of race and ethnicity in the United States.

Race and ethnicity have torn at the fabric of American society ever since the time of Christopher Columbus, when an estimated 1 million Native Americans populated the eventual United States. By 1900, their numbers had dwindled to about 240,000, as tens of thousands were killed by white settlers and U.S. troops and countless others died from disease contracted from people with European backgrounds. Scholars say this mass killing of Native Americans amounted to genocide (Brown 2009).[5]

African Americans also have a history of maltreatment that began during the colonial period, when Africans were taken from their homelands to be sold as slaves in the Americas. From 1525 to 1866, an estimated 12.5 million Africans were sent to the New World, with almost 2 million dying en route (Gates 2014).[6] One-fourth of these Africans were children. At the dawn of the U.S. Civil War in 1860, 4.4 million African Americans, including 3.9 million who were enslaved, lived in this nation. To say that the enslaved were mistreated would be a grievous understatement. Slavery was horrific. Enslaved persons were often whipped or beaten by their masters, many were raped and sexually assaulted, and thousands died from their mistreatment and living conditions (Glymph 2008).[7]

 Slavery in the U.S., by the Numbers

The United States has a history of maltreatment of people of color. When the Civil War began in 1860, there were nearly 4 million enslaved African Americans. They lived a miserable existence, living with whippings and other types of abuse, rape, and sexual assault as a common occurrence.

View the video online at: http://www.youtube.com/embed/RV1TZx_xqNo?rel=0

Slavery, of course, continued in the United States until the North's victory in the Civil War ended it. Many of the African Americans outside the South were not enslaved, but were still victims of racial prejudice. During the 1830s, white mobs attacked free African Americans in cities throughout the nation, including Philadelphia, Cincinnati, Buffalo, and Pittsburgh. The mob violence stemmed from a "deep-seated racial prejudice... in which whites saw blacks as 'something less than human'" (Brown 1975:206)[8] and continued well into the twentieth century when white mobs attacked African Americans in several cities, with at least seven antiblack riots occurring in 1919 that left dozens dead. Meanwhile, the era of Jim Crow racism in the South led to the lynching of thousands of African Americans, segregation in all facets of life, and other kinds of abuses (Litwack 2009).[9]

African Americans were not the only targets of native-born white mobs back then (Dinnerstein and Reimers 2009).[10] As immigrants from Ireland, Italy, Eastern Europe, Mexico, and Asia flooded into the United States during the nineteenth and early twentieth centuries, they, too, were beaten, denied jobs, and otherwise mistreated. During the 1850s, mobs beat and sometimes killed Catholics in cities such as Baltimore and New Orleans. During the 1870s, whites rioted against Chinese immigrants in cities in California and other states. Hundreds of Mexicans were attacked and/or lynched in California and Texas during this period.

Nazi racism in the 1930s and 1940s helped awaken Americans to the evils of prejudice in their own country. Against this backdrop, a monumental two-volume work by Swedish social scientist Gunnar Myrdal (1944)[11] attracted much attention when it was published. The book, *An American Dilemma: The Negro Problem and Modern Democracy*, documented the various forms of discrimination facing blacks back then. The "dilemma" referred to by the book's title was the conflict between the American democratic ideals of egalitarianism and liberty and justice for all and the harsh reality of prejudice, discrimination, and lack of equal opportunity.

The Kerner Commission's 1968 report reminded the nation that little, if anything, had been done since Myrdal's book to address this conflict. Sociologists and other social scientists have warned since then that the status of people of color has actually been worsening in many ways since this report was issued (Massey 2007; Oliver and Shapiro 2019; Wilson 2009).[12] Evidence of this status appears in the remainder of this chapter.

During the era of Jim Crow racism in the South, several thousand African Americans were lynched.

Source: Image courtesy of U.S. Library of Congress, http://loc.gov/pictures/resource/npcc.12928.

Key Takeaways

- U.S. history is filled with violence and other maltreatment against Native Americans, blacks, and immigrants.
- Social scientists warn that the status of people of color has been worsening.

For Your Review

1. Describe why Myrdal said U.S. race relations were an "American dilemma."
2. How much did you learn in high school about the history of race and ethnicity in the United States? Do you think you should have learned more?

3.2 The Meaning of Race and Ethnicity

Learning Objectives

1. Critique the biological concept of race.
2. Discuss why race is a social construction.
3. Explain why ethnic heritages have both good and bad consequences.

To begin our understanding of racial and ethnic inequality, we first need to understand what *race* and *ethnicity* mean. These terms may seem easy to define but are much more complex upon further consideration.

Race

race

A category of people who share certain inherited physical characteristics, such as skin color, facial features, and stature.

Let's start first with **race**, which refers to a category of people who share certain inherited physical characteristics, such as skin color, facial features, and stature. A key question about race is whether it is more of a biological category or a social category. Most people think of race in biological terms; for more than three hundred years, or ever since white Europeans began colonizing nations filled with people of color, people have been identified as belonging to one race or another based on certain biological features.

It is easy to see that people in the United States and around the world differ physically in some obvious ways. The most noticeable difference is skin tone: Some groups of people have very dark skin tones, while others have very light skin tones. Other differences also exist. Some people have very curly hair, while others have very straight hair. Some have thin lips, while others have thick lips. Some groups of people tend to be relatively tall, while others tend to be relatively short. Using such physical differences as their criteria, scientists at one point identified as many as nine races: African, American Indian or Native American, Asian, Australian Aborigine, European (more commonly called "white"), Indian, Melanesian, Micronesian, and Polynesian (Smedley and Smedley 2018/ 2012).[13]

Although people certainly do differ in these physical ways, anthropologists, sociologists, and many biologists question the value of these distinctions and thus the value of the biological concept of race (Smedley and Smedley 2018/2012).[14] For one thing, we often see more physical differences *within* a race than *between* races. For example, some people we call "white" (or European), such as those with Scandinavian backgrounds, have very light skins, while others, such as those from some Eastern European backgrounds, have much darker skin tones. In fact, some "whites" have darker skin tones than some "blacks," or African Americans. Some whites have very straight hair, while others have very curly hair; some have blonde hair and blue eyes, while others have dark hair and brown eyes. Because of interracial reproduction going back to the days of slavery, African Americans also differ in the darkness of their skin and in other physical characteristics. It is estimated that one-fourth of African Americans have some white (i.e., European) ancestry; that 4 percent of whites have African ancestry; and that Latinxs on the average have 6 percent African ancestry, 18 percent Native American ancestry, and 65 percent white ancestry (Bryc et al. 2015).[15] If clear racial differences ever existed thousands of years ago (and many scientists doubt such differences ever existed), in today's world these differences have become increasingly blurred.

Another reason to question the biological concept of race is that an individual or a group of individuals is often assigned to a race arbitrarily. A century ago, for example, Irish, Italians, and Eastern European Jews who left their homelands were not regarded as white once they reached the United States but rather as a different, inferior (if unnamed) race (Painter 2010).[16] The belief in their inferiority helped justify the harsh treatment they suffered in their new country. Today, of course, we call people from all three backgrounds white or European.

In this context, consider someone in the United States who has a white parent and a black parent. What race is this person? American society usually calls this person black or African American, and the person may adopt this identity (as does President Barack Obama, who had a white mother and African father). But where is the logic for doing so? This person, as well as President Obama, is as much white as black in terms of parental ancestry.

Or consider someone with one white parent and another parent who is the child of one black parent and one white parent. This person thus has three white grandparents and one black grandparent. Even though this person's ancestry is 75 percent white and 25 percent black, she or he is likely to be considered black in the United States and may well adopt this racial identity. This practice reflects the antiquated *one-drop rule* in the United States that defines someone as black if she or he has at least one drop of *black blood*, and that was used in the antebellum South to keep the enslaved population as large as possible (Staples 2005).[17] Yet in many Latin American nations, this person would be considered white (see "Lessons from Other Societies"). With such arbitrary designations, race is more of a social category than a biological one.

President Barack Obama had an African father and a white mother. Although his ancestry is equally black and white, Obama considers himself an African American. Most Americans also consider him an African American. In several Latin American nations, however, Obama would be considered white because of his white ancestry.

Source: Image courtesy of Steve Jurvetson, http://www.flickr.com/photos/jurvetson/2175936409.

Lessons from Other Societies

The Concept of Race in Brazil

As the text discusses, race was long considered a fixed, biological category, but today it is now regarded as a social construction. The experience of Brazil provides comparative evidence for this more accurate way of thinking about race.

When the enslaved were first brought to the Americas almost five hundred years ago, many more were taken to Brazil, where slavery was not abolished until 1888, than to the land that eventually became the United States. Because Brazil was then a colony of Portugal, the Portuguese used Africans as slave labor. Just as in the United States, a good deal of interracial reproduction has occurred since those early days, much of it initially the result of the rape of enslaved women by their owners, and Brazil over the centuries has had many more racial intermarriages than the United States. But in a significant departure from the United States, Brazil uses different criteria to consider the race to which a person belongs.

Brazil uses the term *preto*, or *black*, for people whose ancestry is solely African. It also uses the term *branco*, or *white*, to refer to people whose ancestry is both African and European. In contrast, as the text discusses, the United States commonly uses the term *black* or *African American* to refer to someone with even a small amount of African ancestry, and *white* for someone who is thought to have solely European ancestry or at least "looks" white. If the United States were to follow Brazil's practice of reserving the term *black* for someone whose ancestry is solely African and the term *white* for someone whose ancestry is both African and European, many of the Americans commonly called "black" would no longer be considered black and instead would be considered white.

As sociologist Edward E. Telles (2006:79)[18] summarizes these differences, "Blackness is differently understood in Brazil than in the United States. A person considered black in the United States is often not so in Brazil. Indeed, some U.S. blacks may be considered white in Brazil. Although the value given to blackness is similarly low [in both nations], who gets classified as black is not uniform." The fact that someone can count on being considered "black" in one society and not "black" in another society underscores the idea that race is best considered a social construction rather than a biological category.

Sources: Barrionuevo and Calmes 2011; Klein and Luno 2009; Telles 2006[19]

A third reason to question the biological concept of race comes from the field of biology itself and more specifically from the studies of genetics and human evolution. Starting with genetics, people from different races are more than 99.9 percent the same in their DNA (Begley 2008).[20] To turn that around, less than 0.1 percent of all DNA in our bodies accounts for the physical differences among people that we associate with racial differences. In terms of DNA, then, people with different racial backgrounds are much, much more similar than dissimilar.

Even if we acknowledge that people differ in the physical characteristics we associate with race, modern evolutionary evidence reminds us that we are all, really, of one human race. According to evolutionary theory, the human race began thousands and thousands of years ago in sub-Saharan Africa. As people migrated around the world over the millennia, natural selection took over. It favored dark skin for people living in hot, sunny climates (i.e., near the equator), because the heavy amounts of melanin that produce dark skin protect against severe sunburn, cancer, and other problems. By the same token, natural selection favored lighter skin tones for people who migrated farther from the equator to cooler, less sunny climates, because darker skin tones there would have interfered with the production of vitamin D (Stone and Lurquin, 2007).[21] Evolutionary evidence thus reinforces the common humanity of people who differ in the rather superficial ways associated with their appearances: We are one human species composed of people who happen to look different.

Race as a Social Construction

social construction

A concept that has no objective reality but rather is what people decide it is.

The reasons for doubting the biological basis for racial categories suggest that race is more of a social category than a biological one. Another way to say this is that race is a **social construction**, a concept that has no objective reality but rather is what people decide it is (Berger and Luckmann 1963).[22] In this view, race has no real existence other than what and how people think of it.

This understanding of race is reflected in the problems, outlined earlier, in placing people with multiracial backgrounds into any one racial category. In addition to the example of President Obama, golfer Tiger Woods was typically called an African American by the news media when he burst onto the golfing scene in the late 1990s, but in fact his ancestry is one-half Asian (divided evenly between Chinese and Thai), one-quarter white, one-eighth Native American, and only one-eighth African American (Leland and Beals 1997).[23]

Historical examples of attempts to place people in racial categories further underscore the social constructionism of race. In the South during the time of slavery, the skin tone of many enslaved lightened over the years as babies were born from the raping of enslaved women by their owners and other whites. As it became difficult to tell who was "black" and who was not, many court battles over people's racial identity occurred. People who were accused of having black ancestry would go to court to prove they were white in order to avoid enslavement or other problems (Staples 1998).[24]

Although race is a social construction, it is also true that race has real consequences because people *do* perceive race as something real. Even though so little of DNA accounts for the physical differences we associate with racial differences, that low amount leads us not only to classify people into different races but also to treat them differently—and, more to the point, unequally—based on their classification. Yet modern evidence shows there is little, if any, scientific basis for the racial classification that is the source of so much inequality.

The Social Construction of Race

Race is best regarded as a social construction, that is, as a concept that has no objective reality but that exists only because people decide it exists. The racial identity assigned to people has important consequences for many aspects of their lives from birth to death.

View the video online at: http://www.youtube.com/embed/jiwieME2tis?rel=0

Ethnicity

Because of the problems in the meaning of *race*, many social scientists prefer the term *ethnicity* in speaking of people of color and others with distinctive cultural heritages. In this context, **ethnicity** refers to the shared social, cultural, and historical experiences, stemming from common national or regional backgrounds, that make subgroups of a population different from one another. Similarly, an **ethnic group** is a subgroup of a population with a set of shared social, cultural, and historical experiences; with relatively distinctive beliefs, values, and behaviors; and with some sense of identity of belonging to the subgroup. So conceived, the terms *ethnicity* and *ethnic group* avoid the biological connotations of the terms *race* and *racial group*.

At the same time, the importance we attach to ethnicity illustrates that it, too, is in many ways a social construction, and our ethnic membership thus has important consequences for how we are treated. In particular, history and current practice indicate that it is easy to become prejudiced against people with different ethnicities from our own. Much of the rest of this chapter looks at the prejudice and discrimination operating today in the United States against people whose ethnicity is not white and European. Around the world today, ethnic conflict continues to rear its ugly head. The 1990s and 2000s were filled with ethnic cleansing and pitched battles among ethnic groups in Eastern Europe, Africa, and elsewhere. Our ethnic heritages shape us in many ways and fill many of us with pride, but they are also the source of much conflict, prejudice, and even hatred, as the hate crime story that began this chapter so sadly reminds us.

ethnicity

The shared social, cultural, and historical experiences, stemming from common national or regional backgrounds, that make subgroups of a population different from one another.

ethnic group

A subgroup of a population with a set of shared social, cultural, and historical experiences; with relatively distinctive beliefs, values, and behaviors; and with some sense of identity of belonging to the subgroup.

3.3 Prejudice

prejudice

A set of negative attitudes, beliefs, and judgments about whole categories of people, and about individual members of those categories, because of their perceived race and/or ethnicity.

racism

The belief that certain racial or ethnic groups are inferior to one's own.

stereotypes

Simplified, mistaken generalizations about people because of their race and/or ethnicity.

Prejudice and *discrimination* (discussed in the next section) are often confused, but the basic difference between them is this: prejudice is the attitude, while discrimination is the behavior. More specifically, racial and ethnic **prejudice** refers to a set of negative attitudes, beliefs, and judgments about whole categories of people, and about individual members of those categories, because of their perceived race and/or ethnicity. A closely related concept is **racism**, or the belief that certain racial or ethnic groups are inferior to one's own. Prejudice and racism are often based on racial and ethnic **stereotypes**, or simplified, mistaken generalizations about people because of their race and/or ethnicity. While cultural and other differences do exist among the various American racial and ethnic groups, many of the views we have of such groups are unfounded and hence are stereotypes. An example of the stereotypes that white people have of other groups appears in Figure 3.1, in which white respondents in the General Social Survey (GSS), a recurring survey of a random sample of the U.S. population, are twice as likely to think blacks are lazy than to think whites are lazy.

FIGURE 3.1 Perceptions by Non-Latinx White Respondents of the Laziness of Black and White Americans

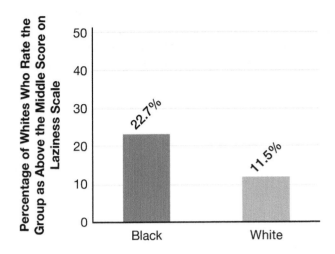

Source: Data from General Social Survey. 2019. Retrieved from http://sda.berkeley.edu/sdaweb/analysis/?dataset=gss18.

Explaining Prejudice

Where does racial and ethnic prejudice come from? Why are some people more prejudiced than others? Scholars have tried to answer these questions at least since the 1940s, when the horrors of Nazism were still fresh in people's minds. Theories of prejudice fall into two camps, social-psychological and sociological. We will look at social-psychological explanations first and then turn to sociological explanations. We will also discuss distorted mass media treatment of various racial and ethnic groups.

Social-Psychological Explanations

One of the first social-psychological explanations of prejudice centered on the **authoritarian personality** (Adorno et al. 1950).[25] According to this view, authoritarian personalities develop in childhood in response to parents who practice harsh discipline. Individuals with authoritarian personalities emphasize such things as obedience to authority, a rigid adherence to rules, and low acceptance of people (*out-groups*) not like oneself. Many studies find strong racial/ethnic and other types of prejudice among such individuals (Miller 2019; Sibley and Duckitt 2008).[26] But whether their prejudice stems from their authoritarian personalities or instead from the fact that their parents were probably prejudiced themselves remains an important question.

authoritarian personality

A personality emphasizing such things as obedience to authority, a rigid adherence to rules, and low acceptance of people not like oneself is said to help account for racial and ethnic prejudice.

frustration theory (or scapegoat theory)

As an explanation of racial and ethnic prejudice, the view that individuals blame the problems they experience on racial and ethnic minorities and thus scapegoat them instead of recognizing the real sources of their own misfortunes.

Another early and still popular social-psychological explanation is called **frustration theory (or scapegoat theory)** (Dollard et al. 1939).[27] In this view, individuals with various problems become frustrated and tend to blame their troubles on groups that are often disliked in the real world (e.g., racial, ethnic, and religious minorities). These minorities are thus scapegoats for the real sources of people's misfortunes. Several psychology experiments find that when people are frustrated, they indeed become more prejudiced. In one early experiment, college students who were purposely not given enough time to solve a puzzle were more prejudiced after the experiment than before it (Cowen et al. 1959).[28]

Authoritarian personalities are said to develop in childhood from harsh parental discipline and to be linked to racial and ethnic prejudice. Although many people with authoritarian personalities are prejudiced, it remains unclear whether their prejudice stems from their personalities or from their parents' own prejudice.

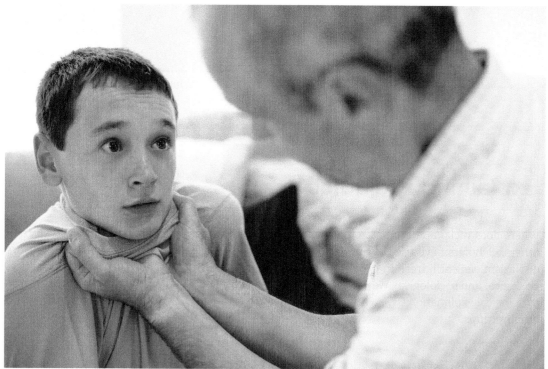

Source: © Thinkstock

Sociological Explanations

A popular sociological explanation emphasizes *conformity* and *socialization* and is called *social learning theory*. In this view, people who are prejudiced are merely conforming to the culture in which they grow up, and prejudice is the result of socialization from parents, peers, the news media, and other various aspects of their culture. Supporting this view, studies have found that people tend to become more prejudiced when they move to areas where people are very prejudiced and less prejudiced when they move to locations where people are less prejudiced (Aronson, 2018).[29] If people in the South today continue to be more prejudiced than those outside the South, as we discuss later, even though legal segregation ended more than four decades ago, the influence of their culture on their socialization may help explain these beliefs.

Children and Our Future

Growing Up as Farmworkers' Kids

Thousands of farmworkers and their families work in the large agricultural fields of California. Adults and children alike live in poor, crowded conditions and do backbreaking work in the hot sun, day after day after day.

Because their parents are migrant workers, many children attend a specific school for only a few weeks or months at most before their parents move to another field in another town, another state, or to Mexico. At Sherwood Elementary School in Salinas, California, in the heart of the state's agricultural sector, 97 percent of students live in or near poverty. With their Latinx backgrounds, more than three-fourths do not speak English well or at all.

At the Sherwood school, according to a news report, many students "sleep beneath carports and live in such cramped quarters that their parents take them to the local truck stop to wash up before school." A local high school teacher said many of his students see little of their parents, who spend most of their waking hours working in the fields. "They have little brothers and sisters to take care of, maybe cook for. Yet they're supposed to turn in a 10-page paper by tomorrow? I mean, it's unreal."

These conditions have grievous consequences for California's migrant farmworker children, almost half of whom fail to complete high school. The principal of the Sherwood Elementary School said the key strategy for her faculty and school was "understanding where the students come from but also having high expectations."

The plight of farmworkers' children is just one aspect of the difficulties facing Latinx children around the country. Thanks to reproduction and immigration, the number of Latinx children nationwide has grown significantly during the past few decades. This growing number underscores the need to pay attention to the health and welfare of Latinx children.

Against this backdrop, it is distressing to note that their health and welfare are not very good at all. About one-fourth of Latinx children live in poverty. Many Latinx children grow up in poor neighborhoods where almost half of the residents do not speak English fluently, where the schools are substandard, and where the high school dropout and teen unemployment rates are high. A number of factors, including their ethnicity, poverty, language barriers, and the immigrant status of many of their parents, limit Latinx children's access to adequate health care and various kinds of social services.

Amid all these problems, however, the situation of California's farmworker children stands out as a national embarrassment for a prosperous country like the United States. As the country struggles to end racial and ethnic inequality, it must not forget the children of Salinas who have to use a truck stop to wash up before school.

Sources: Bazaz 2019; Brown 2011; Landale et al. 2011[30]

The mass media play a key role in how many people learn to be prejudiced by presenting people of color in a negative light. For example, even though poor people are more likely to be white than any other race or ethnicity (see Chapter 2), the news media use pictures of African Americans far more often than those of whites in stories about poverty. In one study, national news magazines, such as *Time* and *Newsweek*, and television news shows portrayed African Americans in almost two-thirds of their stories on poverty, even though only about one-fourth of poor people are African Americans. In the magazine stories, only 12 percent of the African Americans had a job, even though in the real world more than 40 percent of poor African Americans were working at the time the stories were written (Gilens 1996).[31] In another study, Chicago television news stories depicted whites fourteen times more often in stories of good Samaritans, even though whites and African Americans live in Chicago in roughly equal numbers (Entman and Rojecki 2001).[32] Many other studies find that newspaper and television stories about crime and drugs feature higher proportions of African Americans as offenders than is true in arrest statistics (Robinson 2018).[33] Studies like these show that the news media "convey the message that black people are violent, lazy, and less civic minded" (Jackson 1997:A27).[34]

During the 1870s and 1880s, whites feared that Chinese immigrants would take away their jobs. This fear led to white mob violence against the Chinese and to an act of Congress that prohibited Chinese immigration. An example of this violence appears in this illustration, which depicts an anti-Chinese riot in Denver, Colorado, that destroyed that city's Chinatown and involved the beatings of several Chinese residents and the lynching of a 28-year-old Chinese man.

Source: Everett Historical/Shutterstock.com

A second sociological explanation emphasizes *economic and political competition* and is commonly called group threat theory or ethnic competition theory (Olzak 1992; Quillian 2006).[35] In this view, prejudice arises from competition over jobs and other resources and from disagreement over various political issues. When groups vie with each other over these matters, they often become hostile toward each other. Amid such hostility, it is easy to become prejudiced toward the group that threatens your economic or political standing.

The competition explanation is the macro equivalent of the frustration/scapegoat theory already discussed. Much of the white mob violence discussed earlier stemmed from whites' concern that the groups they attacked threatened their jobs and other aspects of their lives. Thus lynchings of African Americans in the South increased when the Southern economy worsened and decreased when the economy improved (Tolnay and Beck 1995).[36] Similarly, white mob violence against Chinese immigrants in the 1870s began after the railroad construction that employed so many Chinese immigrants slowed and the Chinese began looking for work in other industries. Whites feared that the Chinese would take jobs away from white workers and that their large supply of labor would drive down wages. Their assaults on the Chinese killed several people and prompted the passage by Congress of the Chinese Exclusion Act in 1882 that prohibited Chinese immigration (Dinnerstein et al. 2015).[37]

Correlates of Prejudice

Since the 1940s, social scientists have investigated the individual correlates of racial and ethnic prejudice (Cowling et al. 2019; Stangor 2009).[38] These correlates help test the theories of prejudice just presented. For example, if authoritarian personalities do produce prejudice, then people with these personalities should be more prejudiced. If frustration also produces prejudice, then people who are frustrated with aspects of their lives should also be more prejudiced. Other correlates that have been studied include age, education, gender, region of country, race, residence in integrated neighborhoods, and religiosity. We can take time here to focus on gender, education, and region of country and discuss the evidence for the racial attitudes of whites, as most studies do in view of the historical dominance of whites in the United States.

The findings on *gender* are rather surprising. Although women are usually thought to be more empathetic than men and thus to be less likely to be racially prejudiced, research indicates that the racial views of (white) women and men are in fact very similar and that the two genders are about equally prejudiced (Hughes and Tuch, 2003).[39] This similarity supports group threat theory, outlined earlier, in that it indicates that white women and men are responding more as whites than as women or men, respectively, in formulating their racial views.

Findings on *education* and *region of country* are not surprising. Focusing again just on whites, less educated people are usually more racially prejudiced than better-educated people, and Southerners are often more prejudiced than non-Southerners (Krysan 2000).[40] Figure 3.2 depicts educational differences in a type of racial prejudice that social scientists call *social distance*, or feelings about interacting with members of other races and ethnicities. The General Social Survey asks respondents how they feel about a "close relative" marrying an African American. In Figure 3.2, whites without a high school diploma are much more likely than those with more education to oppose these marriages. To recall the sociological perspective (see Chapter 1), our social backgrounds certainly do seem to affect our attitudes.

FIGURE 3.2 Education and Opposition by Non-Latinx Whites to a Close Relative Marrying an African American

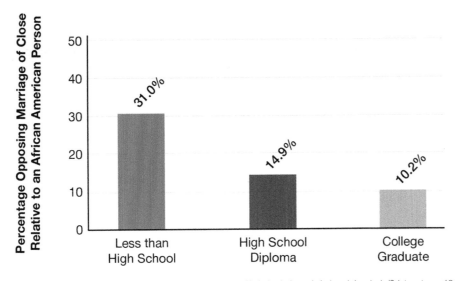

Source: Data from General Social Survey. (2018). Retrieved from http://sda.berkeley.edu/sdaweb/analysis/?dataset=gss18

The Changing Nature of Prejudice

Although racial and ethnic prejudice still exists in the United States, its nature has changed during the past half-century. Studies of these changes focus on whites' perceptions of African Americans. Back in the 1940s and before, the era of overt *Jim Crow* racism (also called *traditional* or *old-fashioned* racism) prevailed, not just in the South but in the entire nation. This racism involved blatant bigotry, firm beliefs in the need for segregation, and the view that blacks were biologically inferior to whites. In the early 1940s, for example, more than half of all whites thought that blacks were less intelligent than whites, more than half favored segregation in public transportation, more than two-thirds favored segregated schools, and more than half thought whites should receive preference over blacks in employment hiring (Schuman et al. 1997).[41]

The Nazi experience and then the civil rights movement led whites to reassess their views, and Jim Crow racism gradually waned. Few whites believe today that African Americans are biologically inferior, and few favor segregation. So few whites now support segregation and other Jim Crow views that national surveys no longer include many of the questions that were asked a half-century ago.

But that does not mean that prejudice has disappeared. Many scholars say that Jim Crow racism has been replaced by a more subtle form of racial prejudice, termed *laissez-faire, symbolic,* or *modern* racism, that amounts to a "kinder, gentler, antiblack ideology" that avoids notions of biological inferiority (Bobo et al. 1997:15; Quillian, 2006; Sears, 1988).[42] Instead, it involves stereotypes about African Americans, a belief that their poverty is due to their cultural inferiority, and opposition to government policies to help them. Similar views exist about Latinxs. In effect, this new form of prejudice blames African Americans and Latinxs themselves for their low socioeconomic standing and involves beliefs such as African Americans and Latinxs simply do not want to work hard.

Prejudice and Public Policy Preferences

If whites do continue to believe in racial stereotypes, say the scholars who study modern prejudice, they are that much more likely to oppose government efforts to help people of color. For example, whites who hold racial stereotypes are more likely to oppose government programs for African Americans (Quillian 2006).[43] We can see an example of this type of effect in Figure 3.3, which compares two groups: whites who attribute blacks' poverty to lack of motivation, and whites who attribute blacks' poverty to discrimination. Those who cite lack of motivation are more likely than those who cite discrimination to believe the government is spending too much to help blacks.

FIGURE 3.3 Racial Stereotyping by Non-Latinx Whites and Their Opposition to Government Spending to Help African Americans

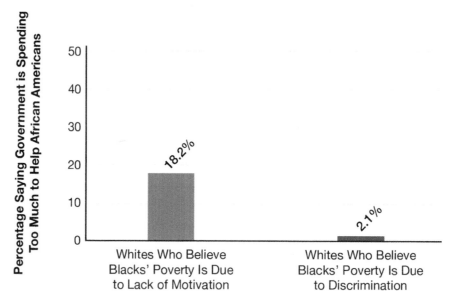

Source: Data from General Social Survey. (2010). Retrieved from http://sda.berkeley.edu/sdaweb/analysis/?dataset=gss18

Racial prejudice influences other public policy preferences as well. In the area of criminal justice, whites who hold racial stereotypes or hostile feelings toward African Americans are more likely to be afraid of crime, to think that the courts are not harsh enough, to support the death penalty, to want more money spent to fight crime, and to favor excessive use of force by police (Unnever 2014).[44]

If racial prejudice influences views on all these issues, then these results are troubling for a democratic society like the United States. In a democracy, it is appropriate for the public to disagree on all sorts of issues, including criminal justice. For example, citizens hold many reasons for either favoring or opposing the death penalty. But is it appropriate for racial prejudice to be one of these reasons? To the extent that elected officials respond to public opinion, as they should in a democracy, and to the extent that racial prejudice affects public opinion, then racial prejudice may be influencing government policy on criminal justice and on other issues. In a democratic society, it is unacceptable for racial prejudice to have this effect.

Whites who are racially prejudiced are more likely to favor harsher treatment of criminals and in particular are more likely to support the death penalty.

Source: © Thinkstock

Key Takeaways

- Social-psychological explanations of prejudice emphasize authoritarian personalities and frustration, while sociological explanations emphasize social learning and group threat.
- Education and region of residence are related to racial prejudice among whites; prejudice is higher among whites with lower levels of formal education and among whites living in the South.
- Jim Crow racism has been replaced by symbolic or modern racism that emphasizes the cultural inferiority of people of color.
- Racial prejudice among whites is linked to certain views they hold about public policy. Prejudice is associated with lower support among whites for governmental efforts to help people of color and with greater support for a more punitive criminal justice system.

For Your Review

1. Think about the last time you heard someone say a remark that was racially prejudiced. What was said? What was your reaction?
2. The text argues that it is inappropriate in a democratic society for racial prejudice to influence public policy. Do you agree with this argument? Why or why not?

3.4 Discrimination

Learning Objectives

1. Discuss Merton's views on whether prejudice and discrimination always coincide.
2. Distinguish between individual discrimination and institutional discrimination.
3. Provide two examples of institutional discrimination.

discrimination

With regard to racial and ethnic inequality, the arbitrary denial of rights, privileges, and opportunities to members of subordinate racial and ethnic groups.

Often racial and ethnic prejudice lead to discrimination against the subordinate racial and ethnic groups in a given society. **Discrimination** in this context refers to the arbitrary denial of rights, privileges, and opportunities to members of these groups. The use of the word *arbitrary* emphasizes that these groups are being treated unequally not because of their lack of merit but because of their race and ethnicity.

Usually prejudice and discrimination go hand-in-hand, but Robert Merton (1949)[45] stressed this is not always so. Sometimes we can be prejudiced and not discriminate, and sometimes we might not be prejudiced and still discriminate. Table 3.1 illustrates his perspective. The top-left cell and bottom-right cell consist of people who behave in ways we would normally expect. The top-left one consists of "active bigots," in Merton's terminology, people who are both prejudiced and discriminatory. An example of such a person is the white owner of an apartment building who dislikes people of color and refuses to rent to them. The bottom-right cell consists of "all-weather liberals," as Merton called them, people who are neither prejudiced nor discriminatory. An example would be someone who holds no stereotypes about the various racial and ethnic groups and treats everyone the same regardless of her or his background.

TABLE 3.1 The Relationship Between Prejudice and Discrimination

	Prejudiced?	
	Yes	*No*
Discriminates?		
Yes	Active bigots	Fair-weather liberals
No	Timid bigots	All-weather liberals

Source: Adapted from Merton, Robert K. 1949. Discrimination and the American Creed. In R. M. MacIver (Ed.), Discrimination and National Welfare (pp. 99–126). New York, NY: Institute for Religious Studies.

The remaining two cells of Table 3.1 are the more unexpected ones. On the bottom left, we see people who are prejudiced but who nonetheless do not discriminate; Merton called them "timid bigots." An example would be white restaurant owners who do not like people of color but still serve them anyway because they want their business or are afraid of being sued if they do not serve them. At the top right, we see "fair-weather liberals," or people who are not prejudiced but who still discriminate. An example would be white store owners in the South during the segregation era who thought it was wrong to treat blacks worse than whites but who still refused to sell to them because they were afraid of losing white customers.

Individual Discrimination

The discussion so far has centered on **individual discrimination**, or discrimination that individuals practice in their daily lives, usually because they are prejudiced but sometimes even if they are not prejudiced. Individual discrimination is common, as Joe Feagin (1991),[46] a former president of the American Sociological Association, found when he interviewed middle-class African Americans about their experiences. Many of the people he interviewed said they had been refused service, or at least received poor service, in stores or restaurants. Others said they had been harassed by the police, and even put in fear of their lives, just for being black. Feagin concluded that these examples are not just isolated incidents but rather reflect the larger racism in American society.

individual discrimination

Discrimination that individuals practice in their daily lives.

Sociologist Joe Feagin's study of middle-class African Americans found that many had been harassed by police and had otherwise experienced various kinds of racial slights.

Source: © Thinkstock

In February 2012, neighborhood watch volunteer George Zimmerman fatally shot 17-year-old Trayvon Martin as Martin was walking back from a 7-Eleven carrying some Skittles and iced tea. Critics said Zimmerman was suspicious of Martin only because Martin was black.

Source: Image courtesy of Sunset Parkerpix, http://www.flickr.com/photos/fleshmanpix/7010115775/.

Sociologist Denise Segura found that more than 40 percent of the Mexican American women she interviewed at a public university had encountered workplace discrimination based on their ethnicity and/or gender.

Source: © Thinkstock

institutional discrimination

Discrimination that pervades the practices of whole institutions, such as housing, medical care, law enforcement, employment, and education, even if such discrimination is not intended.

To many observers, the fatal shooting of Trayvon Martin in February 2012, one of the most newsworthy events of this century so far, was a deadly example of individual discrimination. Martin, a 17-year-old African American, was walking in a gated community in Sanford, Florida, as he returned from a 7-Eleven with a bag of Skittles and some iced tea. An armed neighborhood watch volunteer, George Zimmerman, called 911 and said Martin looked suspicious. Although the 911 operator told Zimmerman not to approach Martin, Zimmerman did so anyway; within minutes Zimmerman shot and killed the unarmed Martin and later claimed self-defense. According to many critics of this incident, Martin's only "crime" was "walking while black." As an African American newspaper columnist observed, "For every black man in America, from the millionaire in the corner office to the mechanic in the local garage, the Trayvon Martin tragedy is personal. It could have been me or one of my sons. It could have been any of us" (Robinson 2012).[47]

Much individual discrimination occurs in the workplace, as sociologist Denise Segura (Segura, 1992)[48] documented when she interviewed 152 Mexican American women working in white-collar jobs at a public university in California. More than 40 percent of the women said they had encountered workplace discrimination based on their ethnicity and/or gender, and they attributed their treatment to stereotypes held by their employers and coworkers. Along with discrimination, they were the targets of condescending comments like "I didn't know that there were any educated people in Mexico that have a graduate degree."

Institutional Discrimination

Individual discrimination is important to address, but at least as consequential in today's world is **institutional discrimination**, or discrimination that pervades the practices of whole institutions, such as housing, medical care, law enforcement, employment, and education. This type of discrimination does not just affect a few isolated people of color. Instead, it affects large numbers of individuals simply because of their race or ethnicity. Sometimes institutional discrimination is also based on gender, disability, and other characteristics.

In the area of race and ethnicity, institutional discrimination often stems from prejudice, as was certainly true in the South during segregation. However, just as individuals can discriminate without being prejudiced, so can institutions when they engage in practices that seem to be racially neutral but in fact have a discriminatory effect. Individuals in institutions can also discriminate without realizing it. They make decisions that turn out, upon close inspection, to discriminate against people of color even if they did not mean to do so.

The bottom line is this: institutions can discriminate even if they do not intend to do so. Consider height requirements for police. Before the 1970s, police forces around the United States commonly had height requirements, say five feet ten inches. As women began to want to join police forces in the 1970s, many found they were too short to meet this requirement. The same was true for people from some racial/ethnic backgrounds, such as Latinxs, whose stature is smaller on the average than that of non-Latinx whites. Of course, even many white males were too short to become police officers, but the point is that even more women, and even more men of certain ethnicities, were too short.

This gender and ethnic difference is not, in and of itself, discriminatory as the law defines the term. The law allows for *bona fide* (good faith) physical qualifications for a job. As an example, we would all agree that someone has to be able to see to be a school bus driver; sight therefore is a *bona fide* requirement for this line of work. Thus even though people who cannot see may not become school bus drivers, the law does not consider such a physical requirement to be discriminatory.

But were the height restrictions for police work in the early 1970s *bona fide* requirements? Women and members of certain ethnic groups challenged these restrictions in court and won their cases, as it was decided that there was no logical basis for the height restrictions then in effect. In short (pun intended), the courts concluded that a person did not have to be five feet ten inches to be an effective police officer. In response to these court challenges, police forces lowered their height requirements, opening the door for many more women, Latinx men, and some other men to join police forces (Appier 1998).[49] Whether police forces back then intended their height requirements to discriminate, or whether they honestly thought their height requirements made sense, remains in dispute. Regardless of the reason, their requirements did discriminate.

Institutional discrimination affects the life chances of people of color in many aspects of life today. To illustrate this, we turn briefly to some examples of institutional discrimination that have been the subject of government investigation and scholarly research.

Institutional discrimination can occur even if this type of discrimination is not intended. Police forces used to have height requirements, but these were deemed by courts to discriminate against women, Latinxs, and other individuals. In response, police forces lowered their height requirements.

Source: © Thinkstock

Health Care

People of color have higher rates of disease and illness than whites, a fact explored further in a discussion on health and medicine in Chapter 12. One question that arises is why their health is worse. One possible answer involves institutional discrimination based on race and ethnicity.

Several studies use hospital records to investigate whether people of color receive optimal medical care, including coronary bypass surgery, angioplasty, and catheterization. After taking the patients' medical symptoms and needs into account, these studies find that African Americans are much less likely than whites to receive the procedures just listed. This is true when poor blacks are compared to poor whites and also when middle-class blacks are compared to middle-class whites (Smedley et al. 2003).[50] In a novel way of studying race and cardiac care, one study performed an experiment in which several hundred doctors viewed videos of African American and white patients, all of whom, unknown to the doctors, were actors. In the videos, each "patient" complained of identical chest pain and other symptoms. The doctors were then asked to indicate whether they thought the patient needed cardiac catheterization. The African American patients were less likely than the white patients to be recommended for this procedure (Schulman et al., 1999).[51]

Why does discrimination like this occur? It is possible, of course, that some doctors are racists and decide that the lives of African Americans just are not worth saving, but it is far more likely that they have *unconscious* racial biases that somehow affect their medical judgments. Regardless of the reason, the result is the same: African Americans are less likely to receive potentially life-saving cardiac procedures simply because they are black. Institutional discrimination in health care, then, is literally a matter of life and death.

After the 2020 pandemic began, evidence emerged of racial bias in the treatment of African Americans with COVID-19 symptoms. To be more specific, a study by a Boston biotechnology company found that African Americans with these symptoms who had visited hospitals in seven states were six times less likely than whites with similar symptoms to have been tested for the coronavirus and to be treated for the disease (Rubix Life Sciences 2020).[52] Evidence like this led the Centers for Disease Control and Prevention to warn health-care professionals against letting unconscious racial bias affect their treatment of COVID-19 patients (Eligon and Burch 2020).[53]

Mortgages, Redlining, and Residential Segregation

When loan officers review mortgage applications, they consider many factors, including the person's income, employment, and credit history. The law forbids them to consider race and ethnicity. Yet African Americans and Latinxs are more likely than whites to have their mortgage applications declined (Blank et al. 2005).[54] Because members of these groups tend to be poorer than whites and to have less desirable employment and credit histories, the higher rate of mortgage rejections may be appropriate, albeit unfortunate.

To control for this possibility, researchers take these factors into account and in effect compare whites, African Americans, and Latinxs with similar incomes, employment, and credit histories. Some studies are purely statistical, and some involve white, African American, and Latinx individuals who independently visit the same mortgage-lending institutions. Both types of studies find that African Americans and Latinxs are still more likely than whites with similar qualifications to have their mortgage applications rejected (Turner et al., 2002).[55] We will probably never know whether loan officers are consciously basing their decisions on racial prejudice, but their practices still amount to racial and ethnic discrimination whether the loan officers are consciously prejudiced or not.

There is also evidence of banks rejecting mortgage applications for people who wish to live in certain urban, supposedly high-risk neighborhoods, and of insurance companies denying homeowner's insurance or else charging higher rates for homes in these same neighborhoods. Practices like these that discriminate against houses in certain neighborhoods are called *redlining*, and they also violate the law (Ezeala-Harrison et al. 2008).[56] Because the people affected by redlining tend to be people of color, redlining, too, is an example of institutional discrimination.

Banks have rejected mortgage applications from people who wish to live in certain urban, high-risk neighborhoods. This practice, called redlining, violates the law. Because many of the loan applicants who experience redlining are people of color, redlining is an example of institutional discrimination.

Source: Image courtesy of Taber Andrew Bain, http://www.flickr.com/photos/88442983@N00/2943913721.

Mortgage rejections and redlining contribute to another major problem facing people of color: residential segregation. Housing segregation is illegal but is nonetheless widespread because of mortgage rejections and other processes that make it very difficult for people of color to move out of segregated neighborhoods and into unsegregated areas. African Americans, in particular, remain highly segregated by residence in many cities, much more so than is true for other people of color. The residential segregation of African Americans is so extensive that it is called *hypersegregation* and has been termed *American apartheid* (Massey and Denton, 1993).[57]

In addition to mortgage rejections, a pattern of subtle discrimination by realtors and homeowners makes it difficult for African Americans to find out about homes in white neighborhoods and to buy them (Pager 2008).[58] For example, realtors may tell African American clients that no homes are available in a particular white neighborhood, but then inform white clients of available homes. The now routine posting of housing listings on the internet has probably reduced this type of housing discrimination, but not all homes and apartments are posted, with some simply sold or rented by word of mouth to avoid certain people learning about them.

The hypersegregation experienced by African Americans cuts them off from the larger society, as many rarely leave their immediate neighborhoods, and results in *concentrated poverty*, where joblessness, crime, and other problems reign. For several reasons, then, residential segregation is thought to play a major role in the seriousness and persistence of African American poverty (Quillian 2012).[59]

Why Cities Are Still So Segregated

Subtle discrimination in the mortgage and real estate industries perpetuates racial segregation in housing. This segregation results in concentrated poverty and its corresponding problems of joblessness, crime, poor health, and other issues.

View the video online at: http://www.youtube.com/embed/O5FBJyqfoLM?rel=0

Employment Discrimination

Title VII of the federal Civil Rights Act of 1964 banned racial discrimination in employment, including hiring, wages, and firing. However, African Americans, Latinxs, and Native Americans still have much lower earnings than whites. Several factors explain this disparity, including the various structural obstacles discussed in the examination of poverty found in Chapter 2. Despite Title VII, however, an additional reason is that people of color continue to face discrimination in hiring and promotion (Jameel and Yerardi 2019).[60] It is again difficult to determine whether such discrimination stems from conscious prejudice or from unconscious prejudice on the part of potential employers, but it is racial discrimination nonetheless.

A now-classic field experiment documented such discrimination. Sociologist Devah Pager (2003)[61] had young white and African American men apply independently in person for entry-level jobs. They dressed the same and reported similar levels of education and other qualifications. Some applicants also admitted having a criminal record, while other applicants reported no such record. As might be expected, applicants with a criminal record were hired at lower rates than those without a record. However, in striking evidence of racial discrimination in hiring, African American applicants *without* a criminal record were hired at the same low rate as the white applicants *with* a criminal record.

Key Takeaways

- People who practice racial or ethnic discrimination are usually also prejudiced, but not always. Some people practice discrimination without being prejudiced, and some may not practice discrimination even though they are prejudiced.
- Individual discrimination is common and can involve various kinds of racial slights. Much individual discrimination occurs in the workplace.
- Institutional discrimination often stems from prejudice, but institutions can also practice racial and ethnic discrimination when they engage in practices that seem to be racially neutral but in fact have a discriminatory effect.

3.5 Dimensions of Racial and Ethnic Inequality

Asian Americans have higher family incomes than whites on the average. Although Asian Americans are often viewed as a "model minority," some Asians have been less able than others to achieve economic success, and stereotypes of Asians and discrimination against them remain serious problems.

Source: © Thinkstock

Racial and ethnic inequality manifests itself in all walks of life. The individual and institutional discrimination just discussed is one manifestation of this inequality. We can also see stark evidence of racial and ethnic inequality in various government statistics. Sometimes statistics lie, and sometimes they provide all too true a picture, as do statistics on racial and ethnic inequality. Table 3.2 presents data on racial and ethnic differences in income, education, and health.

TABLE 3.2 Selected Indicators of Racial and Ethnic Inequality in the United States

	African American	Asian	Latinx	Native American	White, Non-Latinx
Median household income, 2017 ($)	40,258	81,331	50,486	39,719	68,256
Persons who are college educated, 2017 (%)	20.6	52.7	15.2	14.3	34.5
Persons in poverty, 2017 (%)	21.1	10.0	18.3	26.2	8.7
Infant mortality (number of infant deaths per 1,000 births), 2016	11.4	3.6	5.0	9.4	4.9
Note: Native American income and poverty data are for 2016.					

Source: Centers for Disease Control and Prevention. 2019. "Infant Mortality." https://www.cdc.gov/reproductivehealth/maternalinfanthealth/infantmortality.htm; Fontenot, Kayla, Jessica Semega and Melissa Kollar. 2018. *Income and Poverty in the United States: 2017*. Washington, DC: U.S. Census Bureau. U.S. Census Bureau. 2019. American Factfinder: https://factfinder.census.gov/faces/nav/jsf/pages/index.xhtml; Wilson, Valerie and Zane Mokhiber. 2017. "2016 ACS Shows Stubbornly High Native American Poverty and Different Degrees of Economic Well-Being for Asian Ethnic Groups." Economic Policy Institute:https://www.epi.org/blog/2016-acs-shows-stubbornly-high-native-american-poverty-and-different-degrees-of-economic-well-being-for-asian-ethnic-groups/.

The picture presented by Table 3.2 is clear: U.S. racial and ethnic groups differ dramatically in their life chances. Compared to whites, for example, African Americans, Latinxs, and Native Americans have much lower household incomes and much higher rates of poverty; they are also much less likely to have college degrees. In addition, African Americans and Native Americans have much higher infant mortality rates than whites: Black infants, for example, are more than twice as likely as white infants to die. Later chapters in this book will continue to highlight various dimensions of racial and ethnic inequality.

Although Table 3.2 shows that African Americans, Latinxs, and Native Americans fare much worse than whites, it presents a more complex pattern for Asian Americans. Compared to whites, Asian Americans have higher family incomes and are more likely to hold college degrees, but they also have a higher poverty rate. Thus many Asian Americans do relatively well, while others fare relatively worse, as just noted. Although Asian Americans are often viewed as a "model minority," meaning that they have achieved economic success despite not being white, some Asians have been less able than others to climb the economic ladder. Moreover, stereotypes of Asian Americans and discrimination against them remain serious problems (Chou and Feagin 2016).[62]

The Increasing Racial/Ethnic Wealth Gap

At the beginning of this chapter, we noted that racial and ethnic inequality has existed since the beginning of the United States. We also noted that social scientists have warned that certain conditions have actually worsened for people of color since the 1960s.

Telling evidence of this worsening involves racial disparities in wealth, which includes a family's total assets (income, savings and investments, home equity, etc.) and debts (mortgage, credit cards, etc.). As Figure 3.4 shows, the median household wealth of African Americans and Latinxs is minuscule compared to that for non-Latinx whites. These racial/ethnic disparities are larger than in the early 1980s, and, African American wealth has in fact declined since the early 1980s (Collins et al. 2019).[63] The economic recession that began in 2008 helps explain this worsening situation for people of color, whom the recession affected more severely than it did whites.

FIGURE 3.4 The Racial/Ethnic Wealth Gap (Median Net Worth of Households in 2016)

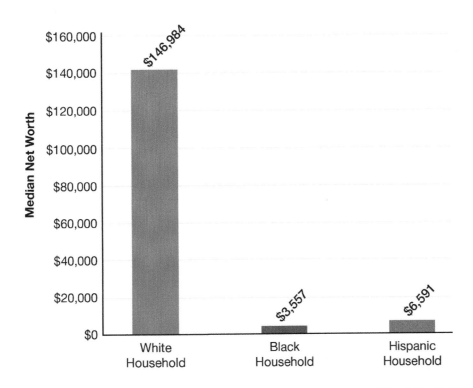

Source: Collins, Chuck, Dedrick Asante-Muhammed, Josh Hoxie and Sabrina Terry. 2019. Dreams Deferred: *How Enriching the 1% Widens the Racial Wealth Divide*. Washington, DC: Institute for Policy Studies.

A large racial/ethnic gap also existed in the percentage of families with negative net worth—that is, those whose debts exceed their assets. One-third of black and Latinx households have zero or negative net worth, compared to only 15.5 percent of white households. Black and Latinx households are thus more than twice as likely as white households to be in debt (Collins et al. 2019).[64]

The Hidden Toll of Racial and Ethnic Inequality

Much evidence suggests that having black or brown skin in a society filled with racial prejudice, discrimination, and inequality takes what has been called a "hidden toll" on the lives of African Americans, Latinxs, and Native Americans (Villarosa 2018).[65] As we shall see in later chapters, these groups have poorer health than whites and die at younger ages; this is especially true for African Americans and Native Americans, but also applies to Latinxs. In fact, every year there are an additional 100,000 African American deaths than would be expected if they lived as long as whites do. One of the many reasons for this situation is the stress of being a person of color in a racist society (Geronimus et al. 2010; Williams et al. 2019).[66]

In this way of thinking, people of color are much more likely than whites to be poor, to live in high-poverty neighborhoods and other settings, and to live in crowded conditions, among many other problems. As this chapter discussed earlier for African Americans, they are also more likely, whether or not they are poor, to experience racial slights, refusals to be interviewed for jobs, and other forms of discrimination in their everyday lives. All these problems mean that African Americans (to focus on the group for which there is the most research on this dynamic) from their earliest ages grow up with a great deal of stress, far more than what most whites experience. This stress, in turn, has certain neural and physiological effects, including hypertension (high blood pressure), that impair African Americans' short-term and long-term health and that ultimately shorten their lives. These effects accumulate over time: Black and white hypertension rates are equal for people in their twenties, but the black rate becomes much higher by the time people reach their forties and fifties. As a news report on evidence of this hidden toll summarized this process, "The long-term stress of living in a white-dominated society 'weathers' blacks, making them age faster than their white counterparts" (Blitstein 2009:48).[67]

Although there is less research on other people of color, many Latinxs and Native Americans also experience the various sources of stress that African Americans experience. To the extent this is true, racial and ethnic inequality also takes a hidden toll on members of these two groups. They, too, experience racial slights, live under disadvantaged conditions, and face other problems that result in high levels of stress, cause various health problems, and shorten their life spans. On a related note, research from the past few years suggests that Donald Trump's presidential campaign and presidency raised stress levels in the general population, and perhaps especially among Latinxs in view of his many harsh comments about immigrants (Hoyt et al. 2018; Wan and Never 2019).[68] These higher stress levels, in turn, may have increased health problems in the Latinx community, including increased premature births and higher levels of hypertension and obesity among Latinx women (Gemmill et al. 2019; Torres et al. 2018).[69]

White Privilege: The Benefits of Being White

Before we leave this section, it is important to discuss the advantages that U.S. whites enjoy in their daily lives simply because they are white. Social scientists term these advantages **white privilege** and say that whites benefit from being white, whether or not they are aware of their advantages (McIntosh, 2007).[70]

This chapter's discussion of the problems facing people of color points to some of these advantages. For example, whites can usually drive a car at night or walk down a street without having to fear that a police officer will stop them simply because they are white. Recalling the Trayvon Martin tragedy, they can also walk down a street without having to fear they will be confronted and possibly killed by a neighborhood watch volunteer. In addition, whites can count on being able to move into any neighborhood they desire to as long as they can afford the rent or mortgage. They generally do not have to fear being passed up for promotion simply because of their race. White students can live in college dorms without having to worry that racial slurs will be directed their way. White people in general do not have to worry about being the victims of hate crimes based on their race. They can be seated in a restaurant without having to worry that they will be served more slowly or not at all because of their skin color. If they are in a hotel, they do not have to think that someone will mistake them for a bellhop, parking valet, or maid. If they are trying to hail a taxi, they do not have to worry about the taxi driver ignoring them because the driver fears he or she will be robbed.

Social scientist Robert W. Terry (1981:120)[71] once summarized white privilege as follows: "*To be white in America is not to have to think about it*. Except for hard-core racial supremacists, the meaning of being white is having the choice of attending to or ignoring one's own whiteness" (emphasis in original). For people of color in the United States, it is not an exaggeration to say that race and ethnicity are a daily fact of their existence. Yet whites do not generally have to think about being white. As all of us go about our daily lives, this basic difference is one of the most important manifestations of racial and ethnic inequality in the United States.

Perhaps because whites do not have to think about being white, many studies find they tend to underestimate the degree of racial inequality in the United States by assuming that African Americans and Latinxs are much better off than they really are (Kraus et al. 2017).[72] As one report summarized these studies' overall conclusion, "Whites tend to have a relatively rosy impression of what it means to be a black person in America. Whites are more than twice as likely as blacks to believe that the position of African Americans has improved a great deal" (Vedantam, 2008:A3).[73] Because whites think African Americans and Latinxs fare much better than they really do, that perception probably reduces whites' sympathy for programs designed to reduce racial and ethnic inequality.

white privilege

The advantages that U.S. whites enjoy in their daily lives simply because they are white, whether or not they are aware of these advantages.

American whites enjoy certain privileges merely because they are white. For example, they usually do not have to fear that a police officer will stop them simply because they are white, and they also generally do not have to worry about being mistaken for a bellhop, parking valet, or maid.

Source: © Thinkstock

Key Takeaways

- Compared to non-Latinx whites, people of color have lower incomes, lower educational attainment, higher poverty rates, and poorer health.
- Racial and ethnic inequality takes a hidden toll on people of color, as the stress they experience impairs their health and ability to achieve.
- Whites benefit from being white, whether or not they realize it. This benefit is called white privilege.

For Your Review

1. Write a brief essay that describes important dimensions of racial and ethnic inequality in the United States.
2. If you are white, describe a time when you benefited from white privilege, whether or not you realized it at the time. If you are a person of color, describe an experience when you would have benefited if you had been white.

3.6 Explaining Racial and Ethnic Inequality

Learning Objectives

1. Understand cultural explanations for racial and ethnic inequality.
2. Describe structural explanations for racial and ethnic inequality.

Why do racial and ethnic inequality exist? Why do African Americans, Latinxs, Native Americans, and some Asian Americans fare worse than whites? In answering these questions, many people have some very strong opinions.

Biological Inferiority

One long-standing explanation is that blacks and other people of color are *biologically inferior*: They are naturally less intelligent and have other innate flaws that keep them from getting a good education and otherwise doing what needs to be done to achieve the American Dream. As discussed earlier, this racist view is no longer common today. However, whites historically used this belief to justify slavery, lynchings of blacks, the harsh treatment of Native Americans in the 1800s, and abuse and lesser forms of discrimination against immigrants from many lands a century ago. In 1994, Richard J. Herrnstein and Charles Murray revived this view in their controversial book, *The Bell Curve* (Herrnstein and Murray 1994),[74] in which they argued that the low IQ scores of African Americans, and of poor people more generally, reflect their genetic inferiority in the area of intelligence. African Americans' low innate intelligence, they said, accounts for their poverty and other problems. Although the news media gave much attention to their book, few scholars agreed with its views, and many condemned the book's argument as a racist way of "blaming the victim" (Gould 1994).[75]

Cultural Deficiencies

Another explanation of racial and ethnic inequality focuses on supposed *cultural deficiencies* of African Americans and other people of color (Murray 1984).[76] These deficiencies include a failure to value hard work and, for African Americans, a lack of strong family ties, and are said to account for the poverty and other problems facing these groups. This view echoes the culture-of-poverty argument presented in Chapter 2 and is certainly popular today. As we saw earlier, many non-Latinx whites think that blacks' poverty is due to their lack of motivation and willpower. Ironically some scholars find support for this cultural deficiency view in the experience of many Asian Americans, whose success is often attributed to their culture's emphasis on hard work, educational attainment, and strong family ties (Min 2005).[77] If that is true, these scholars say, then the lack of success of other people of color stems from the failure of their own cultures to value these attributes.

How accurate is the cultural deficiency argument? Whether people of color have "deficient" cultures remains hotly debated (Bonilla-Silva 2018).[78] Many social scientists find little or no evidence of cultural problems in minority communities and say the belief in cultural deficiencies is an example of symbolic racism that blames the victim. Citing survey evidence, they say that poor people of color value work and education for themselves and their children at least as much as wealthier white people do (Puchner and Markowitz 2015).[79] Yet other social scientists, including those very aware of the structural problems facing people of color, believe that certain cultural problems do exist, but they are careful to say that these cultural problems arise out of the structural problems. For example, Elijah Anderson (1999)[80] wrote that a "street culture" or "oppositional culture" exists among African Americans in urban areas that contributes to high levels of violent behavior, but he emphasized that this type of culture stems from the segregation, extreme poverty, and other difficulties these citizens face in their daily lives and helps them deal with these difficulties. Thus even if cultural problems do exist, they should not obscure the fact that structural problems are responsible for the cultural ones.

Structural Problems

A third explanation for U.S. racial and ethnic inequality is based in conflict theory and reflects the blaming-the-system approach outlined in Chapter 1. This view attributes racial and ethnic inequality to the many structural problems just mentioned, including institutional and individual discrimination, a lack of opportunity in education and other spheres of life, and the absence of jobs that pay an adequate wage (Bonilla-Silva 2018).[81] Segregated housing, for example, prevents African Americans from escaping the inner city and from moving to areas with greater employment opportunities. Employment discrimination keeps the salaries of people of color much lower than they would be otherwise. The schools that many children of color attend every day are typically overcrowded and underfunded. As these problems continue from one generation to the next, it becomes very difficult for people already at the bottom of the socioeconomic ladder to climb up it because of their race and ethnicity (see "Applying Social Research").

Applying Social Research

The Poor Neighborhoods of Middle-Class African Americans

In a society that values equal opportunity for all, scholars have discovered a troubling trend: African American children from middle-class families are much more likely than their white counterparts to move *down* the socioeconomic ladder by the time they become adults. In fact, almost half of all African American children born during the 1950s and 1960s to middle-class parents ended up with lower incomes than their parents by adulthood. Because these children had parents who had evidently succeeded despite all the obstacles facing them in a society filled with racial inequality, we have to assume they were raised with the values, skills, and aspirations necessary to stay in the middle class and even to rise beyond it. What, then, explains why some end up doing worse than their parents?

According to a study by sociologist Patrick Sharkey, an important answer lies in the neighborhoods in which these children are raised. Because of racial segregation in housing, many middle-class African American families find themselves having to live in poor urban neighborhoods. About half of African American children born between 1955 and 1970 to middle-class parents grew up in poor neighborhoods, but hardly any middle-class white children grew up in such neighborhoods. Sharkey found that neighborhood poverty was a much more important factor than variables like parents' education and marital status in explaining this huge racial difference. An additional finding by Sharkey underscored the importance of neighborhood poverty for adult socioeconomic status: African American children raised in poor neighborhoods in which the poverty rate declined significantly ended up with higher incomes as adults than those raised in neighborhoods where the poverty rate did not change.

Why do poor neighborhoods have this effect? It is difficult to pinpoint the exact causes, but several probable reasons come to mind. In these neighborhoods, middle-class African American children often receive inadequate schooling at run-down schools, and they come under the influence of youths who care much less about schooling and who get into various kinds of trouble. The various problems associated with living in poor neighborhoods also likely cause a good deal of stress, which, as discussed elsewhere in this chapter, can cause health problems and impair learning ability.

Even if the exact reasons remain unclear, this study showed that poor neighborhoods make a huge difference in how children end up as adults. One implication of this and similar studies is clear: To help reduce African American poverty, it is important to do everything possible to improve the quality and economy of the poor neighborhoods in which many African American children, middle-class or poor, grow up.

Sources: Morsy and Rothstein 2019; Sharkey 2009[82]

As we assess the importance of structure versus culture in explaining why people of color have higher poverty rates, it is interesting to consider the economic experience of African Americans and Latinxs since the 1990s. During that decade, the U.S. economy thrived. Along with this thriving economy, unemployment rates and poverty rates for African Americans and Latinxs declined. During the economic recession that began in 2008, both these rates then increased.

To explain these trends, does it make sense to assume that African Americans and Latinxs somehow had fewer cultural deficiencies during the 1990s and more cultural deficiencies beginning in 2008? Or does it make sense to assume that their economic success or lack of it depended on the opportunities afforded them by the U.S. economy? Economic writer Joshua Holland (2011)[83] provided the logical answer by attacking the idea of cultural deficiencies: "That's obviously nonsense. It was exogenous economic factors and changes in public policies, not manifestations of 'black culture' [or 'Latinx culture'], that resulted in those widely varied outcomes... While economic swings this significant can be explained by economic changes and different public policies, it's simply impossible to fit them into a cultural narrative."

The COVID-19 pandemic further illustrates the value of a structural explanation of racial and ethnic inequality. Recall that rates of disease and death from COVID-19 have been much higher for African Americans and Latinx than for whites. Scholars and other observers point to several structural conditions as the reasons for this situation (Blow 2020; Farmer 2020; Gibbons 2020; Spicuzza et al. 2020).[84] Compared to whites, for example, African Americans and Latinx are:

- More likely to live in poverty and thus to have chronic health problems that make them more vulnerable to contracting COVID-19 and to dying from it
- More likely to need and use public transportation, increasing their exposure to the coronavirus
- Less likely to be able to work at home, and more likely to work in grocery stores and other settings that increase their exposure to the coronavirus
- More likely to live in dense urban areas, again, increasing their exposure
- More likely to live in polluted areas, which weakens their immune systems and makes them more vulnerable to contracting COVID-19 and to dying from it
- Less likely to have access to health care
- More likely to experience discrimination and microaggressions that weaken their immune systems and, again, makes them more vulnerable to COVID-19

- Although a belief in biological inferiority used to be an explanation for racial and ethnic inequality, this belief is now considered racist.
- Cultural explanations attribute racial and ethnic inequality to certain cultural deficiencies among people of color.
- Structural explanations attribute racial and ethnic inequality to problems in the larger society, including discriminatory practices and lack of opportunity.

For Your Review

1. Which of the three explanations of racial and ethnic inequality makes the most sense to you? Why?
2. Why should a belief in the biological inferiority of people of color be considered racist?

3.7 Reducing Racial and Ethnic Inequality

Learning Objectives

1. Summarize the debate over affirmative action.
2. Describe any three policies or practices that could reduce racial and ethnic inequality in the United States.

Now that we have examined race and ethnicity in the United States, what have we found? Where do we stand in the third decade of the twenty-first century?

On the one hand, there is cause for hope. Legal racial segregation is gone. The vicious, Jim Crow racism that was so rampant in this country into the 1960s has declined dramatically since that tumultuous time. People of color have made important gains in several spheres of life, and people of color occupy important elected positions in and outside the South, a feat that would have been unimaginable a generation ago. Perhaps most notably, Barack Obama has African ancestry and identifies as an African American, and on his 2008 election night people across the country wept with joy at the symbolism of his victory. Certainly progress has been made in U.S. racial and ethnic relations.

On the other hand, there is also cause for despair. Jim Crow racism has been replaced by a modern, symbolic racism that still blames people of color for their problems and reduces public support for government policies to deal with their problems. Institutional and individual discrimination remain pervasive, and hate crimes remain all too common. So does suspicion of people based solely on the color of their skin, as the Trayvon Martin tragedy again reminded us. The apparent racism of President Obama's successor, Donald Trump, is further cause for despair, as there is no place for racism in the highest office in the land.

As this chapter discussed, much evidence points to continuing racial and ethnic inequality. If adequately funded and implemented, several types of programs and policies show strong promise of reducing this inequality. We turn to these in a moment, but first let's discuss affirmative action, an issue that has aroused controversy since its inception.

People Making a Difference

College Students and the Southern Civil Rights Movement

The first chapter of this book included this famous quotation by anthropologist Margaret Mead: "Never doubt that a small group of thoughtful, committed citizens can change the world. Indeed, it is the only thing that ever has." The beginnings of the Southern civil rights movement provide an inspirational example of Mead's wisdom and remind us that young people can make a difference.

Although there had been several efforts during the 1950s by African Americans to end legal segregation in the South, the start of the civil rights movement is commonly thought to have begun on February 1, 1960. On that historic day, four brave African American students from the Agricultural and Technical College of North Carolina, dressed in coats and ties, sat down quietly at a segregated lunch counter in a Woolworth's store in the city of Greensboro and asked to be served. When they were refused service, they stayed until the store closed at the end of the day, and then went home. They returned the next day and were joined by some two dozen other students. They were again refused service and sat quietly the rest of the day. The next day some sixty students and other people joined them, followed by some three hundred on the fourth day. Within a week, sit-ins were occurring at lunch counters in several other towns and cities inside and outside of North Carolina. In late July, 1960, the Greensboro Woolworth's finally served African Americans, and the entire Woolworth's chain desegregated its lunch counters a day later. Although no one realized it at the time, the civil rights movement had "officially" begun thanks to the efforts of a small group of college students.

During the remaining years of the heyday of the civil rights movement, college students from the South and North joined thousands of other people in sit-ins, marches, and other activities to end legal segregation. Thousands were arrested, and at least forty-one were murdered. By risking their freedom and even their lives, they made a difference for millions of African Americans. And it all began when a small group of college students sat down at a lunch counter in Greensboro and politely refused to leave until they were served.

Sources: Branch 1988; Southern Poverty Law Center, n.d.[85]

Affirmative Action

affirmative action

Special consideration for minorities and women in employment and education to compensate for the discrimination and lack of opportunities they experience in the larger society.

Affirmative action refers to special consideration for minorities and women in employment and education to compensate for the discrimination and lack of opportunities they experience in the larger society. Affirmative action programs were begun in the 1960s to provide African Americans and, later, other people of color and women access to jobs and education to make up for past discrimination. President John F. Kennedy was the first known official to use the term, when he signed an executive order in 1961 ordering federal contractors to "take affirmative action" in ensuring that applicants are hired and treated without regard to their race and national origin. Six years later, President Lyndon B. Johnson added sex to race and national origin as demographic categories for which affirmative action should be used.

Although many affirmative action programs remain in effect today, court rulings, state legislation, and other efforts have limited their number and scope. Despite this curtailment, affirmative action continues to spark much controversy, with scholars, members of the public, and elected officials all holding strong views on the issue.

One of the major court rulings just mentioned was the U.S. Supreme Court's decision in *Regents of the University of California v. Bakke*, 438 US 265 (1978). Allan Bakke was a 35-year-old white man who had twice been rejected for admission into the medical school at the University of California, Davis. At the time he applied, UC–Davis had a policy of reserving sixteen seats in its entering class of one hundred for qualified people of color to make up for their underrepresentation in the medical profession. Bakke's college grades and scores on the Medical College Admission Test were higher than those of the people of color admitted to UC–Davis either time Bakke applied. He sued for admission on the grounds that his rejection amounted to reverse racial discrimination on the basis of his being white (Stefoff, 2005).[86]

The case eventually reached the Supreme Court, which ruled 5–4 that Bakke must be admitted into the UC–Davis medical school because he had been unfairly denied admission on the basis of his race. As part of its historic but complex decision, the Court thus rejected the use of strict racial quotas in admission, as it declared that no applicant could be excluded based solely on the applicant's race. At the same time, however, the Court also declared that race may be used as one of the several criteria that admissions committees consider when making their decisions. For example, if an institution desires racial diversity among its students, it may use race as an admissions criterion along with other factors such as grades and test scores.

Two later Supreme Court cases both involved the University of Michigan: *Gratz v. Bollinger*, 539 US 244 (2003), which involved the university's undergraduate admissions, and *Grutter v. Bollinger*, 539 US 306 (2003), which involved the university's law school admissions. In *Grutter* the Court reaffirmed the right of institutions of higher education to take race into account in the admissions process. In *Gratz*, however, the Court invalidated the university's policy of awarding additional points to high school students of color as part of its use of a point system to evaluate applicants; the Court said that consideration of applicants needed to be more individualized than a point system allowed. In a more recent case, *Fisher v. University of Texas*, 570 US 297 (2013), the Court approved the use by the University of Texas of a procedure that involved admitting the top ten percent of every Texas graduating high school class and then considering race and other factors in admitting the rest of the entering group of students.

Drawing on these Supreme Court rulings, then, affirmative action in higher education admissions on the basis of race/ethnicity is permissible as long as it does not involve a rigid quota system and as long as it does involve an individualized way of evaluating candidates. Race may be used as one of several criteria in such an individualized evaluation process, but it must not be used as the only criterion.

The Debate over Affirmative Action

The debate over affirmative action involves several competing arguments (Okechukwu 2019; Quinlan 2015).[87] Affirmative action, opponents say, is reverse discrimination and, as such, is both illegal and immoral. The people benefiting from affirmative action are less qualified than many of the whites with whom they compete for employment and college admissions. In addition, opponents say, affirmative action implies that the people benefiting from it need extra help and thus are indeed less qualified. This implication stigmatizes the groups benefiting from affirmative action.

In response, proponents of affirmative action give several reasons for favoring it. Many say it is needed to make up not just for past discrimination and a lack of opportunities for people of color but also for ongoing discrimination and a lack of opportunity. For example, because of their social networks, whites are much better able than people of color to find out about and to get jobs (Reskin 1998).[88] If this is true, people of color are automatically at a disadvantage in the job market, and some form of affirmative action is needed to give them an equal chance at employment. Proponents also say that affirmative action helps add diversity to the workplace and to the campus. Many colleges, they note, give some preference to high school students who live in a distant state in order to add needed diversity to the student body; to "legacy" students—those with a parent who went to the same institution—to reinforce alumni loyalty and to motivate alumni to donate to the institution; and to athletes, musicians, and other applicants with certain specialized talents and skills. If all these forms of preferential admission make sense, proponents say, it also makes sense to take students' racial and ethnic backgrounds into account as admissions officers strive to have a diverse student body.

Proponents add that affirmative action has indeed succeeded in expanding employment and educational opportunities for people of color, and that individuals benefiting from affirmative action have generally fared well in the workplace or on the campus.

As this brief discussion indicates, several reasons exist for and against affirmative action. A cautious conclusion is that affirmative action may not be perfect, but that some form of it is needed to make up for past and ongoing discrimination and lack of opportunity in the workplace and on campuses. Without the extra help that affirmative action programs give disadvantaged people of color, the discrimination and other difficulties they face are certain to continue.

Other Programs and Policies

As indicated near the beginning of this chapter, one message from DNA evidence and studies of evolution is that we are all part of one human race. If we fail to recognize this lesson, we are doomed to repeat the experiences of the past, when racial and ethnic hostility overtook good reason and subjected people who happened to look different from the white majority to legal, social, and violent oppression. In the democracy that is America, we must try to do better so that there will truly be "liberty and justice for all."

As the United States attempts, however haltingly, to reduce racial and ethnic inequality, sociology has much insight to offer in its emphasis on the structural basis for this inequality. This emphasis strongly indicates that racial and ethnic inequality has much less to do with any personal faults of people of color than with the structural obstacles they face, including ongoing discrimination and lack of opportunity. Efforts aimed at such obstacles, then, are in the long run essential to reducing racial and ethnic inequality. Some of these efforts resemble those for reducing poverty discussed in Chapter 2, given the greater poverty of many people of color, and include the following:

1. Adopt a national "full employment" policy involving federally funded job training and public works programs.
2. Increase federal aid for the working poor, including earned income credits and child-care subsidies for those with children.
3. Establish and expand well-funded early childhood intervention programs, including home visitation by trained professionals, for poor families, as well as adolescent intervention programs, such as Upward Bound, for low-income teenagers.
4. Improve the schools that poor children attend and the schooling they receive, and expand early childhood education programs for poor children.
5. Provide better nutrition and health services for poor families with young children.
6. Strengthen efforts to reduce teenage pregnancies.
7. Strengthen affirmative action programs within the limits imposed by court rulings.
8. Strengthen legal enforcement of existing laws forbidding racial and ethnic discrimination in hiring and promotion.
9. Strengthen efforts to reduce residential segregation.

Key Takeaways

- There is reason to be both hopeful and less hopeful in regard to the future of racial and ethnic relations and inequality in the United States.

- Affirmative action continues to be a very controversial issue. Proponents think it is necessary to compensate for past and continuing racial and ethnic discrimination and lack of opportunity, while opponents think it discriminates against qualified whites.
- A variety of policies and practices hold strong potential for reducing racial and ethnic inequality, providing they are adequately funded and successfully implemented.

For Your Review

1. How hopeful are you in regard to the future of race and ethnicity in the United States? Explain your answer.
2. Do you favor or oppose affirmative action? Why?

3.8 End-of-Chapter Material

Summary

1. Racial and ethnic prejudice and discrimination have been an "American dilemma" in the United States ever since the colonial period. Slavery was only the ugliest manifestation of this dilemma. The urban riots of the 1960s led to warnings about the racial hostility and discrimination confronting African Americans and other groups, and these warnings continue to the present.

2. Social scientists today tend to consider race more of a social category than a biological one for several reasons. Race is thus best considered a social construction and not a fixed biological category.

3. Ethnicity refers to a shared cultural heritage and is a term increasingly favored by social scientists over race. Membership in ethnic groups gives many people an important sense of identity and pride but can also lead to hostility toward people in other ethnic groups.

4. Prejudice, racism, and stereotypes all refer to negative attitudes about people based on their membership in racial or ethnic categories. Social-psychological explanations of prejudice focus on scapegoating and authoritarian personalities, while sociological explanations focus on conformity and socialization or on economic and political competition. Jim Crow racism has given way to modern or symbolic racism that considers people of color to be culturally inferior.

5. Discrimination and prejudice often go hand in hand, but not always. People can discriminate without being prejudiced, and they can be prejudiced without discriminating. Individual and institutional discrimination both continue to exist in the United States.

6. Racial and ethnic inequality in the United States is reflected in income, employment, education, and health statistics. In their daily lives, whites enjoy many privileges denied to their counterparts in other racial and ethnic groups. The COVID-19 pandemic illustrates this situation, as people of color experience many disadvantages that have led them to have much higher rates than whites of disease and death from the coronavirus.

7. On many issues, Americans remain sharply divided along racial and ethnic lines. One of the most divisive issues is affirmative action. Its opponents view it among other things as reverse discrimination, while its proponents cite many reasons for its importance, including the need to correct past and present discrimination against racial and ethnic minorities.

Using What You Know

As a person of color, you obtain a job in a medium-sized city in the Midwest and rent an apartment in a house about two miles from your workplace so that you can commute by bus. One day someone boarding the bus walks past you. As he does so, he snarls, "Go back where you came from!" You're first startled and then angry to hear this racist comment. What do you decide to do? Why?

What You Can Do

To help reduce racial and ethnic inequality, you may wish to do any of the following:

1. Contribute money to a local, state, or national organization that tries to help youths of color at their schools, homes, or other venues.
2. Volunteer for an organization that focuses on policy issues related to race and ethnicity.
3. Volunteer for any programs at your campus that aim at enhancing the educational success of new students of color; if no such programs exist, start one.

Endnotes

1. Dickson, EJ. (2019, July 15). Man Who Killed Heather Heyer at Charlottesville Sentenced to Life In Prison, Plus 419 Years. *Rolling Stone*. Retrieved from: https://www.rollingstone.com/culture/culture-news/heather-heyer-james-fields-charlottesville-murderer-859182/.

2. Kijakazi, Kilolo. 2020. "Covid-19 Racial Health Disparities Highlight Why We Need to Address Structural Racism." *Urban Institute*. Retrieved from https://www.urban.org/urban-wire/covid-19-racial-health-disparities-highlight-why-we-need-address-structural-racism.

3. Artiga, Samantha and Kendal Orgera. 2020. Covid-19 Presents Significant Risks for American Indian and Alaska Native People. San Francisco: Kaiser Family Foundation.

4. Kerner Commission. (1968). *Report of the National Advisory Commission on civil disorders*. New York, NY: Bantam Books.

5. Brown, Drr. A. 2009. *Bury My Heart at Wounded Knee: An Indian History of the American West*. New York, NY: Sterling Innovation.

6. Gates, Henry Louis, Jr. 2014. "Slavery, by the Numbers." *The Root* February 10:https://www.theroot.com/slavery-by-the-numbers-1790874492.

7. Glymph, Thavolia. 2008. *Out of the House of Bondage: The Transformation of the Plantation Household*. New York: Cambridge University Press.

8. Brown, Richard M. 1975. *Strain of Violence: Historical Studies of American Violence and Vigilantism*. New York: Oxford University Press.

9. Litwack, Leon F. 2009. *How Free is Free? The Long Death of Jim Crow*. Cambridge, MA: Harvard University Press.

10. Dinnerstein, L., & Reimers, D. M. 2009. *Ethnic Americans: A History of Immigration*. New York, NY: Columbia University Press.

11. Myrdal, Gunnar. 1944. *An American Dilemma: The Negro Problem and Modern Democracy*. New York: Harper and Brothers.

12. Massey, Douglas S. 2007. *Categorically Unequal: The American Stratification System*. New York: Russell Sage Foundation; Oliver, Melvin L. and Thomas M. Shapiro. 2019. "Disrupting the Racial Wealth Gap." *Contexts* May 7:https://contexts.org/articles/disrupting-the-racial-wealth-gap/. Wilson, William J. 2009. "The Economic Plight of Inner-city Black Males. In E. Anderson (Ed.), *Against the Wall: Poor, Young, Black, and Male* (pp. 55–70). Philadelphia: University of Pennsylvania Press.

13. Smedley, Audrey and Brian D. Smedley. 2018/2012. *Race in North America: Evolution of a Worldview*. Boulder, CO: Westview Press.

14. Smedley, Audrey and Brian D. Smedley. 2018/2012. *Race in North America: Evolution of a Worldview*. Boulder, CO: Westview Press.

15. Bryc, Katarzyna, Eric Y. Durand, J. Michael Macpherson, David Reich and Joanna L. Mountain. 2015. "The Genetic Ancestry of African Americans, Latinos, and European Americans across the United States." *American Journal of Human Genetics* 96(1):37-53.

16. Painter, Nell Irvin. (2010). *The History of White People*. New York: W. W. Norton.

17. Staples, Brent. 2005. Why Race Isn't as "Black" and "White" as We Think. *The New York Times* October 21:A18.

18. Telles, Edward E. 2006. *Race in Another America: The Significance of Skin color in Brazil*. Princeton, NJ: Princeton University Press.

19. Barrionuevo, A., & Calmes, J. 2011. *President Underscores Similarities with Brazilians, But Sidesteps One*. New York Times March 21:A8; Klein, H. S., & Luno, F. V. 2009. *Slavery in Brazil*. New York, NY: Cambridge University Press; Telles, Edward E. (2006). *Race in Another America: The Significance of Skin Color in Brazil*. Princeton, NJ: Princeton University Press.

20. Begley, Sharon. 2008. Race and DNA. *Newsweek* February 29:http://www.thedailybeast.com/newsweek/blogs/lab-notes/2008/02/29/race-and-dna.html .

21. Stone, L., & Lurquin, P. F. 2007. *Genes, Culture, and Human Evolution: A Synthesis*. Malden, MA: Blackwell.

22. Berger, Peter., & Luckmann, Thomas. 1963. *The Social Construction of Reality*. New York, NY: Doubleday.

23. Leland, J., & Beals, G. 1997. In living colors: Tiger Woods is the exception that rules. *Newsweek* May 5:58–60.

24. Staples, Brent. 1998. The Shifting Meanings of 'Black' and 'White.' *The New York Times* November 13:WK14.

25. Adorno, T. W., Frenkel-Brunswick, E., Levinson, D. J., & Sanford, R. N. (1950). *The Authoritarian Personality*. New York, NY: Harper.

26. Miller, Audrey K. 2019. "A Dilemma of Dogma: Specifying the Personality Root of Sexual Prejudice." *Journal of Homosexuality* Forthcoming:https://doi.org/10.1080/00918369.2019.1624454; Sibley, C. G., and Duckitt, J. 2008. Personality and Prejudice: A Meta-analysis and Theoretical Review. *Personality and Social Psychology Review* 12:248–279.

27. Dollard, J., Doob, L. W., Miller, N. E., Mowrer, O. H., & Sears, R. R. (1939). *Frustration and Aggression*. New Haven, CT: Yale University Press.

28. Cowen, E. L., Landes, J., & Schaet, D. E. 1959. The Effects of Mild Frustration on the Expression of Prejudiced Attitudes. *Journal of Abnormal and Social Psychology* 64:33–38.

29. Aronson, Elliot. 2018. *The Social Animal*. New York: Worth Publishers.

30. Bazaz, Aggie Ebrahimi. 2019. "Missing School Is a Given for Children of Migrant Farmworkers." *Truthout* May 6:https://truthout.org/articles/missing-school-is-a-given-for-children-of-migrant-farmworkers/; Brown, P. L. 2011. Itinerant Life Weighs on Farmworkers' Children. *The New York Times* March 13:A18; Landale, N. S., McHale, S., & Booth, A. (Eds.). 2011. *Growing Up Hispanic: Health and Development of Children of Immigrants*. Washington, DC: Urban Institute Press.

31. Gilens, Martin. 1996. Race and Poverty in America: Public Misconceptions and the American News Media. *Public Opinion Quarterly*, 60:515–541.

32. Entman, R. M., and Rojecki, A. 2001. *The Black Image in the White Mind*. Chicago, IL: University of Chicago Press.

33. Robinson, Matthew B. 2018. *Media Coverage of Crime and Criminal Justice*. Durham, NC: Carolina Academic Press.

34. Jackson, D. Z. 1997. Unspoken During Race Talk. *The Boston Globe* December 5:A27.

35. Olzak, Susan. 1992. *The Dynamics of Ethnic Competition and Conflict*. Stanford: Stanford University Press. Quillian, Lincoln 2006. New Approaches to Understanding Racial Prejudice and Discrimination. *Annual Review of Sociology*, 32:299–328.

36. Tolnay, S. E., and Beck, E. M. 1995. *A Festival of Violence: An Analysis of Southern Lynchings, 1882-1930*. Urbana, IL: University of Illinois Press.

37. Dinnerstein, Leonard, Roger L. Nichols and David M. Reimers. 2015. *Natives and Strangers: A History of Ethnic Americans*. New York: Oxford University Press.

38. Cowling, Misha Mei, Joel R. Anderson and Rose Ferguson. 2019. "Prejudice-Relevant Correlates of Attitudes Towards Refugees: A Meta-Analysis." *Journal of Refugee Studies* Forthcoming: https://doi.org/10.1093/jrs/fey062; Stangor, Charles. 2009. "The Study of Stereotyping, Prejudice, and Discrimination within Social Psychology: A Quick History of Theory and Research." Pp. 1-22 in *Handbook of Prejudice, Stereotyping, and Discrimination*, edited by T. D. Nelson. New York: Psychology Press.

39. Hughes, M., & Tuch, S. A. 2003. Gender Differences in Whites' Racial Attitudes: Are Women's Attitudes Really More Favorable? *Social Psychology Quarterly* 66:384–401.

40. Krysan, Maria. 2000. Prejudice, Politics, and Public Opinion: Understanding the Sources of Racial Policy Attitudes. *Annual Review of Sociology* 26:135–168.

41. Schuman, H., Steeh, C., Bobo, L., & Krysan, M. 1997. *Racial Attitudes in America: Trends and Interpretations* (Rev. ed.). Cambridge, MA: Harvard University Press.

42. Bobo, L., Kluegel, J. R., & Smith, R. A. 1997. *Laissez-faire Racism: The Crystallization of a Kinder, Gentler, Antilock Ideology*. In S. A. Tuch & J. K. Martin (Eds.), *Racial Attitudes in the 1990s: Continuity and Change* (pp. 15–44). Westport, CT: Praeger; Quillian, Lincoln. 2006. New Approaches to Understanding Racial Prejudice and Discrimination. *Annual Review of Sociology*, 32, 299–328; Sears, D. O. (1988). *Symbolic Racism*. In P. A. Katz & D. A. Taylor (Eds.), *Eliminating Racism: Profiles in Controversy* (pp. 53–84). New York, NY: Plenum.

43. Quillian, Lincoln. 2006. New Approaches to Understanding Racial Prejudice and Discrimination. *Annual Review of Sociology*, 32:299–328.

44. Unnever, James D. 2014. "Race, Crime, and Public Opinion." *The Oxford Handbook of Ethnicity, Crime, and Immigration*, edited by S. Bucerius and M. Tonry. New York: Oxford University Press.

45. Merton, Robert K. 1949. Discrimination and the American Creed. In R. M. MacIver (Ed.), *Discrimination and National Welfare* (pp. 99–126). New York, NY: Institute for Religious Studies.

46. Feagin, Joe R. (1991). The Continuing Significance of Race: Antiblack Discrimination in Public Places. *American Sociological Review* 56:101–116.

47. Robinson, Eugene. (2012, March 23). Perils of Walking While Black. *The Washington Post*, p.A19. Also retrieved from: https://www.washingtonpost.com/opinions/to-be-black-in-america-/2012/03/22/gIQAEKr4TS_story.html.

48. Segura, D. A. (1992). Chicanas in white-collar jobs: "You have to prove yourself more." In C. G. Ellison & W. A. Martin (Eds.), *Race and ethnic relations in the United States: Readings for the 21st century* (pp. 79–88). Los Angeles, CA: Roxbury.

49. Appier, J. (1998). *Policing Women: The Sexual Politics of Law Enforcement and the LAPD*. Philadelphia, PA: Temple University Press.

50. Smedley, B. D., Stith, A. Y., & Nelson, A. R. 2003. *Unequal Treatment: Confronting Racial and Ethnic Disparities in Health Care*. Washington, DC: National Academies Press.

51. Schulman, Kevin A., Jesse A. Berlin, William Harless, Jon F. Kerner, Shryl Sistrunk, Bernard J. Gersh, Ross Dubé, Christopher K. Taleghani, Jennifer E. Burke, Sankey Williams, John M. Eisenberg and José J. Escarce. 1999. "The Effect of Race and Sex on Physicians' Recommendations for Cardiac Catheterization." *The New England Journal of Medicine* 340:618-26.

52. Rubix Life Sciences. 2020. "Covid-19 and Minority Health Access." March:https://rubixls.com/wp-content/uploads/2020/04/COVID-19-Minority-Health-Access-6.pdf.

53. Eligon, John and Audra D.S. Burch. 2020. "Questions of Bias in Covid-19 Treatment Haunt Mourning Black Families." *The New York Times* May 11:A1.

54. Blank, E. C., Venkatachalam, P., McNeil, L., & Green, R. D. 2005. Racial Discrimination in Mortgage Lending in Washington, DC: A Mixed Methods Approach. *The Review of Black Political Economy*, 33(2), 9–30.

55. Turner, M. A., Freiberg, F., Godfrey, E., Herbig, C., Levy, D. K., & Smith, R. R. 2002. *All Other Things Being Equal: A Paired Testing Study of Mortgage Lending Institutions*. Washington, DC: Urban Institute Press.

56. Ezeala-Harrison, F., Glover, G. B., & Shaw-Jackson, J. 2008. Housing Loan Patterns toward Minority Borrowers in Mississippi: Analysis of Some Micro Data Evidence of Redlining. *The Review of Black Political Economy*, 35(1):43–54.

57. Massey, D. S., & Denton, N. A. (1993). *American apartheid: Segregation and the making of the underclass*. Cambridge, MA: Harvard University Press.

58. Pager, Devah. 2008. The Dynamics of Discrimination. In A. C. Lin & D. R. Harris (Eds.), *The Colors of Poverty: Why Racial and Ethnic Disparities Exist* (pp. 21–51). New York, NY: Russell Sage Foundation.

59. Quillian, Lincoln. 2012. "Segregation and Poverty Concentration: The Role of Three Segregations." *American Sociological Review* 77(3):354-79.

60. Jameel, Maryam and Joe Yerardi. 2019. "Workplace Discrmination Is Illegal. But Our Data Shows It's Still a Huge Problem." *Vox.com* February 28:https://www.vox.com/policy-and-politics/2019/2/28/18241973/workplace-discrimination-cpi-investigation-eeoc.

61. Pager, Devah. 2003. The Mark of a Criminal Record. *American Journal of Sociology*, 108:937–975.

62. Chou, Rosalind S. and Joe R. Feagin. 2016. *The Myth of the Model Minority: Asian Americans Facing Racism*. New York: Routledge.

63. Collins, Chuck, Dedrick Asante-Muhammed, Josh Hoxie and Sabrina Terry. 2019. *How Enriching the 1% Widens the Racial Wealth Divide*: Institute for Policy Studies.

64. Collins, Chuck, Dedrick Asante-Muhammed, Josh Hoxie and Sabrina Terry. 2019. *How Enriching the 1% Widens the Racial Wealth Divide*: Institute for Policy Studies.

65. Villarosa, Linda. 2018. "The Hidden Toll: Why America's Black Mothers and Babies Are in a Life-or-Death Crisis." *The New York Times* April 11:https://www.nytimes.com/2018/04/11/magazine/black-mothers-babies-death-maternal-mortality.html.

66. Geronimus, A. T., Hicken, M., Pearson, J., Seashols, S., Brown, K., & Cruz, T. D. 2010. *Do US Black Women Experience Stress-related Accelerated Biological Aging? Human Nature: An Interdisciplinary Biosocial Perspective*, 21:19–38; Williams, David R., Jourdyn A. Lawrence and Brigette A. Davis. 2019. "Racism and Health: Evidence and Needed Research." *Annual Review of Public Health* 40:105-25.

67. Blitstein, Ryan. 2009. "Weathering the Storm." *Miller-McCune* 2(July-August):48-57.

68. Hoyt, Lindsay T., Katharine H. Zeiders, Natasha Chaku, Russell B. Toomey and Rajni L. Nairc. 2018. "Young Adults' Psychological and Physiological Reactions to the 2016 U.S. Presidential Election"; *Psychoneuroendocrinology* 92:162-69. Wan, William and Lindsey Bever. 2019. "Trump's Presidency May Be Making Latinos Sick." *The Washington Post* July 19:https://wapo.st/3cHeCyA.

69. Torres, J. M. , J. Deardorff, R. B. Gunier, K. G. Harley, a. Alkon, K. Kogut and B. Eskenazi. 2018. "Worry About Deportation and Cardiovascular Disease Risk Factors among Adult Women: The Center for the Health Assessment of Mothers and Children of Salinas Study." *Annals of Behavioral Medicine* 52(2):186-93; Gemmill, Alison, Ralph Catalano, Joan A. Casey, Deborah Karasek, Héctor E. Alcalá, Holly Elser and Jacqueline M. Torres. 2019. "Association of Preterm Births among Us Latina Women with the 2016 Presidential Election." *Jama Network Open* 2(7):doi:10.1001/jamanetworkopen.2019.7084.

70. McIntosh, P. (2007). White privilege and male privilege: A personal account of coming to see correspondence through work in women's studies. In M. L. Andersen & P. H. Collins (Eds.), *Race, class, and gender: An anthology* (6th ed.). Belmont, CA: Wadsworth.

71. Terry, Robert W. 1981. "The Negative Impact on White Values." Pp. 119-51 in *Impacts of Racism on White Americans*, edited by B. P. Bowser and R. G. Hunt. Beverly Hills: Sage Publications.

72. Kraus, Michael W., Julian M. Rucker and Jennifer A. Richeson. 2017. "Americans Misperceive Racial Economic Equality." *PNAS* 114(39):10324-31.

73. Vedantam, Shankar. (2008, March 24). Unequal Perspectives on Racial Equality. *The Washington Post*, p.A3. Also retrieved from: https://www.washingtonpost.com/wp-dyn/content/article/2008/03/23/AR2008032301417.html

74. Herrnstein, Richard J. and Charles Murray. 1994. *The Bell Curve: Intelligence and Class Structure in American Life*. New York: Free Press.

75. Gould, Stephen Jay. 1994. "Curveball." *The New Yorker* November 28:139-49.

76. Murray, C. 1984. *Losing Ground: American Social Policy, 1950–1980*. New York: Basic Books.

77. Min, P. G. (Ed.). 2005. *Asian Americans: Contemporary Trends and Issues* (2nd ed.). Thousand Oaks, CA: Sage Publications.

78. Bonilla-Silva, Eduardo. 2018. *Racism without Racists: Color-Blind Racism and the Persistence of Racial Inequality in the United States*. Lanham, MD: Rowman & Littlefield.

79. Puchner, Laurel and Linda Markowitz. 2015. "Do Black Families Value Education? White Teachers, Institutional Cultural Narratives, & Beliefs About African Americans." *Multicultural Education* 23(1):9-16.

80. Anderson, Elijah. 1999. *Code of the Street: Decency, Violence, and the Moral Life of the Inner City*. New York: W.W. Norton.

81. Bonilla-Silva, Eduardo. 2018. *Racism without Racists: Color-Blind Racism and the Persistence of Racial Inequality in the United States*. Lanham, MD: Rowman & Littlefield.

82. Morsy, Leila and Richard Rothstein. 2019. "Toxic Stress and Children's Outcomes." *Economic Policy Institute*:https://www.epi.org/publication/toxic-stress-and-childrens-outcomes-african-american-children-growing-up-poor-are-at-greater-risk-of-disrupted-physiological-functioning-and-depressed-academic-achievement/; Sharkey, Patrick. 2009. *Neighborhoods and the Black-White Mobility Gap*. Washington DC: Pew Charitable Trusts.

83. Holland, Joshua. 2011. Debunking the Big Lie Right-wingers Use to Justify Black Poverty and Unemployment. *AlterNet July 29*: http://www.alternet.org/teaparty/151830/debunking_the_big_lie_right-wingers_use_to_justify_black_poverty _and_unemployment_.

84. Blow, Charles M. 2020. "Social Distancing Is a Privilege." *The New York Times* April 5:https://www.nytimes.com/2020/04/05/opinion/coronavirus-social-distancing.html; Farmer, Blake. 2020. "Long-Standing Racial and Income Disparities Seen Creeping into Covid-19 Care." *Modern Healthcare* April 6(https://www.modernhealthcare.com/safety-quality/long-standing-racial-and-income-disparities-seen-creeping-covid-19-care); Gibbons, Ann. 2020. "How Can We Save Black and Brown Lives During a Pandemic? Data from Past Studies Can Point the Way." *Science* April 10:https://www.sciencemag.org/news/2020/04/how-can-we-save-black-and-brown-lives-during-pandemic-data-past-studies-can-point-way#; Spicuzza, Mary, Ashley Luthern and Alison Dirr. 2020. "'A Perfect Storm': African Americans in Milwaukee, Already Facing Health Disparities, Hit Hard by Coronavirus." *Milwaukee Journal Sentinel* April 3:https://www.jsonline.com/story/news/2020/04/03/african-americans-milwaukee-hit-hard-coronavirus/5111950002/.

85. Branch, Taylor. 1988. *Parting the Waters: America in the King Years, 1954-1963*. New York: Simon and Schuster; Southern Poverty Law Center. n.d., "Civil Rights Martyrs". (https://www.splcenter.org/what-we-do/civil-rights-memorial/civil-rights-martyrs).

86. Stefoff, R. (2005). *The Bakke case: Challenging affirmative action*. New York, NY: Marshall Cavendish Benchmark.

87. Quinlan, Casey. 2015. "7 Criticisms of Affirmative Action That Have Been Thoroughly Disproved." *Think Progress* December 9:https://thinkprogress.org/7-criticisms-of-affirmative-action-that-have-been-thoroughly-disproved-4283499521b8/; Okechukwu, Amaka. 2019. *To Fulfill These Rights: Political Struggle over Affirmative Action and Open Admissions* New York: Columbia University Press.

88. Reskin, Barbara F. 1998. *Realities of Affirmative Action in Employment*. Washington, DC: American Sociological Association.

CHAPTER 4

Gender Inequality

Social Problems in the News

"Reports of Sexual Harassment Wane at Work, Possibly Thanks to #MeToo," the headline said. In the wake of the #MeToo movement that brought down prominent men in politics, entertainment, and industry over charges of sexual assault and sexual harassment, new survey data reported by a study were suggesting that the movement had helped decrease workplace sexual harassment. Two similar surveys of more than 500 women taken in 2016 and then in 2018 showed a decline in sexual harassment. In one particular result, the number of women who reported being pressured by someone in their workplace to engage in unwanted sexual activity declined by 10 percent between the two surveys. Women in the later survey also reported being more supported and empowered to report any sexual harassment. Applauding these changes, one of the study's authors said, "So many people put themselves out there and made themselves vulnerable during the #MeToo movement—and it's working." At the same time, the second survey registered a greater amount of non-sexual harassment based on the women's gender, perhaps reflecting a backlash against this movement.

Source: Sullivan 2019[1]

Thanks to the contemporary women's rights movement that began in the late 1960s, much has changed for women and men in American society during the past half-century. Still, as this news story about the #MeToo movement reminds us, much more needs to be done. Despite tremendous advancements for women since the 1960s, gender inequality persists and manifests itself in many ways. This chapter examines the major forms of gender inequality and the reasons for its existence, and it outlines various steps our society should take to help ensure equality between the sexes. It will also discuss certain dimensions of gender inequality that appeared during the first months of the COVID-19 pandemic in early 2020. Our discussion begins with a critical look at the concepts of sex and gender.

4.1 Understanding Sex and Gender

Learning Objectives

1. Define sex, gender, femininity, and masculinity.
2. Critically assess the evidence on biology, culture and socialization, and gender.
3. Discuss agents of gender socialization.

Although the terms *sex* and *gender* are sometimes used interchangeably and do complement each other, they nonetheless refer to different aspects of what it means to be a woman or man in any society.

sex

The anatomical and other biological differences between females and males that are determined at the moment of conception and develop in the womb and throughout childhood and adolescence.

primary sex characteristics

Anatomical and other biological differences between females and males that begin developing in the womb.

secondary sex characteristics

Biological differences between females and males that emerge during puberty.

Sex refers to the anatomical and other biological differences between females and males that are determined at the moment of conception and develop in the womb and throughout childhood and adolescence. Females, of course, have two X chromosomes, while males have one X chromosome and one Y chromosome. From this basic genetic difference spring other biological differences. The first to appear are the genitals that boys and girls develop in the womb. The genitalia are called **primary sex characteristics**, while the other differences that develop during puberty are called **secondary sex characteristics** and stem from hormonal differences between the two sexes. Boys generally acquire deeper voices, more body hair, and more muscles from their flowing testosterone. Girls develop breasts and wider hips and begin menstruating as nature prepares them for possible pregnancy and childbirth. For better or worse, these basic biological differences between the sexes affect many people's perceptions of what it means to be female or male, as we next discuss.

Babies are born with anatomical and other biological differences that are determined at the moment of conception. These biological differences define the baby's sex.

Source: Katrina Elena/Shutterstock.com

Gender as a Social Construction

If sex is a biological concept, then **gender** is a social concept. It refers to the social and cultural differences a society assigns to people based on their (biological) sex. A related concept, **gender roles**, refers to a society's expectations of people's behavior and attitudes based on whether they are biologically female or male. Understood in this way, gender, like race as discussed in Chapter 3, is a *social construction*. How we think and behave as females and males is not etched in stone by our biology but rather is a result of how society expects us to think and behave based on what sex we are. As we grow up, we learn these expectations as we develop our **gender identity**, or our beliefs about ourselves as females or males.

These expectations are called *femininity* and *masculinity*. **Femininity** refers to the cultural expectations we have of girls and women, while **masculinity** refers to the expectations we have of boys and men. A familiar nursery rhyme nicely summarizes these two sets of traits:

What are little boys made of?

Snips and snails,

And puppy dog tails,

That's what little boys are made of.

What are little girls made of?

Sugar and spice,

And everything nice,

That's what little girls are made of.

As this rhyme suggests, our traditional notions of femininity and masculinity indicate that we think females and males are fundamentally different from each other. In effect, we think of them as two sides of the same coin of being human. What we traditionally mean by femininity is captured in the adjectives, both positive and negative, we traditionally ascribe to women: gentle, sensitive, nurturing, delicate, graceful, cooperative, decorative, dependent, emotional, passive, and weak. Thus, when we say that a girl or woman is very feminine, we have some combination of these traits in mind: She is soft, dainty, and pretty. What we traditionally mean by masculinity is captured in the adjectives, again both positive and negative, our society traditionally ascribes to men: strong, assertive, brave, active, independent, intelligent, competitive, insensitive, unemotional, and aggressive. When we say that a boy or man is very masculine, we have some combination of these traits in mind: He is tough, strong, and assertive.

These traits might sound like stereotypes of females and males in today's society, and indeed they are, but differences between women and men in attitudes and behavior do, in fact, exist (Aulette et al. 2019).[2] For example, women cry more often than men do. Men are more physically violent than women. Women take care of children more than men do. Women smile more often than men. Men curse and spit more often than women. When women talk with each other, they are more likely to talk about their personal lives than men are when they talk with each other. The two sexes even differ when they hold a cigarette (not that anyone should smoke!). When a woman holds a cigarette, she usually has the palm of her cigarette-holding hand facing upward; when a man holds a cigarette, he usually has his palm facing downward.

gender

The social and cultural differences a society assigns to people based on their biological sex.

gender roles

A society's expectations of people's behavior and attitudes based on whether they are females or males.

gender identity

Individuals' beliefs about themselves as either females or males.

femininity

Cultural expectations of girls and women, including gentleness and attractiveness.

masculinity

Cultural expectations of boys and men, including toughness and bravery.

What's the Difference between Sex and Gender?

Like race, gender is best regarded as a social construction that represents the social and cultural differences a society assigns to people based on their biological sex.

View the video online at: http://www.youtube.com/embed/dYEZd3Tq6JI?rel=0

The Development of Gender Differences

What accounts for differences in female and male behavior and attitudes? Do the biological differences between the sexes account for these other differences? Or do these latter differences stem, as most sociologists think, from cultural expectations and from differences in the ways in which the sexes are socialized? These are critical questions, for they ask whether the differences between boys and girls and women and men stem more from biology or from society. If we think behavioral and other differences between the sexes are due primarily to their respective biological makeups, we imply that these differences are inevitable or nearly so, and that any attempt to change them goes against biology and will likely fail.

For example, consider the biological fact that women bear and nurse children and men do not. Couple this with the common view that women are also more gentle and nurturing than men, and we end up with a "biological recipe" for women to be the primary caretakers of children. As Figure 4.1 depicts, many people, more than one-third of the public, do think that women are better suited to take care of a family's children and that men should be the breadwinners. A belief in a strong biological basis for differences between women and men implies there is little we can or should do to change these roles. It implies that "anatomy is destiny," and destiny is, of course, by definition inevitable.

FIGURE 4.1 Belief That Women Should Stay at Home

Agreement or disagreement with the statement that "it is much better for everyone involved if the man is the achiever outside the home and the woman takes care of the home and family."

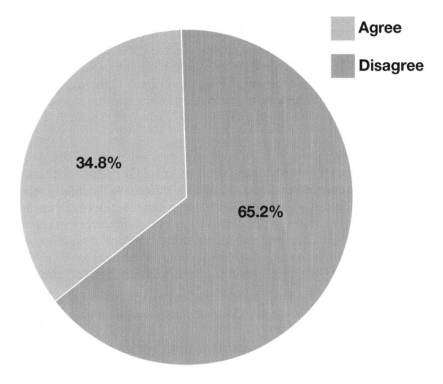

Source: Data from General Social Survey. 2019. Retrieved from http://sda.berkeley.edu/cgi-bin/hsda?harcsda+gss18.

This implication makes it essential to understand the extent to which gender differences do, in fact, stem from biological differences between the sexes or, instead, stem from cultural and social influences. If biology is paramount, then gender differences are perhaps inevitable and the status quo will remain. If culture and social influences matter much more than biology, then gender differences can change and the status quo may give way. With this backdrop in mind, let's turn to the biological evidence for behavioral and other differences between the sexes and then examine the evidence for their social and cultural roots.

Biology and Gender

Several biological explanations for gender roles exist, and we discuss two of the most important ones here. One explanation is from the field of evolutionary psychology (Buss 2019)[3] and argues an evolutionary basis for traditional gender roles.

Scholars advocating this view reason as follows (Saini 2017).[4] In prehistoric societies, two major social roles existed (1) hunting or gathering food to relieve hunger, and (2) bearing and nursing children. Because only women could perform the latter role, they were also the primary caretakers for children for several years after birth. And because women were frequently pregnant, their roles as mothers confined them to the home. Meanwhile, men were better suited than women for hunting because they were stronger and quicker than women. In prehistoric societies, then, biology was indeed destiny: For biological reasons, men in effect worked outside the home (hunted), while women stayed at home with their children.

Evolutionary reasons also explain why men are more violent than women. In prehistoric times, men who were more willing to commit violence against and even kill other men would "win out" in the competition for female mates. They thus were more likely than less violent men to produce offspring, who would then carry these males' genetic violent tendencies.

If the human race evolved along these lines, evolutionary psychologists continue, natural selection favored those societies where men were stronger, braver, and more aggressive and where women were more fertile and nurturing. Such traits over the millennia became fairly instinctual, meaning that men's and women's biological natures evolved differently. To these scholars, traditional gender roles for women and men thus make sense from an evolutionary standpoint, and attempts to change them go against the sexes' biological natures. This in turn implies that existing gender inequality must continue because it is rooted in biology. The title of a book presenting the evolutionary psychology argument summarizes this implication: *Biology at Work: Rethinking Sexual Equality* (Browne 2002).[5]

According to some evolutionary psychologists, today's gender differences in strength and physical aggression are ultimately rooted in certain evolutionary processes that spanned millennia.

Source: © Thinkstock

Critics challenge the evolutionary explanation on several grounds (Fine 2011; Saini 2017).[6] First, much greater gender variation in behavior and attitudes existed in prehistoric times than the evolutionary explanation assumes. Second, even if biological differences did influence gender roles in prehistoric times, these differences are largely irrelevant in modern societies, in which, for example, physical strength is not necessary for survival. Third, human environments throughout the millennia have simply been too diverse to permit the simple, straightforward biological development that the evolutionary explanation assumes. Fourth, evolutionary arguments implicitly justify existing gender inequality by implying the need to confine women and men to their traditional roles.

Anthropological evidence also challenges the evolutionary argument that men's tendency to commit violence was biologically transmitted. This evidence instead finds that violent men have trouble finding female mates who would want them and that the female mates they find and the children they produce are often killed by rivals to the men (Begley 2009).[7]

A second biological explanation for traditional gender roles attributes males' higher levels of aggression to their higher levels of testosterone (Dekkers et al. 2019).[8] Even though some research finds that males with higher levels of testosterone tend to have higher levels of aggression, it is possible that their violence increased their testosterone rather than the reverse. Because studies of human males cannot for ethical and practical reasons manipulate their testosterone levels, the exact meaning of the results from this line of research must remain unclear, and it cannot be assumed that higher levels of testosterone do produce higher levels of aggression (Carré and Olmstead 2015).[9]

Another line of research on the biological basis for sex differences in aggression involves children as young as ages 1 or 2 (Card et al. 2008).[10] They might be playing with each other, interacting with adults, or writing down solutions to hypothetical scenarios given to them by a researcher. In most of these studies, boys are more physically aggressive in thought or deed than girls, even at a very young age. Other studies are more experimental in nature. In one type of study, a toddler will be playing with a toy, only to have it removed by an adult. Boys typically tend to look angry and try to grab the toy back, while girls tend to just sit there and whimper. Because these gender differences are found at very young ages, researchers say they must have some biological basis. However, critics counter that even young children have already been socialized along gender lines (Begley 2009; Fine 2011).[11] To the extent this is true, gender differences in children's aggression may reflect socialization rather than biology.

In sum, biological evidence for gender differences remains controversial. It must be weighed against the evidence, to which we next turn, of cultural variations in the experience of gender and of socialization differences by gender. One thing is clear: Biological explanations for gender imply that existing gender differences and gender inequality must continue to exist. As sociologist Linda L. Lindsey (2011:52)[12] notes, "Biological arguments are consistently drawn upon to justify gender inequality and the continued oppression of women." In contrast, cultural and social explanations of gender differences and gender inequality promise some hope for change. Let's examine the evidence for these explanations.

Culture and Gender

Some of the most compelling evidence against a strong biological determination of gender roles comes from anthropologists, whose work on preindustrial societies demonstrates some striking gender variation from one culture to another. This variation underscores the impact of culture on how females and males think and behave.

Extensive evidence of this impact comes from anthropologist George Murdock (1937),[13] who created the Standard Cross-Cultural Sample of almost two hundred preindustrial societies studied by anthropologists. Some tasks in these societies, such as hunting and trapping, are almost always done by men, while other tasks, such as cooking and fetching water, are almost always done by women. These patterns provide evidence for the evolutionary argument presented earlier, as they probably stem from the biological differences between the sexes. Even so, there were at least some societies in which women hunted and men cooked and fetched water.

More important, there was much greater gender variation in several of the other tasks Murdock studied, including planting crops, milking, and generating fires. Men primarily performed these tasks in some societies, women primarily performed them in other societies, and in still other societies both sexes performed them equally. Murdock's findings illustrate how gender roles differ from one culture to another and imply they are not biologically determined.

Anthropologists continue to investigate cultural differences in gender. Some of their most interesting findings concern gender and sexuality (Brettell and Sargent 2017).[14] Although all societies distinguish "femaleness" and "maleness," additional gender categories exist in some societies. The Native Americans known as the Mohave, for example, recognize four genders: a woman, a woman who acts like a man, a man, and a man who acts like a woman. In some societies, a third, intermediary gender category is recognized. Anthropologists call this category the *berdache*, who is usually a man who takes on a woman's role. This intermediary category combines aspects of both femininity and masculinity of the society in which it is found and is thus considered an **androgynous** gender. Although some people in this category are born as *intersexed* individuals (formerly known as *hermaphrodites*), meaning they have genitalia of both sexes, many are born biologically as one sex or the other but adopt an androgynous identity.

The androgynous genders found by anthropologists remind us that gender is a social construction and not just a biological fact. If culture does affect gender roles, socialization is the process through which culture has this effect. What we experience as girls and boys strongly influences how we develop as women and men in terms of behavior and attitudes. To illustrate this important dimension of gender, let's turn to the evidence on socialization.

Anthropological research finds a good deal of variation in gender roles for certain tasks, including planting crops, milking, and generating fires. Other tasks, such as hunting and trapping, are typically done by men while tasks such as cooking and fetching water are typically done by women.

Source: Nolte Lourens/ Shutterstock.com

androgynous

Containing aspects of both femaleness and maleness, or of both femininity and masculinity.

socialization

The process whereby individuals learn the culture of their society.

Socialization and Gender

Socialization is the process whereby individuals learn the culture of their society. Several agents of socialization exist, including the family, peers, schools, the mass media, and religion, and all these institutions help to socialize people into their gender roles and also help them develop their gender identity.

The Family

Socialization into gender roles begins in infancy, as almost from the moment of birth parents begin to socialize their children as boys or girls without even knowing it (Aulette et al. 2019).[15] Parents commonly describe their infant daughters as pretty, soft, and delicate and their infant sons as strong, active, and alert, even though neutral observers find no such gender differences among infants when they do not know the infants' sex. From infancy on, parents play with and otherwise interact with their daughters and sons differently. They play more roughly with their sons—for example, by throwing them up in the air or by gently wrestling with them—and more quietly with their daughters. When their infant or toddler daughters cry, they warmly comfort them, but they tend to let their sons cry longer and to comfort them less. They give their girls dolls to play with and their boys action figures and toy guns. While these gender differences in socialization are probably smaller now than a generation ago, they certainly continue to exist. Visit the toy section of Walmart or another big-box store and you will likely see pink aisles of dolls and cooking sets and blue aisles of action figures, toy guns, and related items.

Peers

Peer influences also encourage gender socialization. As they reach school age, children begin to play different games based on their gender. Boys tend to play sports and other competitive team games, while girls tend to play smaller, cooperative games such as hopscotch and jumping rope. Although girls are much more involved in sports now than a generation ago, these gender differences in their play persist and encourage boys to be competitive and girls to be cooperative and trusting. The patterns we see in adult males and females thus have some roots in their play as young children (Lindsey 2015)[16] (see "Children and Our Future").

Children and Our Future

Girls and Boys at Play

The text discusses how the types of games that girls and boys play influence their gender-role socialization. Let's take a closer look at two early sociological studies that provided important evidence for this process.

Janet Lever (1978)[17] studied fifth-grade children in three different communities in Connecticut. She watched them play and otherwise interact in school and also had the children keep diaries of their play and games outside school. Lever found that boys' games were typically more complex than girls' games: The boys' games had a greater number of rules and more specialized roles, and they also involved more individuals playing. She attributed these differences to socialization by parents, teachers, and other adults and argued that the complexity of boys' play and games helped them to be better able than girls to learn important social skills such as dealing with rules and coordinating actions to achieve goals.

A second sociologist, Barrie Thorne (1993),[18] studied fourth- and fifth-graders in California and Michigan. The boys tended to play team sports and other competitive games, while the girls tended to play cooperative games such as jump rope. These differences led Thorne to conclude that gender-role socialization stems not only from practices by adults but also from the children's own activities without adult involvement. She also concluded that "girls against the boys" contests in such activities as classroom spelling contests and games like tag helped the children learn that boys and girls are two different and antagonistic sexes. Boys also tended to disrupt girls' games more than the reverse and in this manner both exerted and learned dominance over females. In all these ways, children were not just the passive recipients of gender-role socialization from adults (their teachers), but they also played an active role in ensuring that such socialization occurred.

These two studies were among the first to emphasize the importance of children's play for the gender-based traits and values that girls and boys learn, which in turn affect the choices they make for careers and other matters later in life. The rise in team sports opportunities for girls and women in the years since Lever and Thorne did their research is a welcome development, but young children continue to play in the ways that Lever and Thorne found. The body of research on gender differences in children's play points to the need for teachers, parents, and other adults to encourage girls and boys alike to have a mixture of both competitive and cooperative games so that both sexes may develop a better balance of values that are now commonly considered to be either feminine or masculine.

Schools

School is yet another agent of gender socialization. School playgrounds provide a location for the gender-linked play activities just described to occur. Research also has found that teachers treat their female and male students differently in subtle ways. They tend to call on boys more often to answer questions in class and to praise them more when they give the right answer. They also give boys more feedback about their assignments and other school work (Sadker and Sadder 1994).[19] Some textbooks and other books still portray people in gender-stereotyped ways. It is true that the newer books do less of this than older ones, but the newer books still contain some stereotypes, and the older books are still used in many schools, especially those that cannot afford to buy newer volumes.

Mass Media

Gender socialization also occurs through the mass media. On children's television shows, the major characters are male. On Nickelodeon, for example, the popular SpongeBob SquarePants is a male, as are his pet snail, Gary; his best friend, Patrick Star; their neighbor, Squidward Tentacles; and SpongeBob's employer, Eugene Krabs. Of the major characters in Bikini Bottom, only Sandy Cheeks is a female. For all its virtues, *Sesame Street* features Bert, Ernie, Cookie Monster, and other male characters. As for adults' prime-time television, more men than women continue to fill more major roles in weekly shows, despite notable women's roles in such recent or ongoing shows as *The Good Wife* and *Grey's Anatomy* (Lauzen 2017).[20] Cosmetics abound in television commercials, suggesting not only that a major task for women is to look good but also that their sense of self-worth stems from looking good. Other commercials show women becoming ecstatic over achieving a clean floor or sparkling laundry. Judging from the world of television commercials, then, women's chief goals in life are to look good and to have a clean house. At the same time, men's chief goals, judging from many commercials, are to drink beer and drive cars.

Women's and men's magazines reinforce these gender images (Frazer and Anderson 2018; Milillo 2008).[21] Most of the magazines intended for teenaged girls and adult women are filled with pictures of thin, beautiful models; advice on dieting; cosmetics ads; and articles on how to win and please your man. Conversely, the magazines intended for teenaged boys and men are filled with ads and articles on cars and sports; advice on how to succeed in careers and other endeavors; and pictures of thin, beautiful (and sometimes nude) women. These magazine images again suggest that women's chief goals are to look good and to please men and that men's chief goals are to succeed, win over women, and live life in the fast lane.

Women's magazines reinforce the view that women need to be slender and wear many cosmetics in order to be considered beautiful.

Source: © Thinkstock

Religion

Another agent of socialization, religion, also contributes to traditional gender stereotypes. Many traditional interpretations of the Bible yield the message that women are subservient to men (Tanenbaum 2009).[22] This message begins in Genesis, where the first human is Adam, and Eve was made from one of his ribs. The major figures in the rest of the Bible are men, and women are for the most part depicted as wives, mothers, temptresses, and prostitutes; they are praised for their roles as wives and mothers and condemned for their other roles. More generally, women are constantly depicted as the property of men. The Ten Commandments include a neighbor's wife with his house, ox, and other objects as things not to be coveted (Exodus 20:17), and many biblical passages say explicitly that women belong to men, such as this one from the New Testament: "Wives be subject to your husbands, as to the Lord. For the husband is the head of the wife as Christ is the head of the Church. As the Church is subject to Christ, so let wives also be subject in everything to their husbands" (Ephesians 5:22–24).

A Final Word on the Sources of Gender

Scholars in many fields continue to debate the relative importance of biology and of culture and socialization for how females and males behave and think. The biological differences between females and males suggest to some scholars and members of the public that masculinity and femininity are biologically determined or at least influenced. In contrast, anthropologists, sociologists, and other social scientists tend to view gender as a social construction. Even if biology does matter for gender, they say, the significance of culture and socialization should not be underestimated. To the extent that gender is indeed shaped by society and culture, it is possible to change gender and to help bring about a society where both men and women have more opportunity to achieve their full potential.

Key Takeaways

- Sex is a biological concept, while gender is a social concept and refers to the social and cultural differences a society assigns to people based on their sex.
- Several biological explanations for gender roles exist, but sociologists think culture and socialization are more important sources of gender roles than biology.
- Families, schools, peers, the mass media, and religion are agents of socialization for the development of gender identity and gender roles.

For Your Review

1. Write a short essay about one or two events you recall from your childhood that reflected or reinforced your gender socialization.
2. Do you think gender roles are due more to biology or to culture and socialization? Explain your answer.

4.2 Dimensions of Gender Inequality

Learning Objectives

1. Summarize the status of women around the world today.
2. Understand the extent of and reasons for gender inequality in income and the workplace in the United States.
3. Understand the extent of and reasons for sexual harassment.

The primary focus of this chapter is gender inequality in the United States, but it is also important to discuss gender inequality worldwide. While American women are unequal to men in many respects, women's situation throughout much of the world is especially dire. Accordingly, we first examine the global inequality of women before turning our attention to the United States.

The Global Inequality of Women

The problem of global poverty first discussed in Chapter 2 is especially severe for women. Although, as Chapter 2 noted, hundreds of millions of people on earth are desperately poor, women account for the majority of the poor. Because women tend to be poorer than men worldwide, they are more likely than men to experience all the problems that poverty causes, including malnutrition and disease. But they also suffer additional problems. Some of these problems derive from women's physiological role of childbearing, and some arise from how they are treated simply because they are women.

Let's first look at childbearing. One of the most depressing examples of how global poverty affects women is maternal mortality, or the number of women who die during pregnancy, childbirth, or shortly after childbirth for every 100,000 live births. More than 300,000 women die worldwide annually in this manner. Maternal mortality usually results from one or more of the following: inadequate prenatal nutrition, disease and illness, and inferior obstetrical care, all of which are much more common in poor nations than in wealthy nations. In wealthy nations, the rate of maternal mortality is 10 deaths per 100,000 births, but in poor nations the rate is a distressingly high 484 per 100,000 births, equivalent to almost 5 deaths for every 1,000 births. Women in poor nations are thus forty-eight times more likely than those in wealthy nations to die from complications during pregnancy or childbirth (World Bank 2019).[23]

In addition to these problems, women in poor nations fare worse than men in other ways because of how they are treated as women. One manifestation of this fact is the violence they experience (World Health Organization 2017).[24] About one-third of women worldwide have been raped or beaten, leading Amnesty International (2004)[25] earlier in this century to call violence against women "the greatest human rights scandal of our times." Although violence against women certainly occurs in wealthy nations, it is more common and extreme in poor and middle-income nations. In India and Pakistan, thousands of women are killed every year in dowry deaths, in which a new wife is murdered by her husband and/or his relatives if she does not pay the groom money or goods (Bundhun 2017).[26] In many countries, young girls routinely have their genitals cut out, often with no anesthesia, in what has been termed *female genital mutilation*, a practice that is thought to affect more than 100 million girls and women across the earth and has been called an act of torture (World Health Organization 2018).[27]

In India and Pakistan, thousands of new wives every year are murdered in dowry deaths because they have not provided their husbands a suitable amount of money and goods.

Source: theodoreAB/Shutterstock.com

Sex trafficking is another major problem in countries like Cambodia, India, Nepal, and Thailand, where young girls are often stolen from their parents and forced to work as prostitutes in what amounts to *sexual slavery*. The number of girls (and sometimes boys) under age 18 who work as sex slaves is thought to reach into the millions and to be larger than the number of enslaved Africans during the eighteenth and nineteenth centuries (Kristoff and WuDunn 2010).[28]

Sex Trafficking in India

Sex trafficking is a major problem in poor nations in Asia and elsewhere, with young girls stolen from their parents or tricked into relocating and then forced to work as prostitutes or sex slaves.

View the video online at: http://www.youtube.com/embed/0vDe6rUFs90?rel=0

Beyond violence, women in poor nations are less likely than their male counterparts to get a higher education, and girls are less likely than boys to attend primary school. Women are also less likely than men to work in jobs that pay a decent wage and to hold political office. In many poor nations, girls are less likely than boys to receive adequate medical care when they become ill and are more likely than boys to die before age 5. In all these ways, women and girls in poor nations especially suffer.

Not surprisingly, the general situation of women in low-income nations became even clearer during the early months of the COVID-19 pandemic. During this period, it is true that women around the world were contracting and dying from this disease somewhat less often than men. Observers attributed this gender difference to factors such as women's stronger immunological systems, men's greater smoking rates, and men's reluctance to seek medical care (Henriques 2020).[29] But women in low-income nations suffered more than men in other ways from the pandemic, prompting David Evans (2020)[30] of the Center for Global Development to note that "most of the other impacts [of the pandemic] affect women negatively and disproportionately." This disproportionate impact applied not only to women in low-income nations, but often to those in wealthier nations.

Several reasons help explain this disproportionate impact (Evans 2020; UN Women 2020):[31]

- First, most nurses in low-income nations, as well as in wealthier nations, are women. Because health-care providers were at great risk for COVID-19 and because nurses greatly outnumber physicians (who tend more often to be men), the risk to health-care workers fell disproportionately on women health-care workers.

- Second, women tend to be the primary caretakers of children generally, but especially so in low-income nations. School closures throughout the world during the early pandemic period thus posed a greater burden on women than on men and had a larger impact on their jobs outside the home than on men's jobs.

- Third, health-care resources during a health crisis tend to be diverted from reproductive health to deal with the crisis. In low-income nations, this sad fact results in higher rates of maternal and neonatal (newborn) mortality.

- Fourth, when schools are closed in low-income nations from health crises, teenage pregnancy rates tend to rise. Teenage pregnancies certainly can have many negative consequences, including for the mother's health.

- Fifth, when family members become sick during a health crisis, women, not men, tend to become their caretakers. This pattern exposes women more than men to disease and also places more of a burden on them regarding their time and energy.
- Finally, health crises in low-income nations and elsewhere often lead to economic crises, which certainly happened after the COVID-19 pandemic began. Partly because women tend to be poorer than men, the impact of these economic crises in low-income nations is often larger for women than for men.

Compared to women in poor nations, women in wealthy democratic nations fare much better. Even so, women in some wealthy nations fare better than those in other wealthy nations. In particular, women in several wealthy nations fare better overall than those in the United States. The "Lessons from Other Societies" box discusses this situation further.

Lessons from Other Societies

Women in the Nordic Nations

The United Nations Development Programme (2018) ranks nations on a Gender Inequality Index that measures women's situation and achievements in such areas as reproductive health, education, and politics and the labor market (United Nations Development Programme 2018).[32] Of the more than 160 nations ranked on the measure, Switzerland ranks first, followed by Denmark and Sweden. The remaining Nordic nations, Finland and Iceland, rank eighth and ninth, respectively. Canada ranks 20th, and the United States ranks only 41st. In trying to understand why the United States ranks this low and what it might be able to do to increase its empowerment of women, the experience of the Nordic nations provides some important lessons.

The Nordic nations rank at the top of the gender empowerment measure largely because they have made a concerted effort to boost women's involvement in the business and political worlds (Åseskog 2018; Sumer et al. 2008).[33] They are all social democratic welfare states characterized by extensive government programs and other efforts to promote full economic and gender equality.

For example, Norway's government provides day care for children and adult care for older or disabled individuals, and it also provides 44 weeks of paid parental leave after the birth of a child. Parents can also work fewer hours without losing income until their child is 2 years of age. All these provisions mean that women are much more likely than their American counterparts to have the freedom and economic means to work outside the home, and they have taken advantage of this opportunity. As one analysis concluded, "It has been extremely important for women that social rights have been extended to cover such things as the caring of young children and elderly, sick and disabled members of society. In the Nordic countries, women have been more successful than elsewhere in combining their dual role as mothers and workers, and social policy arrangements are an integral part of the gender equality policy" (Kangas and Palme 2009:565).[34]

The lesson for the United States is clear: An important reason for the Nordic nations' high gender empowerment ranking is government policy that enables women to work outside the home if they want to. The experience of these nations indicates that greater gender equality might be achieved in the United States if it adopted policies similar to those found in these nations that make it easier for women to join and stay in the labor force.

Gender Inequality in the United States

We have said that the women's movement changed American life in many ways but that gender inequality persists in the United States. Let's look at examples of such inequality, much of it taking the form of institutional discrimination, which, as we saw in Chapter 3, can occur even if it is not intended to happen. We start with gender inequality in income and the workplace and then move on to a few other spheres of life.

The Gender Gap in Income

Women have earned less money than men ever since records started being kept. Women now earn about 81 percent of what men earn.

Source: © Thinkstock

In the last several decades, women have entered the workplace in increasing numbers, partly or mostly out of economic necessity, and partly out of desire for the sense of self-worth and other fulfillment that comes with work. In 2017, 54.6 percent of U.S. women aged 16 or older were in the labor force, compared to only 43.3 percent in 1970; comparable figures for men were 66.0 percent in 2017 and 79.7 percent in 1970 (Bureau of Labor Statistics 2018).[35] Thus, while women's labor force participation continues to lag behind men's, this gender gap has narrowed. The figures just cited include women of retirement age. When we just look at younger women, labor force participation is even higher. For example, 72.2 percent of women aged 35–44 were in the labor force in 2017, compared to only 46.8 percent in 1970.

Despite the workplace gains women have made, problems persist. Perhaps the major problem is a gender gap in income. Women have earned less money than men ever since records started being kept (Reskin and Padavic 2002).[36] In the United States in the early 1800s, full-time women workers in agriculture and manufacturing earned less than 38 percent of what men earned. By 1885, they were earning about 50 percent of what men earned in manufacturing jobs. As the 1980s began, full-time women workers' median weekly earnings were about 65 percent of men's. Women have narrowed the gender gap in earnings since then: Their weekly earnings now (2017) are 81.8 percent of men's among full-time workers aged 16 and older (Bureau of Labor Statistics 2018).[37] Still, this means that for every $10,000 men earn, women earn only about $8,180. To turn that around, for every $10,000 women earn, men earn $12,225. This gap amounts to hundreds of thousands of dollars over a lifetime of working.

As Table 4.1 shows, this gender gap exists for all levels of education. On the average, women with a bachelor's degree or higher and working full time earn almost $18,200 less per year than their male counterparts.

TABLE 4.1 Median Annual Earnings of Full-Time, Year-Round Workers Aged 25 and Older by Educational Attainment, 2017*

	High school dropout	High school diploma	Some college or associate's degree	Bachelor's degree or higher
Men	30,368	41,444	47,684	77,012
Women	23,244	31,720	36,400	58,812
Difference	7,124	9,724	11,284	18,200
Gender gap (%; women ÷ men)	76.5	76.5	75.3	76.3
* Median weekly earnings × 52 weeks				

Source: U.S. Bureau of Labor Statistics. 2018. *Highlights of Women's Earnings in 2017*. Washington, DC: U.S. Department of Labor.

sex segregation

In the workplace, the concentration of women in a relatively few low-paying clerical and service jobs.

What accounts for the gender gap in earnings? A major reason is **sex segregation** in the workplace, which accounts for much of the gender gap (Blau and Kahn 2016).[38] Although women have increased their labor force participation, the workplace remains segregated by gender. Almost half of all women work in a few low-paying clerical and service (e.g., restaurant server) jobs, while men work in a much greater variety of jobs, including high-paying ones. Part of the reason for this segregation is that socialization affects what jobs young men and women choose to pursue, and part of the reason is that women and men do not want to encounter difficulties they may experience if they took a job traditionally assigned to the other sex. As well, sex-segregated jobs may discriminate against applicants who are not the "right" sex for that job: Employers may either consciously refuse to hire someone who is the "wrong" sex for the job or have job requirements (e.g., height requirements) and workplace rules (e.g., working at night) that unintentionally make it more difficult for women to qualify for certain jobs. Although such discrimination is illegal, it continues. Whatever the reasons for sex segregation, occupations dominated by women tend to have lower wages and salaries. Because women are concentrated in low-paying jobs, their earnings are much lower than men's.

This fact raises an important question: Why do women's jobs pay less than men's jobs? Is it because their jobs are not important and require few skills (recalling the functional theory of stratification discussed in Chapter 2)? The evidence indicates otherwise: Women's work is devalued precisely because it is women's work, and women's jobs thus pay less than men's jobs because they are women's jobs (Magnusson 2009).[39]

Studies of **comparable worth** support this argument (Levanon et al. 2009; Newton 2018).[40] Researchers rate various jobs in terms of their requirements and attributes that logically should affect the salaries they offer: the importance of the job, the degree of skill it requires, the level of responsibility it requires, the degree to which the employee must exercise independent judgment, and so forth. They then use these dimensions to determine what salary a job should offer. Some jobs might rank better on some dimensions and worse on others but still end up with the same predicted salary if everything evens out.

When researchers do their calculations, they find that certain women's jobs pay less than men's, even though their comparable worth is equal to or even higher than the men's jobs. For example, a social worker may earn less money than a probation officer, even though calculations based on comparable worth would predict that a social worker should earn at least as much. The comparable worth research demonstrates that women's jobs pay less than men's jobs of comparable worth and that the average working family would earn several thousand dollars more annually if pay scales were reevaluated based on comparable worth and women were paid more for their work.

Even when women and men work in the same jobs, women often earn less than men, and men are more likely than women to hold leadership positions in these occupations. Government data provide ready evidence of the lower incomes women receive even in the same occupations. For example, among full-time employees, female marketing and sales managers earn only 75 percent of what their male counterparts earn; female human resource managers earn only 73 percent of what their male counterparts earn; female accountants earn only 77 percent; female elementary and middle school teachers earn only 87 percent; and even female secretaries and administrative assistants earn only 86 percent (U.S. Bureau of Labor Statistics, 2018).[41]

One reason for these differences, and for women's lower earnings in general, is their caregiving responsibilities (Chang 2010).[42] Women are more likely than men to have the major, and perhaps the sole, responsibility for taking care of children and aging parents or other adults who need care. This responsibility limits their work hours and often prompts them to drop out of the labor force. If women rejoin the labor force after their children start school, or join for the first time, they are already several years behind men who began working at an earlier age.

We can see evidence of this "hit" when we examine the gender gap in earnings by age. Women earn close to men during their early 20s, but the gender gap rises rises during the next 2 decades of age as more and more women bear and raise children (see Figure 4.2).

comparable worth

The idea that women's and men's jobs may be of roughly equal value and thus deserve the same pay, even though women's jobs typically pay less than men's jobs.

Some women's jobs pay less than men's jobs even though their comparable worth is equal to or even higher than the men's jobs. For example, a social worker, depicted here, may earn less money than a probation officer, even though calculations based on comparable worth would predict that a social worker should earn at least as much.

Source: © Thinkstock

FIGURE 4.2 Gender, Age, and Women's Earnings as a Percentage of Men's Earnings, 2017

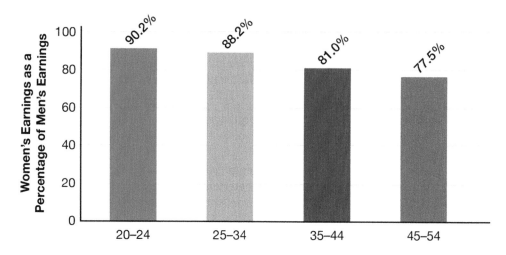

Source: U.S. Bureau of Labor Statistics. 2018. *Highlights of Women's Earnings in 2017*. Washington, DC: U.S. Department of Labor.

A "glass ceiling" limits women's opportunities for promotion in corporations, schools, and other settings.

Source: © Thinkstock

glass ceiling

The invisible barrier facing women as they try to advance in the workplace.

glass escalator

The smooth path afforded men in promotion in the workplace, especially in occupations primarily filled by women.

sexual harassment

Unwelcome sexual advances, requests for sexual favors, or physical conduct of a sexual nature that is used as a condition of employment or promotion or that interferes with an individual's job performance and creates an intimidating or hostile environment.

Still, when variables like number of years on the job, number of hours worked per week, and size of firm are taken into account, gender differences in earnings diminish but do not disappear altogether. Sex discrimination (conscious or unconscious) by employers probably accounts for much of the remaining disparity.

Some of the sex discrimination in employment reflects the existence of two related phenomena, the **glass ceiling** and the **glass escalator**. Women may be promoted in a job only to find they reach an invisible "glass ceiling" beyond which they cannot get promoted, or they may not get promoted in the first place. Men, on the other hand, can often ride a "glass escalator" to the top, even in female occupations. This dynamic characterizes corporations, schools, and other settings. For example, although men constitute only about 23 percent of all public school (elementary and secondary) teachers, they account for about 46 percent of all public school principals (McFarland et al. 2019).[43]

Whatever the reasons for the gender gap in income, the fact that women make so much less than men means that female-headed families are especially likely to be poor, a phenomenon termed the *feminization of poverty* (see Chapter 2). In 2017, about 26 percent of these families lived in poverty, compared to only 12 percent of male-headed families and 5 percent of married-couple families (Fontenot et al. 2018).[44] The gendering of poverty in this manner is one of the most significant manifestations of gender inequality in the United States.

Sexual Harassment

Another workplace problem (including schools) is **sexual harassment**, which, as defined by federal guidelines and legal rulings and statutes, consists of unwelcome sexual advances, requests for sexual favors, or physical conduct of a sexual nature that is used as a condition of employment or promotion or that interferes with an individual's job performance and creates an intimidating or hostile environment. The #MeToo movement, discussed in this chapter's opening news story, reminds us of the frequency and seriousness of this problem.

Although men can be, and are, sexually harassed, women are more often the targets of sexual harassment. This gender difference exists for at least two reasons, one cultural and one structural. The cultural reason centers on the depiction of women and the socialization of men. As our discussion of the mass media and gender socialization indicated, women are still depicted in our culture as sexual objects that exist for men's pleasure. At the same time, our culture socializes men to be sexually assertive. These two cultural beliefs combine to make men believe that they have the right to make verbal and physical advances to women in the workplace. When these advances fall into the guidelines listed here, they become sexual harassment.

The second reason that most targets of sexual harassment are women is more structural. Reflecting the gendered nature of the workplace and of the educational system, typically the men doing the harassment are in a position of power over the women they harass. A male boss harasses a female employee, or a male professor harasses a female student or employee. These men realize that subordinate women may find it difficult to resist their advances for fear of reprisals: A female employee may be fired or not promoted, and a female student may receive a bad grade.

How common is sexual harassment? This is difficult to determine, as the men who do the sexual harassment are not about to shout it from the rooftops, and the women who suffer it often keep quiet because of the repercussions just listed. Combining the results of many anonymous surveys of women employees in corporate and other settings, an average of 58 percent of women reported being harassed in the workplace (National Academies of Sciences, Engineering, and Medicine 2018).[45] In a recent study of college students, 62 percent of women undergraduates reported being sexually harassed, most often by another student (Cantor et al. 2017).[46] In earlier research, almost one-third of women undergraduates and about 40 percent of women graduate students reported being sexually harassed by a faculty member (Clodfelter et al. 2010).[47]

Studies of people who have been sexually harassed find that they often experience various psychological problems. The "Applying Social Research" box discusses this body of research further.

Sexual harassment in the workplace is a common experience. In surveys of women employees, up to two-thirds of respondents report having been sexually harassed.

Source: © Thinkstock

Applying Social Research

The Long-Term Mental Health Consequences of Sexual Harassment

Despite the fact that sexual harassment is illegal, most women (and men) who are sexually harassed do not bring court action or at least report their harassment. Several reasons explain their decision not to sue: They may fear being fired or incurring other negative outcomes, they may worry they will not be believed, and/or they may not want the publicity possibly resulting from going public in this way.

But another reason has to do with the mental and emotional consequences of being sexually harassed. These consequences include relationship problems, a loss of self-esteem, fatigue, depression, anxiety, sleeplessness, and a feeling of powerlessness. These effects are similar to those for posttraumatic stress disorder and are considered symptoms of what has been termed *sexual harassment trauma syndrome*. This syndrome, and perhaps especially the feeling of powerlessness, help explain why sexual harassment victims often do not bring court action and otherwise keep quiet. Unfortunately, if they do report harassment only a long time after first experiencing it, it is too easy for judges, juries, and other parties to think that the woman originally did not mind the behavior that she now says is harassment.

Should the legal system begin to make better use of social science research on sexual harassment trauma syndrome, a study by sociologist Jason N. Houle and colleagues provides important new evidence for legal officials to consider. The authors note two faults in prior sexual harassment research. First, most studies have focused on workers in a single occupation, such as lawyers, or in a single organization, such as a university campus, rather than in a diverse set of occupations and organizations. Second, because most studies have examined workers at only one point in time, they have been unable to study the long-term psychological consequences of sexual harassment.

To correct these deficiencies, Houle et al. analyzed data from a study of 1,010 ninth-graders in St. Paul, Minnesota, that followed them from 1988 to 2004, when they were 30 or 31 years old. The study included measures of the respondents' experience of sexual harassment at several periods over the study's 16-year time span, their level of psychological depression, and their sociodemographic background. Focusing on depression at ages 30 or 31, the authors found that sexual harassment at ages 14–18 did not affect the chances of depression at ages 30–31, but that sexual harassment during any of the other three age periods *did* increase the chances of depression at ages 30–31. These results held true for both women and men who had been harassed. The authors concluded that the "effects of harassment are indeed lasting, as harassment experiences early in the career were associated with heightened depressive symptoms nearly 10 years later."

In finding long-term effects of sexual harassment on women and men in a variety of occupations and organizational settings, Houle et al.'s study made an important contribution to our understanding of the psychological consequences of sexual harassment. Its findings underscore the need for workplaces and campuses to do everything possible to eliminate this illegal and harmful behavior and ideally will prove useful in sexual harassment lawsuits.

Sources: Fitzgerald and Cortina 2017; Houle et al. 2011 [48]

Women of Color: A Triple Burden

Much research finds that women of color experience difficulties for three reasons: their gender, their race, and, often, their social class, which is frequently near the bottom of the socioeconomic ladder. They thus face a *triple burden* that manifests itself in many ways.

For example, women of color experience extra income inequality. Earlier we discussed the gender gap in earnings, with women earning 81.8 percent of what men earn, but women of color face both a gender gap *and* a racial/ethnic gap. Table 4.2 depicts this double gap for full-time workers. We see a racial/ethnic gap among both women and men, as African Americans and Latinxs of either gender earn less than whites. We also see a gender gap between men and women, as women earn somewhat less than men within any race/ethnicity. These two gaps combine to produce an especially high gap between African American and Latinx women and white men: African American women earn only about 70 percent of what white men earn, and Latinx women earn only 67.5 percent of what white men earn.

TABLE 4.2 The Race/Ethnicity and Gender Gap in Annual Earnings for Full-Time, Year-Round Workers, 2017*

	Annual earnings ($)	Percentage of white male earnings
Men		
White (non-Latinx)	50,492	—
Black	36,920	73.1
Latinx	35,880	71.1
Women		
White (non-Latinx)	41,340	81.9
Black	35,464	70.2
Latinx	34,060	67.5
* Median weekly earnings × 52 weeks		

Source: U.S. Bureau of Labor Statistics. 2018. *Highlights of Women's Earnings in 2017*. Washington, DC: U.S. Department of Labor.

These differences in income mean that African American and Latinx women are poorer than white women. We noted earlier that 26 percent of all female-headed families are poor. This figure masks race/ethnic differences among such families: 21 percent of families headed by non-Latinx white women are poor, compared to 33 percent of families headed by African American women and 34 percent of families headed by Latinx women (Fontenot et al. 2018).[49] While white women are poorer than white men, African American and Latinx women are clearly poorer than white women.

Household Inequality

Gender inequality occurs within families and households. We will talk more about this aspect of family life in Chapter 10, but briefly discuss here one significant dimension of gender-based household inequality: housework. Someone has to do housework, and that someone is usually a woman. It takes many hours a week to clean the bathrooms, cook, shop in the grocery store, vacuum, and do everything else that needs to be done. On the average, women spend almost 1 more hour daily than men spend on housework and other household activities, or nearly 7 more hours weekly (Bureau of Labor Statistics 2016).[50] Women spend more time on housework even when they also work outside the home, leading sociologist Arlie Hochschild (1989)[51] to observe in a widely cited book that women engage in a "second shift" of unpaid work when they come home from their paying job.

The good news is that gender differences in housework time are smaller than a generation ago. The bad news is that a large gender difference remains. In the realm of household work, then, gender inequality persists.

Gender Inequality in the COVID-19 Pandemic

As discussed earlier, men were contracting and dying from COVID-19 at higher rates than women during the early pandemic. But just as the pandemic fell more heavily in other ways on women in low-income nations, so did it fall more heavily on women in the United States. As two women's rights advocates explained, "A gender lens highlights the specific risks and vulnerabilities girls and women face [during the pandemic] because of deep-rooted inequalities and traditional gender roles" (Papp and Hersh 2020).[52]

Much of this extra burden on women reflected their reproductive health and role. Pregnant women seemed to be contracting COVID-19 at similar rates to non-pregnant women (Rettner 2020).[53] But because pregnancy may weaken the immune system, this disease was thought to be potentially more threatening to pregnant women and the fetuses they carried (Hopper and Robison 2020).[54] According to news reports, pregnant women were also reluctant to obtain their normal obstetrical care for fear of exposure to the coronavirus and, especially, to have births at hospitals; some began considering home births, which can sometimes be more risky (Zephyrin 2020).[55] In all these ways, COVID-19 affected women more directly and more severely than it affected men.

There were also signs during the early pandemic of a rise in domestic violence. The confinement at home due to the stay-at-home practices that were encouraged to stop the spreading of the virus apparently lead to greater stress and increased domestic violence. Based on preliminary evidence, calls to police and domestic violence hotlines and shelters increased worldwide and also in the United States. As a news report summarized this sad situation, "Movement restrictions aimed to stop the spread of the coronavirus may be making violence in homes more frequent, more severe and more dangerous" (Taub 2020:A9).[56] Compounding this problem, domestic violence experts worried that fear of coronavirus infection was making women at risk of domestic violence less likely to want to or to be able to leave the home to seek help (Godin 2020).[57]

A third problem stemmed from women's caretaking role. As in low-income nations, women in the United States tend to be the caretakers of children and senior citizens. After stay-at-home practices began and children were no longer in school or daycare, the burden of childcare fell more heavily on women than on men. When elders became ill with COVID-19 or developed another health problem, women spent more time on their care than men did. This care could be both mentally and physically exhausting and also exposed these caretakers to the coronavirus (Schnall 2020).[58]

A related problem involved women's roles in health-care and service occupations. Again, as in low-income nations, women are much more involved in these occupations than men are: nurses greatly outnumber physicians, and women are the majority of America's service workers. In health-care settings, grocery stores, and other venues across the nation, more women than men were thus on the frontlines of the coronavirus and more vulnerable to contracting COVID-19 (Gupta 2020).[59] While acknowledging this fact, it is important not to neglect law enforcement and some other occupations dominated by males that were also on the frontlines. Overall, however, gender-based occupational segregation exposed more women than men to the coronavirus during the pandemic.

Key Takeaways

- Among full-time workers, women earn about 79.4 percent of men's earnings. This gender gap in earnings stems from several factors, including sex segregation in the workplace and the lower wages and salaries found in occupations that involve mostly women.
- Sexual harassment results partly from women's subordinate status in the workplace and may involve up to two-thirds of women employees.
- Women of color may face a "triple burden" of difficulties based on their gender, their race/ethnicity, and their social class.

For Your Review

1. Do you think it is fair for occupations dominated by women to have lower wages and salaries than those dominated by men? Explain your answer.
2. If you know a woman who works in a male-dominated occupation, interview her about any difficulties she might be experiencing as a result of being in this sort of situation.

4.3 Violence against Women: Rape and Sexual Assault

Learning Objectives

1. Describe the extent of rape and sexual assault.
2. Explain why rape and sexual assault occur.

Susan Griffin (1971:26)[60] began a classic essay on rape in 1971 with this startling statement: "I have never been free of the fear of rape. From a very early age I, like most women, have thought of rape as a part of my natural environment—something to be feared and prayed against like fire or lightning. I never asked why men raped; I simply thought it one of the many mysteries of human nature."

When we consider interpersonal violence of all kinds—homicide, assault, robbery, and rape and sexual assault—men are more likely than women to be victims of violence. While true, this fact obscures another fact: Women are far more likely than men to be raped and sexually assaulted. They are also much more likely to be portrayed as victims of pornographic violence on the internet and in videos, magazines, and other outlets. Finally, women are more likely than men to be victims of *domestic violence*, or violence between spouses and others with intimate relationships. The gendered nature of these acts against women distinguishes them from the violence men suffer. Violence is directed against men not because they are men per se, but because of anger, jealousy, and the sociological reasons discussed in Chapter 8. But rape and sexual assault, domestic violence, and pornographic violence are directed against women precisely because they are women. These acts are thus an extreme manifestation of the gender inequality women face in other areas of life. We discuss rape and sexual assault here but will leave domestic violence for Chapter 10 and pornography for Chapter 9.

The Extent and Context of Rape and Sexual Assault

Our best knowledge about the extent and context of rape and sexual assault and reasons for these crimes comes from surveys of and interviews with women and men conducted by academic researchers. From these sources we have a fairly good if not perfect idea of how much rape and sexual assault occur, the context in which they occur, and the reasons for them. What do we know?

National survey evidence finds that nearly one-fifth of U.S. women will experience a rape or attempted rape during their lifetime, and that about one-third will experience a rape or sexual assault, including attempts, during their lifetime (Breiding et al. 2014; Tjaden and Thoennes 2000).[61] A study of a random sample of 420 Toronto women involving intensive interviews yielded an even higher figure: Two-thirds said they had experienced at least one rape or sexual assault, including attempts. The researchers, Melanie Randall and Lori Haskell (1995:22),[62] concluded that "it is more common than not for a woman to have an experience of sexual assault during their lifetime."

Studies of college students also find a high amount of rape and sexual assault. Between about 20 percent and 25 percent of women undergraduates in anonymous surveys report being raped or sexually assaulted (including attempts), usually by a male student they knew beforehand (Fisher et al. 2000; Gross et al. 2006; Mellins et al. 2017).[63] In related research, anonymous surveys given to male students ask them to report whether they have committed sexual violence perpetration (ranging from unwanted sexual contact to rape). Across these surveys, an average of 29 percent of male students admit to such perpetration, including 6.5 percent who admit to having committed rape (Anderson et al. 2019).[64] The "People Making a Difference" box describes what one group of college students did to help reduce rape and sexual assault at their campus.

Up to one-third of U.S. women experience a rape or sexual assault, including attempts, at least once in their lives.

Source: © Thinkstock

🎥 Battling Campus Sexual Assaults

Survey evidence indicates that between about 20 percent and 25 percent of women undergraduates in the United States have been sexually assaulted, usually by a male student acquaintance.

View the video online at: http://www.youtube.com/embed/pVwiGU7AEpc?rel=0

People Making a Difference

College Students Protest against Sexual Violence

Swarthmore College is a small liberal arts campus in a suburb of Philadelphia, Pennsylvania. But in the fight against sexual violence, it loomed huge in April 2019, when dozens of students calling themselves the Coalition to End Fraternity Violence conducted a sit-in at one of the college's two fraternity houses. They did this after a leak of more than 100 pages of documents in which the fraternity's members bragged about a "rape attic" and about sexual assaults they had committed. Although most of the assaults occurred in 2013, before the current fraternity members had arrived on campus, the protesters said the documents pointed to a continuing fraternity rape culture, and they called on college officials to shut down the two fraternities. Several days after the sit-in began, members of both fraternities decided to voluntarily disband their respective fraternity and to release their house to the college for more general use. Upon hearing this news, one of the protesters exclaimed, "Everyone kind of thought there was nothing we could do to get rid of them. So this sit-in and the result of the sit-in was just a shocking and tremendously celebratory event." On this small campus in a small town outside of Philadelphia, a few dozen college students had made a difference.

Source: Turkewitz 2019[65]

The public image of rape is of the proverbial stranger attacking a woman in an alleyway. While such rapes do occur, most rapes actually happen between people who know each other. A wide body of research finds that someone the woman knows (including husbands, ex-husbands, boyfriends, and ex-boyfriends) commit 60–80+ percent of all rapes and sexual assaults against women (Barkan 2018; Breiding et al. 2014).[66] A woman is thus two to four times more likely to be raped by someone she knows than by a stranger.

Explaining Rape and Sexual Assault

Sociological explanations of rape fall into cultural and structural categories similar to those presented earlier for sexual harassment. Various "rape myths" in our culture support the absurd notion that women somehow enjoy being raped, want to be raped, or are "asking for it" (Shaw et al. 2017).[67] One of the most famous scenes in movie history occurs in the classic film *Gone with the Wind*, when Rhett Butler carries a struggling Scarlett O'Hara up the stairs. She is struggling because she does not want to have sex with him. The next scene shows Scarlett waking up the next morning with a satisfied, loving look on her face. The not-so-subtle message is that she enjoyed being raped (or, to be more charitable to the film, was just playing hard to get).

A related cultural belief is that women somehow ask or deserve to be raped by the way they dress or behave. If she dresses attractively or walks into a bar by herself, she wants to have sex, and if a rape occurs, well, then, what did she expect? In the award-winning film *The Accused*, based on a true story, actress Jodie Foster played a woman who was raped by several men on top of a pool table in a bar. The film recounted how members of the public questioned why she was in the bar by herself if she did not want to have sex and blamed her for being raped.

A third cultural belief is that a man who is sexually active with a lot of women is a stud and thus someone admired by his male peers. Although this belief is less common in this era of HIV and other STDs, it is still with us. A man with multiple sex partners continues to be the source of envy among many of his peers. At a minimum, men are still the ones who have to "make the first move" and then continue making more moves. There is a thin line between being sexually assertive and sexually aggressive (Shafer et al. 2018).[68]

These three cultural beliefs—that women enjoy being forced to have sex, that they ask or deserve to be raped, and that men should be sexually assertive or even aggressive—combine to produce a cultural recipe for rape. Although most men do not rape, the cultural beliefs and myths just described help account for the rapes that do occur. Recognizing this, the contemporary women's movement began attacking these myths back in the 1970s, and the public is much more conscious of the true nature of rape than a generation ago. That said, much of the public still accepts these cultural beliefs and myths, and prosecutors continue to find it difficult to win jury convictions in rape trials unless the woman who was raped had suffered visible injuries, had not known the man who raped her, and/or was not dressed attractively (Lave 2016).[69]

Structural explanations for rape emphasize the power differences between women and men similar to those outlined earlier for sexual harassment. In male-dominated societies, rape and other violence against women is a likely outcome, as they allow men to demonstrate and maintain their power over women. Supporting this view, studies of preindustrial societies and of the fifty states of the United States find that rape is more common in societies where women have less economic and political power (Baron and Straus 1989; Sanday 1981).[70] Poverty is also a predictor of rape: Although rape in the United States transcends social class boundaries, it does seem more common among poorer segments of the population than among wealthier segments, as is true for other types of violence (Morgan and Truman 2018).[71] Scholars think the higher rape rates among the poor stem from poor men trying to prove their "masculinity" by taking out their economic frustration on women (Martin et al. 2006).[72]

Key Takeaways

- Up to one-third of U.S. women experience a rape or sexual assault, including attempts, in their lifetime.
- Rape and sexual assault result from a combination of structural and cultural factors. In states and nations where women are more unequal, rape rates tend to be higher.

For Your Review

1. What evidence and reasoning indicate that rape and sexual assault are not just the result of psychological problems affecting the men who engage in these crimes?
2. Write a brief essay in which you critically evaluate the cultural beliefs that contribute to rape and sexual assault.

4.4 The Benefits and Costs of Being Male

Learning Objectives

1. List some of the benefits of being male.
2. List some of the costs of being male.

Most of the discussion so far has been about women, and with good reason: In a sexist society such as our own, women are the subordinate, unequal sex. But *gender* means more than *female*, and a few comments about men are in order.

Benefits

We have already discussed gender differences in occupations and incomes that favor men over women. In a patriarchal society, men have more wealth than women and more influence in the political and economic worlds more generally.

Men profit in other ways as well. In Chapter 3, we talked about white privilege, or the advantages that whites automatically have in a racist society whether or not they realize they have these advantages. Many scholars also talk about **male privilege**, or the advantages that males automatically have in a patriarchal society whether or not they realize they have these advantages (McIntosh 2007).[73]

A few examples illustrate male privilege. Men can usually walk anywhere they want or go into any bar they want without having to worry about being raped or sexually harassed. Susan Griffin was able to write "I have never been free of the fear of rape" because she was a woman; it is no exaggeration to say that few men could write the same thing and mean it. Although some men are sexually harassed, most men can work at any job they want without having to worry about sexual harassment. Men can walk down the street without having strangers make crude remarks about their looks, dress, and sexual behavior. Men can ride the subway system in large cities without having strangers grope them, flash them, or rub their bodies against them. Men can apply for most jobs without worrying about being rejected because of their gender, or, if hired, not being promoted because of their gender. We could go on with many other examples, but the fact remains that in a patriarchal society, men automatically have advantages just because they are men, even if race/ethnicity, social class, and sexual orientation and gender identity affect the degree to which they are able to enjoy these advantages.

Costs

Yet it is also true that men pay a price for living in a patriarchy. Without trying to claim that men have it as bad as women, scholars point to the problems men face in a society that promotes male domination and traditional standards of masculinity such as assertiveness, competitiveness, and toughness (Parent et al. 2019).[74] Socialization into masculinity is thought to underlie many of the emotional problems men experience, which stem from a combination of their emotional inexpressiveness and reluctance to admit to, and seek help for, various personal problems (Addis and Hoffman 2017).[75] Sometimes these emotional problems build up and explode, as mass shootings by males at schools and elsewhere indicate, or express themselves in other ways. Compared to girls, for example, boys are much more likely to be diagnosed with emotional disorders, learning disabilities, and attention deficit disorder, and they are also more likely to commit suicide and to drop out of high school.

Men experience other problems that put themselves at a disadvantage compared to women. They commit much more violence than women do and, apart from rape and sexual assault, also suffer a much higher rate of violent victimization. They die earlier than women and are injured more often. Because men are less involved than women in child rearing, they also miss out on many joys of parenting that women are more likely to experience.

Growing recognition of the problems males experience because of their socialization into masculinity has led to increased concern over what is happening to American boys. Citing the strong linkage between masculinity and violence, some writers urge parents to raise their sons differently in order to help our society reduce its violent behavior (Reichert 2019).[76] In all these respects, boys and men—and our nation as a whole—are paying a very real price for being male in a patriarchal society.

Key Takeaways

- In a patriarchal society, males automatically have certain advantages, including a general freedom from fear of being raped and sexually assaulted and from experiencing job discrimination on the basis of their gender.
- Men also suffer certain disadvantages from being male, including higher rates of injury, violence, and death and a lower likelihood of experiencing the joy that parenting often brings.

For Your Review

1. What do you think is the most important advantage, privilege, or benefit that men enjoy in the United States? Explain your answer.
2. What do you think is the most significant cost or disadvantage that men experience? Again, explain your answer.

4.5 Reducing Gender Inequality

Learning Objectives

1. Describe any three policies or programs that should help reduce gender inequality.
2. Discuss possible ways of reducing rape and sexual assault.

Gender inequality is found in varying degrees in most societies around the world, and the United States is no exception. Just as racial/ethnic stereotyping and prejudice underlie racial/ethnic inequality (see Chapter 3), so do stereotypes and false beliefs underlie gender inequality. Although these stereotypes and beliefs have weakened considerably since the 1970s thanks in large part to the contemporary women's movement, they obviously persist and hamper efforts to achieve full gender equality.

A sociological perspective reminds us that gender inequality stems from a complex mixture of cultural and structural factors that must be addressed if gender inequality is to be reduced further than it already has been since the 1970s. Despite changes during this period, children are still socialized from birth into traditional notions of femininity and masculinity, and gender-based stereotyping incorporating these notions continues. Although people should certainly be free to pursue whatever family and career responsibilities they desire, socialization and stereotyping still combine to limit the ability of girls and boys and women and men alike to imagine less traditional possibilities. Meanwhile, structural obstacles in the workplace and elsewhere continue to keep women in a subordinate social and economic status relative to men.

To reduce gender inequality, then, a sociological perspective suggests various policies and measures to address the cultural and structural factors that help produce gender inequality. These steps include, but are not limited to, the following:

1. Reduce socialization by parents and other adults of girls and boys into traditional gender roles.
2. Confront gender stereotyping by the popular and news media.

3. Increase public consciousness of the reasons for, extent of, and consequences of rape and sexual assault, sexual harassment, and pornography.

4. Increase enforcement of existing laws against gender-based employment discrimination and against sexual harassment.

5. Increase funding of rape crisis centers and other services for girls and women who have been raped and/or sexually assaulted.

6. Increase government funding of high-quality day-care options to enable parents, and especially mothers, to work outside the home if they so desire, and to do so without fear that their finances or their children's well-being will be compromised.

7. Increase mentorship and other efforts to boost the number of women in traditionally male occupations and in positions of political leadership.

As we consider how best to reduce gender inequality, the impact of the contemporary women's movement must be neither forgotten nor underestimated. Since it began in the late 1960s, the women's movement has generated important advances for women in almost every sphere of life. Brave women (and some men) challenged the status quo by calling attention to gender inequality in the workplace, education, and elsewhere, and they brought rape and sexual assault, sexual harassment, and domestic violence into the national consciousness. For gender inequality to continue to be reduced, it is essential that a strong women's movement continue to remind us of the sexism that persists in American society and the rest of the world.

Reducing Rape and Sexual Assault

As we have seen, gender inequality also manifests itself in the form of violence against women. A sociological perspective tells us that cultural myths and economic and gender inequality help lead to rape and sexual assault, and that this serious problem goes far beyond a few psychopathic men who attack women. A sociological perspective thus tells us that our society cannot just stop at doing something about these men. Instead, it must make more far-reaching changes by changing people's beliefs about rape and by making every effort to reduce poverty and to empower women. This last task is especially important, for as Randall and Haskell (1995:22),[77] the authors of the Toronto study discussed earlier, observed, a sociological perspective on rape "means calling into question the organization of sexual inequality in our society."

Aside from this fundamental change, other remedies, such as additional and better funded rape crisis centers, would help women who experience rape and sexual assault. Yet even here women of color face an additional barrier. Because the antirape movement was begun by white, middle-class feminists, the rape crisis centers they founded tended to be near where they live, such as college campuses, and not in the areas where women of color live, such as inner cities and Native American reservations. This meant that women of color who experienced sexual violence lacked the kinds of help available to their white, middle-class counterparts (Matthews 1989),[78] and despite some progress, this is still true today.

Key Takeaways

- Certain government efforts, including increased financial support for child care, should help reduce gender inequality.
- If gender inequality lessens, rape and sexual assault should decrease as well.

1. To reduce gender inequality, do you think efforts should focus more on changing socialization practices or on changing policies in the workplace and schools? Explain your answer.

2. How hopeful are you that rape and sexual assault will decrease significantly in your lifetime?

4.6 End-of-Chapter Material

Summary

1. *Sex* is a concept that refers to biological differences between females and males, while *gender* is a concept that refers to a society's expectations of how females and males should think and behave.

2. In understanding gender differences, scholars continue to debate the value of biological explanations. Biological explanations are provocative but ultimately imply that gender differences are inevitable and that the status quo must be maintained. In contrast, cultural and socialization explanations imply some hope for changing gender roles and for reducing gender inequality.

3. Many studies emphasize that socialization leads children in the United States to adopt the gender roles associated with femininity and masculinity. Parents view and interact with their daughters and sons differently, and children continue to learn their gender roles from their peers, schools, the mass media, and religion.

4. Feminism refers to the belief that women should be equal to men. With feminism defined in this way, many more people hold feminist beliefs than might be willing to admit to it.

5. Gender inequality in the workplace is manifested through the gender gap in earnings and through sexual harassment. Women earn only about 80 percent of what men earn. Several reasons account for this gap, including sex segregation in the workplace, women's caring roles, the devaluing of women's work, and outright sex discrimination by employers. Sexual harassment against women is quite common and stems from cultural beliefs about women's and men's roles and structural differences in the workplace in power between women and men.

6. Women of color experience a triple burden based on their gender, race/ethnicity, and social class. Even though white women earn less money and are poorer than white men, women of color earn less money and are poorer than white women.

7. The COVID-19 pandemic killed more men than women but fell more heavily on women in other ways. In particular, it threatened pregnant women, it probably increased domestic violence, and it exposed many women to the coronavirus because of their caretaking roles and great numbers in health-care and service occupations.

8. Violence against women is another manifestation of gender inequality. Research shows that up to one-third of U.S. women will be raped or sexually assaulted and that about 70–80 percent of their assailants will be men they know.

9. In a patriarchal society men enjoy privileges just for being male, whether or not they recognize these privileges. At the same time, men also experience disadvantages, including violent behavior and victimization and higher rates of certain emotional problems than those experienced by women.

Using What You Know

A friend of yours is working 20 hours per week in a local restaurant during the academic year to earn money for her tuition. She tells you that her manager has pressured her to go out on a date with him and has hinted she could be fired if she refuses. Your friend likes working there otherwise and makes good tips, but she is now dreading having to go to work. With the tight job market, she fears not being able to find other work if she quits, and she's afraid of being fired or not believed if she complains to state authorities. She asks you what she should do. What do you tell her?

What You Can Do

To help reduce gender inequality, you may wish to do any of the following:

1. Contribute money to a local, state, or national organization that provides treatment to adolescent girls with drug, alcohol, or other problems.
2. Volunteer at a rape crisis center or for a rape hotline.
3. Start or join a group on your campus that focuses on gender issues.
4. Start or join a group on your campus or in the local community that focuses on getting middle school girls more interested in math and the sciences.

Endnotes

1. Sullivan, Kaitlin. 2019. "Reports of Sexual Harassment Wane at Work, Possibly Thanks to #Metoo." *NBCnews* July 17:https://www.nbcnews.com/health/womens-health/sexual-harassment-losing-its-effect-women-workplace-possibly-thanks-metoo-n1030871.
2. Aulette, Judy Root, Judith Wittner and Kristen Barber. 2019. *Gendered Worlds*. New York: Oxford University Press.
3. Buss, David M. 2019. *Evolutionary Psychology: The New Science of the Mind*. New York: Routledge.
4. Saini, Angela. 2017. *Inferior: How Science Got Women Wrong-and the New Research That's Rewriting the Story*. Boston: Beacon Press.
5. Browne, Kingsley. 2002. *Biology at Work: Rethinking Sexual Equality*. New Brunswick, NJ: Rutgers University Press.
6. Fine, Cordella. 2011. *Delusions of Gender: The Real Science Behind Sex Differences*. New York: W.W. Norton & Company. Saini, Angela. 2017. *Inferior: How Science Got Women Wrong-and the New Research That's Rewriting the Story*. Boston: Beacon Press.
7. Begley, Sharon. 2009. "Don't Blame the Caveman." *Newsweek* June 29:52-62.
8. Dekkers, Tycho J., Joost A. Agelink van Rentergem, Bren Meijer, Arne Popma, Eline Wagemaker and Hilde M. Huizenga. 2019. "A Meta-Analytical Evaluation of the Dual-Hormone Hypothesis: Does Cortisol Moderate the Relationship between Testosterone and Status, Dominance, Risk Taking, Aggression, and Psychopathy." *Neuroscience & Biobehavioral Reviews* 96(January):250-71.
9. Carré, Justin M. and N. A. Olmstead. 2015. "Social Neuroendocrinology of Human Aggression: Examining the Role of Competition-Induced Testosterone Dynamics." *Neuroscience* 286:171-91.
10. Card, Noel A., Brian D. Stucky, Gita M. Sawalani and Todd D. Little. 2008. "Direct and Indirect Aggression During Childhood and Adolescence: A Meta-Analytic Review of Gender Differences, Intercorrelations, and Relations to Maladjustment." *Child Development* 79(5):1185-229. doi: 10.1111/j.1467-8624.2008.01184.x.
11. Begley, Sharon. 2009. "Pink Brain, Blue Brain: Claims of Sex Differences Fall Apart." *Newsweek* September 14:28; Fine, Cordella. 2011. *Delusions of Gender: The Real Science Behind Sex Differences*. New York: W.W. Norton & Company.
12. Lindsey, Linda L. 2011. *Gender Roles: A Sociological Perspective* (5th ed.). Upper Saddle River, NJ: Prentice Hall.
13. Murdock, George. 1937. "Comparative Data on the Division of Labor by Sex." *Social Forces* 15:551-53.
14. Brettell, Caroline B. and Carolyn F. Sargent, eds. 2017. *Gender in Cross-Cultural Perspective*. New York: Routledge.
15. Judy Root Aulette, Judith Wittner and Kristen Barber. 2019. *Gendered Worlds*. New York: Oxford University Press.
16. Lindsey, Linda L. 2015. *Gender Roles: A Sociological Perspective*. Upper Saddle River, NJ: Prentice Hall.
17. Lever, Janet. 1978. "Sex Differences in the Complexity of Children's Play and Games." *American Sociological Review* 43:471-83.
18. Thorne, Barrie. 1993. *Gender Play: Girls and Boys in School*. New Brunswick, NJ: Rutgers University Press.
19. Sadker, Myra and David Sadker. 1994. *Failing at Fairness: How America's Schools Cheat Girls*. New York: Charles Scribner's.
20. Lauzen, Martha M. 2017. *Boxed in 2016-17: Women on Screen and Behind the Scenes in Television*. San Diego: Center for the Study of Women in Television & Film, San Diego State University.
21. Frazer, R. Lee and Kelsey Anderson. 2018. "Media Representations of Race, Ability, and Gender in Three Outdoor Magazines: A Content Analysis of Photographic Images." *Journal of Outdoor Recreation, Education, and Leadership* 10(3):https://js.sagamorepub.com/jorel/article/view/9051; Milillo, Diana. 2008. "Sexuality Sells: A Content Analysis of Lesbian and Heterosexual Women's Bodies in Magazine Advertisements." *Journal of Lesbian Studies* 12(4):381-92.
22. Tanenbaum, Leora. 2009. *Taking Back God: American Women Rising up for Religious Equality*. New York: Farrar, Straus and Giroux.
23. The World Bank. 2019. "Maternal Mortality Ratio."https://data.worldbank.org/indicator/SH.STA.MMRT?most_recent_year_desc=false&view=chart.
24. World Health Organization. 2017. "Violence against Women."https://www.who.int/news-room/fact-sheets/detail/violence-against-women.
25. Amnesty International. (2004). *It's in our hands: Stop violence against women. Summary*. London, United Kingdom: Author.
26. Bundhun, Rebecca. 2017. "Dowries and Death Continue Apace in India." *The National* February 10:https://www.thenational.ae/world/dowries-and-death-continue-apace-in-india-1.81522.
27. World Health Organization. 2018. "Female Genital Mutilation."https://www.who.int/news-room/fact-sheets/detail/female-genital-mutilation.
28. Kristoff, Nicholas D. and Sheryl WuDunn. 2010. *Half the Sky: Turning Oppression into Opportunity for Women Worldwide*. New York: Vintage Books.
29. Henriques, Martha. 2020. "Why Covid-19 Is Different for Men and Women." *BBC.com* April 12:https://www.bbc.com/future/article/20200409-why-covid-19-is-different-for-men-and-women.
30. Evans, David. 2020. "How Will Covid-19 Affect Women and Girls in Low- and Middle-Income Countries?". *Center for Global Development*:https://www.cgdev.org/blog/how-will-covid-19-affect-women-and-girls-low-and-middle-income-countries.

31. UN Women. 2020. *Policy Brief: The Impact of COVID-19 on Women.* New York: UN Women, United Nations.

32. United Nations Development Programme. 2018. *Human Developmentindices and Indicators: 2018 Statistical Update.* New York: United Nations Development Programme.

33. Åseskog, Birgitta. 2018. "National Machinery for Gender Equality in Sweden and Other Nordic Countries." Pp. 146-66 in *Mainstreaming Gender, Democratizing the State*, edited by S. M. Rai. Manchester, UK: Manchester University Press; Sumer, Sevil, Janet Smithson, Maria das Dores Guerreiro and Lise Granlund. 2008. "Becoming Working Mothers: Reconciling Work and Family at Three Particular Workplaces in Norway, the Uk, and Portugal." *Community, Work & Family* 11(4):365-84.

34. Kangas, Olli and Joakim Palme. 2009. "Making Social Policy Work for Econonic Development: The Nordic Experience." *International Journal of Social Welfare* 18(s1):S62-S72.

35. Bureau of Labor Statistics. 2018. *2018 Employment and Earnings Online.* Washington, DC: Author. Retrieved from https://www.bls.gov/opub/ee/2018/cps/annual.htm#empstat.

36. Reskin, Barbara and Irene Padavic. 2002. *Women and Men at Work.* Thousand Oaks, CA: Pine Forge Press.

37. Bureau of Labor Statistics. 2018. *2018 Employment and Earnings Online.* Washington, DC: Author. Retrieved from https://www.bls.gov/opub/ee/2018/cps/annual.htm#empstat.

38. Blau, Francine D. and Lawrence M. Kahn. 2016. "The Gender Wage Gap: Extent, Trends, and Explanations." Cambridge, MA: National Bureau of Economic Research.

39. Magnusson, Charlotta. 2009. "Gender, Occupational Prestige, and Wages: A Test of Devaluation Theory." *European Sociological Review* 25(1):87-101.

40. Levanon, Asaf, Paula England and Paul Allison. 2009. "Occupational Feminization and Pay: Assessing Causal Dynamics Using 1950-2000 U.S. Census Data." *Social Forces* 88(2):865-91; Newton, Jess. 2018. "Job Analysis, Job Evaluation and Comparable Worth: Closing the Gender Pay Gap." *ToughNickel.com*:https://toughnickel.com/business/Job-Analysis-Job-Evaluation-and-Comparable-Worth.

41. U.S. Bureau of Labor Statistics. 2018. *Highlights of Women's Earnings in 2017.* Washington, DC: U.S. Department of Labor.

42. Chang, Mariko Lin. 2010. *Shortchanged: Why Women Have Less Wealth and What Can Be Done About It.* New York: Oxford University Press.

43. McFarland, J., Hussar, B., Zhang, J., Wang, X., Wang, K., Hein, S., Diliberti, M., Forrest Cataldi, E., Bullock Mann, F., and Barmer, A. 2019. *The Condition of Education 2019(NCES 2019-144).* U.S. Department of Education. Washington, DC: National Center for Education Statistics. Retrieved from https://nces.ed.gov/pubsearch/pubsinfo.asp?pubid=2019144.

44. Fontenot, Kayla, Jessica Semega and Melissa Kollar. 2018. *Income and Poverty in the United States: 2017.* Washington, DC: U.S. Census Bureau.

45. National Academies of Sciences, Engineering, and Medicine 2018. *Sexual Harassment of Women: Climate, Culture, and Consequences in Academic Sciences, Engineering, and Medicine.* Washington, DC: The National Academies Press.

46. Cantor, David, Bonnie Fisher, Susan Chibnall, Reanne Townsend, Hyunshik Lee, Carol Bruce and Gail Thomas. 2017. *Report on the Aau Campus Climate Survey on Sexual Assault and Sexual Misconduct.* Washington, DC: Association of American Universities.

47. Clodfelter, Tammatha A., Michael G. Turner, Jennifer L. Hartman and Joseph B. Kuhns. 2010. "Sexual Harassment Victimization During Emerging Adulthood." *Crime & Delinquency* 56(3):455-81.

48. Fitzgerald, Louise F., and Lilia M. Cortina. 2017. "Sexual Harassment in Work Organizations: A View from the 21st Century." In *Handbook of the Psychology of Women*, edited by Cheryl B. Travis and Jacquelyn W. White. Washington, DC: American Psychological Association; Houle, Jason N., Jeremy Staff, Jeylan T. Mortimer, Christopher Uggen and Amy Blackstone. 2011. "The Impact of Sexual Harassment on Depressive Symptoms During the Early Occupational Career." *Society and Mental Health* 1:89-105.

49. Fontenot, Kayla, Jessica Semega and Melissa Kollar. 2018. *Income and Poverty in the United States: 2017.* Washington, DC: U.S. Census Bureau.

50. Bureau of Labor Statistics. 2016. *American Time Use Survey.* https://www.bls.gov/tus/charts/household.htm

51. Hochschild, Arlie. 1989. *The Second Shift: Working Parents and the Revolution at Home.* New York: Viking.

52. Papp, Susan and Marcy Hersh. 2020. "A Gender Lens for Covid-19." *Ms. Magazine* March 31:https://msmagazine.com/2020/03/31/a-gender-lens-for-covid-19/.

53. Rettner, Rachael. 2020. "Surprising Number of Pregnant Women at Nyc Hospitals Test Positive for Covid-19." *Livescience.com* April 15. https://www.livescience.com/coronavirus-in-pregnant-woman-high-nyc.html.

54. Hopper, Leigh and Gabriella Robison. 2020. "Do Pregnant Women Face Special Risks from Covid-19?". *USCNews* April 7:https://news.usc.edu/167968/pregnancy-covid-19-women-risks-breastfeeding-milk/.

55. Zephryn, Laurie. 2020. "The Challenges of Giving Birth in the Time of Covid-19." *Statnews* April 10:https://www.statnews.com/2020/04/10/birth-in-the-time-of-covid-19/.

56. Taub, Amanda. 2020. "Locked Down, and More Vulnerable to Abuse." *The New York Times* April 7:A9.

57. Godin, Melissa. 2020. "As Cities around the World Go on Lockdown, Victims of Domestic Violence Look for a Way Out." *Time* March 18:https://time.com/5803887/coronavirus-domestic-violence-victims/.

58. Schnall, Marianne. 2020. "Putting a Gender Lens on Covid-19: Thought Leaders Weigh In." *Forbes* April 17:https://www.forbes.com/sites/marianneschnall/2020/04/17/putting-a-gender-lens-on-covid-19-thought-leaders-weigh-in/#72acc5235b23.

59. Gupta, Alisha Haridasani. 2020. "Why Women May Face a Greater Risk of Catching Coronavirus." *The New York Times* March 12:https://www.nytimes.com/2020/03/12/us/women-coronavirus-greater-risk.html.

60. Griffin, Susan. 1971. Rape: The All-American Crime. *Ramparts 10, 26–35.*

61. Breiding, Matthew J., Sharon G. Smith, Kathleen C. Basile, Mikel L. Walters, Jieru Chen and Melissa T. Merrick. 2014. "Prevalence and Characteristics of Sexual Violence, Stalking, and Intimate Partner Violence Victimization—National Intimate Partner and Sexual Violence Survey, United States, 2011." *Morbidity and Mortality Weekly Report* 63(SS08):1-18; Tjaden, Patricia and Nancy Thoennes. 2000. *Full Report of the Prevalence, Incidence, and Consequences of Violence against Women.* Washington, DC: National Institute of Justice and the Centers for Disease Control and Prevention.

62. Randall, Melanie and Lori Haskell. 1995. "Sexual Violence in Women's Lives: Findings from the Women's Safety Project, a Community-Based Survey." *Violence Against Women* 1:6-31.

63. Fisher, Bonnie S., Francis T. Cullen and Michael G. Turner. 2000. *The Sexual Victimization of College Women.* Washington, DC: National Institute of Justice and Bureau of Justce Statistics, U.S. Department of Justice; Gross, Alan M., Andrea Winslett, Miguel Roberts and Carol L. Gohm. 2006. "An Examination of Sexual Violence against College Women." *Violence Against Women* 12:288-300; Mellins, Claude A. and and thirteen other authors. 2017. "Sexual Assault Incidents among College Undergraduates: Prevalence and Factors Associated with Risk." *PLOS One* 12(11):doi: 10.1371/journal.pone.0186471.

64. Anderson, RaeAnn E., Kristin E. Silver, Alyssa M. Ciampaglia, Amanda M. Vitale and Douglas L. Delahanty. 2019. "The Prevalence of Sexual Perpetration in College Men: A Systematic Review of Reported Prevalence Rates from 2000 to 2017." *Trauma, Violence, & Abuse*:doi: 10.1177/1524838019860619.

65. Julie Turkewitz. 2019. "Fraternities Move to Disband After Uproar at Swarthmore." *The New York Times* May 2:A19.

66. Barkan, Steven E. 2018. *Criminology: A Sociological Understanding.* Upper Saddle River, NJ: Pearson; Breiding, Matthew J., Sharon G. Smith, Kathleen C. Basile, Mikel L. Walters, Jieru Chen and Melissa T. Merrick. 2014. "Prevalence and Characteristics of Sexual Violence, Stalking, and Intimate Partner Violence Victimization—National Intimate Partner and Sexual Violence Survey, United States, 2011." *Morbidity and Mortality Weekly Report* 63(SS08):1-18.

67. Shaw, Jessica, Rebecca Campbell, Debi Cain and Hannah Feeney. 2017. "Beyond Surveys and Scales: How Rape Myths in Sexual Assault Police Records." *Psychology of Violence* 7(4):602-14.

68. Shafer, Autumn, Rebecca R. Ortiz, Bailey Thompson and Jennifer Huemmer. 2018. "The Role of Hypermasculinity, Token Resistance, Rape Myth, and Assertive Sexual Consent Communication among College Men." *Journal of Adolescent Health* 62(3):S44-S50.

69. Lave, Tamara Rice. 2016. "The Prosecutor's Duty to 'Imperfect' Rape Victims." *Texas Tech Law Review* 49:219-48.

70. Baron, Larry and Murray A. Straus. 1989. Four Theories of Rape in American Society: A State-Level Analysis. New Haven: Yale University Press; Sanday, Peggy Reeves. 1981. "The Socio-Cultural Context of Rape: A Cross-Cultural Study." *Journal of Social Issues* 37:5-27.

71. Morgan, Rachel E. and Jennifer L. Truman. 2018. *Criminal Victimization, 2017.* Washington, DC: Bureau of Justice Statistics, U.S. Department of Justice.

72. Martin, Kimberly, Lynne M. Vieraitis and Sarah Britto. 2006. "Gender Equality and Women's Absolute Status: A Test of the Feminist Models of Rape." *Violence Against Women* 12:321-39.

73. McIntosh, Peggy. 2007. White Privilege and Male Privilege: A Personal Account of Coming to See Correspondence Through Work in Women's Studies. In Margaret L. Andersen & Patricia Hill Collins (Eds.), *Race, Class, and Gender: An Anthology* (6th ed.). Belmont, CA: Wadsworth.

74. Parent, Mike C., Teresa D. Gobble and Aaron Rochlen. 2019. "Social Media Behavior, Toxic Masculinity, and Depression." *Psychology of Men & Masculinities* 20(3):277-87.

75. Addis, M. E. and E. Hoffman. 2017. "Men's Depression and Help-Seeking through the Lenses of Gender." Pp. 171-96 in *The Psychology of Men and Masculinities*, edited by R. F. Levant and Y. J. Wong. Washington, DC: Amereican Psychological Association.

76. Reichert, Michael C. 2019. *How to Raise a Boy: The Power of Connection to Build Good Men.* New York: TarcherPerigee.

77. Randall, Melanie and Lori Haskell. 1995. "Sexual Violence in Women's Lives: Findings from the Women's Safety Project, a Community-Based Survey." *Violence Against Women* 1:6-31.

78. Matthews, Nancy A. 1989. "Surmounting a Legacy: The Expansion of Racial Diversity in a Local Anti-Rape Movement." *Gender & Society* 3:518-32.

CHAPTER 5
Sexual Orientation, Gender Identity, and Inequality

Social Problems in the News

"Pride Parade: 50 Years After Stonewall, a Joyous and Resolute Celebration," the headline said. On June 30, 2019, the annual Pride parade to celebrate the gay rights movement marched exuberantly with rainbow colors down the streets of New York City. This year's parade marked the 50th anniversary of the momentous Stonewall Inn uprising, when police raided a gay bar, the Stonewall Inn, in Greenwich Village on June 28, 1969. A crowd of bar patrons and bystanders began throwing things at the police, who ironically took refuge in the inn. Protests against the raid and the harsh treatment of the LGBTQ community (not then known by that acronym) continued for several days and marked the beginning of the gay rights movement. Now, 50 years later, the latest Pride March in New York was remembering the Stonewall events and celebrating the gains made by the gay rights movement. A drag queen marching in the parade said, "Fifty years ago, this is where the revolution began. Fifty years ago was when we decided enough was enough." But amid the celebration, people were also soberly reflecting on the work that still needed to be done, with a moment of silence shortly before the parade began recalling lives lost to AIDS and hate crimes. As an activist in an alternative Queer Liberation March elsewhere in the city explained, "There is much to celebrate today, and still so much to fight for."

Source: Barron 2019 [1]

From 1933 to 1945, Adolf Hitler's Nazi regime exterminated six million Jews in the Holocaust, but it also persecuted millions of other people, including gay men. Nazi officials alleged that these men harbored what they termed a "degeneracy" that threatened Germany's "disciplined masculinity." Calling gay men "antisocial parasites" and "enemies of the state," the Nazi government arrested more than 100,000 men for violating a law against homosexuality, although it did not arrest lesbians because it valued their child-bearing capacity. At least five thousand gay men were imprisoned, and many more were put in mental institutions. Several hundred other gay men were castrated, and up to fifteen thousand were placed in concentration camps, where most died from disease, starvation, or murder. As the United States Holocaust Memorial Museum (2019)[2] summarizes these events, "Nazi Germany did not seek to kill all homosexuals. Nevertheless, the Nazi state, through active persecution, attempted to terrorize German homosexuals into sexual and social conformity, leaving thousands dead and shattering the lives of many more."

This terrible history reminds us that sexual orientation has often resulted in inequality of many kinds and, in the extreme case of the Nazis, inhumane treatment that included castration, imprisonment, and death. The news story that began this chapter reminds us that despite the many gains made by the LGBTQ community in the past half century, inequality on the basis of sexual orientation and gender identity continues. This chapter examines the many forms of inequality linked to sexual orientation and gender identity today. It begins with a discussion of these two concepts before turning to other matters.

5.1 Understanding Sexual Orientation and Gender Identity

Learning Objectives

1. Define sexual orientation and gender identity.
2. Describe what percentage of the U.S. population is estimated to be LGBTQ.
3. Summarize the history of sexual orientation.
4. Evaluate the possible reasons for sexual orientation.

sexual orientation

Preference for sexual relationships with individuals of the opposite sex, the same sex, or both sexes.

gender identity

The personal conception of oneself as female, male, both, or neither.

transgendered

Those whose gender identity and/or expression departs from the cultural norms based on their birth sex.

To help understand sexual orientation and gender identity, some definitions are first in order. **Sexual orientation** refers to a person's preference for sexual relationships with individuals of the other sex (*heterosexuality*), one's own sex (*homosexuality*), or both sexes (*bisexuality*), while **gender identity** refers to the personal conception of oneself as female, male, both, or neither. **Transgendered** people are those whose gender identity and/or expression departs from the cultural norms based on their birth sex. These people include *transvestites* (those who dress in the clothing of the opposite sex) and *transsexuals* (those whose gender identity differs from their physiological sex and who sometimes undergo sex-confirming surgery. A *transgender woman* is a person who was born biologically as a male and becomes a woman, while a *transgender man* is a person who was born biologically as a woman and becomes a man. As you almost certainly know, *gay* is the common term now used for any homosexual individual; *gay men* or *gays* is the common term used for homosexual men, while *lesbian* is the common term used for homosexual women. All the types of orientation and gender identity just outlined are often collectively referred to by the shorthand *LGBTQ* (lesbian/gay/bisexual/transgender/queer). As you almost certainly also know, the term straight is used today as a synonym for heterosexual.

Counting Sexual Orientation and Gender Identity

We will probably never know precisely how many people are LGBTQ. One problem is conceptual. For example, what does it mean to be gay or lesbian? Does one need to actually have sexual relations with a same-sex partner to be considered gay? What if someone is attracted to same-sex partners but does not actually engage in sex with such persons? What if someone identifies as heterosexual but engages in homosexual sex for money (as in certain forms of prostitution) or for power and influence (as in much prison sex)? What if a biological woman thinks of herself as a man but lives her life fully as a woman? Is this a transgender person? These conceptual problems make it difficult to determine the numbers of LGBTQ people (Gates 2018).[3]

A second problem is empirical. Even if we can settle on clear definitions of the categories defined just earlier, how do we then determine how many people fit these definitions? For better or worse, our best evidence of the number of LGBTQ people in the United States comes from surveys that ask random samples of Americans various questions about their sexuality and/or gender identity. Although these are anonymous surveys, some individuals may be reluctant to disclose their sexual activities, thoughts, and identities to an interviewer. Still, scholars think estimates from these surveys are fairly accurate but also that they probably do underestimate somewhat the actual number of LGBTQ people.

During the 1940s and 1950s, sex researcher Alfred C. Kinsey carried out the first notable attempt to estimate the number of gays and lesbians (Kinsey et al. 1953).[4] His project interviewed more than eleven thousand white women and men about their sexual experiences, thoughts, and attractions. While most interviewees had experiences and feelings that were exclusively straight, a significant number had experiences and feelings that were either exclusively gay or both gay and straight in varying degrees. These findings led Kinsey to reject the popular idea back then that a person is necessarily either heterosexual or homosexual (or straight or gay, to again use the common modern terms). Perhaps Kinsey's most significant and controversial finding was that gradations in sexual orientation did, in fact, exist. To reflect these gradations, he developed the well-known *Kinsey Scale*, which ranks individuals on a continuum ranging from 0 (exclusively heterosexual) to 6 (exclusively homosexual). Kinsey found that 4 percent of males and a slightly lower percentage of females had exclusively same-sex relations after adolescence began, with greater percentages having had at least one same-sex experience or reporting being attracted to persons of the same sex.

More recent research updates Kinsey's early findings and, more important, uses nationally representative samples of Americans (which Kinsey did not use). One such survey in the early 1990s found that 2.8 percent of men and 1.4 percent of women self-identified as gay/lesbian or bisexual, with greater percentages again reporting having had sexual relations with same-sex partners or being attracted to same-sex persons. In a 2016 Gallup poll, 4.4 percent of women and 3.7 percent of men identified as LGBTQ (Gates 2017).[5] For both sexes combined, 4.1 percent so identified, equivalent to more than ten million adults overall. Among millennials (respondents born between 1980 and 1998), 7.3 percent identified as LGBTQ. As these numbers suggest, millennials are more likely than older people to identify as LGBTQ, perhaps because they feel more comfortable in doing so. Other Gallup data suggest that 8.2 percent of Americans have engaged in same-sex relations and that 11 percent have at least some attraction to same-sex persons (Gates 2011).[6] Finally, in the 2018 General Social Survey (GSS), 2.1 percent of men and 7.5 percent of women self-identified as gay/lesbian or bisexual, or 5 percent of women and men combined.

These are all a lot of numbers, but these and other data suggest that between 4 percent and 5 percent of American adults identify as LGBTQ, with women somewhat more likely than men to do so, and that somewhat greater numbers have engaged in same-sex relations and have been attracted to same-sex persons. The overall picture from these estimates is clear: Self-identified LGBTQ people comprise a small percentage of the U.S. population, but they amount to more than ten million adults and undoubtedly a significant number of adolescents. In addition, the total number of people who, regardless of their sexual orientation, have had a same-sex experience is probably at least nineteen million, and the number who have had same-sex attraction is probably at least twenty-five million, when we extrapolate the survey percentages to the adult population.

It is difficult for several reasons to know exactly how many people are LGBTQ.

Source: © Thinkstock

Up to 5 percent of the U.S. adult population identify as LGBTQ. This figure amounts to more than ten million people.

Source: © Thinkstock

How Gay Is America?

It is difficult to measure sexual orientation and gender identity, but survey evidence finds that between about 4 percent and 5 percent of Americans identify as LGBTQ.

View the video online at: http://www.youtube.com/embed/-LwCfpWoY2g?rel=0

Sexual Orientation in Historical Perspective

Based on what is known about homosexuality in past societies, it should be no surprise that so many people in the United States identify as LGBTQ or have had same-sex experiences. This historical record is clear: Homosexuality has existed since ancient times and in some societies has been rather common or at least fully accepted as a normal form of sexual expression.

In the great city of Athens in ancient Greece, male homosexuality (to be more precise, sexual relations between a man and a teenaged boy and, less often, between a man and a man) was not only approved but even encouraged. According to classical scholar K. J. Dover (1989:12),[7] Athenian society "certainly regarded strong homosexual desire and emotion as normal," in part because it also generally "entertained a low opinion of the intellectual capacity and staying-power of women." Louis Crompton (2003:2),[8] who wrote perhaps the definitive history of homosexuality, agrees that male homosexuality in ancient Greece was common and notes that "in Greek history and literature…the abundance of accounts of homosexual love overwhelms the investigator."

Male homosexuality in ancient Rome was also common and accepted as normal sexuality, but it took a different form from that in ancient Greece. Ancient Romans disapproved of sexual relations between a man and a freeborn male youth, but they approved of relations between a slave master and his enslaved youthful male. Sexual activity of this type was common. As Crompton (2003:80)[9] wryly notes, "Opportunities were ample for Roman masters" because the enslaved comprised about 40 percent of the population of ancient Rome. However, these "opportunities" are best regarded as violent domination by slave masters over their enslaved.

By the time Rome fell in 476 CE, Europe had become a Christian continent as the Middle Ages began. Influenced by biblical passages that condemn homosexuality, Europeans considered homosexuality a sin, and their governments outlawed same-sex relations. If discovered, male homosexuals (or any men suspected of homosexuality) were vulnerable to execution for the next 14 centuries, and many did lose their lives. During the Middle Ages, gay men and lesbians were stoned, burned at the stake, hanged, or beheaded, and otherwise abused and mistreated. Crompton (2003:539)[10] calls these atrocities a "routine of terror" and a "kaleidoscope of horrors." Hitler's persecution of gay men several centuries after the Middle Ages ended had ample precedent in European history.

In contrast to the European treatment of gay men and lesbians, China and Japan from ancient times onward viewed homosexuality much more positively, in what Crompton (2003:215)[11] calls an "unselfconscious acceptance of same-sex relations." He adds that male love in Japan during the 1500s was "a national tradition—one the Japanese thought natural and meritorious" (Crompton, 2003:412)[12] and very much part of the *samurai* (military nobility) culture of preindustrial Japan. In China, both male and female homosexuality were seen as normal and even healthy sexual outlets. Because Confucianism, the major Chinese religion when the Common Era began, considered women inferior, it considered male friendships very important and thus may have unwittingly promoted same-sex relations among men. Various artistic and written records indicate that male homosexuality was fairly common in China over the centuries, although the exact numbers can never be known. When China began trading and otherwise communicating with Europe during the Ming dynasty, its tolerance for homosexuality shocked and disgusted Catholic missionaries and other Europeans. Some European clergy and scientists even attributed earthquakes and other natural disasters in China to this tolerance.

In addition to this historical work, anthropologists have also studied same-sex relations in small, traditional societies. In many of these societies, homosexuality is both common and accepted as normal sexual behavior. In one overview of seventy-six societies, the authors found that almost two-thirds regarded homosexuality as "normal and socially acceptable for certain members of the community" (Ford and Beach 1951:130).[13] Among the Azande of East Africa, for example, young warriors live with each other and are not allowed to marry. During this time, they often have sex with younger boys. Among the Sambia of New Guinea, young males live separately from females and have same-sex relations for at least a decade. It is felt that the boys would be less masculine if they continued to live with their mothers and that the semen of older males helps young boys become strong and fierce (Edgerton 1976).[14]

This brief historical and anthropological overview provides ready evidence of what was said at its outset: Homosexuality has existed since ancient times and in some societies has been rather common or at least fully accepted as a normal form of sexual expression. In the great ancient civilizations of Greece, China, and Japan until the industrial age, male homosexuality was fairly common, and female homosexuality was far from unknown. Same-sex relations are also fairly common in many of the societies that anthropologists have studied. Although Western societies, influenced by the Judeo-Christian tradition, have long viewed homosexuality very negatively, the historical and anthropological record demonstrates that same-sex relationships must be regarded as normal expressions of sexuality.

In fact, some of the most famous individuals in Western political, literary, and artistic history certainly or probably engaged in same-sex relations, either sometimes or exclusively: Alexander the Great, Hans Christian Andersen, Marie Antoinette, Aristotle, Sir Francis Bacon, James Baldwin, Leonard Bernstein, Lord Byron, Julius Caesar, Ralph Waldo Emerson, Frederick the Great, Leonardo da Vinci, Herman Melville, Michelangelo, Plato, Cole Porter, Richard the Lionhearted, Eleanor Roosevelt, Socrates, Gertrude Stein, Pyotr Tchaikovsky, Henry David Thoreau, Walt Whitman, Tennessee Williams, Oscar Wilde, and Virginia Woolf, to name just a few. Regardless of or perhaps in some cases because of their sexuality, they all made great contributions to the societies in which they lived.

Explaining Sexual Orientation

We have seen that it is difficult to determine the number of people who are LGBTQ. It is even more difficult to know why some people are LGBTQ while most are not. Determining the origins of sexual orientation and gender identity is not just an academic exercise. When people believe that the roots of LGBTQ status are biological, so that LGBTQ people do not choose to be LGBTQ, they are more likely to have positive or at least tolerant views of this status. When they believe that this status is instead merely a personal choice, they are more likely to disapprove of it (Sheldon et al.

2007).[15] For this reason if for no other, it is important to know why some people are LGBTQ while most are not. Because most research on this topic concerns sexual orientation rather than gender identity, this section focuses on sexual orientation.

Studies of the origins of sexual orientation focus mostly on biological factors and on social and cultural factors, and a healthy scholarly debate exists on the relative importance of these two sets of factors.

Biological Factors

Research points to certain genetic and other biological roots of sexual orientation but is by no means conclusive (Bailey et al. 2016).[16] A major line of research concerns genetics. Although no "gay gene" has been discovered, studies of identical twins find they are more likely to have the same sexual orientation (gay or straight) than would be expected from chance alone. Because identical twins have the same DNA, this similarity suggests a genetic basis for sexual orientation. Keep in mind, however, that any physical or behavioral trait that is *totally* due to genetics should show up in both twins or in neither twin. Because many identical twins still do *not* have the same sexual orientation, this dissimilarity suggests that genetics are far from the only cause of sexual orientation, to the extent they cause it at all, and that other biological and/or social factors must play a role (Ganna et al. 2019; Watts et al. 2018).[17]

Another line of research concerns brain anatomy, as some studies find differences in the size and structure of the hypothalamus, which controls many bodily functions, in the brains of gays versus the brains of straights. However, other studies find no such differences (Lasco et al. 2002).[18] Further, because sexual behavior can affect the hypothalamus, it is difficult to determine whether any differences that might be found reflect the influence of the hypothalamus on sexual orientation, or instead the influence of sexual orientation on the hypothalamus (Sheldon et al. 2007).[19]

A third line of biological research concerns hormonal balance in the womb, with scientists speculating that the level of prenatal androgen affects which sexual orientation develops. Because prenatal androgen levels cannot be measured, studies typically measure it only indirectly in the bodies of gays and straights by comparing the lengths of certain fingers and bones that are thought to be related to prenatal androgen. Some of these studies suggest that gay men had lower levels of prenatal androgen than straight men and that lesbians had higher levels of prenatal androgen than straight women, but other studies find no evidence of this connection (Bailey et al. 2016).[20] A review of this line of research concluded that "the notion that non-heterosexual preferences may reflect [deviations from normal prenatal hormonal levels] is not supported by the available data" (Rahman 2005:1057).[21]

Social and Cultural Factors

Sociologists usually emphasize the importance of socialization over biology for the learning of many forms of human behavior. In this view, humans are born with "blank slates" and thereafter shaped by their society and culture. More specifically, children are shaped by their parents, teachers, peers, and other aspects of their immediate social environment while they are growing up.

Given this standard sociological position, one might think that sociologists generally believe that people are gay or straight not because of their biology but because they learn to be gay or straight from their society, culture, and immediate social environment. This, in fact, was a common belief of sociologists about a generation ago (Engle et al. 2006).[22] In a 1988 review article, for example, two sociologists concluded that "evidence that homosexuality is a social construction [learned from society and culture] is far more powerful than the evidence for a widespread organic [biological] predisposition toward homosexual desire" (Risman and Schwartz 1988:143).[23]

Despite scholarly speculation, sexual orientation does not appear to be affected by the level of prenatal hormones.

Source: © Thinkstock

However, sociologists' views of the origins of sexual orientation have apparently changed since this passage was written. In a more recent national survey of a random sample of sociologists, 22 percent said male homosexuality results from biological factors, 38 percent said it results from both biological and environmental (learning) factors, and 39 percent said it results from environmental factors (Engle et al. 2006).[24] Thus, 60 percent (= 22 + 38) thought that biology totally or partly explains male homosexuality, almost certainly a much higher figure than would have been found a generation ago.

In this regard, it is important to note that 77 percent (= 38 + 39) of the sociologists still felt that environmental factors, or socialization, matter as well. Scholars who hold this view believe that sexual orientation is partly or totally learned from one's society, culture, and immediate social environment. In this way of thinking, we learn "messages" from all these influences about whether it is OK or not OK to be sexually attracted to someone from our own sex and/or to someone from the opposite sex. If we grow up with positive messages about same-sex attraction, we are more likely to acquire this attraction. If we grow up with negative messages about same-sex attraction, we are less likely to acquire it and more likely to have heterosexual desire.

It is difficult to do the necessary type of research to test whether socialization matters in this way, but the historical and cross-cultural evidence discussed earlier provides at least some support for this process. Homosexuality was generally accepted in ancient Greece, ancient China, and ancient Japan, and it also seemed rather common in those societies. The same connection holds true in many of the societies that anthropologists have studied. In contrast, homosexuality was condemned in Europe from the very early part of the first millennium CE, and it seems to have been rather rare (although it is very possible that many gays hid their sexual orientation for fear of persecution and death).

So where does this leave us? What are the origins of sexual orientation? The most honest answer is that we do not yet know its origins, as a recent review concluded: "No causal theory of sexual orientation has yet gained widespread support. The most scientifically plausible causal hypotheses are difficult to test. However, there is considerably more evidence supporting nonsocial causes of sexual orientation than social causes" (Bailey et al. 2016:46).[25] As this conclusion implies, sexual orientation is best understood as resulting from still unknown biological factor(s) over which individuals have no control, just as individuals do not decide whether they are left-handed or right-handed. Supporting this view, many gays say they realized they were gay during adolescence, just as straights would say they realized they were straight during their own adolescence; moreover, evidence (from toy, play, and clothing preferences) of future sexual orientation even appears during childhood (Bailey et al. 2016).[26] Other scholars say that cultural norms at least partly influence sexual orientation, so that people are more likely to identify as gay or straight and to be attracted to their same sex or opposite sex depending on the cultural views of sexual orientation into which they are socialized as they grow up. At best, perhaps all we can say is that sexual orientation stems from a complex mix of biological and cultural factors that remain to be determined.

The official stance of the American Psychological Association (APA) is in line with this view. According to the APA, "There is no consensus among scientists about the exact reasons that an individual develops a heterosexual, bisexual, gay, or lesbian orientation. Although much research has examined the possible genetic, hormonal, developmental, social, and cultural influences on sexual orientation, no findings have emerged that permit scientists to conclude that sexual orientation is determined by any particular factor or factors. Many think that nature and nurture both play complex roles; most people experience little or no sense of choice about their sexual orientation" (American Psychological Association 2019).[27]

Key Takeaways

- An estimated 4 percent to 5 percent, or more than ten million, American adults identify as LGBTQ.

- Homosexuality seems to have been fairly common and very much accepted in some ancient societies as well as in many societies studied by anthropologists.
- Scholars continue to debate the extent to which sexual orientation stems more from biological factors or from social and cultural factors and the extent to which sexual orientation is a choice or not a choice.

For Your Review

1. Do you think sexual orientation is a choice, or not? Explain your answer.
2. Write an essay that describes how your middle school and high school friends talked about sexual orientation generally and homosexuality specifically.

5.2 Public Attitudes about Sexual Orientation

Learning Objectives

1. Understand the extent and correlates of heterosexism.
2. Understand the nature of public opinion on other issues related to sexual orientation.
3. Describe how views about LGBTQ issues have changed since a few decades ago.

As noted earlier, views about gays and lesbians have certainly been very negative over the centuries in the areas of the world, such as Europe and the Americas, that mostly follow the Judeo-Christian tradition. There is no question that the Bible condemns homosexuality, with perhaps the most quoted Biblical passages in this regard found in Leviticus:

- "Do not lie with a man as one lies with a woman; that is detestable" (Leviticus 18:22).
- "If a man lies with a man as one lies with a woman, both of them have done what is detestable. They must be put to death; their blood will be on their own heads" (Leviticus 20:13).

The important question, though, is to what extent these passages should be interpreted literally. Certainly very few people today believe that male homosexuals should be executed, despite what Leviticus 20:13 declares. Still, many people who condemn homosexuality cite passages like Leviticus 18:22 and Leviticus 20:13 as reasons for their negative views.

This is not a theology text, but it is appropriate to mention briefly two points that many religious scholars make about what the Bible says about homosexuality (Martin 2016; Sprinkle 2016).[28] First, English translations of the Bible's antigay passages may distort their original meanings, and various contextual studies of the Bible suggest that these passages did not, in fact, make blanket condemnations about homosexuality.

Second, and perhaps more important, most people "pick and choose" what they decide to believe from the Bible and what they decide not to believe. Although the Bible is a great source of inspiration for many people, most people also are inconsistent when it comes to choosing which Biblical beliefs to believe. For example, if someone chooses to disapprove of homosexuality because the Bible condemns it, why does this person not also choose to believe that gay men should be exe-

The Bible contains several passages that appear to condemn homosexuality.

Source: © Thinkstock

cuted, which is precisely what Leviticus 20:13 dictates? Further, the Bible specifies many practices and penalties that even very devout people do not follow or believe. For example, most people do not keep kosher, even though the Bible says that everyone should do this, and most people certainly think that people who commit adultery, engage in premarital sex, or work on the Sabbath should not be executed, even though the Bible says that such people should be executed. Citing these inconsistencies, many religious scholars say it is inappropriate to base public views and policy about homosexuality on what the Bible says about it.

We now turn our attention to social science evidence on views about LGBTQ behavior and people. We first look at negative attitudes and then discuss a few other views.

The Extent of Heterosexism in the United States

We saw in earlier chapters that *racism* refers to negative views about, and practices toward, people of color, and that *sexism* refers to negative views about, and practices toward, women. **Heterosexism** is the analogous term for negative views about, and discriminatory practices toward, LGBTQ individuals and their sexual behavior.

There are many types of negative views about LGBTQ status and thus many ways to measure heterosexism. The General Social Survey (GSS), given regularly to a national sample of U.S. residents, asks whether respondents think that "sexual relations between two adults of the same sex" are always wrong, almost always wrong, sometimes wrong, or not wrong at all. In 2018, 32 percent of respondents said same-sex relations are "always wrong," and 58 percent responded they are "not wrong at all" (see Figure 5.1).

heterosexism

Negative views about, and discriminatory practices toward, LGBTQ individuals and their sexual behavior.

FIGURE 5.1 Opinion about "Sexual Relations between Two Adults of the Same Sex," 2018

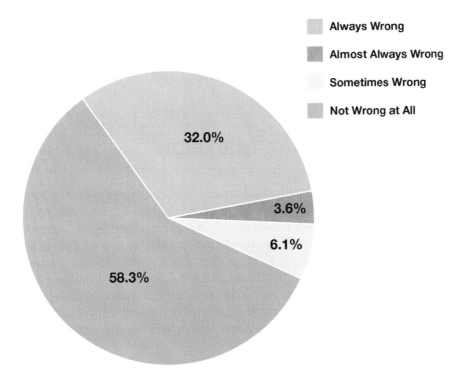

- Always Wrong
- Almost Always Wrong
- Sometimes Wrong
- Not Wrong at All

32.0%

3.6%

6.1%

58.3%

Source: Data from General Social Survey. (2018). Retrieved from https://sda.berkeley.edu/sdaweb/analysis/?dataset=gss18.

As another way of measuring heterosexism, the Gallup poll asks whether "gay or lesbian relations" are "morally acceptable or morally wrong" (Gallup 2019).[29] In 2019, 64 percent of Gallup respondents answered "morally acceptable," while 35 percent replied "morally wrong."

Although Figure 5.1 shows that 42 percent of Americans consider same-sex relations at least sometimes wrong (adding up all the "wrong" responses), public views of these relations have become much more positive over the past few decades. We can see evidence of this trend in Figure 5.2, which shows that the percentage of GSS respondents who say same-sex relations are "always wrong" has dropped considerably since the GSS first asked this question in 1973, while the percentage who respond "not wrong at all" has risen considerably, with both these changes occurring since the early 1990s.

FIGURE 5.2 Changes in Opinion about "Sexual Relations between Two Adults of the Same Sex," 1973–2018

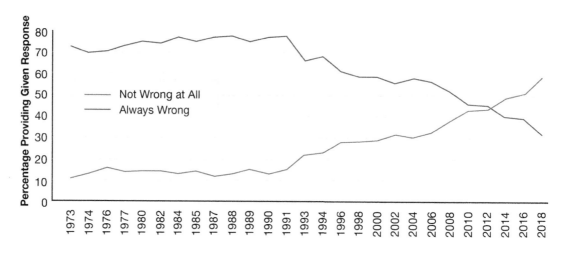

Source: Data from General Social Surveys. (1973–2018). Retrieved from http://sda.berkeley.edu/cgi-bin/hsda?harcsda+gss10.

Trends in Gallup data confirm that public views regarding homosexuality have become more positive in recent times. Recall that 64 percent of Gallup respondents in 2019 called same-sex relations "morally acceptable," while 35 percent replied "morally wrong." Ten years earlier in 2009, these percentages were 49 percent and 47 percent, respectively, representing a marked shift in public opinion during that decade.

Views on Same-Sex Marriage

The next section discusses several issues that demonstrate inequality based on sexual orientation. Because these issues are so controversial, public opinion polls have included many questions about them. One of these issues is same-sex marriage, which was prohibited by law a generation ago but is now legal throughout the United States thanks to a U.S. Supreme Court ruling. Because same-sex marriage nonetheless continues to be controversial, it is worth examining attitudes about it. The 2018 General Social Survey asked whether respondents agree that "homosexual couples should have the right to marry one another." More than 58 percent of respondents expressing an opinion agreed with this statement, and 32 percent disagreed, indicating a 2-1 majority in favor of legal same-sex marriage. As Figure 5.3 shows, the percentage in favor has risen considerably since 1988.

FIGURE 5.3 Changes in Opinion about Same-Sex Marriage, 1988–2018 (Percentage Agreeing That Same-Sex Couples Should Have the Right to Marry; Those Expressing No Opinion Excluded from Analysis)

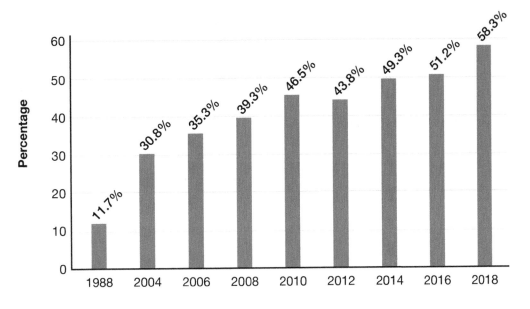

Source: Data from General Social Surveys. 1988–2018. Retrieved from http://sda.berkeley.edu/cgi-bin/hsda?harcsda+gss18.

 When America Legalized Same-Sex Marriage

Jubilation by many Americans greeted the legalization of same-sex marriage in 2015, thanks to a U.S. Supreme Court ruling. Survey evidence finds that Americans' approval of same-sex marriage has increased dramatically during the past 3 decades.

View the video online at: http://www.youtube.com/embed/z9jM1rk1N_o?rel=0

A Brief Conclusion on Public Attitudes

We have had limited space to discuss public views on LGBTQ topics, but a brief conclusion is apparent from the discussion: Although some 32 percent of the public remains heterosexist as measured by the GSS "always wrong" question, views about LGBTQ behavior and certain rights of the LGBTQ community have become markedly more positive in recent decades. This trend matches what we saw in earlier chapters regarding views concerning people of color and women. The United States has without question become less racist, less sexist, and less heterosexist since the 1970s.

Key Takeaways

- Views about LGBTQ behavior have improved markedly since a generation ago. More than half the U.S. public now supports same-sex marriage.
- According to the General Social Survey, about 58 percent of the public say that same-sex relations are "not wrong at all," and the same percentage agrees that same-sex couples "should have the right to marry one another."

For Your Review

1. Reread this section and indicate how you would have responded to every survey question discussed in the section. Drawing on the discussion of correlates of heterosexism, explain how knowing about these correlates helps you understand why you hold your own views.
2. Why do you think public opinion about LGBTQ behavior and issues has become more positive during the past few decades?

5.3 Inequality Based on Sexual Orientation and Gender Identity

Learning Objectives

1. Understand the behavioral, psychological, and health effects of bullying and other mistreatment of the LGBTQ community.
2. Evaluate the arguments for and against same-sex marriage.
3. Provide three examples of heterosexual privilege.

Until the Supreme Court's *Lawrence v. Texas* ruling in 2003, individuals who engaged in consensual same-sex relations could be arrested in many states.

Until a few decades ago, individuals who engaged in consensual same-sex relations could be arrested in many states for violating so-called sodomy laws. The U.S. Supreme Court, which had upheld such laws in 1986, finally outlawed them in 2003 in *Lawrence v. Texas*, 539 US 558, by a 6–3 vote. The majority opinion of the court declared that individuals have a constitutional right under the Fourteenth Amendment to engage in consensual, private sexual activity.

Despite this landmark ruling, the LGBTQ community continues to experience many types of problems. In this regard, sexual orientation is a significant source of social inequality, just as race/ethnicity, gender, and social class are sources of social inequality. We examine manifestations of inequality based on sexual orientation in this section.

Source: © Thinkstock

Bullying and Violence

Bullying and violence against adolescents and adults thought or known to be LGBTQ constitute perhaps the most serious manifestation of inequality based on sexual orientation. According to the Federal Bureau of Investigation (2018),[30] 1,130 hate crimes (violence and/or property destruction) against gays and lesbians occurred in 2017, although this number is very likely an underestimate because many hate crime victims do not report their victimization to the police. An estimated 25 percent of gay men have been physically or sexually assaulted because of their sexual orientation (Egan 2010),[31] and some have been murdered.

LGBTQ teenagers and those teenagers thought to be LGBTQ are very often the targets of taunting, bullying, physical assault, and other abuse in schools and elsewhere. In federal survey data, 60 percent of LGB youths report being bullied on school property or cyberbullied during the past year, a rate twice higher than that for their straight counterparts (stopbulling.gov 2017).[32] Other survey evidence indicates that 85 percent of LGBTQ students report being verbally harassed at school, and 40 percent report being physically harassed; 72 percent report hearing anti-gay slurs frequently or often at school; 61 percent feel unsafe at school, with 30 percent missing at least one day of school in the past month for fear of their safety; and 17 percent are physically assaulted to the point they need medical attention (Kosciw et al. 2010).[33]

The bullying, violence, and other mistreatment experienced by LGBTQ teens have significant educational and mental health effects. The most serious consequence is suicide, but LGBTQ youths are also much more likely to skip school; to do poorly in their studies; to drop out of school; to experience depression, anxiety, and low self-esteem; and to engage in risky and/or unhealthy behaviors such as smoking and using alcohol or other drugs (HealthyPeople.gov 2019).[34]

LGBTQ youths are more likely than other youths to be bullied and assaulted. As a result, they are also more likely to do poorly in school and to experience mental and physical health problems, among other consequences.

Source: Pattie Steib/Shutterstock.com

🎥 LGBTQ High School Students Share Their Experiences

Bullying of LGBTQ teens and those thought to be LGBTQ remains common and may have significant consequences for their mental health and educational performance.

View the video online at: http://www.youtube.com/embed/iAwJQYs7pKM?rel=0

Children and Our Future

The Homeless Status of LGBTQ Teens

Many LGBTQ teens are taunted, bullied, and otherwise mistreated at school. As the text discusses, this mistreatment affects their school performance and psychological well-being, and some even drop out of school as a result. We often think of the home as a haven from the realities of life, but the lives of many LGBTQ teens are often no better at home. If they come out to their parents, one or both parents often reject them. Sometimes they kick their teen out of the home, and sometimes the teen leaves because the home environment becomes intolerable. Regardless of the reason, a large number of LGBTQ teens become homeless. They may be living in the streets, but they may also be living with a friend, at a homeless shelter, or at some other venue. But the bottom line is that they are not living at home with a parent.

The actual number of homeless LGBTQ teens will probably never be known. However, it is estimated that they are more than twice as likely as cisgender and heterosexual teens to experience homelessness. In a related estimate, even though these teens constitute only about 7 percent of all teens, they comprise about 40 percent of all homeless teens. Their higher degree of homelessness adds to the problems, discussed in the text, they already experience from being LGBTQ (Morton et al. 2017).[35] That is because homeless people of all ages are at greater risk for victimization by robbers and other offenders, hunger, substance abuse, and mental health problems. The homeless problem among LGBTQ youths underscores the need to provide many types of services to help LGBTQ teens, homeless or not, deal with the many issues that arise in their personal lives.

Source: Morton et al. 2017[36]

Discrimination in Employment, Housing, and Public Accommodations

Federal law prohibits discrimination in employment, housing, and public accommodations (hotels, etc.) based on race, nationality, sex, or religion. Notice that this list does *not* include sexual orientation or gender identity. It is entirely legal under federal law for employers to refuse to hire LGBTQ people or those perceived as LGBTQ, to fire an employee who is openly LGBTQ or perceived as LGBTQ, or to refuse to promote such an employee. It is likewise entirely legal for LGBTQ people to be denied housing and public accommodations. Twenty-four states do prohibit all such discrimination (but only for sexual orientation in one of these states), but that leaves twenty-six states that do not prohibit it. An estimated 44 percent of the LGBTQ population lives in these latter states (Movement Advancement Project 2019).[37] In these states, employers are entirely free to refuse to hire, fire, or to refuse to promote them; homeowners and lessors are entirely free to refuse to sell or rent homes and apartments to them; and owners and managers of public accommodations are entirely free to refuse to let them stay in their establishments.

The Employment Non-Discrimination Act (ENDA), which would prohibit job discrimination based on sexual orientation or gender identity, has been proposed in Congress but has not come close to passing. In response to the absence of legal protection for LGBTQ employees, many companies have instituted their own policies. As of 2018, 83 percent of the *Fortune* 500 companies, the largest 500 corporations in the United States, had policies prohibiting discrimination based on LGBTQ status (Human Rights Campaign 2019).[38]

National survey evidence shows that many LGBTQ people have, in fact, experienced workplace discrimination and mistreatment. In the 2008 and 2012 General Social Surveys, 29.1 percent of LGB respondents said they had ever been harassed at work because someone thought they were LGB, compared to only 2.8 percent of straight respondents. In a 2018 survey, 46 percent of LGBTQ employees said they were closeted at work, 18 percent had heard sexually inappropriate comments at work, 53 percent had heard jokes about gays and lesbians, 20 percent said they lost out on job opportunities because they were LGBTQ, nearly one-third felt unhappy or depressed at work, one-fourth avoided specific people in their workplace, and one-fifth had searched for a different job because of these experiences (Fidas and Cooper 2018).[39] Scholars have also conducted field experiments in which they send out resumes or job applicants to prospective employers. The resumes are identical except that some mention or imply the applicant is LGBTQ, while the others do not indicate sexual orientation. The job applicants similarly either say they are LGBTQ or do not say this. The LGBTQ resumes and applicants are less likely than their non-LGBTQ counterparts to receive a positive response from prospective employers (Mishel 2016).[40]

LGBTQ people who experience workplace harassment and discrimination suffer in other ways as well (Sears and Mallory 2011).[41] Compared to LGBTQ employees who do not experience these problems, they are more likely to have various mental health issues, to be less satisfied with their jobs, and to have more absences from work.

Applying Social Research

How Well Do the Children of Same-Sex Couples Fare?

More than 100,000 same-sex couples are raising children (Goldberg and Conron 2018).[42] Although same-sex marriage is now legal throughout the United states, one-third of Americans still oppose same-sex marriage, as discussed in the text, and many people probably believe that children are better off if they are raised by both a mother and a father instead of by a same-sex couple.

To address this issue, social scientists have studied the children of same-sex couples and compared them to the children of heterosexual parents. Although it is difficult to have random, representative samples of same-sex couples' children, a number of studies find that these children fare at least as well psychologically and in other respects as heterosexual couples' children (Bailey et al. 2016).[43]

A notable analysis earlier in this century reviewed almost two dozen studies of same-sex couples' children (Stacey and Biblarz 2001).[44] These studies yielded the central conclusion that the psychological well-being of these children is at least as good as that of heterosexual couples' children. As the authors summarized this conclusion and its policy implications, "Because every relevant study to date shows that parental sexual orientation per se has no measurable effect on the quality of parent-child relationships or on children's mental health or social adjustment, there is no evidentiary basis for considering parental sexual orientation in decisions about children's 'best interest.'"

The authors of this analysis did a later review of almost three dozen studies published that compared the children of same-sex couples (most of them lesbian parents) to those of heterosexual couples (Biblarz and Stacey 2010).[45] They again found that the psychological well-being and social adjustment of same-sex couples' children was at least as high as those of heterosexual couples' children, and they even found some evidence that children of lesbian couples fare better in some respects than those of heterosexual couples. As they summarized the body of research on this issue: "Research consistently has demonstrated that despite prejudice and discrimination children raised by lesbians develop as well as their peers. Across the standard panoply of measures, studies find far more similarities than differences among children with lesbian and heterosexual parents, and the rare differences mainly favor the former."

This body of research contributed in important ways to the national debate on same-sex marriage that preceded its legalization. Although opponents of same-sex marriage may feel otherwise, the research evidence strongly suggests that children of same-sex couples indeed fare well.

Same-Sex Marriage

As noted earlier, same-sex marriage is now legal throughout the United States, and more than two-thirds of Americans agree same-sex couples should have the right to marry. Because nearly one-third of Americans still believe these couples should not be allowed to marry, same-sex marriage remains a controversial issue. To help understand this controversy, it is worth considering the arguments against and for same-sex marriage.

The issue of same-sex marriage remains controversial even though same-sex couples are now allowed to marry throughout the United States.

Source: © Thinkstock

Arguments against same-sex marriage. Opponents of same-sex marriage have made at least three central points (Silliman 2015; Lopez 2016).[46] First, and in no particular order, marriage is intended to procreate the species, and same-sex couples cannot reproduce. Second, the children that same-sex couples do have through adoption or artificial means experience various psychological problems because their parents are gay or lesbian and/or because they do not have both a father and a mother. Third, allowing gays and lesbians to marry would undermine the institution of marriage.

Arguments for same-sex marriage. In reply, proponents of same-sex marriage make their own points (Baume 2016; Hart-Brinson 2018).[47] First, many heterosexual couples are allowed to marry even though they will not have children, either because they are not able to have them, because they do not wish to have them, or because they are beyond childbearing age. Second, studies show that children of same-sex couples are at least as psychologically healthy as the children of opposite-sex couples (see "Children and Our Future"). Third, there is no evidence that legalizing same-sex marriage has weakened the institution of marriage, either in the United States or in other nations that have legalized it (see "Lessons from Other Societies").

Lessons from Other Societies

Same-Sex Marriage in the Netherlands

Many nations have by now made same-sex marriage legal. All these nations have legalized it since 2001, when the Netherlands became the first country to do so. Given the Netherlands' landmark status in this respect, it is informative to examine how, if at all, legalization has affected the lives of gays and lesbians and the institution of marriage itself in that nation.

One thing is clear: There is no evidence that the institution of marriage in the Netherlands has in any respect become weaker because same-sex couples have been allowed to marry since 2001. Heterosexual couples continue to marry, and the institution appears at least as strong as it was before 2001. It also seems clear that same-sex marriages are working and that same-sex married couples' unions are accepted as normal features of contemporary Dutch life.

In an interesting development, same-sex couples did not exactly rush to marry after the Netherlands gave them the right to marry. There was an initial spurt in 2001, and many such couples have married since. However, the Dutch government estimates that same-sex couples are still less likely than heterosexual couples to marry.

Three reasons may account for this disparity. First, there is less pressure from family and friends for same-sex couples to marry than for heterosexual couples to marry. Second, fewer same-sex couples than heterosexual couples decide to marry in order to have children. Third, gays and lesbians in the Netherlands are thought to be somewhat more individualistic than their heterosexual counterparts.

The available evidence shows that same-sex couples who have married in the Netherlands seem happy to have done so. The institution of marriage is thus thriving in the Netherlands at least as well as in nations that have not yet allowed same-sex couples to marry. The experience of the Netherlands, as well as that of the United States and other nations that now permit same-sex couples to marry, demonstrates that allowing same-sex couples to marry does not at all threaten the institution of marriage and, in fact, may strengthen it by adding to the ranks of the married.

Sources: Ames 2011; Badgett 2009; Dittrich 2011; Taylor 2015[48]

Although the children of same-sex couples fare at least as well as those of heterosexual couples, it is still difficult in some states for same-sex couples to adopt a child. As of early 2019, ten states permitted child welfare agencies to refuse to place children for adoption or foster care with same-sex couples or LGBTQ individuals if doing so would violate the agency's moral or religious convictions (Moreau 2019).[49] Still, adoptions by same-sex couples have become more numerous in recent years because of the legalization of same-sex marriage and because public opinion about these marriages and about LGBTQ status more generally has become more favorable.

Military Service

LGBTQ individuals traditionally were not permitted to serve in the U.S. military. If they remained closeted, of course, they could serve with impunity, but many gays and lesbians in the military were given dishonorable discharges when their sexual orientation was discovered. LGBTQ military members who successfully remained in the closet lived under continual fear that their status would become known and they would be ousted from the military.

As a presidential candidate in 1992, Bill Clinton said he would end the ban on LGBTQ people in the military. After his election, his intention to do so ignited fierce opposition by military leaders, much of the Congress, and considerable public opinion. As a compromise, in 1993 the government established the so-called don't-ask, don't-tell (DADT) policy. DADT protected members of the military from being asked about their sexual orientation, but it also stipulated that they would be discharged from the military if they made statements or engaged in behavior that indicated an LGBTQ orientation. Because DADT continued the military ban on LGBTQ people, proponents of allowing them to serve in the military opposed the policy and continued to call for the elimination of any restrictions regarding sexual orientation for military service.

In response to a lawsuit, a federal judge in 2010 ruled that DADT was unconstitutional. Meanwhile, Barack Obama had also called for the repeal of DADT, both as a presidential candidate and then as president. In late 2010, Congress passed legislation repealing DADT, and President Obama signed the legislation, which took effect in September 2011 and officially ended discrimination against LGBTQ troops. However, in April 2019 the Pentagon, acting under a directive from the Trump administration, prohibited transgender people from enlisting, required current troops diagnosed with gender dysphoria in the future to serve in their biological sex, and prohibited these troops from receiving hormone treatment or undergoing gender-affirming surgery. At the time of this writing, several lawsuits against this new policy were pending.

Physical and Mental Health

It is well known that HIV (human immunodeficiency virus) and AIDS (acquired immunodeficiency syndrome) wracked the LGBTQ community beginning in the 1980s. Many eventually died from AIDS-related complications, and HIV and AIDS remain serious illnesses for gays and straights alike. An estimated 1.1 million Americans now have HIV (2017 data). Nearly 39,000 Americans are newly diagnosed with HIV annually, with about two-thirds of these new cases involving men who have had sex with other men; nearly 18,000 Americans are newly diagnosed with AIDS annually. Fortunately, HIV can now be controlled fairly well by appropriate medical treatment (Centers for Disease Control and Prevention 2019).[50]

It is less well known that LGBTQ adults have higher rates than other adults of other physical health problems and also of mental health problems (HealthyPeople.gov 2019).[51] These problems are thought to stem from the stress that LGBTQ people experience from living in a society in which they frequently encounter verbal and physical harassment, job discrimination, a need for some to conceal their sexual identity, and lack of equal treatment arising from the illegality of same-sex marriage. We saw earlier that LGBTQ secondary school students experience various kinds of educational and mental health issues because of the mistreatment they encounter. By the time LGBTQ individuals reach their adult years, the various stressors they have experienced at least since adolescence have begun to take a toll on their physical and mental health.

The stress of being LGBTQ in a society that disapproves of this status is thought to account for the greater likelihood of LGBTQ people having physical and mental health problems.

Source: © Thinkstock

Because stress is thought to compromise immune systems, LGBTQ people on the average have lower immune functioning and lower perceived physical health than other people. Because stress impairs mental health, they are also more likely to have higher rates of depression, loneliness, low self-esteem, and other psychiatric and psychological problems, including a tendency to attempt suicide (Jackson et al. 2016).[52] Among all LGBTQ individuals, those who have experienced greater levels of stress related to their sexual orientation have higher levels of physical and mental health problems than those who have experienced lower levels of stress. It is important to keep in mind that these various physical and mental health problems do not stem from an LGBTQ status itself, but rather from the experience of living as LGBTQ in a society in which many people still hold negative views about LGBTQ status and in which discrimination and mistreatment occur against LGBTQ people.

An additional reason for the health problems of LGBTQ people is discrimination against them in health care settings and/or neglect and ignorance of their health-care needs (Mirza and Rooney 2018).[53] Sometimes health-care professionals have simply refused to treat LGBTQ patients; other times these professionals are insufficiently familiar with these patients' health-care needs and issues. In national survey evidence, between 6 percent and 9 percent of LGBTQ people report each of the following problems stemming from their LGBTQ status: (a) a health-care professional refused to see them or provide them health-care; (2) a physician made negative comments about them or their LGBTQ status; (c) a health-care provider engaged in sexual misconduct, including sexual assault; corresponding percentages for transgender people range between 12 percent and 29 percent (Mirza and Rooney 2018).[54] This situation leads many LGBTQ people to delay seeking health-care or to decide not to seek it at all.

Heterosexual Privilege

In earlier chapters, we discussed the related concepts of *white privilege* and *male privilege*. To recall, simply because they are white, whites can go through their daily lives without worrying about or experiencing the many kinds of subtle and not-so-subtle negative events that people of color experience. Moreover, simply because they are male, men can go through their daily lives without worrying about or experiencing the many kinds of subtle and not-so-subtle negative events that women experience. Whether or not they are conscious of it, therefore, whites and men are automatically privileged compared to people of color and women, respectively.

heterosexual privilege

The many advantages that heterosexuals (or people perceived as heterosexuals) enjoy simply because their sexual orientation is not LGBTQ.

An analogous concept exists in the study of sexual orientation and inequality. This concept is **heterosexual privilege**, which refers to the many advantages that heterosexuals (or people perceived as heterosexuals) enjoy simply because their sexual orientation is not LGBTQ. There are many such advantages, and we have space to list only a few:

- Heterosexuals can be out day or night or at school or workplaces without fearing that they will be verbally harassed or physically attacked because of their sexuality or that they will hear jokes about their sexuality.

- Heterosexuals do not have to worry about not being hired for a job, about being fired, or not being promoted because of their sexuality.

- Heterosexuals can legally marry everywhere in the United States and receive all the federal, state, and other benefits that married couples receive.

- Heterosexuals can express a reasonable amount of affection (holding hands, kissing, etc.) in public without fearing negative reactions from onlookers.

- Heterosexuals do not have to worry about being asked why they prefer opposite-sex relations, being criticized for choosing their sexual orientation, or being urged to change their sexual orientation.

- Heterosexual parents do not have to worry about anyone questioning their fitness as parents because of their sexuality.

- Heterosexuals do not have to feel the need to conceal their sexual orientation.

- Heterosexuals do not have to worry about being accused of trying to "push" their sexuality onto other people.

Gay Men and Blood Donations during the COVID-19 Pandemic

This section has discussed discrimination against the LGBTQ community in several aspects of life. After the COVID-19 pandemic emerged, an additional form of discrimination involving blood donation arose (Morrison 2020). When the pandemic began, the nation's blood supply severely dwindled because blood donations dropped, and a call went out for people to donate blood. Not long thereafter, another call went out for people who had recovered from COVID-19 to donate their blood plasma for research on coronavirus antibodies.

To answer these twin calls, many people did donate blood and blood plasma, but gay and bisexual men were turned away. The reason for this goes back to the HIV/AIDS crisis of the 1980s and 1990s, when new federal policy prohibited any man who had ever had sex with any other men from donating blood. In 2015, the Food and Drug Administration changed this policy to a twelve-month deferral period, such that gay and bisexual men were allowed to donate blood if they had not had sex with another man for at least twelve months prior. Meanwhile, heterosexual men who may have had multiple sex partners were allowed to donate blood without a similar deferral-period restriction.

By 2020, because technological advances had made it possible to detect HIV in donated blood rather quickly, LGBTQ advocates said that any restrictions on blood donations by gay and bisexual men should be removed. In early April 2020, the FDA shortened the twelve-month deferral period to three months to help maximize blood donations. LGBTQ advocates said this policy change did not go far enough and that it still amounted to stigmatizing discrimination against gay and bisexual men. As one physician said, "There's really no scientific reason anymore, in my opinion, to have this ban at all since our testing capacity has been truly revolutionized" (Morrison 2020). A gay man who had recovered from COVID-19 and was not allowed to donate his blood plasma agreed. "We don't need old stigma dictating the way that we make medical and scientific decisions," he said. "That's not how it's supposed to work. Science is supposed to inform the way we make decisions" (Morrison 2020).[55]

People Making a Difference

Improving the Family Lives of LGBTQ Youth

Many organizations and agencies around the country aim to improve the lives of LGBTQ teens. One of them is the Family Acceptance Project (FAP) at San Francisco State University, which focuses on the family problems that LGBTQ teens often experience. According to its website, FAP is a "research, intervention, education and policy initiative that works to prevent health and mental health risks for lesbian, gay, bisexual and transgender (LGBT) children and youth, including suicide, homelessness and HIV—in the context of their families, cultures and faith communities. We use a research-based, culturally grounded approach to help ethnically, socially and religiously diverse families to support their LGBT children."

To accomplish its mission, FAP engages in two types of activities: research and family support services. In the research area, FAP has published some pioneering studies of the effects of school victimization and of family rejection and acceptance on the physical and mental health of

LGBTQ teens during their adolescence and into their early adulthood. In the family support services area, FAP provides confidential advice, information, and counseling to families with one or more LGBTQ children or adolescents, and it also has produced various educational materials for these families and for professionals who deal with LGBTQ issues.

Through its pioneering efforts, the Family Acceptance Project is one of many organizations making a difference in the lives of LGBTQ youth. For further information about FAP, visit http://familyproject.sfsu.edu.

Key Takeaways

- Bullying, taunting, and violence are significant problems for the LGBTQ community.
- LGBTQ people are at greater risk for behavioral and physical and mental health problems because of the many negative experiences they encounter.
- Federal law does not protect LGBTQ individuals from employment discrimination.
- The children of same-sex couples fare at least as well as children of heterosexual couples.

For Your Review

1. Do you know anyone who has ever been bullied and taunted for being LGBTQ or for being perceived as LGBTQ? If so, describe what happened.
2. Write a brief essay in which you summarize the debate over same-sex marriage, provide your own view, and justify your view.

5.4 Improving the Lives of the LGBTQ Community

Learning Objective

1. Understand which measures show promise of reducing inequality based on sexual orientation.

The inequality arising from sexual orientation and gender identity stems from long-standing and deep-rooted prejudice against non-heterosexual attraction and behavior and nonconforming gender identity. We have seen in this chapter that attitudes related to LGBTQ status have become markedly more positive since a generation ago. Much of this improvement must be credited to the gay rights movement that began after the Stonewall Inn raid in 1969, as discussed in this chapter's opening news story.

Despite the advances this movement has made and despite the improvement in public attitudes about LGBTQ issues, this chapter showed that LGBTQ people continue to experience many types of inequality and other problems. As with inequality based on race and/or ethnicity, social class, and gender, much work still needs to be done to reduce inequality based on LGBTQ status.

For this inequality to be reduced, it is certainly essential that heterosexuals and cisgender people do everything possible in their daily lives to avoid any form of mistreatment of LGBTQ individuals and to treat them as they would treat anyone else. Beyond this, certain other measures should help address LGBTQ inequality. These measures include, but are not limited to, the following:

1. Parents should make clear to their children that all sexual orientations and gender identities are equally valid. Parents whose child happens to be LGBTQ should love that child at least as much as they would love a child who was not LGBTQ.

2. School programs should continue and strengthen their efforts to provide students a positive environment in regard to sexual orientation and to educate them about LGBTQ issues. Bullying and other harassment of LGBTQ students must not be tolerated. In early 2019, New Jersey joined California in requiring the teaching of gay and lesbian history; the 48 other states should follow their example.

3. Federal law should prohibit all discrimination against LGBTQ people.

4. Police should continue to educate themselves about LGBTQ issues and should strengthen their efforts to ensure that physical attacks on LGBTQ people are treated at least as seriously as attacks on other people.

Key Takeaways

- Although the gay rights movement has made significant advances, many types of inequality based on LGBTQ status continue to exist.
- Several measures should be begun or continued to reduce inequality based on LGBTQ status.

For Your Review

1. Is there a gay rights advocacy group on your campus? If so, what is your opinion of it?
2. How do you think parents should react if their teenaged daughter or son comes out to them? Explain your answer.

5.5 End-of-Chapter Material

Summary

1. Sexual orientation refers to a person's preference for sexual relationships with individuals of the other sex, one's own sex, or both sexes. Transgender people are those whose behavior, appearance, and/or gender identity departs from conventional norms.

2. According to national survey evidence, between 4 percent and 5 percent of American adults identify as LGBTQ (lesbian/gay/bisexual/transgender/queer), a figure equivalent to more than ten million adults.

3. Male homosexuality in ancient Greece and Rome seems to have been accepted and rather common, but Europe, the Americas, and other areas influenced by the Judeo-Christian

tradition have long viewed homosexuality very negatively. In many societies studied by anthropologists, homosexuality is rather common and considered a normal form of sexuality.

4. Scholars continue to debate whether sexual orientation and gender identity are more the result of biological factors or social and cultural factors.

5. Sexual orientation is a significant source of inequality. LGBTQ people experience bullying, taunting, and violence; they may also experience employment discrimination and other types of discrimination. Because of the stress of living as LGBTQ, they are at greater risk for several types of physical and mental health problems. During the early period of the COVID-19 pandemic, many gay men were prohibited from donating blood to help replenish the nation's blood supply or blood plasma to aid research on coronavirus antibodies.

Using What You Know

As an LGBTQ individual, you're working in a medium-sized office and generally like your coworkers. Even though your coworkers know you are LGBTQ and treat you well enough, occasionally you still hear them make jokes about LGBTQ people. You certainly never laugh at these jokes, but neither have you ever said anything critical about them, because you worry that if you tell your supervisor or coworkers that their joking makes you feel uncomfortable, they may get angry with you and even stop talking to you. What do you decide to do?

What You Can Do

To help reduce inequality based on sexual orientation and gender identity, you may wish to do any of the following:

1. Start or join an LGBTQ advocacy group on your campus.

2. Write a letter to the editor in favor of federal legislation to ban discrimination based on LGBTQ status.

3. Urge your U.S. senators and representative to pass legislation prohibiting such discrimination.

4. Work for a social service agency in your local community that focuses on the needs of LGBTQ teens.

Endnotes

1. Barron, James. 2019. "Pride Parade: 50 Years after Stonewall, a Joyous and Resolute Celebration." *The New York Times* June 30:https://www.nytimes.com/2019/06/30/nyregion/nyc-pride-parade.html.

2. United States Holocaust Memorial Museum. 2019. *Nazi Persecution of Homosexuals 1933–1945.* Retrieved July 23, 2019, from https://www.ushmm.org/exhibition/persecution-of-homosexuals/.

3. Gates, Gary. 2018. "The Challenge of Measuring the U.S. Lgbt Population." *Gallup Podcast* (May 25):https://news.gallup.com/podcast/234872/challenge-measuring-lgbt-population.aspx.

4. Kinsey, Alfred C., Wardell B. Pomeroy, Clyne E. Martin and Paul H. Gebhard. 1953. *Sexual Behavior in the Human Female.* Philadelphia: W.B. Saunders Co.

5. Gates, Gary J. 2017. "In U.S., More Adults Identifying as Lgbt." Gallup News January 11:https://news.gallup.com/poll/201731/lgbt-identification-rises.aspx.

6. Gates, Gary J. 2011. *How Many People Are Lesbian, Gay, Bisexual, and Transgender?* Los Angeles: The Williams Institute, UCLA School of Law.

7. Dover, K. J. (1989). *Greek homosexuality.* Cambridge, MA: Harvard University Press.

8. Crompton, Louis. 2003. *Homosexuality and Civilization.* Cambridge, MA: Belknap Press.

9. Crompton, Louis. 2003. *Homosexuality and Civilization.* Cambridge, MA: Belknap Press.

10. Crompton, Louis. 2003. *Homosexuality and Civilization.* Cambridge, MA: Belknap Press.

11. Crompton, Louis. 2003. *Homosexuality and Civilization.* Cambridge, MA: Belknap Press.

12. Crompton, Louis. 2003. *Homosexuality and Civilization.* Cambridge, MA: Belknap Press.

13. Ford, Clellan S. and Frank A. Beach. 1951. *Patterns of Sexual Behavior.* New York: Harper and Row.

14. Edgerton, Robert. 1976. *Deviance: A Cross-Cultural Perspective.* Menlo Park, CA: Cummings Publishing Company.

15. Sheldon, Jane P., Carla A. Pfeffer, Toby Epstein Jayaratne, Merle Feldbaum and Elizabeth M. Petty. 2007. "Beliefs About the Etiology of Homosexuality and About the Ramifications of Discovering Its Possible Genetic Origin." *Journal of Homosexuality* 52(3/4):111-50.

16. Bailey, J. Michael, Paul L. Vasey, Lisa M. Diamond, S. Marc Breedlove, Eric Vilain and Marc Epprecht. 2016. "Sexual Orientation, Controversy, and Science." *Psychological Science in the Public Interest* 17(2):45-101.

17. Ganna, Andrea, Karin J. H. Verweij, Michel G. Nivard, Robert Maier, Robbee Wedow, Alexander S. Busch, Abdel Abdellaoui, Shengru Guo, J. Fah Sathirapongsasuti, Paul Lichtenstein, Sebastian Lundström, Niklas Långström, Adam Auton, Kathleen Mullan Harris, Gary W. Beecham, Eden R. Martin, Alan R. Sanders, John R. B. Perry, Benjamin M. Neale and Brendan P. Zietsch. 2019. "Large-Scale Gwas Reveals Insights into the Genetic Architecture of Same-Sex Sexual Behavior." *Science* 365(6456):DOI: 10.1126/science.aat7693; Watts, Tuesday M., Luke Holmes, Jamie Raines, Sheina Orbell and Gerulf Rieger. 2018. "Sexual Arousal Patterns of Identical Twins with Discordant Sexual Orientations." *Nature Scientific Reports* 8:https://www.nature.com/articles/s41598-018-33188-2.

18. Lasco, M.A., T. J. Jordan, M. A. Edgar, C. K. Petito and W. Byne. 2002. "A Lack of Dimporphism of Sex or Sexual Orientation in the Human Anterior Commissure." *Brain Research* 986:95-98.

19. Sheldon, Jane P., Carla A. Pfeffer, Toby Epstein Jayaratne, Merle Feldbaum and Elizabeth M. Petty. 2007. "Beliefs About the Etiology of Homosexuality and About the Ramifications of Discovering Its Possible Genetic Origin." *Journal of Homosexuality* 52(3/4):111-50.

20. Bailey, J. Michael, Paul L. Vasey, Lisa M. Diamond, S. Marc Breedlove, Eric Vilain and Marc Epprecht. 2016. "Sexual Orientation, Controversy, and Science." *Psychological Science is in the Public Interest* 17(2):45-101.

21. Rahman, Q. 2005. "The Neurodevelopment of Human Sexual Orientation." *Neuroscience Biobehavioral Review* 29(7):1057-66.

22. Engle, Michael J., Joseph A. McFalls, Jr., Bernard J. Gallagher, III and Kristine Curtis. 2006. "The Attitudes of American Sociologists toward Causal Theories of Male Homosexuality." *The American Sociologist* 37(1):68-76.

23. Risman, Barbara and Pepper Schwartz. 1988. "Sociological Research on Male and Female Homosexuality." *Annual Review of Sociology* 14:125-47.

24. Engle, Michael J., Joseph A. McFalls, Jr., Bernard J. Gallagher, III and Kristine Curtis. 2006. "The Attitudes of American Sociologists toward Causal Theories of Male Homosexuality." *The American Sociologist* 37(1):68-76.

25. Bailey, J. Michael, Paul L. Vasey, Lisa M. Diamond, S. Marc Breedlove, Eric Vilain and Marc Epprecht. 2016. "Sexual Orientation, Controversy, and Science." *Psychological Science is in the Public Interest* 17(2):45-101.

26. Bailey, J. Michael, Paul L. Vasey, Lisa M. Diamond, S. Marc Breedlove, Eric Vilain and Marc Epprecht. 2016. "Sexual Orientation, Controversy, and Science." *Psychological Science is in the Public Interest* 17(2):45-101.

27. American Psychological Association. (2019). Answers to Your Questions: For a Better Understanding of Sexual Orientation and Homosexuality. Retrieved from https://www.apa.org/topics/lgbt/orientation.

28. Martin, Colby. 2016. *Unclobber: Rethinking Our Misuse of the Bible on Homosexuality.* Louisville, KY: Westminster John Knox Press; Sprinkle, Preston, ed. 2016. Grand Rapids, MI: Zondervan.

29. Gallup 2019. Gay and Lesbian Rights.Retrieved July 24, 2019 from http://www.gallup.com/poll/1651/gay-lesbian-rights.aspx .

30. Federal Bureau of Investigation. 2018. *Crime in the United States, 2017.* Washington, DC: Author.

31. Egan, Patrick J. 2010. "Within Reach: Reducing Lgbt Inequality in the Age of Obama." *Pathways: A Magazine on Poverty, Inequality, and Social Policy* Spring:22-25.

32. stopbullying.gov. (2017). LGBTQ Youth. Retrieved from https://www.stopbullying.gov/at-risk/groups/lgbt/index.html.

33. Kosciw, Joseph G., Emily A. Greytak, Elizabeth M. Diaz and Mark J. Bartkiewicz. 2010. *The 2009 National School Climate Survey: The Experiences of Lesbian, Gay, and Transgender Youth in Our Nation's Schools.* New York: Gay, Lesbian and Straight Education Network.

34. HealthyPeople.gov. 2019. *Lesbian, Gay, Bisexual, and Transgender Health.* Retrieved from https://www.healthypeople.gov/2020/topics-objectives/topic/lesbian-gay-bisexual-and-transgender-health.

35. Morton, M.H., A. Dworsky and G.M. Samuels. 2017. *Missed Opportunities: Youth Homelessness in America.* Chicago: Chapin Hall at the University of Chicago.

36. Morton, M.H., A. Dworsky and G.M. Samuels. 2017. *Missed Opportunities: Youth Homelessness in America.* Chicago: Chapin Hall at the University of Chicago.

37. Movement Advancement Project. 2019. *Non-Discrimination Laws.* Retrieved from http://www.lgbtmap.org/equality-maps/non_discrimination_laws.

38. Human Rights Campaign. 2019. *Workplace Discrimination Laws and Policies.* Retrieved from https://www.hrc.org/resources/Workplace-Discrimination-Policies-Laws-and-Legislation.

39. Fidas, Deena and Liz Cooper. 2018. *A Workplace Divided: Understanding the Climate for Lgbtq Workers Nationwide.* Washington, DC: Human Rights Campaign Foundation.

40. Mishel, Emma. 2016. "Discrimination against Queer Women in the U.S. Workforce: A Résumé Audit Study." *Socius: Sociological Research for a Dynamic World*:DOI: 10.1177/2378023115621316.

41. Sears, Brad and Christy Mallory. 2011. *Documented Evidence of Employment Discrimination & Its Effects on Lgbt People.* Los Angeles: The Williams Institute, UCLA School of Law.

42. Goldberg, Shoshana K. and Kerith J. Conron. 2018. "How Many Same-Sex Couples in the U.S. Are Raising Children?" *The Williams Institute*:https://williamsinstitute.law.ucla.edu/research/parenting/how-many-same-sex-parents-in-us/.

43. Bailey, J. Michael, Paul L. Vasey, Lisa M. Diamond, S. Marc Breedlove, Eric Vilain and Marc Epprecht. 2016. "Sexual Orientation, Controversy, and Science." *Psychological Science is in the Public Interest* 17(2):45-101.

44. Stacey, Judith and Timothy J. Biblarz. 2001. "(How) Does the Sexual Orientation of Parents Matter?". *American Sociological Review* 66(2):159-83.

45. Biblarz, Timothy J. and Judith Stacey. 2010. "How Does the Gender of Parents Matter?" Journal of Marriage and Family 72(1):3-22.

46. Silliman, Daniel. 2015. "Supreme Court Briefs Reveal Religious Groups Don't Agree on How to Oppose Same-Sex Marriage." *The Washington Post* April 27:https://www.washingtonpost.com/news/acts-of-faith/wp/2015/04/27/supreme-court-briefs-reveal-religious-groups-dont-agree-on-how-to-oppose-gay-marriage/?utm_term=.56adc65fa79a; Lopez, German. 2016. "The Strongest Argument against Same-Sex Marriage: Traditional Marriage is in the Public Interest." *Vox.com* March 31:https://www.vox.com/2015/6/26/17937580/same-sex-gay-marriage-argument-traditional-marriage.

47. Baume, Matt. 2016. "The Top Arguments for and against Same-Sex Marriage at the Supreme Court." *Huffington Post* February 2:https://www.huffpost.com/entry/the-top-arguments-for-and-against-marriage-at-the-supreme-court_b_7172008?guccounter=1&guce_referrer=aHR0cHM6Ly93d3cuZ29vZ2xlLmNvbS8&guce_referrer_sig=AQAAALjb4Rxs_ZsV1jiPTE0UK5K_79U_ahMW2tl5X9HW64b-m280oW7aJR281uf5XoUQgKHHZVDv-TvTQN8-zhBQOc4DCCXIzFzc-SlyteQFlFL9e5sENoa-uKTeFSjAn3Rp6O9xpB3i14QvPIK4zd-Y2Qj0mKPl-HfEqu1GoKe7OFvRiP. Hart-Brinson, Peter. 2018. *The Gay Marriage Generation: How the Lgbtq Movement Transformed American Culture.* New York: NYU Press.

48. Ames, Paul. 2011. "Dutch Gays Don't Take Advantage of Opportunity to Marry." *GlobalPost* April 20:http://www.globalpost.com/dispatch/news/regions/europe/benelux/110419/netherlands-gay-rights-same-sex-marriage; Badgett, M.V. Lee. 2009. *When Gay People Get Married: What Happens When Societies Legalize Same-Sex Marriage.* New York: NYU Press; Dittrich, Boris O. 2011. "Gay Marriage's Diamond Anniversary: After the Netherlands Acted, Civilization as We Know It Didn't End." *Los Angeles Times* April 17:http://articles.latimes.com/2011/apr/17/opinion/la-oe-dittrich-gay-marriage-20110417; Taylor, Adam. 2015. "What Was the First Country to Legalize Gay Marriage?". *The Washington Post* June 26:https://www.washingtonpost.com/news/worldviews/wp/2015/06/26/what-was-the-first-country-to-legalize-gay-marriage/?utm_term=.8a4c1b8a1ef8.

49. Moreau, Julie. 2019. "Lgbtq Parents Face 'State-Sanctioned Discrimination,' American Bar Association Says." *NBCnews* February 6:https://www.nbcnews.com/feature/nbc-out/lgbtq-parents-face-state-sanctioned-discrimination-american-bar-association-says-n968456.

50. Centers for Disease Control and Prevention. 2019, "Hiv/Aids: Statistis Overview", https://www.cdc.gov/hiv/statistics/overview/index.html. (http://www.cdc.gov/hiv/topics/basic/index.htm).

51. HealthyPeople.gov. 2019. "Lesbian, Gay, Bisexual, and Transgender Health." https://www.healthypeople.gov/2020/topics-objectives/topic/lesbian-gay-bisexual-and-transgender-health.

52. Jackson, Chandra L., Madina Agénor, Dayna A. Johnson, Bryn Austin and Ichiro Kawachi. 2016. "Sexual Orientation Identity Disparities in Health Behaviors, Outcomes, and Services Use among Men and Women in the United States: A Cross-Sectional Study." *BMC Public Health* 16:doi: 10.1186/s12889-016-3467-1.

53. Mirza, Shabab Ahmed and Caitlin Rooney. 2018. "Discrimination Prevents Lgbtq People from Accessing Health Care." *Center for American Progress*:https://www.americanprogress.org/issues/lgbt/news/2018/01/18/445130/discrimination-prevents-lgbtq-people-accessing-health-care/.

54. Mirza, Shabab Ahmed and Caitlin Rooney. 2018. "Discrimination Prevents Lgbtq People from Accessing Health Care." *Center for American Progress*:https://www.americanprogress.org/issues/lgbt/news/2018/01/18/445130/discrimination-prevents-lgbtq-people-accessing-health-care/.

55. Morrison, Tony. 2020. "Fda 'Commencing a Study' That Could Lead to the Removal of a Once-Lifetime Ban on Gay Men Donating Blood as Covid-19 Survivor Says He Was Turned Away from Blood Center for Being Gay." *ABC News* April 24:https://abcnews.go.com/US/fda-reveals-generating-scientific-evidence-lead-removal-lifetime/story?id=70251561.

CHAPTER 6
Aging and Ageism

Social Problems in the News

"Seniors Return to Workforce at Habitat for Humanity Store," the headline said. In the summer of 2019, retirees in Idaho Falls, Idaho, who needed more money than their Social Security payments and savings were providing them had found employment at a store run by Habitat for Humanity, the national organization that builds homes for low-income families. One of these employees was an 81-year-old woman, who said, "Working keeps you sharp. I'm ringing up prices at the register, answering questions about what we have and what we can get for people." She and the other retirees working at the store were placed there by a company named Experience Works, which helps older Americans find work in eleven states. An Experience Works official said, "Our seniors need to keep going and employers see the drive that exists in them." In addition to the extra income, the Habitat for Humanity store employee also appreciated being busy outside her home and interacting with customers. As she explained, "I could just stay at home if I wanted to and pay my bills, but what kind of life would that be?"

Source: Kauffman 2019[1]

The number of older Americans is growing rapidly. As this news story suggests, they have much to contribute to our society. Yet they also encounter various problems because of their advanced age. We appreciate our elderly but also consider them something of a burden. We also hold unfortunate stereotypes of them and seemingly view old age as something to be shunned. Television commercials and other advertisements extol the virtues of staying young by coloring hair and by removing all facial wrinkles. In our youth-obsessed culture, older people seem to be second-class citizens. This chapter discusses views about aging and how and why old age is a source of inequality. The coronavirus pandemic that began in early 2020 reminds us older people are vulnerable in many ways.

6.1 The Concept and Experience of Aging

Learning Objectives

1. Define social gerontology.
2. Distinguish biological aging, psychological aging, and social aging.

Because we all want to live into old age, the study of age and aging helps us understand something about ourselves and a stage in the life course we all hope to reach.

Source: © Thinkstock

gerontology

The study of aging.

chronological age

The number of years since we were born.

biological aging

The physical changes that "slow us down" as we get into our middle and older years.

psychological aging

The psychological changes, including those involving mental functioning and personality, that occur as we age.

social aging

The changes in roles and relationships that occur as people age.

Here is why you should want to know about aging and the problems older people face: *You will be old someday*. At least you will be old if you do not die prematurely from an accident, cancer, a heart attack, some other medical problem, murder, or suicide. Although we do not often think about aging when we are in our late teens and early twenties, one of our major goals in life is to become old. By studying age and aging and becoming familiar with some of the problems facing older people now and in the future, we are really studying something about ourselves and a stage in the life course we all hope to reach.

The study of aging is so important and popular that it has its own name, **gerontology**. *Social gerontology* is the study of the social aspects of aging. The scholars who study aging are called *gerontologists*. The people they study go by several names, most commonly "older people," "elders," "seniors," and "the elderly." The latter term is usually reserved for those 65 or older, while "older people" and "elders" often include people in their 50s as well as those 60 or older.

Dimensions of Aging

Age and aging have four dimensions. The dimension most of us think of is **chronological age**, defined as the number of years since someone was born. A second dimension is **biological aging**, which refers to the physical changes that "slow us down" as we get into our middle and older years. For example, our arteries might clog up, or problems with our lungs might make it more difficult for us to breathe. A third dimension, **psychological aging**, refers to the psychological changes, including those involving mental functioning and personality, that occur as we age. Gerontologists emphasize that chronological age is not always the same thing as biological or psychological age. Some people who are 65, for example, can look and act much younger than some who are 50.

The fourth dimension of aging is social. **Social aging** refers to changes in a person's roles and relationships, both within their networks of relatives and friends and in formal organizations such as the workplace and houses of worship. Although social aging can differ from one individual to another, it is also profoundly influenced by the *perception* of aging that is part of a society's culture. If a society views aging positively, the social aging experienced by individuals in that society will be more positive and enjoyable than in a society that views aging negatively. As we shall see, though, the perception of aging in the United States is not very positive, with important consequences for our older citizens.

Key Takeaways

- The study of the elderly and aging helps us understand problems in a state of the life course we all hope to reach.
- Biological aging refers to the physical changes that accompany the aging process, while psychological aging refers to the psychological changes that occur.
- Social aging refers to the changes in a person's roles and relationships as the person ages.

For Your Review

1. Think about an older person whom you know. To what extent has this person experienced psychological aging? To what extent has this person experienced social aging?
2. The text states that the perception of aging in the United States is not very positive. What do you think accounts for this?

6.2 Perspectives on Aging

Learning Objectives

1. State the assumptions of disengagement, activity, and conflict theories of aging.
2. Critically assess these three theories.

Recall that social aging refers to changes in people's roles and relationships in a society as they age. Social gerontologists have tried to explain how and why the aging process in the United States and other societies occurs. Their various explanations, summarized in Table 6.1, help us understand patterns of social aging. They fall roughly into the functionalist, symbolic interactionist, or conflict approaches discussed in Chapter 1.

TABLE 6.1 Theory Snapshot

Theoretical perspective	Major assumptions
Disengagement theory	To enable younger people to assume important roles, a society must encourage its older people to disengage from their previous roles and take on roles more appropriate to their physical and mental decline. This theory is considered a functionalist explanation of the aging process.
Activity theory	Older people benefit themselves and their society if they continue to be active. Their positive perceptions of the aging process are crucial to their ability to remain active. This theory is considered an interactionist explanation of the aging process.
Conflict theory	Older people experience age-based prejudice and discrimination. Inequalities among the aged exist along the lines of gender, race/ethnicity, and social class. This theory falls into the more general conflict theory of society.

One of the first explanations was called **disengagement theory** (Cumming and Henry 1961).[2] This approach assumed that all societies must find ways for older people's authority to give way to younger people. A society thus encourages its elderly to disengage from their previous roles and to take on roles more appropriate to their physical and mental decline. In this way, a society effects a smooth transition of its elderly into a new, more sedentary lifestyle and ensures that their previous roles will be undertaken by a younger generation that is presumably more able to perform these roles. Because disengagement theory assumes that social aging preserves a society's stability and that a society needs to ensure that disengagement occurs, it is often considered a functionalist explanation of the aging process.

A shortcoming of this theory was its assumption that older people are no longer capable of adequately performing their previous roles. However, older people in many societies continue to perform their previous roles quite well. In fact, society may suffer if its elderly do disengage, as it loses their insight and wisdom. Then too, many elders cannot afford to disengage from their previous roles: If they leave their jobs, they are also leaving needed sources of income, as the opening news story discussed, and if they leave their jobs and other roles, they also reduce their social interaction and the benefits it brings.

disengagement theory

The view, now largely abandoned, by some past social gerontologists that a society needs to encourage its elderly to disengage from their previous roles and to take on roles more appropriate to their declining physical and mental abilities.

activity theory

The view by social gerontologists that older people will benefit both themselves and their society if they remain active and try to continue to perform the roles they had before they aged.

Today most social gerontologists prefer **activity theory**, which assumes that older people benefit both themselves and their society if they remain active and try to continue to perform the roles they had before they aged (Winstead et al. 2014).[3] As they perform their roles, their perception of the situations they are in is crucial to their perception of their aging and thus to their self-esteem and other aspects of their psychological well-being. Because activity theory focuses on the individual and her or his perception of the aging process, it is often considered a social interactionist explanation of social aging.

A criticism of activity theory is that it overestimates the ability of the elderly to maintain their level of activity: Although some elders can remain active, others cannot. Another criticism is that activity theory is too much of an individualistic approach, as it overlooks the barriers many societies place to successful aging. Some elders are less able to remain active because of their poverty, gender, and social class, as these and other structural conditions may adversely affect their physical and mental health. Activity theory overlooks these conditions.

conflict theory

The view by social gerontologists that ageism and structural obstacles pose several problems for the elderly and prevent them from realizing their potential and for achieving the best physical and mental health possible.

Explanations of aging grounded in conflict theory put these conditions at the forefront of their analyses. A **conflict theory** of aging, then, emphasizes the impact of **ageism**, or negative views about old age and prejudice and discrimination against the elderly. According to this view, older workers are devalued because they are no longer economically productive and because their higher salaries (because of their job seniority), health benefits, and other costs drive down capitalist profits. Conflict theory also emphasizes inequality among the aged along gender, race/ethnicity, and social class lines. Reflecting these inequalities in the larger society, some elders are quite wealthy, but many others are very poor.

ageism

Negative views about and prejudice and discrimination against older people.

 ### Ageism Is a Major Roadblock for Older Job Seekers

Conflict theory emphasizes the impact of ageism on older people. One consequence of ageism is discrimination in employment, as older people may face discrimination in hiring and promotion.

View the video online at: http://www.youtube.com/embed/mK_PDYtJI-U?rel=0

One criticism of conflict theory is that it blames ageism on modern, capitalist economies. However, negative views of the elderly also exist to some extent in modern, socialist societies and in preindustrial societies. Capitalism may make these views more negative, but such views can exist even in societies that are not capitalistic.

Key Takeaways

- Disengagement theory assumes that all societies must find ways for older people's authority to give way to younger people. A society thus encourages its elderly to disengage from their previous roles and to take on roles more appropriate to their physical and mental decline.
- Activity theory assumes that older people will benefit both themselves and their society if they remain active and try to continue to perform the roles they had before they aged.

For Your Review

1. Which theory of aging—disengagement theory, activity theory, or conflict theory—makes the most sense to you? Why?

6.3 Life Expectancy and the Graying of Society

Learning Objectives

1. Describe the differences in life expectancy around the world.
2. List the potential problems associated with the growing proportion of older individuals in poor nations.
3. Explain the evidence for inequality in U.S. life expectancy.

When we look historically and cross-culturally, we see that *old age* is a relative term, since few people in preindustrial times or in poor countries today reach the age range that most Americans would consider to be old, say 65 or older. When we compare contemporary societies, we find that **life expectancy**, or the average age to which people can be expected to live, varies dramatically across the world. As Figure 6.1 illustrates, life expectancy in North America, most of Europe, and Australia averages 75 years or more, while life expectancy in most of Africa averages less than 65 years (Population Reference Bureau 2011).[4]

What accounts for these large disparities? The major factor is the wealth or poverty of a nation, as the wealthiest nations have much longer life expectancies than the poorest ones. This is true because, as Chapter 2 noted, the poorest nations by definition have little money and few other resources. They suffer from hunger, AIDS, and other diseases, and they lack indoor plumbing and other modern conveniences found in almost every home in the wealthiest nations. As a result, they have high rates of infant and childhood mortality, and many people who make it past childhood die prematurely from disease, starvation, and other problems.

life expectancy

The average age to which people can be expected to live.

FIGURE 6.1 Average Life Expectancy across the Globe (Years)

< 59.31

59.31 - 64.88

64.88 - 69.62

69.62 - 74.36

> 74.36

Source: Adapted from World Bank. (2017). Life Expectancy at Birth, Total. Retrieved from: https://data.worldbank.org/indicator/SP. DYN.LE00.IN?end=2017&start=2017&type=shaded&view=map. Reproduced via Creative Commons Attribution 4.0 International (CC BY 4.0) license: https://creativecommons.org/licenses/by/4.0/.

These differences mean that few people in these societies reach the age of 65 that Western nations commonly mark as the beginning of old age. Figure 6.2 depicts the percentage of selected nations' population that is 65 or older. Not surprisingly, the nations of Africa have very low numbers of people 65 or older. In Uganda, for example, only 2 percent of the population is at least 65, compared to 16 percent of Americans and 22–23 percent of Germans and Italians.

FIGURE 6.2 Percentage of Population Aged 65 or Older, 2017

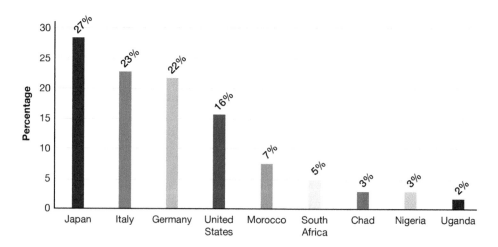

Source: Adapted from World Bank. 2017. Population Ages 65 and Above. Retrieved from https://data.worldbank.org/indicator/SP. POP.65UP.TO.ZS.

Despite these international disparities, life expectancy overall has been increasing around the world. It was only 46 years worldwide in the early 1950s but is now 72 (Population Reference Bureau 2018).[5] This means that the number of people 65 or older is growing rapidly; they are expected to reach almost 1.5 billion worldwide by 2050, twice their number today and five times their number just 20 years ago (United Nations Population Division 2019).[6] Despite international differences in life expectancy and the elderly percentage of the population, the world as a whole is decidedly "graying," with important implications for the cost and quality of elder care and other issues.

Older people worldwide will likely double their numbers by 2050. This trend has important implications for many issues, including the cost and quality of elder care.

Source: © Thinkstock

As life expectancy rises in poor nations, these nations will experience special problems (United Nations 2017).[7] One problem will involve paying for the increased health care that older people in these nations will require. Because these nations are so poor, they will face even greater problems than the industrial world in paying for such care and for other programs and services their older citizens will need. Another problem stems from the fact that many poor nations are slowly industrializing and urbanizing. As they do so, traditional family patterns, including respect for the elderly and the continuation of their roles and influence, may weaken. One reason for this is that urban families have smaller dwelling units in which to accommodate their elderly relatives and lack any land onto which they can build new housing. Families in poor nations will thus find it increasingly difficult to accommodate their elders.

Life Expectancy in the United States

Life expectancy has been increasing in the United States along with the rest of the world (see Figure 6.3). It rose rapidly in the first half of the 20th century and has increased steadily since then. From a low of 47.3 years in 1900, it rose to about 71 years in 1970 and 77 years in 2000 and to 78.7 years in 2016. Americans born in 2016 will thus be expected to live about 31 years longer than those born a century earlier. It is worth noting, however, that life expectancy peaked at 78.9 years in 2014 and has declined slightly since then, as of this writing. Increases in opioid deaths and suicide rates help account for this troubling trend (Devitt 2018).[8] It is likely that the coronavirus pandemic will further reduce life expectancy to some extent.

During the next few decades, the numbers of the elderly will increase rapidly thanks to the large baby boom generation born after World War II (from 1946 to 1964) that has now been entering its 60s and 70s. Elders numbered about 3.1 million in 1900 (4.1 percent of the population), number about 48 million today, and are expected to reach 89 million by 2050. The large increase in older Americans overall has been called the *graying of America* and will have important repercussions for elderly care and other aspects of old age in the United States, as we discuss later.

FIGURE 6.3 Changes in U.S. Life Expectancy at Birth, 1900–2016

Sources: Data from Arias, Elizabeth, Jiaquan Xu, and Kenneth D. Kochanek. 2019. United States Life Tables, 2016. National Vital Statistics Reports, 68(4):1–65.

Healthy Aging: Promoting Well-Being in Older Americans

As the number of older Americans continues to increase, this growing segment of the population will face a number of challenges, including the need to provide for their health care as they age and become more infirm.

View the video online at: http://www.youtube.com/embed/G5Z4JAcCfIM?rel=0

Inequality in Life Expectancy

We have seen that inequality in life expectancy exists around the world, with life expectancy lower in poor nations than in wealthy nations. Inequality in life expectancy also exists *within* a given society along gender, race/ethnicity, and social class lines.

For gender, the inequality is in favor of women, who for both biological and social reasons outlive men across the globe. In the United States, for example, girls born in 2016 could expect to live to about 81 years on the average, but boys only 76 years.

In most countries, race and ethnicity combine with social class to produce longer life expectancies for the (wealthier) dominant race, which in the Western world is almost always white. The United States again reflects this international phenomenon: Whites (non-Latinx) born in 2016 could expect to live almost 79 years on the average, but African Americans only 75 years. In fact, gender and race combine in the United States to put African American males at a particular disadvantage, as they can expect to live only 71.6 years (see Figure 6.4). The average African American male will die 10.4 years earlier than the average white woman.

FIGURE 6.4 Sex, Race, and Life Expectancy for U.S. Residents Born in 2016 (African Americans and non-Latinx Whites)

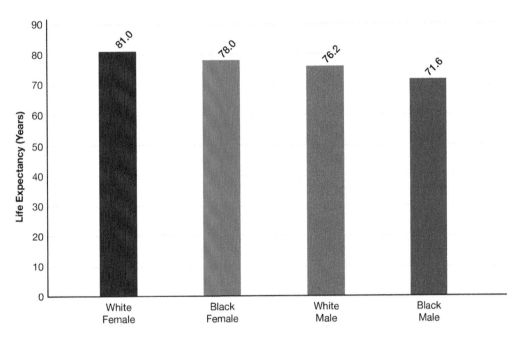

Source: Data from Arias, Elizabeth, Jiaquan Xu, and Kenneth D. Kochanek. 2019. United States Life Tables, 2016. *National Vital Statistics Reports, 68*(4):1–65.

Key Takeaways

- Life expectancy differs widely around the world and is much higher in wealthy nations than in poor nations.
- Life expectancy has also been increasing around the world, including in the United States, and the increasing number of older people in the decades ahead will pose several serious challenges.
- Inequality in life expectancy exists within a given society along gender, race/ethnicity, and social class lines.

For Your Review

1. As our nation and the world both "gray," what do you think is the most important problem that will stem from the increasing number of older people?
2. Write a short essay in which you discuss the problems that an elderly person you know, perhaps a grandparent, has experienced related to being older.

6.4 Biological and Psychological Aspects of Aging

Learning Objectives

1. Describe any four biological changes associated with aging.
2. List any three steps that individuals can try to undertake to achieve successful aging.

Like many other societies, the United States has a mixed view of aging and older people. While we generally appreciate our elderly, we have a culture oriented toward youth, as evidenced by the abundance of television characters in their 20s and lack of those in their older years. As individuals, we do our best not to look old, as the many ads for wrinkle creams and products to darken gray hair attest. Moreover, when we think of the elderly, negative images often come to mind. We often think of someone who has been slowed by age both physically and mentally. She or he may have trouble walking up steps, picking up heavy grocery bags, standing up straight, or remembering recent events. The term *senile* often comes to mind, and phrases like "doddering old fool," "geezer," and other disparaging remarks sprinkle our language when we talk about them. Meanwhile, despite some improvement, the elderly are often portrayed in stereotypical ways on television and in movies (Smith et al. 2017).[9]

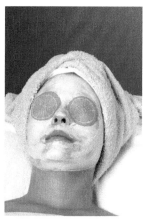

Because our society values youthfulness, many people try their best not to look old.

Source: © Thinkstock

How true is this negative image? What do we know of physical and psychological changes among the elderly? How much of what we think we know about aging and the elderly is a myth, and how much is reality? Gerontologists have paid special attention to answering these questions (Novak 2018).[10]

Biological changes certainly occur as we age. The first signs are probably in our appearance. Our hair begins to turn gray, male hairlines recede, and a few wrinkles set in. The internal changes that often accompany aging are more consequential, among them being that (a) fat replaces lean body mass, and many people gain weight; (b) bone and muscle loss occur; (c) lungs lose their ability to take in air, and our respiratory efficiency declines; (d) the functions of the cardiovascular and renal (kidney) systems decline; (e) the number of brain cells declines, as does brain mass overall; and (f) vision and hearing decline. Cognitive and psychological changes also occur. Learning and memory begin declining after people reach their 70s; depression and other mental and/or emotional disorders can set in; and dementia, including Alzheimer's disease, can occur.

Still, the nature and extent of all these changes vary widely among older people. Some individuals are frail at 65, while others remain vigorous well into their 70s and beyond. People can be "old" at 60 or even 50, while others can be "young" at 80. Many elders are no longer able to work, but others remain in the labor force. All in all, then, most older people do not fit the doddering image myth and can still live a satisfying and productive life.

Enhancing Vitality for Successful Aging

To what extent are the effects of biological and psychological aging the inevitable results of chronological aging? Gerontologists are still trying to understand what causes these effects, and their explanations center on such things as a declining immune system, the slowing of cellular replication, and other processes that need not concern us here.

One thing is clear: We can all take several steps to help us age better, because what we do as we enter our older years matters much more than genetics (Novak 2018).[11] To the extent this is true, the effects of biological and psychological aging are not necessarily inevitable, and "successful aging" is possible. The steps highlighted in the gerontological literature are by now almost a cliché, but regular exercise, good nutrition, and stress reduction stand at the top of most gerontologists' recommendations for continued vitality in later life. In fact, Americans live about 10 years less than an average set of genes should let them live because they do not exercise enough and because they eat inadequate diets.

Research by social gerontologists suggests at least two additional steps older people can take if they want "successful aging." The first is involvement in informal, personal networks of friends, neighbors, and relatives. The importance of such networks is one of the most thoroughly documented in the social gerontological literature (George and Ferraro 2016)[12] (see "Applying Social Research"). Networks enhance successful aging for at least two reasons. First, they provide practical support, such as help buying groceries and visiting the doctor, to the elderly who need it. Second, they help older people maintain their self-esteem, meet their desire for friendships, and satisfy other emotional needs.

Children and Our Future

Grandparents Raising Grandchildren

An estimated 2.7 million grandparents are now raising their grandchildren as their primary caregivers. This situation, which has been growing, reflects several factors: The parents may have died, they may be in jail or prison or have been unable to deal with substance abuse, a child may have been removed from a parent because of parental abuse, or a child may have been abandoned. With the great increase in deaths from opioids during this century, the number of children who have lost a parent has increased, and these children have ended up in the care of a grandparent. As well, many grandparents provide daily or regular day care for one or more children because their parent(s) cannot afford day care. In addition to this situation, several million additional grandparents live in a household with children and may help take care of them but are not the primary caregivers.

Whatever the reason, many grandparents find it very difficult to raise a child. Parenting is taxing even for people in their 20s; for people much older, it can be especially taxing. As with caregiving in general, the stress of raising one or more children may affect a grandparent's mental and/or physical health. It may also prove financially burdensome, because many grandparents live on fixed incomes and did not have much money even before their grandchild ended up with them.

Many grandparents consider the caregiving and financial support they provide for a grandchild to be both a joy and a privilege. But as their numbers grow, many such grandparents are also finding their involvement to also be somewhat of a physical, mental, and/or financial burden. As their numbers continue to grow, it will be important for the federal and state governments to provide them the assistance they need to help them and their grandchildren to flourish as much as possible.

Sources: Lent and Otto 2018; Sexena and Brotherson 2013[13]

A second step for successful aging suggested by scholarly research is religious involvement (Malone and Dadswell 2018)[14] which enhances psychological well-being for at least two reasons. As people worship in a congregation, they interact with other congregants, which enhances their social support networks. Moreover, as they practice their religious faith, they reduce their stress and can cope better with personal troubles. For both these reasons, attendance at religious services and the practice of prayer are thought to enhance psychological well-being among older people. Some elders cannot attend religious services regularly because they have health problems or are no longer able to drive a car. But prayer and other private devotional activities remain significant for many of them. To the extent that religion makes a difference for elders' well-being, health-care facilities and congregations should do what they can to enable older adults to attend religious services and to otherwise practice their religious faith.

Applying Social Research

Friendships and Successful Aging

As the text discusses, social networks improve the lives of older Americans by providing both practical and emotional support. Early research on social networks and aging focused more on relatives than on friends. Rebecca G. Adams, former president of the Southern Sociological Society, was one of the first sociologists to emphasize the role that friends can also play in the lives of the elderly. She interviewed seventy older women who lived in a Chicago suburb and asked them many questions about the extent and quality of their friendships.

In one of her most important findings, Adams discovered that the women reported receiving more help from friends than researchers previously realized. The women were somewhat reluctant to ask friends for help but did so when family members were not available and when they would not overly inconvenience these friends. Adams also found that "secondary" friendships—those involving friends that a woman spent time with but with whom she was not especially close—were more likely than "primary" friendships (very close friendships) to contribute to her interviewees' psychological well-being, as these friendships enabled the women to meet new people, to become involved in new activities, and thus to be engaged with the larger society. These findings led Adams to conclude that researchers should recognize the importance of friends for older people, particularly the elderly without family.

Adams also asked the women about their friendships with men. The seventy women she interviewed reported a combined 670 friendships, of which only 3.6 percent were with men. (About 91 percent were with other women, and 6 percent were with couples.) Although prior research had assumed that the number of these male friendships is small because there are so few unmarried elderly men compared to the number of unmarried elderly women, Adams discovered additional reasons. Her respondents interpreted *any* friendship with a man as a courting or romantic friendship, which they thought would be viewed negatively by their children and by their peers. Adopting a traditional gender-role orientation, they also expected any man they might marry to be able to protect them physically and financially. Yet they also realized that any elderly man they might know would be very likely unable to do so. These reasons led them to shy away from male friendships.

Work by Adams and other social scientists on the friendships and other aspects of the social support systems for older Americans has contributed greatly to our understanding of the components of successful aging. Practically speaking, it points to the need for programs and other activities to make it easier for the elderly to develop and maintain friendships with both sexes to improve their ability to meet both their practical and emotional needs.

Sources: Adams 1985, 1986[15]

Key Takeaways

- Certain biological, cognitive, and psychological changes occur as people age. These changes reinforce the negative view of the elderly, but this view nonetheless reflects stereotypes and myths about aging and the elderly.
- Regular exercise, good nutrition, stress reduction, involvement in personal networks, and religious involvement all enhance successful aging.

For Your Review

1. Do you think the negative view of older people that is often found in our society is an unfair stereotype, or do you think there is actually some truth to this stereotype? Explain your answer.
2. Referring back to Chapter 1's discussion of Émile Durkheim, how does research that documents the importance of personal networks for successful aging reflect Durkheim's insights?

6.5 Problems Facing Older Americans

Learning Objectives

1. Discuss the several problems experienced by the U.S. elderly.
2. Describe how the social attitudes of older Americans generally differ from those of younger Americans.

Although many older Americans do not fit the negative image with which they are portrayed, it is still true that they face special problems because of their age and because of ageism. We examine some of these problems here.

Physical and Mental Health

Perhaps the problem that comes most readily to mind is health, or, to be more precise, poor health. As noted earlier, it is true that many older people remain in good health and are fully able to function mentally and physically. Still, and as also noted earlier, the biological and psychological effects of aging do lead to greater physical and mental health problems among the elderly than in younger age groups. Examples of these problems include: (1) almost two-thirds of people 65 and older report having at least some difficulty in such things as walking, seeing even if wearing glasses, and hearing even if using hearing aids; (2) about two-thirds have high blood pressure; and (3) more than one-fourth have heart disease (National Center for Health Statistics 2018).[16] Similarly, 62 percent of elders report having at least two chronic conditions (from a list including high blood pressure and heart disease, but also arthritis, cancer, diabetes, stroke, and several others), compared to only 18 percent of people under age 65. These problems mean that elders are more likely than younger age groups to report that their general health is only fair or poor (see Figure 6.5).

FIGURE 6.5 Age and Self-Reported Health

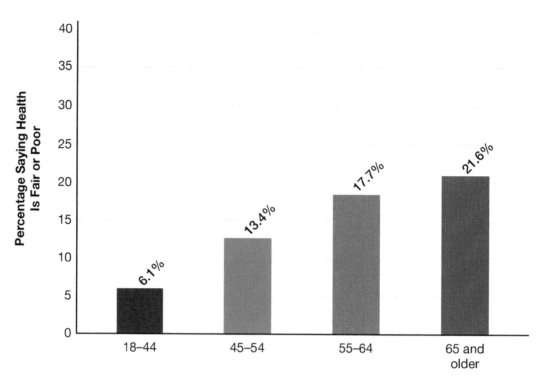

Source: National Center for Health Statistics. 2018. Health, United States, 2017: With Special Feature on Mortality. Hyattsville, MD: U. S. Department of Health and Human Services.

As is well known, the poorer health of older Americans contributed mightily to their much higher death rate from COVID-19 during the spring of 2020. As of mid-April 2020, people age 75 or older accounted for 57 percent of all COVID-19 deaths despite making up less than 7 percent of the national population (National Vital Statistics System 2020).[17]

The elderly also suffer from dementia, including Alzheimer's disease, which affects 5.5 million people 65 or older, or more than 10 percent (Alzheimer's Association 2019).[18] Another mental health problem is depression, which affects almost 15 percent of women 65 or older and 10 percent of men 65 or older. Because of mental or physical disability, 44 percent of elders have difficulty performing daily living activities such as bathing, dressing, doing housework, and preparing a meal (Federal Interagency Forum on Aging-Related Statistics 2016).[19]

Living with Alzheimer's and Dementia

Older people may experience dementia, including Alzheimer's. This health problem not only affects their lives, but also the lives of their family and friends, especially any caregivers they may have.

View the video online at: http://www.youtube.com/embed/q2tpIDKQ9JU?rel=0

If the elderly have more health problems, then adequate care for them is of major importance. They visit the doctor and hospital more often than younger people do. Medicare covers about one-half of their health-care costs; this is a substantial amount of coverage but still forces many seniors to pay thousands of dollars annually themselves. Some physicians and other health-care providers do not accept Medicare "assignment," meaning that the patient must pay an even higher amount. Moreover, Medicare pays little or nothing for long-term care in nursing homes and other institutions and for mental health services. All these factors mean that older Americans can still face high medical expenses or at least pay high premiums for private health insurance.

Older people visit the doctor and hospital more often than younger people. Partly for this reason, adequate health care for the elderly is of major importance.

Source: fizkes/Shutterstock.com

Nursing Home Care

While most older Americans live by themselves or with their families, a small minority live in group settings. A growing type of group setting is the *continuous care retirement community*, a setting of private rooms, apartments, and/or condominiums that offers medical and practical care to those who need it. In some such communities, residents eat their meals together, while in others they cook for themselves. Usually these communities offer above-average recreational facilities and can be very expensive, as some require a lifetime contract or at least monthly fees that can run into the thousands of dollars.

Nursing homes are often understaffed to save costs and are also generally not subject to outside inspection. These conditions help contribute to the neglect of nursing home residents.

Source: © Thinkstock

For elders who need high-level medical care or practical support, nursing homes are the primary option. About 15,650 nursing homes exist: Nearly 3 percent of Americans 65 or older live in them, and 10 percent of Americans 85 or older live in them (Federal Interagency Forum on Aging-Related Statistics 2016; Harris-Kojetin et al. 2019).[20] About two-thirds of all nursing home residents are women. Almost all residents receive assistance in bathing and showering, 88 percent receive help in using the bathroom, and 58 percent receive help in eating.

As noted earlier, Medicare does not pay for long-term institutional care for most older Americans. Because nursing home care costs up to $100,000 yearly, residents can quickly use up all their assets and then, ironically, become eligible for payments from *Medicaid*, the federal insurance program for people with low incomes.

If one problem of nursing homes is their expense, another problem is the quality of care they provide. Because their residents are typically in poor physical and/or mental health, their care must be the best possible, as they can do little to help themselves if their care is substandard. As more people enter nursing homes in the years ahead, the quality of nursing home care will become even more important. Yet there is much evidence that nursing home care is often substandard and is replete with neglect and abuse (Allen 2014; Harrington et al. 2017).[21]

The problems of nursing homes were exposed during the COVID-19 pandemic in spring 2020. As the pandemic swept the nation, it especially devastated many nursing homes and other senior facilities. Perhaps this was bound to occur to some extent given the frail condition of the residents of these facilities. However, investigations revealed that some nursing homes had been unforgivably lax in their observance of safety precautions against the pandemic. As a news report summarized this situation, "Government records reveal how supply shortages, lapses in care, a lack of transparency and inadequate infection control precautions are fueling the spread of Covid-19 within America's nursing homes" (Ellis and Hicken 2020).[22] A news headline captured this situation bluntly: "Nursing Homes Were a Disaster Waiting to Happen" (Mollot 2020).[23]

Financial Security and Employment

Earlier we noted that the elderly are less likely than younger age groups to live in poverty and that their financial status is much better than that of previous generations of older people. One reason for this is Social Security: If Social Security did not exist, the poverty rate of the elderly would be 36 percent, or four times higher than the actual rate (Romig 2019).[24] Without Social Security, then, more than one-third of all people 65 or older would be living in official poverty, and this rate would be higher still for women and persons of color. However, this brief summary of their economic well-being obscures some underlying problems (Carr 2010; Cubanski et al. 2018).[25]

First, recall Chapter 2's discussion of *episodic poverty*, which refers to the drifting of many people into and out of poverty as their jobs and other circumstances change. Once they become poor, older people are more likely than younger ones to *stay* poor, as younger people have more job and other opportunities to move out of poverty. Recall also that the official poverty rate obscures the fact that many people live just above it and are "near poor." This is especially true of the elderly, who, if hit by large medical bills or other expenses, can hardly afford to pay them.

Second, the extent of older Americans' poverty varies by sociodemographic factors and is much worse for some groups than for others. Older women, for example, are more likely than older men to live in poverty for at least two reasons. Because women earn less than men and are more likely to take time off from work during their careers, they have lower monthly Social Security benefits than men and smaller pensions from their employers. As well, women outlive men and thus use up their savings. Racial and ethnic disparities also exist among the elderly, reflecting poverty disparities in the entire population, as older people of color are much more likely than older whites to live in poverty.

Third, monthly Social Security benefits are tied to people's earnings before retirement: The higher the earnings, the higher the monthly benefit. Thus a paradox occurs: People who earn low wages will get lower Social Security benefits after they retire, even though they need *higher* benefits to make up for their lower earnings. In this manner, the income inequality that exists before retirement continues to exist after it.

This paradox reflects a wider problem involving Social Security. However helpful it might be in aiding older Americans, the aid it provides lags far behind comparable programs in other wealthy Western nations (see "Lessons from Other Societies"). Social Security payments are low enough that many older Americans who receive no other income assistance live in official poverty. For all these reasons, Social Security is certainly beneficial for many older Americans, but it remains inadequate compared to what other nations provide.

Because many older Americans do live in poverty or near poverty, many face *food insecurity*, meaning that they sometimes lack any food or at least proper nutrition because they cannot afford it. Needless to say, the malnutrition resulting from food insecurity may lead to health problems among seniors or aggravate health problems they may already have. It is estimated that 8 percent of adults age 60 and older were food insecure in 2017; this percentage amounts to 5.5 million seniors who were going hungry at least part of the time that year. This problem is most prevalent in southern and southwestern states; for example, Louisiana's 12 percent rate of food insecurity among elders is the highest such state rate in the nation, and Memphis, Tennessee, leads all major cities with a 17 percent rate (Ungar and Lieberman 2019).[26]

Older women are more likely than older men to live in poverty.

Source: © Thinkstock

Lessons from Other Societies

Aging Policy and Programs in the Netherlands and Sweden

The experience of the Netherlands and Sweden, both of which have longer life expectancies than the United States, points to strategies the United States should pursue to improve the lives of older Americans. In the Netherlands, everyone at age 65 receives a full pension that does not depend on how much money they earned while they were working, and everyone thus gets the same amount. This amount is larger than the average American gets, because Social Security does depend on earnings, and many Americans earn fairly low amounts during their working years. As a result, Dutch elderly are much less likely than their American counterparts to be poor. The Dutch elderly (and also the nonelderly) have generous government insurance for medical problems and for nursing home care; this financial help is much higher than older Americans obtain through Medicare.

The Netherlands also helps its elderly in other ways. For example, many of that nation's elderly receive regular government-subsidized home visits by health-care professionals and/or housekeepers; this practice enables the elderly to remain independent and avoid having to enter a nursing home.

Sweden has a home-care visitation program that is similar to the Netherlands' program. Many elderly are visited twice a day by a care assistant who helps them bathe and dress in the morning and go to bed at night. The care assistant also regularly cleans their residence and takes them out for exercise. The Swedish government pays about 80 percent of the costs of this assistance and subsidizes the remaining cost for elderly who cannot afford it. Like the Netherlands' program, Sweden's program helps the elderly to remain independent and live at home rather than enter a nursing institution.

Compared to the United States, then, other democracies generally provide their elderly less expensive or free health care, greater financial support during their retirement, and home visits by health-care professionals and other assistants. In these and other ways, these other governments encourage "active aging." Adoption of similar policies in the United States would improve the lives of older Americans and perhaps prolong their life spans.

Sources: Davey et al. 2014; Slaets 2019; Smits et al. 2014[27]

Workplace Ageism

Older people who want to work may have trouble finding employment because of age discrimination and other factors.

Source: © Thinkstock

Older Americans also face problems in employment. More than one-fifth of people 65 and older remain in the labor force. Some of these are unemployed even though they are looking for work, because several obstacles make it difficult for them to find jobs. First, many workplaces do not permit the part-time working arrangements that many seniors favor. Second, the rise in high-tech jobs over the last generation means that older workers would need to be retrained for many of today's jobs, and few retraining programs exist. Third, although federal law prohibits age discrimination in employment, it exists anyway, as employers do not think older people are "up to" the job, even though the evidence indicates they are good, productive workers (Baker 2017).[28] Finally, earnings above a certain level reduce Social Security benefits before full retirement age, leading some older people to avoid working at all or to at least limit their hours. All these obstacles lead seniors to drop out of the labor force or to remain unemployed.

Age discrimination in the workplace merits some further discussion. According to sociologist Vincent J. Roscigno (2010),[29] survey evidence suggests that more than half of older workers have experienced or observed age discrimination in the workplace, and more than 80 percent of older workers have experienced or observed jokes, disrespect, or other prejudicial comments about old age. Roscigno notes that workplace ageism receives little news media attention and has also been neglected by social scientists. This is so despite the related facts that ageism in the workplace is common and that the older people who experience this discrimination suffer financial loss and emotional problems. Roscigno (2010:17)[30] interviewed several victims of age discrimination and later wrote, "Many conveyed fear of defaulting on mortgages or being unable to pay for their children's college after being pushed out of their jobs. Others expressed anger and insecurity over the loss of affordable health insurance or pension benefits...Just as prevalent and somewhat surprising to me in these discussions were the less-tangible, yet deeper social-psychological and emotional costs that social science research has established for racial discrimination or sexual harassment, for instance, but are only now being considered in relation to older workers."

One of the people Roscigno interviewed was a maintenance worker who was laid off after more than 2 decades of working for his employer. This worker was both hurt and angry. "They now don't want to pay me my pension," he said. "I was a good worker for them and always did everything they asked. I went out of my way to help train people and make everything run smoothly, so everybody was happy and it was a good place to work. And now this is what I get, like I never really mattered to them. It's just not right" (Roscigno 2010:17).[31]

Bereavement and Social Isolation

Most older Americans have adequate social support networks, which, as we saw earlier, are important for their well-being. However, a significant minority of elders live alone and do not see friends and relatives as often as they wish. Bereavement takes a toll, as elders who might have been married for many years suddenly find themselves living alone. Here a gender difference again exists.

Because women outlive men and are generally younger than their husbands, they are much more likely than men to be widowed and thus more likely to live alone (see Table 6.2).

TABLE 6.2 Living Arrangements of Noninstitutionalized Older Americans, 2018

	Men (%)	Women (%)
Living alone	21	34
Living with spouse/partner	72	48
Other arrangement	7	18

Source: Data from from Living, Administration for Community. 2018. *2018 Profile of Older Americans*. Washington, DC: Administration for Community Living, U.S. Department of Health and Human Services.

Many elders have at least one adult child living within driving distance, and such children are an invaluable resource. At the same time, however, some elders have no children, because either they outlived their children or they never had any. As baby boomers began reaching their older years, more of them have had no children because they were more likely than previous generations to not marry and/or to not have children if they did marry. Baby boomers thus face a relative lack of children to help them when they enter their "old-old" years (Leland 2010).[32]

Bereavement is always a difficult experience, but because so many elders lose a spouse or partner, it is a particular problem in their lives. The grief that usually follows bereavement can last several years and, if it becomes extreme, can involve anxiety, depression, guilt, loneliness, and other problems. Of all these problems, loneliness is perhaps the most common and the most difficult to overcome.

Elder Abuse

Some seniors fall prey to their own relatives who commit **elder abuse** against them. Such abuse involves one or more of the following: physical or sexual violence, psychological or emotional abuse, neglect of care, or financial exploitation (Novak 2018).[33] Accurate data are hard to come by since few elders report their abuse, but estimates say that at least 10 percent of older Americans have suffered at least one form of abuse, amounting to hundreds of thousands of cases annually. However, few of these cases come to the attention of the police or other authorities (National Center on Elder Abuse 2019).[34]

Although we may never know the actual extent of elder abuse, it poses a serious health problem for the elders who are physically, sexually, and/or psychologically abused or neglected, and it may even raise their chances of dying. One study of more than 2,800 elders found that those who were abused or neglected were three times more likely than those who were not mistreated to die during the next 13 years. This difference was found even after injury and chronic illness were taken into account (Horn 1998).[35]

A major reason for elder abuse seems to be stress. The adult children and other relatives who care for elders often find it an exhausting, emotionally trying experience, especially if the person they are helping needs extensive help with daily activities. Faced with this stress, elders' caregivers can easily snap and take out their frustrations with physical violence, emotional abuse, or neglect of care.

elder abuse

Physical violence, mental and emotional abuse, neglect of care, and financial exploitation committed against the elderly, most often by their relatives who are caring for them.

Senior Power: Older Americans as a Political Force

Older Americans often hold strong views on issues that affect them directly, such as Medicare and Social Security. In turn, politicians often work to win the older vote and shape their political stances accordingly.

During the past few decades, older people have become more active politically on their own behalf.

Source: © Thinkstock

To help address all the problems discussed in the preceding pages, several organizations have been established since the 1980s to act as interest groups in the political arena on behalf of older Americans. One of the most influential groups is AARP (formerly called the American Association of Retired Persons), which is open to people 50 or older. AARP provides travel and other discounts to its members and lobbies Congress and other groups extensively on elderly issues. Its membership numbers about thirty-eight million, or about one-third of the 50 and older population. AARP is an influential force in the political arena because of its numbers and resources.

A very different type of political organization of the elderly was the Gray Panthers, founded by the late Maggie Kuhn in 1970 (Kuhn et al. 1991).[36] Although this group has been less newsworthy since Kuhn's death in 1995, at its height it had some eighty-five local chapters across the nation and seventy thousand members and supporters. A more activist organization than AARP and other lobbying groups for the elderly, the Gray Panthers took more liberal stances. For example, it urged the establishment of a national health-care service and programs to increase affordable housing for the elderly.

generational equity

The argument by critics of political activism on behalf of older Americans that programs for the elderly threaten to take money from programs to help younger Americans either now or as they age.

As older Americans have engaged the political process on their own behalf, critics have charged that programs for the elderly are too costly to the nation, that the elderly are better off than groups like AARP claim, and that new programs for the elderly will take even more money from younger generations and leave them insufficient funds for their own retirement many years from now. Their criticism, which began during the 1980s, came to be called the **generational equity** argument (Williamson et al. 2003).[37]

Advocates for the elderly say the generational equity critics exaggerate the financial well-being of older Americans and neglect the fact that many older Americans, especially women and those of color, are poor or near poor and thus need additional government aid. Anything we can do now to help the aged, they continue, will also help future generations of the elderly. As Lenard W. Kaye (1994:346)[38] observed in an early critique of the generational equity movement, "In the long run, all of us can expect to live into extended old age, barring an unexpected fatal illness or accident. To do injustice to our current generation of elders, by means of policy change, can only come back to haunt us as each and every one of us—children, young families, and working people—move toward the latter stages of the life course."

People Making a Difference

Saving the Life of a Senior Citizen

Many young people volunteer to help senior citizens with housecleaning and other activities, and many also spend time with residents of nursing homes and retirement communities by reading and talking with them. Every so often, they also save a senior citizen's life.

One such example occurred in June 2019 in Sapulpa, Oklahoma. When four teenaged boys walking down a residential street saw a house on fire, they called 911 and rushed inside to see if anyone was there. One of the boys found a 90-year-old woman overcome by smoke and carried her outside. The woman's daughter later wrote in a blog post, "Thank you for your selfless acts of heroism and courage. Thank you for not allowing this to be the tragic end to our mother's amazing life. Thank you for staying with her, hugging her, and helping her feel less alone until we could get to her."

There are many ways to make a difference in the lives of senior citizens, but actually saving their lives is not an action that comes immediately to mind. But these four boys did not hesitate in this emergency, and the many children and grandchildren of the senior citizen they saved will be forever grateful.

Source: O'Kane 2019[39]

Key Takeaways

- The U.S. elderly experience several health problems, including arthritis, high blood pressure, heart disease, hearing loss, vision problems, diabetes, and dementia.
- Nursing home care in the United States is very expensive and often substandard; neglect and abuse of nursing home residents is fairly common. These problems contributed to the scourge of COVID-19 in nursing homes in spring 2020.
- Despite help from Social Security, many older Americans face problems of financial security.
- It is difficult to determine the actual extent of elder abuse, but elder abuse often has serious consequences for the health and lives of older Americans.
- During the last few decades, older Americans have been active in the political process on their own behalf and today are an important political force in the United States.

For Your Review

1. What do you think is the worst or most serious problem facing the U.S. elderly? Explain your answer.
2. The text suggests that the lives of the U.S. elderly would be improved if the United States were to adopt some of the policies and practices that other nations have for their elderly. Explain why you agree or disagree with this suggestion.

6.6 Reducing Ageism and Helping Older Americans

Learning Objectives

1. Understand the contradictory impulses that make it difficult to predict the future for older Americans.
2. Discuss any two programs or policies that should help address some of the problems facing older Americans.

We have seen some contradictory impulses that make it difficult to predict the status of older Americans in the decades ahead. On the one hand, the large number of baby boomers will combine with increasing longevity to swell the ranks of the elderly; this process has already begun and will accelerate during the coming years. The inevitable jump in the size of the aged population may strain Social Security, Medicare, and other programs for the aged. On the other hand, the baby boomer generation will reach its old age as a much better educated and more healthy and wealthy group than any previous generation. It will likely participate in the labor force, politics, and other arenas more than previous generations of elders and, as has been true for some time, exert a good deal of influence on national political and cultural affairs.

Although this sounds like a rosier picture, several concerns remain. Despite the relative affluence of the baby boomers, segments of the group, especially among women and people of color, remain mired in poverty, and these segments will continue to be once they reach their older years. Moreover, the relative health of the baby boomers means that they will outlive previous generations of the aged. Yet as more of them reach the ranks of the "old-old," they will become frailer and require care from health-care professionals and organizations and from social support networks. As noted earlier, some may not have children and will be in even more need of help.

Although older Americans fare much better than their counterparts in poor nations, they fare not nearly as well as their counterparts in other wealthy democracies, which generally provide many more extensive and better-funded programs and services for their elderly. Older Americans also continue to confront stereotypes and prejudicial attitudes that add to the burden many of them already face from the biological process of aging.

A sociological understanding of aging and ageism reminds us that many of the problems that older Americans face are ultimately rooted not in their chronological age but rather in the stereotypes about them and in the lack of adequate social programs like those found in other Western democracies. This understanding also reminds us that the older Americans who face the most severe problems of health, health care, and financial security are women and people of color, and that their more severe problems reflect the many inequalities they have experienced throughout the life course, long before they reached their older years. These inequalities accumulate over the years to leave them especially vulnerable when they finally arrive into their 60s.

With this understanding, it becomes clear that efforts to improve the lives of older Americans must focus on providing them with more numerous and more extensive social services and programming of many kinds and on reducing the stereotypes and prejudicial attitudes that many Americans hold of older people. Possibilities involving improved social services and programming might be drawn from the example provided by other Western nations and include the following (National Council on Aging 2019; Rowe et al. 2010):[40]

1. An expansion of Social Security to provide a much more comfortable life for all older Americans, regardless of their earnings history, and thus regardless of their gender and race/ethnicity.

2. An expansion of Medicare and other health aid for older Americans to match the level of health-care assistance provided by many other Western nations. In one particular area that needs attention, Medicaid pays for nursing home care only after nursing home patients use up most of their own assets, leaving a patient's spouse with severe financial problems. Other Western nations pay for nursing home care from the outset, and the United States should adopt this practice.

3. The establishment of more flexible work hours, job-sharing arrangements, and other policies that would enhance the ability of older people to work part-time or full-time.

4. Increase paid and volunteer opportunities for older adults to help take care of young children and adolescents, especially those who are poor or otherwise disadvantaged, in schools and other settings, creating a win-win situation for both the older adults and the children.

5. As with stereotypical and prejudicial views based on gender and race/ethnicity, greater educational efforts should be launched to reduce stereotyping and prejudicial attitudes based on aging. Like sexism and racism, ageism has no place in a nation like the United States, which has historically promised equality and equal opportunity for all.

Beyond all these measures, aging scholars emphasize the need to help *future* older populations by investing in younger people. As a group of several scholars has noted, "Many of the key determinants of successful aging are cumulative, occurring throughout the lifetime and, importantly, starting in early childhood. The people who will turn 65 between 2050 and 2070 have already been born. If we want to promote their health and well-being into old age, we need to begin now, when they are infants and children. Childhood and early adolescent experiences leave a footprint for many functions in older age. Failing to invest in education and health throughout childhood and young adulthood is short-sighted" (Rowe et al. 2010:24).[41]

Key Takeaways

- Although the number of older Americans will be increasing in the years ahead, the baby boomers who are now reaching old age will be better educated and wealthier than older Americans of past generations.
- Efforts to help older Americans would benefit from relying on the models practiced by other Western democracies.

For Your Review

1. What do you think is the most important action the United States should take to help older Americans?
2. Does it make sense for the United States to follow the example of other democracies as it tries to help older Americans, or is the United States different enough from these nations that it does not make sense to do so? Explain your answer.

6.7 End-of-Chapter Material

Summary

1. Gerontology is the study of aging. Gerontologists study the biological, psychological, and social dimensions of aging. Social gerontologists focus on social aging and distinguish several dimensions of aging, which refers to changes in people's roles and relationships as they age.
2. The perception and experience of aging vary from one society to another and within a given society over time.
3. Sociological explanations of aging include disengagement theory, activity theory, and conflict theory. Disengagement theory emphasizes the need of society to disengage its elders from their previous roles to pave the way for a younger and presumably more able generation to take over those roles. In contrast, activity theory assumes that elders need to remain active to enhance their physical and mental health. Conflict theory emphasizes ageism, or discrimination and prejudice against the elderly, and the structural barriers society poses to elders' economic and other aspects of overall well-being.
4. Life expectancy differs dramatically around the world and within the United States, where it's lower for men and lower for people of color. Because life expectancy has increased, people are living longer, resulting in a "graying of society." In the United States, the imminent entrance of the baby boom generation into its older years will further fuel a large rise in the number of older Americans. This graying of society may strain traditional economic and medical programs for their care and affect views of aging and the elderly.
5. Although aging involves several physiological and psychological changes, negative stereotypes of aging and the elderly exaggerate the extent and impact of these changes. Proper

exercise, nutrition, and stress reduction can minimize the effects of aging, as can religious involvement and informal social support networks.

6. As a diverse group, older Americans differ greatly in terms of wealth and poverty, education, health, and other dimensions. They face several problems because of their age, including illness and disability, financial security, employment obstacles, and elder abuse. The COVID-19 pandemic exposed some of these problems, as death rates for senior citizens were much higher than those for younger Americans. For several reasons, older Americans generally hold more conservative views on social and moral issues. At the same time, groups working on behalf of older Americans in the political arena have succeeded in bringing elder issues to the attention of public officials and political parties.

7. As the ranks of older Americans swell in the years ahead, elders will be better educated and wealthier than their predecessors, but their sheer numbers may impose considerable strain on social institutions. Already there are signs of perceived conflict between the needs of the elderly and those of younger generations. However, advocates for older Americans believe that efforts to help elders now will in the long run help younger Americans when they finally reach their old age.

Using What You Know

It is about 20 years from now, and a close friend of yours is facing a difficult decision. Her mother is in failing health and might have the onset of dementia. It has become increasingly apparent that she can no longer live alone, and your friend is trying to decide whether to have her mother come live with her, to arrange for in-home care for her, or to place her into residential care. What advice do you give to your friend?

What You Can Do

To help reduce inequality based on aging and ageism and the problems facing older people, you may wish to do any of the following:

1. Volunteer at a senior citizens' center, residential care facility, or nursing home.
2. Write a letter to the editor about media stereotypes about older people.
3. Start a group on your campus to educate students about the problems facing senior citizens.

Endnotes

1. Kauffman, Brennen. 2019. "Seniors Return to Workforce at Habitat for Humanity." *Post Register* July 22:https://www.postregister.com/news/local/seniors-return-to-workforce-at-habitat-for-humanity-store/article_669a808a-b48c-5d3d-95e4-a0c1640542b9.html.
2. Cumming, Elaine and William E. Henry. 1961. *Growing Old: The Process of Disengagement*. New York: Basic Books.
3. Winstead, Vicki, Elizabeth A. Yost, Shelia R. Cotten, Ronald W. Berkowsky and William A. Anderson. 2014. "The Impact of Activity Interventions on the Well-Being of Older Adults in Continuing Care Communities." Journal of Applied Gerontology 33(7):888-911.
4. Population Reference Bureau. 2011. *2011 world population data sheet*. Washington, DC: Author.
5. Population Reference Bureau. 2018. *World Population Data Sheet*. Washington, DC: Author.
6. United Nations Population Division. 2019. *World Population Prospects 2019*. Retrieved from https://population.un.org/wpp/Graphs/Probabilistic/POP/65plus/900.
7. United Nations. 2017. *World Population Ageing 2017—Highlights*. New York: Department of Economic and Social Affairs, United Nations.
8. Devitt, Michael. 2018. "CDC Data Show U.S. Life Expectancy Continues to Decline ". *American Academy of Family Physicians News* December 10:https://www.aafp.org/news/health-of-the-public/20181210lifeexpect-drop.html.
9. Smith, Stacy L., Katherine Pieper, Marc Choueiti, Artur Tofan, Anne-Marie Depauw and Ariana Case. 2017. *Seniors on the Small Screen: Aging in Popular Television Content*. Pasadena, CA: Annenberg School for Communication and Journalism, University of Southern California.
10. Novak, Mark. 2018. *Issues in Aging* 4th ed. New York: Routledge.
11. Novak, Mark. 2018. *Issues in Aging*. New York: Routledge.
12. George, Linda K. and Kenneth F. Ferraro, eds. 2016. *Handbook of Aging and the Social Sciences*. San Diego: Academic Press.
13. Lent, Jaia Peterson and Adam Otto. 2018. "Grandparents, Grandchildren, and Caregiving: The Impacts of America's Substance Use Crisis." *American Society on Aging*:https://www.asaging.org/blog/grandparents-grandchildren-and-caregiving-impacts-americas-substance-use-crisis; Saxena, Divya and Sean Brotherson. 2013. "When Grandparents Become Parents to Their Grandchildren." https://www.ag.ndsu.edu/publications/home-farm/when-grandparents-become-parents-to-their-grandchildren.
14. Malone, Joanna and Anna Dadswell. 2018. "The Role of Religion, Spirituality and/or Belief in Positive Ageing for Older Adults." *Geriatrics* 3(2):doi: 10.3390/geriatrics3020028.
15. Adams, Rebecca G. 1985. "People Would Talk: Normative Barriers to Cross-Sex Friendships for Elderly Women." *The Gerontologist* 25:605-11; Adams, Rebecca G. 1986. "Secondary Friendship Networks and Psychological Well-Being among Elderly Women." *Activities, Adaptation, and Aging* 8:59-72.

16. National Center for Health Statistics. 2018. *Health, United States, 2017: With Special Feature on Mortality*. Hyattsville, MD: U.S. Department of Health and Human Services.

17. National Vital Statistics System. 2020. "Provisional Death Counts for Coronavirus Disease (Covid-19)."https://www.cdc.gov/nchs/nvss/vsrr/covid19/index.htm.

18. Alzheimer's Association. 2019. *2019 Alzheimer's Disease Facts and Figures*. Chicago: Alzheimer's Association.

19. Federal Interagency Forum on Aging-Related Statistics. 2016. *Older Americans 2016: Key Indicators of Well-Being*. Washington, DC: U.S. Government Printing Office.

20. Federal Interagency Forum on Aging-Related Statistics. 2016. *Older Americans 2016: Key Indicators of Well-Being*. Washington, DC: U.S. Goverment Printing Office; Harris-Kojetin, L., M. Sengupta, J.P. Lendon, V. Rome, R. Valverde, C. Caffrey and National Center for Health Statistics. *Vital Health Stat* 3(43). 2019. 2019. *Long-Term Care Providers and Services Users in the United States, 2015-2016*. Washington, DC: National Center for Health Statistics.

21. Allen, Marshall. 2014. "One Third of Skilled Nursing Patients Harmed in Treatment." *ProPublica* March 3:http://www.propublica.org/article/one-third-of-skilled-nursing-patients-harmed-in-treatment; Harrington, Charlene, Joshua M. Wiener, Leslie Ross and MaryBeth Musumeci. 2017. "Key Issues in Long-Term Services and Supports Quality." *Kaiser Family Foundation*:https://www.kff.org/medicaid/issue-brief/key-issues-in-long-term-services-and-supports-quality/view/footnotes/#footnote-240687-27.

22. Ellis, Blake and Melanie Hicken. 2020. "Covid-19 Is Ravaging Nursing Homes. Government Records Show Why." *CNN* April 24:https://www.cnn.com/2020/04/24/us/nursing-homes-coronavirus-invs/index.html.

23. Mollot, Richard. 2020. "Nursing Homes Were a Disaster Waiting to Happen." *The New York Times* April 28:https://www.nytimes.com/2020/04/28/opinion/coronavirus-nursing-homes.html.

24. Romig, Kathleen. 2019. "Social Security Lifts More Americans above Poverty Than Any Other Program." *Center on Budget and Policy Priorities*:https://www.cbpp.org/research/social-security/social-security-lifts-more-americans-above-poverty-than-any-other-program.

25. Carr, Deborah. 2010. "Golden Years? Poverty among Older Americans." *Contexts* 9(1):62-63; Cubanski, Juliette, Wyatt Koma, Anthony Damico and Tricia Neuman. 2018. "How Many Seniors Live in Poverty?". *Kaiser Family Foundation*:https://www.kff.org/report-section/how-many-seniors-live-in-poverty-issue-brief/.

26. Ungar, Laura and Trudy Lieberman. 2019. "Starving Seniors: How America Fails to Feed Its Aging." *Kaiser Health News*(September 3):https://khn.org/news/starving-seniors-how-america-fails-to-feed-its-aging/?utm_campaign=KFF-2019-The-Latest&utm_source=hs_email&utm_medium=email&utm_content=76448806&_hsenc=p2ANqtz-900NUIB-BxjqvY5yA0qKCarhsR0VNPUUo7uGdB_bWorE9yNc-Ft_2ei0X-layfLeH0uGYXokbtyqVFk55PjTigYH7GaKA&_hsmi=06.

27. Davey, Adam, Bo Malmberg and Gerdt Sundström. 2014. "Aging in Sweden: Local Variation, Local Control." *The Gerontologist* 54(4):525-32; Slaets, Joris. 2019. "Aging in the Netherlands." *AARP International*:https://www.google.com/search?client=firefox-b-1-d&q=aging+netherlands; Smits, Carolien H. M., Hugo K. van den Beld, Marja J. Aartsen and Johannes J. F. Schroots. 2014. "Aging in the Netherlands: State of the Art and Science." *The Gerontologist* 54(3):335-43.

28. Baker, Edith S. 2017. "Is There Age Discrimination in Hiring?". *Monthly Labor Review* April:1-2.

29. Roscigno, Vincent J. 2010. "Ageism in the American Workplace." *Contexts* 9(1):16-21.

30. Roscigno, Vincent J. 2010. "Ageism in the American Workplace." *Contexts* 9(1):16-21.

31. Roscigno, Vincent J. 2010. "Ageism in the American Workplace." *Contexts* 9(1):16-21.

32. Leland, John. 2010. "A Graying Population, a Graying Work Force." *The New York Times* April 25:A14.

33. Novak, Mark. 2018. *Issues in Aging*. New York: Routledge.

34. National Center on Elder Abuse. 2019. "Statistics/Data."https://ncea.acl.gov/About-Us/What-We-Do/Research/Statistics-and-Data.aspx#prevalence.

35. Horn, Dara. 1998. "Bad News on Elder Abuse." *Time*, August 17, pp. 82.

36. Kuhn, Maggie, Christina Long and Laura Quinn. 1991. *No Stone Unturned: The Life and Times of Maggie Kuhn*. New York: Ballantine Books.

37. Williamson, John B., Tay K. McNamara and Stephanie A. Howling. 2003. "Generational Equity, Generational Interdependence, and the Framing of the Debate over Social Security Reform." *Journal of Sociology and Social Welfare* 30(3):3-14.

38. Kaye, Lenard W. 1994. "Generational Equity: Pitting Young against Old." Pp. 343-47 in *Perspectives in Social Gerontology*, edited by J. Robert B. Enright. Boston: Allyn and Bacon.

39. O'Kane, Caitlin. 2019. "Four Teenage Boys Save 90-Year-Old Woman from Burning House." *KHOU.com* June 7:https://www.khou.com/article/news/four-teenage-boys-save-90-year-old-woman-from-burning-house/285-a8f139af-1206-4571-8685-fc5db385689a.

40. Naitonal Council on Aging. 2019. "Public Policy & Action."https://www.ncoa.org/public-policy-action/; Rowe, John W., Lisa F. Berkman, Robert Binstock, Axel Boersch-Supan, John Cacioppo, Laura Carsternsen, Dana Goldman, Linda Fried, James Jackson, Martin Kohli, Jay Olshansky and John Rother. 2010. "Policies and Politics for an Aging America." *Contexts* 9(1):22-27.

41. Rowe, John W., Lisa F. Berkman, Robert Binstock, Axel Boersch-Supan, John Cacioppo, Laura Carsternsen, Dana Goldman, Linda Fried, James Jackson, Martin Kohli, Jay Olshansky and John Rother. 2010. "Policies and Politics for an Aging America." *Contexts* 9(1):22-27.

PART 3

Problems of Well-Being and Behavior

Source: Africa Studio/Shutterstock

CHAPTER 7

Alcohol and Other Drugs

Social Problems in the News

"Ohio Opens School for Students with Addiction," the headline said. A new high school in Columbus, Ohio, opened specifically for students who were abusing alcohol and/or other drugs. One of these students had started using alcohol and other drugs when she was 13. As she recalled, "Drugs was what I thought was curing my depression and really helping me through those times, which you know, turns out only made it worse." After she tried to commit suicide, she went to a substance abuse program in Utah and became sober. But when she returned to Ohio, peer pressure led her to start drinking and using other drugs again. She remembers that other students were saying to her, "What's wrong with you, why don't you want to party, why don't you want to be a normal high schooler?" She started using drugs again and eventually overdosed on pills. This relapse led this student to enroll in the new Columbus school, and she was eager to start attending. "You put me in a sober environment and I hear all these sobriety terms and recovery words and that's what I'm going to want, ya know?" she said. "That's what I'm excited to want."

Source: Pfleger 2019[1]

This news story points to three basic facts that are often forgotten in discussions about alcohol and other drugs. First, because of a combination of physiological, psychological, and social factors, drugs make us feel good. Second, because drugs make us feel good, many people want to use them. Third, peer pressure often leads to drug use. To acknowledge these three facts is not meant to excuse the use of alcohol and other drugs, which cause serious individual and societal problems. But it is meant to indicate why the United States and other nations have found it so difficult to deal with drug use.

This difficulty in turn points to the need to understand why people use alcohol and other drugs, including the influence of our sociodemographic backgrounds on the likelihood of using them. This chapter examines these and other aspects of drug use before turning to the important issue of social and political policy regarding drug use.

7.1 Drug Use in History

Learning Objectives

1. Discuss the presence of drugs in ancient times.
2. Summarize the use of drugs in the United States during the 19th century.
3. Explain the racial basis for decisions to ban opium, cocaine, and marijuana in the United States.

Shakespeare once wrote that "what's past is prologue." This familiar phrase means that what happened in the past provides a context for, and can help to understand and predict, the future. To the extent that the past is prologue, the history of drug use provides a sobering lesson: Drug use has been common since ancient times and has been common in almost every society. As three drug scholars have written, "People have used chemicals to alter their state of mind since before there were written records" (Kleiman et al. 2011:xviii).[2] If past is indeed prologue, then it is no surprise that drug use remains common in contemporary nations despite considerable efforts to reduce it.

Ancient Greeks drank poppy juice, which contained opium, around 300 BCE. Use of other drugs was also common in ancient times.

Source: © Thinkstock

Examples of drug use thousands of years ago abound (Faupel et al. 2014; Goodman et al. 2007).[3] Mead, an alcoholic drink made from fermented honey, was first used about 8000 BCE, and beer and berry wines were first used about 6000 BCE. The ancient Sumerians used opium starting about 5000 BCE. Ancient Egypt used alcohol in 3500 BCE, while ancient China used cannabis (the source of marijuana) around 3000 BCE. Ancient people in what is now Switzerland ate poppy seeds (the source of opium) in 2500 BCE. Coca leaves (the source of cocaine) have been chewed for thousands of years. Folk medicines made from plants and herbs have also been used since ancient times. People in ancient Palestine drank wine in 350 BCE. Ancient Greeks drank poppy juice in 300 BCE. In about the same period, South American tribes used a hallucinogen called *cohoba*, made from mimosa beans. The Chinese and other Asians were using opium regularly by 1000 CE. The use of various drugs has also been common in the many societies that anthropologists have studied (Page and Singer 2010).[4]

Sociologist Erich Goode (2008:176)[5] once summarized the history of drug use as follows: "Humans have been ingesting drugs for thousands of years. And throughout recorded time, significant numbers of nearly every society on earth have used one or more drugs to achieve certain desired physical or mental states. Drug use comes close to being a universal, both worldwide and throughout history."

Drug Use in U.S. History

This history of drug use includes the United States, where past is again prologue. During the colonial era, tobacco was a major crop in Virginia and other colonies, thanks to slave labor. After being processed, it was commonly used by colonists and also exported to Europe in great quantities (Gately 2001).[6] From the earliest colonial days, alcohol was another drug used in great quantities, as "Americans were drinkers right from the start" (Genzlinger 2011:C1).[7] The Mayflower, the celebrated ship that brought the first Puritans to what eventually became the United States, was filled with barrels of beer. In colonial New England, rum manufacturing was a major industry, and rum drinking was common. During the early 1770s, New England had more than 140 rum distilleries, and rum consumption in the colonies averaged 7.5 million gallons annually. This massive drinking has led one author to call rum "the real spirit of 1776" (Williams 2006).[8] In addition to rum, colonists routinely drank beer and hard cider.

During the 19th century, Americans began to use drugs other than alcohol in great quantities. One popular drug was coffee. Before the Civil War, Americans who drank coffee had to buy green (unroasted) coffee beans in bulk and roast their own coffee. Then in 1865, John Arbuckle, a Pittsburgh grocer, began selling roasted coffee inside a new invention—the paper bag. His bagged coffee was an instant hit across the nation, other coffee manufacturers followed suit, and coffee use by Americans greatly increased.

Alcohol also remained a very popular drug, and use of this drug during the 1800s was probably greater than during colonial America. Two reasons help account for this trend (Faupel et al. 2014).[9] One reason was the western frontier. As the nation moved west, many of the explorers and settlers who led the way were men who were unmarried or who had left their families behind. To put it mildly, they drank a lot, fought a lot, and gambled a lot. A second reason was that many Irish immigrants came to the United States during a great wave of immigration that began in the mid-19th century. Although it might sound like a stereotype, the Irish drank a lot of alcohol back in their homeland, and they continued to do so once they reached the United States. Regardless of who was drinking, heavy alcohol use contributed greatly to poverty, to physical assaults and homicides, and to domestic violence and other family problems.

Three other popular drugs in this era were opium, cocaine, and marijuana. Use of these drugs was so common that 19th-century America has been called a "dope fiend's paradise" (Brecher 1973:3).[10] A brief discussion of these drugs' histories will underscore the widespread use of drugs in the American past and also racial issues that arose when laws were passed to ban these drugs (Musto 1999).[11]

Opium

During the decades before and after the Civil War, the use of opium was extremely common. It was a staple in many patent medicines, elixirs, and tonics sold back then in apothecaries, general stores, and other venues. Large numbers of people from all social backgrounds used these opium-laced medicines for problems such as chronic pain, depression, headaches, menstrual cramps, and toothaches. It is not much of an exaggeration to say that the United States was a nation of opium users during this period. As anthropologist Robert B. Edgerton (1976:57–58)[12] summarizes the situation, "The use of opium was widespread in all segments of American society. Children were calmed with opium derivatives, women used many popular patent medicines which were liberally larded with opiates, and 'opium dens' were probably present in all cities and most towns as well."

Opium was a common ingredient in 19th-century tonics and elixirs that were sold widely to the public.

Source: © Thinkstock

Patronage of opium dens (the equivalent of today's bar or tavern, with opium the drug of choice rather than alcohol) was a popular activity for the Chinese immigrants who began coming to the United States during the 1850s to help build railroads and perform other jobs. White workers viewed these immigrants as a threat to their jobs, and racial prejudice against the Chinese increased. Politicians, labor unions, and other parties warned that the Chinese were kidnapping little white children, taking them to the opium dens, and turning them into "opium fiends." This campaign had two effects: It increased prejudice against the Chinese, and it increased public concern about opium. As a result, San Francisco in 1875 became the first city to ban opium dens. Other California cities did the same, and the state itself banned opium dens in 1881. Three decades later, the federal government banned the manufacture, sale, and use of opium (except for use with a physician's prescription) when it passed the Harrison Narcotics Act in 1914.

Cocaine

Cocaine was another drug that was very popular in the 19th century, beginning in the 1880s, thanks in part to enthusiastic claims by Sigmund Freud and American physicians that cocaine could help relieve asthma, depression, hay fever, sexual impotence, toothache pain, and a host of other problems. Like opium, cocaine was a popular ingredient in the many patent medicines, and the U.S. Army Surgeon General advocated its medical use. Cocaine was a major ingredient in a new beverage introduced in 1886, Coca-Cola, which became an instant hit because people felt so good when they drank Coke! During the next 2 decades, however, concern grew about cocaine's effects. Some of this concern was fueled by the absurd, racist belief that African Americans who used cocaine became extra strong, dangerous, and even invulnerable to bullets. Cocaine was heavily taxed by the 1914 Harrison Narcotics Act and later banned.

Coca-Cola Was Invented Using Cocaine

When Coca-Cola was introduced in 1886, it became very popular. A major reason for its popularity was that this new product contained cocaine, and people who drank it felt so good as a result.

View the video online at: http://www.youtube.com/embed/2HZ_r66lKSo?rel=0

Marijuana

A third legal drug during the late 19th century was marijuana. It joined opium and cocaine in being a common ingredient in patent medicines for problems like migraine headaches, menstrual cramps, and toothache pain. After the Mexican Revolution of 1910, Mexicans moved to the United States in increased numbers and brought with them their habit of marijuana use. Fearing that Mexicans would take their jobs, whites began to charge that Mexicans who used marijuana would become violent and more likely to rape and murder innocent white victims. This racist claim increased concern about marijuana and helped lead to the federal Marihuana Tax Act of 1937 that banned its use.

This brief history shows that drug use has been part of the American culture ever since the nation began. If past is prologue, it should come as no surprise that drugs remain part of the American culture today, and it should also come as no surprise that efforts to reduce or eliminate drug use often meet with much resistance and little success. As the United States continues to try to deal with drug use, the historical record should not be forgotten.

Key Takeaways

- Drug use has been common since ancient times.
- Alcohol was widely drunk in colonial America. During the latter 19th century, opium, marijuana, and cocaine were legal drugs that were also widely used.
- Racial prejudice played an important role in decisions during the late 19th century and early 20th century to ban opium, marijuana, and cocaine.

For Your Review

1. Were you surprised to read that mind-altering drug use has been common since ancient times? Why or why not?
2. Were you surprised to read that racial prejudice helped lead to bans on opium, marijuana, and cocaine? Why or why not?

7.2 Drugs and Drug Use Today

Learning Objectives

1. Summarize the different types of drugs.
2. Explain the various harms caused by alcohol and tobacco.
3. Understand the effects of marijuana, cocaine, and other illegal drugs.

A **drug** may be defined as any substance other than food that, when taken into the body, affects the structure and/or functioning of the body. Defined this way, many common substances contain drugs or are drugs: coffee, NoDoz, and other products to keep us alert; aspirin, acetaminophen, ibuprofen, and other pain relievers; Tums, Rolaids, and other products that reduce heartburn; Metamucil and other products that reduce constipation; Robitussin, Sudafed, and other cold medicines; and so forth. If you have ever used one of these products, you are technically a drug user, however silly that might sound.

Many prescription drugs also certainly exist: Prozac and other antidepressants; Valium and other tranquilizers; Lipitor and other cholesterol drugs; Yasmin, Yaz, and other birth control pills; Viagra and other products that relieve erectile dysfunction; and so forth. Sales of these prescription drugs amount to tens of billions of dollars annually.

The following substances are also drugs: alcohol, ecstasy, cocaine, heroin, marijuana, LSD, methamphetamine, PCP, and tobacco. Much has been written about these drugs, and we will discuss them further later in this section. But note that two of these drugs, alcohol and tobacco, are legal after a certain age, while the remaining drugs are illegal everywhere in the nation, except for marijuana, which is now legal in several states.

One of the problems in deciding how to deal with drugs is that this distinction between legal drugs and illegal drugs has no logical basis. It makes sense to assume that the illegal drugs should be the ones that are the most dangerous and cause the most physical and social harm, but this assumption is not true. Rather, alcohol and tobacco cause the most harm even though they are legal. As Kleiman et al. (2011:xviii)[13] note about alcohol, "When we read that one in twelve adults suffers from a substance abuse disorder or that 8 million children are living with an addicted parent, it is important to remember that alcohol abuse drives those numbers to a much greater extent than does dependence on illegal drugs." Tobacco kills more than 480,000 Americans annually, while alcohol kills about 88,000 annually through its effects on the liver and other body organs and through its involvement in traffic accidents, homicides, and other situations (Centers for Disease Control and Prevention 2018, 2019).[14]

drug

Any substance other than food that, when taken into the body, affects the structure and/or functioning of the body.

Tips from Former Smokers

Smoking cigarettes and other use of tobacco kill more than 480,000 Americans every year, a number much higher than the number of deaths from all other drugs combined.

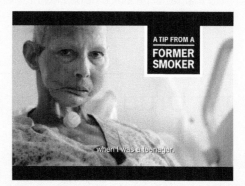

View the video online at: http://www.youtube.com/embed/_th5U5hRu8k?rel=0

Putting these numbers together, some 568,000 Americans die annually from alcohol and tobacco use. Meanwhile, overdoses of illegal drugs and prescription drugs (including opioids, which caused a well-publicized drug crisis during the past decade) killed about 74,000 Americans in 2017 (Kochanek et al. 2019).[15] Figure 7.1 depicts the huge difference between deaths from alcohol and tobacco as legal drugs and from illegal and prescription drug overdoses.

FIGURE 7.1 Annual Deaths from Legal Drugs, Illegal Drugs, and Prescription Drugs

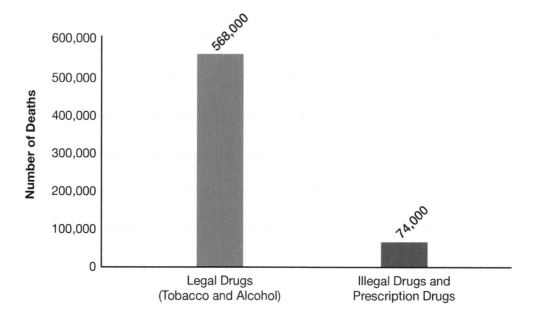

Sources: Kochanek, Kenneth D., Sherry L. Murphy, Jiaquan Xu, and Elizabeth Arias. 2019. "Deaths: Final Data for 2017." *National Vital Statistics Reports* 68(9):1−76. Centers for Disease Control and Prevention. 2018. "Alcohol and Public Health: Fact Sheets—Alcohol Use and Your Health." https://www.cdc.gov/alcohol/fact-sheets/alcohol-use.htm; Centers for Disease Control and Prevention. 2019. "Smoking & Tobacco Use: Fast Facts." https://www.cdc.gov/tobacco/data_statistics/fact_sheets/fast_facts/index.htm.

We return to the issue of the relative harm of legal and illegal drugs toward the end of the chapter when we discuss drug policy. In the meantime, keep in mind two related facts: (1) all drugs can be dangerous, and (2) some drugs are much more dangerous than others. Two aspirins are safe to take, but a bottle of aspirin can kill someone. Two cups of coffee a day are fine, but drinking too many cups a day can cause anxiety, insomnia, and headaches. One drink of alcohol is safe to take, but several drinks in a short time amount to binge drinking, and long-term use of alcohol can kill someone. One snort of cocaine is usually safe, but even one snort can result in a sudden fatal heart attack, and long-term use often has serious health consequences.

Types of Drugs

Drugs are commonly classified into certain categories according to their physiological effects. All drugs may make us feel good, but they do so in different ways. Partly because many drugs have multiple effects, many different classifications of drugs exist. A common classification includes the following categories: depressants, hallucinogens, marijuana, narcotics, and stimulants.

Depressants

Depressants slow down the activity of the central nervous system. Depending on the specific drug, they help induce drowsiness and relaxation, and they can reduce anxiety and pain. Several types of depressants exist. *Analgesics* reduce pain and include over-the-counter products such as aspirin, acetaminophen (the major ingredient in Tylenol), and ibuprofen (the major ingredient in Advil and Motrin), and many prescription medicines that contain acetaminophen. *Sedatives* help people relax and include alcohol, barbiturates, and sleep medicines such as Sominex and Tylenol PM (both over-the-counter) and Ambien and Valium (both prescription). Large doses of depressants may lead to physical dependence and sometimes death.

depressants

Drugs that slow down the activity of the central nervous system; depending on the specific drug, they help induce drowsiness and relaxation, and they can reduce anxiety and pain.

Hallucinogens

Hallucinogens are mind-altering drugs that cause delusions or hallucinations. Their ranks include ecstasy, LSD, mescaline, and PCP. Many people who use a hallucinogen report that the mind-altering effects of the drug provide them a truly wonderful experience, but many also find the effects to be troubling at best and horrible and terrifying at worst. Long-term effects include hallucinations that occur without any drug use preceding them.

hallucinogens

Mind-altering drugs that cause delusions or hallucinations.

Marijuana

Because marijuana's effects do not fit neatly into any other category of drug, marijuana (along with its close cousin, hashish) is often considered to be its own category. As we will see later, it is by far the most popular illegal drug in the United States. Its effects include distortion of time and space, euphoria, hunger, increased sensory perception, and relaxation.

Marijuana is by far the most popular illegal drug in the United States.

Source: © Thinkstock

Narcotics

narcotics

Drugs derived from opium that slow down the central nervous system, relieve pain, and induce drowsiness, euphoria, and relaxation.

Narcotics are sometimes classified under depressants because they slow down the central nervous system, but they are often still considered as their own category. They are highly effective at relieving pain and are a common substance in prescription medicines for severe pain. By definition, all narcotics are derived from opium, either in its natural form or in a synthesized form. Examples of narcotics include codeine, heroin, methadone, and morphine. In addition to relieving pain, narcotics may induce drowsiness, euphoria, and relaxation. Although narcotics do not damage bodily organs, they are very physically addictive, and high doses can be fatal, as the opioid crisis of the last decade poignantly reminds us.

Stimulants

stimulants

Drugs that speed up the central nervous system and increase alertness and energy and possibly produce euphoria or anxiety.

Stimulants have the opposite effect of depressants by speeding up the central nervous system. They increase alertness and energy and can produce euphoria or anxiety. Some are legal and some are illegal, and many very different drugs are considered stimulants: caffeine, cocaine, methamphetamine and other amphetamines, nicotine (tobacco), and Ritalin. Stimulants can be very physically addictive, and nicotine is thought to be more addictive than heroin. While caffeine is very safe in normal amounts, many other stimulants may have dangerous short-term or long-term side effects on the cardiovascular system.

Not all drugs can be discussed in one chapter. In choosing which drugs to discuss in a book on social problems, it makes sense to discuss the drugs that have probably most concerned Americans during the past half century. We thus focus in the remainder of this section mostly on alcohol, tobacco, marijuana, cocaine, and heroin.

Legal Drugs

As noted earlier, alcohol and tobacco (nicotine) are two legal drugs that are very common and that together kill hundreds of thousands of Americans annually. According to national survey evidence collected by the Substance Abuse and Mental Health Services Administration (SAMHSA) of the federal government, most people 12 and older (many younger than 18) have tried alcohol, and over half the public drinks currently (defined as having had at least one drink in the past month). While many people have tried tobacco, less than one-fifth of the public uses it currently (at least once during the past month). Table 7.1 summarizes the prevalence of alcohol and nicotine use. Translating some of these percentages into actual numbers, about 60 million Americans ages 12 and older are current tobacco users (mostly by smoking cigarettes), and 140 million are current alcohol users.

TABLE 7.1 Prevalence of Alcohol and Tobacco Use, Ages 12 and Older, 2017*

	Lifetime	Past year	Past month
Alcohol	80.9	65.7	51.7
Tobacco	62.7	27.5	22.4
* Percentage using in designated time period			

Source: Substance Abuse and Mental Health Services Administration. 2018. *Results from the 2017 National Survey on Drug Use and Health: Detailed Tables*. Rockville, MD: Author.

With this backdrop, we now discuss these two legal but very harmful drugs in greater detail.

Alcohol

Moderate alcohol use (more than one drink per day for an adult female and two drinks per day for an adult male) is relatively safe for most people and may even have health benefits (Harvard T.H. Chan School of Public Health 2019).[16] The problem is that many people drink much more than moderately.

SAMHSA survey data show the extent of such problem drinking, as its survey measures both **binge drinking** (five or more drinks on the same occasion—within 2 hours of each other—on at least 1 day in the past month) and **heavy drinking** (binge drinking on at least 5 days in the past month). Table 7.2 presents the relevant data for people 12 and older and also for those aged 18–25, who have higher rates than the rest of the population.

binge drinking

Five or more drinks on the same occasion—within 2 hours of each other—on at least 1 day in the past month.

heavy drinking

Binge drinking on at least 5 days in the past month.

TABLE 7.2 Prevalence of Binge and Heavy Alcohol Use, 2017*

	Ages 12 and older	Ages 18–25
Binge use	24.5	36.9
Heavy use	6.1	9.6
* Percentage engaging in alcohol use		

Source: Source: Substance Abuse and Mental Health Services Administration. 2018. *Results from the 2017 National Survey on Drug Use and Health: Detailed Tables.* Rockville, MD: Author.

As Table 7.2 indicates, almost one-fourth of all people 12 and older and slightly more than one-third of those aged 18–25 engage in binge drinking, while about 6 percent and almost 10 percent, respectively, engage in heavy drinking. The figures for those 12 and older translate to about sixty-six million binge drinkers and sixteen million heavy drinkers. These numbers show that tens of millions of people abuse alcohol annually and underscore the problem of dealing with problem drinking.

The amount of alcohol consumed annually by occasional, moderate, and heavy drinkers is staggering. The relevant data appear in Table 7.3. Americans aged 14 or older drink 7.9 billion gallons of alcohol annually, equivalent to 137.3 billion standard drinks. This number of drinks works out to about 487 drinks per person annually for the 14 and older population and 726 drinks per person for the 14 and older population that drinks at all. Keep in mind that this is just an average. The heavy drinkers identified in Table 7.2 have many more than 726 drinks every year, while light drinkers have only a relative handful of drinks.

TABLE 7.3 Alcohol Consumption in the United States, Ages 14 or Older, 2016

	Number of gallons	Equivalent number of standard drinks*
Beer	6.4 billion	68.2 billion
Wine	898.7 million	23.1 billion
Spirits	539.3 million	46.0 billion
Total	7.9 billion	137.3 billion
* One drink = 12 ounces of beer, 5 ounces of wine, or 1.5 ounces of spirits		

Source: Haughwout, Sarah P. and Megan E. Slater. 2018. *Apparent Per Capita Alcohol Consumption: National, State, and Regional Trends, 1977-2016.* Washington, DC: National Institute on Alcohol Abuse and Alcoholism.

The Drinking Culture and the Alcohol Industry

As noted earlier, alcohol has a long history in the United States and an even longer history in much of the rest of the world. When we think about the tens of millions of Americans who drink at least occasionally, the ads for beer and wine and hard liquor that appear regularly in the popular media, and the thousands of bars and related venues across the country, it is certainly no exaggeration to say that we have a drinking culture.

Once upon a time, the federal and state governments tried to eliminate this culture. We are speaking, of course, about Prohibition. The passage of the Eighteenth Amendment to the U.S. Constitution in January 1919 banned the manufacture, sale, and transportation of alcohol; the ban took effect a year later. For reasons we will discuss later, the ban was eventually deemed a failure, and the passage of the Twenty-First Amendment in 1933 repealed the Eighteenth Amendment.

Alcohol manufacturing and sales are a major industry worldwide today. Several alcohol companies rank among the largest corporations in the world as well as in the United States. U.S. alcohol sales amounted to almost $254 billion in 2018 (Morris 2019).[17] The amount of money the public spends on alcohol equals 13.4 percent of what it spends on food (U.S. Department of Agriculture 2018).[18] The alcohol industry provides more than two million jobs annually and almost $50 billion in taxes, and it contributes more than $122 billion in direct impact to the annual national economy (American Beverage Licensees 2018).[19] All these figures show that the alcohol industry plays a significant role in the U.S. economy.

The alcohol industry is a major part of the U.S. and worldwide economies and provides about two million jobs annually in the United States.

Source: © Thinkstock

Despite this role, if the United States does indeed have a drinking culture, the alcohol industry bears a major share of the responsibility. As the American Medical Association (2004)[20] has stated,

Like the tobacco industry, the alcohol industry produces a legal, widely consumed drug; is dominated by relatively few producers; and utilizes a powerful combination of advertising dollars, savvy marketing, political campaign contributions, and sophisticated lobbying tactics to create and maintain an environment favorable to its economic and political interests. It requires the recruitment of new, youthful drinkers to maintain and build its customer base...As a chemical that affects our bodies, alcohol is a powerful drug resulting in more premature deaths and illnesses than all illicit drugs combined. Yet the industry has shaped public opinion and forced government to treat it not as a drug but as a cultural artifact, a valued legal commodity, almost a food, even a necessity of life.

Consequences of Alcohol Abuse

Despite alcohol's immense popularity, the fact remains that millions of Americans abuse it. This abuse means that alcohol has serious personal and social consequences. One set of consequences involves personal health. We noted earlier that alcohol abuse is responsible for about eighty-eight thousand deaths annually through the physiological damage it does and its involvement in fatal injuries and accidents. Heavy alcohol use can destroy the liver, increase blood pressure, weaken the heart and immune system, and cause sexual dysfunction. It can lead to neurological problems and also raises the risk of incurring several kinds of cancer. Binge drinking can cause serious immediate health problems because it may lead to someone overdosing on alcohol. About five million Americans visit the emergency room every year for alcohol overdoses and other alcohol-related problems (White et al. 2018).[21]

In addition to these health problems, alcohol use is responsible for about 10,500 traffic fatalities annually (2016 data), accounting for 28 percent of all these fatalities, and it plays an important role in violent crime (Centers for Disease Control and Prevention 2019; Ford 2017).[22] As almost anyone with an alcoholic family member can attest, alcohol abuse can also cause many problems for families, including domestic violence and divorce and the stress that results from having to deal with someone's alcoholism on a daily basis. (The "Children and Our Future" box discusses the impact of parental alcoholism on children.) Alcohol abuse costs the United States $250 billion each year in medical expenses, lost workplace productivity, lost earnings because of alcohol-related illness or premature death, lost earnings by victims of violent crime, and alcohol-caused traffic accidents (Sacks et al. 2015).[23]

After social distancing began in early 2020 with the onset of the COVID-19 pandemic, alcohol experts worried about its consequences for recovering alcoholics. Although social distancing was absolutely necessary to reduce the spread of the coronavirus, it is also true that recovering alcoholics normally rely heavily on interpersonal contact in Alcoholics Anonymous and other group settings and on interpersonal contact with supportive friends and family. As one news report summarized this problem, "For millions of people in recovery or looking for help for alcohol use, in-person group meetings can be a source of relief. But social distancing measures that were put in place to help curb the coronavirus have disrupted the support networks people rely upon for help" (Santhanam 2020). Recovering alcoholics turned to video meetings for their social support, but alcohol experts said it would take many months before they could assess the impact of this change on recovering alcoholics' drinking behavior and health. They also worried that the stress of the pandemic would cause recovering alcoholics to relapse and resume their heavy drinking (Santhanam 2020).[24]

Children and Our Future

Children of Alcoholics

As with so many social problems, one of the saddest consequences of alcohol abuse involves children. About one-tenth of children live with with an alcoholic parent. Whether because alcoholism is partly inherited or because children tend to use their parents as role models, children of alcoholics are much more likely than children of nonalcoholics to become alcoholics themselves by the time they reach adulthood.

Because living with an alcoholic parent is often both chaotic and unpredictable, it is no surprise that children of alcoholics often experience a great deal of stress and other difficulties that may also account for their greater tendency to become alcoholics. Compared to other children, they are more likely to be neglected and/or abused by their parents, and they are also more likely to miss school, have lower grades, and engage in disruptive behavior. In addition, they are at great risk for eating disorders and substance abuse other than alcohol abuse. The stress they experience can also harm their neurological development and immune system and put them at greater risk for different kinds of illness and disease. Children of alcoholics are also at greater risk for several kinds of psychological and emotional problems. These include (1) *guilt*, because they may blame themselves for their parent's drinking; (2) *anxiety*, because they worry about their parent's health and may see their parents arguing and fighting; (3) *embarrassment* that leads them not to invite friends over to visit nor to ask another adult for help; (4) *lack of trust* in other people, because they have learned not to trust their alcoholic parent; and (5) *anger, confusion*, and *depression*.

One special problem that children of alcoholics face is that they are "forced into adulthood." They often find themselves having to care for younger siblings and even for their alcoholic parent. By taking on such a heavy responsibility, they in effect become adults at too tender an age. This responsibility weighs on them and helps account for the psychological and emotional difficulties they often experience.

Mental health professionals strongly advise that children of alcoholics receive counseling and other kinds of support to help them deal with their family experiences. Perhaps the best known program for these children is Alateen, which also serves teenagers who want help dealing with an alcoholic friend. Teenagers at Alateen meetings share their experiences, learn how to deal with their situation, and provide emotional support for each other. They also learn that they are in no way responsible for the alcoholism of their parent, other relative, or friend.

Young children and teenagers are resilient, but children of alcoholics have to be especially resilient. Programs like Alateen help give them a second chance.

Sources: Lipari and Van Horn 2017; Tagliareni 2018[25]

College Students

Alcohol abuse is also a problem on college and university campuses across the United States. Based on national survey evidence, more than one-third of full-time college students ages 18–22 have been binge drinkers during the past month (Lipari and Jean-Francois 2016).[26]

Binge drinking by college students has many serious consequences (Center for Science in the Public Interest 2008; National Center on Addiction and Substance Abuse 2007).[27] Binge drinkers are much more likely than other students to miss class, get poor grades, be injured, have unprotected sex, and to drive after drinking. More than 1,500 college students die every year from alcohol-related injuries incurred in motor vehicle crashes and other accidents. In other consequences, some 700,000 students are assaulted annually by a student who has been drinking, and heavy alcohol use plays a role in an estimated 97,000 rapes and sexual assaults of college students annually.

Tobacco and Nicotine

Nicotine, the major drug in tobacco, is another legal but very dangerous drug. Based on the annual death numbers mentioned earlier, tobacco use kills 5.5 times as many people every year as those killed by alcohol use. Tobacco is a slow poison. If it were not already a legal drug used by millions, and a company had just manufactured cigarettes for the first time, the Food and Drug Administration would never approve this product. Fortunately for tobacco companies, nicotine does not distort perception the way that alcohol and many other psychoactive drugs do. Someone smoking or otherwise using tobacco can safely drive a car, operate machinery, and so forth, and someone "under the influence" of tobacco does not become violent.

If you have ever watched any number of movies or television shows that portray life before the 1970s, you know that the United States used to have a tobacco culture the way it now has an alcohol culture. Many, many people smoked cigarettes, and a large number smoked cigars or pipes. This particular drug culture began to abate in the 1970s after much evidence mounted about the deaths and other serious health effects of tobacco use and especially about the dangers of second-hand smoke. Whereas college students a generation ago often sat in smoke-filled classrooms and Americans generally sat in smoke-filled restaurants and other venues, today most Americans can count on being in enclosed public spaces in which smoking is banned.

Even so, we have already seen that more than one-fifth of Americans 12 and older, or some sixty million people, are still current users (past month) of tobacco; most of these users are cigarette smokers. Thanks to the greater knowledge about tobacco's health effects, public education campaigns about these effects, heavy taxes on cigarettes, and changing attitudes about tobacco, these numbers represent a significant decline from a generation ago. Still, the advent of vaping among young people in the last decade has alarmed many public health experts, because inhaled vapors contain toxic chemicals that may cause heart disease, respiratory problems, and cancer (American Heart Association 2020).[28]

Tobacco use causes more preventable death and illness in the United States than any other cause of death; if no one used tobacco, the more than 480,000 tobacco-related deaths each year would not occur. As we think about tobacco, this startling statistic needs to be kept in mind: *About half of all cigarette smokers will one day die from a premature death caused by a smoking-related illness* (King et al. 2011).[29] Another startling statistic is this: *On the average, cigarette smokers die 10 years sooner than non-smokers* (Centers for Disease Control and Prevention 2019).[30] To repeat what was said just earlier, tobacco is a slow poison.

Tobacco kills in several ways. Smoking causes 80–90 percent of all lung cancers, and it greatly increases the risk of emphysema and other lung disease, coronary heart disease, and stroke. In addition to lung cancer, tobacco use also causes several other cancers, including bladder cancer, cervical cancer, esophageal cancer, stomach cancer, and throat cancer. Women who smoke are at greater risk for lower bone density and hip fracture when they get older.

One interesting and very important fact about cigarette smoking is what happens when the cost of cigarettes is increased. Most smokers begin their deadly habit during adolescence or young adulthood. Because this is a period of their lives when they do not have much money, increases in the cost of cigarettes are particularly useful in persuading some of these young people not to buy cigarettes. Government data indicate that every 10 percent increase in the price of cigarettes reduces cigarette consumption among young people by 4 percent (Centers for Disease Control and Prevention 2011).[31] A similar but smaller effect occurs among older smokers.

Earlier we said that the alcohol industry plays a major role in the amount of drinking that occurs in the United States. The same is true of the tobacco industry and smoking. This industry spends about $8.6 billion annually—or an average of $24 million daily—in advertising, sponsorship of public events, and other activities to promote its deadly product, and for many years hid or distorted data about the deadly effects of cigarette smoking (Centers for Disease Control and Prevention 2019).[32]

Tobacco is a slow poison. If it were a new drug, it would not be approved for public consumption.

Source: © Thinkstock

Illegal Drugs

Government survey data also provide a picture of illegal drug use. Table 7.4 presents these data for several illegal drugs.

TABLE 7.4 Prevalence of Illegal Drug Use, Ages 12 and Older, 2017*

	Lifetime	Past year	Past month
Any illegal drug	49.5	19.0	11.2
Marijuana	45.2	15.0	9.6
Cocaine/crack	14.9	2.2	0.8
Hallucinogens	15.5	1.9	0.5
Heroin	1.9	0.3	0.2
Misuse of prescription drugs	not measured	6.6	2.2
Methamphetamine	5.4	0.6	0.3
Opioids (heroin/pain relievers)	not measured	4.2	1.3
* Percentage using in designated time period			

Source: Substance Abuse and Mental Health Services Administration. 2018. *Results from the 2017 National Survey on Drug Use and Health: Detailed Tables*. Rockville, MD: Substance Abuse and Mental Health Services Administration.

The following figure from Table 7.4 is striking: 49.5 percent of all Americans ages 12 and older have used an illegal drug at least once in their lifetimes. This percentage translates to about 135 million people. In terms of lifetime use, the single most popular illegal drug is easily marijuana, which is now legal in several states, but millions of Americans have used an illegal drug other than marijuana.

Despite the prevalence of lifetime illegal drug use, most public health experts are primarily concerned with current (past month) illegal drug use. The percentages for past-month (and also past-year) use in Table 7.4 are noticeably smaller than those for lifetime use. They indicate that most people who have used illegal drugs in their lifetimes are no longer using them, or at least have not used them in the past year or past month. Most of these lifetime users tried their illegal drug once, twice, or a few times and then stopped using it, and some may have used it more often but then stopped. In any event, it is the current, past-month users who raise the most concern for our society in general and for the public health and legal communities and other sectors of our society that deal with illegal drug use and its effects.

In looking at current illegal drug use, we see that 11.2 percent of the public falls into this category. The drug of choice here is marijuana, but very small percentages have used an illegal drug other than marijuana in the past month. These small percentages, though, still translate to many people nationwide. For example, the 0.3 percent who have used meth in the last month is equivalent to 800,000 people.

The percentages in Table 7.4 underestimate the problem of illegal drug use in at least two respects. First, the government survey does not include people whose illegal drug use is especially high: the homeless, runaway teenagers, jail and prison inmates, and youths in detention centers. Second, and conversely, the survey includes people whose illegal drug use is relatively low—namely, young adolescents and people in their middle age and older years. Illegal drug use is somewhat higher for the 18–25 age group, although the illegal drug of choice is again marijuana.

With this backdrop in mind, we now discuss a few illegal drugs in further detail.

Marijuana

As we have seen, marijuana is easily the most widely used illegal drug in the United States. Marijuana use can cause several problems (National Institute on Drug Abuse 2019).[33] Marijuana distorts perception, impairs coordination, and can cause short-term memory loss, and people who are high from marijuana may be unable to safely drive a motor vehicle or operate machinery. In addition, regular pot smokers may be at risk for respiratory problems, and teen marijuana users may suffer cognitive impairment. Chronic marijuana use is also associated with absence from school and the workplace and with social relationship problems, although this association might exist because someone with personal problems begins using marijuana regularly.

Despite these problems, marijuana is almost certainly the most benign illegal drug in terms of health and social consequences, and it is also much more benign than either alcohol or tobacco (Faupel et al. 2014).[34] As noted earlier, these latter two drugs kill about 568,000 Americans annually. In contrast, marijuana has probably never killed anyone, and its use has not been clearly associated with any cancers. Alcohol use is a risk factor for violent behavior, but marijuana use is a risk factor for mellow behavior: If everyone who now uses alcohol instead smoked marijuana, our violent crime rate would probably drop significantly! Despite some popular beliefs, marijuana is generally not physiologically addictive, it does not reduce ambition and motivation, and it does not act as a "gateway drug" that leads to the use of more dangerous drugs (Hanson et al. 2012).[35]

While not entirely safe, then, marijuana is much safer, both on an individual basis and on a societal basis, than either alcohol or tobacco. Even so, it remains an illegal drug for recreational use in most states. This fact underscores our earlier observation that the legality or illegality of drugs has no logical basis. If the personal and social harm caused by a drug determined whether it is legal or not, then it would be logical for marijuana to be legal and for alcohol or tobacco to be illegal.

Cocaine

Cocaine produces a high that is considered more pleasurable than that for any other drug. According to Erich Goode (2008:288),[36] "Cocaine's principal effects are exhilaration, elation, and euphoria—voluptuous, joyous feelings accompanied by a sense of grandiosity." As a stimulant, cocaine also increases energy, alertness, and a sense of self-confidence. It is not physiologically addictive, but it is considered psychologically addictive: The high it produces is so pleasurable that some users find they need to keep using it.

Cocaine most often appears in a powdered form that is sniffed (or, to use the more common term, snorted). The high it produces may last up to 30 minutes once it arrives. A more potent form, crack cocaine (or, more commonly, crack), is made by heating a mixture of powdered cocaine, baking soda, and water. A user then heats this mixture and breathes in the resulting vapors. Crack produces an immediate, intense high and is a relatively inexpensive drug. These features made crack a very popular drug when it was first introduced into U.S. cities in the 1980s, with street gangs fighting each other to control its distribution and sale.

Cocaine and crack use has declined since the 1970s and 1980s, but, as Table 7.4 showed, almost 15 percent of the public has used cocaine at least once. Still, past-year use is only 2.2 percent, and past-month (current) use is only 0.8 percent. Cocaine use thus must be considered rare in percentage terms. At the same time, these percentages translate to 5.9 million and 2.2 million Americans, respectively.

In terms of health risks, cocaine is a much more dangerous drug than marijuana. As a stimulant, cocaine speeds up the central nervous system. Because it does so much more intensely than most other stimulants, its use poses special dangers for the cardiovascular system (National Institute on Drug Abuse 2016).[37] In particular, it can disrupt the heart's normal rhythm and cause ventricular fibrillations, and it can speed up the heart and raise blood pressure. An overdose of cocaine can thus be deadly, and long-term use produces an increased risk of stroke, seizure, and heart disease. Because cocaine also constricts blood vessels in the brain, long-term use raises the risk of attention deficit, memory loss, and other cognitive problems. Long-term abuse has also caused panic attacks, paranoia, and even psychosis.

Cocaine is a particularly addictive drug because of the high degree of pleasurable feelings it causes.

Source: © Thinkstock

Heroin

Heroin is derived from opium. It was one of the popular opiate drugs that, as discussed earlier, were used so widely during the late 19th century. Heroin was first marketed as a painkiller and cough suppressant by the company that makes Bayer aspirin. As the United States became more concerned about opium use, Bayer Laboratories discontinued heroin marketing in 1910, and heroin, like other opiates, was banned under the 1914 Harrison Narcotics Act.

Like other narcotics, heroin use produces a feeling of euphoria. After it is injected, "the user feels a flash, a rush, which has been described as an intense, voluptuous, orgasmlike sensation. Following this is the feeling of well-being, tranquility, ease, and calm, the sensation that everything in the user's life is just fine. Tensions, worries, problems, the rough edges of life—all seem simply to melt away" (Goode 2008:308–309).[38]

Users typically take heroin into their body by injecting it into a vein. This mode of administration is undoubtedly a major reason for the public's very negative image of heroin users. Indeed, the image of a heroin addict "shooting up" is one that has appeared in many movies and television shows past and present. Many heroin addicts share their needles, a practice that increases their risk of contracting HIV and hepatitis.

The public's image and concern about heroin is partly deserved in some ways and partly undeserved in other ways. Like other opiates, heroin is extremely physiologically addictive, although not as addictive as nicotine. But also like other opiates, heroin does not damage body organs. The emaciated look we often associate with heroin users stems not from the drug itself but from the low-caliber lifestyles that heroin addicts tend to live and their decisions to spend the little money they have on heroin rather than on food and a healthier lifestyle. An overdose of heroin can certainly kill, just as overdoses of other drugs can kill. One reason heroin overdoses occur is that heroin users cannot know for sure the purity of the heroin they buy illegally and thus may inject an unsafe dose to get high.

Prescription Drug Abuse

Table 7.4 showed that about 6.6 percent Americans misused prescription drugs during the past year and 2.2 percent during the past month. This type of use is illegal. It constitutes the most widespread illegal drug use other than marijuana use and has grown in recent years, especially among adolescents. The prescription drugs that are most often abused are those containing narcotics, tranquilizers, and stimulants; two of the most common brands that are abused are OxyContin and Vicodin. The flooding of the drug market with OxyContin and similar drugs earlier in this century led to the opioid crisis of the past decade. Because prescription drugs, including opioids, can benefit many people who use them legally under the care of a health professional, our nation faces a special difficulty in dealing with the abuse of these drugs. As the head of the National Institute on Drug Abuse once said, "The challenges we face are much more complex because we need to address the needs of patients in pain, while protecting those at risk for substance use disorders" (Zuger 2011:D1).[39]

Most prescription drug abusers have their own prescriptions or obtain their drugs from friends, acquaintances, or relatives who have their own prescriptions. Whatever the source, some of these prescriptions are obtained legitimately—for actual medical conditions—and then abused, and some are obtained after feigning a medical condition. Many experts fault physicians for over-prescribing painkillers and other prescription drugs.

The "Applying Social Research" box discusses the roots of adolescent prescription drug abuse in family and school factors. The importance of these factors reinforces the sociological view that the origins of drug use often lie beyond the individual and in the social environment.

Many prescription drug abusers use drugs obtained from their own prescriptions or from prescriptions of friends or relatives.

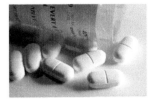

Source: © Thinkstock

Applying Social Research

Prescription Drug Abuse by Adolescents

Despite the importance of prescription drug abuse, social science research on its causes is relatively sparse. In one of the first studies to examine the social origins of adolescent prescription drug abuse, sociologist Jason A. Ford analyzed data on adolescents in the national survey conducted by the Substance Abuse and Mental Health Services Administration that is discussed elsewhere in this chapter. Drawing on the large body of work that attributes drug use in part to weak social bonds, Ford reasoned that prescription drug abuse should be higher among adolescents who have weaker bonds to their parents and also weaker bonds to their schools.

For his measure of parental bonds, Ford used several questions that asked adolescents about their relationship with their parents, including whether parents feel proud of them and praise them for doing a good job, and whether their parents help them with their homework and limit their time out with friends on a school night. For his measure of school bonds, he used several questions that asked adolescents such things as whether they liked going to school and whether they found their schooling meaningful and important. His measure of prescription drug abuse relied on the adolescents' self-reports of whether they had used any prescription drug for nonmedical purposes in the past year.

Controlling for gender, race, and other factors, Ford found support for his hypotheses: Prescription drug abuse was higher among adolescents with weaker bonds to their parents and also weaker bonds to their schools.

These results have important implications for efforts to reduce prescription drug abuse by adolescents. They suggest that efforts by our society to strengthen families and to improve our schools may well have a significant, beneficial side-effect: lower prescription drug abuse by adolescents.

Source: Ford 2009[40]

Key Takeaways

- The distinction between legal drugs and illegal drugs has no logical basis; legal drugs cause much more harm than illegal drugs.
- Alcohol and tobacco kill more than 500,000 Americans annually. Binge drinking on campuses results in accidents and assaults involving several hundred thousand college students annually.
- Marijuana is by far the most commonly used illegal drug. The low prevalence of other illegal drugs still amounts to millions of people using these drugs annually.

7.3 Social Patterning of Drug Use

Learning Objectives

1. Outline the nature of gender differences in drug use.
2. Understand whether racial and ethnic differences in drug use exist.
3. Explain whether education and religiosity are related to drug use.

It is a sociological truism that our sociodemographic backgrounds—gender, race and ethnicity, social class, and so forth—influence many of our behaviors and attitudes. Drug use is no different. By examining the social patterning of drug use, we can see which kinds of people, in terms of their sociodemographic backgrounds, are more or less at risk for using drugs. And by understanding these sociodemographic differences, we begin to understand why some people are more likely than others to use drugs. Our examination of these differences will rely heavily on government survey data and focus on past-month differences in alcohol, tobacco, and illegal drug use (all illegal drugs combined).

Gender

On the average, males drink alcohol more often and more heavily than females, and they are also more likely to use other types of drugs.

Source: © Thinkstock

Gender predicts drug use, with males somewhat more likely than females to use drugs of various types. Figure 7.2 depicts this difference for current (past month) use among the 18–25 age group for alcohol, tobacco, and illegal drugs; the largest difference appears for tobacco. In related data, males are also more likely than females to engage in both binge drinking and heavy drinking.

Why do these gender differences exist? A major reason is *masculinity* (Aulette et al. 2019).[41] Compared to girls, boys are raised to be more active, assertive, and daring, and to care less about the effects of their behavior on others. As they grow older, these traits make them more likely to use drugs and to engage in crime and other risky behaviors.

FIGURE 7.2 Gender and Prevalence of Alcohol, Tobacco, and Illegal Drug Use, Ages 18–25, 2017 (Percentage Using in Past Month)

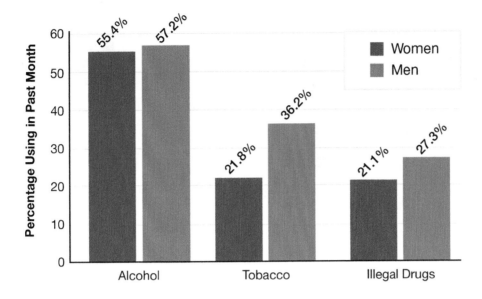

Source: Substance Abuse and Mental Health Services Administration. 2018. *Results from the 2017 National Survey on Drug Use and Health: Detailed Tables.* Rockville, MD: Author.

Race and Ethnicity

Racial and ethnic differences in drug use of various types exist to some extent but exhibit no clear pattern in the 18–25 age group (see Figure 7.3). For alcohol use, whites have the highest rate of drinking; for tobacco use, Native Americans have the highest rate; and for illegal drug use, no group really stands out as having the highest rate. Note that African Americans have roughly the same illegal drug use rate as whites, and have lower rates of alcohol and tobacco use than whites do. Although many people believe that African Americans are more likely than whites to use drugs, research data show that this belief is a myth. Similarly, despite the popular image that Native Americans are heavy drinkers, the data do not support that image.

FIGURE 7.3 Race/Ethnicity and Prevalence of Alcohol, Tobacco, and Illegal Drug Use, Ages 18–25, 2017 (Percentage Using in Past Month)

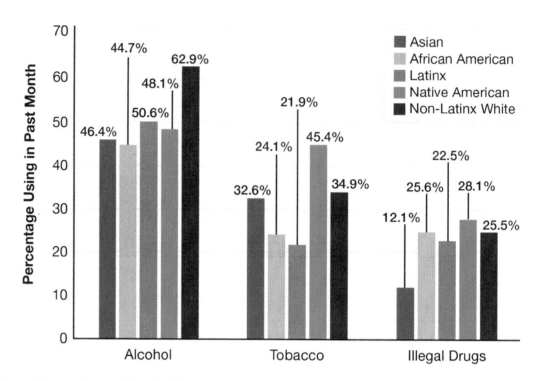

Source: Substance Abuse and Mental Health Services Administration. 2018. *Results from the 2017 National Survey on Drug Use and Health: Detailed Tables.* Rockville, MD: Author.

Education

Education differences in drug use depend on the type of drug (see Figure 7.4). For alcohol, higher levels of education are associated with a higher likelihood of drinking. One possible reason for this association is that people with lower levels of education are more likely to be religious, and people who are religious are less likely to drink. For tobacco, higher levels of education are associated with lower levels of tobacco use. In particular, college graduates are much less likely to use tobacco than people without a college degree. For illegal drugs, there is no clear association between education and use of these drugs, although college graduates report somewhat lower past-month use.

FIGURE 7.4 Education and Prevalence of Alcohol, Tobacco, and Illegal Drug Use, Ages 18–25, 2017 (Percentage Using in Past Month)

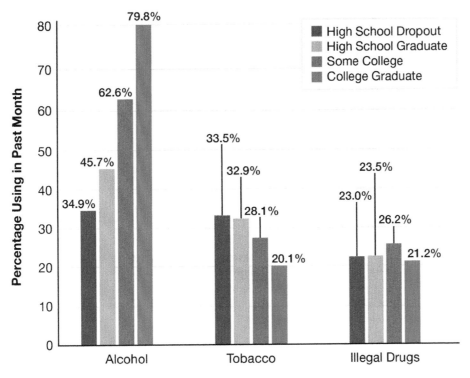

Source: Substance Abuse and Mental Health Services Administration. 2018. *Results from the 2017 National Survey on Drug Use and Health: Detailed Tables.* Rockville, MD: Author.

Religiosity

Much research finds that **religiosity**—how religious someone is—affects how often people use various drugs: The more religious people are, the lower their drug use; conversely, the less religious they are, the higher their drug use (Ransome and Gilman 2016).[42] We can see evidence of this relationship in Figure 7.5, which presents data for a nationwide sample of youths ages 17–18. Those who say religion is important in their lives report less drinking (i.e., on only 0–2 days in the past year) than those who say religion is unimportant in their lives.

religiosity

How religious someone is, in terms of how often the person attends religious service, prays, and reads scripture.

FIGURE 7.5 Religiosity and Drinking among Youths Ages 17–18 (Percentage Saying They Drank Alcohol on Only 0–2 Days in the Past Year)

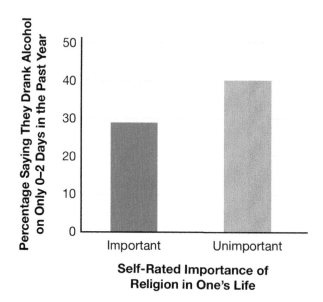

Source: National Longitudinal Study of Adolescent Health, Wave I. (2012). Retrieved from http://www.icpsr.umich.edu/cgi-bin/SDA/DSDR/hsda?dsdr+21600-0001.

Key Takeaways

- Drug use is socially patterned: Aspects of our sociodemographic backgrounds affect our likelihood of using various drugs.
- Perhaps the clearest social pattern involves gender, with males more likely than females to use and abuse alcohol, tobacco, and illegal drugs.
- Despite common beliefs, the rate of illegal drug use is lower for African Americans than for whites.

For Your Review

1. The text discusses five social patterns of drug use: gender, race/ethnicity, education, and religiosity. Taking into account these five sets of patterns, write a short essay in which you use this information to understand your own level of use (or nonuse) of alcohol, tobacco, and illegal drugs.
2. Did it surprise you to read that illegal drug use is lower among African Americans than among whites? Why or why not?

7.4 Explaining Drug Use

To know how to reduce drug use, we must first know what explains it. The major explanations for drug use come from the fields of biology, psychology, and sociology.

Biological Explanations

To explain drug use, the field of biology assumes that some people are particularly vulnerable to the effects of drugs. Because these people are more likely to experience very intense effects, they become physiologically and/or psychologically addicted to a particular drug. To the extent this process occurs, the people in question are assumed to have a biological predisposition for drug addiction that is thought to be a genetic predisposition.

Most research on genetic predisposition has focused on alcohol and alcoholism, but much research on other drugs also exists (Dick 2016).[43] Studies of twins find that identical twins are more likely than fraternal twins (who are not genetically identical) to both have alcohol and other substance abuse problems or not to have them. In addition, studies of children of alcoholic parents who are adopted by nonalcoholic parents find that these children are more likely than those born to nonalcoholic parents to develop alcohol problems themselves. Although this research points to genetic factors, it has not identified the specific gene(s) that might be responsible. Many nonbiological factors also explain the use of, and addiction to alcohol and other drugs. We now turn to these factors.

Research on identical twins suggests that alcoholism has a genetic basis.

Source: © Thinkstock

Psychological Explanations

Psychological explanations join biological explanations in focusing on why certain individuals are more likely than others to use drugs and to be addicted to drugs (Hanson et al. 2018).[44] Some popular psychological explanations center on personality differences between drug users and nonusers. These explanations assume that users have personality traits that predispose them to drug use. These traits include low self-esteem and low self-confidence, low trust in others, and a need for thrills and stimulation. In effect, drug users have personality problems that make them prone to drug use, and once they start using drugs, their personality problems multiply.

One problem with research on personality explanations is methodological: If we find personality differences between drug users and nonusers, should we conclude that personality problems cause drug use, or is it possible that drug use causes personality problems? Much research on personality and drug use cannot answer this question adequately, since it studies drug users and nonusers at one point in time (*cross-sectional research*). To answer this question adequately, *longitudinal research*, which examines the same people over time, is necessary. Among initial drug abstainers at Time 1, if those with the personality traits mentioned earlier turn out to be more likely than those without the traits to be using drugs at Time 2, then we can infer that personality problems affect drug use rather than the reverse. Longitudinal research on personality and drug use that studies adolescents and college students does indeed find this causal sequence (Fehrman et al. 2019).[45]

Other psychological explanations are based on the classic concept of *operant conditioning:* the idea that people and animals are more likely to engage in a behavior when they are rewarded, or reinforced, for it. These explanations assume that people use drugs because drugs are positive reinforcers in two respects. First, drugs provide pleasurable effects themselves and thus provide *direct reinforcement.* Second, drug use often is communal: People frequently use drugs (alcohol is certainly a prime example, but so are many other drugs) with other people, and they enjoy this type of social activity. In this manner, drug use provides *indirect reinforcement.*

Sociological Explanations

Sociological explanations emphasize the importance of certain aspects of the social environment—social structure, social bonds to family and school, social interaction, and culture—for drug use, depending on the type of drug. For drugs like heroin and crack that tend to be used mostly in large urban areas, the social structure, or, to be more precise, social inequality, certainly seems to matter. As sociologist Elliott Currie (1994:3)[46] once observed, the use of these drugs by urban residents, most of them poor and of color, reflects the impact of poverty and racial inequality: "Serious drug use is not evenly distributed: it runs 'along the fault lines of our society.' It is concentrated among some groups and not others, and has been for at least half a century." This fact helps explain why heroin use rose in the inner cities during the 1960s, as these areas remained poor even as the U.S. economy was growing. Inner-city youths were attracted to heroin because its physiological effects helped them forget about their situation and also because the heroin subculture—using an illegal drug with friends, buying the drug from dealers, and so forth—was an exciting alternative to the bleakness of their daily lives. Crack became popular in inner cities during the 1980s for the same reasons.

Social bonds to families and schools also make a difference. Adolescents with weak bonds to their families and schools, as measured by such factors as the closeness they feel to their parents and teachers, are more likely than those with stronger bonds to use various drugs. Their weaker bonds prompt them to be less likely to accept conventional norms and more likely to use drugs and engage in other delinquent behavior.

Regarding social interaction, sociologists emphasize that *peer influences* greatly influence one's likelihood of using alcohol, tobacco, and a host of other drugs (Hanson et al. 2018).[47] Much and probably most drug use begins during adolescence, when peer influences are especially important. When our friends during this stage of life are drinking, smoking, or using other drugs, many of us want to fit in with the crowd and thus use one of these drugs ourselves. In a related explanation, sociologists also emphasize that society's "drug culture" matters for drug use. For example, because we have a culture that so favors alcohol, many people drink alcohol. And because we have a drug culture in general, it is no surprise, sociologically speaking, that drug use of many types is so common.

To the extent that social inequality, social interaction, and a drug culture matter for drug use, sociologists say, it is a mistake to view most drug use as stemming primarily from an individual's biological or psychological problems. Although these problems do play a role for some individuals' use of some drugs, drug use as a whole stems to a large degree from the social environment and must be understood as a social problem, and not just as an individual problem.

Beyond these general explanations of why people use drugs, sociological discussions of drug use reflect the three sociological perspectives introduced in Chapter 1—functionalism, conflict theory, and symbolic interactionism—as we shall now discuss. Table 7.5 summarizes this discussion.

TABLE 7.5 Theory Snapshot

Theoretical perspective	Contributions to understanding of drug use
Functionalism	Drug use is functional for several parties in society. It provides drug users the various positive physiological effects that drugs have; it provides the sellers of legal or illegal drugs a source of income; and it provides jobs for the criminal justice system and the various other parties that deal with drug use. At the same time, both legal drugs and illegal drugs contribute to dysfunctions in society.
Conflict theory	Much drug use in poor urban areas results from the poverty, racial inequality, and other conditions affecting people in these locations. Racial and ethnic prejudice and inequality help determine why some drugs are illegal as well as the legal penalties for these drugs. The large multinational corporations that market and sell alcohol, tobacco, and other legal drugs play a powerful role in the popularity of these drugs and lobby Congress to minimize regulation of these drugs.
Symbolic interactionism	Drug use arises from an individual's interaction with people who engage in drug use. From this type of social interaction, an individual learns how to use a drug and also learns various attitudes that justify drug use and define the effects of a drug as effects that are enjoyable.

Functionalism

Recall that functionalist theory emphasizes the need for social stability, the functions that different aspects of society serve for society's well-being, and the threats (or dysfunctions) to society's well-being posed by certain aspects of society. In line with this theory, sociologists emphasize that drug use may actually be functional for several members of society. For the people using legal or illegal drugs, drug use provides them the various positive physiological effects that drugs have. For the people selling drugs, drug use provides them a major source of income and jobs for people working in the legal (alcohol and tobacco) drug industry. Illegal drug use is even functional for the criminal justice system, as it helps provide jobs for the police, court officials, and prison workers who deal with illegal drugs. Legal and illegal drugs also provide jobs for the social service agencies and other organizations and individuals whose work focuses on helping people addicted to a drug. At the same time, drugs, whether legal or illegal, have the many dysfunctions for society that this chapter discussed earlier, and this fact must not be forgotten as we acknowledge the functions of drugs.

Conflict Theory

Conflict theory, which stresses the negative effects of social inequality and the efforts of society's elites to maintain their position, helps us understand drug use in at least three respects. First, and as noted just earlier, much drug use in poor urban areas results from the poverty, racial inequality, and other conditions affecting people in these locations. They turn to illegal drugs partly to feel better about their situation, and partly because the illegal drug market is a potentially great source of income that does not require even a high school diploma.

Second, racial/ethnic prejudice and inequality help determine why some drugs are illegal as well as the criminal penalties for these drugs. For example, the legal penalties for crack have been much harsher, gram for gram, than those for powder cocaine, even though the two drugs are pharmacologically identical. Crack users traditionally have tended to be poor, urban, African Americans, while powder cocaine users have tended to be whites, many of them at least fairly wealthy. Other evidence for this argument of conflict theory is seen in the history of American drug use. As we discussed earlier, racial/ethnic prejudice led common drugs in the 19th century to become illegal: prejudice against Chinese immigrants for opium, prejudice against African Americans for cocaine, and prejudice against Mexican Americans for marijuana.

Third, conflict theory emphasizes the huge impact that multinational corporations have by marketing and selling the legal drugs—alcohol, tobacco, and many prescription drugs—that often have harmful individual and societal consequences. They also spend billions of dollars to lobby Congress. These actions illustrate conflict theory's critical view of the role that corporations play in today's society.

Symbolic Interactionism

Given its focus on social interaction, symbolic interactionism understands drug use as a behavior arising from an individual's interaction with people who engage in drug use. From this type of social interaction, an individual learns how to use a drug and also learns various attitudes that justify drug use and define the effects of a drug as effects that are enjoyable.

A classic study reflecting this approach is Howard S. Becker's (1953)[48] "Becoming a Marihuana User." Becker wrote that someone usually begins smoking marijuana in the presence of friends who are experienced marijuana users. This social interaction, he argued, is critical for new users to wish to continue using marijuana. To want to do so, they must learn three behaviors or perceptions from friends who are "turning them on" to marijuana use. First, they must learn how to smoke a joint (marijuana cigarette) by deeply inhaling its smoke and holding in the smoke before exhaling. Second, they must perceive that the effects they feel after smoking enough marijuana (spatial distortion, hunger pangs, short-term memory loss) signify that they are *stoned* (under the influence of marijuana); their friends typically tell them that if they are feeling these effects, they are indeed stoned. Third, they must learn to define these effects as pleasurable; if people suddenly experience spatial distortion, intense hunger, and memory loss, they might very well worry they are having huge problems! To prevent this from happening, their friends say things to them such as, "Doesn't that feel great!" This and similar comments help reassure the new users that the potentially worrisome effects they are experiencing are in fact very enjoyable effects.

Key Takeaways

- Biological theories assume that some people are especially vulnerable to drug addiction for genetic reasons.
- A popular set of psychological theories assumes that drug addiction results from certain personality traits and problems.
- Sociological theories attribute drug use to various aspects of the social environment, including peer influences, weak social bonds, and the larger drug culture.

For Your Review

1. When you think about the reasons for drug use and addiction, do you think biological factors, psychological factors, or the social environment play the most important role? Explain your answer.
2. Write a brief essay in which you discuss a time when your friends influenced you, or someone else you know, to use a legal or illegal drug.

7.5 Drug Policy and the War on Illegal Drugs

Learning Objectives

1. Explain whether the DARE program is effective.
2. Outline the goals and examples of a harm reduction approach to drug use.
3. List the problems arising from the current legal war on illegal drugs.

For many decades, the United States has used several strategies to try to deal with drugs. These strategies generally fall into four categories: treatment, prevention, harm reduction, and, for certain drugs, criminalization and the use of the criminal justice system or, as we will call it, the war on illegal drugs. We now turn to these strategies.

Treatment

Treatment programs are intended for people who already are using drugs, perceive they have a drug problem, and want to reduce or eliminate their drug use. This strategy is probably familiar to most readers, even if they have not used drugs themselves or at least have not had the benefit of a treatment program. Treatment programs often involve a group setting, but many drug users also receive individual treatment from a psychiatrist, psychologist, or drug counselor. Perhaps the most famous treatment program is Alcoholics Anonymous, a program that involves alcoholics meeting in a group setting, acknowledging their drinking problem and its effects on family members and other loved ones, and listening to each other talk about their situations. Other group settings are residential settings, sometimes called *detox units*. In these settings, people check themselves into an institution and stay there for several weeks until they and the professionals who treat them are satisfied that they can leave.

The various forms of treatment can be very effective for some addicts and less effective or not effective at all for other addicts; most treatment programs have a high failure rate (Goode 2012).[49] A sociological perspective suggests that however effective treatment might be for some people, the origins of drug use ultimately lie in the larger society—its social structure, social interaction, and the drug culture—and that these roots must be addressed for serious reductions in drug use to occur.

The Betty Ford Center, named after First Lady Betty Ford, who acknowledged her alcoholism, is a residential detox unit for people with alcohol and other drug problems.

Source: Image courtesy of Betty Ford Center. Retrieved from: https://commons.wikimedia.org/wiki/File:BETTYFORD.jpg.

Prevention

Because it is always best to try to prevent a problem before it begins, an important strategy to deal with drug use involves prevention. The major prevention strategies involve drug education or drug testing (Faupel et al. 2014).[50] Many education-based prevention programs focus on children and adolescents. This focus reflects the fact that use of most drugs begins during adolescence, and that if adolescents do not begin using drugs during this period of their lives, they are much less likely to do so when they become adults. Some education strategies follow what is called an *informational model*: They involve public service advertising, the distribution of drug pamphlets in medical offices, and other such efforts. Several studies question the effectiveness of strategies based on this model (Faupel et al. 2014).[51]

Other education programs take place in the secondary school system and on college campuses. The most famous such program is almost certainly DARE (Drug Abuse Resistance Education), which involves police officers speaking to young children, usually those in fifth and sixth grade. DARE programs have been carried out in several thousand schools across the nation. However, several studies find that DARE programs do not generally reduce subsequent drug use among the children who attend them compared to children who do not attend them (Ingraham 2017).[52]

Drug testing is very common in today's society, and you may well have been required to have a drug test as part of an application for a job, involvement in a school sport, or other activity. Drug testing is expensive, and many critics say it is not cost-effective in view of the low prevalence of illegal drug use in the United States (Faupel et al. 2014).[53]

Harm Reduction

harm reduction

A strategy that attempts to minimize the harm caused by drugs; an example includes the provision of sterile needles to heroin users.

A third strategy involves **harm reduction**. As this term implies, this strategy attempts to minimize the harm caused by drugs. It recognizes that many people will use drugs despite efforts, including arrest and prosecution for illegal drugs, to prevent them from doing so. Our nation is currently using a harm reduction approach with regard to alcohol and tobacco. It recognizes that tens of millions of people use these products, and designated-driving programs and other efforts try to minimize the considerable harm these two drugs cause.

A specific harm reduction strategy with regard to illegal drugs is the provision of clean, sterile needles for people who inject themselves with heroin, cocaine/crack, or other drugs. Many of these users share needles, and this sharing spreads HIV, hepatitis, and other diseases. If they have a supply of sterile needles, the reasoning goes, the transmission of these diseases will be reduced even if use of the drugs is not reduced.

drug courts

Courts in which drug offenders who have been arrested and found guilty are sentenced to drug treatment and counseling rather than to jail or prison.

Another harm reduction strategy involves the use of **drug courts**, which began in the 1990s and now number more than 2,500 across the United States. In these courts, drug offenders who have been arrested and found guilty are sentenced to drug treatment and counseling rather than jail or prison. Evaluation studies show that the courts save much money compared to imprisoning drug offenders and that they are more effective than imprisonment in reducing the offenders' drug habit (Cheesman et al. 2016).[54]

People Making a Difference

The Law Enforcement Action Partnership

The Law Enforcement Action Partnership (LEAP), formerly called Law Enforcement Against Prohibition, is an organization of current and former police and other criminal justice professionals, including prosecutors, judges, and FBI agents, who advocate for decriminalizing and regulating illegal drugs as part of a larger strategy of criminal justice reform. Because many of these professionals were on the front lines in the war against drugs and often put their lives in danger, their views about drug policy cannot be dismissed lightly.

According to LEAP's website, it "recognizes that drugs can be dangerous and addictive. Reasonable regulation should protect public health and include age restrictions on drug sales and use." It also "argues that as the government ends prohibition, it should release drug offenders, expunge their records, and restore their civil rights. However, we believe that people using alcohol or other drugs must be held accountable for the harms caused to others while under the influence."

One LEAP member is MacKenzie Allen, a retired deputy sheriff who worked in Los Angeles and Seattle, including time as an undercover agent who bought illegal drugs and made countless arrests for drug offenses. Although Allen strongly disapproves of drug use, he also says that the drug problem is best understood as a public health problem, not a legal problem. He notes that the United States has lowered cigarette use through public education and without outlawing cigarettes. "Can you imagine the mayhem had we outlawed cigarettes?" he once wrote. "Can you envision the 'cigarette cartels' and the bloodbath that would follow? Yet, thanks to a public awareness campaign we've made a huge dent in tobacco use without arresting a single cigarette smoker."

Allen adds that most of the problems associated with illegal drug use are actually the result of the laws against drugs. These laws create a huge illegal market, much of it involving violent cartels, he says, that promises strong profits for the manufacturers and sellers of illegal drugs. He thinks that the war on drugs has been far too expensive and has overcrowded the nation's jails and prisons.

As Allen's comments indicate, the legal war on drugs has had many costs. It is difficult to know what to do about illegal drugs, but in bringing these costs to the attention of elected officials and the American public, the Law Enforcement Action Partnership is making a difference. For further information about LEAP, visit https://lawenforcementactionpartnership.org/.

Sources: Allen 2017; Law Enforcement Action Partnership, 2019[55]

The Legal War on Illegal Drugs

The most controversial drug strategy involves the legal war on illegal drugs, involving the use of the police and the rest of the criminal justice system to arrest and punish the users, manufacturers, and sellers of illegal drugs. As the brief history of drug use at the beginning of this chapter indicated, the United States has banned certain drugs since the late 19th century, and it accelerated this effort during the 1970s and 1980s as concern grew about heroin, crack, and other drugs.

In judging this long-standing approach, two considerations should be kept in mind (Meier and Geis 2006).[56] One consideration is the *philosophical* question of the extent to which the government in a free society should outlaw behaviors that may be harmful even if people (let's assume we are talking about legal adults) want to engage in them. Americans do all kinds of things that may harm themselves and that may directly or indirectly harm other people. For example, many Americans eat high amounts of candy, ice cream, potato chips, hamburgers, and other high-fat and processed food that causes obesity, great harm to individual health, premature death and bereavement, and tens of billions of dollars in health costs and lost productivity annually. Although obesity almost certainly causes more harm overall than illegal drugs, no one is about to say that consumption of these food items should be banned or restricted for adults. Americans also engage in many other activities that can be very harmful, including downhill skiing, contact sports, skydiving, and any number of other activities, but no one is about to say that we should be prohibited from engaging in these efforts. Where is the logic, then, in allowing all these behaviors and in not allowing the use of certain drugs? A philosophical argument can be made that all drug use should, in fact, be allowed in a free society (Husak 2002),[57] and perhaps this is an issue you and your classmates will want to discuss.

The second consideration is the *social science* question of whether laws against drugs do more good than harm, or more harm than good. In a rational society, if a law or policy does more good than harm, then we should have the law or policy. However, if it does more harm than good, however much good it might do, then we should not have it, because the harm outweighs the good.

In considering this issue, critics of drug laws say they do much more harm than good, and they often cite Prohibition as an example of this dynamic. Prohibition was repealed because our society decided it was doing much more harm than good and was thus a "triumphant failure," as one author has called this period of our history (Okrent 2011:67).[58] Prohibition caused several harms: (1) the rise of organized crime to earn illegal profits from the manufacture, distribution, and sale of alcohol; (2) the violence and murder among organized crime gangs that fought each other over drug "turf"; (3) the wounding and death of innocent bystanders from gunfights between organized crime gangs; (4) the wounding and murder of police officers who enforced Prohibition; (5) rampant corruption among police officers and political officials who took money from organized crime to ignore violations of Prohibition; and (6) the expenditure of much time, money, and energy by the criminal justice system to enforce Prohibition.

Prohibition did reduce drinking and the violence associated with drinking. But some scholars say that the organized crime violence caused by Prohibition was so common and deadly that the homicide rate grew during Prohibition rather than lessening (Jensen 2000),[59] though other scholars dispute this finding (Caulkins et al. 2016).[60] In yet another problem, many people during Prohibition became sick and/or died from drinking tainted liquor. Because alcohol was no longer regulated, illegal alcohol often contained, by accident or design, dangerous substances. As an example, fifteen thousand people in the Midwest became sick with a severe neurological problem after drinking an illegal alcohol laced with a paint thinner chemical (Genzlinger 2011).[61]

Critics of today's legal war on illegal drugs say it has reproduced the same problems that Prohibition produced (Drug Policy Alliance 2017).[62] Among these problems are the following:

One of the harms associated with the war on drugs is that police officers die in the line of duty when they are killed by drug sellers or users.

Source: © Thinkstock

- Drug gangs and individual drug sellers engage in deadly fights with each other and also kill or wound police officers and other law enforcement personnel who fight the war on drugs.

- Many innocent bystanders, including children, are wounded or killed by stray bullets.

- Many police officers take bribes to ignore drug law violations and/or sell drugs confiscated from dealers.

- The criminal justice system and other agencies spend much time, money, and energy in the war against illegal drugs, just as they did during Prohibition. Enforcing drug laws costs more than $47 billion annually. Police and other law enforcement personnel make more than 1.6 million arrests annually for drug offenses, including 1.4 million only for possession; 600,000 of these possession arrests involved marijuana possession. Some 450,000 people are in prison or jail for drug offenses (Drug Policy Alliance 2019).[63]

- The drug war has focused disproportionately on African Americans and Latinxs and greatly increased their numbers who have gone to jail or prison. Even though illegal drug use is no more common among African Americans than among whites, the arrest rate for drug offenses is much higher for African Americans than the rate for whites. Partly because of the drug war, about one-third of young African American men have prison records.

- Many of the annual deaths from illegal drug use stem from the fact that the drugs are illegal. Because they are illegal, they may contain dangerous substances that can be fatal, just as in Prohibition. In addition, some illegal drug users overdose because they underestimate the purity of a drug.

Because of all these problems, drug law critics say, the United States should legalize marijuana, the most benign illegal drug, and seriously consider legalizing some or all other illegal drugs.

The War on Drugs Is Racist

One problem of the legal war against illegal drugs is that it has focused disproportionately on African Americans and Latinxs, even though these populations do not have higher rates of illegal drug use than white Americans have.

View the video online at: http://www.youtube.com/embed/wONAqaxgloo?rel=0

Proponents of the drug war reply that if drugs were legalized or decriminalized (still against the law, but violations would be treated like traffic offenses), many more people would use the newly legal drugs, and the problems these drugs cause would increase. Responding to this argument, drug law critics say it is not at all certain that drug use would increase if drugs were legalized. To support their view, they cite two pieces of evidence.

First, illegal drugs are already relatively easy to obtain and use without fear of arrest. If people have decided not to use illegal drugs now, it is unlikely they will use them if the drugs were legalized.

Second, marijuana use in the United States decreased in the 1970s and 1980s after several states decriminalized it. International evidence is also instructive: Marijuana use also declined in the Netherlands after they decriminalized the drug in the 1970s, and after Portugal decriminalized possession of all drugs in 2001, teenage drug use declined (see "Lessons from Other Societies").

At this point, it is impossible to know how much, if at all, the use of illegal drugs would rise if they were legalized. Critics of the drug war say that even if the use of drugs did rise, the benefits of legalizing or decriminalizing them would still outweigh the disadvantages (Feiling 2010),[64] which is evidently what the United States decided when it repealed Prohibition.

Lessons from Other Societies

What Happened after the Netherlands and Portugal Decriminalized Drugs?

As the United States ponders its drug policy, the experiences of the Netherlands and Portugal provide some provocative lessons.

The Netherlands decriminalized drugs in 1976. Under the Netherlands' policy, although criminal penalties remain for possessing hard drugs (cocaine, heroin, etc.) and large quantities of marijuana, drug users are not normally arrested for possessing drugs, but they must receive drug treatment if they are arrested for another reason. Drug sellers are not normally arrested for selling small amounts of drugs, but they may be arrested for selling them in large amounts. Marijuana use in the Netherlands dropped in the immediate years after it was decriminalized, and the rate of its use is lower than the U.S. rate.

In 2001, Portugal became the first European nation to remove all criminal penalties for drug possession. Portugal took this step because it reasoned that fear of arrest keeps drug addicts from seeking help and because it recognized that drug treatment costs far less than imprisonment. Anyone convicted of drug possession is sent for drug treatment, but the person may refuse treatment without any penalty.

In the first 5 years after Portugal decriminalized all drug possession, teenaged illegal drug use declined, new HIV infections from sharing needles declined, the prison population declined, deaths from drug overdoses declined, and the number of drug addicts receiving treatment increased.

Although the Netherlands, Portugal, and other Western European nations certainly differ from the United States in many ways, their experience strongly suggests that decriminalization of drugs may cause much more good than harm. If so, the United States has important lessons to learn from their experiences.

Sources: Ingraham 2015; MacCoun 2011; Drug Policy Alliance 2019[65]

Key Takeaways

- To deal with drugs, the United States has used several strategies, including treatment, prevention, harm reduction, and the legal war on illegal drugs.
- According to its critics, the war on illegal drugs has done much more harm than good and in this respect is repeating the example of Prohibition.

For Your Review

1. Do you think the United States should make sterile needles and syringes freely available to people who are addicted to drugs that are injected? Why or why not?
2. Do you agree or disagree that the war on illegal drugs is doing more harm than good? Explain your answer.

7.6 Reducing Drug Use

Learning Objectives

1. Explain the problems associated with arresting hundreds of thousands of people for drug possession.
2. List any three specific measures that may help deal with the drug problem.

As you may have already noticed and will notice again, the other chapters in this book usually present a fairly optimistic assessment when they discuss prospects for addressing the social problem discussed in each chapter. They point to the experience of other nations that do a good job of addressing the social problem, they cite social science evidence that points to solutions for addressing the problem, and they generally say that the United States could address the problem if it had the wisdom to approach it appropriately and to spend sufficient sums of money.

This chapter will not end with an optimistic assessment for addressing the drug problem. The reason for this lack of optimism is that what's past is prologue: People have enthusiastically used drugs since prehistoric times and show no signs of reducing their drug use. Many and perhaps most scholars think the legal war on drugs has had little, if any, impact on drug use (Caulkins and Reuter 2017; Walker 2015),[66] and many scholars recognize that this war brought with it the many disadvantages cited in the previous section. As Kleiman et al. (2011:xvi)[67] observe, "Our current drug policies allow avoidable harm by their ineffectiveness and create needless suffering by their excesses."

A growing number of people in the political world agree. In 2011, the Global Commission on Drug Policy issued a major report on the world's antidrug efforts. The commission comprised nineteen members, including a former United Nations secretary general, a former U.S. secretary of state, a former chair of the U.S. Federal Reserve, and former presidents or prime ministers of Brazil, Colombia, Greece, Mexico, and Switzerland. The commission's report called for a drastic rethinking of current drug policy: "The global war on drugs has failed, with devastating consequences for individuals and societies around the world...Fundamental reforms in national and global drug control policies are urgently needed" (Global Commission on Drug Policy 2011:3).[68] Decriminalization and even legalization of illegal drugs should be seriously considered, the report concluded.

Given this backdrop, many drug experts question whether our current drug policies make sense. They add that the best approach our society could take would be to expand the prevention, treatment, and harm reduction approaches discussed earlier: Because drugs will always be with us, our society should do what it can to minimize the many harms that drugs cause. Drug education prevention and drug treatment programs should thus be expanded, sterile needles should be made available for drug addicts, and drug courts should be used for a greater number of drug offenders.

Beyond these approaches, some experts say marijuana use should be decriminalized and that decriminalization of other drugs should be seriously considered. If marijuana were not only decriminalized but also legalized and taxed, it is estimated that this new tax revenue would amount to $8.7 billion annually and that about $8.7 billion annually would also be saved in reduced law enforcement costs, for a total of more than $17 billion in new funds that could be used for drug prevention, drug treatment, and other needs (Kristof 2010).[69] Many Americans agree with these experts: In a 2018 national survey, 62 percent of the public favored legalizing marijuana, while 34 percent opposed legalizing it (Geiger 2019).[70]

More generally, these experts say, it makes little sense to arrest some 1.4 million people each year for drug possession and to put many of them in jail or prison. We do not arrest and imprison alcoholics and cigarette smokers; instead we try to offer them various kinds of help, and we should do the same for people who are addicted to other kinds of drugs. If arrest and imprisonment must continue, these measures should be reserved for sellers of large quantities of illegal drugs, not for the people who use the drugs or for those who sell only small quantities. When low-level drug dealers are imprisoned, they are simply replaced on the street by new dealers. Providing low-level dealers with alternative sentencing would greatly reduce the number of imprisoned dealers, saving considerable incarceration costs, without making illegal drugs more available.

In addition to all these measures, several other steps might well reduce certain kinds of drug use or at least reduce the harm that both drugs and our current drug policies cause (Caulkins and Reuter 2017; Kleiman et al. 2011).[71] These steps include the following:

1. *Providing legally prescribed heroin and/or substitute opiates, including methadone, for heroin addicts.* This provision has proven effective in several other nations.

2. *Encouraging primary care physicians and other health-care providers to screen more carefully for substance abuse.*

3. *Basing drug sentencing less on the quantity of illegal drugs sold and more on the level of violence in which some drug sellers engage.*

4. *Abandoning DARE.* According to Kleiman et al. (2011:201),[72] "The continued dominance in school-based drug education of DARE—a program that has never been shown to actually reduce drug use—is a scandal." They instead recommend school-based programs that help

children develop self-control and prosocial behavior, as these programs have also been shown to reduce children's subsequent drug use.

5. *Following the psychological principle of operant conditioning by providing drug addicts small cash payments for clean drug tests, as these rewards have been shown to be effective.*

6. *Fully reintegrating former drug dealers and recovering drug addicts into society.* They should have full access to public housing, educational loans, and other benefits, and they should be allowed to vote in states that now do not let them vote.

7. *Raising alcohol taxes.* According to Kleiman et al. (2011),[73] tripling the alcohol tax would especially reduce drinking by heavy drinkers and by minors, and it would reduce the number of homicides by 1,000 annually and the number of motor vehicle accidents by 2,000 annually. The new tax money could also help fund alcohol treatment and prevention programs. "In the entire field of drug-abuse control," Kleiman et al. (2011:204)[74] write, "there is no bargain as attractive as a higher alcohol tax."

8. *Prohibiting alcohol sales to anyone who has engaged in drunk driving or who has committed violence under the influence of alcohol.* For this ban to work, everyone who wants to buy alcohol would have to show an ID, and those prohibited from buying alcohol would have that indicated on their ID. This ban would certainly be unpopular among the many drinkers who drink responsibly, but it would reduce the great harm that alcohol causes.

9. *Allowing marijuana users to grow their own cannabis or to buy it from small growers.* This would reduce the sales of cannabis, and thus its profits, from the organized crime groups and the Mexican cartels that now provide much of the marijuana used in the United States.

10. *Raising the cigarette tax.* Some states already have high cigarette taxes, but several states have low cigarette taxes. Raising the taxes in the low-tax states would reduce cigarette smoking in these states. The new tax revenue could be used to fund treatment programs that help reduce smoking.

Key Takeaways

- Critics of the war on drugs say that people who use illegal drugs should be treated, not arrested, just as people who use alcohol and tobacco are treated, if they seek treatment, rather than arrested.
- Specific measures that could help address the drug problem include providing legally prescribed heroin or substitute opiates for heroin addicts and raising the alcohol tax.

For Your Review

1. Do you think that alcohol taxes should be raised? Why or why not?
2. Do you favor decriminalization of marijuana? Explain your answer.

7.7 End-of-Chapter Material

Summary

1. Humans have used drugs of various types since prehistoric times. Alcohol has been a common drug in the United States since the colonial period, and opium, marijuana, and heroin were common legal drugs in the late 19th century.

2. The distinction between legal and illegal drugs lacks a logical basis. Alcohol and tobacco kill many more people than all illegal drugs combined. In the wake of the COVID-19 pandemic, alcohol experts worried that social distancing, however necessary, would put recovering alcoholics at risk for relapsing into heavy drinking.

3. The use of several drugs is socially patterned. Males are more likely than females to use drugs, and religious people are less likely to use them than those who are less religious. The differences that race/ethnicity, education, and region of country make for drug use depends on the type of drug.

4. Biological theories assume that drug addiction results from a genetic predisposition, while psychological theories attribute drug use to certain personality traits and to positive reinforcement.

5. Sociological theories attribute drug use to peer and cultural influences. A sociological perspective suggests that the ultimate roots of drug use lie in the social environment rather than inside the individual.

6. Major approaches to dealing with drugs include treatment, prevention, harm reduction, and the use of the criminal justice system for illegal drugs. Critics of the war on drugs say that it does more harm than good, and they urge that serious consideration be given to decriminalizing marijuana and perhaps other drugs.

Using What You Know

A college friend of yours seems to drink a lot most nights and even goes to class some mornings hung over. You are concerned about your friend, and have begun to suggest that your friend have only a couple drinks when you're both out for the evening. Unfortunately, your friend has just laughed you off. What, if anything, do you do?

What You Can Do

To help deal with the societal and individual problems caused by alcohol and other drugs, you may wish to do any of the following:

1. Volunteer for a local agency that helps teenagers or adults who have a problem with alcohol or other drugs.

2. Start or join in efforts on your campus to encourage responsible drinking.

3. Start a group to encourage your state to raise taxes on alcohol and cigarettes.

Endnotes

1. Pfleger, Paige. (2019, July 29). "Ohio Opens School for Students with Addiction." *Side Effects Public Media*. Retrieved from: https://www.sideeffectspublicmedia.org/post/ohio-opens-school-students-addiction.

2. Kleiman, Mark A.R., Jonathan P. Caulkins and Angela Hawken. 2011. *Drugs and Drug Policy: What Everyone Needs to Know*. New York: Oxford University Press.

3. Faupel, Charles E., Alan M. Horowitz and Greg S. Weaver. 2014. The Sociology of American Drug Use, 3rd Ed. New York: Oxford University Press; Goodman, Jordan, Andrew Sherratt and Paul e. Lovejoy, eds. 2007. *Consuming Habits: Drugs in History and Anthropology*. New York: Routledge.

4. Page, Bryan and Merrill Singer. 2010. *Comprehending Drug Use: Ethnographic Research at the Social Margins*. New Brunswick, NJ: Rutgers University Press.

5. Goode, Erich. 2008. *Deviant Behavior*, 8th ed. Upper Saddle River, NJ: Prentice Hall

6. Gately, Iain. 2001. *Tobacco: The Story of How Tobacco Seduced the World*. New York: Grove Press.

7. Genzlinger, Neil. 2011. "Bellying up to the Time When America Went Dry." *The New York Times* October 1:C1.

8. Williams, Ian. 2006. *Rum: A Social and Sociable History of the Real Spirit of 1776*. New York: Nation Books.

9. Faupel, Charles E., Alan M. Horowitz and Greg S. Weaver. 2014. *The Sociology of American Drug Use*, 3rd Ed. New York: Oxford University Press.

10. Brecher, Edward M. 1973. *Licit and Illicit Drugs*. Boston: Little, Brown.

11. Musto, David F. 1999. *The American Disease: Origins of Narcotic Control*. New York: Oxford University Press.

12. Edgerton, Robert. 1976. *Deviance: A Cross-Cultural Perspective*. Menlo Park, CA: Cummings Publishing Company.

13. Kleiman, Mark A.R., Jonathan P. Caulkins and Angela Hawken. 2011. *Drugs and Drug Policy: What Everyone Needs to Know*. New York: Oxford University Press.

14. Centers for Disease Control and Prevention. 2018. "Alcohol and Public Health: Fact Sheets-Alcohol Use and Your Health."https://www.cdc.gov/alcohol/fact-sheets/alcohol-use.htm; Centers for Disease Control and Prevention. 2019. "Smoking & Tobacco Use: Fast Facts."https://www.cdc.gov/tobacco/data_statistics/fact_sheets/fast_facts/index.htm.

15. Kochanek, Kenneth D., Sherry L. Murphy, Jiaquan Xu and Elizabeth Arias. 2019. "Deaths: Final Data for 2017." *National Vital Statistics Reports* 68(9):1-76.

16. Harvard T.H. Chan School of Public Health. 2019. *Alcohol: Balancing Risks and Benefits*. Retrieved from https://www.hsph.harvard.edu/nutritionsource/healthy-drinks/drinks-to-consume-in-moderation/alcohol-full-story/.

17. Morris, Seren. 2019. US Alcohol Sales Increased by 5.1% in 2018. *The Drinks Business* January 17:https://www.thedrinksbusiness.com/2019/01/us-alcohol-sales-increased-by-5-1-in-2018/

18. U.S. Department of Agriculture. 2018. *Food Expenditure Series*. Retrieved from https://www.ers.usda.gov/data-products/food-expenditure-series/.

19. American Beverage Licensees. 2018. *America's Beer, Wine & Spirits Retailers Create 2.03 Million Jobs & $122.63 Billion in Direct Economic Impact*. October 23: https://www.ablusa.org/americas-beer-wine-spirits-retailers-create-2-03-million-jobs-122-63-billion-in-direct-economic-impact/.

20. American Medical Association. 2004. *Alcohol Industry 101: Its Structure & Organization*. Chicago, IL: Author.

21. White, Aaron M., Megan E. Slater, Grace Ng, Ralph Hingson and Rosalind Breslow. 2018. "Trends in Alcohol-Related Emergency Department Visits in the United States: Results from the Nationwide Emergency Department Sample, 2006 to 2014." *Alcoholism: Clinical & Experimental Research* 42(2):352-59.

22. Centers for Disease Control and Prevention. 2019. "Impaired Driving: Get the Facts." https://www.cdc.gov/motorvehiclesafety/impaired_driving/impaired-drv_factsheet.html; Ford, Jessie V. 2017. "Sexual Assault on College Hookups: The Role of Alcohol and Acquaintances." *Sociological Forum* 32(2):381-405. doi: 10.1111/socf.12335.

23. Sacks, Jeffrey J., Katherine R. Gonzales, Ellen E. Bouchery, Laura E. Tomedi and Robert D. Brewer. 2015. "2010 National and State Costs of Excessive Alcohol Consumption." *American Journal of Preventive Medicine* 49(5):e73-e79.

24. Santhnam, Laura. 2020. "Why Covid-19 Can Be 'Toxic' for People in Alcohol Recovery." *PBS* April 23:https://www.pbs.org/newshour/health/why-covid-19-can-be-toxic-for-people-in-alcohol-recovery.

25. Lipari, Rachel N. and Struther L. Van Horn. 2017. "Children Living with Parents Who Have a Substance Use Disorder." *The CBHSQ Report* August 24: https://www.samhsa.gov/data/sites/default/files/report_3223/Short-Report-23.html; Tagliareni, Sonia. 2018. "Alateen." *DrugRehab.com* May 31:https://www.drugrehab.com/support/alateen/.

26. Lipari, Rachel N. and Beda Jean-Francois. 2016. "A Day in the Life of College Students Aged 18-22: Substance Use Facts." *The CBHSQ Report* May 26:https://www.samhsa.gov/data/sites/default/files/report_2361/ShortReport-61.html.

27. Center for Science in the Public Interest. (2008). *Binge drinking on college campuses*. Retrieved September 20, 2011, from http://www.cspinet.org/booze/collfact1.htm; National Center on Addiction and Substance Abuse. (2007). *Wasting the best and the brightest: Substance abuse at America's colleges and universities*. New York, NY: Author.

28. American Heart Association. 2020. "The Ugly Truth about Vaping." Retrieved on March 20, 2020 from https://www.heart.org/en/healthy-living/healthy-lifestyle/quit-smoking-tobacco/the-ugly-truth-about-vaping.

29. King, B., Dube, S., Kaufmann, R., Shaw, L., & Pechacek, T. (2011). Vital signs: Current cigarette smoking among adults aged ≥18 years—United States, 2005–2010. *Morbidity and Mortality Weekly Report, 60*(35), 1207–1212.

30. Centers for Disease Control and Prevention. 2019. "Smoking & Tobacco Use: Fast Facts."https://www.cdc.gov/tobacco/data_statistics/fact_sheets/fast_facts/index.htm.

31. Centers for Disease Control and Prevention. 2011. *Economic Facts about US Tobacco Production and Use*. Retrieved from http://www.cdc.gov/tobacco/data_statistics/fact_sheets/economics/econ_facts/.

32. Centers for Disease Control and Prevention. 2019. "Economic Trends in Tobacco."https://www.cdc.gov/tobacco/data_statistics/fact_sheets/economics/econ_facts/index.htm.

33. National Institute on Drug Abuse. 2019. *Marijuana*. Retrieved from https://www.drugabuse.gov/publications/research-reports/marijuana/letter-director.

34. Faupel, Charles E., Alan M. Horowitz and Greg S. Weaver. 2014. *The Sociology of American Drug Use*, 3rd Ed. New York: Oxford University Press.

35. Hanson, Glen R., Peter J. Venturelli and Annette E. Fleckenstein. 2012. *Drugs and Society*. Burlington, MA: Jones & Bartlett.

36. Goode, E. 2008. *Drugs in American Society*, 7th ed. New York: McGraw Hill.

37. National Institute on Drug Abuse. 2016. "Cocaine." https://www.drugabuse.gov/publications/research-reports/cocaine/what-cocaine.

38. Goode, Erich. 2008. *Drugs in American Society*, 7th ed. New York: McGraw Hill.

39. Zuger, Abigail. 2011. "A General in the Drug War." *The New York Times* June 14:D1.

40. Ford, Jason A. 2009. "Nonmedical Prescription Drug Use among Adolescents: The Influence of Bonds to Family and School." *Youth & Society* 40(3):336-52.

41. Aulette, Judy Root, Judith Wittner and Kristen Barber. 2019. *Gendered Worlds*. New York: Oxford University Press.

42. Ransome, Yusuf and Stephen E. Gilman. 2016. "The Role of Religious Involvement in Black-White Differences in Alcohol Use Disorders." *Journal of Studies on Alcohol & Drugs* 77(5):792-801.

43. Dick, Danielle M. 2016. "The Genetics of Addiction: Where Do We Go from Here?" *Journal of Studies on Alcohol and Drugs* 77(5):673-75.

44. Hanson, Glen R., Peter J. Venturelli and Annette E. Fleckenstein. 2018. *Drugs and Society*. Burlington, MA: Jones & Bartlett.

45. Fehrman, Elaine, Vincent Egan, Alexander N. Gorban, Jeremy Levesley, Evgeny M. Mirkes and Awaz K. Muhammad. 2019. *Personality Traits and Drug Consumption: A Story Told by Data*. New York: Springer.

46. Currie, Elliott. 1994. *Reckoning: Drugs, the Cities, and the American Future*. New York: Hill and Wang.

47. Hanson, Glen R., Peter J. Venturelli and Annette E. Fleckenstein. 2018. *Drugs and Society*. Burlington, MA: Jones & Bartlett.

48. Becker, H. S. (1953). Becoming a Marihuana User. *American Journal of Sociology*, 59, 235–242.

49. Goode, Erich. 2012. *Drugs in American Society*, 8th ed. New York: McGraw-Hill.

50. Faupel, Charles E., Alan M. Horowitz and Greg S. Weaver. 2014. *The Sociology of American Drug Use*, 3rd Ed. New York: Oxford University Press.

51. Faupel, Charles E., Alan M. Horowitz and Greg S. Weaver. 2014. *The Sociology of American Drug Use*, 3rd Ed. New York: Oxford University Press.

52. Ingraham, Christopher. 2017. "A Brief History of Dare, the Anti-Drug Program Jeff Sessions Wants to Revive." *The Washington Post* July 12:https://www.washingtonpost.com/news/wonk/wp/2017/07/12/a-brief-history-of-d-a-r-e-the-anti-drug-program-jeff-sessions-wants-to-revive/?utm_term=.f7c5e5755fe3.

53. Faupel, Charles E., Alan M. Horowitz and Greg S. Weaver. 2014. *The Sociology of American Drug Use*, 3rd Ed. New York: Oxford University Press.

54. Cheesman, Fred L., Scott E. Graves, Kathryn Holt, Tara L. Kunkel, Cynthia G. Lee and Michelle T. White. 2016. "Drug Court Effectiveness and Efficiency: Findings for Virginia." *Alcoholism Treatment Quarterly* 34(2):143-69. doi: 10.1080/07347324.2016.1148486.

55. Allen, MacKenzie. 2017. "Why This Cop Asked the President About Legalizing Drugs." *The Huffington Post* February 23: http://www.huffingtonpost.com/mackenzie-allen/why-this-cop-asked-the-pr_b_827338.html; Law Enforcement Action Partnership. 2019. *Drug Policy: Our Principles*. Retrieved from https://lawenforcementactionpartnership.org/our-issues/drug-policy/.

56. Meier, Robert F. and Gilbert Geis. 2006. *Criminal Justice and Moral Issues*. New York: Oxford University Press.

57. Husak, Douglas. 2002. *Legalize This! The Case for Decriminalizing Drugs*. New York: Verso Books.

58. Okrent, Daniel. 2011. *Last Call: The Rise and Fall of Prohibition*. New York: Scribner.

59. Jensen, Gary F. 2000. "Prohibition, Alcohol, and Murder: Untangling Counterveiling Mechanisms." *Homicide Studies* 4:18-36.

60. Caulkins, Jonathan P., Beau Kilmer and Mark A. R.Kleiman. 2016. *Marijuana Legalization: What Everyone Needs to Know*. New York: Oxford University Press.

61. Genzlinger, Neil. 2011. "Bellying up to the Time When America Went Dry." *The New York Times* October 1:C1.

62. Drug Policy Alliance. 2017. *It's Time for the U.S. To Decriminalize Drug Use and Possession*. Washington, DC: Drug Policy Alliance.

63. Drug Policy Alliance. 2019. *Drug War Statistics*. Retrieved from http://www.drugpolicy.org/issues/drug-war-statistics.

64. Feiling, Thomas. 2010. *Cocaine Nation: How the White Trade Took over the World*. New York: Pegasus.

65. Drug Policy Alliance. 2019. *Drug Decriminalization in Portugal: Learning from a Health and Human-Centered Approach*. Washington, DC: Drug Policy Alliance; Ingraham, Christopher. 2015. "Why Hardly Anyone Dies from a Drug Overdose in Portugal." *The Washington Post* June 5:https://www.washingtonpost.com/news/wonk/wp/2015/06/05/why-hardly-anyone-dies-from-a-drug-overdose-in-portugal/; MacCoun, Robert J. 2011. "What Can We Learn from the Dutch Cannabis Coffeeshop System?". *Addiction* 106(11):1899-910.

66. Caulkins, Jonathan P. and Peter Reuter. 2017. "Dealing More Effectively and Humanely with Illegal Drugs." *Crime and Justice* 46:95-158; Walker, Samuel. 2015. *Sense and Nonsense About Crime, Drugs, and Communities*. Stamford, CT: Cengage Learning.

67. Kleiman, Mark A.R., Jonathan P. Caulkins and Angela Hawken. 2011. *Drugs and Drug Policy: What Everyone Needs to Know*. New York: Oxford University Press.

68. Global Commission on Drug Policy. 2011. *War on Drugs: Report of the Global Commission on Drug Policy*. Rio de Janeiro, Brazil: Author.

69. Kristof, Nicholas D. 2010. "End the War on Pot." *The New York Times* October 28:A33.

70. Geiger, A. W. 2019. "5 Facts About Marijuana." *Pew Research Center*(June 26):https://www.pewresearch.org/fact-tank/2019/06/26/facts-about-marijuana/.

71. Caulkins, Jonathan P. and Peter Reuter. 2017. "Dealing More Effectively and Humanely with Illegal Drugs." *Crime and Justice* 46:95-158; Kleiman, M. A. R., Caulkins, J. P., & Hawken, A. (2011). *Drugs and drug policy: What everyone needs to know*. New York, NY: Oxford University Press.

72. Kleiman, Mark A.R., Jonathan P. Caulkins and Angela Hawken. 2011. *Drugs and Drug Policy: What Everyone Needs to Know*. New York: Oxford University Press.

73. Kleiman, Mark A.R., Jonathan P. Caulkins and Angela Hawken. 2011. Drugs and Drug Policy: What Everyone Needs to Know. New York: Oxford University Press.

74. Kleiman, Mark A.R., Jonathan P. Caulkins and Angela Hawken. 2011. *Drugs and Drug Policy: What Everyone Needs to Know*. New York: Oxford University Press.

CHAPTER 8
Crime and Criminal Justice

Social Problems in the News

"After Shooting, a Family Mourns Loss of a 2nd Son," the headline said. In Boston, Massachusetts, a young man was murdered in July 2019 only a week before he would have turned 21. The fatal shooting occurred in front of an apartment building in a low-income neighborhood. An older brother of the victim was also fatally shot a decade earlier, only 2 miles from the more recent shooting. Four days before the younger brother's death, he had paid their father a visit. The father recalled, "I walked him home and that was the last time I've seen my son. My son was a good kid. I don't know why this happened to him. This gotta stop. This really got to stop."

Source: Lotan and Ellement 2019[1]

Crime rates apparently declined after the COVID-19 pandemic began in early 2020, because so many people, offenders and non-offenders alike, were staying home (Coyne 2020).[2] Even so, this poignant news account from Boston reminds us that crime continued to afflict many people across the nation during the year before the pandemic and will continue to do so in the years ahead. As a result, you may know several people, perhaps including yourself, who have been victims of a crime. The study of crime bears directly on this book's theme of continuity and change: Crime seems to have always been with us, yet sound social science research points to many programs and policies with great promise for reducing crime if only our nation would undertake them. We begin with some conceptual issues in understanding crime before turning to the types of crime, explanations for crime, and some aspects of the criminal justice system.

8.1 The Problem of Crime

Learning Objectives

1. Understand the extent of public concern about crime.
2. Explain how the news media contribute to myths about crime.
3. Describe how crime in the United States is measured.

Put most simply, **crime** is behavior that is prohibited by the criminal law because it is considered especially harmful or offensive. This simple definition, however, raises many questions:

- Who decides what is offensive or harmful?

- Are some harmful behaviors not considered crimes, and are some crimes not that harmful?

- Are some people more likely than others to be considered criminals because of their gender, race and ethnicity, social class, age, or other aspect of their social backgrounds?

crime

Behavior considered so harmful or offensive that it is banned by the criminal law.

deviance

Behavior that violates norms and arouses negative social reactions.

These questions lie at the heart of the sociological study of deviance, of which crime is a special type. **Deviance** is behavior that violates social norms and arouses strong social disapproval. This definition reflects the common sociological view that deviance is not a quality of a behavior itself but rather the result of what other people think about the behavior. This view is reflected in a famous quote from sociologist Howard S. Becker (1963:9),[3] who wrote several decades ago that "deviance is not a quality of the act the person commits, but rather a consequence of the application by others of rules or sanctions to an 'offender.' The deviant is one to whom that label has been successfully applied; deviant behavior is behavior that people so label."

This definition reminds us that some harmful behaviors, such as white-collar crime, may not be considered deviant and fail to result in severe legal punishment, perhaps because wealthy individuals perform them. It also reminds us that some less harmful behaviors, such as prostitution, may be considered very deviant because the public deems the behavior immoral and because poor people engage in them. As these possibilities suggest, the application of a criminal label to an offender is *problematic*: People arrested and/or convicted of a crime may not have engaged in a very harmful behavior or even in the behavior of which they are suspected, and some people with no criminal record have in fact engaged in harmful and even criminal behavior.

Media Myths of Crime

Although crime is a serious social problem, the news media distort the true nature of crime and thus public perceptions of crime in certain ways (Robinson 2018; Surette 2015).[4]

First, if the television news and newspapers suddenly have several stories about a few sensational crimes, public concern about crime may jump, even though crime in general has not risen at all.

Second, the news media overdramatize crime by reporting it in many news stories. Crime dominates news coverage in many newspapers and television newscasts, and, as just noted, the media may devote much coverage to a few sensational crimes and create the false impression that a "crime wave" is occurring when the crime rate may even be declining.

The news media feature violent crime, even though violent crime comprises only a small portion of all crime.

Source: © Thinkstock

Third, the media devote particularly heavy coverage to violent crime, reflecting the common saying that "if it bleeds, it leads." Reflecting this coverage, many media stories about crime concern homicide, even though homicide comprises less than 1 percent of all crime. More generally, the media's heavy focus on violent crime occurs even though violent crime comprises only about 12–14 percent of all street crimes combined. Media attention to violent crime thus gives the public the false impression that most crime is violent when in fact most crime involves a theft of some sort (*property crime*).

Fourth, the media tend to highlight crimes committed by African Americans or other people of color and crimes with white victims. A greater percentage of crime stories involve people of color as offenders than is true in arrest statistics, and a greater percentage of crime stories also involve whites as victims than is actually true. Reflecting these two trends, crimes in which African Americans are the offenders and whites are the victims also receive disproportionate media coverage, even though most crimes involve offenders and victims of the same race. In all these ways, the news media exaggerate the extent to which people of color commit crimes and the extent to which whites are victims of crimes.

Measuring Crime

It is surprisingly difficult to know how much crime occurs. Crime is not like the weather, when we all can see whether it is raining, snowing, or sunny. Usually when crime occurs, only the criminal and the victim, and sometimes an occasional witness, know about it. We thus have an incomplete picture of the crime problem, but because of various data sources we still have a pretty good understanding of how much crime exists and of who is most likely to commit it and be victimized by it.

The government's primary source of crime data is the **Uniform Crime Reports (UCR)**, published annually by the Federal Bureau of Investigation. The FBI gathers its data from police departments around the country, who tell the FBI about crimes that have come to their attention. The police also tell the FBI whether someone is arrested for the crime and, if so, the person's age, gender, and race. The FBI gathers all these UCR data and reports them in an annual volume called *Crime in the United States.*

Most UCR data concern the so-called **Part I Crimes**, eight felonies that the FBI considers the most serious. Four of these are violent crimes—homicide, rape, aggravated assault, and robbery—and four are property crimes—burglary, larceny (e.g., shoplifting, pickpocketing, purse-snatching), motor vehicle theft, and arson.

According to the FBI, 1,247,321 violent crimes and 7,694,086 property crimes occurred in 2017, for a total of more than 8.9 million offenses. This is the nation's official crime count, and by any standard it is a lot of crime. However, this number is much lower than it should be because *more than half of all crime victims do not report their crimes to the police*, and the police thus do not know about them. These unreported crimes represent "hidden" crimes or, as they are often called, the **dark figure of crime**. Thus, the true crime problem is much greater than suggested by the UCR.

This underreporting of crime represents a major problem for the UCR's validity. Several other problems exist. First, the UCR excludes white-collar crimes and thus diverts attention away from their harm. Second, police practices affect the number of crimes listed in the UCR. For example, the police do not record every report they hear from a citizen as a crime. Sometimes they do not have the time to do so, and sometimes they do not believe the citizen. If they do not record the report, the FBI does not count it as a crime. If the police start recording more reports or fail to record even more reports, the official crime rate will rise or fall, respectively, even though the actual number of crimes has not changed. Third, if crime victims become more or less likely to report their crimes to the police (e.g., the advent of the 911 emergency number may have increased calls to the police), the official crime rate will again change, even if the actual number of crimes has not.

A more accurate picture of crime comes from the **National Crime Victimization Survey (NCVS)**, administered annually to tens of thousands of randomly selected U.S. households. People in the households are asked whether they or their residence has been the victim of several different types of crimes in the past half year. Their responses are then extrapolated to the entire U.S. population to yield fairly accurate estimates of the actual number of crimes occurring in the nation. These estimates are thought to be more accurate than the UCR's figures, even if it is true that victims sometimes might not want to tell NCVS interviewers what happened to them.

Table 8.1 lists the number of street crimes as reported by the UCR and estimated by NCVS. Note that these two crime sources do not measure exactly the same crimes. For example, the NCVS excludes commercial crimes such as shoplifting, while the UCR includes them. The NCVS also includes simple assaults (where someone receives only a minor injury), while the UCR excludes them. These differences notwithstanding, we can still see that the NCVS estimates about twice as many crimes as the UCR reports to us. The *dark figure* of crime is large indeed.

TABLE 8.1 Number of Crimes: Uniform Crime Reports (UCR) and National Crime Victimization Survey (NCVS), 2017

	UCR	NCVS
Violent crime	1,247,321	5,612,670
Property crime	7,694,086	13,340,220
Total	8,941,407	18,952,890

Source: Federal Bureau of Investigation. 2018. *Crime in the United States, 2017*. Washington, DC: Federal Bureau of Investigation; Morgan, Rachel E. and Jennifer L. Truman. 2018. *Criminal Victimization, 2017*. Washington, DC: Bureau of Justice

Uniform Crime Reports (UCR)

The FBI's regular compilation of crime statistics, most of them on Part I crimes.

Part I Crimes

The FBI's term for the major crimes included in the Uniform Crime Reports, including homicide, rape, robbery, aggravated assault, burglary, larceny, motor vehicle theft, and arson.

dark figure of crime

The large number of crimes that do not come to the attention of the police and thus also not to the public.

National Crime Victimization Survey (NCVS)

An annual survey conducted by the U.S. Department of Justice that asks a representative sample of the American public about crimes they have suffered.

Statistics, U.S. Department of Justice.

self-report survey

A survey given to individuals, usually adolescents, that asks them about offenses they have committed and usually about their families and other aspects of their lives.

A third source of crime information is the **self-report survey**. Here subjects, usually adolescents, indicate on an anonymous questionnaire whether and how often they committed various offenses in, say, the past year. Typically, they also answer questions about their family relationships, school performance, and other aspects of their backgrounds. Self-report studies have yielded valuable information about delinquency and explanations of crime. Like the NCVS, they underscore how much crime is committed that does not come to the attention of the police.

Key Takeaways

- Much of the American public is concerned about crime, and many people worry about becoming a victim of various types of crime.
- The news media overdramatize the nature and amount of crime, and they give more attention to crimes involving African Americans and Latinxs as offenders and whites as victims.
- The nation's major source of crime data is the Uniform Crime Reports (UCR). However, many people do not report their crimes to the police, and police practices affect the number of "official" crimes reported by the UCR.

For Your Review

1. Why do you think so many Americans are afraid of crime even though the crime rate has greatly declined since the early 1990s?
2. Why is it difficult to measure crime accurately? Why is the measurement of crime by the FBI inaccurate?

8.2 Types of Crime

Learning Objectives

1. Describe the major aspects of homicide.
2. Discuss evidence indicating that white-collar crime is more serious than street crime.
3. Explain the major issues raised by the concept of consensual crime.

Many types of crime exist. Criminologists commonly group crimes into several major categories: (1) violent crime; (2) property crime; (3) white-collar crime; (4) organized crime; and (5) consensual or victimless crime. Within each category, many more specific crimes exist. For example, violent crime includes homicide, aggravated and simple assault, rape and sexual assault, and robbery, while property crime includes burglary, larceny, motor vehicle theft, and arson. Because a full discussion of the many types of crime would take several chapters or even an entire book or more, we highlight here the most important dimensions of the major categories of crime and the issues they raise for public safety and crime control.

Violent Crime

Even if, as our earlier discussion indicated, the news media exaggerate the problem of violent crime, it remains true that violent crime plagues many communities around the country and is the type of crime that most concerns Americans. The news story that began this chapter reminds us that violent crime is all too real for too many people; it traps some people inside their homes and makes others afraid to let their children play outside or even walk to school. Rape and sexual assault are a common concern for many women, who often must take precautions that men do not think about doing.

Certain aspects of homicide are worth noting (Fox et al. 2019).[5] First, although some homicides are premeditated, most in fact are relatively spontaneous and the result of intense emotions like anger, hatred, or jealousy. Two people may begin arguing for any number of reasons, and things escalate. A fight or use of a weapon may then ensue that results in a fatal injury.

Second, and related to the first aspect, most homicide offenders and victims knew each other before the homicide occurred. Indeed, about three-fourths of all homicides involve nonstrangers, and only one-fourth involve strangers. Although fear of a deadly attack by a stranger dominates the American consciousness, we in fact are much more likely on average to be killed by someone we know than by someone we do not know.

Third, about two-thirds of homicides involve firearms. To be a bit more precise, just over half involve a handgun, and the remaining firearm-related homicides involve a shotgun, rifle, or another undetermined firearm. Combining these first three aspects, then, the most typical homicide involves nonstrangers who have an argument that escalates and then results in the use of deadly force when one of the antagonists uses a handgun.

About two-thirds of homicides involve firearms, and half involve a handgun.

Source: © Thinkstock

Fourth, most homicides (as most violent crime in general) are **intraracial**, meaning that they occur within the same race; the offender *and* victim are of the same race. For single offender/single victim homicides where the race of both parties is known, nearly 90 percent of African American victims are killed by African American offenders, and about 80 percent of white victims are killed by white offenders (Federal Bureau of Investigation 2018).[6] Although whites fear victimization by African Americans more than by whites, whites in fact are much more likely to be killed by other whites than by African Americans. While African Americans do commit about half of all homicides, most of their victims are also African American.

intraracial

In criminology, the commission of crime by offenders against members of their own race or ethnicity.

Fifth, males commit nearly 90 percent of all homicides and females commit only 10 percent. Most sociologists attribute this huge difference to gender socialization and other social factors rather than to biological differences between the sexes.

Sixth, the homicide rate is much higher in large cities than in small towns. In 2017, the homicide rate (number of homicides per 100,000 population) in cities with a population at or over 250,000 was 11.0 percent, compared to only 3.1 percent in towns with a population between 10,000 and 24,999. Thus, the risk for homicide is about 3.5 times in large cities than in small towns. While most people in large cities certainly do *not* die from homicide, where we live still makes a difference in our chances of being victimized by homicide and other crime.

Finally, the homicide rate (and also the violent crime rate more generally) rose in the late 1980s and peaked during the early 1990s before declining sharply until the early 2000s and then leveling off and fluctuating since then. Although debate continues over why the homicide rate declined during the 1990s, many criminologists attribute the decline to a strong economy, an ebbing of gang wars over drug trafficking, and a decline of people in the 15–25 age group that commits a disproportionate amount of crime. These scholars tend to say that rising imprisonment rates played only a small role, if that, in the declining homicide rate (Travis et al. 2014).[7]

Rape and sexual assault were included in Chapter 4's discussion of violence against women as a serious manifestation of gender inequality. As that chapter noted, it is estimated that at least one-fifth of American women have been been raped or sexually assaulted. Like homicide, about three-fourths of all rapes and sexual assaults involve individuals who know each other, not strangers. Women thus have more to fear in this regard from someone they know than from someone they do not know.

Property Crime

As noted earlier, the major property crimes are burglary, larceny, motor vehicle theft, and arson. These crimes are quite common in the United States and other nations and, as Table 8.1 indicated, millions occur annually in this country. Many Americans have installed burglar alarms and other security measures in their homes and similar devices in their vehicles. While property crime by definition does not involve physical harm, it still makes us concerned, in part because it touches so many of us. Although property crime has in fact declined along with violent crime since the early 1990s, it still is considered a major component of the crime problem, because it is so common and produces losses of billions of dollars annually.

Much property crime can be understood in terms of the roles and social networks of property criminals. In this regard, many scholars distinguish between *amateur theft* and *professional theft*. Most property offenders are amateur offenders: They are young and unskilled in the ways of crime, and the amount they gain from any single theft is relatively small. They also do not plan their crimes and instead commit them when they see an opportunity for quick illegal gain. In contrast, professional property offenders tend to be older and quite skilled in the ways of crime, and the amount they gain from any single theft is relatively large. Not surprisingly, they often plan their crimes well in advance. The so-called *cat burglar*, someone who scales tall buildings to steal jewels, expensive artwork, or large sums of money, is perhaps the prototypical example of the professional property criminal. Many professional thieves learn how to do their crimes from other professional thieves, and in this sense they are mentored by the latter just as students are mentored by professors, and young workers by older workers.

White-Collar Crime

If you were asked to picture a criminal in your mind, what image would you be likely to think of first: a scruffy young male with a scowl or sneer on his face, or a handsome, middle-aged man dressed in a three-piece business suit? No doubt the former image would come to mind first, if only because violent crime and property crime dominate newspaper headlines and television newscasts and because many of us have been victims of violent or property crime. Yet white-collar crime is arguably much more harmful than street crime, both in terms of economic loss and of physical injury, illness, and even death.

white-collar crime

Crime committed by people in the course of their occupations; Edwin Sutherland's definition emphasized crime by people of high social status.

What exactly is **white-collar crime**? The most famous definition comes from Edwin Sutherland (1949:9),[8] a sociologist who coined the term in the 1940s and defined it as "a crime committed by a person of respectability and high social status in the course of his occupation." Sutherland examined the behavior of the seventy largest U.S. corporations and found that they had violated the law hundreds of times among them. Several had engaged in crimes during either World War I or II: They provided defective weapons and spoiled food to American troops and even sold weapons to Germany and other nations the United States was fighting.

Although white-collar crime as studied today includes auto shop repair fraud and employee theft by cashiers, bookkeepers, and other employees of relatively low status, most research follows Sutherland's definition by focusing on crime committed by people of "respectability and high social status." Thus, much of the study of white-collar crime today focuses on fraud by physicians, attorneys, and other professionals and on illegal behavior by executives of corporations designed to protect or improve corporate profits (*corporate crime*).

In the study of professional fraud, health-care fraud stands out for its extent and cost (Rosoff et al. 2020).[9] Health-care fraud is thought to amount to tens of billions of dollars annually, compared to around $20 billion for all property crime combined. For example, some physicians bill Medicare and private insurance for services that patients do not really need and may never receive, and medical supply companies sometimes furnish substandard equipment. To compensate for the economic loss it incurs, health-care fraud drives up medical expenses and insurance costs. In this sense, it steals from the public even though no one ever breaks into your house or robs you at gunpoint.

Although health-care and other professional fraud are serious, corporate crime dwarfs all other forms of white-collar crime in the economic loss it incurs and in the death, injury, and illness it causes. Corporate financial crime involves such activities as fraud, price fixing, and false advertising that again cost the public billions of dollars annually. Even worse is **corporate violence**—actions by corporations that kill or maim people or leave them ill. The victims of corporate violence include corporate employees, consumers of corporate goods, and the public as a whole. Annual deaths from corporate violence exceed the number of deaths from homicide, and illness and injury from corporate violence affect an untold number of people every year (Barkan 2018).[10]

corporate violence

Actions by corporations that cause death, injury, or illness.

Employees of corporations suffer from unsafe workplaces in which they are exposed to hazardous conditions and chemicals because their companies fail to take adequate measures to reduce or eliminate this exposure. Such exposure may result in illness, and exposure over many years can result in death. According to a recent estimate, some than 50,000 people die each year from this situation (AFL-CIO 2019),[11] a figure about three times greater than the number of annual homicides. A notorious example of this problem involves the asbestos industry, which industry learned during the 1930s that asbestos exposure could cause fatal lung disease and cancer. Even so, asbestos companies hid evidence of this hazard for more than 3 decades: They allowed their workers to continue to work with asbestos and marketed asbestos as a fire retardant that was widely installed in schools and other buildings. More than 200,000 asbestos workers and members of the public either have already died or are expected to die from asbestos exposure; most or all of these deaths could have been prevented if the asbestos industry had acted responsibly when it first discovered it was manufacturing a dangerous product (Lilienfeld 1991).[12]

The asbestos industry learned in the 1930s that asbestos was a major health hazard, but it kept this discovery a secret for more than 3 decades.

Source: © Thinkstock

Unsafe products also kill or maim consumers. One of the most notorious examples of deaths from an unsafe product involved the Ford Pinto, a car first sold in the early 1970s that was vulnerable to fire and explosion when hit from behind in a minor rear-end collision (Cullen et al. 2006).[13] Ford knew before the Pinto went on the market that its gas tank was unusually vulnerable in a rear-end collision and determined it would take about $11 per car to fix the problem. It then did a cost-benefit analysis to determine whether it would cost more to fix the problem or instead to settle lawsuits after Pinto drivers and passengers died or were burned and injured in rear-end collisions. This analysis indicated that Ford would save about $87 million if it did *not* fix the problem and instead paid out compensation after Pinto drivers and passengers died or got burned. Because Ford made this decision, about five hundred people eventually died in Pinto rear-end collisions and many others were burned. In a more recent example involving vehicles, General Motors and Toyota were both fined a few years ago for hiding evidence of defects that killed dozens of drivers and passengers. In GM vehicles, vehicles suddenly lost power from defective ignition switches, while in Toyotas, defective gas pedals caused sudden acceleration. No executives from either company were imprisoned because of their deadly deceit, and their fines of more than $2 billion combined amounted to only a minuscule fraction of their annual revenues (Harwell 2015; Ivory and Vlasic 2015).[14]

The toll of white-collar crime, both financial and violent, is difficult to estimate, but by all accounts it exceeds the economic loss and death and injury from all street crime combined. White-collar crime is thought to involve an annual economic loss of almost $600 billion annually from corporate fraud, professional fraud, employee theft, and tax evasion and an annual toll of almost 100,000 deaths from workplace-related illness or injury, unsafe products, and preventable environmental pollution. These figures compare to an economic loss of about $20 billion from property crime and a death toll of about 17,000 from homicide (Barkan 2018).[15] Even so, the typical corporate criminal receives much more lenient punishment, if any, than the typical street criminal (Rosoff et al. 2020).[16]

Organized Crime

organized crime

Criminal activity by groups or organizations whose major purpose for existing is to commit such crime.

Organized crime refers to criminal activity by groups or organizations whose major purpose for existing is to commit such crime. When we hear the term "organized crime," we almost automatically think of the so-called Mafia, vividly portrayed in the *Godfather* movies and other films, that comprises several highly organized and hierarchical Italian American "families." Although Italian Americans have certainly been involved in organized crime in the United States, so have Irish Americans, Jews, African Americans, and other ethnicities over the years. The emphasis on Italian domination of organized crime overlooks these other involvements and diverts attention from the actual roots of organized crime.

What are these roots? Simply put, organized crime exists and even thrives because it provides goods and/or services that the public demands. Organized crime flourished during the 1920s because it was all too ready and willing to provide an illegal product, alcohol, that the public continued to demand even after Prohibition began. Today, organized crime earns its money from products and services such as illegal drugs, prostitution, pornography, loan sharking, and gambling. It also began long ago to branch out into legal activities such as trash hauling and the vending industry.

Government efforts against organized crime since the 1920s have focused on arrest, prosecution, and other law-enforcement strategies. Organized crime has certainly continued despite these efforts. This fact leads some scholars to emphasize the need to reduce public demand for the goods and services that organized crime provides. However, other scholars say that reducing this demand is probably a futile or mostly futile task, and they instead urge consideration of legalizing at least some of the illegal products and services (e.g., drugs and prostitution) that organized crime provides. Doing so, they argue, would weaken the influence of organized crime.

Consensual Crime

consensual crime

Illegal behavior in which people participate voluntarily, including drug use, prostitution, and gambling.

Consensual crime (also called *victimless crime*) refers to behaviors in which people engage voluntarily and willingly even though these behaviors violate the law. Illegal drug use, discussed in Chapter 7, is a major form of consensual crime; other forms include prostitution, gambling, and pornography. People who use illegal drugs, who hire themselves out as prostitutes or employ the services of a prostitute, who gamble illegally (although much gambling today is entirely legal), and who use illegal pornography are all doing so because they want to. These behaviors are not entirely victimless, as illegal drug users, for example, may harm themselves and others, and that is why the term *consensual crime* is often preferred over *victimless crime*. As just discussed, organized crime provides some of the illegal products and services that compose consensual crime, but these products and services certainly come from sources other than organized crime.

This issue aside, the existence of consensual crime raises two related questions that Chapter 7 first discussed. First, to what degree should the government ban behaviors that people willingly commit and that generally do not have unwilling victims? Second, do government attempts to ban such behaviors do more good than harm or more harm than good? Chapter 7's discussion of these questions focused on illegal drugs, and in particular on the problems caused by laws against certain drugs, but similar problems arise from laws against other types of consensual crime. For example, laws against prostitution enable pimps to control prostitutes and help ensure the transmission of sexual diseases because condoms are not regularly used.

Critics of consensual crime laws say we are now in a new prohibition and that our laws against illegal drugs, prostitution, and certain forms of gambling are causing the same problems now that the ban on alcohol did during the 1920s and, more generally, cause more harm than good. Proponents of these laws respond that the laws are still necessary as an expression of society's moral values and as a means, however imperfect, of reducing involvement in harmful behaviors.

Key Takeaways

- Most homicides are committed for relatively emotional, spontaneous reasons and between people who knew each other beforehand.
- White-collar crime involves more death, injury, and economic loss than street crime, but the punishment of white-collar crime is relatively weak.
- Consensual crime raises two related issues: (a) To what extent should the government prohibit people from engaging in behavior in which there are no unwilling victims, and (b) do laws against consensual crime do more good than harm or more harm than good?

For Your Review

1. If homicide is a relatively emotional, spontaneous crime, what does that imply for efforts to use harsh legal punishment, including the death penalty, to deter people from committing homicide?
2. Do you think consensual crimes should be made legal? Why or why not?

8.3 Who Commits Crime?

Learning Objectives

1. Explain why males commit more crime than females.
2. Discuss whether social class differences exist in crime rates.
3. Discuss whether racial/ethnic differences exist in crime rates.

While people from all walks of life commit street crime, some people are still more likely than others to break the law because of their social backgrounds. These social backgrounds include their gender, age, social class, urban/rural residence, and race and ethnicity. Despite their inaccuracies, the three data sources discussed in the first section of this chapter all provide a similar picture of what kinds of people, in terms of their social backgrounds, are more or less likely to commit street crime. We briefly discuss each background in turn.

Gender

Simply put, males commit much more crime than females. In UCR data, men comprise about 80 percent of all arrests for violent crime and about 65 percent of all arrests for property crime. (See Figure 8.1.) In the NCVS, victims report that males commit most of the violent crimes they experienced, and self-report studies find that males far outpace females in the commission of serious street offenses. When it comes to breaking the law, crime is a man's world.

FIGURE 8.1 Gender and Arrest (Percentage of All Arrests)

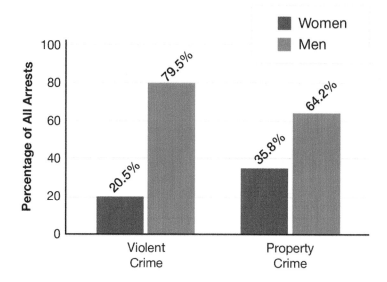

Source: Data from Federal Bureau of Investigation. 2018. *Crime in the United States, 2017.* Washington, DC: Author.

The key question is why such a large gender difference exists (Kruttschnitt 2016).[17] As noted earlier for homicide, most criminologists attribute this difference to gender socialization and other social factors. One of these other factors is the opportunity to commit crime. Studies find that parents watch their daughters more closely than they watch their sons, who are allowed to stay out later at night and thus have more opportunity to break the law.

Age

Age also makes a difference in criminal behavior: Offending rates are highest in the late teens and early 20s and decline thereafter. Accordingly, people in the 15–24 age range account for about one-third or more of all arrests even though they comprise only about 14 percent of the population.

Several factors again seem to account for this pattern (Steffensmeier and Allan 2000; Monahan et al. 2015).[18] First, peer relationships matter more during this time of one's life than later, and peers are also more likely during this period than later to be offenders themselves. For both reasons, our peer relationships during our teens and early 20s are more likely than those in our later years to draw us into crime. Second, adolescents and young adults are more likely than older adults to lack full-time jobs; for this reason, they are more likely to need money and thus to commit offenses to obtain money and other possessions. Third, as we age out of our early 20s, our ties to conventional society increase: Many people marry, have children, and begin full-time employment, though not necessarily in that order. These events and bonds increase our stakes in conformity, to use some social science jargon, and thus reduce our desire to break the law. Fourth, the prefrontal cortex, which governs self-control, in adolescent brains is still biologically immature.

 19-Year-Old Man Arrested in Homicide

Young people, those in the 15–24 age range, commit crime at higher rates than older people. The arrest of a 19-year-old man depicted in this video illustrates this basic fact of criminal behavior.

View the video online at: http://www.youtube.com/embed/MmzytsHQMhk?rel=0

Social Class

Findings on social class differences in crime are less clear than they are for gender or age differences. Arrest statistics and much research indicate that poor people are much more likely than wealthier people to commit street crime. However, some scholars attribute the greater arrests of poor people to social class bias against them. Despite this possibility, most criminologists would probably agree that low-income people are more likely than wealthier people to commit street crime (Bjerk 2007).[19] Reflecting this conclusion, a sociologist once noted, with tongue only partly in cheek, that social scientists know they should not "stroll the streets at night in certain parts of town or even to park there" and that areas of cities that frighten them are "not upper-income neighborhoods" (Stark 1987:894).[20]

Explanations of this relationship center on the effects of poverty, which produces anger, frustration, and economic need and is associated with a need for respect and with poor parenting skills and other problems. All these factors help make low-income children more likely to commit antisocial behavior, including street crime, when they reach adolescence and beyond. These effects combine to lead poor people to be more likely than wealthier people to commit street crime, even if it is true that most poor people do not commit street crime at all.

Although the poor are more likely than the wealthy to commit street crime, it is also true that the wealthy are much more likely to commit white-collar crime, which, as argued earlier, can be much more harmful than street crime. If we consider both street crime and white-collar crime, then there does not appear to be a social class-crime relationship, since the poor have higher rates of the former and the wealthy have higher rates of the latter.

Urban versus Rural Residence

Where we live also makes a difference for our likelihood of committing crime. We saw earlier that big cities have a much higher homicide rate than small towns. This trend exists for violent crime and property crime more generally. Urban areas have high crime rates in part because they are poor, but poverty by itself does not completely explain the urban-rural difference in crime, since many rural areas are poor as well. A key factor that explains the higher crime rates of urban areas is their greater population density (Stark 1987).[21] When many people live close together, they come into contact with one another more often. This fact means that teenagers and young adults have more peers to influence them to commit crime, and it also means that potential criminals have more targets (people and homes) for their criminal activity. Urban areas also have many bars, convenience stores, and other businesses that can become targets for potential criminals; bars, taverns, and other drinking settings may also become settings where tempers flare and violence ensues.

The significance of population density for urban crime rates mirrors that for COVID-19 rates during the 2020 pandemic. During the first few months of the pandemic, these rates were much higher in cities like New York and Detroit than in smaller towns and rural areas (Lopez 2020).[22] If crime is higher in cities because of the greater social interaction that occurs from their population density, then COVID-19 rates were similarly higher in cities partly because of their greater social interaction, which more easily spread the coronavirus amid crowded streets, buses, subways, and other settings. To some extent, then, crime and COVID-19 (as well as other infectious diseases) have the same social roots, even if COVID-19 as a disease was originally a biological phenomenon.

Race and Ethnicity

In discussing who commits crime, any discussion of race and ethnicity is bound to arouse controversy because of the possibility of racial and ethnic stereotyping. But if we can say that men and younger people have relatively high crime rates without necessarily sounding biased against individuals who are male or younger, then it should be possible to acknowledge that certain racial and ethnic groups have higher crime rates without sounding biased against them.

Keeping this in mind, race and ethnicity do seem to be related to criminal offending. In particular, much research finds that African Americans and Latinxs have higher rates of street crime than non-Latinx whites (Barkan 2019),[23] even if almost all African Americans and Latinxs commit no street crime at all. For example, although African Americans comprise about 14 percent of the U.S. population, they account for about 37 percent of all arrests for violent crime (Federal Bureau of Investigation 2018).[24] Similarly, although Latinxs comprise about 17 percent of the population, they account for almost 24 percent of violent crime arrests.

Latinxs also have higher crime rates than non-Latinx whites, but lower rates than those for African Americans. Although racial and ethnic bias by the criminal justice system may account for some of these racial/ethnic differences in offending, most criminologists agree that such differences do in fact exist for serious street crimes (Barkan 2019; Walker et al. 2018).[25]

Why do these differences exist? A racist explanation would attribute them to biological inferiority of the groups, African Americans and Latinxs, with the relatively high rates of offending. Such explanations were popular several generations ago but fortunately lost favor as time passed and attitudes changed. Today, scholars attribute racial/ethnic differences in offending to several sociological factors (Gabbidon and Greene 2019).[26] First, African Americans and Latinxs are much poorer than whites on the average, and poverty contributes to higher crime rates. Second, they are also more likely to live in urban areas, which, as we have seen, also contributes to higher crime rates. Third, the racial and ethnic discrimination they experience leads to anger and frustration that in turn can promote criminal behavior. Although there is less research on Native Americans' criminality, they, too, appear to have higher crime rates than whites because of their much greater poverty and experience of racial discrimination (McCarthy and Hagan 2003).[27]

In appreciating racial/ethnic differences in street crime rates, it is important to keep in mind that whites commit most white-collar crime, and especially corporate crime, as it is white people who lead and manage many corporations. Just as social class affects the type of crime that people do, so do race and ethnicity. Wealthy, white people commit much crime, but it is white-collar crime they tend to commit, not street crime.

FIGURE 8.2 Race, Ethnicity, and Arrest for Violent Crime (Percentage of All Violent Crime Arrests)

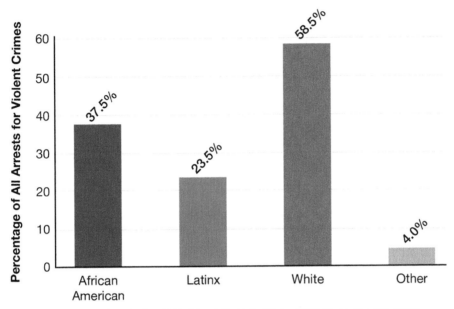

Source: Data from Federal Bureau of Investigation. 2018. *Crime in the United States, 2017*. Washington, DC: Author.

Key Takeaways

- Males commit more street crime than females, in part because of gender role socialization that helps make males more assertive and aggressive.
- Young people commit a disproportionate amount of street crime, in part because of the influence of their peers and their lack of stakes in conformity.
- The disproportionate involvement of African Americans and Latinxs in street crime arises largely from their poverty and urban residence.

For Your Review

1. If we say that males commit more crime than females, does that imply that we are prejudiced against males? Why or why not?
2. Write a brief essay that outlines social class and racial/ethnic differences in street crime and explains the reasons for these differences.

8.4 Explaining Crime

Learning Objectives

1. Understand social structure theories of crime.
2. Explain the social bonding theory of crime.
3. Describe the general assumptions of conflict theories of crime.

If we want to be able to reduce crime, we must first understand why it occurs. Sociologists generally discount explanations rooted in the individual biology or psychology of criminal offenders. While some offenders may suffer from biological defects or psychological problems that lead them to commit crime, most do not. Further, biological and psychological explanations cannot adequately explain the social patterning of crime discussed earlier: why higher crime rates are associated with certain locations and social backgrounds. For example, if California has a higher crime rate than Maine, and the United States has a higher crime rate than Canada, it would sound silly to say that Californians and Americans have more biological and psychological problems than Mainers and Canadians, respectively. Biological and psychological explanations also cannot easily explain why crime rates rise and fall, nor do they lend themselves to practical solutions for reducing crime.

California has a higher crime rate than many other states, but it is difficult to argue that Californians have more biological or psychological problems than the residents of other states.

Source: © Thinkstock

In contrast, sociological explanations do help understand the social patterning of crime and changes in crime rates, and they also lend themselves to possible solutions for reducing crime. A brief discussion of these explanations follows, and a summary appears in Table 8.2.

TABLE 8.2 Sociological Explanations of Crime

Major perspective	Related explanation	Summary of explanation
Functional (social structure theories)	Social disorganization	Certain social characteristics of urban neighborhoods contribute to high crime rates. These characteristics include poverty, dilapidation, population density, and population turnover.
	Anomie	According to Robert Merton, crime by the poor results from a gap between the cultural emphasis on economic success and the inability to achieve such success through the legitimate means of working.
Interactionist (social process theories)	Differential association	Edwin H. Sutherland argued that criminal behavior is learned by interacting with close friends who teach us how to commit various crimes and also the values, motives, and rationalizations we need to adopt in order to justify breaking the law.
	Social bonding	Travis Hirschi wrote that delinquency results from weak bonds to conventional social institutions, such as families and schools.
	Labeling	Deviance and crime result from being officially labeled; arrest and imprisonment increase the likelihood of reoffending.
Conflict (conflict theories)	Group conflict	Criminal law is shaped by the conflict among the various social groups in society that exist because of differences in race and ethnicity, social class, religion, and other factors.

Major perspective	Related explanation	Summary of explanation
	Radical	The wealthy try to use the law and criminal justice system to reinforce their power and to keep the poor and people of color at the bottom of society.
	Feminist	Gender plays an important role in the following areas: (1) the reasons girls and women commit crime; (2) the reasons female crime is lower than male crime; (3) the victimization of girls and women by rape, sexual assault, and domestic violence; and (4) the experience of women professionals and offenders in the criminal justice system.

The Functional Perspective: Social Structure Theories

Social structure theories all stress that crime results from the breakdown of society's norms and social organization and in this sense fall under the functional perspective outlined in Chapter 1. They trace the roots of crime to problems in the society itself rather than to biological or psychological problems inside individuals. By doing so, they suggest the need to address society's social structure in order to reduce crime. Several social structure theories exist.

Social Disorganization Theory

A popular explanation is **social disorganization theory**. This approach originated primarily in the work of Clifford R. Shaw and Henry D. McKay (1942),[28] two social scientists at the University of Chicago who studied that city's delinquency rates during the early 20th century. During this time, the ethnic composition of Chicago changed considerably, as the city's inner zones were first occupied by English, German, and Irish immigrants, then by Eastern European immigrants, and then by African Americans who moved there from southern states. Shaw and McKay found that the inner zones of Chicago consistently had the highest delinquency rates regardless of which ethnic group lived there, and they also found that the ethnic groups' delinquency rates declined as they moved to outer areas of Chicago. To explain these related patterns, Shaw and McKay reasoned that the inner zones of Chicago suffered from *social disorganization*: A weakening of social institutions such as the family, school, and religion that in turn weakens the strength of social bonds and norms and the effectiveness of socialization. Research today confirms that crime rates are highest in neighborhoods with several kinds of structural problems, including high rates of residential mobility, population density, poverty, and single-parent families (Goodson and Bouffard 2019).[29]

social disorganization theory

The view that the weakening of social bonds and conventional social institutions in a community raises its crime rates.

Anomie Theory

Another popular explanation is **anomie theory**, first formulated by Robert K. Merton (1938)[30] in a classic article. Writing just after the Great Depression, Merton focused on the effects of poverty in a nation like the United States that places so much emphasis on economic success. With this strong cultural value, wrote Merton, the poor who do not achieve the American dream feel especially frustrated. They have several ways or adaptations of responding to their situation (see Table 8.3).

anomie theory

Robert Merton's view that deviance is caused by a failure to achieve the American goal of financial success through the conventional means of working.

TABLE 8.3 Anomie Theory

	Goal of economic success	
	Accept	*Reject*

Value of working		
Accept	Conformity	Ritualism
Reject	Innovation	Retreatism

First, said Merton, they may continue to accept the goal of economic success and also the value of working at a job to achieve such success; Merton labeled this adaptation *conformity*. Second, they may continue to favor economic success but reject the value of working and instead use new, illegitimate means, for example theft, to gain money and possessions; Merton labeled this adaptation *innovation*. Third, they may abandon hope of economic success but continue to work anyway because work has become a habit. Merton labeled this adaptation *ritualism*. Finally, they may reject both the goal of economic success and the means of working and withdraw from society either by turning to drugs or by becoming hobos; Merton labeled this adaptation *retreatism*. He also listed a fifth adaptation, which he called *rebellion*, which involves people rejecting economic success and working and trying instead to bring about a new society with new values and a new economic system.

Merton's theory was very influential for many years but eventually lost popularity, partly because many crimes, such as assault and rape, are not committed for the economic motive his theory assumed, and partly because many people use drugs and alcohol without dropping out of society, as his retreatism category suggested. In recent years, however, scholars have rediscovered and adapted his theory, and it has regained favor as new attention is being paid to the frustration resulting from poverty and other strains in one's life that in turn may produce criminal behavior (Agnew 2015; De Coster and Thompson 2017).[31]

The Interactionist Perspective: Social Process Theories

Social process theories stress that crime results from social interaction. In particular, our friends influence our likelihood of committing crime or not committing crime.

Source: Tracy Whiteside/Shutterstock.com

differential association theory

Edwin Sutherland's view that deviance stems from interacting with primary group members who commit deviance and have values conducive to deviance.

Social process theories all stress that crime results from the social interaction of individuals with other people, particularly their friends and family, and thus fall under the interactionist perspective outlined in Chapter 1. They trace crime to the influence that our friends and family have on us and to the meanings and perceptions we derive from their views and expectations. By doing so, they indicate the need to address the peer and family context to reduce crime.

Differential Association Theory

One of the most famous criminological theories is **differential association theory**, first formulated at about the same time as Merton's anomie theory by Edwin H. Sutherland and published in its final form in an edition of a criminology text he wrote (Sutherland 1947).[32] Rejecting the idea that crime has strong biological roots, Sutherland said crime instead grows out of interaction with others. Specifically, he wrote that adolescents and other individuals learn that it is acceptable to commit crime and also how to commit crime from their interaction with their close friends. Adolescents become delinquent if they acquire more and stronger attitudes in favor of breaking the law than attitudes opposed to breaking the law. Crime and delinquency, then, result from a very normal social process, social interaction. Adolescents are more or less at risk for delinquency partly depending on who their friends are and what their friends do or do not do and what they think or do not think.

Many scholars today consider peer influences to be among the most important contributors to delinquency and other misbehavior (Akers et al 2017).[33] One problem with differential association theory is that it does not explain behavior, like rape, that is usually committed by a lone offender and that is generally not the result of attitudes learned from close friends.

Social Bonding Theory

In a 1969 book, *Causes of Delinquency*, Travis Hirschi (1969)[34] asked not what prompts people to commit crime, but rather what keeps them from committing crime. This question was prompted by his view that human nature is basically selfish and that society needs to tame this selfishness. He wrote that an adolescent's bonds to society, and specifically the bonds to family and school, help keep the adolescent from breaking the law.

Hirschi identified several types of social bonds, but generally thought that the closer adolescents feel to their family and teachers, the more they value their parents' beliefs and school values, and the more time they spend with their families and on school activities, the less likely they are to be delinquent. Turning that around, they are more likely to be delinquent if they feel more distant from their parents and teachers, if they place less value on their family's and school's values, and if they spend less time with these two very important aspects of their lives.

Hirschi's **social bonding theory** became one of the influential criminological theories today. Much research based on this theory focuses on the relationship between parents and children. When this relationship is warm and harmonious and when children respect their parents' values and parents treat their children firmly but fairly, children are less likely to commit antisocial behavior during childhood and delinquency during adolescence. Schools also matter: Students who do well in school and are very involved in extracurricular activities are less likely than other students to engage in delinquency (Payne and Welch 2016).[35]

social bonding theory

Travis Hirschi's view that deviance results from weak bonds to conventional social institutions such as the family and schools.

Children and Our Future

Saving Children from a Life of Crime

Millions of children around the nation live in circumstances that put them at risk for a childhood, adolescence, and adulthood filled with antisocial behavior, delinquency, and crime, respectively. Although most of these children in fact will not suffer this fate, some will. These circumstances thus must be addressed to save these children from a life of crime. As social scientists Brandon C. Welsh and David P. Farrington observe, "Convincing research evidence exists to support a policy of saving children from a life of crime by intervening early in childhood to tackle key risk factors."

What are these risk factors? They include being born to a teenaged, single mother; living in poverty or near poverty; attending poor, dilapidated schools; and living in high-crime urban areas. These risk factors are all related, as most children born to teenaged, single mothers live in poverty or near poverty, and many such children live in high-crime urban areas.

What can be done to help save such children from a life of crime? Ideally, our nation would lift them and their families entirely out of poverty with employment and social payment policies. Although this sort of national policy will not occur in the foreseeable future, a growing amount of rigorous social science evaluation evidence points to several effective programs and policies that can still help at-risk children. These include: (1) at the individual level, certain types of preschool programs and social skills training programs for older children; (2) at the family level, home visiting by trained professionals and parenting training programs; and (3) at the school and community levels, certain types of after-school and community-mentoring programs in which local adults spend time with children at risk for delinquency and other problems.

As Welsh and Farrington note, "Early prevention is by no means a panacea. But it does represent an integral part of any plan to reduce the nation's crime rate." They add that several other Western democracies have national agencies devoted to improving behavioral and other outcomes among those nations' children, and they call for the United States to establish a similar national agency, the National Council on Early Prevention, as part of a nationwide strategy to prevent delinquency and other antisocial behaviors among American youth. Other scholars and writers emphasize the need to provide poor families income subsidies and free or heavily subsidized child care among other measures, as poverty itself is a risk factor for children's antisocial behavior and also contributes to many other risk factors for this behavior.

Sources: Duncan and Le Menestrel 2019; Kirp 2018; Welsh and Farrington 2007[36]

Another social institution, religion, has also been the subject of research. Many studies find that religious involvement seemingly helps keep adolescents from using alcohol and other drugs (see Chapter 7), from engaging in frequent sexual activity, and from engaging in delinquency generally (Guo 2018).[37]

Labeling Theory

labeling theory

The view that being labeled deviant increases the chances of future deviance.

Our criminal justice system is based on the idea that the prospect of quick arrest and harsh punishment should deter criminal behavior. **Labeling theory** has the opposite idea, as it assumes that labeling someone as a criminal or deviant, which arrest and imprisonment certainly do, makes the person *more* likely to continue to offend. This result occurs, argues the theory, because the labeling process gives someone a negative self-image, reduces the potential for employment, and makes it difficult to have friendships with law-abiding individuals.

When this man is released from prison, he will probably face difficulties in finding a job and starting friendships with law-abiding people. These difficulties will make him more likely to commit new crimes.

Suppose, for example, that you were just released from prison after serving a 5-year term for armed robbery. If you apply for a job and list your prison term on the application, how likely are you to get hired? If you are at a bar and meet someone who interests you and then tell the person where you were for the previous 5 years, what are the chances that the conversation will continue? Faced with bleak job prospects and few people who want to spend time with you, what are your alternatives? Might you not succumb to the temptation to hang out with other offenders and even to commit new crime yourself?

In line with labeling theory, several studies find that arrest and imprisonment increase future offending (Klement 2015; Nagin et al. 2009).[38] To the extent this undesired consequence occurs, efforts to stem juvenile and adult crime through harsher punishment may sometimes have the opposite result from their intention.

Source: © Thinkstock

The Conflict Perspective

group conflict theory

The assumption that criminal law is shaped by the conflict among the various social groups in society that exist because of differences in race and ethnicity, social class, religion, and other factors.

Several related theories fall under the conflict perspective outlined in Chapter 1. Although they all have something to say about why people commit crime, their major focus is on the use and misuse of the criminal law and criminal justice system to deal with crime. Three branches of the conflict perspective exist in the study of crime and criminal justice.

The first branch is called **group conflict theory**, which assumes that criminal law is shaped by the conflict among the various social groups in society that exist because of differences in race and ethnicity, social class, religion, and other factors. The more powerful groups try to pass laws that ban behaviors in which subordinate groups tend to engage, and they try to use the criminal justice system to suppress subordinate group members. A widely cited historical example of this view is Prohibition, which resulted from years of effort by temperance advocates, most of them from white, Anglo-Saxon, rural, and Protestant backgrounds, to ban the manufacture, sale, and use of alcohol. Although these advocates thought alcohol use was a sin and incurred great social costs, their hostility toward alcohol also reflected their hostility toward the types of people back then who tended to use alcohol: poor, urban, Catholic immigrants (Gusfield 1963).[39]

The second branch of the conflict perspective is called **radical theory**. Compared to group conflict theory, radical theory theory highlights the importance of economic social class and power more than the importance of religion, ethnicity, and other social group characteristics. In this way, radical theory evokes the basic views of Karl Marx on the exploitation and oppression of the poor and working class by the ruling class (DeKeseredy and Dragiewicz 2012).[40]

Dutch criminologist Willem Bonger (1916)[41] presented an early but still influential radical explanation of crime. He blamed the high U.S. crime rate on its economic system, capitalism. As an economic system, he said, capitalism emphasizes the pursuit of profit. Yet, if someone gains profit, someone else is losing it. This emphasis on self-gain creates an egoistic culture in which people look out for themselves and are quite willing to act in a way that disadvantages other people. Amid such a culture, Bonger said, crime is an inevitable outcome. Bonger thought crime would be lower in socialist societies because they place more emphasis on the welfare of one's group than on individual success.

Feminist approaches comprise the third branch of the conflict perspective on the study of crime and criminal justice (Mallicoat 2019).[42] Several such approaches exist, but they generally focus on at least one of four areas: (1) the reasons girls and women commit crime; (2) the reasons female crime is lower than male crime; (3) the victimization of girls and women by rape, sexual assault, and domestic violence; and (4) the experience of women professionals and offenders in the criminal justice system.

Regarding the first area, the research generally finds that girls and women commit crime for the same reasons that boys and men commit crime: poverty, parental upbringing, and so forth. But it also finds that both women and men "do gender" when they commit crime. That is, they commit crime according to gender roles, at least to some extent. Thus, one study found that women robbers tend to rob other women and not to use a gun when they do so (Miller and Brunson 2000).[43]

In addressing the second area, on why female crime is less common than male crime, scholars often cite two reasons discussed earlier: gender role socialization and gender-based differences in parental supervision. One additional reason derives from social bonding theory: Girls feel closer to their parents than boys do, and thus are less delinquent (Lanctôt and Le Blanc 2002).[44]

We have already commented on the victimization of women from rape, sexual assault, and domestic violence, but the study of this topic began with work by feminist criminologists during the 1970s. Since that time, innumerable works have addressed this type of victimization, which is also thought to contribute to girls' delinquency and, more generally, female drug and alcohol abuse (Chesney-Lind and Shelden 2014).[45]

The final area for feminist work addresses women professionals and offenders in the criminal justice system. This body of research documents the many blatant and subtle forms of discrimination that women face as offenders, police, attorneys, judges, prison guards, and other professionals (Mallicoat 2019).[46]

radical theory

A view that highlights the importance of (economic) social classes more than the importance of religion, ethnicity, and other social group characteristics in shaping the creation and operation of criminal law.

One important area of feminist-inspired work on crime and criminal justice involves studies of women police officers.

Source: © Thinkstock

Key Takeaways

- Social structure theories stress that crime results from economic and other problems in how society is structured and from poverty and other problems in neighborhoods.
- Interactionist theories stress that crime results from our interaction with family members, peers, and other people, and from labeling by the criminal justice system.
- Conflict theories stress that social groups with power and influence try to use the law and criminal justice system to maintain their power and to keep other groups at the bottom of society.

For Your Review

1. What are any two criminogenic (crime-causing) social or physical characteristics of urban neighborhoods?
2. According to labeling theory, why are arrest and imprisonment sometimes counterproductive?

8.5 The Criminal Justice System

Learning Objectives

1. Describe what is meant by the "working personality" of the police.
2. Discuss the quality of legal representation of criminal defendants.
3. Explain whether incarceration reduces crime in an effective and cost-efficient manner.

The U.S. criminal justice system faces two major tasks: (1) keeping the public safe by apprehending criminals and, ideally, reducing crime; and (2) doing so while protecting individual freedom from the abuse of power by law enforcement agents and other government officials. The latter goal is a key feature that distinguishes a democracy from a dictatorship.

How well does the U.S. criminal justice system work in both respects? How well does it control and reduce crime, and how well does it observe individual rights and not treat people differently based on their social class, race and ethnicity, gender, and other social characteristics? What are other problems in our criminal justice system? Although whole books have been written about these topics, we have space here to discuss only some of this rich literature.

Police

Police officers realize that their lives may be in danger at any time, and they also often interact with suspects and other citizens whose hostility toward the police is quite evident. For these reasons, officers typically develop a *working personality* that, in response to the danger and hostility police face, tends to be authoritarian and suspicious (Skolnick 1994).[47] Indeed, it is not too far-fetched to say that police-citizen relations are characterized by mutual hostility and suspicion.

Officer Gets Shot in Leg During Shootout with Robbery Suspect

Police work can be very dangerous, and police officers realize their lives may be at risk any time they are on the job. This realization helps explain why police usually develop a working personality that tends to be authoritarian and suspicious of the public.

View the video online at: http://www.youtube.com/embed/xz-hG26ZPy0?rel=0

Two aspects of police behavior are especially relevant for a textbook on social problems. The first is police *corruption*. No one knows for sure how much police corruption occurs, but low-level corruption (e.g., accepting small bribes and stealing things from stores while on patrol) is thought to be fairly common, while high-level corruption (e.g., accepting large bribes and confiscating and then selling illegal drugs) is thought to be far from rare (Barkan and Bryjak 2018).[48] Several notorious police scandals have called attention to rampant corruption amid some police forces. One such scandal involved the so-called Rampart Division in Los Angeles and involved dozens of officers who beat and shot suspects, stole drugs and money, and lied at the trials of the people they arrested (Glover and Lait 2000).[49]

The other relevant behavior is *police brutality* or, to use a less provocative term, the *use of undue* (also called *unjustified* or *excessive*) force by police. Police, of course, are permitted and even expected to use physical force when necessary to subdue suspects, but some use excessive force. How much police brutality occurs? Based on national survey data of people (drivers, pedestrians, and others) stopped by police who felt that excessive force was used (Langton and Durose 2013),[50] an estimated 267,000 incidents of excessive force occur annually nationwide, for an average of 731 daily (Barkan and Bryjak 2018).[51] (Note that this estimate assumes that these citizens' beliefs about excessive force were accurate.)

Do police commit more brutality against African Americans and other people of color than against non-Latinx whites? To best answer this question, we need to distinguish between fatal shootings and nonfatal use of police force. Regarding fatal shootings, the best evidence suggests that African Americans fatally shot by police are slightly more likely than their white counterparts to have been unarmed (Sullivan et al. 2018).[52] This evidence points to a racial disparity in victims of unjustified police shootings of civilians, but not to a strong such disparity. Regarding nonfatal police brutality, the best evidence points to a significant racial disparity. In the national survey data just mentioned, African Americans are 2.6 times more likely to report having excessive force used against them (Hyland et al. 2015).[53] Research analyzing actual instances of excessive force also finds that African Americans are significantly more likely than whites to be victimized by this behavior (Fridell and Lim 2016; Goff et al. 2016; Paoline et al. 2016).[54] However, some research of this type still does not find this form of racial disparity (Miller et al. 2017).[55]

Another issue in policing concerns the following question: How well do the police prevent crime? To answer this question, let us be clear what it is asking. The relevant question is not whether having the police we do have keeps us safer than having no police at all. Rather, the relevant question is whether hiring more police or making some specific change in police practice would lower the crime rate. The evidence on this issue is complex, but certain conclusions are in order.

In terms of crime reduction, the ways in which police are deployed matter more than the actual number of police.

Source: © Thinkstock

First, simply adding more officers to a city's existing police force will probably not reduce crime, or will reduce it only to a very small degree and at great expense (Walker 2015).[56] Why do additional police not seem to matter in this way? Much violence takes place indoors or in other locations far from police purview, and practical increases in police numbers still would not yield numbers high enough to guarantee a police presence in every public location where crime might happen. Because criminals typically think they can commit a crime with impunity if no police are around, the hiring of additional police is not likely to deter them.

Additional police may not matter, but how police are deployed *does* matter. In this regard, a second conclusion from the policing and crime literature is that *directed patrol* involving the consistent deployment of large numbers of police in high-crime areas ("hot spots") can reduce crime significantly (Braga and Weisburd 2015).[57] However, *crackdowns*—in which the police flood a high-crime and -drug neighborhood, make a lot of arrests, and then leave—have at most a short-term effect, with crime and drug use eventually returning to their previous levels or simply becoming displaced to other neighborhoods.

We cannot leave our discussion of police without mentioning two facts about their circumstances. First, police do have good reason to believe that their lives may be in danger at any moment. Dozens of police die in the line of duty every year, and many more officers suffer nonfatal injuries from being shot or assaulted or being involved in a motor vehicle accident. This situation prompts the U.S. Department of Labor (2018)[58] to conclude that "police officers have a higher risk of incurring a work-related injury than most other occupations." As evidence, an estimated 4 percent of all law enforcement officers suffer nonfatal injuries that require time off from work, compared to only 1 percent for all occupations.

Second, during the early 2020 pandemic, many police contracted COVID-19. As of mid-April 2020, for example, more than 4,000 New York City police officers had the disease, and 29 had died from it (Waldrop 2020).[59] Similarly, 347 Chicago police officers had the disease, and 3 had died from it (NBC Chicago 2020).[60] The close physical contact that police have with other officers and with members of the public contributed to this disturbing situation.

Criminal Courts

In the U.S. legal system, suspects and defendants enjoy certain rights and protections guaranteed by the Constitution and Bill of Rights and provided in various Supreme Court rulings. Even so, the criminal courts in reality often fail to achieve the high standards by which they should be judged (Kohler-Hausmann 2018; Van Cleve 2016).[61]

A basic problem is the lack of adequate counsel for the poor. Wealthy defendants can afford the best attorneys and get what they pay for: excellent legal defense. An oft-cited example here is O. J. Simpson, the former football star and television and film celebrity who was arrested and tried during the mid-1990s for allegedly killing his ex-wife and one of her friends (Barkan 1996).[62] Simpson hired a "dream team" of nationally famous attorneys and other experts, including private investigators, to defend him at an eventual cost of some $10 million. A jury acquitted him, but a poor defendant in similar circumstances almost undoubtedly would have been found guilty and perhaps received a death sentence.

Almost all criminal defendants are poor or near poor. Although they enjoy the right to free legal counsel, in practice they receive ineffective counsel or virtually no counsel at all. The poor are defended by public defenders or by court-appointed private counsel, and either type of attorney simply has far too many cases to handle them adequately. Many poor defendants see their attorneys for the first time just moments before a hearing before the judge. Because of their heavy caseloads, these defense attorneys simply do not have the time to consider the complexities of any one case. The famed image from novels, films, and TV shows of defense attorneys vigorously contesting the guilt of their clients is in fact a myth for almost all criminal defendants. Instead, these defendants receive "assembly line justice," in which their cases are disposed of quickly and efficiently through guilty pleas, even when the evidence against them is weak (Zeidman 2017).[63]

A related problem is **plea bargaining**, in which a defendant agrees to plead guilty, usually in return for a reduced sentence. Under our system of justice, criminal defendants are entitled to a trial by jury if they want one. In reality, however, most defendants plead guilty, and criminal trials are very rare, with only about 3 percent to 6 percent of felony cases going to trial. Prosecutors favor plea bargains because they help ensure convictions while saving the time and expense of jury trials, while defendants favor plea bargains because they help ensure a lower sentence than if they were convicted after a jury trial. However, this practice in effect means that defendants are punished if they do exercise their right to have a trial. Critics of this aspect say that defendants are being coerced into pleading guilty even if they might have a good chance of winning an acquittal if their case went to trial (Zeidman 2017).[64]

plea bargaining

An agreement between the prosecution and defense that a criminal defendant will plead guilty, usually in return for a reduced sentence.

The Problem of Prisons and Mass Incarceration

The United States now (2017 data) houses about 1.5 million people in state and federal prisons and 750,000 in local jails. This total of more than 2.2 million people behind bars yields an incarceration rate that is by far the highest rate of any Western democracy. This rate is about four times higher than the rate 5 decades ago and represents a tough-on-crime approach that began during the 1970s and that has since put millions of Americans behind bars and created a situation now called *mass incarceration*. This situation is troubling, and so is the racial composition of American prisoners (Hinton et al. 2018).[65] Some 56 percent of all state and federal prisoners are African American or Latinx, even though these two groups comprise only about 31 percent of the national population. As Chapter 7 noted, African Americans and Latinxs have been arrested and imprisoned for drug offenses far out of proportion to their actual use of illegal drugs. This racial/ethnic disparity, along with the generally harsher sentencing of the tough-on-crime approach, has contributed to what law professor Michelle Alexander (2012)[66] terms the "new Jim Crow" of mass incarceration. Reflecting her concern, about one of every three young African American males are under correctional supervision (in jail or prison or on probation or parole).

The corrections system costs the nation tens of billions of dollars annually. What does the expenditure of this huge sum accomplish? It would be reassuring to know that the high U.S. incarceration rate keeps the nation safe and even helps reduce the crime rate, and it is certainly true that the crime rate would be much higher if we had no prisons at all. However, many and perhaps most criminologists think the surge in imprisonment during the last few decades has not helped reduce the crime rate appreciably and has not achieved any such gain in a cost-efficient manner (Travis et al. 2014).[67] Greater crime declines would be produced, many criminologists say, if equivalent funds were instead spent on crime prevention programs instead of on incarceration, a point returned to in Section 6.

Criminologists also worry that prison may be a breeding ground for crime because rehabilitation programs such as vocational training and drug and alcohol counseling are lacking and because prison conditions are substandard. They note that hundreds of thousands of prisoners are released every year and come back into their communities ill equipped to resume a normal life. There they face a lack of job opportunities (how many employers want to hire an ex-con?) and a lack of friendships with law-abiding individuals, as our earlier discussion of labeling theory indicated.

Living conditions behind bars merit further discussion. A common belief of Americans is that many prisons and jails are like country clubs, with exercise rooms and expensive video and audio equipment abounding. However, this belief is a myth (Kappeler and Potter 2018).[68] Although some minimum-security federal prisons may have clean, adequate facilities, state prisons and local jails are typically squalid places, with substandard ventilation, plumbing, heating, and cooling, among other problems.

Some Americans probably feel that criminals deserve to live amid these conditions, while many Americans are probably at least not very bothered by this situation. But this situation increases the odds that inmates will leave prison and jail as *more* of a threat to public safety than when they were first incarcerated. Treating inmates humanely would be an important step toward successful reentry into mainstream society.

Before leaving this topic, it is worth noting that prison and jail living conditions contributed mightily to high rates of COVID-19 among the incarcerated population in early 2020. Because of their severe overcrowding, poor health care, and other conditions, the nation's prisons and jails became what were called "petri dishes" for the spread of the coronavirus (Williams et al. 2020).[69] As just one example, more than 80 percent of the incarcerated population at a large state prison in Ohio tested positive for the coronavirus, along with 160 correctional officers and other staff (Volpenhein and Star 2020).[70] This situation not only threatened the lives of all these people, but it also set the stage for spread into the larger community after prisoners served their sentences and as correctional staff returned home every day to their families. To help reduce infections, many jurisdictions released low-level offenders from their jails and prisons or gave newly convicted offenders fines and/or probation in lieu of incarceration.

People Making a Difference

Making a Difference in the Lives of Released Prisoners

The text notes that hundreds of thousands of prisoners are released every year. Many of them are burdened with drug, alcohol, and other problems and face bleak prospects for employment, friendships, and stable lives, in general. Since 1967, The Fortune Society has been making a difference in the lives of ex-convicts in and near New York City.

The Fortune Society's website (http://www.fortunesociety.org) describes the group's mission: "The Fortune Society's mission is to support successful reentry from prison and promote alternatives to incarceration, thus strengthening the fabric of our communities." About 70 percent of its more than 190 employees are ex-prisoners and/or have histories of substance abuse or homelessness. It is fair to say that The Fortune Society was working on prisoner reentry long before scholars discovered the problem in the late 1990s and early 2000s.

Former prisoners receive many services from the Fortune Society. One of the most important services is transitional and permanent housing. The organization also provides drug and alcohol counseling, family services, adult education and career development programs, and classes in anger management, parenting skills, and health care. An unusual service is providing professional photographic headshots for formerly incarcerated people to help them find a job. A recipient of this service was grateful, saying, "It is a beginning, a stepping stone to stay out of the street system."

The Fortune Society has received national recognition for its efforts. Two federal agencies, the Department of Justice and the Department of Housing and Urban Development, have featured The Fortune Society as a model program for helping formerly incarcerated people. The Urban Institute featured this model in a video it developed about prisoner reentry programs. And in 2005, the American Society of Criminology presented the society its President's Award for "Distinguished Contributions to the Cause of Justice." These and other examples of the national recognition won by The Fortune Society indicate that for more than 5 decades it has indeed been making a difference.

Sources: Kaden 2019; The Fortune Society 2018[71]

Focus on the Death Penalty

The death penalty remains one of the most controversial issues in the criminal justice system. The United States is the only Western democracy that sentences common criminals to death, as other democracies decided decades ago that civilized nations should not execute anyone, even if the person took a human life. Although a majority of Americans support capital punishment, research and evidence yield a powerful case against it (Bohm 2017; Death Penalty Information Center 2019).[72]

First, capital punishment does not deter homicide: Almost all studies on this issue fail to find a deterrent effect. An important reason for this stems from the nature of homicide. As discussed earlier, it is a relatively spontaneous, emotional crime. Most people who murder do not sit down beforehand to calculate their chances of being arrested, convicted, and executed. Instead, they lash out. Premeditated murders do exist, but the people who commit them do not think they will get caught and so, once again, are not deterred by the potential for execution.

Second, the death penalty is racially discriminatory. While some studies find that African Americans are more likely than whites who commit similar homicides to receive the death penalty, the clearest evidence for racial discrimination involves the race of the victim: Homicides with white victims are more likely than those with African American victims to result in a death sentence. Although this difference is not intended, it suggests that the criminal justice system values white lives more than African American lives.

The death penalty is racially discriminatory and does not deter homicide.

Source: © Thinkstock

Third, many people have been mistakenly convicted of capital offenses, raising the possibility of *wrongful executions*. Sometimes defendants are convicted out of honest errors, and sometimes they are convicted because the police and/or prosecution fabricated evidence or engaged in other legal misconduct. Whatever their source, wrongful convictions of capital offenses raise the ugly possibility that a defendant will be executed even though he was actually innocent of any capital crime. During the past 5 decades, more than one hundred sixty people have been released from death row after DNA or other evidence cast serious doubt on their guilt.

Fourth, executions are expensive. Keeping a murderer in prison for life costs about $1.4 million in current dollars (say 40 years at $35,000 per year), while the average death sentence costs the state about $2 million to $3 million in legal expenses.

This diverse body of evidence leads most criminologists to oppose the death penalty. In 1989, the American Society of Criminology formally declared that it "condemns this form of punishment, and urges its members to use their professional skills in legislatures and courts to seek a speedy abolition of this form of punishment."

If the Victim Is White, Death Penalty Is Much More Likely

Several studies find that the death penalty is more likely to be imposed when the victim of a homicide is white than when the victim is a person of color. This finding suggests that jurors and the criminal justice system place more value on white people's lives than on African Americans' lives.

View the video online at: http://www.youtube.com/embed/mIlNsihUkyM?rel=0

Key Takeaways

- Partly because the police often fear for their lives, they tend to have a "working personality" that is authoritarian and suspicious. Police corruption and use of undue force remain significant problems in many police departments.
- Although criminal defendants have the right to counsel, the legal representation of such defendants, most of whom are poor or near poor, is very inadequate.
- Prisons are squalid places, and incarceration has not been shown to reduce crime in an effective or cost-efficient manner. During the 2020 pandemic, the jail and prison incarcerated population and staff were especially vulnerable to contracting COVID-19, threatening both them and the outside public.
- Most criminologists agree that capital punishment does not deter homicide, and they worry about racial discrimination in the use of the death penalty and about the possibility of wrongful executions.

For Your Review

1. Have you ever had an encounter with a police officer? If so, how would you describe the officer's personality? Was it similar to what is described in the text?
2. The text argues that improvement in prison conditions would help reduce the probability of reoffending after inmates leave prison. Do you agree or disagree with this statement? Explain your answer.

8.6 Reducing Crime and Improving Criminal Justice

Learning Objective

1. Describe five strategies that criminologists have proposed to reduce crime.

As noted earlier, the United States has been using a **get-tough approach** to fight crime. This approach has involved longer prison terms and the building of many more prisons and jails. Scholars doubt that this surge in imprisonment has achieved significant crime reduction at an affordable cost, and they worry that it may be leading to greater problems in the future as hundreds of thousands of prison inmates are released back into their communities every year.

Many of these scholars favor an approach to crime borrowed from the field of public health. In the areas of health and medicine, a **public health approach** tries to treat people who are already ill, but it especially focuses on preventing disease and illness before they begin. While physicians try to help people who already have cancer, medical researchers constantly search for the causes of cancer so that they can try to prevent it before it affects anyone. Applying this model to criminal behavior, criminologists have advanced several ideas that, if implemented with sufficient funds and serious purpose, hold great potential for achieving significant, cost-effective reductions in crime and improving criminal justice (Barkan and Rocque 2020; Tonry and Nagin 2017; Welsh et al. 2014).[73] Many of their strategies rest on the huge body of theory and research on the factors underlying crime in the United States, which we had space only to touch on earlier, while other proposals call for criminal justice reforms. We highlight some of these many strategies here.

get-tough approach

The use of longer prison terms and other law enforcement measures to reduce crime.

public health approach

A strategy that highlights the need to prevent illness or disease; in criminology, a strategy that highlights the need to address the factors that lead to criminal behavior.

Applying Social Research

Immigrants and Crime Rates

Many people, including President Donald Trump, firmly believe that immigrants have higher crime rates than native-born Americans and in particular pose a significant danger of criminal violence. This belief has motivated calls to reduce immigration and efforts to deport undocumented immigrants who are already in the United States.

Given the considerable controversy over immigration and crime, it is not surprising that sociologists, criminologists, and other social scientists have tried to find out whether immigrants, do, in fact, have higher crime rates, and especially higher violent crime rates, than native-born Americans. During the past 2 decades, many studies have examined this issue. This research yields consistent results and this conclusion: Immigrants' crime rates, violent or otherwise, are no higher than the rates of native-born Americans and may in fact be lower than the latter rates. There is even some evidence that immigration has contributed to the decline in crime that has occurred in the nation since the early 1990s.

In view of this body of research, the belief that immigrants have higher violent crime rates must be considered nothing more than a myth, because the research evidence simply does not support it. Some immigrants do commit crime, of course, just as some native-born Americans do. But overall they are clearly not the dangerous menace that many people, including the president of the United States, say they are, and any belief to the contrary is misguided.

Sources: Adelman et al. 2017; Ousey and Kubrin 2018[74]

A first strategy involves serious national efforts to reduce poverty and to improve neighborhood living conditions. It is true that most poor people do not commit crime, but it is also true that most street crime is committed by the poor or near poor for reasons discussed earlier. Efforts that create decent-paying jobs for the poor, enhance their vocational and educational opportunities, and improve their neighborhood living conditions should all help reduce poverty and its attendant problems and thus to reduce crime.

A second strategy involves changes in how American parents raise their boys. To the extent that the large gender difference in serious crime stems from male socialization patterns, changes in male socialization should help reduce crime. This will certainly not happen any time soon, but if American parents can begin to raise their boys to be less aggressive and less dominating, they will help reduce the nation's crime rate. As two feminist criminologists once wrote, "A large price is paid for structures of male domination and for the very qualities that drive men to be successful, to control others, and to wield uncompromising power....Gender differences in crime suggest that crime may not be so normal after all. Such differences challenge us to see that in the lives of women, men have a great deal more to learn" (Daly and Chesney-Lind 1988:527).[75]

Lessons from Other Societies

Preventing Crime and Treating Prisoners in Western Europe

The text suggests the get-tough approach that the United States has been using to reduce crime has not worked in a cost-effective manner and has led to other problems, including a flood of inmates returning to their communities every year. In fighting crime, the United States has much to learn from Western Europe. In contrast to the U.S. get-tough approach, Western European nations tend to use a public health model that comprises two components. The first is a focus on crime prevention that uses early childhood intervention programs and other preventive measures to address the roots of crime and other childhood and family problems. The second is a criminal justice policy that involves sentencing defendants and treating prisoners in a manner more likely to rehabilitate offenders and reduce their repeat offending than the more punitive approach in the United States.

The overall Western European approach to offenders is guided by the belief that imprisonment should be reserved for the most dangerous violent offenders, and that probation, community service, and other forms of community corrections should be used for other offenders. Because violent offenders comprise only a small proportion of all offenders, the Western European approach saves a great deal of money while still protecting public safety. Western European prisons also generally have much better living conditions and programming than their American counterparts, partly because it is felt that prisoners will be less likely to reoffend if they are treated humanely while incarcerated and receive the many services they need.

The experience of Denmark and the Netherlands is illustrative. Like the United States, Denmark had to deal with rapidly growing crime rates during the 1960s. Whereas the United States responded with the get-tough approach involving longer and more certain prison terms and the construction of more and more prisons, Denmark took the opposite approach: It adopted shorter prison terms for violent offenders and used the funds saved from the reduced prison costs to expand community corrections for property offenders. Finland and the Netherlands have also adopted a similar approach that favors community corrections and relatively short prison terms for violent offenders over the get-tough approach the United States adopted.

All these nations save great sums of money in prison costs and other criminal justice expenses because they chose not to adopt the U.S. get-tough approach. Even so, their citizens overall are at least as safe as Americans from crime. Their approach should be kept in mind as the United States evaluates its get-tough policies. There may be much to learn from their less punitive strategy: While the United States got tough, perhaps they got sensible.

Sources: Dammer and Albanese 2014; Duran 2018; Waller and Welsh 2007[76]

A third and very important strategy involves expansion of early childhood intervention (ECI) programs and nutrition services for poor mothers and their children, as the "Children and Our Future" box discussed earlier. ECI programs generally involve visits by social workers, nurses, or other professionals to young, poor mothers shortly after they give birth, as these mother's children are often at high risk for later behavioral problems. These visits may be daily or weekly and last for several months, and they involve parenting instruction and training in other life skills. These programs have been shown to be very successful in reducing childhood and adolescent misbehavior in a cost-effective manner (Greenwood 2006).[77] In the same vein, nutrition services would also reduce the risk of neurological impairment among newborns and young children and thus their likelihood of developing later behavioral problems.

A fourth strategy calls for a national effort to improve the nation's schools and schooling. This effort would involve replacing large, older, and dilapidated schoolhouses with smaller, nicer, and better equipped ones. For many reasons, this effort should help improve student academic achievement and school commitment and thus lower delinquent and later criminal behavior.

A final set of strategies involves changes in the criminal justice system that should help reduce repeat offending and save much money that could be used to fund the ECI programs and other efforts just outlined. Placing nonviolent property and drug offenders in community corrections (e.g., probation, daytime supervision) would reduce the number of prison and jail inmates by hundreds of thousands annually without endangering Americans' safety and save billions of dollars in prison costs. These funds could also be used to improve prison and jail vocational and educational programming and drug and alcohol services, all of which are seriously underfunded. If properly funded, such programs and services hold great promise for rehabilitating many inmates (Cullen 2013).[78] Elimination of the death penalty would also save much money while also eliminating the possibility of wrongful executions.

This is not a complete list of strategies, but it does suggest the kinds of efforts that would help address the roots of crime and, in the long run, help to reduce it. Although the United States may not be interested in pursuing this crime-prevention approach, strategies like the ones just mentioned would in the long run be more likely than our current get-tough approach to create a safer society and at the same time save us billions of dollars annually.

Note that none of these proposals addresses white-collar crime, which should not be neglected in a discussion of reducing the nation's crime problem. One reason white-collar crime is so common is that the laws against it are weakly enforced; more consistent enforcement of these laws should help reduce white-collar crime, as would the greater use of imprisonment for convicted white-collar criminals (Rosoff et al. 2020).[79]

Key Takeaways

- The get-tough approach has not been shown to reduce crime in an effective and cost-efficient manner. A sociological explanation of crime thus suggests the need to focus more resources on the social roots of crime in order to prevent crime from happening in the first place.
- Strategies suggested by criminologists to reduce crime include: (a) reducing poverty and improving neighborhood living conditions, (b) changing male socialization patterns, (c) expanding early childhood intervention programs, (d) improving schools and schooling, and (e) reducing the use of incarceration for drug and property offenders.

For Your Review

1. The text notes that social science research has not shown the get-tough approach to be effective or cost-efficient. If this is true, why do you think this approach has been so popular in the United States since the 1970s?
2. Of the five strategies outlined in the text to reduce crime, which one strategy do you think would be most effective if it were implemented with adequate funding? Explain your answer.

8.7 End-of-Chapter Material

Summary

1. Crime is a major concern for many Americans. More than one-third fear walking alone at night in their neighborhoods, and even larger percentages worry about specific types of crimes. News media coverage of crime contributes to these fears. The media overdramatize crime by covering so much of it and by giving especially heavy attention to violent crime even though most crime is not violent. In other problems, the news media disproportionately depict young people and people of color as offenders and whites as victims.

2. The nation's major source of crime statistics is the FBI's Uniform Crime Reports (UCR). Because many people do not tell the police about crimes they have experienced, the UCR underestimates the actual level of crime in the United States. It is also subject to changes in police reporting practices and in particular to deliberate efforts by police to downplay the amount of crime. To help correct these problems, the National Crime Victimization Survey (NCVS) measures crime every year in a national survey that asks residents to report their criminal victimization. The NCVS is thought to yield a more accurate estimate of crime than the UCR, and it also provides much information on the circumstances under which victimization occurs. Self-report surveys, typically given to adolescents, are a final form of crime measurement and provide much information on the adolescents' social backgrounds and thus on the context of their offending.

3. The major categories of crime are violent crime, property crime, white-collar crime, and consensual crime. Much violent crime is relatively spontaneous and emotional, and a surprising amount involves victims and offenders who knew each other before the violent act occurred. Despite popular perceptions, most violent crime is also intraracial. A major distinction in the understanding of property crime is that between professional thieves, who are very skilled and steal valuable possessions or large sums of money, and amateur thieves, who are unskilled and whose theft is petty by comparison. Corporate crime and other kinds of white-collar crime arguably cost the nation more than street crime in economic loss, health problems, and death; corporate violence involves unsafe working conditions, unsafe products, and environmental pollution. Consensual crime, such as illegal drug use and prostitution, raises two important questions: (1) Which consensual but potentially harmful behaviors should the state ban and which should it not ban, and (2) does banning such behaviors do more harm than good or more good than harm?

4. Crime is socially patterned. Males commit more serious crimes than females. African Americans and Latinxs have higher crime rates than whites, poor people have higher crime rates than the wealthy, and youths in their teens and early 20s have higher crime rates than older people. In addition, crime is higher in urban areas than in rural areas.

5. Many sociological theories of criminal behavior exist. Social structure theories highlight poverty and weakened social institutions as important factors underlying crime. Social process theories stress the importance of peer relationships, social bonding, and social reaction. Conflict theories call attention to the possible use of the legal system to punish behavior by subordinate groups, while feminist theories examine gender differences in criminality, the victimization of women by rape, sexual assault, and domestic violence, and the experiences of women professionals and offenders in the criminal justice system.

6. The criminal justice system costs tens of billions of dollars annually, yet scholars question the potential of this system to reduce crime. How police are deployed seems a more important factor regarding their potential for crime reduction than the actual numbers of police. The surge in imprisonment of the last few decades may have accounted for a relatively small drop in crime, but whatever reduction it has achieved has not been cost-effective, and hundreds of thousands of prison inmates are now returning every year to their communities. Several problems also exist in the criminal justice system itself. Police corruption and brutality remain serious concerns, while indigent defendants receive inadequate legal representation or none at all. Despite public perceptions, prisons and jails are squalid places, and rape and other violence are daily concerns. During the 2020 pandemic, the incarcerated population incurred

high rates of COVID-19 because of the severe overcrowding of their facilities and other living conditions.

7. The United States is the only Western democracy to use the death penalty for common criminals. Social science evidence finds that the death penalty does not deter homicide, is racially discriminatory, may involve wrongful convictions, and costs considerably more than life imprisonment.

8. Many proposals for reducing crime derive from sociological evidence. These proposals aim to reduce poverty and improve neighborhood living conditions; to change male socialization patterns; to expand early childhood intervention programs and nutrition services; to improve the nation's schools and schooling; and to reduce the number of prison inmates by placing nonviolent property and drug offenders in community corrections. The funds saved by this last proposal could be used to improve prison and jail rehabilitation programming.

Using What You Know

Suppose you are the Democratic Party governor of a Midwestern state and that you are up for reelection in 2 years. You were a political science major in college but had a sociology minor with a focus in criminal justice. The crime rate in your state has risen slightly since you took office, and there is growing sentiment in the state's major newspapers and from the Republican Party opposition in the state legislature to lengthen prison terms for serious crime and to build two more prisons for the greater number of prisoners that will be expected. Because of your studies in college, you are skeptical that this approach will reduce crime, and you recognize it will cost millions of dollars. But you also realize that your opponents and some members of the news media are beginning to say that you are soft on crime. What do you do?

What You Can Do

To help deal with the problem of crime, you may wish to do any of the following:

1. Volunteer at an agency that helps troubled teenagers.

2. Volunteer with an organization that helps ex-offenders.

3. Work for an organization that provides early childhood intervention services for at-risk children.

Endnotes

1. Lotan, Gal Tziperman, and Ellement, John R. 2019. After Shooting, a Family Mourns Loss of a 2nd Son. *The Boston Globe* July 30: B1.

2. Coyne, Marley. 2020. "Crime Rates across U.S. Drop Amid the Coronavirus Pandemic." *Forbes* April 11:https://www.forbes.com/sites/marleycoyne/2020/04/11/crime-rates-across-us-drop-amid-the-coronavirus-pandemic/#19f8ddda311e.

3. Becker, Howard S. 1963. *Outsiders: Studies in the Sociology of Deviance.* New York: Free Press.

4. Robinson, Matthew B. 2018. *Media Coverage of Crime and Criminal Justice.* Durham, NC: Carolina Academic Press; Surette, Ray. 2015. *Media, Crime, and Criminal Justice: Images, Realities, and Policies.* Belmont, CA: Wadsworth Publishing Co.

5. Fox, James Alan, Jack Levin and Kenna Quinet. 2019. *The Will to Kill: Making Sense of Senseless Murder.* Thousand Oaks, CA: Sage Publications.

6. Federal Bureau of Investigation. 2018. *Crime in the United States, 2017.* Washington, DC: Federal Bureau of Investigation.

7. Travis, Jeremy, Bruce Western and Steve Redburn, eds. 2014. *The Growth of Incarceration in the United States: Exploring Causes and Consequences.* Washington, DC: National Academies Press.

8. Sutherland, Edwin H. 1949. *White Collar Crime.* New York, NY: Holt, Rinehart, and Winston.

9. Rosoff, Stephen M., Henry N. Pontell and Robert Tillman. 2020. *Profit without Honor: White Collar Crime and the Looting of America.* Hoboken, NJ: Pearson.

10. Barkan, Steven E. 2018. *Criminology: A Sociological Understanding.* Upper Saddle River, NJ: Pearson.

11. AFL-CIO. 2019. *Death on the Job: The Toll of Neglect, 2019.* Washington, DC: AFL-CIO.

12. Lilienfeld, David E. 1991. "The Silence: The Asbestos Industry and Early Occupational Cancer Research—a Case Study." *American Journal of Public Health* 81:791-800.

13. Cullen, Francis T., William J. Maakestad and Gray Cavender. 2006. *Corporate Crime under Attack: The Fight to Criminalize Business Violence.* Cincinnati: Anderson Publishing Company.

14. Harwell, Drew. 2015. "Why General Motors' $900 Million Fine for a Deadly Defect Is Just a Slap on the Wrist." *The Washington Post* September 17:https://www.washingtonpost.com/news/business/wp/2015/09/17/why-general-motors-900-million-fine-for-a-deadly-defect-is-just-a-slap-on-the-wrist/' Ivory, Danielle and Bill Vlasic. 2015. "$900 Million Penalty for G.M.'S Deadly Defect Leaves Many Cold." *The New York Times* September 18:B1.

15. Barkan, Steven E. 2018. *Criminology: A Sociological Understanding.* Upper Saddle River, NJ: Pearson.

16. Rosoff, Stephen M., Henry N. Pontell and Robert Tillman. 2020. *Profit without Honor: White Collar Crime and the Looting of America.* Hoboken, NJ: Pearson.

17. Kruttschnitt, Candace. 2016. "The Politics, and Place, of Gender in Research on Crime." *Criminology* 54(1):8-29.

18. Steffensmeier, Darrell and Emilie Allan. 2000. "Looking for Patterns: Gender, Age, and Crime." Pp. 85-127 in *Criminology: A Contemporary Handbook*, edited by J. F. Sheley. Belmont, CA: Wadsworth; Monahan, Kathryn, Laurence Steinberg and Alex R. Piquero. 2015. "Juvenile Justice Policy and Practice: A Developmental Perspective." *Crime and Justice* 44(1):577-619. doi: doi:10.1086/681553.

19. Bjerk, David. 2007. "Measuring the Relationship between Youth Criminal Participation and Household Economic Resources." *Journal of Quantitative Criminology* 23:23-39.

20. Stark, Rodney. 1987. "Deviant Places: A Theory of the Ecology of Crime." *Criminology* 25:893-911.

21. Stark, Rodney. 1987. "Deviant Places: A Theory of the Ecology of Crime." *Criminology* 25:893-911.

22. Lopez, German. 2020. "Why New York Has 14 Times as Many Coronavirus Deaths as California." *Vox.com* April 13:https://www.vox.com/2020/4/7/21205890/coronavirus-covid-19-pandemic-new-york-california.

23. Barkan, Steven E. 2019. *Race, Crime, and Justice: The Continuing American Dilemma*. New York: Oxford University Press.

24. Federal Bureau of Investigation. 2018. *Crime in the United States, 2017*. Washington, DC: Federal Bureau of Investigation.

25. Barkan, Steven E. 2019. *Race, Crime, and Justice: The Continuing American Dilemma*. New York: Oxford University Press; Walker, Samuel, Cassia Spohn and Miriam DeLone. 2018. *The Color of Justice: Race, Ethnicity, and Crime in America*. Belmont, CA: Wadsworth Publishing Company.

26. Gabbidon, Shaun L. and Helen Taylor Greene. 2019. *Race and Crime*. Thousand Oaks, CA: Sage Publications.

27. McCarthy, Bill and John Hagan. 2003. "Sanction Effects, Violence, and Native North American Street Youth." Pp. 117-37 in *Violent Crime: Assessing Race and Ethnic Differences*, edited by D. F. Hawkins. Cambridge: Cambridge University Press.

28. Shaw, Clifford R. and Henry D. McKay. 1942. *Juvenile Delinquency and Urban Areas*. Chicago: University of Chicago Press.

29. Goodson, Amanda and Leana A. Bouffard. 2019. "Social Disorganization and Gender Equality as Correlates of Family Violence and Rape." *Journal of Crime & Justice* 42(3):274-87.

30. Merton, Robert K. 1938. Social Structure and Anomie. *American Sociological Review* 3:672–682.

31. Agnew, Robert. 2015. "The Role of the Social Environment in General Strain Theory." *The Nurture Versus Biosocial Debate in Criminology: On the Origins of Criminal Behavior and Criminality*, Vol. 184-198, edited by K. M. Beaver, J. C. Barnes and B. B. Boutwell. Thousand Oaks, CA: Sage Publications; De Coster, Stacy and Maxine S. Thompson. 2017. "Race and General Strain Theory: Microaggressions as Mundane Extreme Environmental Stresses." *Justice Quarterly* 34(5):903-30.

32. Sutherland, Edwin H. 1947. *Principles of Criminology*, 4th ed.. Philadelphia: J. P. Lippincott.

33. Akers, Ronald L., Christine S. Sellers and Wesley G. Jennins. 2017. *Criminological Theories: Introduction, Evaluation, and Application*. New York: Oxford University Press.

34. Hirschi, Travis. 1969. *Causes of Delinquency*. Berkeley: University of California Press.

35. Payne, Allison Ann and Kelly Welch. 2016. "The Centrality of Schools in the Lifecourse: The Case for Focusing on School-Related Influences in Developmental Theory and Research." *Deviant Behavior* 37(7):748-60.

36. Duncan, Greg and Suzanne Le Menestrel, eds. 2019. *A Roadmap to Reducing Child Poverty*. Washington, DC: The National Academies Press;. Kirp, David L. 2018. "To Make America Richer, Help Poor Children." *The New York Times* December 6:https://www.nytimes.com/2018/12/06/opinion/medicaid-immigrants-food-stamps-trump.html?rref=collection/sectioncollection/opinion; Welsh, Brandon C. and David P. Farrington. 2007. "Save Children from a Life of Crime." *Criminology & Public Policy* 6(4):871-79.

37. Guo, Siying. 2018. "A Model of Religious Involvement, Family Processes, Self-Control, and Juvenile Delinquency in Two-Parent Families." *Journal of Adolescence* 63:175-90.

38. Klement, Christian. 2015. "Comparing the Effects of Community Service and Imprisonment on Reconviction: Results from a Quasi-Experimental Danish Study." *Journal of Experimental Criminology* 11(2):237-61; Nagin, Daniel S., Francis T. Cullen and Cheryl Lero Jonson. 2009. "Imprisonment and Reoffending." *Crime and Justice: A Review of Research* 38:115-200.

39. Gusfield, Joseph R. 1963. *Symbolic Crusade: Status Politics and the American Temperance Movement*. Urbana, IL: University of Illinois Press.

40. DeKeseredy, Walter S. and Molly Dragiewicz, eds. 2012. *Routledge Handbook of Critical Criminology*. New York: Routledge.

41. Bonger, Willem. 1916. *Criminality and Economic Conditions*. Translated by H. P. Horton. Boston: Little, Brown.

42. Mallicoat, Stacy L. 2019. *Women, Gender, and Crime: Core Concepts*. Thousand Oaks, CA: Sage Publications.

43. Miller, Jody and Rod K. Brunson. 2000. "Gender Dynamics in Youth Gangs: A Comparison of Males' and Females' Accounts." *Justice Quarterly* 17:419-48.

44. Lanctôt, Nadine and Marc Le Blanc. 2002. "Explaining Deviance by Adolescent Females." *Crime and Justice: A Review of Research* 29:113-202.

45. Chesney-Lind, Meda and Randall G. Shelden. 2014. *Girls, Delinquency, and Juvenile Justice*. Malden, MA: Wiley-Blackwell.

46. Mallicoat, Stacy L. 2019. *Women, Gender, and Crime: Core Concepts*. Thousand Oaks, CA: Sage Publications.

47. Skolnick, Jerome H. 1994. *Justice without Trial: Law Enforcement in Democratic Society*. New York: Macmillan.

48. Barkan, Steven E. and George Bryjak. 2018. *Fundamentals of Criminal Justice*. Boston: FlatWorld.

49. Glover, Scott and Matt Lait. 2000. "Police in Secret Group Broke Law Routinely, Transcripts Say." Pp. A1 in *The Los Angeles Times*.

50. Langton, Lynn and Matthew Durose. 2013. *Police Behavior During Traffic and Street Stops, 2011*. Washington, DC: Bureau of Justice Statistics, U.S. Department of Justice.

51. Barkan, Steven E. and George Bryjak. 2018. *Fundamentals of Criminal Justice*. Boston: FlatWorld.

52. Sullivan, John, Julie Tate and Jennifer Jenkins. 2018. "Fatal Police Shootings of Unarmed People Have Significantly Declined, Experts Say." *The Washington Post* May 7:https://www.washingtonpost.com/investigations/fatal-police-shootings-of-unarmed-people-have-significantly-declined-experts-say/2018/05/03/d5eab374-4349-11e8-8569-26fda6b404c7_story.html.

53. Hyland, Shelley, Lynn Langton and Elizabeth Davis. 2015. *Police Use of Nonfatal Force, 2002–11*. Washington, DC: Bureau of Justice Statistics, U.S. Department of Justice.

54. Fridell, Lorie and Hyeyoung Lim. 2016. "Assessing the Racial Aspects of Police Force Using the Implicit- and Counter-Bias Perspectives." *Journal of Criminal Justice* 44:36-48; Goff, Phillip Atiba, Tracey Lloyd, Amanda Geller, Steven Raphael and Jack Glaser. 2016. *The Science of Justice: Race, Arrests, and Police Use of Force*. New York: Center for Policing Equity, John Jay College of Criminal Justice; Paoline, Eugene A., III, Jacinta M. Gau and William Terrill. 2016. "Race and the Police Use of Force Encounter in the United States." *British Journal of Criminology*:https://doi.org/10.1093/bjc/azw089.

55. Miller, Ted R, Bruce A Lawrence, Nancy N Carlson, Delia Hendrie, Sean Randall, Ian R H Rockett and Rebecca S Spicer. 2017. "Perils of Police Action: A Cautionary Tale from Us Data Sets." *Injury Prevention* 23:27-32.

56. Walker, Samuel. 2015. *Sense and Nonsense About Crime, Drugs, and Communities*. Stamford, CT: Cengage Learning. .

57. Braga, Anthony A. and David L. Weisburd. 2015. "Focused Deterrence and the Prevention of Violent Gun Injuries: Practice, Theoretical Principles, and Scientific Evidence." *Annual Review of Public Health* 36:55-68.

58. Bureau of Labor Statistics. 2018. "Occupational Employment Statistics, Police and Sheriff's Patrol Officers." https://www.bls.gov/OES/current/oes333051.htm.

59. Waldrop, Theresa. 2020. "New York City Police Department Has Lost 29 Members to Covid-19." *CNN* April 19:https://www.cnn.com/2020/04/19/us/new-york-city-police-covid-19-deaths/index.html.

60. NBC Chicago. 2020. "Chicago Police Reveal 50 More Positive Covid-19 Tests in Department."https://www.nbcchicago.com/news/local/chicago-police-reveal-50-more-positive-covid-19-tests-in-department/2259742/.

61. Kohler-Hausmann, Issa. 2018. *Misdemeanorland: Criminal Courts and Social Control in an Age of Broken Windows Policing* Princeton: Princeton University Press; Van Cleve, Nicole Gonzalez. 2016. *Crook County: Racism and Injustice in America's Largest Criminal Court*. Stanford: Stanford University Press.

62. Barkan, Steven E. 1996. "The Social Science Significance of the O.J. Simpson Case." Pp. 36-42 in *Representing O.J.: Murder, Criminal Justice and Mass Culture*, edited by G. Barak. Albany, NY: Harrow and Heston.

63. Zeidman, Steven. 2017. "Eradicating Assembly-Line Justice: An Opportunity Lost by the Revised American Bar Association Criminal Justice Standards." *Hofstra Law Review* 46:293-328.

64. Zeidman, Steven. 2017. "Eradicating Assembly-Line Justice: An Opportunity Lost by the Revised American Bar Association Criminal Justice Standards." *Hofstra Law Review* 46:293-328.

65. Hinton, Elizabeth Kai, LaShae Henderson and Cindy Reed. 2018. *An Unjust Burden: The Disparate Treatment of Black Americans in the Criminal Justice System*. New York: Vera Institute of Justice.

66. Alexander, Michelle. 2012. *The New Jim Crow: Mass Incarceration in the Age of Colorblindness*. New York: The New Press.

67. Travis, Jeremy, Bruce Western and Steve Redburn, eds. 2014. *The Growth of Incarceration in the United States: Exploring Causes and Consequences*. Washington, DC: National Academies Press.

68. Kappeler, Victor E. and Gary W. Potter. 2018. *The Mythology of Crime and Criminal Justice*. Prospect Heights, IL: Waveland Press.

69. Williams, Timothy, Benjamin Weiser and William K. Rashbaum. 2020. "Social Distancing Isn't an Option, So Prisons Free Inmates to Try to Slow Infection." *The New York Times* March 31:A9.

70. Volpenhein, Sarah and Marion Star. 2020. "Marion Prison's Virus Outbreak Seeps into Public." *Columbus Dispatch* April 25:https://www.dispatch.com/news/20200425/marion-prisonrsquos-virus-outbreak-seeps-into-public.

71. Kaden, Allison. 2019. From Mugshots to Headshots: Nonprofit Works to Help the Formerly Incarcerated. *WPIX*: https://pix11.com/2019/07/24/from-mugshots-to-headshots-nonprofit-works-to-help-the-formerly-incarcerated/; The Fortune Society. 2018. 2017-2018 Annual Report. New York: The Fortune Society

72. Bohm 2017; Death Penalty Information Center. 2019. *Facts About the Death Penalty*. Washington, DC: Death Penalty Information Center.

73. Barkan, Steven E. and Michael Rocque. 2020. *Crime Prevention: Programs, Policies, and Practices*. Thousand Oaks, CA: Sage Publications; Tonry, Michael and Daniel S. Nagin, eds. 2017. *Reinventing American Criminal Justice, Vol. 46*. Chicago: University of Chicago Press; Welsh, Brandon C., Anthony A. Braga and Christopher J. Sullivan. 2014. "Serious Youth Violence and Innovative Prevention: On the Emerging Link between Public Health and Criminology." *JQ: Justice Quarterly* 31(3):500-23. doi: 10.1080/07418825.2012.690441.

74. Adelman, Robert, Lesley Williams Reid, Gail Markle, Saskia Weiss and Charles Jaret. 2017. "Urban Crime Rates and the Changing Face of Immigration: Evidence across Four Decades." *Journal of Ethnicity in Criminal Justice* 15(1):52-77; Ousey, Graham C. and Chris E. Kubrin. 2018. "Immigration and Crime: Assessing a Contentious Issue." *Annual Review of Criminology* 1:63-84.

75. Daly, Kathleen and Meda Chesney-Lind. 1988. "Feminism and Criminology." *Justice Quarterly* 5:497-538.

76. Dammer, Harry R. and Jay S. Albanese. 2014. *Comparative Criminal Justice Systems*. Belmont, CA: Wadsworth Publishing Company; Duran, Jack W. 2018. "What German Prisons Do Differently." *Vera Institute of Justice*(August 23):https://www.vera.org/blog/dispatches-from-germany/what-german-prisons-do-differently; Waller, Irvin and Brandon C. Welsh. 2007. "Reducing Crime by Harnessing International Best Practices." Pp. 208-16 in *Solutions to Social Problems: Lessons from Other Societies*, edited by D. S. Eitzen. Boston: Allyn & Bacon.

77. Greenwood, Peter W. 2006. *Changing Lives: Delinquency Prevention as Crime-Control Policy*. Chicago: University of Chicago Press.

78. Cullen, Francis T. 2013. "Rehabilitation: Beyond Nothing Works." *Crime and Justice* 42(1):299-376.

79. Rosoff, Stephen M., Henry N. Pontell and Robert Tillman. 2020. *Profit without Honor: White Collar Crime and the Looting of America*. Hoboken, NJ: Pearson.

CHAPTER 9
Sexual Behavior

Social Problems in the News

"Rewrite of Texas Sex Education Standards Could Include Lessons on Contraception," the head-line said. Across Texas, sex education in the public schools is either absent or, when present, typically emphasizes the need for abstinence and ignores the concept of safe sex. But in the summer of 2019, the Texas State Board of Education was considering whether to require a sex education curriculum that includes age-appropriate material on contraception and sexuality. A pro-sex education activist said that Texas needs to "come into the 21st century. . . . If we teach abstinence-only sex education, we're ignoring the nearly 60 percent of students who say that they are sexually active before they graduate from high school. We're ignoring LGBTQ students because our abstinence-only sex education does not deal with sexual orientation or gender iden-tity." Disagreeing with this view, an anti-sex education activist said that abstinence is the best strategy for children to practice and that parents need to have the final say regarding when their children receive sex education and what they are taught about it.

Against this debate backdrop lay the stark reality that the teen birth rate in Texas has been the fourth highest in the United States, with about 30,000 teen pregnancies annually and with 3 per-cent of girls ages 15–19 giving birth in 2017.

Sources: Rivera 2019; Zelinski 2019[1]

This news story reminds us that sexual behavior is often cause for concern and the basis for certain social problems. It should come as no surprise that social scientists study many aspects of sexual behavior and have provided a good deal of insight on sexual issues. This chapter discusses the social scientific evidence for various types of sexual behavior and issues relating to them: teenage sex and pregnancy, abortion, prostitution, and pornography. Although people often have strong views about these issues, we will see that the social scientific evidence sometimes challenges the views that many people hold.

9.1 An Overview of Heterosexuality

Learning Objectives

1. Explain what happened as a result of the sexual revolution.
2. Describe current views on sexual behavior.
3. Understand the prevalence of certain sexual behaviors today.

Because Chapter 5 discussed sexual orientation and gender identity, this chapter's discussion of sexual behavior focuses mostly on issues concerning heterosexual sex. To provide a backdrop for these issues, we first provide an overview of heterosexual behavior and views about such behavior.

The Sexual Revolution: Changing Attitudes and Changing Behavior

The youth counterculture of the 1960s emphasized that sexual intercourse need not be delayed until marriage. Their views helped fuel the so-called sexual revolution.

Source: © Thinkstock

sexual revolution

A substantial change during the 1960s and 1970s in many aspects of Americans' sexual behavior and in how they thought about sex.

The 1960s were a time of major change in the United States. The Southern civil rights movement and Vietnam antiwar movements shook the nation, and the women's rights, gay rights, and environmental movements began. Another major change was the **sexual revolution**, which saw a substantial change in many aspects of Americans' sexual behavior and in how they thought about sex. Thanks in large part to the introduction of the birth control pill, women became freer to have sex without fear of pregnancy. The hippies of the youth counterculture of the 1960s emphasized *free love*, the idea that sexual intercourse need not be delayed until marriage, and a popular slogan heard during the Vietnam war years was "make love, not war." A highlight (or lowlight, depending on one's view) of the era was the Summer of Love in 1967, when tens of thousands of young people gathered in the Haight-Ashbury neighborhood of San Francisco to do drugs, have sex, and engage in other counterculture activities. The appearance of HIV and AIDS during the 1980s reversed some of the trends of the sexual revolution, as people became more concerned about the consequences of unprotected sex, but the effects of this revolution largely remain: Many more people now have sex before marriage than before the 1960s, and views about certain sexual behaviors have become less conservative since the 1960s and 1970s (Pampel 2016).[2]

We can see evidence of changing views about sex in data from the General Social Survey (GSS), which has been administered nationally since the early 1970s. One of the questions the GSS asks is about premarital sex: "There's been a lot of discussion about the way morals and attitudes about sex are changing in this country. If a man and woman have sex relations before marriage, do you think it is always wrong, almost always wrong, wrong only sometimes, or not wrong at all?" In 1972, only 27.2 percent of the public replied it was "not wrong at all," but by 2018, this percentage had more than doubled to 61.8 percent (see Figure 9.1).

FIGURE 9.1 Change in Views about Premarital Sex (Percentage Saying Premarital Sex Is "Not Wrong at All")

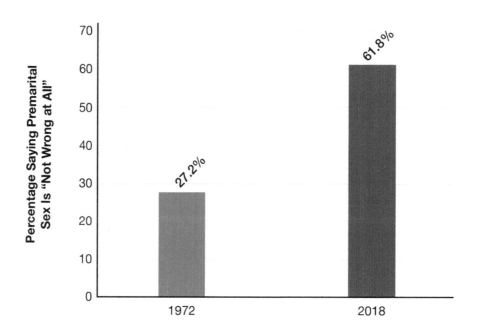

Source: Data from General Social Surveys. 1972 and 2018. Retrieved from https://sda.berkeley.edu/sdaweb/analysis/
;jsessionid=E87D6F2B568F883F6138D2CBA1BE95DC?dataset=gss18.

On two other issues, extramarital sex and sex between teenagers ages 14–16, views have not changed from a generation ago or have hardly changed. Very few Americans today, fewer than 3 percent, think that extramarital sex is "not wrong at all," and very few thought it was not wrong a generation ago when the GSS asked about this behavior. Regarding teenage sex, 3 percent of GSS respondents thought it not wrong during the mid-1980s, while 9 percent held this view in 2018. Although this change represents an increase, the vast majority of Americans still think that teenage sex is at least sometimes wrong. As all these trend data indicate, the sexual revolution changed certain sexual attitudes but did not affect other attitudes. In this respect, then, the sexual revolution was only partly revolutionary.

Certain changes in sexual behavior also occurred as part of the sexual revolution. In particular, many more people began having sex before age eighteen during and after the 1960s than before the 1960s and, in a related trend, to have more sexual partners before age eighteen (Laumann et al. 1994).[3] We can see evidence of the former trend in national survey data reported in Table 9.1, which shows the percentage of people born in different decades (*birth cohorts*) who had sex before age eighteen. Among women, less than one-third of those in the 1933–1942 and 1943–1952 birth cohorts (who would all have reached age eighteen *before* the sexual revolution) had sex before age eighteen. These low figures jumped to 47.6 percent for those in the 1953–1962 birth cohort (who became teenagers in the 1960s and 1970s, *during* the sexual revolution) and then grew further to 58.2 percent in the next birth cohort. In the twenty-year span, then, between the 1943–1952 and 1963–1974 birth cohorts, women became almost twice as likely (58.2/30.0) to have sex before age eighteen. Men, too, became more likely to have sex before age eighteen, though at a slightly smaller rate of increase over the thirty-year span shown in the table. In related figures, only 30 percent of teenaged girls in 1972 were sexually experienced; by 1988, this figure had jumped to 51 percent (Martinez et al. 2011).[4] The remarkable increase in teenage sex for both females and males since the 1960s has had important repercussions down to the present, as we shall see in the section on teenage sex and pregnancy later in this chapter.

TABLE 9.1 Percentage Who Had Heterosexual Sex before Age Eighteen

Birth cohort	1933–1942	1943–1952	1953–1962	1963–1974
Women	32.2	30.0	47.6	58.2
Men	42.5	47.9	56.8	61.3

Source: Laumann, E.O., J.H. Gagnon, R.T. Michael, and S. Michaels, 1994. *The Social Organization of Sexuality* (p. 328). Chicago: University of Chicago Press.

Heterosexuality Today: Attitudes and Behavior

Americans' attitudes today about heterosexual behavior are very diverse. On some issues, Americans are fairly united, either in a more tolerant and accepting direction or in a less tolerant and unaccepting direction. On other issues, Americans are fairly divided, with large numbers of people feeling one way and large numbers feeling another way. The American public is probably even more diverse in its sexual behavior: Some people have a lot of sex and engage in a variety of sexual activities, while other people have less sex and limit their sexual activity to vaginal intercourse. To gain a sense of what Americans are thinking and doing in the area of heterosexual activity, national surveys provide some important evidence.

Attitudes

As noted earlier, the GSS asks respondents to indicate their views on several types of heterosexual behavior and issues related to this behavior. We'll first look again at their views about sexual behavior that we examined earlier in the discussion about the sexual revolution. This time we will focus on the percentage who say the behaviors are wrong ("always wrong," "almost always wrong," or "sometimes wrong") (see Figure 9.2).

FIGURE 9.2 Views on Sexual Behavior (Percentage Saying the Behavior Is Wrong)

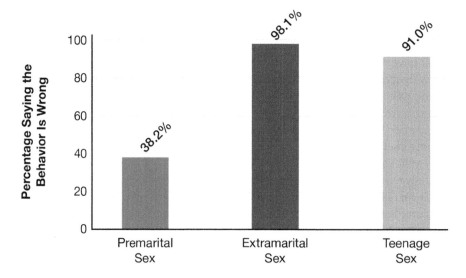

Source: Data from General Social Survey. 2020. Retrieved from https://sda.berkeley.edu/sdaweb/analysis/?dataset=gss18.

Figure 9.2 shows that Americans almost unanimously think that adultery (extramarital sex) and teenage sex are wrong, but that they are rather split on whether premarital sex is wrong, with somewhat more than one-third saying it is wrong and two-thirds saying it is not wrong at all.

Certain aspects of our social backgrounds predict our views about premarital sex. In particular, women, older people, and those who are more religious are more likely than their counterparts to disapprove of it. We see evidence of one of these trends in Figure 9.3, which focuses on religiosity and the percentage of GSS respondents who say that premarital sex is wrong (always wrong, almost always wrong, or sometimes wrong). Religiosity is strongly related to this belief, with very religious respondents six to eight times more likely than those who are slightly or not religious to say premarital sex is wrong.

FIGURE 9.3 Religiosity and Disapproval of Premarital Sex (Percentage Saying Premarital Sex between a Woman and a Man Is Wrong)

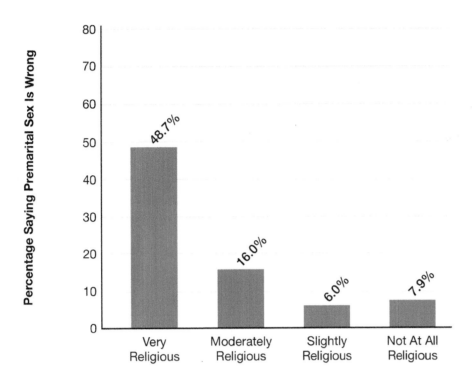

Source: Data from General Social Survey. 2020. Retrieved from https://sda.berkeley.edu/sdaweb/analysis/?dataset=gss18.

Behavior

A good understanding of Americans' sexual behaviors comes from the 2011–2013 National Survey of Family Growth (NSFG), which was administered to 10,416 Americans ages 15–44 nationwide. Although this survey omits people older than 44, it still yields valuable information about people in their prime reproductive years.

Table 9.2 reports some NSFG gender-based data on several kinds of sexual behaviors for young people ages 18–24. Although many people think that males are much more sexually active than females, the data in Table 9.2 show that the gender differences in heterosexual contact are practically nonexistent. Reflecting a conclusion from Chapter 5's discussion of sexual orientation, however, females are more likely than males to have had same-sex sexual contact. In one other gender difference not reported in the table, males are more likely than females to have had multiple heterosexual sex partners. Specifically, and looking at ages 15–44, 5.0 percent of males have had at least five heterosexual partners during the past year, compared to only 1.7 percent of females; similarly, 21.1 percent of males say they have had at least fifteen heterosexual partners in their lifetime, compared to only 10.1 percent of females (Centers for Disease Control and Prevention 2017).[5] In this specific sexual aspect, then, males are indeed more active than females.

TABLE 9.2 Lifetime Prevalence of Sexual Behaviors, Ages 18–24*

	Females	Males
Any opposite-sex contact	85.6	83.5
Any opposite-sex contact: vaginal intercourse	81.7	79.9
Any opposite-sex contact: gave or received oral sex	77.3	77.6
* Percentage engaging in behavior at least once		

	Females	Males
Any opposite-sex contact: anal sex	28.4	29.3
Any same-sex behavior	19.4	6.2
* Percentage engaging in behavior at least once		

Source: Source: Copen, C.E., A. Chandra, and I. Febo-Vazquez, 2016. Sexual Behavior, Sexual Attraction, and Sexual Orientation among Adults Aged 18–44 in the United States: Data from the 2011–2013 National Survey of Family Growth. National Health Statistics Reports; no 88. Hyattsville, MD: National Center for Health Statistics.

Although women and men in the United States are equally sexually active, unmarried men tend to have more sexual partners than unmarried women.

Source: © Thinkstock

We saw earlier that higher degrees of religiosity are strongly associated with greater disapproval of premarital sex. Does this mean that religiosity should also be associated with a lower likelihood of actually engaging in premarital sex? The answer is clearly yes, as many studies of adolescents find that those who are more religious are more likely to still be virgins and, if they have had sex, more likely to have had fewer sexual partners (Hayward 2019).[6] Survey data on adults yield a similar finding: Among all never-married adults in the GSS, those who are more religious are also more likely to have had fewer sexual partners (Barkan 2006).[7] We see evidence of this relationship in Table 9.3, which shows that among never-married adults ages 21–39, those who are very religious are more likely to have had no sexual partners in the past five years and, if they have had any partners, less likely to have had at least two partners. Although it is hypothetically possible that not having sexual partners leads someone to become more religious, it is much more likely that being very religious reduces the number of sexual partners that never-married adults have.

TABLE 9.3 Self-Rated Religiosity and Number of Sexual Partners in Past Five Years among Never-Married Adults Ages 21–39 (%)

Number of sexual partners	Very religious	Moderately religious	Slightly religious or not at all religious
0	22.3	13.1	8.9
1	33.2	26.3	24.3
2 or more	44.5	60.6	66.8

Source: Data from General Social Surveys (2014–2018). Retrieved from https://sda.berkeley.edu/sdaweb/analysis/?dataset=gss18.

Key Takeaways

- The sexual revolution liberalized some views about sexual behavior and increased participation in some forms of sexual behavior, particularly premarital sex.
- Gender, age, and religiosity predict attitudes about premarital sex.
- There are few or no gender differences today in the prevalence of various heterosexual behaviors, but men are more likely than women to have had multiple sex partners.

For Your Review

1. Do you think the sexual revolution was a good thing or a bad thing? Explain your answer.
2. Did it surprise you to learn that women and men are equally sexually active today? Why or why not?

9.2 Teenage Sex and Pregnancy

Learning Objectives

1. Describe how many teenagers have had sex.
2. List several problems associated with teenage pregnancy and birth.
3. Discuss how to reduce teenage pregnancy and help teenage mothers.

We saw earlier that the percentage of teenagers who have sex greatly increased during the 1960s and 1970s. Regardless of what one thinks about premarital sex, this increase had at least two important practical consequences: It greatly increased the risk of teenage pregnancy, and it greatly increased the risk of getting HIV and other sexually transmitted diseases (STDs). For these and other reasons, teenage sex rightly arouses much concern. This section examines trends in teenage sex and pregnancy, the reasons for these trends, and possible measures for reducing teenage pregnancy. As part of this examination, it also discusses STDs, which affects sexually active teens but also older sexually active people.

Teenage Sexual Activity

As noted earlier, teenagers are much more sexually active today than they were before the sexual revolution. Among never-married teens ages 15–19, 42.4 percent of females and 44.2 percent of males have had sexual intercourse, or about 43 percent overall (Abma and Martinez 2017).[8] This percentage represents a drop from its highest point, in 1988, of 51 percent for females and of 60 percent for males. About 79 percent of sexually experienced girls and 84 percent of experienced boys used contraception, most often a condom, the first time they ever had sex. In their most recent act of sexual intercourse, about 90 percent of girls and 95 percent of boys used contraception, again most often a condom.

The birth rate for females aged 15–19 is 18.8 births per 1,000 females (2017 data). This rate represents a substantial decline from the early 1990s, when it reached a peak of almost 60 per 1,000 females. However, it remains much higher today than the rate in other Western democracies (Centers for Disease Control and Prevention 2019).[9]

If 43 percent of teens have had sexual intercourse, that means the majority of teens, 57 percent, have never had intercourse. It is interesting to examine their reasons for this status. Table 9.4 shows the relevant data. The top reasons for both sexes are religion/morals and not having found the right person yet; concern about pregnancy ranks third.

TABLE 9.4 Main Reason Given for Never Having Sexual Intercourse, Ages 15–19 (%)

	Females	Males
Against religion or morals	35	28
Don't want to get (a female) pregnant	19	21
Haven't found the right person yet	22	28
Don't want to get an STD	7	5
In a relationship, but waiting for the right time	6	7
Other reason	10	11

Source: Abma, Joyce C. and Gladys M. Martinez. 2017. "Sexual Activity and Contraceptive Use among Teenagers in the United States, 2011–2015." *National Health Statistics Reports* June 22(104):1–22.

The Problem of Teenage Pregnancy

The number of teen births today is much, much lower than four decades ago. This huge decline is a notable development.

Source: © Thinkstock

Most teenage pregnancies and births are unplanned and are part of a more general problem for all women in their childbearing years. About 45 percent of all pregnancies in the United States, or some 2.8 million pregnancies annually, are unplanned (2011 data, the latest at the time of this writing). Of these unplanned pregnancies and excluding miscarriages, 42 percent end in abortion, and 58 percent end in birth. Putting all these numbers together, about 1.6 million births happen each year from unplanned pregnancies. Without publicly funded family planning services, an estimated 2 million additional unplanned pregnancies, 900,000 births, and 700,000 abortions would occur annually.[10]

Planned or unplanned, nearly 450,000 teenage pregnancies occurred in 2013, resulting in some 273,000 live births, 110,000 abortions, and 66,000 miscarriages and stillbirths (Kost et al. 2017).[11] By 2017, the number of teen births had declined to 194,000, down tremendously from a peak of almost 1.2 million in 1980 (Martin et al. 2018).[12] Pregnancy and birth rates for the past several decades have been higher for African American, Native American, and Latinx teens than for non-Latinx white or Asian teens, and that trend remains true today. In 2017, the birth rates for the first three groups were all at least 27.5 per 1,000 females in this age group, compared to rates of 13.2 for non-Latinx white teens and 3.3 for Asian teens (Centers for Disease Control and Prevention 2019).[13]

Although teenaged pregnancies (and births from these pregnancies) are far from the majority of all pregnancies, unplanned or planned, they pose special problems (Carey and Seladi-Schulman 2018; Centers for Disease Control and Prevention 2019).[14] On the individual level, pregnant teenagers are more at risk than older pregnant women for high blood pressure and anemia, and they are also more likely to experience early labor, premature birth, and low birth weight. In addition, because teenagers are more likely than adults to have STDs, pregnant teenagers are more likely than older pregnant women to have an STD while they are pregnant, either because they already had an STD when they conceived or because they incur an STD from having sex during pregnancy.

Many pregnant teenagers decide to drop out of school. In a telling statistic, only 53 percent of women in their twenties who gave birth as a teenager have a high school diploma, compared to 90 percent of their counterparts who did not have a teenage birth (Manlove and Lantos 2018).[15] If pregnant teens stay in school, they often must deal with the embarrassment of being pregnant, and the physical and emotional difficulties accompanying their teenage pregnancy can affect their school performance and mental health. Once the baby is born, child care typically becomes an enormous problem, whether or not the new mother is in school. Because pregnant teenagers disproportionately come from families that are poor or near poor, they have few financial resources and often have weak social support networks, either before or after the baby is born.

Can the U.S. End Teen Pregnancy?

Although teenage pregnancies and births have declined greatly from the early 1980s, tens of thousands of teenagers still become pregnant and give birth every year. Pregnant teenagers are at risk for several problems, including pregnancy complications.

View the video online at: http://www.youtube.com/embed/iRGPjWQOh4c?rel=0

At the societal level, teenage pregnancy and motherhood are very costly in at least two important respects. First, because pregnancy and childbirth complications are more common among teenagers, their health-care expenses during and after pregnancy and childbirth are often higher than the expenses incurred by older women. Medicaid, the federal government's national health plan for poor families, often covers much of these expenses, and the premiums that private health insurance companies charge are higher than otherwise because of their expenses when they insure the families of pregnant teenagers.

Second, the children of teenage mothers are at risk for several kinds of behavioral and developmental problems. The "Children and Our Future" box discusses these problems further.

Children and Our Future

Kids Having Kids: The Children of Teenage Mothers

Teenage mothers (ages 15–19) are often unprepared emotionally or practically to raise a child. They often have poor parenting skills and, for example, do not take the time to read daily to their children and otherwise stimulate their cognitive development. They are also less likely than older mothers to provide proper emotional support for their children. In addition, the stress they experience as very young mothers puts them at risk for neglecting or abusing their children. The fact that teenage mothers tend to come from low-income families and continue to live in poverty or near poverty after they become mothers compounds all these problems.

For all these reasons, the children of teenage mothers are at greater risk for several kinds of problems. These problems include impaired neurological development, behavioral problems, and poor school performance.

In particular, when compared to children born to older mothers, the children of teen mothers have lower cognitive scores on the average when they start kindergarten, and they continue to have lower math, reading, and vocabulary test scores as they grow older. These problems persist into their own adolescence, as they are less likely than children of older mothers to graduate from high school. Children of teen mothers are also somewhat more likely to have chronic health problems during childhood and adolescence. When the children of teenage mothers become adolescents, they are also more at risk for delinquency and drug use and to have a prison record by the time they reach young adulthood.

The teenage pregnancy and birth rates in the United States are by far the highest of all Western democracies. The problems that children of teen mothers experience underscore the need for our nation to do everything possible to prevent teenage pregnancy.

Sources: Cook and Cameron 2015; Mollborn 2017[16]

Sexually Transmitted Diseases

Teens and young adults ages 15–24 compose one-fourth of all sexually active people, but they account for one-half of new sexually transmitted diseases.

Source: © Thinkstock

In addition to pregnancy and birth, another problem associated with teenage sexual activity is the transmission of sexually transmitted diseases (STDs). This is a problem during the teenage years, but it is even more of a problem during young adulthood, when sexual activity is greater than during adolescence. Although young people ages 15–24 comprise only about one-fourth of all sexually active people, they account for half of the 20 million new STDs annually. In a related statistic, one-fourth of sexually active adolescent females have an STD. The overall STD rate for young people is higher for females than for males, but young males have a higher rate of syphilis than young females (Centers for Disease Control and Prevention 2018).[17] Despite the high prevalence of STDs among young people, many who test positive for an STD did not believe they were at risk for getting an STD (Wildsmith et al. 2010).[18]

In addition to the gender differences just mentioned, racial/ethnic differences for incurring STDs also exist. We can illustrate this for chlamydia among women of all ages. In 2017, the rate for new chlamydia cases for African American females was about 1,420 cases per 100,000 population, while the rate for Native American females was 1,148. The Latinx rate was 564, while the non-Latinx white rate was 283 and the Asian rate 160. According to the CDC, the higher rates for women of color in this example and for people of color for STDs more generally reflect their life circumstances (including higher rates of poverty and lack of health insurance) more than behavioral differences: "Inequities in the burden of disease for chlamydia, gonorrhea, syphilis and other STDs by race and Hispanic ethnicity continue to persist at unacceptable levels in the United States. These disparities are not explained by individual or population-level behavioral differences; rather they result in large measure from stubbornly entrenched systemic, societal, and cultural barriers to STD diagnoses, treatment and preventive services accessible on a routine basis" (Centers for Disease Control and Prevention 2018).[19]

Reducing Teenage Pregnancy and Helping Teenage Mothers

Teenage pregnancies cannot occur in either of these two situations: (1) Teenagers do not have sex, or (2) they use effective contraception if they do have sex. If we could wave a magic wand or turn the clock back to before the 1960s, it might be possible to greatly reduce the number of teenagers who have sex, but that day is long past. Teenage sex increased during the 1960s and 1970s and remains more common today despite declines after HIV and AIDS became a worldwide problem during the 1980s and 1990s and concern also grew about teenage pregnancies and STD. Many states require abstinence education in the public schools, which they believe will delay teens' first sexual encounters and reduce their numbers of sexual partners, pregnancies, births, and STDs. However, most sexual behavior researchers believe that pleas for abstinence, as well as sex education programs that focus solely or almost entirely on abstinence, do not have these impacts. As the Kaiser Family Foundation (2018)[20] summarizes this expert opinion, "There is currently no strong body of evidence to support that abstinence-only programs have these effects on the sexual behavior of youth and some have documented negative impacts on pregnancy and birth rates."

If this is true, say sexual behavior researchers, then the best strategy is to use *a harm reduction* approach. We first encountered this term in Chapter 7's discussion of illegal drugs. A harm reduction approach recognizes that because certain types of harmful behavior are inevitable, our society should do its best to minimize the various kinds of harm that these various behaviors generate. In regard to teenage sex and pregnancy, a harm reduction approach has two goals: (1) to help reduce the risk for pregnancy among sexually active teens and (2) to help teenage mothers and their children.

Reducing Pregnancy

To achieve the first goal, parents, sex education classes, family planning clinics, youth development programs, and other parties must continue to emphasize the importance of waiting to have sex but also the need for teenagers to use contraception if they are sexually active. In addition, effective contraception (birth control pills, other hormonal control, and also condoms, which protect against STDs) must be made available for teenagers at little or no cost. Efforts in all these areas have contributed greatly to the dramatic drop in teenage pregnancy and birth rates since the early 1980s. Studies indicate that these strategies do not lead to more teenage sex and that consistent contraceptive use greatly reduces the risk of teenage pregnancy. As one writer has summarized these studies' conclusions, "Contraceptives no more cause sex than umbrellas cause rain...When contraception is unavailable, the likely consequences is not less sex, but more pregnancy" (Kristof 2011:A31).[21] If all women had access to the most effective contraception, it is estimated that the United States would save $12 billion in health-care costs each year from the reduced numbers of unintended pregnancies and births that would result (Welti and Manlove 2017).[22]

People Making a Difference

Helping Teenagers Reduce the Risk of Pregnancy

The Metro Council for Teen Potential (MCTP) is a membership coalition in Rochester, New York, that "promotes a comprehensive and community-wide approach to foster youth assets and youth health and to prevent teen pregnancy," according to its website. To do so, MCTP provides various kinds of information to its member agencies and organizations, including the latest data on pregnancy and other problems facing teens and the latest information on the "best practices" to use to help teens. It has also developed a youth curriculum and media campaign aimed at informing youths about risky behaviors, sexuality, and other aspects of their lives. Its member groups include the Rochester School District and youth development organizations throughout Rochester.

An important focus of MCTP's efforts is teen pregnancy, and MCTP has received substantial funding from the U.S. Centers for Disease Control and Prevention to formulate and implement strategies to prevent teen pregnancies. Its website includes survey results of Rochester-area teens' sexual behavior, views about teen pregnancy, substance use, and other behaviors and attitudes.

MCTP supports several initiatives in Rochester that focus on teenage sexuality and pregnancy. One of these is a program called In-Control, which provides reproductive health care, education, and other services through Planned Parenthood.

For all its efforts, MCTP has won the Organizational Award from the Youth Services Quality Council for the high quality of its work for youths and their families. In helping to reduce teen pregnancy and address other problems facing teenagers in Rochester, the Metro Council for Teen Potential is making a difference. For further information, visit its website at https://metrocouncilrochester.org/.

Another strategy to prevent teenage pregnancy involves the use of **early childhood intervention programs (ECIP)**. Many such programs exist, but they generally involve visits by social workers, nurses, and other professionals to the homes of children who are at risk for neurological, emotional, and/or behavioral problems during their first several years and also as they grow into adolescents and young adults (Kahn and Moore 2010).[23] It might sound like a stereotype, but these children are disproportionately born to single, teenage mothers and/or to slightly older parents who live in poverty or near poverty. Long-term evaluation studies show that the best of these programs reduce the likelihood that the very young children they help will become pregnant or have children of their own after they become teenagers (Kahn and Moore 2010).[24] In effect, helping young children today helps prevent teenage pregnancy tomorrow.

Helping Teen Mothers

Because teen pregnancies occur despite the best prevention efforts, the second goal of a harm reduction approach is to help teens during their pregnancies and after childbirth. This strategy has the immediate aim of providing practical and emotional support for these very young mothers; it also has the longer-term aims of reducing repeat pregnancies and births and of preventing developmental and behavior problems among their children.

Second-chance homes provide many kinds of services for pregnant teenagers and teen mothers, many of whom are unable to continue living with their own parents.

Source: Photographee.eu/Shutterstock.com

To achieve these aims, ECIP are again helpful. Another type of program to help teen mothers involves the use of **second-chance homes**, which are maternity group homes for unmarried teen mothers (Andrews and Moore 2011; Hudgins et al. 2014).[25] One of the many sad facts of teenage motherhood is that teen mothers often have nowhere to live. A teen mother's parent(s) may refuse to let her and her infant live with them, either because they are angry at her pregnancy or because they simply do not have the room or financial means to house and take care of a baby. Or a pregnant teen may decide to leave her parents' home because of the parents' anger or because they refuse to let her continue seeing the child's father. In another possibility, a teen mother may begin living with the father, but these unions are typically unstable and often end, again leaving her and her child without a home. As well, many teen mothers were runaways from home before they became pregnant or were living in foster care. Because of all these situations, many teen mothers find themselves without a place to live.

In second-chance homes (which, depending on the program, are in reality one large house, a set of apartments, or a network of houses), mothers and children (as well as pregnant teens) receive shelter and food, but they also receive important services, such as childrearing help, educational and vocational counseling and training, family planning counseling, and parenting classes. Although rigorous evaluation studies do not yet exist of the effectiveness of second-chance homes, they do seem to offer a valuable resource for teen mothers and their children (Hudgins et al. 2014).[26]

Addressing Poverty

A final strategy for addressing the problem of teenage sex and pregnancy is to address a more general societal condition that helps produce teenage sex and pregnancy. This condition is poverty. As noted earlier, teenage mothers tend to have grown up in poor or near poor families; relatedly, they also tend to live in disadvantaged neighborhoods—those with high rates of poverty, unemployment, high school dropouts, and so forth. Efforts that reduce poverty (see Chapter 2) and improve the conditions of disadvantaged neighborhoods will also reduce the collateral effects of poverty, including teenage pregnancy and birth.

9.3 Abortion

A major consequence of unplanned pregnancy, during or after the teen years, is abortion. As noted earlier, some 42 percent of all unplanned pregnancies end with an abortion. The more we can reduce unplanned pregnancies through the various strategies just discussed, the fewer abortions we will have. This section presents some additional information on abortion while acknowledging the incredibly strong passions that abortion raises. Many people believe that abortion represents a woman's right to control her own body, while many other people believe that abortion is murder. We will not review these arguments, which should be very familiar by now, but we will look at the history of abortion and examine some public opinion data about abortion and public health data on its prevalence. We end with a brief discussion of abortion policy.

A Brief History of Abortion

Like drug use discussed in Chapter 7 and prostitution discussed later in this chapter, abortion has a very long history. In fact, sex historians Vern Bullough and Bonnie Bullough (1977:92)[27] note that abortion has "been widely practiced since the beginning of recorded history." Although early Christianity regarded abortion as murder, there was no general agreement regarding how old the fetus must be for an abortion to be considered murder. During the Middle Ages, most religious scholars thought abortion was not murder unless quickening (when a woman begins to feel the fetus moving) had occurred, which is usually about four to five months into a pregnancy. In a notable development, Pope Pius IX declared in 1869 that abortion was murder no matter how young the fetus was, and that remains the belief of the Catholic Church.

During the nineteenth century, many countries passed new laws that banned abortion, and most U.S. states did so as well. Bullough and Bullough (1977:111)[28] say these new laws were intended to protect pregnant women from unskilled abortionists, but that the laws backfired because "desperate women turned to illegal practitioners." Many illegal abortionists were simply unskilled to perform abortions, but even doctors and midwives who provided abortions illegally did not have access to hospitals or medical clinics if something went wrong. After antibiotics came into use during the twentieth century, illegal abortion providers also did not have access to these miracle drugs and thus could not treat any infection occurring after an abortion. By the early 1960s, the only legal abortions in most states were those done to save the mother's life, with about 8,000 such *therapeutic abortions* performed annually.

In addition to these legal abortions, an estimated 400,000–650,000 illegal abortions were also being performed annually by the early 1960s. For the reasons just given, these abortions were often risky procedures and resulted in a "very high maternal mortality rate" (Bullough and Bullough 1977:112).[29] In plain English, many women died from illegal abortions.

The sheer number of illegal abortions and maternal death and health complications helped ignite a new abortion rights movement. This movement also believed that women had the right to control their own bodies without government interference. By 1970, sixteen states had legalized abortion or had made abortions easier to receive under certain circumstances. Some courts began to rule that laws against abortion violated women's constitutional right to privacy. Finally, the U.S. Supreme Court supported legal abortion in its famous 1973 decision *Roe v. Wade*. This decision allowed all abortions during the first trimester (a roughly three-month period of pregnancy) and permitted states to regulate abortion during the second trimester to protect the mother's health, but states could still not prohibit abortion during this trimester. For the remaining trimester, states were allowed to prohibit abortion except when the mother's life or health was at stake.

The legalization of abortion by the *Roe* decision was controversial from the beginning and remains so today (see "Applying Social Research"). Amid all this controversy, it is important to keep in mind that the *Roe* decision protected the health and lives of many pregnant women. As the Guttmacher Institute (Cohen 2009:2)[30] has explained, "The United States legalized abortion nationwide in 1973, in part because of the clear evidence that restrictive laws were not ending abortion but were exacting a significant public health toll, notably on lower-income women who could not travel or pay for safe services. Almost immediately afterward, pregnancy-related deaths and hospitalizations due to complications of unsafe abortion effectively ended. The United States was not the first country and has been far from the last to recognize this relationship and move to liberalize its law."

Applying Social Research

The Abortion and Crime Rate Controversy

In 2001, two scholars published an article on abortion and crime rates. The article concluded that the legalization of abortion after the Supreme Court's *Roe v. Wade* decision in 1973 lowered the crime rate two decades later. They reasoned that the *Roe* decision increased the number of abortions among poor teenagers, whose children are at risk for delinquency and crime when they reach adolescence and young adulthood. Because the increased number of abortions meant that these children were never born, the crime rate in the late 1980s and 1990s was lower than it would have been because of the *Roe* decision.

This article set off a firestorm of controversy, with people on both sides of the abortion debate appalled at the implication that abortions should be promoted to lower the crime rate many years later. The article also set off a wave of social science research to determine the validity of the article's conclusion. These same two scholars much more recently conducted an update to their original study that repeats their original conclusions.

The research that has been published since their original article yielded mixed results. Some studies found that legal abortion did lower the crime rate; other studies have found that it did not lower the crime rate; and some studies have even found that it raised the crime rate. Even if abortion might have lowered the crime rate during the 1990s, most criminologists think that the crime rate decline during that decade mostly stemmed from other reasons, including more effective policing and a thriving economy.

It remains highly debatable whether any possible crime-reducing effect of abortion is a relevant factor for the debate over legal abortion. Regardless of its possible relevance, however, the social science research on this issue is so equivocal that it is premature to assume that abortion does, in fact, lower the crime rate.

Sources: Chamlin et al. 2008; Donohue and Levitt 2001, 2019; Kahane et al. 2008; Shoesmith 2017[31]

Despite the fact that *Roe v. Wade* reduced the health risks of unsafe abortions, access to abortion has weakened in the years since this case was decided in 1973. In a 1992 ruling, *Planned Parenthood v. Casey*, the Supreme Court weakened *Roe* by ruling that states could ban abortions after the fetus became viable at twenty-two or twenty-three weeks, which is before the end of the second trimester. This ruling also allowed states to require a twenty-four-hour waiting period, the signing of an informed consent form, and the signing of a parental consent form for minors. Various acts by Congress have also made it more difficult to receive an abortion. In particular, congressional legislation in 1976 banned Medicaid funding of abortions.

The legalization of abortion in the United States after the 1973 *Roe v. Wade* decision of the Supreme Court reduced the number of unsafe abortions.

Source: © Thinkstock

Many states have passed various laws to make it more difficult for a woman to get an abortion. As of August 2019, these selected laws were in effect (Guttmacher Institute 2019)[32]:

- Thirty-three states prohibit the use of state funds for abortions unless the woman's life is in danger or the pregnancy resulted from rape or incest.

- Eighteen states require that a woman receive counseling before an abortion that includes information on one or more of the following topics: the ability of a fetus to feel pain, mental health consequences following an abortion, the availability of ultrasound, or the claimed link between abortion and breast cancer.

- Twenty-seven states require a waiting period between receiving counseling and receiving an abortion.

- Twenty-six states require consent from one or both parents for a minor to receive an abortion, and fifteen states require that one or both parents be notified; included in these numbers are four states that require both consent and notification.

- Nineteen states require an abortion to occur in a hospital after a specified number of weeks of pregnancy.

This widespread effort to limit abortion access accelerated in the weeks after the COVID-19 pandemic began in early 2020. States across the nation prohibited or provided guidelines against nonurgent medical visits. Although these actions were necessary to protect the public's health, some states took advantage of the situation to pass measures that also ended or severely limited abortion access; these states included Alabama, Arkansas, Iowa, Ohio, Oklahoma, and Texas. A lawsuit filed by the ACLU against Arkansas's effort declared that "prohibiting abortion during the pandemic will not achieve any of the State's public-health objectives and is in fact likely to exacerbate the crisis" (Gold and Lampen 2020).[33]

Missouri the Latest State to Advance Strict Anti-Abortion Legislation

Many states have passed legislation that restricts women's access to legal abortions. This legislation has meant that women either have to travel much longer distances to obtain an abortion or endure an unwanted pregnancy.

View the video online at: http://www.youtube.com/embed/CL9MO3cAucg?rel=0

Abortion Data

Some basic facts about the number of abortions in the United States are essential for a complete understanding of the abortion issue. (Data are for 2014 and come from Guttmacher Institute 2018.)[34] One of the most important facts is that one-fourth of American women have an abortion by age 45. This fact is important because it underscores how common abortion is and suggests the huge impact that will occur if the U.S. Supreme Court ever outlaws abortion nationwide. Another fact is that 926,000 abortions occurred in 2014 in the United States, down from a peak of 1.6 million abortions in 1990. This decrease is thought to stem from a drop in unwanted pregnancies (see earlier discussion) and from a decline in facilities that provide abortions because of harassment from abortion opponents, from reduced public funding, and from legal restrictions. Still another fact is that 75 percent of abortion patients are poor or near poor. In addition, half of abortion patients were using contraception during the month they became pregnant.

Yet another important fact is that in many parts of the nation, it is very difficult and even practically impossible for women to get an abortion. Only 10 percent of the more than 3,000 counties in the United States have an abortion provider; 39 percent of women of childbearing age (15–44) live in the 90 percent of counties that lack any abortion providers. These women must travel relatively long distances to a provider and may lack the money or transportation to do so, effectively preventing many and perhaps most of them from obtaining an abortion.

Public Views about Abortion

People tend to hold very strong views about abortion, and the news media regularly report on rallies and other events carried out by both sides of the abortion controversy. This news coverage obscures an important fact about public opinion on abortion: The public largely supports abortions that occur under certain circumstances, while it is divided over abortions that occur under other circumstances. On some types of abortions, then, there is a strong public consensus in a favor of abortion, while on other types of abortions there is much disagreement.

The circumstances for which the public largely supports abortions are those where the physical health of the mother is at stake, where the pregnancy resulted from a rape or act of incest, or where the baby is likely to have a serious defect. The circumstances for which the public is divided on abortion are those where a woman wants an abortion for any other reason, including her wish not to have any more children.

We see evidence of these two patterns of abortion opinion in data from the GSS. The GSS regularly asks a series of questions that begin with the following statement: "Please tell me whether or not you think it should be possible for a pregnant woman to obtain a legal abortion if…" After this initial statement, the question lists a circumstance or reason for an abortion. These scenarios are as follows: (a) The woman's own health is seriously endangered by the pregnancy; (b) she became pregnant as a result of rape; (c) there is a strong chance of serious defect in the baby; (d) she is married and does not want any more children; (e) the family has a very low income and cannot afford any more children; (f) she is not married and does not want to marry the man; and (g) the woman wants it for any reason.

As Figure 9.4 shows, strong majorities of the public support a legal abortion for the first three scenarios: the women's health is endangered; the pregnancy resulted from a rape; or the baby is likely to have a serious defect. On the other hand, only 45–50 percent of the public support a legal abortion for the remaining scenarios: a married woman does not want more children; the family cannot afford more children; an unmarried woman does not want to marry; or a woman wants an abortion for any reason.

FIGURE 9.4 Support for Legal Abortion, 2018

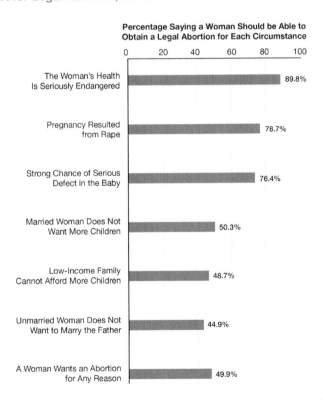

Percentage Saying a Woman Should be Able to Obtain a Legal Abortion for Each Circumstance

Circumstance	Percentage
The Woman's Health Is Seriously Endangered	89.8%
Pregnancy Resulted from Rape	78.7%
Strong Chance of Serious Defect in the Baby	76.4%
Married Woman Does Not Want More Children	50.3%
Low-Income Family Cannot Afford More Children	48.7%
Unmarried Woman Does Not Want to Marry the Father	44.9%
A Woman Wants an Abortion for Any Reason	49.9%

Source: Data from General Social Survey. 2018. Retrieved from https://sda.berkeley.edu/sdaweb/analysis/?dataset=gss18.

Correlates of Public Views

Religiosity is a strong predictor of abortion views. In particular, very religious people are much less likely than not-religious people to support legal abortion for any reason.

Source: © Thinkstock

Reflecting the sociological principle that our social backgrounds influence our attitudes and behaviors, several aspects of people's social backgrounds are associated with their views on abortion.

One of these aspects is religiosity, as you might already know. In the 2018 GSS, about 74 percent of people who say they are not religious support legal abortion "for any reason," compared to only 26 percent of people who say they are very religious. Not-religious people are thus about three times more likely than very religious people to support legal abortion for any reason.

Because pregnancy and childbirth affect women more directly than men, it might make sense to think that women are more likely than men to favor legal abortion. However, there is no gender difference in this regard: In the 2018 GSS, about 50 percent of each sex favored legal abortion. This surprising result apparently reflects the fact that women are more religious than men, a circumstance that lowers their overall support for legal abortion from what otherwise would be expected (Barkan 2014).[35]

Three other aspects of our social backgrounds are rather strongly associated with abortion views: education, our political views, and region of country. People with college degrees are much more likely than those with lower education levels to support legal abortion for any reason; liberals are much more likely than conservatives to favor legal abortion (see Figure 9.5); and people in the South are less likely than those in other U.S. regions to support legal abortion.

FIGURE 9.5 Self-Described Political Views and Support for Legal Abortion for Any Reason, 2018 (%)

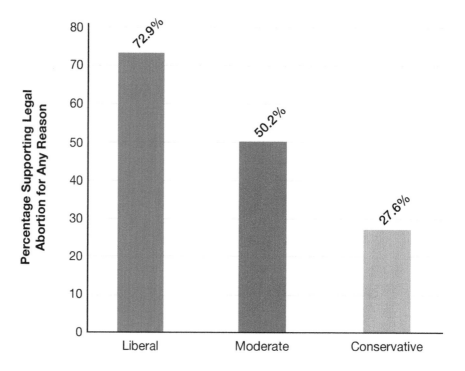

Source: Data from General Social Survey. 2018. Retrieved from https://sda.berkeley.edu/sdaweb/analysis/?dataset=gss18.

Reducing Abortions and Making Them Safe

No one likes abortions. Abortion rights opponents liken them to murder, and abortion rights proponents are certainly not gleeful when abortions occur. Rather, they recognize that abortions will occur whether they are legal or illegal, and they think that legal abortion protects women from the dangers of illegal abortions and recognizes women's right to control their own bodies.

Chapter 7's discussion of illegal drugs emphasized that "what's past is prologue": Because drugs have been used since prehistoric times, it is no surprise that illegal drug use remains common today even despite possible arrest and punishment. The long history of abortion suggests that "what's past is prologue" is again a relevant theme for this particular behavior. Since the beginning of recorded history, women have tried to end their pregnancies. Whatever we might think of abortion, the fact remains that many women will continue to try to end their pregnancies whether abortion is legal or whether it is illegal. As with teenage pregnancy and the use of illegal drugs, a *harm reduction* approach to abortion again makes sense in view of this basic fact, as we shall now explain.

Around the world, the rate of abortion is *unrelated* to whether it is legal or illegal: Abortion rates are as high in nations that ban abortion as in nations that allow them (Sedgh et al. 2016).[36] Laws against abortions thus do not reduce abortions, but they do cause another very serious problem: unsafe abortions. As the Guttmacher Institute (2018)[37] explains, these laws "make the abortions that do occur more likely to be unsafe." When abortion is illegal, women either must have an abortion from an unskilled provider in unhygienic conditions, or they may try to induce their own abortion by inserting an object into their uterus or by ingesting a toxic substance. Not surprisingly, all these illegal abortions are very risky and can lead to many complications, including severe bleeding, serious infection, or organ damage, any of which can be fatal. Unsafe abortion around the world is a significant cause of maternal mortality, along with childbirth-related infection and hemorrhaging. For abortion to be safe, then, it must be legal. Making abortion illegal does not make abortions disappear, but it does make them dangerous.

Both sides of the abortion debate want to see abortions reduced. How then can this goal be achieved? The most promising strategy is to reduce unintended pregnancies, as discussed in the previous section on teenage pregnancy, through the consistent use of effective contraception. The reason for this strategy is simple: Almost all abortions result from unintended pregnancies, and if we can reduce unintended pregnancies, we will reduce the number of abortions (Dreweke 2016).[38] As the Guttmacher Institute explains, "Extensive research shows that behind almost every abortion is an unintended pregnancy, and the most effective way to prevent unintended pregnancy is through correct and consistent use of contraceptives."[39]

Ironically, opponents of legal abortion also tend to be opposed to sex education that emphasizes safe sex and, as well, to providing contraceptives at no cost or low cost to sexually active teenagers and young adults. During the past few years, many state governments led by conservative governors and/or state legislatures have reduced or eliminated funding for Planned Parenthood and other family planning agencies whose clients are largely low-income women (Guttmacher Institute 2018).[40]

These funding cuts and other efforts to reduce contraceptive counseling and provision have two consequences. First, they help ensure that many more unwanted babies are born, at a cost of thousands of dollars in birthing costs for each baby and many dollars more in the societal problems (discussed in the teenage pregnancy section) associated with unwanted births to poor mothers.

Efforts to reduce contraceptive counseling and the use of contraceptives help increase the number of unplanned pregnancies and, in turn, the number of abortions.

Source: © Thinkstock

Second, these efforts also help ensure that more unintended pregnancies and thus more abortions will occur. Because almost all abortions result from unintended pregnancies, any efforts by political and religious forces that make it less likely that sexually active people use contraception ironically help increase the number of abortions. Because abortion opponents want to reduce abortions, they should favor additional funding for family planning agencies and for other efforts that increase contraceptive use.

Beyond these considerations, it is also important that public funds be available to pay for abortions by low-income women. As noted earlier, Medicaid funding cannot be used for abortions that are not meant to protect the mother's health or to end a pregnancy from rape or incest, and most states do not fund these abortions. This situation means that although low-income women have a legal right to receive an abortion, this lack of funding denies them this right in practice.

Although people on both sides of the abortion debate have sincere, strongly held views, a dispassionate analysis based on the discussion in this section leads to the following conclusions. First, if we want abortions to be rare, efforts to promote safe sex and the consistent use of effective contraception must be applauded and funded, not condemned and unfunded. Second, abortions will occur whether or not they are legal; recognizing this fact, if we want abortions to be safe, they must be legal, and restrictions on access to them should be removed.

Key Takeaways

- Abortion continues to be one of the most controversial issues in the United States. Many states have implemented laws and policies that make it difficult to obtain abortions.
- Several aspects of our social backgrounds predict views on legal abortion. In particular, religiosity is associated with opposition to legal abortion, while education is associated with approval of legal abortion.
- To reduce the number of abortions, it is necessary to reduce unwanted pregnancies. To ensure that abortions will be safe, they must be legal.

For Your Review

1. Do you favor or oppose legal abortion? Does your answer depend on the reasons for which a woman desires an abortion? Write an essay in which you explain your answer.
2. A major principle of sociology is that social backgrounds influence attitudes and behavior. Write an essay in which you illustrate this principle with regard to attitudes about abortion.

9.4 Prostitution

Learning Objectives

1. Summarize the history of prostitution in the United States.

Prostitution, the selling of sexual services, is yet another controversial sexual behavior. Many people, especially those with conservative religious views, believe prostitution is immoral because it involves sex for money, and they consider prostitution a sign of society's moral decay. Many feminists believe that prostitution is degrading to women and provides a context in which prostitutes are robbed, beaten, and/or raped. These two groups of people might agree on little else, but they both hold strong negative views about prostitution. Regardless of their other beliefs, many people also worry that prostitution spreads STDs. All these groups think prostitution should remain illegal, and they generally prefer stricter enforcement of laws against prostitution.

prostitution

The selling of sexual services.

Other people also do not like prostitution, but they believe that the laws against prostitution do more harm than good. They think that legalizing prostitution would reduce the various harms prostitution causes, and they believe that views about the immorality of prostitution should not prevent our society from dealing more wisely with it than it does now.

This section presents a short history of prostitution before turning to the various types of prostitution, reasons for prostitution, and policy issues about how best to deal with it. Because most prostitution involves female prostitutes and male customers, our discussion will largely focus on this form.

History of Prostitution

Often called the world's oldest profession, prostitution has been common since ancient times (Ringdal 2004).[41] In ancient Mesopotamia, priests had sex with prostitutes. Ancient Greece featured legal *brothels* (houses of prostitution) that serviced political leaders and common men alike. Prostitution was also common in ancient Rome, and in the Old Testament it was "accepted as a more or less necessary fact of life and it was more or less expected that many men would turn to prostitutes" (Bullough and Bullough 1977:137–138).[42] During the Middle Ages and through the nineteenth century, prostitution was tolerated as a necessary evil, as legal brothels operated in much of Europe and were an important source of tax revenue. As the dangers of venereal disease became known, some cities shut down their brothels, but other cities required regular medical exams of their brothels' prostitutes.

Prostitution was also common in the United States through the nineteenth century (Bullough and Bullough 1987).[43] Poor women became prostitutes because it provided a source of income at a time when they had few job prospects. Some prostitutes worked for themselves on streets and in hotels and inns, and other prostitutes worked in legal brothels in many U.S. cities. During the Civil War, prostitutes found many customers among the soldiers of the Union and the Confederacy; the term *hooker* for prostitute comes from their relations with soldiers commanded by Union General Joseph Hooker. After the Civil War, camps of prostitutes would set up at railroad construction sites. When the railroad workers would visit the camps at night, they hung their red signal lamps outside the prostitutes' tents so they could be found if there was a railroad emergency. The term "red-light district" for a prostitution area originated in the red glow that resulted from this practice.

Many U.S. cities had legal brothels into the early 1900s. Beginning in about 1910, however, religious groups and other parties increasingly spoke out about the immorality of prostitution, and in addition claimed that middle-class girls were increasingly becoming prostitutes. Their efforts succeeded in shutting down legal brothels nationwide. Some illegal brothels continued, and among their number was a San Francisco brothel run during the 1940s by a *madam* (brothel manager and/or owner) named Sally Stanford. Her clientele included many leading politicians and businessmen of San Francisco and nearby areas. Like other earlier brothels, Stanford's brothel required regular medical exams of her employees to help prevent the spread of venereal diseases (Stanford 1966).[44] Despite or perhaps because of her fame from being a madam, Stanford was later elected mayor of Sausalito, a town across the bay from San Francisco.

Prostitution in the United States Today

Estimates of the number of prostitutes in the United States range widely between 70,000 and 500,000. Streetwalkers comprise about one-fifth of all prostitutes.

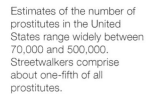

Source: © Thinkstock

No one really knows how many prostitutes we now have. Prostitutes are not eager to be studied, and because their work is illegal, the federal government does not compile statistics on their numbers as it does for physicians, plumbers, teachers, and hundreds of other legal occupations. A well-analyzed estimate at the beginning of this century put the number of female prostitutes at 70,000 and further concluded that they engage in an average of 700 acts of prostitution with male customers annually, or almost 50 million acts of prostitution overall each year (Brewer et al. 2000).[45] However, other estimates put the number of prostitutes as high as 500,000, with many of these prostitutes working part-time, whether or not they also work in a legal occupation (Clinard and Meier 2011).[46]

Regardless of the actual number, prostitution is very common. The GSS asks, "Thinking about the time since your eighteenth birthday, have you ever had sex with a person you paid or who paid you for sex?" In 2018, 9.1 percent of men and 2.4 percent of women answered "yes" to this question. These figures translate to about 11 million men eighteen and older who have engaged in prostitution, usually as the customer, and 3 million women.

In 2017, police and other law enforcement agents made 28,490 arrests for prostitution and commercialized vice (Federal Bureau of Investigation 2018).[47] Most of these arrests were of prostitutes, but some were of customers. Women accounted for 61 percent of the arrests in this entire category.

Types of Prostitutes

streetwalkers

Prostitutes who typically find their customers, or are found by their customers, on a street and who then have a quick act of sex in the customer's car, in an alleyway or other secluded spot, or in a cheap hotel.

call girls

Prostitutes who work as independent operators in their homes or fancy hotels and charge higher rates for their services.

escorts

Prostitutes who work for escort agencies and may operate out of an apartment rented by their agency or come to a client's hotel room or other location.

Several types of prostitutes exist. At the bottom of the prostitution "hierarchy" are **streetwalkers** (also called *street prostitutes*), who typically find their customers, or are found by their customers, somewhere on a street. They then have a quick act of sex in the customer's car, in an alleyway or other secluded spot, or in a cheap hotel. They are often controlled by pimps who find them clients and may take a large chunk of their earnings. Although streetwalkers are the subjects in most studies of prostitutes, they in fact compose only about one-fifth of all prostitutes (Weitzer 2012).[48]

The remaining 80 percent of prostitutes generally work indoors. **Call girls** work as independent operators in their homes or fairly fancy hotels and charge a lot of money for their services, which include sex but also talking and dining. Their clients are typically businessmen or other wealthy individuals. Many call girls earn between $200 and $500 per hour, and some earn between $1,000 and $6,000 per hour or per session (Weitzer 2009).[49] **Escorts** work for escort agencies, which often advertise heavily in phone books and on the internet. They may operate out of an apartment rented by their agency or come to a client's hotel room or other location. Although they may actually act as an escort to a dinner or show, typically their services include sexual acts. They, too, are generally well paid for their work, but do not earn nearly as much as call girls because they have to give at least 30 percent of their earnings to their agency.

Call girls and escorts rank at the top of the prostitution hierarchy. Below them, but above streetwalkers, are three other types of prostitutes. **Brothel workers**, as the name implies, are prostitutes who work in brothels. The only legal brothels in the United States today are found in several rural counties in Nevada, which legalized prostitution in these counties in 1971. Workers in these brothels pay income tax. Because their employers require regular health exams and condom use, the risk of sexually transmitted disease in Nevada's brothels is low. **Massage parlor workers**, as their name also implies, work in massage parlors. Many massage parlors, of course, involve no prostitution at all, and are entirely legal. However, some massage parlors are in fact fronts for prostitution, where the prostitute masturbates a man and brings him to what is often termed a "happy ending." A final category of prostitution involves prostitutes who work in bars, casinos, or similar establishments (**bar or casino workers**). They make contact with a customer in these settings and then have sex with them elsewhere.

The lives and welfare of streetwalkers are much worse than those of the five types of indoor workers just listed (Weitzer 2012).[50] In particular, many streetwalkers are exploited or abused by pimps, use heroin or other drugs, and are raped, robbed, and/or beaten by their clients. A good number of streetwalkers also began their prostitution careers as runaway teenagers and were abused as children.

In contrast, indoor workers begin their trade when they are older and are less likely to have been abused as children. Their working conditions are much better than those for streetwalkers, they are less likely to be addicted to drugs and to have STDs, they are better paid, and they are much less likely to be victimized by their clients. Studies that compare indoor prostitutes with nonprostitutes find that they have similar levels of self-esteem, physical health, and mental health. Many indoor prostitutes even report a rise in self-esteem after they begin their indoor work (Weitzer 2012).[51]

Explaining Prostitution

By definition, prostitution involves the selling of sex. This means that money is the key feature of prostitution. As such, money is also the major motivation for women who become prostitutes, as most of them come from low-income backgrounds. For indoor workers, and especially call girls, prostitution is a potentially well-paying occupation. Streetwalkers hardly get rich from prostitution and suffer the many problems listed earlier, but prostitution still provides them a source of income that they are unlikely to receive through legal occupations because they have few marketable job skills.

Despite this financial motivation, most women do not become prostitutes, and scholars have tried to understand why some women do so. Because prostitutes are not eager to be studied, as noted earlier, we do not yet have studies of random samples of prostitutes, and probably never will have such studies. As also noted earlier, most studies of prostitutes involve streetwalkers, even though they compose only about 20 percent of all prostitutes. Several of these studies cite high rates of child abuse in the backgrounds of streetwalkers, but other studies find that their rates of child abuse are similar to those of women from similar sociodemographic backgrounds who are not prostitutes (Weitzer 2009).[52] Although some studies find certain psychological problems among streetwalkers, it is unclear whether these problems existed before they became streetwalkers or developed (as is very possible) after they became streetwalkers. Methodologically, the best way to clarify this causal question would be to randomly assign young women to become prostitutes or not to become prostitutes, and then to study what happens to their psychological health afterward. For many reasons, this type of study would be highly unethical and will never be done. In the absence of studies of this type, it is difficult to determine what exactly prompts some women to become prostitutes.

brothel workers

Prostitutes who work in brothels (houses of prostitution).

massage parlor workers

Prostitutes who work in massage parlors.

bar or casino workers

Prostitutes who work in bars, casinos, or similar establishments.

Customers

There is an old saying that "it takes two to tango." Prostitution obviously cannot occur unless a customer wants to pay for the services of a prostitute. Despite this essential fact of prostitution, there are very few studies of why men choose to become customers. The implicit message from this lack of studies is that it is normal for men to have sex with a prostitute but abnormal for women to charge these men for this sex. The few studies we do have do not find any substantial differences between customers and noncustomers (Weitzer 2009).[53] Just as men come from various social backgrounds, so do the men who choose to have sex with a prostitute.

Customers of prostitutes tend to come from the same kinds of social backgrounds as do noncustomers. They have certain motivations for wanting to be with a prostitute, but many noncustomers have the same motivations yet still do not pay for prostitution.

Source: © Thinkstock

Customers do have certain motivations for choosing to pay for prostitution (Weitzer 2009).[54] These motivations include (1) the desire to have sex with someone with a certain physical appearance (age, race, body type); (2) the lack of a sexual partner or dissatisfaction with a sexual partner, including a desire to have unconventional sex that the partner does not share; (3) the thrill of having sex with a prostitute; and (4) the desire to have sex without having to make an emotional commitment. Although one or more of these motivations may be necessary for a man's decision to seek prostitution, they do not entirely explain this decision. For example, many men may not have a sexual partner or may be dissatisfied with a partner they do have, but they still do not decide to pay for a prostitute.

Sociological Perspectives

Beyond explaining why individual women and men are more likely than others to pay for sex or to receive pay for sex, the three sociological perspectives outlined in Chapter 1—functionalist theory, conflict theory, and symbolic interactionism—offer more general insights on prostitution. Table 9.5 provides a summary of these insights.

TABLE 9.5 Theory Snapshot

Theoretical perspective	Contributions to understanding prostitution
Functionalism	Prostitution is functional for several parties in society. It provides prostitutes a source of income, and it provides a sexual alternative for men who lack a sexual partner or are dissatisfied with their current sexual partner. According to Kingsley Davis, prostitution also helps keep the divorce rate lower than it would be if prostitution did not exist.
Conflict theory	Prostitution arises from women's poverty in a patriarchal society. It also reflects the continuing cultural treatment of women as sex objects who exist for men's pleasure.
Symbolic interactionism	Prostitutes and their customers have various understandings of their behavior that help them justify why they engage in this behavior. Many prostitutes believe they are performing an important service for their customers, and this belief is perhaps more common among indoor prostitutes than among street prostitutes.

According to *functionalist theory*, prostitution exists because it serves several important functions for society generally and for certain people in society. As we have already mentioned, it provides a source of income for many women who otherwise might be jobless, and it provides a sexual alternative for men with the motivations listed earlier. More than eighty years ago, sociologist Kingsley Davis (1937)[55] wrote that prostitution even lowers the divorce rate. He reasoned that many married men are unhappy with their sex life with their wives. If they do not think this situation can improve, some men start an affair with another woman and may fall in love with that woman, threatening these men's marriages. Other men turn to a prostitute. Because prostitution is generally impersonal, these men do not fall in love with their prostitutes, and their marriages are not threatened. Without prostitution, then, more men would have affairs, and more divorces would result. Although Davis's hypothesis is provocative, there are no adequate studies to test it.

According to *conflict theory*, prostitution reflects the economic inequality in society. Many poor women feel compelled to become prostitutes because of their lack of money; because wealthier women have many other sources of income, the idea of becoming a prostitute is something they never have to consider. Sad but interesting historical support for this view comes from an increase in prostitution in the second half of the nineteenth century. Many women lost husbands and boyfriends in the Civil War and were left penniless. Lacking formal education and living in a society that at the time offered few job opportunities to women, many of these bereaved women were forced to turn to prostitution to feed their families and themselves. As American cities grew rapidly during the last decades of the nineteenth century, thousands of immigrant women and other poor women also turned to prostitution as a needed source of income (Rosen 1983).[56] This late nineteenth-century increase in prostitution, then, occurred because of women's poverty.

According to the *feminist* version of conflict theory, prostitution results not only from women's poverty but also from society's patriarchal culture that still views men as the dominant figure in heterosexual relationships and that still treats women as "sex objects" who exist for men's pleasure (Barry 1996).[57] In such a culture, it is no surprise and even inevitable that men will want to pay for sex with a woman and that women will be willing to be paid for sex. In this feminist view, the oppression and exploitation that prostitution inherently involves reflects the more general oppression and exploitation of women in the larger society.

Symbolic interactionism moves away from these larger issues to examine the everyday understandings that prostitutes and their customers have about their behavior. These understandings help both prostitutes and customers justify their behavior. Many prostitutes, for example, believe they are performing an important service for the men who pay them. Indoor prostitutes are perhaps especially likely to feel they are helping their customers by providing them not only sex but also companionship (Weitzer 2009).[58] A woman who once owned a massage parlor named "The Classic Touch" echoed this view. Her business employed fourteen women who masturbated their customers and offered a senior citizen discount. Claiming that her employees were performing an important service, the owner said that many of her customers were senior citizens or divorced or disabled men. She further argued that her setting was safe from the HIV virus and that husbands who came there obtained a "stress release" that helped their marriages (Ordway 1995:1).[59]

Dealing with Prostitution

With prostitution, past is once again prologue. It has existed since ancient times, and it has continued throughout the United States long since prostitution was banned in the United States by 1920. The legal brothels that now exist in rural counties in Nevada are the exception in this nation, not the rule. Yet prostitution remains common outside of Nevada.

As with illegal drugs (see Chapter 7), as we think about how to deal with prostitution, we should consider both a philosophical question and a social science question (Meier and Geis 2006).[60] The philosophical question is whether two people should be allowed to engage in a behavior, in this case prostitution, in which both want to participate. Many people may dislike this behavior for various reasons, but is that sufficient justification for the behavior to be banned if both people (let's assume they are legal adults) want to engage in it? In this regard, and without at all meaning to equate prostitution with same-sex sexual behavior, an analogy with homosexuality is worth considering. Homosexual sex used to be illegal because many people thought it was immoral. When the U.S. Supreme Court finally invalidated all laws against homosexual sex in its 2003 case, *Lawrence v. Texas*, the majority opinion declared that "the fact that a State's governing majority has traditionally viewed a particular practice as immoral is not a sufficient reason for upholding a law prohibiting the practice." It further asserted, "The petitioners are entitled to respect for their private lives. The State cannot demean their existence or control their destiny by making their private sexual conduct a crime. Their right to liberty under the Due Process Clause gives them the full right to engage in their conduct without intervention of the government." Although the majority opinion specifically said its decision did not apply to prostitution, a reasonable argument may be made that respect for privacy of consensual sexual conduct also means that prostitution, too, should be legal.

Here it may be argued that prostitution still victimizes and objectifies women even if they want to engage in it. This is a reasonable argument, but there are many occupations that victimize employees, either because the occupations are dangerous (such as coal mining and construction work) or because the job requirements objectify women as sex objects (such as fashion modeling and cheerleading). Because hardly anyone would say these occupations should be illegal, is it logical to say that prostitution should be illegal? Former U.S. Surgeon General Joycelyn Elders once said it makes no sense to ban prostitution simply because it objectifies women: "Why are we so upset about sex workers selling sexual acts to consenting adults?" she asks. "We say that they are selling their bodies, but how different is that from what athletes do? They're selling their bodies. Models? They're selling their bodies. Actors? They're selling their bodies" (McCaslin 1999:A8).[61]

 ### Legalizing Prostitution in New York State?

Although prostitution remains very controversial and unpopular, legalizing it would arguably help protect prostitutes from abuse by pimps and customers and provide tax revenues to states.

View the video online at: http://www.youtube.com/embed/KWJ0q9JfLhQ?rel=0

The social science question concerning laws against prostitution is whether these laws do more good than harm, or more harm than good. If they do more good than harm, they should be maintained and even strengthened; if they do more harm than good, they should be repealed. Some and perhaps many scholars, along with other observers, believe that the laws against prostitution do more harm than good, and they say that the best way to deal with prostitution might be to legalize and regulate it (McKinley 2019; Weitzer 2011).[62]

Proponents of legalization argue as follows. Although many people cite the horrible lives of many streetwalkers as a major reason for their support of laws against prostitution, these laws ironically cause the problems that streetwalkers experience. When U.S. prostitution was legal a century ago in brothels across the nation, brothel prostitutes were safer than streetwalkers are now. Prostitutes working today in Nevada's legal brothels are safer than streetwalkers. Whatever we might think of their behavior, legal brothel workers are relatively safe from being robbed, beaten, or raped, and their required regular medical exams leave them relatively free of sexually transmitted disease. The health problems and criminal victimization that many streetwalkers experience happen *because* their behavior is illegal, and legalizing and regulating prostitution would reduce these problems.

In this regard, legalization of prostitution is yet another *harm reduction* approach to a social problem. As Weitzer (2012:227)[63] observes, "Research suggests that, under the right conditions, legal prostitution can be organized in a way that increases workers' health, safety, and job satisfaction.

Mandatory condom use and other safe-sex practices are typical in legal brothels, and the workers face much lower risk of abuse from customers."

Legalization of prostitution would also yield a considerable amount of tax revenue, as is now true in Nevada. Let's assume that 50 million acts of prostitution occur annually in the United States, to cite our earlier estimate that may be too low, and that each of these acts costs an average $30. Putting these numbers together, prostitutes receive $1.5 billion annually in income. If they paid about one-third of this amount (admittedly a rough estimate) in payroll taxes, the revenue of state and federal governments would increase by $500 million. Because arrests for prostitution and commercialized vice annually would reduce significantly if prostitution were legalized, the financial savings from this reduction could be used for other pursuits.

Legalizing prostitution would add the United States to the lengthy list of other Western democracies that have already legalized it. Although their models of legalization vary, the available evidence indicates that legalizing prostitution does, in fact, reduce the many problems now associated with illegal prostitution (see "Lessons from Other Societies").

Workers in legal brothels are relatively safe from victimization by customers and from the risk of incurring and transmitting sexual diseases.

Source: "Brothel in Elko, NV," Wikipedia, last modified January 11, 2012, http://commons.wikimedia.org/wiki/File:Inez's.JPG.

Lessons from Other Societies

Legal Brothels in Other Western Democracies

In many other Western democracies, prostitution is legal to varying degrees that depend on the specific nation. In some nations, streetwalking is permitted, but in other nations, only brothels are permitted.

The legal brothel model is what the United States had a century ago and has today only in rural Nevada. As in Nevada, nations that permit legal brothels usually require regular health exams and the use of condoms to prevent STDs. They also license the brothels so that the brothels must fulfill various standards, including the safe-sex practices just mentioned, to receive a license. In addition, brothels pay taxes on their revenues, and brothel workers pay taxes on their incomes. According to a recent news report on Switzerland, which legalized prostitution in the 1940s, "The Swiss have taken this pragmatic approach to prevent exploitation, sexually transmitted diseases, links with criminal networks and other problems common in countries where sex commerce is banned."

As in rural Nevada, brothel workers in these other nations are unlikely to be abused by their customers. A major reason for their relative safety is that they work indoors and that any abuse by customers might be heard or witnessed by someone else inside the brothel. In addition, brothels in many nations have implemented certain measures to ensure workers' safety, including the provision of panic buttons, the use of listening devices, and screening of customers when they enter the brothel.

A report by the Ministry of Justice in the Netherlands, where legal brothels operate, concluded that most brothel workers say that they feel safe. A government report in New Zealand, which legalized prostitution in 2003, concluded that legalization made it more likely that prostitutes report any problems to the police and also increased their self-esteem because their behavior was now legal. A government commission in Australia that evaluated legal brothels in the northeastern state of Queensland said, "There is no doubt that licensed brothels provide the safest working environment for sex workers in Queensland…Legal brothels now powering in Queensland provide a sustainable model for a healthy, crime-free, and safe legal licensed brothel industry."

Assessing all these nations' experiences, sociologist Ronald Weitzer concluded that "legal prostitution, while no panacea, is not inherently dangerous and can be structured to minimize risks and empower workers." The United States, then, has much to learn from the other Western democracies that have legalized prostitution.

Sources: Bachmann 2018; Chagnon 2017; Weitzer 2009, 2012[64]

Key Takeaways

- Prostitution has existed since ancient times and continues to be common today around the world. The United States had legal brothels before 1920, and legal brothels are found today in rural counties in Nevada.
- Many people oppose prostitution because they feel it is immoral or because they feel it degrades and victimizes women. Because prostitution usually involves consensual behavior, some scholars say it should not be illegal in a society that values a right to privacy.
- Some scholars also say that laws against prostitution do more harm than good and in particular account for the various problems that streetwalkers experience.

For Your Review

1. Do you think prostitution should become legal and regulated? Why or why not?
2. The major difference between prostitution and sex resulting from a casual pickup involves whether money is exchanged. Write an essay in which you first take the "pro" side on the following debate question, and then take the "con" side: that prostitution is worse than sex from a casual pickup.

9.5 Pornography

Learning Objectives

1. Explain why pornography is difficult to define.
2. Describe evidence indicating that pornography is popular.
3. Discuss whether pornography contributes to violence against women.

pornography

Printed or visual materials that are sexually explicit and that are intended to arouse sexual excitement rather than artistic appreciation.

Pornography may be defined as printed or visual materials that are sexually explicit and that are intended to arouse sexual excitement rather than artistic appreciation. This definition is fine as far as it goes, but it does raise many questions that underscore the difficulty of dealing with pornography. For example, how "explicit" must a printed or visual material be for it to be explicit? Is a picture of a woman in a skimpy negligee explicit, or must she be fully unclothed? If a woman in a photo is wearing an evening gown that is very low-cut, is that explicit? If a young male gets aroused by seeing her cleavage, does that make the photo of her pornographic? If two people on network television are apparently beginning to have consensual sex just before a commercial begins (this is network television, after all), is that explicit and arousing enough to constitute pornography? If you answered no to this last question, what if some viewers do find this short portrayal of consensual sex to be explicit and arousing? Is their reaction enough for us to have to conclude that the scene they saw was indeed pornographic? How many people in fact have to find a printed or visual material explicit and arousing for it to be considered pornographic?

These questions suggest that it is not very easy to define pornography after all. Back in the 1950s, young males in the United States would leaf through *National Geographic* magazine to peek at photos of native women who were partially nude. Those photos, of course, were not put there to excite boys across the country; instead they were there simply to depict native people in their natural habitat. Another magazine began about the same time that also contained photos of nude women. Its name was *Playboy*, and its photos certainly had a much different purpose: to excite teenage boys and older men alike. Other, more graphic magazines grew in its wake, and today television shows and PG-13 and R-rated movies show more nudity and sex than were ever imaginable in the days when *National Geographic* was a boy's secret pleasure. Beyond these movies and television shows, a powerful pornography industry now exists on the internet, in porn stores, and elsewhere. Yesterday's very controversial *Playboy* appears quite tame compared to what else is now available.

If things as different as *National Geographic*, *Playboy*, R-rated movies, and hard-core pornography show nudity and can be sexually arousing, what, then, should be considered pornography? Are at least some of the tamer pictures in *Playboy* really that different from the great paintings in art history that depict nude women? This question is not necessarily meant to defend *Playboy*; rather, it is meant to have you think about what exactly is and is not pornography and what, if anything, our society can and should do about it.

However we define pornography, sexually explicit materials, along with drugs, prostitution, and abortion, have been common since ancient times (Bullough and Bullough 1977).[65] Archeologists have uncovered sexually explicit drawings, pottery, and other artifacts from China, Greece, Japan, Persia, Peru, and other locations; these artifacts depict sexual organs and sexual behavior. Sexually explicit material appears in much writing left from ancient Greece and ancient Rome. "Vast quantities of material dealing with sex" (Bullough and Bullough 1977:161)[66] remain from medieval Europe. The huge amount of pornography that exists today represents a centuries-old tradition.

Public Opinion about Pornography

Many people oppose pornography, but two very different groups have been especially outspoken over the years, as is true about prostitution. One of these groups consists of religious organizations and individuals who condemn pornography as a violation of religious values and as an offense to society's moral order. The other group consists of feminists who condemn pornography for its sexual objectification of women and especially condemn the hard-core pornography that glorifies horrible sexual violence against women. Many feminists also charge that pornography promotes rape by reinforcing the cultural myths discussed earlier. As one writer put it in a famous phrase some forty years ago, "Pornography is the theory, and rape the practice" (Morgan 1980:139).[67]

The GSS asks, "Which of these statements comes closest to your feelings about pornography laws: (1) There should be laws against the distribution of pornography whatever the age; (2) There should be laws against the distribution of pornography to persons under eighteen; or (3) There should be no laws forbidding the distribution of pornography." In 2018, 30.5 percent of the public thought that pornography should be illegal for everyone, and 63.9 percent thought it should be illegal for people under eighteen; 5.6 percent thought there should be no laws against pornography. Adding the last two percentages together, 69.5 percent thought pornography should be legal for everyone eighteen and older.

Certain aspects of our social backgrounds predict our views about pornography laws. Two of the strongest predictors are gender and religiosity. Focusing on the percentage who favor laws against pornography regardless of age, there is a strong gender difference in this view (see Figure 9.6), with women almost twice as likely as men to favor these laws. Religiosity also predicts support for pornography laws regardless of age: People who consider themselves very religious are five times more likely than those who consider themselves not religious to favor these laws (see Figure 9.7).

FIGURE 9.6 Gender and Support for Laws against Pornography Regardless of Age, 2018 (%)

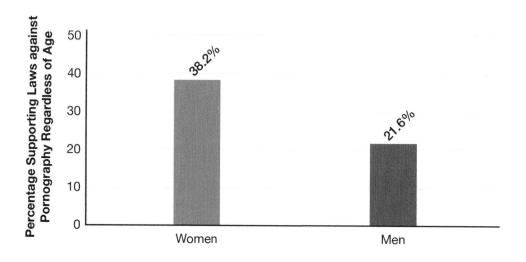

Source: Data from General Social Survey. 2018. Retrieved from https://sda.berkeley.edu/sdaweb/analysis/?dataset=gss18.

FIGURE 9.7 Self-Rated Religiosity and Support for Laws against Pornography Regardless of Age, 2018 (%)

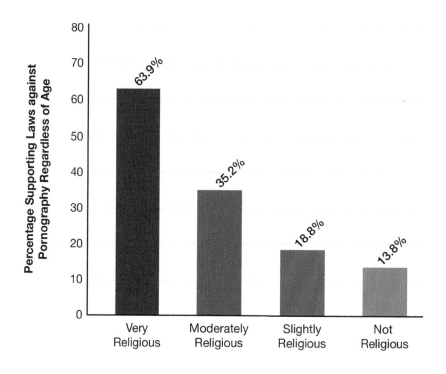

Source: Data from General Social Survey. 2018. Retrieved from https://sda.berkeley.edu/sdaweb/analysis/?dataset=gss18.

The Popularity of Pornography

Pornography is so widespread and easy to access on the internet and elsewhere that many people must be viewing it, reading it, and in general "using" it. Although this assumption makes sense, it is very difficult to determine how much revenue the pornography industry generates annually. This difficulty largely stems from the fact that most pornography these days is online, and online purveyors of pornography generally do not file financial statements nor even keep financial records (Tarrant 2016).[68] That said, estimates during the last decade or so of annual pornography revenue worldwide range from between about $5 billion and $14 billion (Tarrant 2016).[69] A very popular online pornography website, Pornhub, has 78 billion page views annually (2014 data). According to the GSS, 29 percent of Americans adults, or about 74 million adults, have seen an X-rated movie in the past year. This overall figure includes 39 percent of men and 20 percent of women.

Effects of Pornography

Many feminists and other people oppose pornography because they believe it causes rape or other violence against women. This belief raises an important question: To what extent does pornography in fact cause such violence? The fairest answer might be that we do not really know. Many scholars believe pornography does cause violence against women and other problems, but other scholars conclude that pornography does not have this effect and may even help reduce sexual violence by providing a sexual outlet for men (Castleman 2016; Diamond 2009; Fagan 2019; Ley 2014; Weitzer 2011).[70]

These divergent views reflect the complexity of the evidence from research on pornography. Many studies do conclude that pornography causes rape. For example, male students who watch violent pornography in experiments later exhibit more hostile attitudes toward women than those watching consensual sex or nonsexual interaction. However, it remains doubtful that viewing pornography in real life has a longer-term effect that lasts beyond the laboratory setting, and several experimental studies do not even find any short-term effects. In other types of research, rape rates have not risen in the U.S. states that have made their pornography laws more lenient; states' rape rates are not related to their circulation rates of pornographic magazines; and rape rates have declined sharply since the early 1990s, even though pornography is much more widely available now than back then thanks to the internet and other technologies.

A review of the research on pornography and rape concluded that pornography does not increase rape (Ferguson and Hartley 2009:323):[71]

> *Evidence for a causal relationship between exposure to pornography and sexual aggression is slim and may, at certain times, have been exaggerated by politicians, pressure groups and some social scientists. Some of the debate has focused on violent pornography, but evidence of any negative effects is inconsistent, and violent pornography is comparatively rare in the real world. Victimization rates for rape in the United States demonstrate an inverse relationship between pornography consumption and rape rates. Data from other nations have suggested similar relationships...It is concluded that it is time to discard the hypothesis that pornography contributes to increased sexual assault behavior.*

Dealing with Pornography

Whatever pornography is or is not, many people find it disgusting, but many other people are more tolerant of it. In our discussion of prostitution, we examined the issue of whether it is proper for a democracy to ban a consensual behavior simply or mostly because many people consider it immoral. The same question may be asked about pornography (to be more precise, pornography that does not involve children), especially because it does not appear to cause violence against women. Even if it did cause such violence, efforts to stop it raise important issues of freedom of speech and censorship. In a free society, civil liberties advocates say, we must proceed very cautiously. Once we ban some forms of pornography, they ask, where do we stop (Strossen 2000).[72]

This issue aside, much of what we call pornography still degrades women by depicting them as objects that exist for men's sexual pleasure and by sometimes portraying them as legitimate targets of men's sexual violence. These images should be troubling for any society that values gender equality. The extent of pornography in the United States may, for better or worse, reflect our historical commitment to freedom of speech, but it may also reflect our lack of commitment to full equality between women and men. Even if women have made great strides in recent decades toward full equality with men, the persistent popularity of pornography shows that our society has a long way to go toward viewing women as equally human as men.

Key Takeaways

- Pornography is notoriously difficult to define. Just as beauty is in the eye of the beholder, to quote the old saying, so is pornography.
- Pornography is a major industry in the United States and around the world and accounts for about $13 billion in U.S. revenues annually.
- A growing conclusion from the research evidence is that pornography does not lead to violence against women. In addition to this consideration, laws against pornography raise questions of freedom of speech.

For Your Review

1. Do you think all pornography should be legal for people age eighteen and older? Why or why not?
2. In your opinion, does pornography promote violence against women? Explain your answer.

9.6 End-of-Chapter Material

Summary

1. The sexual revolution of the 1960s and 1970s involved changes in Americans' attitudes on certain sexual issues and an increase in premarital sex.
2. Although teenagers are more sexually active today than before the sexual revolution, teenage pregnancy and birth rates have declined sharply since the early 1990s. Teenage pregnancy and birth cause several problems for the teenage mother and for society as a whole.
3. To reduce teenage pregnancy further, the United States should expand publicly funded family planning programs and increase the provision of contraceptives at little or no cost.
4. Abortion has been common since ancient times and remains one of the most controversial issues in the United States. Since the U.S. Supreme Court's *Roe v. Wade* decision legalized all abortions during the first two trimesters, subsequent court rulings and various state actions have made abortions more difficult to obtain. Abortion rates differ by region of the nation and reflect the presence or absence of abortion providers. After the pandemic began

in early 2020, several states passed legislation to ban or severely limit access to legal abortions during the pandemic.

5. Around the world, abortion rates do not depend on whether abortion is legal or illegal, and they occur in great numbers even when they are illegal. For abortions to be as safe as possible, they must be legal.

6. Prostitution has also been common since ancient times. Until the second decade of the twentieth century it was legal in much of the United States in the form of legal brothels.

7. Streetwalkers comprise about one-fifth of all prostitutes. Compared to indoor prostitutes, they are more likely to be victims of violence and to obtain and transmit sexual diseases.

8. When prostitution is legal, prostitutes fare much better than when prostitution is illegal. The problems that streetwalkers experience generally stem from the fact that their behavior is illegal.

9. Pornography has also been around since ancient times. It does not appear to cause sexual violence against women, and efforts to ban it raise freedom of speech issues.

Using What You Know

A college friend of yours has become pregnant after a casual sexual encounter. She is in the second semester of her junior year and was planning to graduate in fifteen months and go on to get a master's degree in a business school. She confides in you that she is considering an abortion and wants your advice on what she should do. What do you tell her?

What You Can Do

To help deal with the sexual behavior problems discussed in this chapter, you may wish to do any of the following:

1. Volunteer for a local agency that helps pregnant teenagers.

2. Start or join in efforts on your campus to encourage safe sex.

3. Volunteer at a family planning agency.

Endnotes

1. Rivera, Madeline, 2019. Texas Wants to Move Away from Abstinence-only Sex Ed, May Teach Sexual Health as Early as Kindergarten. *Fox News* June 26: https://www.foxnews.com/us/texas-health-standards-review-includes-broadening-sex-education-curriculum; Zelinski, Andrea. 2019. Rewrite of Texas Sex Education Standards Could Include Lessons on Contraception. *Houston Chronicle* June 18: https://www.houstonchronicle.com/news/houston-texas/houston/article/Rewrite-of-Texas-sex-education-standards-could-13990300.php.

2. Pampel, Fred C. 2016. "Cohort Changes in the Social Distribution of Tolerant Sexual Attitudes." *Social Forces* 95(2):753-77.

3. Laumann, Edward O., John H. Gagnon, Robert T. Michael and Stuart Michaels. 1994. *The Social Organization of Sexuality*. Chicago: University of Chicago Press.

4. Martinez, Gladys, Casey E. Copen and Joyce C. Abma. 2011. "Teenagers in the United States: Sexual Activity, Contraceptive Use, and Childbearing, 2006–2010 National Survey of Family Growth." *Vital and Health Statistics* 23(31):1-35.

5. Centers for Disease Control and Prevention. 2017. "Key Statistics from the National Survey of Family Growth—N Listing."https://www.cdc.gov/nchs/nsfg/key_statistics/n.htm#number12months.

6. Hayward, George M. 2019. "Religiosity and Premarital Sexual Behaviors among Adolescents: An Analysis of Functional Form." *Journal for the Scientific Study of Religion*: https://doi.org/10.1111/jssr.12588.

7. Barkan, Steven E. 2006. "Religiosity and Premarital Sex During Adulthood." *Journal for the Scientific Study of Religion* 45:407-17.

8. Abma, Joyce C. and Gladys M. Martinez. 2017. "Sexual Activity and Contraceptive Use among Teenagers in the United States, 2011–2015." *National Health Statistics Reports* June 22(104):1-22.

9. Centers for Disease Control and Prevention. 2019. "About Teen Pregnancy." Retrieved from https://www.cdc.gov/teenpregnancy/about/index.htm.

10. Guttmacher Institute. 2019. "Unintended Pregnancy in the United States." Retrieved from https://www.guttmacher.org/fact-sheet/unintended-pregnancy-united-states.

11. Kost, Kathryn, Isaac Maddow-Zimet and Alex Arpaia. 2017. *Pregnancies, Births and Abortions among Adolescents and Young Women in the United States, 2013: National and State Trends by Age, Race and Ethnicity*. New York: Guttmacher Institute.

12. Martin, J.A., B.E. Hamilton and M.J.K Osterman. 2018. "Births in the United States, 2017." *NCHS Data Brief* 2018(318):1-8.

13. Centers for Disease Control and Prevention. 2019. "About Teen Pregnancy." Retrieved from https://www.cdc.gov/teenpregnancy/about/index.htm.

14. Carey, Elea and Jill Seladi-Schulman. 2018. "Teenage Pregnancy." *Healthline.com* July 30:https://www.healthline.com/health/adolescent-pregnancy; Centers for Disease Control and Prevention. 2019. "About Teen Pregnancy."https://www.cdc.gov/teenpregnancy/about/index.htm.

15. Manlove, Jennifer and Hannah Lantos. 2018. "Data Point: Half of 20- to 29-Year Old Women Who Gave Birth in Their Teens Have a High School Diploma." *Child Trends* January 11:https://www.childtrends.org/half-20-29-year-old-women-gave-birth-teens-high-school-diploma.

16. Cook, Sinead M.C. and Sharon T. Cameron. 2015. "Social Issues of Teenage Pregnancy." *Obstetrics, Gynaecology & Reproductive Medicine* 25(9):243-48; Mollborn, Stefanie. 2017. "Teenage Mothers Today: What We Know and How It Matters." *Child Development Perspectives* 11(1):63-69.

17. Centers for Disease Control and Prevention. 2018. *Sexually Transmitted Disease Surveillance 2017*. Atlanta: Centers for Disease Control and Prevention.

18. Wildsmith, Elizabeth, Erin Schelar, Kristen Peterson and Jennifer Manlove. 2010, "Sexually Transmitted Diseases among Young Adults: Prevalence, Perceived Risk, and Risk-Taking Behavior." Retrieved October 15, 2011, (http://www.childtrends.org/Files//Child_Trends-2010_05_01_RB_STD.pdf).

19. Centers for Disease Control and Prevention. 2018. *Sexually Transmitted Disease Surveillance 2017*. Atlanta: Centers for Disease Control and Prevention.

20. Kaiser Family Foundation. 2018. *Abstinence Education Programs: Definition, Funding, and Impact on Teen Sexual Behavior*. Retrieved from https://www.kff.org/womens-health-policy/fact-sheet/abstinence-education-programs-definition-funding-and-impact-on-teen-sexual-behavior/.

21. Kristof, Nicholas D. 2011. "The Birth Control Solution." *The New York Times* November 3:A31.

22. Welti, Kate and Jennifer Manlove. 2017. "How Increasng the Use of Effective Contraception Could Reduce Untended Pregnancy and Public Health Care Costs." *Child Trends*:https://www.childtrends.org/publications/increasing-use-effective-contraception-reduce-unintended-pregnancy-public-health-care-costs.

23. Kahn, Jordan and Kristin A. Moore. 2010, "What Works for Home Visiting Programs: Lessons from Experimental Evaluations of Programs and Interventions." Retrieved October 16, 2011, (http://www.childtrends.org/Files//Child_Trends-2010_7_1_FS_WWHomeVisitpdf.pdf).

24. Kahn, Jordan and Kristin A. Moore. 2010, "What Works for Home Visiting Programs: Lessons from Experimental Evaluations of Programs and Interventions." Retrieved October 16, 2011, (http://www.childtrends.org/Files//Child_Trends-2010_7_1_FS_WWHomeVisitpdf.pdf).

25. Andrews, Kristine M. and Kristin A. Moore. 2011, "Second Chance Homes: A Resource for Teen Mothers." Retrieved October 15, 2011, (http://www.childtrends.org/Files//Child_Trends-2011_04_15_RB_2ndChanceHomes.pdf); Hudgins, Rebekah, Steve Erickson and Dion Walker. 2014. "Everyone Deserves a Second Chance: A Decade of Supports for Teenage Mothers." *Health & Social Work* 39(2):101-08.

26. Hudgins, Rebekah, Steve Erickson and Dion Walker. 2014. "Everyone Deserves a Second Chance: A Decade of Supports for Teenage Mothers." *Health & Social Work* 39(2):101-08.

27. Bullough, Vern L. and Bonnie Bullough. 1977. *Sin, Sickness, and Sanity: A History of Sexual Attitudes*. New York: New American Library.

28. Bullough, Vern L. and Bonnie Bullough. 1977. *Sin, Sickness, and Sanity: A History of Sexual Attitudes*. New York: New American Library.

29. Bullough, Vern L. and Bonnie Bullough. 1977. *Sin, Sickness, and Sanity: A History of Sexual Attitudes*. New York: New American Library.

30. Cohen, Susan A. 2009. "Facts and Consequences: Legality, Incidence and Safety of Abortion Worldwide." *Guttmacher Policy Review* 12(4):2-6.

31. Chamlin, M. B., A. J. Myer and B. A. Sanders. 2008. "Abortion as Crime Control: A Cautionary Tale." *Criminal Justice Policy Review* 19(2):135-52; Donohue, John J. and S.D. Levitt. 2001. "The Impact of Legalized Abortion on Crime." *Quarterly Journal of Economics* 116:379-420; Donohue, John J. and Steven D. Levitt. 2019. "The Impact of Legalized Abortion on Crime over the Last Two Decades." *NBER* Working Paper No. 25863(May):https://www.nber.org/papers/w25863.pdf; Kahane, L. H., D. Paton and R. Simmons. 2008. "The Abortion-Crime Link: Evidence from England and Wales." *Economica* 75(1):1-21; Shoesmith, Gary L. 2017. "Crime, Teenage Abortion, and Unwantedness." *Crime & Delinquency* 63(11):1458-90.

32. Guttmacher Institute. 2019. An Overview of Abortion Laws. Retrieved from https://www.guttmacher.org/state-policy/explore/overview-abortion-laws.

33. Gold, Hannah and Claire Lampen. 2020. "Every State That's Tried to Ban Abortion over The Coronavirus." *The Cut* April 14:https://www.thecut.com/2020/04/every-state-thats-tried-to-ban-abortion-over-coronavirus.html.

34. Guttmacher Institute. 2018. Induced Abortion in the United States. Retrieved from https://www.guttmacher.org/fact-sheet/induced-abortion-united-states.

35. Barkan, Steven E. 2014. "Gender and Abortion Attitudes: Religiosity as a Suppressor Variable." *Public Opinion Quarterly* 78:940-950.

36. Sedgh, Gilda, Jonathan Bearak, Susheela Singh, Akinrinola Bankole, Anna Popinchalk, Bela Ganatra, Clémentine Rossier, Caitlin Gerdts, Özge Tunçalp, Brooke Ronald Johnson, Heidi Bart Johnston and Leontine Alkema. 2016. "Abortion Incidence between 1990 and 2014: Global, Regional, and Subregional Levels and Trends." *Lancet* 388(10041):258-67.

37. Guttmacher Institute. 2018. Highly Restrictive Laws Do Not Eliminate Abortion. Retrieved from https://www.guttmacher.org/infographic/2018/highly-restrictive-laws-do-not-eliminate-abortion.

38. Dreweke, Joerg. 2016. "New Clarity for the U.S. Abortion Debate: A Steep Drop in Unintended Pregnancy Is Driving Recent Abortion Declines." Retrieved from https://www.guttmacher.org/gpr/2016/03/new-clarity-us-abortion-debate-steep-drop-unintended-pregnancy-driving-recent-abortion.

39. Barot, Sneha. 2011. "Unsafe Abortion: The Missing Link in Global Efforts to Improve Maternal Health." *Guttmacher Policy Review* 14(2):24-28.

40. Guttmacher Institute. 2018. "Family Planning Funding Restrictions." Retrieved from https://www.guttmacher.org/evidence-you-can-use/family-planning-funding-restrictions.

41. Ringdal, Nils Johan. 2004. *Love for Sale: A World History of Prostitution*. Translated by R. Daly. New York: Grove Press.

42. Bullough, Vern L. and Bonnie Bullough. 1977. *Sin, Sickness, and Sanity: A History of Sexual Attitudes*. New York: New American Library.

43. Bullough, Vern L. and Bonnie Bullough. 1987. *Women and Prostitution: A Social History*. Buffalo: Prometheus.

44. Stanford, Sally. 1966. *The Lady of the House*. New York: G.P. Putnam.

45. Brewer, Devon D., John J. Potterat, Sharon B. Garrett, Stephen Q. Muth, Jr. John M. Roberts, Danuta Kasprzyk, Daniel E. Montano and William W. Darrow. 2000. "Prostitution and the Sex Discrepancy in Reported Number of Sexual Partners." *Proceedings of the National Academy of Sciences* 97:12385-88.

46. Clinard, Marshall B. and Robert F. Meier. 2011. *Sociology of Deviant Behavior*. Fort Worth: Harcourt Brace.

47. Federal Bureau of Investigation. 2018. *Crime in the United States, 2017*. Washington, DC: Author.

48. Weitzer, Ronald. 2012. "Prostitution: Facts and Fictions." Pp. 223-30 in *The Contexts Reader*, edited by D. Hartmann and C. Uggen. New York: W.W. Norton & Company.

49. Weitzer, Ronald. 2009. "Sociology of Sex Work." *Annual Review of Sociology* 35:213-13-34.

50. Weitzer, Ronald. 2012. "Prostitution: Facts and Fictions." Pp. 223-30 in *The Contexts* Reader, edited by D. Hartmann and C. Uggen. New York: W.W. Norton & Company.

51. Weitzer, Ronald. 2012. "Prostitution: Facts and Fictions." Pp. 223-30 in *The Contexts Reader*, edited by D. Hartmann and C. Uggen. New York: W.W. Norton & Company.

52. Weitzer, Ronald. 2009. "Sociology of Sex Work." *Annual Review of Sociology* 35:213-13-34.

53. Weitzer, Ronald. 2009. "Sociology of Sex Work." *Annual Review of Sociology* 35:213-13-34.

54. Weitzer, Ronald. 2009. "Sociology of Sex Work." *Annual Review of Sociology* 35:213-13-34.

55. Davis, Kingsley. 1937. "The Sociology of Prostitution." *American Sociological Review* 2:744-55.

56. Rosen, Ruth. 1983. *The Lost Sisterhood: Prostitution in America, 1900-1918*. Baltimore: Johns Hopkins Univesity Press.

57. Barry, Kathleen. 1996. *The Prostitution of Sexuality*. New York: NYU Press.

58. Weitzer, Ronald. 2009. "Sociology of Sex Work." *Annual Review of Sociology* 35:213-13-34.

59. Ordway, Rennee. 1995. "Relaxation Spas Perplex Officials." Pp. 1 in *The Bangor Daily News*. Bangor, Maine.

60. Meier, Robert F. and Gilbert Geis. 2006. *Criminal Justice and Moral Issues*. New York: Oxford University Press.

61. McCaslin, John. 1999. "Vaginal Politics." *Washington Times* October 13:A8.

62. McKinley, Jesse. 2019. "Push to End Penalties for Oldest Profession." *The New York Times* June 1:A21. Weitzer, Ronald. 2011. *Legalizing Prostitution: From Illicit Vice to Lawful Business*. New York: NYU Press.

63. Weitzer, R. (2007). Prostitution: Facts and Fictions. *Contexts*, 6(4), 28–33. https://doi.org/10.1525/ctx.2007.6.4.28. Retrieved from: https://journals.sagepub.com/doi/pdf/10.1525/ctx.2007.6.4.28

64. Bachman, Helena. 2019. "Sex in the City: Zurich Prostitution 'Sex Boxes' Deemed Success in Switzerland." *USA Today* August 24:https://www.usatoday.com/story/news/world/2018/08/24/sex-boxes-make-legal-prostitution-safe-zurich-switzerland-europe/1083444002/; Chagnon, Marianne. 2017. "Prostitution in the Netherlands: What Is Really Happening Here." *DutchReview* February 10:https://dutchreview.com/featured/prostitution-in-the-netherlands-what-is-really-happening-here/; Weitzer, Ronald. 2009. "Sociology of Sex Work." *Annual Review of Sociology* 35:213-13-34; Weitzer, Ronald. (2009). "Sociology of Sex Work." *Annual Review of Sociology* 35:213-13-34; Weitzer, R. (2007). "Prostitution: Facts and Fictions." *Contexts*, 6(4), 28–33. https://doi.org/10.1525/ctx.2007.6.4.28. Retrieved from: https://journals.sagepub.com/doi/pdf/10.1525/ctx.2007.6.4.28.

65. Bullough, Vern L. and Bonnie Bullough. 1977. *Sin, Sickness, and Sanity: A History of Sexual Attitudes*. New York: New American Library.

66. Bullough, Vern L. and Bonnie Bullough. 1977. *Sin, Sickness, and Sanity: A History of Sexual Attitudes*. New York: New American Library.

67. Morgan, Robin. 1980. "Theory and Practice: Pornography and Rape." Pp. 134-40 in *Take Back the Night*, edited by L. Lederer. New York: William Morrow.

68. Tarrant, Shira. 2016. *The Pornography Industry: What Everyone Needs to Know*. New York: Oxford University Press.

69. Tarrant, Shira. 2016. *The Pornography Industry: What Everyone Needs to Know*. New York: Oxford University Press.

70. Castleman, Michael. 2016. "Evidence Mounts: More Porn, Less Sexual Assault." *Psychology Today* January 14:https://www.psychologyto-day.com/us/blog/all-about-sex/201601/evidence-mounts-more-porn-less-sexual-assault; Diamond, Milton. 2009. "Pornography, Public Acceptance and Sex Related Crime: A Review." *International Journal of Law & Psychiatry* 32(5):304-14; Fagan, Pat. 2019. "The Effects of Pornography on Individuals, Marriage, Family and Community." *Family Research Council*:https://www.frc.org/issuebrief/the-effects-of-pornography-on-individuals-marriage-family-and-community; Ley, David J. 2014. "Common Sense About the Effects of Pornography." *Psychology Today* February 3:https://www.psychologytoday.com/us/blog/women-who-stray/201402/common-sense-about-the-effects-pornography; Weitzer, Ronald. 2011. "Review Essay: Pornography's Effects: The Need for Solid Evidence." *Violence Against Women* 17(5):666-75.

71. Ferguson, Christopher J. and Richard D. Hartley. 2009. "The Pleasure Is Momentary...the Expense Damnable?: The Influence of Pornography on Rape and Sexual Assault." *Aggression & Violent Behavior* 14(5):323-29. doi: 10.1016/j.avb.2009.04.008.

72. Strossen, Nadine. 2000. *Defending Pornography: Free Speech, Sex, and the Fight for Women's Rights*. New York: New York University Press.

PART 4

Problems of Social Institutions

Source: ESB Professional/Shutterstock.com

CHAPTER 10
The Changing Family

Social Problems in the News

"Domestic Violence Victims Can Now Bring Pets to Choices Shelter," the headline said. In Columbus, Ohio, a new domestic violence shelter called Choices for Domestic Violence Victims had just opened a kennel for cats, dogs, and other small pets. Abusers often threaten to harm or kill a woman's pet, and women may decide not to try to flee their abusers if they cannot take their pet with them. The new kennel would enable these pets to continue to live with Choices residents and any children they might have with them, although the pets stay in the kennel to avoid disturbing any residents with animal allergies or fears. A Choices resident recalled the day her puppy was delivered to the new kennel. "I was so excited, I jumped up and ran down to see her right away," she said. "I'm so full of joy now that she's here. She lifts me up. I always feel better when we come out and play."

Although this Columbus shelter's kennel was a welcome development, only 3 percent of the 3,000 domestic violence shelters nationwide accept pets. The CEO of the National Coalition Against Domestic Violence lamented this situation: "For many survivors, at some point it becomes 'my life or the pet's life.' That's a really sad decision to have to make."

Source: Neese 2019[1]

Once upon a time, domestic violence did not exist, or so the popular television shows of the 1950s would have had us believe. Neither did single-parent households, same-sex couples, interracial couples, mothers working outside the home, heterosexual spouses deciding not to have children, or other family forms and situations that are increasingly common today. Domestic violence existed, of course, but it was not something that television shows and other popular media back then depicted. The other family forms and situations also existed to some degree but have become much more common today.

The 1950s gave us *Leave It to Beaver* and other television shows that depicted loving, happy, "traditional" families living in the suburbs. The father worked outside the home, the mother stayed at home to take care of the kids and do housework, and their children were wholesome youngsters who rarely got into trouble and certainly did not use drugs or have sex. Today we have many TV shows featuring single parents, same-sex couples, divorced couples or individuals, domestic violence, and teenagers doing drugs, being sexually active, or committing crime.

In the real world, we hear that parents are too busy working at their jobs to raise their kids properly. We hear of domestic violence, as in the story from Columbus at the start of this chapter. We hear of kids living without fathers because their parents are divorced or never were married in the first place. We hear of young people having babies, using drugs, and committing violence. We hear that the breakdown of the nuclear family, the entrance of women into the labor force, and the growth of single-parent households are responsible for these problems. Some observers urge women to work only part-time or not at all so they can spend more time with their children. Some yearn wistfully for a return to the 1950s, when everything seemed so much easier and better. Children had what they needed back then: one parent (almost always the father) to earn the money, and another parent (almost always the mother) to take care of them full-time until they started kindergarten, when this parent would be there for them when they came home from school.

Families have indeed changed, but this yearning for the 1950s falls into what historian Stephanie Coontz (2016)[2] calls the "nostalgia trap." The 1950s television shows did depict what some families were like back then, but they failed to show what many other families were like. More-

Families shown in today's television shows are very different from the traditional family depicted in popular television shows of the 1950s. Television families from the 1950s consisted of two heterosexual parents, with the father working outside the home and the mother staying at home with two or more wholesome children.

Source: © Thinkstock

over, the changes in families since that time have probably not had all the harmful effects that many observers allege. Historical and cross-cultural evidence even suggests that the *Leave It to Beaver*-style family of the 1950s was a relatively recent and atypical phenomenon and that many other types of families can thrive just as well as the 1950s television families did.

This chapter expands on these points and looks at today's families and the changes they have undergone. It also examines some of the controversies and problems now surrounding families and relationships and discusses some of the initial effects on families of the 2020 COVID-19 pandemic.

10.1 Overview of the Family

Learning Objectives

1. Describe why many children throughout history have not lived in a nuclear family.
2. Understand the status of the nuclear family in the United States since the colonial period.
3. Describe the major marriage and family arrangements in the United States today.

family

A group of two or more people who are related by blood, marriage, adoption, or a mutual commitment and who care for one another.

nuclear family

A family composed of two parents and their children living in the same household.

extended family

A family in which parents, children, and other relatives live in the same household.

A **family** is a group of two or more people who are related by blood, marriage, adoption, or a mutual commitment and who care for one another. Defined in this way, the family is universal or nearly universal: Some form of the family has existed in every society, or nearly every society, that we know about (Starbuck and Lundy 2015).[3] Yet it is also true that many types of families have existed, and the cross-cultural and historical record indicates that these different forms of the family can all "work": They provide practical and emotional support for their members, and they socialize their children.

It is important to keep this last statement in mind, because Americans until the last few decades thought of only one type of family, and that is the **nuclear family**: A married heterosexual couple and their young children living by themselves under one roof. The nuclear family has existed in most societies with which scholars are familiar. An **extended family**, which consists of parents, their children, and other relatives, has a nuclear family at its core and was quite common in prehistoric societies. Many *one-parent* families begin as (two-parent) nuclear families that dissolve upon divorce or separation or, more rarely, the death of one of the parents. In recent decades, one-parent families have become more common in the United States because of divorce and births out of wedlock, but they were actually very common throughout most of human history because many spouses died early in life and because many babies were born out of wedlock.

Although many prehistoric societies featured nuclear families, a few societies studied by anthropologists have not had them. In these societies, a father does not live with a woman after she has his child and sees them either irregularly or not at all. Despite the absence of a father and the lack of a nuclear family, this type of family arrangement seems to have worked well in these societies. In particular, children are cared for and grow up to be productive members of their societies (Smith 1996).[4]

These examples do not invalidate the fact that nuclear families are almost universal. But they do indicate that the functions of the nuclear family can be achieved through other family arrangements. If that is true, perhaps the oft-cited concern over the "breakdown" of the 1950s-style nuclear family in modern America is at least somewhat undeserved. As indicated by the examples just given, children can and do thrive without two parents. To say this is meant neither to extol divorce, births out of wedlock, and fatherless families nor to minimize the problems they may involve.

Rather, it is meant simply to indicate that the nuclear family is not the only viable form of family organization (Seccombe 2020).[5]

In fact, although nuclear families remain the norm in most societies, in practice they are something of a historical rarity: Until about a century ago, many spouses died by their mid-forties, and many babies were born out of wedlock. In medieval Europe, for example, people died early from disease, malnutrition, and other problems. One consequence of early mortality was that many children often outlived at least one of their parents and thus essentially were raised in one-parent families or in stepfamilies (Gottlieb 1993).[6]

Although the nuclear family is a common family arrangement today, historically many children lived with only one parent because spouses died early and many babies were born out of wedlock.

Source: fizkes/Shutterstock.com

During the American colonial period, different family types abounded, and the nuclear family was by no means the only type (Coontz 1995).[7] Nomadic Native American groups had relatively small nuclear families, while nonnomadic groups had larger extended families. Because nuclear families among enslaved African Americans were difficult to achieve, those who were enslaved adapted by developing extended families, adopting orphans, and taking in other people not related by blood or marriage. Many European parents of colonial children died because average life expectancy was only forty-five years. The one-third to one-half of children who outlived at least one of their parents lived in stepfamilies or with just their surviving parent. Mothers were so busy working the land and doing other tasks that they devoted relatively little time to child care, which instead was entrusted to older children or servants.

Moving much forward in U.S. history, an important change in American families occurred during the 1940s after World War II ended. As men came home after serving in the military, books, magazines, and newspapers exhorted women to have babies, and babies they did have: People got married at younger ages and the birth rate soared, resulting in the *baby boom generation*. Meanwhile, divorce rates dropped. The national economy thrived as auto and other factory jobs multiplied, and many families for the first time could dream of owning their own homes. Suburbs sprang up, and many families moved to them. Many families during the 1950s did indeed fit the *Leave It to Beaver* model of the breadwinner-homemaker suburban nuclear family. Following the Depression of the 1930s and the war of the 1940s, the 1950s seemed an almost idyllic decade.

Even so, fewer than 60 percent of American children during the 1950s lived in breadwinner-homemaker nuclear families. Moreover, many lived in poverty, as the poverty rate then was almost twice as high as it is today. Teenage pregnancy rates were much higher than today's rates. Although not publicized back then, alcoholism and violence in families were common. Historians have found that many women in this era were unhappy with their homemaker roles, Mrs. Cleaver (Beaver's mother) to the contrary, suffering from what Betty Friedan (1963)[8] famously called the "feminine mystique."

During the 1960s and 1970s, women began to enter the labor force. They did so to increase their families' incomes and to achieve greater self-fulfillment. More than 60 percent of married women with children under six years of age are now in the labor force, compared to less than 19 percent in 1960. At about the same time, divorce rates increased for several reasons that we examine later in this chapter. Changes in the American family had begun, and along with them various controversies and problems.

Marriage and the Family in the United States Today

In the United States today, marriage remains an important institution, with about 50 percent of adults eighteen and older currently married. However, this figure was 72 percent in 1960. The lower figure today reflects three trends: (1) people are marrying later in life than in 1960; (2) the divorce rate is higher now than in 1960; and (3) more people are unmarried because they prefer to live with someone and not to marry that person (Parker and Stepler 2017).[9] Still, when we examine General Social Survey data just for people aged 45–60, who are past the traditional marrying age and thus "old enough" to have gotten married, 88 percent are currently married or had been married at some point in their lives before becoming divorced, separated, or widowed. At the same time, however, it is estimated that one-fourth of young adults today will not have married by the time they reach age fifty (Schoppe-Sullivan 2017).[10] These figures indicate that marriage continues to be an important aspect of American life, even if not all marriages succeed and even if more people than two generations ago are not marrying.

To the extent that marriage rates have declined, this decline is greatest for people without a college education. This situation has been called the "education gap in marital status" (Parker and Stepler 2017).[11] For example, almost two-thirds (65 percent) of college graduates ages twenty-five and older are currently married (2015 data), compared to only 50 percent of those with a high school diploma.

 ## Why Are Fewer Americans Getting Married?

Marriage rates in the United States have declined in recent decades. However, most Americans continue to get married, even if they do so at later ages than just a few decades ago.

View the video online at: http://www.youtube.com/embed/8djXpoTl200?rel=0

This education gap in marriage rates worsens the financial situation that people with lower education already face. As one writer observed, "As marriage increasingly becomes a phenomenon of the better-off and better-educated, the incomes of two-earner married couples diverge more from those of struggling single adults" (Marcus 2011).[12] An important consequence of this education gap is that the children of one-parent households are less likely than those of two-parent households to graduate high school and to attend college. In this manner, a parent's low education helps to perpetuate low education among the parent's children.

In view of the general decline in marriage rates, it is worth noting that the 2020 COVID-19 pandemic threatened to lower marriage rates further, at least temporarily. That is because many couples were apparently delaying their wedding plans either because their states banned large gatherings or because they did not wish to expose themselves and their wedding party and guests to the coronavirus (Halleck 2020).[13] Most of these couples would probably marry later when it was safe to do so, but it is also likely that some of them would never marry or even end their relationship. Couples that did marry during the pandemic had downscaled weddings with many fewer, if any, guests. Not surprisingly, the wedding industry suffered a devastating blow from the pandemic along with the rest of the economy (Testa 2020).[14]

Children and Families

Almost two-thirds (65.4 percent) of the nation's 74 million children under age eighteen live with two parents (2018 data), while slightly more than one-fourth (26.6 percent) live with one parent, usually their mother. The proportion of families with just with one parent varies significantly by race and ethnicity: Latinx and African American families are more likely than white families to be headed by only one parent (see Figure 10.1).

FIGURE 10.1 Race, Ethnicity, and Percentage of Families with Only One Parent, 2018

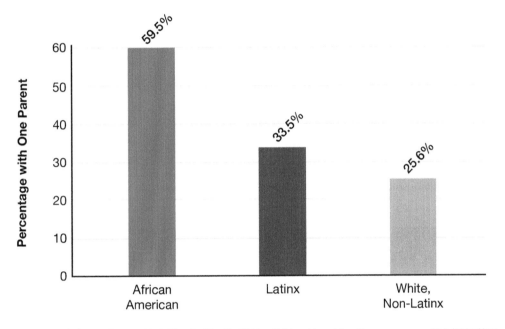

Source: Data from U.S. Census Bureau. 2019. Historical Families Tables. Retrieved from https://www.census.gov/data/tables/time-series/demo/families/families.html.

We will discuss several other issues affecting children later in this chapter. But before we move on, it is worth noting that children, despite all the joy and fulfillment they so often bring to parents, also often reduce parents' emotional well-being, especially that of mothers (Nelson et al. 2014; Gillihan 2017).[15] Children have these effects because raising them can be both stressful and expensive. Depending on household income, the average child costs parents between about $170,000 and $370,000 from birth until age eighteen (Fiorillo 2018).[16] College education obviously can cost tens of thousands of dollars beyond that. Robin W. Simon (2008)[17] argues that American parents' stress would be reduced if the government provided better and more affordable day care and after-school options, flexible work schedules, and tax credits for various parenting costs. She also thinks that the expectations Americans have of the joy of parenthood are unrealistically positive and that parental stress would be reduced if expectations became more realistic.

After the 2020 COVID-19 pandemic began, parents and children sheltered at home. Parents who could do so worked from home, and almost all children could no longer go to school. Many other parents still had to go to work outside the home or had to cut back their hours so they could stay home with their children, who were often attending school online or trying to do schoolwork remotely. All these trying experiences cast light on certain aspects of children and family life. As discussed by Pulitzer Prize-winning reporter Claire Cain Miller (2020),[18] the lessons learned about these aspects are:

- *Parenting happens at all hours.* Although many employers expect full-time availability from their employees, that is not possible for many parents. The pandemic family situation exhibited the conflicting demands faced by many employees between work and parenting.

- *Raising children is not just a personal choice.* Because children are the future of the country, raising children is a benefit for all of society. For this reason, employers should give their employees more flexible time, and the federal government should provide paid parental leave, as most other democracies do, and heavily subsidize high-quality childcare, as many democracies also do.

- *Working parents cannot do it alone.* Childcare became a crisis during the pandemic because schools and childcare facilities closed. Parents trying to work from home had to also take care of their children, while parents working outside the home needed childcare to do so. Employers and the federal and state governments again need to provide flexible work schedules, paid parental leave, and affordable, high-quality childcare.

Key Takeaways

- Although the nuclear family has been very common, many children throughout history have not lived in a nuclear family, in part because a parent would die at an early age.
- Most Americans eventually marry. This fact means that marriage remains an important ideal in American life, even if not all marriages succeed.
- More than one-fourth of children live with only one parent, usually their mother.
- The childcare crisis that emerged in the wake of the 2020 pandemic made very clear that working parents need paid parental leave, flexible work schedules, and heavily subsidized, high-quality childcare.

For Your Review

1. The text argues that the childcare crisis after the 2020 pandemic emerged emphasized the need for our society to provide flexible work hours for parents, subsidized childcare, and paid parental leave. Do you agree or disagree with this argument? Explain your answer.
2. The text notes that most people eventually marry. In view of the fact that so many marriages end in divorce, why do you think that so many people continue to marry?
3. Some of the children who live only with their mothers were born out of wedlock. Do you think the parents should have married for the sake of their child? Why or why not?

10.2 Sociological Perspectives on the Family

Learning Objective

1. Summarize understandings of the family as presented by functional, conflict, and social interactionist theories.

Sociological views on today's families and their problems generally fall into the functional, conflict, and social interactionist approaches introduced in Chapter 1. Let's review these views, which are summarized in Table 10.1.

TABLE 10.1 Theory Snapshot

Theoretical perspective	Major assumptions
Functionalism	The family performs several essential functions for society. It socializes children, it provides emotional and practical support for its members, it helps regulate sexual activity and sexual reproduction, and it provides its members with a social identity. Family problems stem from sudden or far-reaching changes in the family's structure or processes; these problems threaten the family's stability and weaken society.
Conflict theory	The family contributes to social inequality by reinforcing economic inequality and by reinforcing patriarchy. Family problems stem from economic inequality and from patriarchal ideology. The family can also be a source of conflict, including physical violence and emotional cruelty, for its own members.
Symbolic interactionism	The interaction of family members and intimate couples involves shared understandings of their situations. Wives and husbands have different styles of communication, and social class affects the expectations that spouses have of their marriages and of each other. Family problems stem from different understandings and expectations that spouses have of their marriage.

Social Functions of the Family

Recall that the functional perspective emphasizes that social institutions perform several important functions to help preserve social stability and otherwise keep a society working. A functional understanding of the family thus stresses the ways in which the family as a social institution helps make society possible. As such, the family performs several important functions.

First, the family is the primary unit for *socializing children*. No society is possible without adequate socialization of its young. In most societies, the family is the major unit in which socialization happens. Parents, siblings, and, if the family is extended rather than nuclear, other relatives all help socialize children from the time they are born.

Second, the family is ideally a major source of *practical and emotional support* for its members. It provides them food, clothing, shelter, and other essentials, and it also provides them love, comfort, and help in times of emotional distress, and other types of support.

Third, the family helps *regulate sexual activity and sexual reproduction*. All societies have norms governing with whom and how often a person should have sex. The family is the major unit for teaching these norms and the major unit through which sexual reproduction occurs. One reason for this is to ensure that infants have adequate emotional and practical care when they are born.

Fourth, the family provides its members with a *social identity*. Children are born into their parents' social class, race and ethnicity, religion, and so forth. Some children have advantages throughout life because of the social identity they acquire from their parents, while others face many obstacles because the social class or race/ethnicity into which they are born is at the bottom of the social hierarchy.

Beyond discussing the family's functions, the functional perspective on the family maintains that sudden or far-reaching changes in conventional family structure and processes threaten the family's stability and thus that of society. For example, most sociology and marriage-and-family textbooks during the 1950s maintained that the male breadwinner–female homemaker nuclear family was the best arrangement for children, as it provided for a family's economic and child-rearing needs. Any shift in this arrangement, they warned, would harm children and, by extension, the family as a social institution and even society

One of the most important functions of the family is the socialization of children. In most societies the family is the major unit through which socialization occurs.

Source: © Thinkstock

itself. Textbooks no longer contain this warning, but many conservative observers continue to worry about the impact on children of working mothers and one-parent families.

The Family and Conflict

Conflict theorists agree that the family serves the important functions just listed, but they also point to problems within the family that the functional perspective minimizes or overlooks altogether.

First, the family as a social institution contributes to social inequality. Because families pass along their wealth to their children, and because families differ greatly in the amount of wealth they have, the family helps reinforce existing inequality. As it developed through the centuries, and especially during industrialization, the family also became more and more of a patriarchal unit (since men made money working in factories while women stayed home), helping to reinforce men's status at the top of the social hierarchy.

Second, the family can also be a source of conflict for its own members. Although many families provide their members emotional comfort and support, many families do just the opposite and are far from the harmonious, happy groups depicted in the 1950s television shows. Instead, they argue, shout, and use emotional cruelty and physical violence. We return to family violence later in this chapter.

The conflict perspective emphasizes that many of the problems we see in today's families stem from economic inequality and from patriarchy. The problems that many families experience reflect the fact that they live in poverty or near poverty. Money does not always bring happiness, but a dire lack of money produces stress and other difficulties that impair a family's functioning and relationships. The "Applying Social Research" box discusses other ways in which social class influences the family.

Conflict within a family also stems from patriarchy. Husbands usually earn more money than wives, and many men continue to feel that they are the head of their families. When women resist this old-fashioned notion, spousal conflict occurs.

Applying Social Research

Social Class and the Family

Social science research documents social class differences in how well a family functions: the quality of its relationships and the cognitive, psychological, and social development of its children. This focus reflects the fact that what happens during the first months and years of life may have profound effects on how well a newborn prospers during childhood, adolescence, and beyond. To the extent this is true, the social class differences that have been found have troublesome implications.

According to sociologist Frank E. Furstenberg, Jr., "steep differences exist across social classes" in mothers' prenatal experiences, such as the quality of their diet and health care, as well as in the health care that their infants receive. As a result, he says, "children enter the world endowed unequally." This inequality worsens after they are born for several reasons.

First, low-income families are much more likely to experience *negative events*, such as death, poor health, unemployment, divorce, and criminal victimization. When these negative events do occur, says Furstenberg, "social class affects a family's ability to cushion their blow...Life is simply harder and more brutish at the bottom." These negative events produce great amounts of stress. As Chapter 2 discussed, this stress in turn causes children to experience various developmental problems.

Second, low-income parents are much less likely to read and speak regularly to their infants and young children, who thus are slower to develop cognitive and reading skills. This problem in turn impairs their school performance when they enter elementary school.

Third, low-income parents are also less able to expose their children to cultural experiences (e.g., museum visits) outside the home, to develop their talents in the arts and other areas, and to otherwise be involved in the many nonschool activities that are important for a child's development. In contrast, wealthier parents keep their children very busy in these activities in a pattern that sociologist Annette Lareau calls *concerted cultivation*. These children's involvement in these activities provides them various life skills that help enhance their performance in school and later in the workplace.

Fourth, low-income children grow up in low-income neighborhoods, which often have inadequate schools and many other problems, including toxins such as lead paint, that impair a child's development. In contrast, says Furstenberg, children from wealthier families "are very likely to attend better schools and live in better neighborhoods. It is as if the playing field for families is tilted in ways that are barely visible to the naked eye."

Fifth, low-income families are less able to afford to send a child to college, and they are more likely to lack the social contacts that wealthier parents can use to help their child get a good job after college.

For all these reasons, social class profoundly shapes how children fare from conception through early adulthood and beyond. Because this body of research documents many negative consequences of living in a low-income family, it reinforces the need for wide-ranging efforts to help such families.

Sources: Furstenberg 2010; Lareau 2011; Sacks and Murphy 2018[19]

Families and Social Interaction

Social interactionist perspectives on the family examine how family members and intimate couples interact on a daily basis and arrive at shared understandings of their situations. Studies grounded in social interactionism give us a keen understanding of how and why families operate the way they do.

Some studies, for example, focus on how husbands and wives communicate and the degree to which they communicate successfully. A classic study by Mirra Komarovsky (1964)[20] found that wives in blue-collar marriages liked to talk with their husbands about problems they were having, while husbands tended to be quiet when problems occurred. Such gender differences are less common in middle-class families, where men are better educated and more emotionally expressive than their working-class counterparts, but gender differences in communication still exist in these families. Another classic study by Lillian Rubin (1976)[21] found that wives in middle-class families say that ideal husbands are ones who communicate well and share their feelings, while wives in working-class families are more apt to say that ideal husbands are ones who do not drink too much and who go to work every day.

According to the symbolic interactionist perspective, family problems often stem from the different understandings, perceptions, and expectations that spouses have of their marriage and of their family. When these differences become too extreme and the spouses cannot reconcile their disagreements, spousal conflict and possibly divorce may occur (Kulik et al 2016).[22]

Key Takeaways

- The family ideally serves several functions for society. It socializes children, provides practical and emotional support for its members, regulates sexual reproduction, and provides its members with a social identity.
- Reflecting conflict theory's emphases, the family may also produce several problems. In particular, it may contribute for several reasons to social inequality, and it may subject its members to violence, arguments, and other forms of conflict.
- Social interactionist understandings of the family emphasize how family members interact on a daily basis. In this regard, several studies find that husbands and wives communicate differently in certain ways that sometimes impede effective communication.

For Your Review

1. As you think how best to understand the family, do you favor the views and assumptions of functional theory, conflict theory, or social interactionist theory? Explain your answer.
2. Do you think the family continues to serve the function of regulating sexual behavior and sexual reproduction? Why or why not?

10.3 Changes and Problems in American Families

Learning Objectives

1. Discuss why the U.S. divorce rate rose during the 1960s and 1970s and summarize the major individual-level factors accounting for divorce today.
2. Describe the effects of divorce for spouses and children.
3. Summarize the evidence on how children fare when their mothers work outside the home.
4. Describe the extent of family violence and explain why it occurs.

American families have undergone many changes since the 1950s. Scholars, politicians, and the public have strong and often conflicting views on the reasons for these changes and their consequences. We now look at some of the most important issues affecting U.S. families through the lens of the latest social scientific evidence. Because Chapter 5 on sexual orientation and inequality discussed same-sex marriage and families, please refer back to that chapter for material on this very important topic.

Cohabitation

Some people who are not currently married nonetheless **cohabit**, or live together, with someone in a romantic relationship. The number of cohabiting adults in the United States has increased somewhat during this century, from 14 million adults in 2007 to 18 million in 2016 (Stepler 2017).[23] About half of these cohabiters are under age thirty-five, but almost one-fourth are fifty and older. Still, only 7 percent of all adults were cohabiting in 2016 at any one time, although this figure rises to about 10 percent of adults ages 18–24 and 14 percent of adults ages 25–34.

Although cohabitation has increased somewhat during this century, it is especially much more common than a half-century ago. Although measurement issues prevent an exact assessment, census data indicate that only 0.1 percent of adults ages 18–24 were cohabiting in 1968, compared to the 10 percent figure just mentioned for this age group for 2016 (Gurrentz 2018).[24] The "at any one time" percentages we have listed mask the fact that cohabitation is now the rule rather than the exception, because three-fourths of young adults will cohabit at some point in their lives (Brown et al. 2017).[25] Moreover, cohabitation now precedes most marriages, with 70 percent of first marriages involving women under age thirty-six beginning in cohabitation (Kupferberg 2019).[26]

The rise in cohabitation reflects the declining marriage rate discussed earlier in this chapter, which in turn reflects a rise during the last half century of divorce rates and never-married rates. Because more people are unmarried than in the past, more people are now "available" for cohabitation. Fortunately for them, cohabitation is undoubtedly considered much more acceptable than in the past. A half century ago, unmarried romantic partners who lived together were said by many people to be "living in sin"; these days, this arrangement seems instead to be a perfectly normal aspect of the life cycle.

cohabit

To live together in a romantic, sexual relationship without being married.

According to the census, roughly 10 percent of people ages 18–24 are currently cohabiting in the United States. This figure represents a steep rise from several decades ago.

Source: © Thinkstock

🎥 What Is a Cohabitation Agreement?

Cohabitation is much more common now than a generation or two ago and has almost become the norm before getting married. This video explains the the content of cohabitation agreements, which are meant to protect both people in the arrangement if they break up.

View the video online at: http://www.youtube.com/embed/GonxbSxsK5A?rel=0

Married couples during the 1980s and 1990s who cohabited with each other before marrying were more likely to divorce than married couples who had not first cohabited (Jose et al. 2010).[27] This difference probably reflected the early cohabiters' lower commitment to the idea of marriage, making them more willing to divorce if they were unhappy in their eventual marriage. However, and controlling for social class and other factors, today's cohabiting couples who marry are not more likely to divorce than married couples who did not cohabit (Brown et al. 2017).[28] This change probably reflects the great growth in cohabitation, which has become so common that people who choose to cohabit before marrying are no less committed to the idea of marriage than people who do not cohabit before marrying. In a corresponding change, early cohabiters were less happy and otherwise had lower psychological well-being than married adults, but today's cohabiters exhibit similar well-being to that of their married counterparts (Brown et al. 2017).[29]

How do children of cohabiting parents fare in terms of physical and mental health and other outcomes? The answer is rather complicated (Brown 2010; Manning, 2015).[30] In general, children of long-term cohabiting couples fare as well as those of married couples. However, most cohabiting couples eventually dissolve their relationship within a few years, and any children they have tend to fare worse than children of married couples.

Divorce and Single-Parent Households

The U.S. divorce rate has risen since the early 1900s, with several peaks and valleys, and is now the highest in the industrial world. It rose sharply during the Great Depression and World War II, probably because of the economic distress of the former and the family disruption caused by the latter, and fell sharply after the war as the economy thrived and as marriage and family were proclaimed as patriotic ideals. It dropped a bit more during the 1950s before rising sharply through the 1960s and 1970s (Cherlin 2009).[31] The divorce rate has since declined somewhat and today is only slightly higher than its peak at the end of World War II. Still, at least 40 percent of all new marriages today are projected to eventually end in divorce (Wilcox 2019).[32]

Reasons for Divorce

We cannot be certain about why the divorce rate rose so much during the 1960s and 1970s, but we can rule out two oft-cited causes. First, there is little reason to believe that marriages became any less happy during this period. We do not have good data to compare marriages then and now, but the best guess is that marital satisfaction did not decline after the 1950s ended. What did change was that people after the 1950s became more willing to seek divorces in marriages that were already unhappy.

Second, although the contemporary women's movement is sometimes blamed for the divorce rate by making women think marriage is an oppressive institution, actual divorce trends suggest this blame is misplaced. This is because the divorce rate began rising in the early 1960s, several years before the women's movement emerged in the late 1960s and early 1970s. If the divorce rate began rising before the women's movement started, it is illogical to blame the women's movement. Instead, other structural and cultural forces must have been at work, just as they were at other times in the last century, as just noted, when the divorce rate rose and fell.

Why, then, did divorce increase during the 1960s and 1970s? One reason is the increasing economic independence of women. As women entered the labor force in the 1960s and 1970s, they became more economically independent of their husbands, even if their jobs typically paid less than their husbands' jobs. When women in unhappy marriages do become more economically independent, they are more able to afford to get divorced than when they have to rely entirely on their husbands' earnings (Hiedemann et al. 1998).[33] When both spouses work outside the home, moreover, it is more difficult to juggle the many demands of family life, and family life can be more stressful. Such stress can reduce marital happiness and make divorce more likely. Spouses may also have less time for each other when both are working outside the home, making it more difficult to deal with problems they may be having.

It is also true that disapproval of divorce has declined since the 1950s, even if negative views of it still remain (Cherlin 2009).[34] Not too long ago, divorce was considered a terrible thing; now it is considered a normal if unfortunate part of life. We no longer say a bad marriage should continue for the sake of the children. When New York Governor Nelson Rockefeller ran for president in the early 1960s, the fact that he had been divorced hurt his popularity, but when California Governor Ronald Reagan ran for president less than two decades later, the fact that he had been divorced was hardly noted. Many presidential candidates and other politicians today have been divorced. But is the growing acceptability of divorce a cause of the rising divorce rate, or is it the result of the rising divorce rate? Or is it both a cause and a result? This important causal order question is difficult to resolve.

Disapproval of divorce has declined since the 1950s, and divorce is now considered a normal if unfortunate part of life.

Source: © Thinkstock

Another reason divorce rose during the 1960s and 1970s may be that divorces became easier to obtain legally. In the past, most states required couples to prove that one or both had committed actions such as mental cruelty, adultery, or other such behaviors in order to get divorced. Today almost all states have no-fault divorce laws that allow a couple to divorce if they say their marriage has failed from irreconcilable differences. Because divorce has become easier and less expensive to obtain, more divorces occur. But are no-fault divorce laws a cause or result of the post-1950s rise in the divorce rate? The divorce rate increase preceded the establishment of most states' no-fault laws, but it is probably also true that the laws helped make additional divorces more possible. Thus no-fault divorce laws are probably one reason for the rising divorce rate after the 1950s, but only one reason (Kneip and Bauer 2009).[35]

We have just looked at possible reasons for divorce rate trends, but we can also examine the reasons why certain marriages are more or less likely to end in divorce within a given time period. Although, as noted earlier, 40 percent of all new marriages today will probably end in divorce, it is also true that some marriages are more likely to end than others (Aughinbaugh et al. 2013; Wilcox 2019).[36] One key predictor of divorce is age at marriage: Teenagers who get married are much more likely to get divorced than people who marry well into their twenties or beyond, partly because they have financial difficulties and are not yet emotionally mature. A second correlate of divorce is social class: People who are poor and have less formal education at the time of their marriage are much more likely to get divorced than people who begin their marriages in economic comfort and with higher levels of education.

Effects of Divorce and Single-Parent Households

Much research exists on the effects of divorce on spouses and their children, and scholars often disagree on what these effects are. One thing is clear: Divorce plunges many women into poverty or near-poverty (Brown and Wright 2017).[37] Many have been working only part-time or not at all outside the home, and divorce takes away their husband's economic support. Even women working full-time often have trouble making ends meet, because many are in low-paying jobs.

Although the economic consequences of divorce seem clear, what are the psychological consequences for husbands, wives, and their children? Are they better off if a divorce occurs, worse off, or about the same?

Effects on Spouses

The research evidence for spouses is conflicting. Many studies find that divorced spouses are, on average, less happy and have poorer mental health after their divorce, but some studies find that happiness and mental health often improve after divorce (Waite et al. 2009).[38] The postdivorce time period that is studied may affect what results are found: For some people psychological well-being may decline in the immediate aftermath of a divorce, given how difficult the divorce process often is, but rise over the next few years. The contentiousness of the marriage also matters. Some marriages ending in divorce have been filled with hostility, conflict, and sometimes violence, while other marriages ending in divorce have not been very contentious at all, even if they have failed. Individuals seem to fare better psychologically after ending a very contentious marriage but fare worse after ending a less contentious marriage (Bourassa et al. 2015).[39]

Effects on Children

What about the children? Parents used to stay together "for the sake of the children," thinking that divorce would cause their children more harm than good. Studies of this issue generally find that children in divorced families are indeed more likely, on average, to do worse in school, to use drugs and alcohol and suffer other behavioral problems, and to experience emotional distress and other psychological problems (Weaver and Schofield 2015; Wilcox 2019).[40] The trauma of the divorce and the difficulties that single parents encounter in caring for and disciplining children are thought to account for these effects.

However, two considerations suggest that children of divorce may fare worse for reasons other than divorce trauma and the resulting single-parent situation. First, most children whose parents divorce end up living with their mothers. As we just noted, many divorced women and their children live in poverty or near poverty. To the extent that these children fare worse in many ways, their mothers' low incomes may be a contributing factor. Studies of this issue find that divorced mothers' low incomes do, in fact, help explain some of the difficulties that their children experience (Demo and Fine 2010).[41] Divorce trauma and single-parenthood still matter for children's well-being in many of these studies, but the worsened financial situation of divorced women and their children also makes a difference.

Second, children may do worse after a divorce because of the parental conflict that led to the divorce, not because of the divorce itself. It is well known that the quality of the relationship between a child's parents affects the child's behavior and emotional well-being (Moore et al. 2011).[42] This fact raises the possibility that children may fare better if their parents end a troubled marriage than if their parents stay married. Researchers have investigated this issue, and their findings generally mirror the evidence for spouses just cited: Children generally fare better if their parents end a highly contentious marriage, but they fare worse if their parents end a marriage that has not been highly contentious (Weaver and Schofield 2015).[43] Commenting on divorces from highly contentious marriages, sociologist Virginia E. Rutter (2010:169)[44] bluntly concludes, "There are times and situations when divorce is beneficial to the people who divorce and to their children."

Marriage and Well-Being

Is marriage good for people? This is the flip side of the question we have just addressed on whether divorce is bad for people. Are people better off if they get married? Or are they better off if they stay single?

In 1972, sociologist Jessie Bernard (1972)[45] famously said that every marriage includes a "her marriage" and a "his marriage." By this she meant that husbands and wives view and define their marriages differently. When spouses from the same marriage are interviewed, they disagree on such things as how often they should have sex, how often they actually do have sex, and who does various household tasks. Women do most of the housework and child care, while men are freer to work and do other things outside the home. Citing various studies, she said that marriage is better for men than for women. Married women, she said, have poorer mental health than unmarried women, while married men have better mental health than unmarried men. In short, she said that marriage was good for men but bad for women.

Critics later said that Bernard misinterpreted her data on women and that married women are also better off than unmarried women (Glenn 1997).[46] More recent research generally finds that marriage does benefit both sexes: Married people, women and men alike, are generally happier than unmarried people (whether never married, divorced, or widowed), score better on other measures of psychological well-being, are physically healthier, have better sex lives, and have lower death rates (Waite et al. 2009; Wilcox 2019).[47] There is even evidence that marriage helps keep men from committing crime (Andersen 2017)![48] Marriage has these benefits for several reasons, including the emotional and practical support spouses give each other, their greater financial resources compared to those of unmarried people, and the sense of obligation they have toward each other.

Four issues qualify the general conclusion that marriage is beneficial. First, it would be more accurate to say that good marriages are beneficial, because bad marriages certainly are not, and stressful marriages can impair physical and mental health (Neff and Karney 2017).[49] Second, although marriage is generally beneficial, it is less beneficial for low-income couples, whose marriages tend to be more stressful, than for wealthier couples (Wadsworth 2016).[50] Third, happier and healthier people may be the ones who get married in the first place and are less apt to get divorced once they do marry. If so, marriage does not promote better mental and physical health; rather, better mental and physical health promote marriage (Kane 2016).[51] Research testing this *selectivity hypothesis* finds that both processes occur: Psychologically healthy people are more apt to get and stay married, but marriage also promotes psychological well-being. Fourth, research over several decades finds that wives experience more stress than husbands because they have greater caregiving responsibilities for children and aging parents and spend more time on housework (Caputo et al. 2016; Hochschild 1989; Jenkins 1997).[52]

Married people are generally happier than unmarried people and score higher on other measures of psychological well-being.

Source: © Thinkstock

Working Mothers and Day Care

As noted earlier, women are now much more likely to be working outside the home than a few decades ago. This is true for both married and unmarried women and also for women with and without children. As women have entered the labor force, the question of who takes care of the children has prompted much debate and controversy. Many observers say young children suffer if they do not have a parent, implicitly their mother, taking care of them full-time until they start school and being there every day when they get home from school. In the 2018 General Social Survey, one-fourth of respondents agreed that "it is much better for everyone involved if the man is the achiever outside the home and the woman takes care of the home and family." What does research say about how young children fare if their mothers work? (Notice that no one seems to worry that fathers work!)

Early studies compared the degree of attachment shown to their mothers by children in day care and that shown by children who stay at home with their mothers. In one type of study, children were put in a laboratory room with their mothers and observed as the mothers left and returned. The day-care kids usually treated their mothers' departure and returning casually and acted as if they did not care that their mothers were leaving or returning. In contrast the stay-at-home kids acted very upset when their mothers left and seemed much happier and even relieved when they returned. Several researchers concluded that these findings indicated that day-care children lacked sufficient emotional attachment to their mothers (Schwartz 1983).[53] However, other researchers reached a very different conclusion: The day-care children's apparent nonchalance when their mothers left and returned simply reflected the fact that they always saw her leave and return every day when they went to day care. The lack of concern over her behavior showed only that they were more independent and self-confident than the stay-at-home children, who were fearful when their mothers left, and not that they were less attached to their mothers (Coontz 1997).[54]

Children in day care exhibit better cognitive skills than stay-at-home children but are also slightly more likely to engage in aggressive behavior that is within the normal range of children's behavior.

Source: © Thinkstock

Some recent research has compared stay-at-home children and day-care children using data from a large study funded by the National Institute of Child Health and Human Development (Rabin 2008).[55] This research finds that day-care children exhibit better cognitive skills (reading and arithmetic) than stay-at-home children but are also slightly more likely to engage in aggressive behavior that is well within the normal range of children's behavior. This research has also yielded two other conclusions. First, the quality of parenting and other factors such as parent's education and income matter much more for children's cognitive and social development than whether or not they are in day care. Second, to the extent that day care is beneficial for children, it is high-quality day care that is beneficial, as low-quality day care can be harmful.

This latter conclusion is an important finding, because many day-care settings in the United States are not high quality. Unfortunately, many parents who use day care cannot afford high-quality care, which can cost thousands of dollars yearly. This problem reflects the fact that the United States lags far behind other Western democracies in providing subsidies for day care (see "Lessons from Other Societies" later in this chapter). Because working women are certainly here to stay and because high-quality day care seems at least as good for children as full-time care by a parent, it is essential that the United States make good day care available and affordable.

 Why Day Care Is So Expensive in America

High-quality day care is vitally important for millions of American families, but such day care is also very expensive. The United States lags far behind other wealthy democracies in providing free or heavily subsidized day care for the families that need it.

View the video online at: http://www.youtube.com/embed/JQNLWyQKLj4?rel=0

Racial and Ethnic Diversity in Marriages and Families

Marriages and families in the United States exhibit a fair amount of racial and ethnic diversity, as we saw earlier in this chapter (Cohen 2018).[56] One notable difference is that African American, Latinx, and Native American children and their families are especially likely to live in poverty. As a result, they are at much greater risk for the many problems that children in poverty experience (see Chapter 2).

Beyond these cold facts lie other racial and ethnic differences in family life (Wright et al. 2012).[57] Studies of Latinx and Asian American families find they have especially strong family bonds and loyalty. Extended families in both groups and among Native Americans are common, and these extended families have proven a valuable shield against the problems all three groups face because of their race/ethnicity and poverty.

Another notable difference involves births to unmarried mothers (*nonmarital births*). About 40 percent of children today are born to unmarried mothers, the majority of them in cohabiting relationships; this 40 percent figure represents an increase from 28 percent in 1990 and only 10.7 percent in 1970. Today's 40 percent figure also masks significant racial-ethnic differences, as African American, Latinx, and Native American children are much more likely than Asian and non-Latinx white children to be born to unmarried mothers (see Figure 10.2).

FIGURE 10.2 Percentage of Births to Unmarried Mothers, by Race/Ethnicity 2017

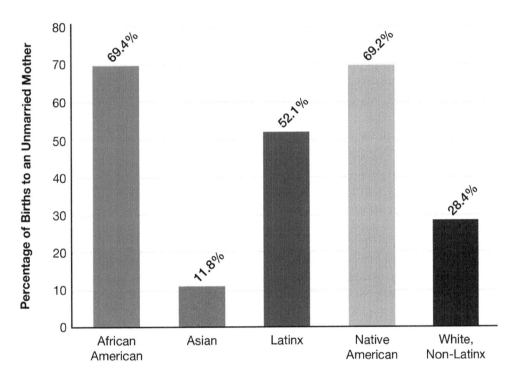

Source: Data from Martin, Joyce A., Brady E. Hamilton, Michelle J.K. Osterman, Anne K. Driscoll, and Patrick Drake. 2018. Births: Final Data for 2017. Retrieved from https://www.cdc.gov/nchs/data/nvsr/nvsr67/nvsr67_08-508.pdf.

Some scholars say the high number of unmarried births to African American mothers contributes to African Americans' poverty, crime, and other problems (Haskins 2009).[58] But other scholars say this blame is misplaced to at least some extent. Extended families and strong female-headed households in the African American community, they say, help compensate for the absence of fathers (Willie and Reddick 2010).[59] The problems African Americans face, they add, stem to a large degree from their experience of racism, segregated neighborhoods, lack of job opportunities, and other structural difficulties (Sampson 2009).[60] Even if fatherless families contribute to these problems, these scholars say, these other factors play a larger role.

Family Violence

Although family violence has received much attention since the 1970s, families were violent long before scholars began studying family violence and the public began hearing about it. Our discussion focuses on two types of family violence: violence against intimates (spouses, live-in partners, boyfriends, or girlfriends) and violence against children. (Violence against elders also occurs and was discussed in Chapter 6.)

Violence against Intimates

intimate partner violence

Violence between spouses, ex-spouses, and current and former sexual partners.

Intimates commit violence against each other in many ways: They can hit with their fists, slap with an open hand, throw an object, push or shove, or use or threaten to use a weapon. When all these acts and others are combined, we find that much **intimate partner violence** occurs. While we can never be certain of the exact number of intimates who are attacked, the U.S. Department of Justice estimates from its National Crime Victimization Survey (NCVS) that about 666,000 acts of violence (2017 data) are committed annually by one intimate against another intimate (Morgan and Truman 2018).[61] Other national survey data find that one-third of U.S. women have been assaulted by an intimate partner (Black et al. 2011).[62] These figures and other evidence indicate that intimate partner violence is very common and affects millions of people, with women much more likely than men to be victimized by it (Miller-Perrin et al. 2018).[63]

According to some estimates, about one-third of U.S. women have been assaulted by a spouse or partner at least once in their lives.

Source: © Thinkstock

Why do men hit their wives, partners, and girlfriends? As with rape and sexual assault (see Chapter 4), sociologists answer this question by citing both structural and cultural factors. Structurally, women are the subordinate gender in a patriarchal society and, as such, are more likely to be victims of violence, whether it is rape or intimate violence. Intimate violence is more common in poor families, and economic inequality thus may lead men to take out their frustration over their poverty on their wives and girlfriends (Miller-Perrin et al. 2018).[64]

Cultural myths also help explain why men hit their wives and girlfriends (Gosselin 2019).[65] Many men continue to believe that their wives should not only love and honor them but also obey them, as the traditional marriage vow says. If they view their wives in this way, it becomes that much easier to hit them. In another myth, many people still ask why women do not leave home if the hitting they suffer is really that bad; the implication is that the hitting cannot be that bad because they do not leave home. This reasoning ignores the fact that many women *do* try to leave home, which often angers their husbands and ironically puts the women more at risk for being hit, or they do not leave home because they have nowhere to go. Battered women's shelters are lacking in many locations and often can accommodate a woman and her children for only two or three weeks. Many battered women also have little money of their own and simply cannot afford to leave home. The belief that battering cannot be that bad if women hit by their husbands do not leave home ignores all these factors and is thus a myth that reinforces spousal violence against women. (See "People Making a Difference" for a profile of the woman who started the first women's shelter.)

As Chapter 4 discussed, the 2020 coronavirus pandemic brought new concerns about domestic violence (Godin 2020; Taub 2020; Whiting).[66] The pandemic caused untold stress, which is a risk factor for domestic violence. As well, women who now had to be sheltered at home with an abuser were reportedly reluctant to leave their homes to seek help for fear of contracting the coronavirus. Because they were group settings, shelters for domestic violence survivors worried about the coronavirus spreading among their clients and staff. For all these and other reasons recounted throughout this social problems text, the pandemic had social effects that extended beyond the disease itself.

What Is Intimate Partner Violence?

Intimate partner violence affects hundreds of thousands of people every year. Survey evidence suggests that up to one-third of American women have been assaulted by an intimate partner.

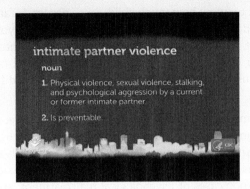

View the video online at: http://www.youtube.com/embed/VuMCzU54334?rel=0

People Making a Difference

The Founder of the First Battered Women's Shelter

Sandra Ramos deserves our thanks because she founded the first known shelter for battered women in North America back in the late 1970s.

Her life changed one night in 1970 when she was only twenty-eight years old and working as a waitress at a jazz club. One night a woman from her church in New Jersey came to her home seeking refuge from a man who was abusing her. Ramos took in the woman and her children and soon did the same with other abused women and their children. Within a few months, twenty-two women and children were living inside her house. "It was kind of chaotic," recalled Maria, forty-seven, the oldest of Ramos's three children. "It was a small house; we didn't have a lot of room. But she reaches out to people she sees suffering. She does everything in her power to help them."

When authorities threatened to arrest Ramos if she did not remove all these people from her home, she conducted sit-ins and engaged in other actions to call attention to the women's plight. She eventually won county funding to start the first women's shelter.

One woman whom Ramos helped was Geraldine Wright, who was born in the Dominican Republic. Wright says she owes Ramos a great debt. "Sandy makes you feel like, OK, you're going through this, but it's going to get better," she says. "One of the best things I did for myself and my children was come to the shelter. She helped me feel strong, which I usually wasn't. She helped me get a job here at the shelter so that I could find a place and pay the rent."

Since that first woman knocked on her door in 1970, Sandra Ramos worked unceasingly for the rights and welfare of abused women. She has fittingly been called "one of the nation's most well-known and tireless advocates on behalf of battered women." For about a half century, Sandra Ramos has made a considerable difference.

Source: Akbary 2016; Llorente 2009[67]

Child Abuse

child abuse

Maltreatment of children in the form of physical or sexual assault, emotional trauma, or neglect.

Child abuse takes many forms. Children can be physically or sexually assaulted, and they may also suffer from emotional abuse and practical neglect. Whatever form it takes, child abuse is a serious national problem.

It is especially difficult to know how much child abuse occurs. Infants obviously cannot talk, and toddlers and older children who are abused usually do not tell anyone about the abuse. They might not define it as abuse, they might be scared to tell on their parents, they might blame themselves for being abused, or they might not know whom they could talk to about their abuse. Whatever the reason, they usually remain silent, thus making it very difficult to know how much abuse takes place.

Using information from child protective agencies throughout the country, the U.S. Department of Health and Human Services (DHHS) estimates that almost 675,000 children (2017 data) are victims of child abuse and neglect annually (Administration on Children, Youth and Families, 2019).[68] This figure includes some 123,000 cases of physical abuse; 58,000 cases of sexual abuse; 505,000 cases of neglect; 39,000 cases of psychological maltreatment; and 15,000 cases of medical neglect. The total figure represents about 1 percent of all children under the age of 18. Obviously this is just the tip of the iceberg, as many cases of child abuse never become known. National survey evidence suggests the following annual rates of child abuse: physical abuse, 4.0 percent; sexual abuse, 2.2 percent; neglect, 4.7 percent; emotional abuse, 5.6 percent (Finkelhor et al. 2014).[69] Taking all these types of abuse into account, the percentage of children who suffer at least one type of abuse is nearly 12 percent, a rate about twelve times higher than the DHHS estimate just mentioned. Whatever the true figure is, most child abuse is committed by parents, stepparents, and other people the children know, not by strangers.

Government data estimate that almost 675,000 children are abused or neglected each year. Because most children do not report their abuse or neglect, the actual number is probably much higher.

Just as the pandemic brought new concerns about domestic violence, so did it bring new concerns about child abuse (Agrawal 2020).[70] The major reason for these concerns was stress: stress from the pandemic itself, stress from losing one's job and/or losing income, and stress from having children home full-time instead of at school or childcare. Because cases of child abuse sometimes come to light due to teachers noticing evidence of abuse on their pupils, the shutting of schools during the pandemic also meant that child abuse would be less likely to be noticed and reported.

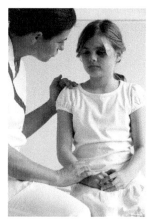

Source: © Thinkstock

Children and Our Future

Is Spanking a Good Idea?

As the text discusses, spanking underlies many episodes of child abuse. Nonetheless, many Americans approve of spanking. In the 2018 General Social Survey, 66.9 percent of respondents agreed that "it is sometimes necessary to discipline a child with a good, hard, spanking." Reflecting this "spare the rod and spoil the child" belief, most parents have spanked their children. National survey evidence finds that 49 percent of children under age ten have been spanked in the past year, with this figure rising to more than 60 percent for children ages 3–4.

The reason that many people approve of spanking and that many parents spank is clear: They believe that spanking will teach a child a lesson and improve a child's behavior and/or attitude. However, most child and parenting experts believe the opposite is true. When children are spanked, these experts say, they are more likely to misbehave as a result. If so, spanking ironically produces the opposite result from what a parent intends. A number of studies reach this negative conclusion, prompting the American Academy of Pediatrics to urge pediatricians to tell parents not to spank their children at all.

Spanking has this effect for several reasons. First, it teaches children that they should behave to avoid being punished. This lesson makes children more likely to misbehave if they think they will not get caught, as they'd not learn to behave for its own sake. Second, spanking also teaches children that it is OK to hit someone to solve an interpersonal dispute and even to hit someone if you love her or him, because that is what spanking is all about. Third, children who are spanked may come to resent their parents and thus be more likely to misbehave because their bond with their parents weakens.

This harmful effect of spanking is especially likely when spanking is frequent. As Alan Kazdin, a former president of the American Psychological Association (APA) has explained, "Corporal punishment has really serious side effects. Children who are hit become more aggressive." When spanking is rare, this effect may or may not occur, according to research on this issue, but this research also finds that other forms of discipline are as effective as a rare spanking in teaching a child to behave. This fact leads Kazin to say that even rare spanking should be avoided. "It suppresses [misbehavior] momentarily. But you haven't really changed its probability of occurring. Physical punishment is not needed to change behavior. It's just not needed."

Sources: Finkelhor et al. 2019; Gershoff et al. 2017; Harder 2007[71]

Why does child abuse occur? Structurally speaking, children are another powerless group and, as such, are easy targets of violence. Moreover, the best evidence indicates that child abuse is more common in poorer families. The stress these families suffer from their poverty is thought to be a major reason for the child abuse occurring within them (Gosselin 2019).[72] As with spousal violence, then, economic inequality is partly to blame for child abuse. Cultural values and practices also matter. In a nation where spanking is common, it is inevitable that physical child abuse will occur, because there is a very thin line between a hard spanking and physical abuse. Not everyone defines a good, hard spanking in the same way. As two family violence scholars once noted, "Although most physical punishment [of children] does not turn into physical abuse, most physical abuse begins as ordinary physical punishment" (Wauchope and Straus 1990:147).[73] (See "Children and Our Future" for a further discussion of spanking.)

Abused children are much more likely than children who are not abused to end up with various developmental, psychological, and behavioral problems throughout their life course. In particular, they are more likely to be aggressive, to use alcohol and other drugs, to be anxious and depressed, and to get divorced if they marry (Child Welfare Information Gateway 2019).[74]

Key Takeaways

- The divorce rate rose for several reasons during the 1960s and 1970s but has generally leveled off since then.
- Divorce often lowers the psychological well-being of spouses and their children, but the consequences of divorce also depend on the level of contention in the marriage that has ended.
- Despite continuing controversy over the welfare of children whose mothers work outside the home, research indicates that children in high-quality day care fare better in cognitive development than those who stay at home.
- Violence between intimates is fairly common and stems from gender inequality, income inequality, and several cultural myths that minimize the harm that intimate violence causes.
- At least 670,000 children are abused or neglected each year in the United States. Because most abused children do not report the abuse, the number of cases of abuse and neglect is undoubtedly much higher.

For Your Review

1. Think of someone you know (either yourself, a relative, or a friend) whose parents are divorced. Write a brief essay in which you discuss how the divorce affected this person.

2. Do you think it is ever acceptable for a spouse to slap or hit another spouse? Why or why not?

10.4 Families in the Future

Learning Objective

1. Understand the implications of social science theory and research for how to address family problems.

As perhaps our most important social institution, the family seems to arouse strong passions from almost everyone. Sociological theory and research, along with research from the other social sciences, have important implications for how our society should address the various family issues discussed in this chapter.

One set of implications concerns the many children and families living in poverty. The households in which they live are mostly headed by women, and the majority of these households are the result of divorce. The programs and policies outlined in Chapter 2 are certainly relevant for any efforts to help these families. These efforts include, but are not limited to, increased government financial support, subsidies for child care, vocational training and financial aid for schooling for women who wish to return to the labor force or to increase their wages, early childhood visitation and intervention programs, and increases in programs providing nutrition and medical care to poor women and their children. In all these efforts, the United States has much to learn from the nations of Western Europe (see "Lessons from Other Societies").

Lessons from Other Societies

Putting Families First: Helping Families in Western Europe

The nations of Western Europe make a much greater effort than the United States to help families with young children. According to sociologist James W. Russell, these nations believe that taking care of their children is a communal responsibility because "society as a whole benefits from having children adequately reared. Children grow up to take over the responsibilities of maintaining the survival of the society. They will also be available to provide needed services to both their own parents and aging adults who did not raise their own children. An aging adult who did not have children may need the services of a younger doctor who was raised by someone else." In contrast, says Russell, the United States tends to believe that families need to be self-reliant and should not expect very much help from the government. This difference in philosophy leads Western European nations to provide much more support than the United States for families with young children.

This support takes several forms whose nature and extent vary among the Western European nations. Most of the nations, for example, provide at least four months of *paid* maternity leave after the birth of a child; in contrast, the United States guarantees only three months of *unpaid* leave, and only for employees who work for companies that employ at least fifty people. Many

European nations also provide paid parental leave after the maternity leave benefits expire; the United States does not provide this benefit. In Sweden, parents share sixteen months of paid leave to care for a new child.

In another striking difference from the United States, all European nations have a family allowance program, which provides cash payments to parents for every child they have after their first child. The intent here is not only to help these families, but also to encourage them to have children to help counter declining birth rates in Europe.

A third very important difference is that European nations provide free or heavily subsidized child care of generally high quality to enable parents to work outside the home. For example, France provides free child care for children ages 2–6 and pays 75 percent of the cost of child care for children under two.

In these and other ways, the nations of Western Europe help their families with young children and thus their societies as a whole. The United States has much to learn from their example.

Sources: Cohn 2014; Russell 2018[75]

Another issue and set of implications from social science research concern family violence. To the extent that much violence against intimates and children is rooted in the frustration and stress accompanying poverty, efforts that reduce poverty will also reduce family violence. And to the extent that gender inequality helps explain violence against women, continuing and strengthening efforts to reduce gender inequality should also reduce violence against intimates, as most of this violence is directed by men against women. Further, if, as many scholars believe, the violent nature of masculinity helps account for violence men commit against their wives and girlfriends, then efforts to change male gender-role socialization should also help.

Turning to child abuse, because so much child abuse remains unknown to child protective authorities, it is difficult to reduce its seriousness and extent. However, certain steps might still help. Because child abuse seems more common among low-income families, efforts that reduce poverty should also reduce child abuse. The home visitation programs that help poor children also help reduce child abuse. Although, as noted earlier, approval of spanking is deeply rooted in our culture, a national educational campaign to warn about the dangers of spanking, including its promotion of children's misbehavior, may eventually reduce the use of spanking and thus the incidence of child physical abuse.

Divorce is a final issue for which research by sociologists and other scholars is relevant. Much evidence suggests that divorce from low-conflict marriages has negative consequences for spouses and children, and some evidence suggests that these consequences arise not from the divorce itself but rather from the conflict preceding the divorce and the poverty into which many newly single-parent households are plunged. There is also evidence that spouses and children fare better after a divorce from a highly contentious marriage. Efforts to help preserve marriages should certainly continue, but these efforts should proceed cautiously or not proceed at all for the marriages that are highly contentious. To the extent that marital conflict partly arises from financial difficulties, once again government efforts that help reduce poverty should also help preserve marriages.

Key Takeaways

- Efforts to help children and families living in poverty or near poverty should be expanded.
- Efforts to help preserve marriages should proceed cautiously or not at all for highly contentious marriages.

For Your Review

1. Why do you think the United States lags behind other democracies in efforts to help families?
2. What do you think is the single most important policy or action that our government should take to help America's families?

10.5 End-of-Chapter Material

Summary

1. As a social institution, the family is a universal or near-universal phenomenon. Yet historical and cross-cultural records indicate that many types of families and family arrangements exist now and have existed in the past. Although the nuclear family has been the norm in many societies, in practice its use has been less common than many people think. Many societies have favored extended families, and in early times children could expect, because of the death of a parent or births out of wedlock, to live at least some part of their childhood with only one parent.

2. Almost one-third of American children live in one-parent families; this percentage varies by race and ethnicity. Some research finds that parents experience more stress and lower psychological well-being than nonparents.

3. Sociological perspectives on the family fall into the more general functional, conflict, and social interactionist approaches guiding sociological thought. Functional theory emphasizes the several functions that families serve for society, including the socialization of children and the economic and practical support of family members. Conflict theory emphasizes the ways in which nuclear families contribute to ongoing gender, class, and race inequality, while social interactionist approaches examine family communication and interaction to make sense of family life.

4. Scholars continue to debate the consequences of divorce and single-parent households for women, men, and their children. Several studies find that divorce and single parenting in and of themselves do not have the dire consequences for children that many observers assume. The low income of single-parent households, and not the absence of a second parent, seems to account for many of the problems that children in such households do experience. Women and children seem to fare better when a highly contentious marriage ends.

5. Despite ongoing concern over the effect on children of day care instead of full-time care by one parent, recent research finds that children in high-quality day care are not worse off than their stay-at-home counterparts. Some studies find that day-care children are more independent and self-confident than children who stay at home and that they perform better on various tests of cognitive ability.

6. Racial and ethnic diversity marks American family life. Controversy also continues to exist over the high number of fatherless families in the African American community. Many observers blame many of the problems African Americans face on their comparative lack of two-parent households, but other observers say this blame is misplaced.

7. Family violence affects millions of spouses and children yearly. Structural and cultural factors help account for the high amount of intimate violence and child abuse. Despite claims to the contrary, the best evidence indicates that women are much more at risk than men for violence by spouses and partners. In the wake of the 2020 COVID-19 pandemic, concerns arose about possible increases in both domestic violence and child abuse, thanks in part to the heightened stress caused by the pandemic.

Using What You Know

You're working for a medium-sized corporation and have become friendly with one of your coworkers, Susan. One day she shows up at work with some bruises on the right side of her face. She looks upset, and when you ask her what happened, Susan replies that she slipped on the stairs at home and took a nasty fall. You suspect that her husband hit her and that she's not telling the truth about how she got hurt. What, if anything, do you say or do?

What You Can Do

To help deal with the family problems discussed in this chapter, you may wish to do any of the following:

1. Volunteer at a day-care center.
2. Volunteer at a battered women's shelter.
3. Start or join a group on your campus that addresses dating violence.

Endnotes

1. Neese, Alissa Widman. 2019. "Domestic Violence Victims Can Now Bring Pets to Choices Shelter." *The Columbus Dispatch* August 9:https://www.dispatch.com/news/20190808/domestic-violence-victims-can-now-bring-pets-to-choices-shelter.

2. Coontz, Stephanie. 2016. *The Way We Never Were: American Families and the Nostalgia Trap*, revised and updated edition. New York: Basic Books.

3. Starbuck, Gene H. and Karen Saucier Lundy. 2015. *Families in Context*. New York: Routledge.

4. Smith, Raymond T. 1996. *The Matrifocal Family: Power, Pluaralism and Politics*. New York: Routledge.

5. Seccombe, Karen. 2020. *Families and Their Social Worlds*. New York: Pearson.

6. Gottlieb, Beatrice. 1993. *The Family in the Western World from the Black Death to the Industrial Age*. New York: Oxford University Press.

7. Coontz, Stephanie. 1995. "The Way We Weren't: The Myth and Reality of the 'Traditional' Family." *National Forum: The Phi Kappa Phi Journal* Summer:11-14.

8. Friedan, Betty. 1963. *The Feminine Mystique*. New York: W. W. Norton.

9. Parker, Kim and Renee Stepler. 2017. "As U.S. Marriage Rate Hovers at 50%, Education Gap in Marital Status Widens." *Pew Research Center*(September 14):https://www.pewresearch.org/fact-tank/2017/09/14/as-u-s-marriage-rate-hovers-at-50-education-gap-in-marital-status-widens/.

10. Schoppe-Sullivan, Sarah. 2017. "Reminder: Marriage Is No Longer the Mode." *Council on Contemporary Families* (September 12):https://contemporaryfamilies.org/singles2017factsheet/.

11. Parker, Kim and Renee Stepler. 2017. "As U.S. Marriage Rate Hovers at 50%, Education Gap in Marital Status Widens." *Pew Research Center*(September 14):https://www.pewresearch.org/fact-tank/2017/09/14/as-u-s-marriage-rate-hovers-at-50-education-gap-in-marital-status-widens/.

12. Marcus, Ruth. 2011. "The Marriage Gap Presents a Real Cost." *The Washington Post* December 18: Retrieved from http://www.washingtonpost.com/opinions/the-marriage-gap-presents-a-real-cost/2011/12/16/gIQAz24DzO_story.html?hpid=z3.

13. Halleck, Rebecca. 2020. "Virus Fears Pose Problems for Wedding Business." *The New York Times* March 8:ST11.

14. Testa, Jessica. 2020. "What Is the Plan When Everyone Postpones?". *The New York Times* April 26:ST11.

15. Nelson, S. Katherine, Kostadin Kushlev and Sonja Lyubomirsky. 2014. "The Pains and Pleasures of Parenting: When, Why, and How Is Parenthoodassociated with More or Less Well-Being?". Psychological Bulletin 140:846-895; Gillihan, Seth J. 2017. "Why Parenthood Often Lowers Well-Being — Especially for Moms." Psychology Today April 5:https://www.psychologytoday.com/us/blog/think-act-be/201704/why-parenthood-often-lowers-well-being-especially-moms.

16. Fiorillo, Steve. 2018. "How Much Does It Cost to Raise a Child in the U.S. In 2018?". *TheStreet* December 19:https://www.thestreet.com/personal-finance/cost-to-raise-child-14814957.

17. Simon, Robin W. 2008. "The Joys of Parenthood, Reconsidered." *Contexts* 7(2):40-45.

18. Miller, Claire Cain. 2020. "Three Things Lockdowns Have Exposed About Working and Parenting." *The New York Times* April 27:https://www.nytimes.com/2020/04/27/upshot/coronavirus-exposes-workplace-truths.html.

19. Furstenberg, Frank E., Jr. 2010. "Diverging Development: The Not-So-Invisible Hand of Social Class in the United States." Pp. 276-94 in *Families as They Really Are*. New York: W.W. Norton. Lareau, Annette. 2011. *Unequal Childhoods: Class, Race, and Family Life*, 2nd Ed. Berkeley: University of California Press; Sacks, Vanessa and David Murphey. 2018. *The Prevalence of Adverse Childhood Experiences, Nationally, by State, and by Race or Ethnicity*. Washington, DC: Child Trends.

20. Komarovsky, Mirra. 1964. *Blue-collar Marriage*. New York: Random House.

21. Rubin, Lillian B. 1976. *Worlds of Pain: Life in the Working-class Family*. New York: Basic Books.

22. Kulik, Liat, Shulamith Walfisch and Gabriel Llberman. 2016. "Spousal Conflict Resolution Strategies and Marital Relaitions in Late Adulthood." Personal Relationships 23(3):456-74.

23. Stepler, Renee. 2017. "Number of U.S. Adults Cohabiting with a Partner Continues to Rise, Especially among Those 50 and Older." *Pew Research Center* April 6:https://www.pewresearch.org/fact-tank/2017/04/06/number-of-u-s-adults-cohabiting-with-a-partner-continues-to-rise-especially-among-those-50-and-older/.

24. Gurrentz, Benjamin. 2018. "Living with an Unmarried Partner Now Common for Young Adults." *US Census Bureau*(November 15):https://www.census.gov/library/stories/2018/11/cohabitaiton-is-up-marriage-is-down-for-young-adults.html.

25. Brown, Susan L., Wendy D. Manning and Krista K. Payne. 2017. "Relationship Quality among Cohabiting Versus Married Couples." *Journal of Family Issues* 38(12):1730-53.

26. Kupferberg, Arielle. 2019. "Premarital Cohabitation and Direct Marriage in the United States: 1956–2015." *Marriage & Family Review* 55(5):447-75.

27. Jose, Anita, K. Daniel O'Leary and Anne Moyer. 2010. "Does Premarital Cohabitation Predict Subsequent Marital Stability and Marital Quality? A Meta-Analysis." *Journal of Marriage & Family* 72(1):105-16. doi: 10.1111/j.1741-3737.2009.00686.x.

28. Brown, Susan L., Wendy D. Manning and Krista K. Payne. 2017. "Relationship Quality among Cohabiting Versus Married Couples." *Journal of Family Issues* 38(12):1730-53.

29. Brown, Susan L., Wendy D. Manning and Krista K. Payne. 2017. "Relationship Quality among Cohabiting Versus Married Couples." *Journal of Family Issues* 38(12):1730-53.

30. Brown, Susan L. 2010. "Marriage and Child Well-Being: Research and Policy Perspectives." *Journal of Marriage & Family* 72(5):1059-77; Manning, Wendy D. 2015. "Cohabitating and Child Wellbeing." *Future of Children* 25(2):51-66.

31. Cherlin, A. J. (2009). The origins of the ambivalent acceptance of divorce. *Journal of Marriage & Family*, 71(2), 226–229.

32. Wilcox, W. Bradford, ed. 2019. *State of Our Unions 2019*. Charlottesville, VA: The National Marriage Project, University of Virginia.

33. Hiedemann, Bridget, Olga Suhomlinova and Angela M. O'Rand. 1998. "Economic Independence, Economic Status, and Empty Nest in Midlife Marital Disruption." *Journal of Marriage and the Family* 60:219-31.

34. Cherlin, Andrew J. 2009. "The Origins of the Ambivalent Acceptance of Divorce." *Journal of Marriage & Family* 71(2):226-29.

35. Kneip, Thorsten and Gerrit Bauer. 2009. "Did Unilateral Divorce Laws Raise Divorce Rates in Western Europe?". *Journal of Marriage & Family* 71(3):592-607. doi: 10.1111/j.1741-3737.2009.00621.x.

36. Aughinbaugh, Alison, Omar Robles and Hugette Sun. 2013. "Marriage and Divorce: Patterns by Gender, Race, and Educational Attainment." *Monthly Labor Review* October: https://www.bls.gov/opub/mlr/2013/article/pdf/marriage-and-divorce-patterns-by-gender-race-and-educational-attainment.pdf; Wilcox, W. Bradford, ed. 2019. State of Our Unions 2019. Charlottesville, VA: The National Marriage Project, University of Virginia.

37. Brown, Susan L. and Matthew R. Wright. 2017. "Marriage, Cohabitation, and Divorce in Later Life." *Innovation in Aging* 1(2):1-11.

38. Waite, Linda J., Ye Luo and Alisa C. Lewin. 2009. "Marital Happiness and Marital Stability: Consequences for Psychological Well-Being." *Social Science Research* 38(1):201-12.

39. Bourassa, Kyle J., David A. Sbarra and Mark A. Whisman. 2015. "Women in Very Low Quality Marriages Gain Life Satisfaction Following Divorce." *Journal of Family Psychology* 29(3):490-99.

40. Weaver, Jennifer M. and Thomas J. Schofield. 2015. "Mediation and Moderation of Divorce Effects on Children's Behavior Problems." *Journal of Family Psychology* 29(1):39-48l Wilcox, W. Bradford, ed. 2019. *State of Our Unions 2019.* Charlottesville, VA: The National Marriage Project, University of Virginia.

41. Demo, D. H., & Fine, M. A. (2010). *Beyond the average divorce.* Thousand Oaks, CA: Sage Publications.

42. Moore, Kristin A., Andrea Kinghorn and Tawana Bandy. 2011. *Parental Relationship Quality and Child Outcomes across Subgroups.* Washington, DC: Child Trends.

43. Weaver, Jennifer M. and Thomas J. Schofield. 2015. "Mediation and Moderation of Divorce Effects on Children's Behavior Problems." *Journal of Family Psychology* 29(1):39-48.

44. Rutter, Virginia E. 2010. "The Case for Divorce." Pp. 159-69 in *Families as They Really Are,* edited by B. J. Risman. New York: W.W. Norton.

45. Bernard, Jessie. 1972. *The Future of Marriage.* New York: Bantam.

46. Glenn, Norval D. 1997. "A Critique of Twenty Family and Marriage and the Family Textbooks." Family Relations 46:197-208.

47. Waite, Linda J., Ye Luo and Alisa C. Lewin. 2009. "Marital Happiness and Marital Stability: Consequences for Psychological Well-Being." *Social Science Research* 38(1):201-12; Wilcox, W. Bradford, ed. 2019. *State of Our Unions 2019.* Charlottesville, VA: The National Marriage Project, University of Virginia.

48. Andersen, Lars Højsgaard. 2017. "Marriage, in-Laws, and Crime: The Case of Delinquent Brothers-in-Law." *Criminology* 55(2):438-64.

49. Neff, Lisa A. and Benjamin R. Karney. 2017. "Acknowledging the Elephant in the Room: How Stressful Environmental Contexts Shape Relationship Dynamics." *Current Opinion in Psychology* 13:107-10.

50. Wadsworth, Tim. 2016. "Marriage and Subjective Well-Being: How and Why Context Matters." *Social Indicators Research* 126(3):1025-48.

51. Kane, Jennifer B. 2016. "Marriage Advantages in Perinatal Health: Evidence of Marriage Selection or Marriage Protection?". *Journal of Marriage & Family* 78(1):212-29.

52. Caputo, Jennifer, Eliza K. Pavalko and Melissa A. Hardy. 2016. "The Long-Term Effects of Caregiving on Women's Health and Mortality." *Journal of Marriage & Family* 78(5):1382-98; Hochschild, Arlie. 1989. *The Second Shift: Working Parents and the Revolution at Home.* New York: Viking; Jenkins, Carol L. 1997. "Women, Work, and Caregiving: How Do These Roles Affect Women's Well-Being?". *Journal of Women and Aging* 9(3):27-45.

53. Schwartz, Pamela. 1983. "Length of Day-Care Attendance and Attachment Behavior in Eighteen-Month-Old Infants." *Child Development* 54:1073-78.

54. Coontz, Stephanie. 1997. *The Way We Really Are: Coming to Terms with America's Changing Families.* New York: Basic Books.

55. Rabin, Roni Caryn. 2008. "A Consensus About Day Care: Quality Counts." *The New York Times* September 15:A1.

56. Cohen, Philip N. 2018. *The Family: Diversity, Inequality, and Social Change.* New York: W.W. Norton.

57. Wright, R. H., Jr., Mindel, C. H., Tran, T. V., & Habenstein, R. W. (Eds.). (2012). *Ethnic families in America: Patterns and variations* (5th ed.). Upper Saddle River, NJ: Pearson.

58. Haskins, Ron. 2009. "Moynihan Was Right: Now What?". *The Annals of the American Academy of Political and Social Science* 621:281-314.

59. Willie, Charles V. and Richard J. Reddick. 2010. *A New Look at Black Families.* Lanham, MD: Rowman & Littlefield.

60. Sampson, Robert J. 2009. "Racial Stratification and the Durable Tangle of Neighborhood Inequality." *The Annals of the American Academy of Political and Social Science* 621:260-80.

61. Morgan, Rachel E. and Jennifer L. Truman. 2018. *Criminal Victimization, 2017.* Washington, DC: Bureau of Justice Statistics, U.S. Department of Justice.

62. Black, M.C., K.C. Basile, M.J. Breiding, S.G. Smith and M.L. Walters. 2011. *The National Intimate Partner and Sexual Violence Survey (Nisvs): 2010 Summary Report.* Atlanta: Centers for Disease Control and Prevention.

63. Miller-Perrin, Cindy L., Robin D. Perrin and Claire M. Renzetti. 2018. *Violence and Maltreatment in Intimate Relationships.* Thousand Oaks, CA: Sage Publications.

64. Miller-Perrin, Cindy L., Robin D. Perrin and Claire M. Renzetti. 2018. *Violence and Maltreatment in Intimate Relationships.* Thousand Oaks, CA: Sage Publications.

65. Gosselin, Denise Kindschi. 2019. *Family & Intimate Partner Violence: Heavy Hands.* New York: Pearson.

66. Godin, Melissa. 2020. "As Cities around the World Go on Lockdown, Victims of Domestic Violence Look for a Way Out." *Time* March 18:https://time.com/5803887/coronavirus-domestic-violence-victims/. Taub, Amanda. 2020. "Locked Down, and More Vulnerable to Abuse." *The New York Times* April 7:A9. Whiting, Jason. 2020. "Trapped at Home: Domestic Abuse During the Pandemic." *Psychology Today* April 10:https://www.psychologytoday.com/us/blog/love-lies-and-conflict/202004/trapped-home-domestic-abuse-during-the-pandemic.

67. Akbary, Zarina. 2016. "Strengthen Our Sisters: The Remarkable Work of Sandra Ramos." *Garden State Woman Education Foundation*(January 13):https://www.gardenstatewoman.com/item/687-strengthen-our-sisters-the-remarkable-work-of-sandra-ramos; Llorente, Elizabeth. 2009. "Strengthening Her Sisters". Retrieved November 2, 2011 from http://www.aarp.org/giving-back/volunteering/info-10-2009/strengthening_her_sisters.html.

68. Administration on Children, Youth and Families. 2019. *Child Maltreatment 2017.* Washington, DC: U.S. Department of Health and Human Services, U.S. Government Printing Office.

69. Finkelhor, David, Jennifer Vanderminden, Heather Turner, Sherry Hamby and Anne Shattuck. 2014. "Child Maltreatment Rates Assessed in a National Household Survey of Caregivers and Youth." *Child Abuse & Neglect* 38:1421-35.

70. Agrawal, Nina. 2020. "The Coronavirus Could Cause a Child Abuse Epidemic." *The New York Times* April 7:https://www.nytimes.com/2020/04/07/opinion/coronavirus-child-abuse.html.

71. Finkelhor, David, Heather Turner, Brittany Kaye Wormuth, Jennifer Vanderminden and Sherry Hamby. 2019. "Corporal Punishment: Current Rates from a National Survey." *Journal of Child and Family Studies*:https://doi.org/10.1007/s10826-019-01426-4. Gershoff, Elizabeth T., Kierra M.P. Sattler and Arya Ansari. 2017. "Strengthening Causal Estimates for Links between Spanking and Children's Externalizing Behavior Problems." *Psychological Science* 29(1):110-20; Harder, Ben. 2007. "Spanking: When Parents Lift Their Hands." *Los Angeles Times* February 19:http://articles.latimes.com/2007/feb/19/health/he-spanking19.

72. Gosselin, Denise Kindschi. 2019. *Family & Intimate Partner Violence: Heavy Hands.* New York: Pearson.

73. Wauchope, Barbara and Murray A. Straus. 1990. "Physical Punishment and Physical Abuse of American Children: Incidence Rates by Age, Gender, and Occupational Class." Pp. 133-48 in Physical Violence in American Families: Risk Factors and Adapatations to Violence in 8,145 Families, edited by M. A. Straus and R. J. Gelles. New Brunswick, NJ: Transaction Books.

74. Child Welfare Information Gateway. 2019. *Long-Term Consequences of Child Abuse and Neglect.* Washington, DC: U.S. Department of Health and Human Services, Administration for Children and Families, Children's Bureau.

75. Cohn, Jonathan. 2014. I'm Insanely Jealous of Sweden's Work-Family Policies. You Should Be, Too. *The New Republic* June 22:https://newrepublic.com/article/118294/us-should-copy-sweden-and-denmarks-work-family-policies; Russell, James W. 2018. *Double Standard: Social Policy in Europe and the United States.* Lanham, MD: Rowman & Littlefield.

CHAPTER 11
Schools and Education

Social Problems in the News

"Detroit Schools Face Tough Choices with Too Many Repairs, Not Enough Money," the headline said. In Detroit, Michigan, the public schools are decrepit, needing more than $540 million worth of repairs. Their many problems include corroded plumbing, malfunctioning boilers, leaking roofs, and hazardous electrical systems. Several schools have had to shut down their drinking water because the water's levels of copper and lead were too high. All these conditions, which a news report said some observers term "deplorable," prompted a lawsuit against the state of Michigan that claimed schoolchildren were being denied a good education. School staff readily admit that their schools are indeed decrepit. For example, an elementary school guidance counselor wrote in a blog that "the odorous smell of mold and mildew hits you like a brick wall when you step through the front doors" of her school. She added that the school's gym had been closed and condemned because of mold caused by a leaky ceiling and that the playground was also closed because "a geyser of searing hot steam explodes out of the ground."

Source: Chambers 2019; Strauss 2016[1]

Charles Dickens's majestic novel *A Tale of Two Cities* begins with this unforgettable passage: "It was the best of times, it was the worst of times, it was the age of wisdom, it was the age of foolishness, it was the epoch of belief, it was the epoch of incredulity, it was the season of Light, it was the season of Darkness, it was the spring of hope, it was the winter of despair, we had everything before us, we had nothing before us, we were all going direct to Heaven, we were all going direct the other way."

These words are timeless, and they certainly apply to the U.S. education system today. In many ways it is the best of systems, but in many ways it is also the worst of systems. It teaches wisdom, but its many problems smack of foolishness. It fills many people with hope, but it also fills many people with despair. Some students have everything before them, but many also have nothing before them. In the wealthiest nation on the face of the earth, students in one of America's large cities, Detroit, attend schools with decrepit and even dangerous conditions. They are hardly alone, as students in cities across the nation could easily speak of similar ills. If Dickens were alive today, he might well look at our schools and conclude that "we were all going direct the other way."

Education is one of our most important social institutions. Youngsters and adolescents spend most of their weekday waking hours in school, doing homework, or participating in extracurricular activities, and many then go on to college. People everywhere care deeply about what happens in our nation's schools, and issues about the schools ignite passions across the political spectrum. Yet, as the opening news story about Detroit's schools illustrates, many schools are poorly equipped to prepare their students for the complex needs of today's world.

This chapter's discussion of education begins with an overview of education in the United States and then turns to sociological perspectives on education. The remainder of the chapter discusses education in today's society. This discussion highlights education as a source and consequence of various social inequalities and examines several key issues affecting the nation's schools and the education of its children.

If anything, these inequalities worsened after the 2020 COVID-19 pandemic began and schools shut down everywhere (Casey 2020; Hoover 2020).[2] As students of all ages suddenly began learning remotely, low-income students and families faced special challenges. Many lacked computers or other devices for remote learning, lacked reliable Internet access, and/or found themselves in crowded homes without a quiet place to do their studies. Many low-income college students also had to find new jobs to pay for their college expenses, with their employment cutting into their study time and often exposing them to the coronavirus because of the nature of their jobs. Educators worried that this unfortunate situation would harm the learning of secondary school and college students alike and cause them to fall further behind their wealthier peers.

11.1 An Overview of Education in the United States

Learning Objectives

1. Explain why compulsory education arose during the nineteenth century.
2. Summarize social class, gender, and racial and ethnic differences in educational attainment.
3. Describe the impact that education has on income.
4. Explain how the U.S. education system ranks internationally.

education

The social institution through which a society teaches its members the skills, knowledge, norms, and values they need to learn to become good, productive members of their society.

formal education

Learning that occurs in schools under teachers, principals, and other specially trained professionals.

informal education

Learning that occurs outside the schools, traditionally in the home.

Education is the social institution through which a society teaches its members the skills, knowledge, norms, and values they need to learn to become good, productive members of their society. As this definition makes clear, education is an important part of socialization. Education is both *formal* and *informal*. **Formal education** is often referred to as *schooling*, and as this term implies, it occurs in schools under teachers, principals, and other specially trained professionals. **Informal education** may occur almost anywhere, but for young children it has traditionally occurred primarily in the home, with their parents as their instructors. Day care and preschool have become increasingly popular venues in industrial societies for young children's instruction, and education from the early years of life is thus more formal than it used to be.

Education in early America was only rarely formal. During the colonial period, the Puritans in what is now Massachusetts required parents to teach their children to read and also required larger towns to have an elementary school, where children learned reading, writing, and religion. In general, though, schooling was not required in the colonies, and only about 10 percent of colonial children, usually just the wealthiest, went to school, although others became apprentices (Rury 2020).[3]

To help unify the nation after the Revolutionary War, textbooks were written to standardize spelling and pronunciation and to instill patriotism and religious beliefs in students. However, these textbooks also included negative stereotypes of Native Americans and certain immigrant groups. The children going to school continued primarily to be those from wealthy families. By the mid-1800s, a call for free, compulsory education had begun, and compulsory education became widespread by the end of the century. This was an important development, as children from all social classes could now receive a free, formal education. Compulsory education was intended to further national unity and to teach immigrants "American" values. It also arose because of industrialization, as an industrial economy demanded reading, writing, and math skills much more than an agricultural economy had.

Free, compulsory education applied only to primary and secondary schools. Until the mid-1900s, very few people went to college, and those who did typically came from fairly wealthy families. After World War II, however, college enrollments soared, and today more people are attending college than ever before, even though college attendance is still related to social class, as we shall discuss shortly.

An important theme emerges from this brief history: Until very recently in the record of history, formal schooling was restricted to wealthy males. This means that boys who were not white and rich were excluded from formal schooling, as were virtually all girls, whose education was supposed to take place informally at home. Today, as we will see, race, ethnicity, social class, and, to some extent, gender continue to affect both educational achievement and the amount of learning occurring in schools.

In colonial America, only about 10 percent of children went to school, and these children tended to come from wealthy families. After the Revolutionary War, new textbooks helped standardize spelling and pronunciation and promote patriotism and religious beliefs, but these textbooks also included negative stereotypes of Native Americans.

Source: Image courtesy of Joel Dorman Steele and Esther Baker Steele, http://commons.wikimedia.org/wiki/File:Spinninginthecolonialkitchen.jpg.

Education in the United States Today

Education in the United States is a massive social institution involving millions of people and billions of dollars. More than 79 million people, almost one-fourth of the U.S. population, attend school at all levels. This number includes more than 59 million in grades pre-K through high school, and almost 20 million in college (including graduate and professional school). They attend some 98,000 public schools, 35,000 private schools (three-fourths of them religious, one-fourth secular), and 4,300 two-year and four-year colleges and universities. More than five million faculty at all levels work in these settings (National Center for Education Statistics 2019).[4]

Correlates of Educational Attainment

educational attainment

How far one gets in school, which has been shown to depend heavily on family income and race/ethnicity.

About 67 percent of U.S. high school graduates enroll in college the following fall. This is a very high figure by international standards, as college in many other industrial nations is reserved for the very small percentage of the population who pass rigorous entrance exams. They are the best of the brightest in their nations, whereas higher education in the United States is open to all who graduate high school. Even though that is true, our chances of achieving a college degree are greatly determined at birth, as social class and race and ethnicity substantially affect who goes to college. They affect whether students drop out of high school, in which case they do not go on to college; they affect the chances of getting good grades in school and good scores on college entrance exams; they affect whether a family can afford to send its children to college; and they affect the chances of staying in college and obtaining a degree versus dropping out. For all these reasons, **educational attainment**—how far one gets in school—depends heavily on family income and race/ethnicity (Goldrick-Rab et al. 2016).[5]

Family Income and Race/Ethnicity

Government data readily show the effects of family income and race/ethnicity on educational attainment. Let's first look at how race and ethnicity affect the likelihood of dropping out of high school. Figure 11.1 shows the percentage of people ages 16–24 who are not enrolled in school and who have not received a high school diploma. The dropout rate is highest for Latinxs and Native Americans and lowest for Asians and whites.

FIGURE 11.1 Race, Ethnicity, and High School Dropout Rate, Persons Ages 16–24, 2017 (Percentage Not Enrolled in School and without a High School Diploma)

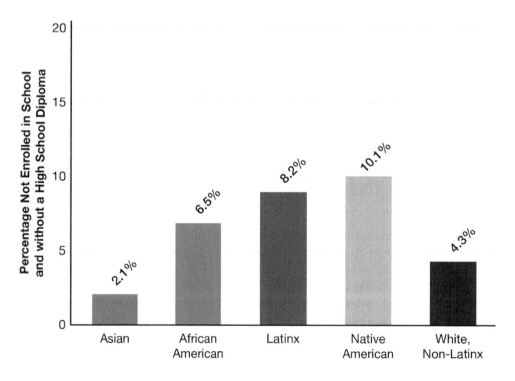

Source: National Center for Education Statistics. 2019. *The Condition of Education 2019*. Washington, DC: National Center for Education Statistics, U.S. Department of Education.

Now let's look at how family income affects the likelihood of attending college, a second benchmark of educational attainment. Figure 11.2 shows the relationship between family income and the percentage of high school graduates who enroll in college immediately following graduation: Students from families in the highest income bracket are the most likely to attend college.

FIGURE 11.2 Family Income and Percentage of High School Graduates Who Attend College Immediately after Graduation, 2016

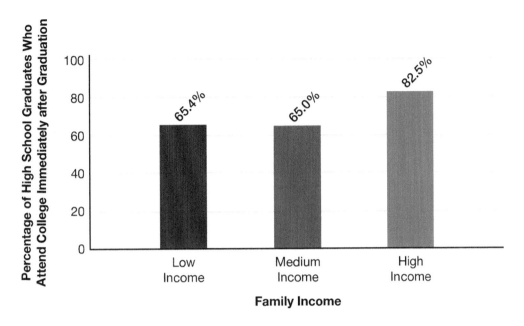

Source: National Center for Education Statistics. 2017. *Digest of Education Statistics: 2017*. Washington, DC: National Center for Education Statistics https://nces.ed.gov/programs/digest/d17/.

Finally, let's examine how race and ethnicity affect the likelihood of obtaining a college degree, a third benchmark of educational attainment. Figure 11.3 shows the relationship between race/ethnicity and the percentage of persons ages 25–29 who have a bachelor's or higher degree. This relationship is quite strong, with African Americans, Latinxs, and Native Americans the least likely to have a four-year degree, and whites and especially Asians most likely to have a degree.

FIGURE 11.3 Race, Ethnicity, and Percentage of Persons Ages 25–29 with a Bachelor's or Higher Degree, 2018

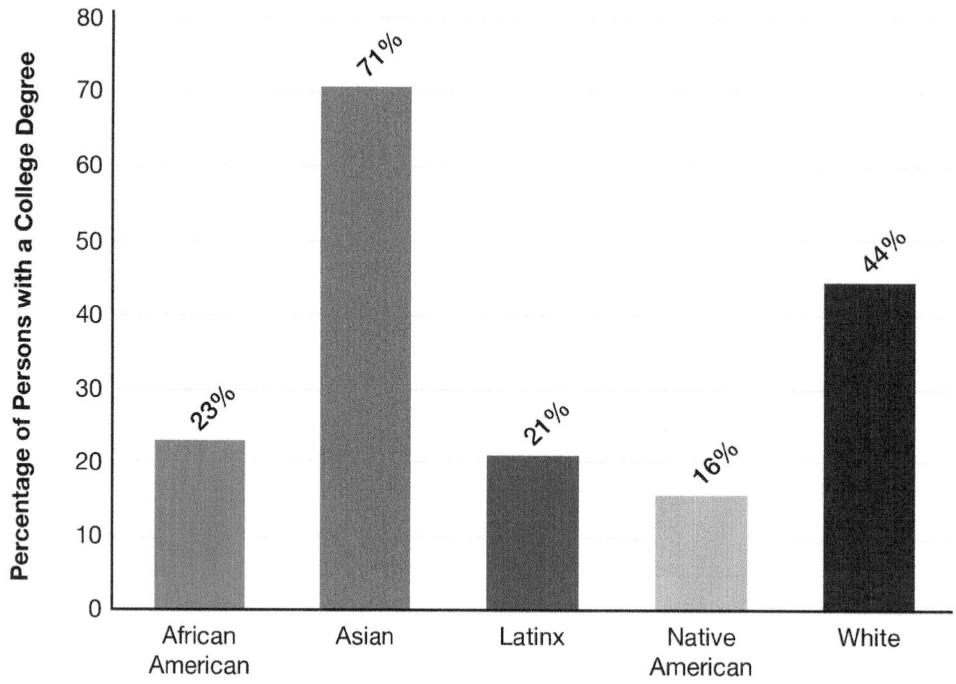

Source: National Center for Education Statistics. 2019. *The Condition of Education 2019*. Washington, DC: National Center for Education Statistics, U.S. Department of Education.

Explaining the Racial/Ethnic Gap in Educational Attainment

Why do African Americans, Latinxs, and Native Americans have lower educational attainment? Four factors are commonly cited: (a) the underfunded and otherwise inadequate schools that children in these groups often attend; (b) the higher poverty of their families and lower education of their parents that often leave children ill prepared for school even before they enter kindergarten; (c) racial/ethnic discrimination; and (d) the fact that these groups' families are especially likely to live in very disadvantaged neighborhoods (Ballantine et al. 2017).[6]

The last two factors, racial/ethnic discrimination and residence in disadvantaged neighborhoods, need additional explanation. At least three forms of racial/ethnic discrimination impair educational attainment (Ballantine et al. 2017; Mickelson 2003).[7] The first form involves tracking. Students tracked into vocational or general curricula tend to learn less and have lower educational attainment than those tracked into a faster-learning, academic curriculum (Ansalone 2010).[8] Because students of color are more likely to be tracked "down" rather than "up," their school performance and educational attainment suffer.

The second form of racial discrimination involves school discipline. Students of color are more likely than white students to be suspended, expelled, or otherwise disciplined for similar types of misbehavior (Payne and Welch 2016).[9] Because such discipline again reduces school performance and educational attainment, this form of discrimination helps explain the lower attainment of students of color.

The third form involves teachers' expectations of students. As our later discussion of the symbolic interactionist perspective on education examines further, teachers' expectations of students affect how much students learn. Research finds that teachers have lower expectations for their students of color, and that these expectations help to lower how much these students learn.

Turning to residence in disadvantaged neighborhoods, it should not be surprising that poor neighborhoods have lower educational attainment because they have inadequate schools, but poor neighborhoods matter for reasons beyond their schools' quality (Kirk and Sampson 2011; Wodtke et al. 2011).[10] First, because many adults in these neighborhoods are high school dropouts and/or unemployed, children in these neighborhoods lack adult role models for educational attainment. Second, poor neighborhoods tend to be racially and ethnically segregated. As a result, Latinx children in these neighborhoods are less likely to speak English well because they lack native English-speaking friends, and African American children are more likely to speak "black English" than conventional English; both language problems impede school success.

Third, poor neighborhoods have higher rates of violence and other deviant behaviors than wealthier neighborhoods (Quillian 2017).[11] Children in these neighborhoods thus are more likely to experience high levels of stress and to be victims of violence (which increases their stress and can impair their neurological development). Crime in these neighborhoods also tends to reduce teacher commitment and parental involvement in their children's schooling. Finally, poor neighborhoods are more likely to have environmental problems such as air pollution and toxic levels of lead paint; these problems lead to asthma and other health problems among children (as well as adults), which impairs the children's ability to learn and do well in school.

 ## How America's Public Schools Keep Kids in Poverty

African Americans, Latinxs, and Native Americans have lower educational attainment, partly because their schools and schooling are inferior. This problem helps prevent them from going to college and attaining a suitable income as adults.

View the video online at: http://www.youtube.com/embed/7O7BMa9XGXE?rel=0

For all these reasons, then, children in poor neighborhoods are at much greater risk for lower educational attainment. As a study of this risk concluded, "Sustained exposure to disadvantaged neighborhoods...throughout the entire childhood life course has a devastating impact on the chances of graduating from high school" (Wodtke et al. 2011:731).[12] If these neighborhoods are not improved, the study added, "concentrated neighborhood poverty will likely continue to hamper the development of future generations of children" (Wodtke et al. 2011:733).[13]

Gender

Gender also affects educational attainment. In earlier generations, women were less likely than men to go to college. But today there is a noticeable gender difference in the other direction, with women more likely than men to earn a four-year degree or higher. Among people ages 25–29, 41 percent of women have at least a bachelor's degree, compared to only 33 percent of men (National Center for Education Statistics 2019).[14] This difference reflects the fact that females are more likely than males to graduate high school, to attend college after high school graduation, and to obtain a degree after starting college.

Impact of Education on Income

On the average, college graduates have much higher annual earnings than high school graduates. How much does this consequence affect why you decided to go to college?

Source: michaeljung/Shutterstock.com

credential society

A society in which higher education is seen as evidence of the attainment of the needed knowledge and skills for various kinds of jobs.

Have you ever applied for a job that required a high school diploma? Are you going to college in part because you realize you will need a college degree for a higher-paying job? As these questions imply, the United States is a **credential society** (Collins 1979).[15] This means at least two things. First, a high school or college degree (or beyond) indicates that a person has acquired the needed knowledge and skills for various jobs. Second, a degree at some level is a requirement for most jobs. As you know full well, a college degree today is a virtual requirement for a decent-paying job. The ante has been upped considerably over the years: In earlier generations, a high school diploma, if even that, was all that was needed, if only because so few people were then graduating from high school. With most people graduating from high school today, a high school diploma is not worth as much. Then too, today's society increasingly requires skills and knowledge that only a college education brings.

A credential society also means that people with more formal education achieve higher incomes. Annual earnings are indeed much higher for people with more education (see Figure 11.4). As earlier chapters indicated, gender and race/ethnicity affect the payoff we get from our education, but education itself still makes a huge difference for our incomes.

FIGURE 11.4 Educational Attainment and Median Annual Earnings, Ages 25–34, 2017

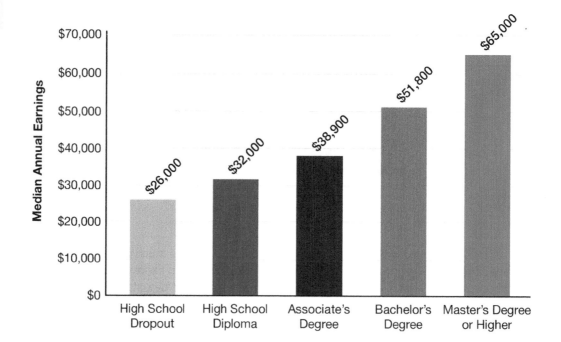

Source: National Center for Education Statistics. 2019. *The Condition of Education 2019*. Washington, DC: National Center for Education Statistics, U.S. Department of Education.

Impact of Education on Mortality

Beyond income, education also affects at what age people tend to die. Simply put, people with higher levels of education tend to die later in life, and those with lower levels tend to die earlier (Buckles et al. 2016).[16] The reasons for this disparity are complex, but two reasons stand out. First, more highly educated people are less likely to smoke and engage in other unhealthy activities, and they are more likely to exercise and engage in other healthy activities and eat healthy diets. Second, they have better access to high-quality health care.

How the U.S. Education System Compares Internationally

The United States has many of the top colleges and universities and secondary schools in the world, and many of the top professors and teachers. But its education system fails in other respects. One kind of evidence for this discouraging assertion comes from international comparisons of secondary school students' proficiency in mathematics, reading, and science. (OECD 2018).[17] In all three areas, the United States ranks below the average for the world's wealthy democracies that are its peer nations. This situation suggests that the United States is far from the world leader in the quality of education. The "Lessons from Other Societies" box examines what the United States might learn from the sterling example of Finland's education system.

Lessons from Other Societies

Successful Schooling in Finland

Finland is widely regarded as having perhaps the top elementary and secondary education system in the world. Its model of education offers several important lessons for U.S. education.

To understand the lessons to be learned from Finland, we should go back several decades to the 1970s, when Finland's education system was below par, with its students scoring below the international average in mathematics and science. Moreover, urban schools in Finland outranked rural schools, and wealthy students performed much better than low-income students. Today, Finnish students rank at the top in international testing, and low-income students do almost as well as wealthy students.

Finland's education system ranks so highly today because it took several measures to improve its education system. First, and perhaps most important, Finland raised teachers' salaries, required all teachers to have a three-year master's degree, and paid all costs, including a living stipend, for the graduate education needed to achieve this degree. These changes helped to greatly increase the number of teachers, especially the number of highly qualified teachers, and Finland now has more teachers for every 1,000 residents than does the United States. Unlike the United States, teaching is considered a highly prestigious profession in Finland, and the application process to become a teacher is very competitive. The college graduates who apply for one of Finland's eight graduate programs in teaching typically rank in the top 10 percent of their class, and only 5–15 percent of their applications are accepted. A leading Finnish educator observed, "It's more difficult getting into teacher education than law or medicine." In contrast, U.S. students who become teachers tend to have lower SAT scores than those who enter other professions, they only need a four-year degree, and their average salaries are lower than other professionals with a similar level of education.

Second, Finland revamped its curriculum to emphasize critical thinking skills, reduced the importance of scores on standardized tests and then eliminated standardized testing altogether, and eliminated academic tracking before tenth grade. Unlike the United States, Finland no longer ranks students, teachers, or schools according to scores on standardized tests because these tests are no longer given.

Third, Finland built many more schools to enable the average school to have fewer students. Today the typical school has fewer than three hundred students, and class sizes are smaller than those found in the United States.

Fourth, Finland increased funding of its schools so that its schools are now well maintained and well equipped. Whereas many U.S. schools are decrepit, Finnish schools are decidedly in good repair.

Finally, Finland provided free medical and dental care for children and their families and expanded other types of social services, including three years of paid maternity leave and subsidized day care, as the country realized that children's health and home environment play critical roles in their educational achievement.

These and other changes helped propel Finland's education system to a leading position among the world's industrial nations. As the United States ponders how best to improve its own education system, it may have much to learn from Finland's approach to how children should learn.

Sources: Abrams 2011; Anderson 2011; Eggers and Calegari, 2011; Hancock 2011; Sahlberg 2011; Strauss 2019[18]

Key Takeaways

- Until very recently in the record of history, formal schooling was restricted to wealthy males.
- Students from low-income backgrounds tend to have lower educational attainment than students from wealthier backgrounds.
- African Americans and Latinxs tend to have lower educational attainment than non-Latinx whites and Asians.
- Gender influences educational attainment in a complex fashion; older women have lower educational attainment than older men, but younger women have greater educational attainment than younger men.
- The United States ranks behind many other industrial nations in the quality of the education its citizens receive.

For Your Review

1. Do you think the government should take steps to try to reduce racial and ethnic differences in education, or do you think it should take a hands-off approach? Explain your answer.
2. Should the government require that children receive a formal education, as it now does, or should it be up to parents to decide whether their children should receive a formal education? Explain your answer.

11.2 Sociological Perspectives on Education

Learning Objectives

1. List the major functions of education.
2. Explain the problems that conflict theory sees in education.
3. Describe how symbolic interactionism understands education.

The major sociological perspectives on education fall nicely into the functional, conflict, and symbolic interactionist approaches (Ballantine et al. 2017).[19] Table 11.1 summarizes what these approaches say.

TABLE 11.1 Theory Snapshot

Theoretical perspective	Major assumptions
Functionalism	Education serves several functions for society. These include (a) socialization, (b) social integration, (c) social placement, and (d) social and cultural innovation. Latent functions include child care, the establishment of peer relationships, and lowering unemployment by keeping high school students out of the full-time labor force. Problems in the educational institution harm society because all these functions cannot be completely fulfilled.
Conflict theory	Education promotes social inequality through the use of tracking and standardized testing and the impact of its "hidden curriculum." Schools differ widely in their funding and learning conditions, and this type of inequality leads to learning disparities that reinforce social inequality.
Symbolic interactionism	This perspective focuses on social interaction in the classroom, on the playground, and in other school venues. Specific research finds that social interaction in schools affects the development of gender roles and that teachers' expectations of pupils' intellectual abilities affect how much pupils learn. Certain educational problems have their basis in social interaction and expectations.

The Functions of Education

Functional theory stresses the functions that education serves in fulfilling a society's various needs. Perhaps the most important function of education is *socialization*. If children are to learn the norms, values, and skills they need to function in society, then education is a primary vehicle for such learning. Schools teach the three Rs (reading, 'riting, 'rithmetic), as we all know, but they also teach many of the society's norms and values. In the United States, these norms and values include respect for authority, patriotism (remember the Pledge of Allegiance?), punctuality, and competition (for grades and sports victories).

A second function of education is *social integration*. For a society to work, functionalists say, people must subscribe to a common set of beliefs and values. As we saw, the development of such common views was a goal of the system of free, compulsory education that developed in the nineteenth century. Thousands of immigrant children in the United States today are learning English,

U.S. history, and other subjects that help prepare them for the workforce and integrate them into American life.

A third function of education is *social placement*. Beginning in grade school, students are identified by teachers and other school officials either as bright and motivated or as less bright and even educationally challenged. Depending on how they are identified, children are taught at the level that is thought to suit them best. In this way, they are presumably prepared for their later station in life. Whether this process works as well as it should is an important issue, and we explore it further when we discuss school tracking later in this chapter.

Social and cultural innovation is a fourth function of education. Our scientists cannot make important scientific discoveries and our artists and thinkers cannot come up with great works of art, poetry, and prose unless they have first been educated in the many subjects they need to know for their chosen path.

FIGURE 11.5 The Functions of Education
Schools ideally perform many important functions in modern society. These include socialization, social integration, social placement, and social and cultural innovation.

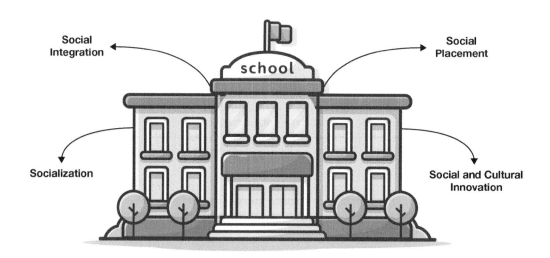

Education also involves several *latent* functions, functions that are by-products of going to school and receiving an education rather than a direct effect of the education itself. One of these is *child care*: Once a child starts kindergarten and then first grade, for several hours a day the child is taken care of for free. The *establishment of peer relationships* is another latent function of schooling. Most of us met many of our friends while we were in school at whatever grade level, and some of those friendships endure the rest of our lives. A final latent function of education is that it *keeps millions of high school students out of the full-time labor force*. This fact keeps the unemployment rate lower than it would be if they were in the labor force.

Because education serves so many manifest and latent functions for society, problems in schooling ultimately harm society. For education to serve its many functions, various kinds of reforms are needed to make our schools and the process of education as effective as possible.

Conflict Theory: Education and Inequality

Conflict theory does not dispute the functions just described. However, it does give some of them a different slant by emphasizing how education also perpetuates social inequality. One example of this process involves the function of social placement. When most schools begin tracking their students in grade school, the students thought by their teachers to be bright are placed in the faster tracks (especially in reading and arithmetic), while the slower students are placed in the slower tracks; in high school, three common tracks are the college track, vocational track, and general track.

Such *tracking* does have its advantages; it helps ensure that bright students learn as much as their abilities allow them, and it helps ensure that slower students are not taught over their heads. But conflict theorists say that tracking also helps perpetuate social inequality by *locking* students into faster and lower tracks. Worse yet, several studies show that students' social class and race and ethnicity affect the track into which they are placed, even though their intellectual abilities and potential should be the only things that matter: White, middle-class students are more likely to be tracked "up," while poorer students and students of color are more likely to be tracked "down." Once they are tracked, students learn more if they are tracked up and less if they are tracked down. The latter tend to lose self-esteem and begin to think they have little academic ability and thus do worse in school because they were tracked down. In this way, tracking is thought to be good for those tracked up and bad for those tracked down. Conflict theorists thus say that tracking perpetuates social inequality based on social class and race and ethnicity (Potter 2019).[20]

Conflict theorists add that standardized tests are culturally biased and thus also help perpetuate social inequality (Grodsky et al. 2008).[21] According to this criticism, these tests favor white, middle-class students, whose socioeconomic status and other aspects of their backgrounds have afforded them various experiences that help them answer questions on the tests.

A third critique by conflict theory involves the quality of schools. As we will see later in this chapter, U.S. schools differ mightily in their resources, learning conditions, and other aspects, all of which affect how much students can learn in them. Simply put, schools are unequal, and their very inequality helps perpetuate inequality in the larger society. Children going to the worst schools in urban areas face many more obstacles to their learning than those going to well-funded schools in suburban areas. Their lack of learning helps ensure they remain trapped in poverty and its related problems.

In a fourth critique, conflict theorists say that schooling teaches a **hidden curriculum**, by which they mean a set of values and beliefs that support the status quo, including the existing social hierarchy (Booher-Jennings 2008).[22] Although no one plots this behind closed doors, our schoolchildren learn patriotic values and respect for authority from the books they read and from various classroom activities.

A final critique is historical and concerns the rise of free, compulsory education during the nineteenth century (Cole 2008).[23] Because compulsory schooling began in part to prevent immigrants' values from corrupting "American" values, conflict theorists see its origins as smacking of *ethnocentrism* (the belief that one's own group is superior to another group). They also criticize its intention to teach workers the skills they needed for the new industrial economy. Because most workers were very poor in this economy, these critics say, compulsory education served the interests of the upper/capitalist class much more than it served the interests of workers.

hidden curriculum

A set of values and beliefs learned in school that support the status quo, including the existing social hierarchy.

Symbolic Interactionism and School Behavior

Symbolic interactionist studies of education examine social interaction in the classroom, on the playground, and in other school venues. These studies help us understand what happens in the schools themselves, but they also help us understand how what occurs in school is relevant for the larger society. Some studies, for example, show how children's playground activities reinforce gender-role socialization. Girls tend to play more cooperative games, while boys play more competitive sports (Thorne 1993)[24] (see Chapter 4).

Applying Social Research

Assessing the Impact of Small Class Size

Do elementary school students fare better if their classes have fewer students rather than more students? It is not easy to answer this important question, because any differences found between students in small classes and those in larger classes might not necessarily reflect class size. Rather, they may reflect other factors. For example, perhaps the most motivated, educated parents ask that their child be placed in a smaller class and their school goes along with this request. Perhaps teachers with more experience favor smaller classes and are able to have their principals assign them to these classes, while new teachers are assigned larger classes. These and other possibilities mean that any differences found between the two class sizes might reflect the qualities and skills of students and/or teachers in these classes, and not class size itself.

For this reason, the ideal study of class size would involve *random assignment* of both students and teachers to classes of different size. (Recall that Chapter 1 discusses the benefits of random assignment.) Fortunately, a notable study of this type exists.

The study, named Project STAR (Student/Teacher Achievement Ratio), began in Tennessee in 1985 and involved 79 public schools and 11,600 students and 1,330 teachers who were all randomly assigned to either a smaller class (13–17 students) or a larger class (22–25 students). The random assignment began when the students entered kindergarten and lasted through third grade; in fourth grade, the experiment ended, and all the students were placed into the larger class size. The students are now certainly much older, and many aspects of their educational and personal lives have been followed since the study began.

Some of the more notable findings of this multiyear study include the following:

- While in grades K–3, students in the smaller classes had higher average scores on standardized tests.
- Students who had been in the smaller classes continued to have higher average test scores in grades 4–7.
- Students who had been in the smaller classes were more likely to complete high school and also to attend college.
- Students who had been in the smaller classes were less likely to be arrested during adolescence.
- Students who had been in the smaller classes were more likely in their twenties to be married and live in wealthier neighborhoods.
- White girls who had been in the smaller classes were less likely to have a teenage birth than white girls who had been in the larger classes.

Why did small class size have these benefits? Two reasons seem likely. First, in a smaller class, there are fewer students to disrupt the class by talking, fighting, or otherwise taking up the teacher's time. More learning can thus occur in smaller classes. Second, kindergarten teachers are better able to teach noncognitive skills (cooperating, listening, sitting still) in smaller classes, and these skills can have an impact many years later.

Regardless of the reasons, it was the experimental design of Project STAR that enabled its findings to be attributed to class size rather than to other factors. Because small class size does seem to help in many ways, the United States should try to reduce class size in order to improve student performance and later life outcomes.

Sources: Chetty et al. 2011; Schanzenbach 2006[25]

Another body of research shows that teachers' views about students can affect how much the students learn. When teachers think students are smart, they tend to spend more time with these students, to call on them, and to praise them when they give the right answer. Not surprisingly, these students learn more because of their teachers' behavior. But when teachers think students are less bright, they tend to spend less time with these students and to act in a way that leads them to learn less.

Robert Rosenthal and Lenore Jacobson (1968)[26] conducted a classic study of this phenomenon. They tested a group of students at the beginning of the school year and told their teachers which students were bright and which were not. They then tested the students again at the end of the school year. Not surprisingly, the bright students had learned more during the year than the less bright ones. But it turned out that the researchers had randomly decided which students would be designated bright and less bright. Because the "bright" students learned more during the school year without actually being brighter at the beginning, their teachers' behavior must have been the reason. In fact, their teachers did spend more time with them and praised them more often than was true for the "less bright" students. This process helps us understand why tracking is bad for the students tracked down.

Other research in the symbolic interactionist tradition focuses on how teachers treat girls and boys. Many studies find that teachers call on and praise boys more often than girls (Jones and Dindia 2004).[27] Teachers do not do this consciously, but their behavior nonetheless sends an implicit message to girls that math and science are not for them and that they are not suited to do well in these subjects. This body of research has stimulated efforts to educate teachers about the ways in which they may unwittingly send these messages and about strategies they could use to promote greater interest and achievement by girls in math and science.

Research guided by the symbolic interactionist perspective suggests that teachers' expectations may influence how much their students learn. When teachers expect little of their students, their students tend to learn less.

Source: © Thinkstock

Key Takeaways

- According to the functional perspective, education helps socialize children and prepare them for their eventual entrance into the larger society as adults.
- The conflict perspective emphasizes that education reinforces inequality in the larger society.
- The symbolic interactionist perspective focuses on social interaction in the classroom, on school playgrounds, and at other school-related venues. Social interaction contributes to gender-role socialization, and teachers' expectations may affect their students' performance.

For Your Review

1. Review how the functionalist, conflict, and symbolic interactionist perspectives understand and explain education. Which of these three approaches do you most prefer? Why?

11.3 Issues and Problems in Elementary and Secondary Education

Learning Objectives

1. Describe how schooling in the United States helps perpetuate social inequality.
2. Explain the difference between de jure segregation and de facto segregation.
3. Describe the extent of school violence and the controversy over zero-tolerance policies.
4. Discuss how and why social inequality in the larger society manifests itself in higher education.

The *elementary* (K–8) and *secondary* (9–12) education system today faces many issues and problems of interest not just to educators and families but also to sociologists and other social scientists. We cannot discuss all these issues here, but we will highlight some of the most interesting and important.

Schools and Inequality

Earlier we mentioned that schools differ greatly in their funding, conditions, and other aspects. Noted author and education critic Jonathan Kozol refers to these differences as "savage inequalities," to quote the title of one of his books (Kozol 1991).[28] Kozol's concern over inequality in the schools stemmed from his experience as a young teacher in a public elementary school in a Boston inner-city neighborhood in the 1960s. Kozol was shocked to see that his school was literally falling apart. The building itself was decrepit, with plaster falling off the walls and bathrooms and other facilities substandard. Classes were large, and the school was so overcrowded that Kozol's fourth-grade class had to meet in an auditorium, which it shared with another class, the school choir, and, for a time, a group of students practicing for the Christmas play. Kozol's observations led to the writing of his first award-winning book, *Death at an Early Age* (Kozol 1967).[29]

Kozol (1991)[30] later traveled around the United States and systematically compared public schools in several cities' inner-city neighborhoods to those in the cities' suburbs. Everywhere he went, he found great discrepancies in school spending and in the quality of instruction. In schools in Camden, New Jersey, for example, spending per pupil was less than half the amount spent in the nearby, much wealthier town of Princeton. Chicago and New York City schools spent only about half the amount that some of the schools in nearby suburbs spent.

These numbers were reflected in other differences Kozol found when he visited city and suburban schools. In East St. Louis, Illinois, where most of the residents are poor and almost all are African American, schools had to shut down once because of sewage backups. The high school's science labs were thirty to fifty years out of date when Kozol visited them; the biology lab had no dissecting kits. A history teacher had 110 students but only twenty-six textbooks, some of which were missing their first one hundred pages. At one of the city's junior high schools, many window frames lacked any glass, and the hallways were dark because light bulbs were missing or not working. Visitors could smell urinals one hundred feet from the bathroom.

Contrast these conditions with those Kozol observed in suburban schools. A high school in a Chicago suburb had seven gyms and an Olympic-sized swimming pool. Students there could take classes in seven foreign languages. A suburban New Jersey high school offered fourteen AP courses, fencing, golf, ice hockey, and lacrosse, and the school district there had ten music teachers and an extensive music program.

From his observations, Kozol concluded that the United States is shortchanging its children in poor rural and urban areas. As we saw in Chapter 2, poor children start out in life with many strikes against them. The schools they attend compound their problems and help ensure that the American ideal of equal opportunity for all remains just that—an ideal—rather than a reality. As Kozol (1991:233)[31] observed, "All our children ought to be allowed a stake in the enormous richness of America. Whether they were born to poor white Appalachians or to wealthy Texans, to poor black people in the Bronx or to rich people in Manhasset or Winnetka, they are all quite wonderful and innocent when they are small. We soil them needlessly." Although the book in which Kozol reported these conditions was published some thirty years ago, ample evidence (including the news story about Detroit's schools that began this chapter) shows these conditions persist today.

Large funding differences in the nation's schools also endure. In Philadelphia, Pennsylvania, for example, annual per-pupil instructional expenditure was $9,061 in 2016–2017; in nearby suburban Lower Merion Township, it was $21,176, or more than twice as high as Philadelphia's expenditure (Tauber 2018).[32]

Teacher salaries are related to these funding differences. Salaries in urban schools in low-income neighborhoods are markedly lower than those in schools in wealthier neighborhoods (García and Weiss 2019).[33] As a result, teachers at the low-income schools tend to be inexperienced teachers just out of college. All things equal, they are less likely than their counterparts at wealthier schools to be effective teachers.

Jonathan Kozol has written movingly of "savage inequalities" in American schools arising from large differences in their funding and in the condition of their physical facilities.

Source: © Thinkstock

People Making a Difference

Teaching Young Students about Science and Conservation

Since 1999, the Ocean Discovery Institute has taught more than 40,000 public school students in a low-income San Diego neighborhood about the ocean and the environment. Most of the students are Latinx, and a growing number are recent immigrants from Southeast Asia and East Africa. By learning about ocean science, the students also learn something about geology, physics, and other sciences. Ocean Discovery's program has grown over the years, and it now services more than 6,000 students annually in thirteen schools.

For example, fifth-grade classes visit Ocean Discovery's Living Lab science education facility, where they use a gel electrophoresis machine to conduct DNA sequencing, while seventh-grade classes go with Ocean Discovery personnel to the nearby Cabrillo National Monument, where they explore the coastal environment and learn about plant biodiversity. First, ODI instructors teach hands-on marine science activities to students in grades 3–6. They also consult closely with the schools' teachers about the science curriculum taught in the schools. Ocean Discovery teachers follow up these activities with classroom visits to help students understand how the science and conservation principles they learned are relevant to their daily lives.

K–12 students may also visit the Living Lab on their own after school or on Saturdays or during the summer. Ocean Discovery staff and volunteers read ocean science books with the youngest children, while older children benefit from having a quiet place to do their homework and from the opportunity to ask staff about their homework. More structured programs also occur during these times, including the Career Explorers program for middle school students, who learn about career paths in the ocean sciences, and the Ocean Adventures program for elementary school students, who learn about sea animals and the ocean. In the Science Empowering Students program, eighth-graders work alongside practicing scientists to learn about field research methods, build content knowledge on the particular subject of research, and participate in data collection and analysis on a long-term project.

In 2011, Ocean Discovery received the Presidential Award for Excellence in Science, Mathematics, and Engineering Mentoring. Several Ocean Discovery staff and students traveled to the White House to take part in various events and accept the award from President Obama. As this award attests, the Ocean Discovery Institute is making a striking difference in the lives of low-income San Diego students. For further information, visit http://www.oceandiscoveryinstitute.org. (Full disclosure: The author's son works for Ocean Discovery.)

Source: Torgan 2016[34]

School Racial Segregation

de jure segregation

School segregation stemming from legal requirements.

A related issue to school inequality is school racial segregation. Before 1954, schools in the South were racially segregated by law (**de jure segregation**). Communities and states had laws that dictated which schools African American children attended and which schools white children attended. Schools were either all African American or all white, and, inevitably, white schools were much better funded than African American schools. Then in 1954, the U.S. Supreme Court outlawed *de jure* school segregation in its famous *Brown v. Board of Education* decision. Southern school districts fought this decision with legal machinations, and *de jure* school segregation did not really end in the South until the civil rights movement won its major victories a decade later.

de facto segregation

School segregation stemming from neighborhood residential patterns.

Meanwhile, Northern schools were also segregated; decades after the *Brown* decision, they have become even more segregated. School segregation in the North stemmed, both then and now, not from the law but from neighborhood residential patterns. Because children usually go to schools near their homes, if adjacent neighborhoods are all black or all white, then the schools for these neighborhoods will also be all black or all white, or mostly so. This type of segregation is called **de facto segregation**.

Today many children continue to go to schools that are segregated because of neighborhood residential patterns, a situation that Kozol (2005)[35] calls "apartheid schooling." More than half of the nation's schoolchildren attend schools that are largely racially segregated. Although such segregation is legal, the schools filled with students of color tend to suffer severely from lack of funding, poor physical facilities, and poorly paid teachers (Mervosh 2019).[36]

Many children today attend schools that are racially segregated because of neighborhood residential patterns.

Source: Monkey Business Images/Shutterstock.com

 ## Why Are Schools Still So Segregated?

Although school racial segregation is illegal, many American children still attend segregated schools because of residential segregation. Segregated schools tend to suffer from lack of funding, dilapidated conditions, and teacher turnover and low salaries.

View the video online at: http://www.youtube.com/embed/v2TG9n0vc-4?rel=0

During the 1960s and 1970s, states, municipalities, and federal courts tried to reduce de facto segregation by busing urban African American children to suburban white schools and, less often, by busing white suburban children to African American urban schools. Busing inflamed passions as perhaps few other issues did during those decades (Lukas 1985).[37] White parents opposed it because they did not want their children bused to urban schools, where, they feared, the children would be unsafe and receive an inferior education. The racial prejudice that many white parents shared heightened their concerns over these issues. African American parents were more likely to see the need for busing, but they, too, wondered about its merits, especially because it was their children who were bused most often and faced racial hostility when they entered formerly all-white schools.

As one possible solution to reduce school segregation, some cities have established *magnet schools*, schools for high-achieving students of all races to which the students and their families apply for admission (Rossell 2017).[38] Although these schools do help some students whose families are poor and of color, their impact on school segregation has been minimal because the number of magnet schools is low and because they are open only to the very best students who, by definition, are also few in number. Some critics also say that magnet schools siphon needed resources from public school systems and that their reliance on standardized tests makes it difficult for African American and Latinx students to gain admission.

School Choice: Education Vouchers and Charter Schools

school choice

Programs in which parents and their children, primarily from low-income families in urban areas, receive public funds to attend a school different from their neighborhood's school.

charter schools

Public schools built and operated by for-profit companies and to which students normally apply for admission.

Children who attend a public school ordinarily attend the school that is designated for the neighborhood in which they live, and they and their parents normally have little choice in the matter. One of the most popular but also controversial components of the school reform movement today is **school choice**, in which parents and their children, primarily from low-income families in urban areas, receive public funds to attend a school different from their neighborhood's school (Fox and Buchanan 2017).[39] School choice has two components. The first component involves *education vouchers*, which parents can use as tuition at private or parochial (religious) schools. The second component involves **charter schools**, which are public schools (because public funds pay for students' tuition) built and operated by for-profit companies. Students normally apply for admission to these schools; sometimes they are accepted based on their merit and potential, and sometimes they are accepted by lottery. Both components have strong advocates and fierce critics. We examine each component in turn.

Education Vouchers

Advocates of school choice programs involving education vouchers say they give low-income families an option for high-quality education they otherwise would be unable to afford. These programs, the advocates add, also help improve the public schools by forcing them to compete for students with their private and parochial counterparts. In order to keep a large number of parents from using vouchers to send their children to the latter schools, public schools have to upgrade their facilities, improve their instruction, and undertake other steps to make their brand of education an attractive alternative. In this way, school choice advocates argue, vouchers induce public schools to make themselves more attractive to prospective students.

Critics of school choice programs say they harm the public schools by decreasing their enrollments and therefore their funding. Public schools do not have the money now to compete with private and parochial ones, nor will they have the money to compete with them if vouchers become more widespread. Critics also worry that voucher programs will lead to a "brain drain" of the most academically motivated children and families from low-income schools.

Charter Schools

Nearly 7,000 charter schools operate across the nation, with about 6 percent of American children attending them. Charter schools and their proponents claim that students fare better in these schools than in conventional public schools because of the charter schools' rigorous teaching methods, strong expectations for good behavior, small classrooms, and other advantages.

Critics say charter schools incur the same problems that education vouchers incur: They take some of the brightest students from a city's conventional public schools and lead to lower funding for these schools. Critics also cite research findings that charter schools do not in fact deliver the strong academic performance claimed by their advocates. For example, a study that compared test scores at charter schools in sixteen states with those at public schools found that the charter schools did worse overall: 17 percent of charter schools had better scores than public schools, 46 percent had scores similar to those of public schools, and 37 percent had lower scores (Center for Research on Education Outcomes 2009).[40] A recent review of charter school research reported mixed results overall regarding these schools' effectiveness (Berends 2015).[41]

Even when charter school test scores are higher, there is the methodological problem that students are not randomly assigned to attend a charter school (Basile 2010).[42] It is thus possible that the students and parents who apply to charter schools are more highly motivated than those who do not. If so, the higher test scores found in some charter schools may reflect the motivation of the students attending these schools, and not necessarily the schools' teaching methods. It is also true that charter schools do not usually enroll students who know little English (because their parents are immigrants) and students with disabilities or other problems. All such students often face difficulties in doing well in school. This is yet another possible reason that a small number of charter schools outperform public schools. Despite the popularity of charter schools, then, the academic case for them remains to be proven.

School Violence

At least since the infamous April 1999 school shootings at Columbine High School in Littleton, Colorado, where two students murdered twelve other students and one teacher before killing themselves, school violence has been a concern to many Americans. Within days after the Littleton massacre, school after school across the nation installed metal detectors, located police at building entrances and in hallways, and began questioning or suspending students joking about committing violence. People everywhere wondered why the schools were becoming so violent and what could be done about it. The more recent massacre in December 2012 of twenty-six people, including twenty students and six staff, at Sandy Hook Elementary School in Newtown, Connecticut, brought new attention to school violence. The shooter this time was an outsider, not a student at the school.

School violence continues to concern many Americans.

Source: Mike Focus/Shutterstock.com

Despite these tragic events and other school shootings that made headlines, school violence has fortunately declined since the 1990s, with fewer students and staff dying in the nation's schools or being physically attacked. As this trend indicates, the risk of school violence should not be exaggerated: Statistically speaking, schools are very safe, especially in regard to fatal violence. Two kinds of statistics illustrate this point. First, fewer than 3 percent of all homicides involving school-aged children take place in or near school; virtually all children's homicides occur in or near a child's home. Second, an average of eighteen students were killed at school yearly between 2009 and 2016; because about 59 million students attend U.S. elementary and secondary schools, the chances are less than one in 3 million that a student will be killed at school. Other types of school violence are admittedly more common. For example, 6 percent of high school students in 2016 reported being threatened or injured with a weapon on school property during the past year (Centers for Disease Control and Prevention 2016).[43] Although this figure is 6 percent too many, it still indicates that 94 percent of high school students that year were free of such violence.

Bullying

Bullying is another problem in the nation's elementary and secondary schools and is often considered a specific type of school violence. However, bullying can take many forms, such as taunting, that do not involve the use or threat of physical violence. As such, we consider bullying here as a separate problem while acknowledging its close relation to school violence.

bullying

Physical and verbal attacks and harassment directed at a victim(s) by one student or a group of students over an extensive period of time.

cyberbullying

The use of the internet, cell phones and smartphones, and other digital technologies to bully others.

First it will be helpful to define **bullying**. A common definition in the research literature is that bullying involves "physical and verbal attacks and harassment directed at a victim(s) by one student or a group of students over an extensive period of time" (Moon et al. 2011).[44] Another definition is also helpful: "The use of one's strength or popularity to injure, threaten or embarrass another person on purpose" (St. George 2011).[45] As these definitions suggest, bullying can be *physical* in nature (violence such as shoving and punching), *verbal* (teasing, taunting, and name calling), and *social* (spreading rumors, breaking up friendships, deliberately excluding someone from an activity). An additional form of bullying that has emerged in the last decade or so is **cyberbullying**. As its name implies, cyberbullying involves the use of the internet, cell phones and smartphones, and other digital technologies to bully others (e.g., rumors can be spread via Facebook).

Bullying is a serious problem for at least two reasons. First, bullying is a common occurrence. About one-fifth of students report being victimized by some form of bullying during the past school year; this rate of victimization is much higher than the rate of school violence victimization (U.S. Department of Health and Human Services 2019).[46]

 13-Year-Old Commits Suicide After Being Bullied at School

One-third of secondary school students report being bullied at school during the past year. As this video illustrates, the consequences of bullying can be very serious. Although most bullying victims do not commit or attempt suicide, they still may suffer mental and physical health problems and have problems with their studies and other aspects of school performance.

View the video online at: http://www.youtube.com/embed/cbwdZBnCe10?rel=0

Second, bullying can have serious consequences (Adams and Lawrence 2011).[47] Students who are bullied often experience psychological problems that can last into adulthood; these problems include anxiety, depression, loneliness, sleeplessness, and suicidal thoughts. Their physical health may also suffer. Their school performance (grades, attendance, and participation in school activities) may also decline. In addition, bullying victims sometimes respond by lashing out in violence; many of the mass school shootings of the 1990s were committed by male students who had been bullied.

School Discipline and Racial Discrimination

To reduce school violence and bullying, many school districts have adopted strict policies that specify harsh punishments. A common policy involves *zero-tolerance* for weapons; this type of policy calls for automatic suspension or expulsion of a student who has anything resembling a weapon for any reason. Zero-tolerance or other very strict policies are also in place in many schools for offenses such as drug use and possession, fighting, and classroom disruption. However well intended these policies may be, the research evidence suggests that they are ineffective in deterring the behavior they are meant to prevent, and may even be counterproductive. As one review of this evidence puts it, "It is not clear that zero tolerance policies are succeeding in improving school safety. In fact, some evidence...suggests that these policies actually may have an adverse effect on student academic and behavioral outcomes" (Boccanfuso and Kuhfeld 2011:1).[48] When students are suspended, their grades may suffer, and their commitment to schooling may lower; these problems in turn increase their likelihood of engaging in delinquency. The expelled students find it difficult to get back into a school and eventually achieve a high school diploma. Their behavior, too, may become more unlawful as a result, and they also are more likely to face unemployment and low-paying jobs. Zero-tolerance school discipline thus seems to do much more harm than good.

In addition to deterrence, another reason for the adoption of strict discipline policies has been to avoid the racial discrimination that occurs when school officials have discretion in deciding which students should be suspended or expelled (Skiba and Rausch 2006).[49] In school districts with such discretion, African American students with weapons or "near weapons" (such as a small penknife) are more likely than white students with the same objects to be punished in this manner. However, research finds that African American and Latinx students are still more likely than white students to be suspended or expelled for similar misbehaviors (having a weapon, fighting, cursing a teacher, etc.) even in school districts with very strict discipline (Payne and Welch 2016).[50] School discipline, then, is often racially discriminatory.

Key Takeaways

- Schools in America are unequal: They differ greatly in the extent of their funding, in the quality of their physical facilities, and in other respects. Jonathan Kozol calls these differences "savage inequalities."
- Although school violence has declined since the 1990s, it continues to concern many Americans. Bullying at school is a common problem and can lead to more serious violence by the children who are bullied.
- School choice programs are popular but also controversial. Charter schools on the average do no better than public schools, and sometimes worse.

For Your Review

1. Do you favor or oppose school vouchers? Why?

11.4 Issues and Problems in Higher Education

Learning Objectives

1. Explain why certain college students flounder.
2. Describe what is meant by legacy admissions and summarize the criticism of this policy.
3. List any two factors that affect college and university graduation rates.
4. Describe the extent of physical and sexual violence on the nation's campuses.

The issues and problems discussed so far in this chapter concern elementary and secondary schools in view of their critical importance for tens of millions of children and for the nation's social and economic well-being. However, higher education has its own issues and problems. Once again, we do not have space to discuss all these matters, but we will examine some of the most interesting and important. (Recall that Chapter 7 discussed alcohol abuse on campus, a very significant higher education problem.)

Cost

Higher education can cost students and their parents tens of thousands of dollars per year. This expense prevents many students from going to college and puts many students and parents into considerable debt.

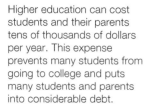

Source: © Thinkstock

Perhaps the most important issue is that higher education, at least at four-year institutions, is quite expensive and can cost tens of thousands of dollars per year. This figure varies by the type of college or university, as private institutions cost much more than public institutions (for in-state students). The average annual cost of tuition, fees, and room and board at four-year public colleges and universities was $19,488 in 2016-2017; this same cost at private colleges and universities was $41,468 (National Center for Education Statistics 2019).[51] Elite institutions cost much more than this average: The annual cost of a Harvard University education, for example, was $74,300 in 2019–2020.

Although financial aid reduces the net cost of a college education for many students, including about half of the student body at many institutions, a college education is still very expensive for many families. Some students are fortunate enough to have their college education paid fully by their parent(s), but many students take out loans and graduate with considerable debt. Of all the college students who graduated in 2018, roughly two-thirds had to take out loans to pay for their various expenses. These students graduated with an average debt of about $30,000 (Hess 2019),[52] which can certainly take many years to pay off. Roughly one-fifth of graduates with student loans are behind on their payments.

America's Student Debt Crisis

About two-thirds of all college students graduate with debt that can take many years to pay off. Of those graduates with loans, approximately one-fifth eventually fall behind on their payments.

JESSIE SUREN
La Salle University, '10

View the video online at: http://www.youtube.com/embed/PqzEcER8AJA?rel=0

Floundering Students

Although college is often said to be the best time of one's life, many students have difficulties during their college years. These students are called *floundering students*. Homesickness during the first semester on campus is common, but a number of students have difficulties beyond homesickness. According to psychiatry professor David Leibow, who has studied troubled students, many floundering students mistakenly believe that they are the only ones who are floundering, and many fail to tell their parents or friends about their problems (Golden 2010).[53] The major cause of floundering, says Leibow, is academic difficulties; other causes include homesickness, relationship problems, family problems including family conflict and the serious illness or death of a family member, personal illness, and financial difficulties.

All these reasons add up to significant mental health problems for many college students. More than 60 percent of students report experiencing "overwhelming anxiety" during the past year, and more than 40 percent say they have felt depressed (Wolverton 2019).[54] Nearly 10 percent of students annually seek psychological counseling on their college campus for one or more of the reasons just listed (Center for Collegiate Mental Health 2016).[55] Many students who seek counseling are given medications to treat their symptoms. Leibow says these medications are often helpful but worries that they are overprescribed. Three reasons underlie his concern. First, although the students given these medications may have problems, often the problems are a normal part of growing into adulthood and not serious enough to justify medication. Second, some of these medications can have serious side effects. Third, students who take medications may be less motivated to address the underlying reasons for their problems.

Social Class and Race in Admissions

Although colleges and universities are making a greater effort to attract and retain low-income students and students of color, these students remain greatly underrepresented at institutions of higher education.

Source: © Thinkstock

We saw earlier in this chapter that students of color and low-income students are less likely to attend college. When these students do attend college, they are much more likely to attend lower-ranking institutions than very selective campuses. As evidence, more than half of the students at the 200 most selective colleges and universities come from the wealthiest one-fourth of U.S. households, while only 15 percent come from the poorest one-fourth of households (Delisle and Cooper 2018).[56] Other research finds that a smaller group of thirty-eight elite colleges has more students who come from the wealthiest 1 percent of families than students who come from the bottom 60 percent of families by income, and that only 14 percent of students at the most selective schools come from the bottom 50 percent of families by income (Smith 2019).[57]

These facts raise important questions about the lack of diversity in college admissions and campus life. Partly because affirmative action is so controversial (see Chapter 3), attention has begun to focus on the low numbers of low-income students at many colleges and universities, and especially at the more selective institutions as ranked by *U.S. News & World Report* and other sources. Many education scholars and policymakers feel that increasing the number of low-income students would not only help these students but also increase campus diversity along the lines of socioeconomic status and race/ethnicity (since students of color are more likely to be from low-income backgrounds). Efforts to increase the number of low-income students, these experts add, would avoid the controversy that has surrounded affirmative action.

In response to this new attention to social class, colleges and universities have begun to increase their efforts to attract and retain low-income students. For example, several selective institutions are now providing financial aid to cover all or most of the students' expenses. Despite these efforts, however, the U.S. higher education system remains very stratified, as the evidence just cited suggests. And when low-income students do attend selective colleges and universities, they face many obstacles, including financial problems and food insecurity, a lack of knowledge of such things as office hours and other aspects of school life with which wealthy students are much more familiar, and disparaging comments about their socioeconomic backgrounds (Jack 2019; Smith, 2019).[58]

Legacy Admissions

legacy admissions

A college admissions policy that gives preference to applicants who are children or other relatives of graduates of the institution.

At highly selective colleges and universities, the policy of **legacy admissions** makes it easier for certain wealthy students to gain admission. Under this policy, students who are daughters or sons (or other relatives) of graduates of the institution are given preference in admissions. Because their parents are very likely to be wealthy, a legacy admissions policy in effect amounts to what critics call "affirmative action for the rich" (Kahlenberg 2010).[59] According to some research, being a child of an alumna or alumnus of one of these institutions increases one's chances of admission by 45 percentage points (Kahlenberg 2011).[60] Thus, if a nonlegacy applicant with certain qualifications would ordinarily have a 40 percent chance of being admitted, a legacy applicant with the same qualifications would have an 85 percent chance of being admitted. Critics say legacy admissions give an unfair advantage to wealthy students and use up valuable spots that should go to more qualified students from more varied socioeconomic backgrounds. The 2019 college admissions scandal, in which several dozen parents allegedly bribed college officials or paid for falsified entrance exam scores to secure their children's admission to top colleges and universities (Medina et al. 2019),[61] reminds us that wealthy families have resources for college admissions that poor families do not have. Although the policy of legacy admissions is legal, it still gives these families the unfair advantage just mentioned.

Graduation Rates

For the sake of students and of their colleges and universities, it is important that as many students as possible go on to earn their diplomas. However, only 60 percent of students at four-year institutions graduate within six years. This figure varies by type of institution. At the highly selective private institutions, an average of 87 percent of students graduate within six years, while at institutions with an open admissions policy, the graduation rate averages only 31 percent (National Center for Education Statistics 2019).[62]

The 60 percent overall rate masks a racial/ethnic difference in graduation rates: While 74 percent of Asian students and 64 percent of white students graduate within six years, only 40 percent of African American students, 54 percent of Latinx students, and 39 percent of Native American students graduate within six years (National Center for Education Statistics 2019).[63] A similar difference exists for income, as the graduation rate for low-income students is much lower than that for wealthier students (Luhby 2011).[64] In fact, students with high test scores and low-income parents are less likely to graduate than those with low test scores and high-income parents (Krugman 2012).[65]

Low-income students drop out at higher rates because of academic and financial difficulties and family problems (Gonzalez 2010).[66] Their academic and financial difficulties are intertwined. Low-income students often have to work many hours per week during the academic year to be able to pay their bills. Because their work schedules reduce the time they have for studying, their grades may suffer. This general problem has been made worse by cutbacks in federal grants to low-income students that began during the 1980s. These cutbacks forced low-income students to rely increasingly on loans, which have to be repaid. This fact leads some to work more hours during the academic year to limit the loans they must take out, and their increased work schedule again may affect their grades.

Low-income students face additional difficulties beyond the financial. Their writing and comprehension skills upon entering college are often weaker than those of wealthier students. If they are first-generation college students (meaning that neither parent went to college), they often have problems adjusting to campus life and living amid students from much more advantaged backgrounds.

As discussed at the beginning of this chapter, low-income students faced special difficulties after campuses shut down in the wake of the 2020 COVID-19 pandemic and changed to remote instruction (Casey 2020).[67] As one headline summarized their situation, "Low-income College Students Already Faced Barriers to Graduating. The Coronavirus Multiplied Them" (Kolodner 2020).[68] Many low-income students returned to homes with unreliable or even no access to the Internet, and/or to homes where they could not find a quiet place to study or participate in classes held by video conference. Many had worked on or near their campuses to help pay for college; now they had to find new jobs at home, which many were not able to do because so much of the economy had shut down. If they were able to find employment, they usually did not end up with a job that would have enabled them to work from home. Instead, their jobs were in the service sector, such as grocery stores, that required them to commute and interact with the public, exposing them to the coronavirus. While all college students had to deal with the implications of the pandemic on their education, low-income students found themselves in a more difficult situation than their wealthier peers.

Campus Violence

Earlier we discussed violence in the elementary and secondary schools. Violence can also happen on college and university campuses, although shootings are very rare. However, some examples from the last two decades illustrate that students and faculty are not immune from gun violence. In April 2019, a former student entered a classroom at the University of North Carolina-Charlotte and fatally shot two students and wounded four others. In April 2012, a former student lined up and then shot and killed seven people and wounded three others at Oikos University in Oakland, California. In February 2010, Amy Bishop, a biology professor at the University of Alabama in Huntsville who had recently been denied tenure, shot and killed three faculty at a department meeting and wounded three others. Almost three years earlier, a student at Virginia Tech went on a shooting rampage and killed thirty-two students and faculty before killing himself.

Other types of violence are more common on the nation's campuses. Chapter 4 noted that at least one-fifth of women students have been raped or sexually assaulted (including attempts), usually by a male student who was an acquaintance, friend, or intimate partner. Beyond rape and sexual assault, students are also sometimes physically assaulted or robbed.

Key Takeaways

- The cost of higher education and other problems make it difficult for low-income students and students of color to enter college and to stay in college once admitted.
- Many college students have academic and personal problems that lead them to flounder and to seek psychological counseling.
- Many campuses continue to lack racial and social class diversity, and affirmative action remains very controversial.
- Physical and sexual violence is a general problem on the nation's campuses. At least one-fifth of college women are raped or sexually assaulted.

For Your Review

1. If you were the director of admissions at a university, what steps would you take to increase the number of applications from low-income students?
2. Do you think alcohol use is to blame for most campus violence, or are there other important factors at work? Explain your answer.

11.5 Improving Schools and Education

Learning Objectives

1. Understand how helpful good schooling can be to improve the lives of low-income children.
2. Discuss the importance of good teachers.
3. List any three strategies that will improve the education of low-income students.

This concluding section focuses mostly on elementary and secondary education, given its critical importance for young people's development. As we consider how to improve the nation's schools, and especially how to improve outcomes for low-income students and students of color, we need to keep in mind an important consideration: Good schooling can make an important difference for these students, and good teachers can greatly help low-income students (Chetty et al. 2011).[69] Even so, students' family and neighborhood backgrounds still matter greatly for their school performance (Downey and Gibbs 2012; Ladd and Fiske 2011).[70] Good schooling, then, can only go so far in overcoming the many strikes that low-income students and those of color have against them even before they enter kindergarten and the problems they continue to experience thereafter. As one education writer observes,

> *Let's be realistic: Teachers aren't miracle workers. There's only so much they can do to address problems that troubled students bring to class every day, including neglect, abuse, and unaddressed medical and mental health issues. The obvious and subtle ways that poverty inhibits a child's ability to learn—from hearing, visual and dental problems to higher asthma rates to diminished verbal interaction in the home—have been well-documented.*
>
> *So let's seek to improve the state of families. Attacking schools and teachers makes everyone feel like a reformer, but the problems begin long before a child steps through the schoolhouse door* (Farhi 2011).[71]

The Need for More General Social Reform

The importance of students' family and neighborhood backgrounds has a significant implication: To improve low-income students' school performance, our society must address the problems of poverty and racial/ethnic inequality (Hanauer 2019).[72] As two sociologists argue this point, "If we are serious about improving American children's school performance, we will need to take a broader view of education policy. In addition to school reform, we must also aim to improve children's lives where they spend the vast majority of their time—with their families and in their neighborhoods" (Downey and Gibbs 2012:85).[73] Chapter 2 and Chapter 3 discussed strategies to reduce poverty and racial/ethnic inequality; these strategies would also help improve the school performance of low-income students and those of color.

A School Reform Agenda

Despite the need to address poverty and racial inequality, schools with decaying buildings, uncommitted teachers, and other problems still cannot be expected to produce students with even adequate levels of academic achievement. It is thus critical, says poverty expert Mark Robert Rank (2004:208),[74] to do everything possible to provide a quality education to the nation's poor children: "To deny children the fundamental right to a decent education is both morally wrong and bad social policy. It flies in the face of the American concept of equality of opportunity...Countless studies have documented the immediate and lingering effects of disparate educational outcomes on later life. Improving public education for low-income children is absolutely essential."

In short, good schools and good teachers do matter. In particular, good elementary and middle school teachers have been shown to have a lifelong impact on their students: Students with good teachers are more likely years later to have lower teenage pregnancy rates and higher college attendance rates, and they are also more likely to have higher salaries in adulthood (Lowrey 2012).[75]

Education experts urge several measures to improve the nation's schools and the education of American children (Addonizio 2019; American University School of Education 2019; King 2018).[76] These measures include the following:

- Have smaller schools and smaller classes.
- Provide more funding for schools, especially those in low-income neighborhoods.
- Repair decaying school buildings.
- Increase teachers' pay to attract more highly qualified applicants.
- Hold teachers more accountable for their students' learning, while recognizing the obstacles that teachers of low-income students must overcome.
- Expand early childhood (preschool) education.

On the national level, these steps will cost billions of dollars, but this expenditure promises to have a significant payoff by saving money in the long run and reducing crime, health problems, and other social ills.

As the United States tries to improve its schools, it is also important to attend to the emotional and physical health needs of low-income children. Because of the many problems these children experience in their families and neighborhoods, including alcohol and drug abuse, hunger, illness, marital conflict, and violence, their emotional and physical health may often suffer. They cannot be expected to do well in school unless they are in good health in both respects. For this reason, many schools are now partnering with community health organizations and other agencies to address the emotional and physical health needs of schoolchildren, often by establishing well-staffed and well-equipped health centers inside the schools.

It is also important for the nation to try to improve parenting skills if it hopes to improve the educational performance and attainment of low-income students (Roksa and Potter 2011).[77] As Chapter 10 discussed, low-income parents seem less likely to read and talk with their young children, and this problem impairs their children's cognitive and neurological development. Home visits and other efforts by professionals to encourage parents of infants and toddlers to engage in these activities regularly hold potential for improving their children's ability to learn and do well in school.

School violence and bullying are two other problems that must also be addressed. Several of the steps just outlined should reduce school violence, but other measures should also help. One example involves antibullying programs, which include regular parent meetings, strengthened playground supervision, and appropriate discipline when warranted. Research indicates that these programs reduce bullying by 20–23 percent on the average (Farrington and Ttofi 2009).[78] More generally, because the roots of school violence are also similar to the roots of youth violence outside the schools, measures that reduce youth violence should also reduce school violence. As discussed in previous chapters, such measures include early childhood prevention programs for youths at risk for developmental and behavioral problems, parenting training programs, and policies that provide income and jobs for families living in poverty.

At the level of higher education, our discussion highlighted the fact that social inequality in the larger society also plays out in colleges and universities. The higher dropout rates for low-income students and for students of color in turn contribute to more social inequality. Colleges and universities need to do everything possible to admit these students and then to help them once they are admitted, as they face many obstacles and difficulties that white students from more advantaged backgrounds are much less likely to encounter.

Key Takeaways

- Good schooling can be very helpful for low-income students, but these students' socioeconomic backgrounds have more impact than schooling on their futures.

- For this reason, more general social reform must accompany effective school reform.
- Several strategies, including smaller classes and better-paid teachers, will help improve the learning of low-income students.

For Your Review

1. Write a short essay in which you outline what a school superintendent might do to improve the learning of the school district's elementary school students.
2. Why do you think the United States has not more vigorously pursued the school reform agenda outlined in this section?

11.6 End-of-Chapter Material

Summary

1. Education is both formal and informal. Formal education occurs in schools under specially trained teachers, while informal education takes place primarily in the home, with parents as instructors.
2. In the early nineteenth century in the United States, a movement for free, compulsory education began. Reasons for interest in such education included the perceived needs to unify the country, to "Americanize" immigrants, and to give members of the working class the skills, knowledge, and discipline they needed to be productive workers.
3. In the United States, social class, race and ethnicity, and gender all affect educational attainment. Poor people end up with less schooling than middle- and upper-class people, and African Americans and Latinxs have lower educational attainment than whites and Asian Americans. Although women had less schooling than men in the past, today they are more likely to graduate from high school and to attend college.
4. Education in the United States has a significant impact on two areas. One is income: the higher the education, the higher the income. The second is attitudes: the higher the education, the greater the tolerance for nontraditional behaviors and viewpoints.
5. Sociological perspectives on education fall into the functionalist, conflict, and symbolic interactionist approaches discussed in earlier chapters. Functional theory stresses the functions education serves for society, including socialization, social placement, social integration, and social and cultural innovation. Conflict theory stresses that education perpetuates and reinforces existing social inequality for several reasons, including the use of tracking and inequality in schooling between rich and poor communities. Symbolic interactionism emphasizes the social interaction that's part of schooling and calls attention to the ways in which the treatment of students as smart or dull can affect how much they end up learning.
6. Several issues and problems affect education in the United States today. Many schools are decrepit and lack sufficient books and equipment, and many are also segregated by race and ethnicity. Increasing interest in school choice has led to controversy over whether the government should provide aid to parents to send their children to private and parochial schools. Finally, school violence is an issue of continuing concern; however, the vast majority of schools are very safe for their students, teachers, and other personnel. Bullying is more common, with about one-third of students bullied every year.
7. At the level of higher education, students of color and those from low-income backgrounds are less likely to attend college at all, and if they do attend, they are less likely to graduate. After campuses shut down in the wake of the 2020 COVID-19 pandemic, many low-income

students, including many students of color, faced several types of challenges as they tried to continue their education via remote learning.

Using What You Know

You are the principal of a middle school in a poor urban neighborhood. Your classrooms lack basic supplies, your roof often leaks, and an ominous odor often arises from your school's water system. You have appealed many times to the school district for additional funds to deal with all these problems, but these funds have not been provided. What, if anything, do you do next?

What You Can Do

To help deal with the education problems discussed in this chapter, you may wish to do any of the following:

1. Volunteer to tutor students at a local school or after-school program.
2. If your college or university has low numbers of low-income students, establish a student group to encourage your school to admit more such students.
3. Start or join a group on your campus to call attention to the need for responsible alcohol use, as drinking is associated with much campus violence.

Endnotes

1. Chambers, Jennifer. 2019. "Detroit Schools Face Tough Choices with Too Many Repairs, Not Enough Money." *The Detroit News* April 29:https://www.detroitnews.com/story/news/local/detroit-city/2019/04/29/detroit-schools-face-tough-choices-too-many-repairs-not-enough-money/3232674002/; Strauss, Valerie. 2016. "How Bad Are Conditions in Detroit Public Schools? This Appalling." *The Washington Post* January 20:https://www.washingtonpost.com/news/answer-sheet/wp/2016/01/20/how-appalling-are-conditions-in-detroit-public-schools-this-appalling/.

2. Casey, Nicholas. 2020. "For Classmates, Zoom Exposes a Class Divide." *The New York Times* April 5:A1; Hoover, Eric. 2020. "Distanced Learning." *The Chronicle of Higher Education* April 24:https://www.chronicle.com/article/Distanced-Learning/248634.

3. Rury, John L. 2020. *Education and Social Change*. New York: Routledge.

4. National Center for Education Statistics. 2019. *The Condition of Education 2019*. Washington, DC: National Center for Education Statistics, U.S. Department of Education.

5. Goldrick-Rab, Sara, Robert Kelchen, Douglas N. Harris and James Benson. 2016. "Reducing Income Inequality in Educational Attainment: Experimental Evidence on the Impact of Financial Aid on College Completion." 121(6):1762-817. doi: 10.1086/685442.

6. Ballantine, Jeanne H., Floyd M. Hammack and Jenny Stuber. 2017. *The Sociology of Education: A Systematic Analysis*. New York: Routledge.

7. Ballantine, Jeanne H., Floyd M. Hammack and Jenny Stuber. 2017. *The Sociology of Education: A Systematic Analysis*. New York: Routledge; Mickelson, R. A. 2003. When are Racial Disparities in Education the Result of Racial Discrimination? A Social Science Perspective. *Teachers College Record* 105:1052–1086.

8. Ansalone, George. 2010. "Tracking: Educational Differentiation or Defective Strategy." *Educational Research Quarterly* 34(2):3-17.

9. Payne, Allison Ann and Kelly Welch. 2016. "The Centrality of Schools in the Lifecourse: The Case for Focusing on School-Related Influences in Developmental Theory and Research." *Deviant Behavior* 37(7):748-60.

10. Kirk, David S. and Robert J. Sampson. 2011. " Crime and the Production of Safe Schools." Pp. 397-418 in *Whither Opportunity?: Rising Inequality, Schools, and Children's Life Chances*, edited by G. J. Duncan and R. J. Murnane. New York: Russell Sage Foundation; Wodtke, Geoffrey T., David J. Harding and Felix Elwert. 2011. "Neighborhood Effects in Temporal Perspective: The Impact of Long-Term Exposure to Concentrated Disadvantage on High School Graduation." American Sociological Review 76(5):713-36. doi: 10.1177/0003122411420816.

11. Quillian, Lincoln. 2017. "Neighborhood and the Intergenrational Transmission of Poverty." *Focus* 33(2):22-24.

12. Wodtke, Geoffrey T., David J. Harding and Felix Elwert. 2011. "Neighborhood Effects in Temporal Perspective: The Impact of Long-Term Exposure to Concentrated Disadvantage on High School Graduation." *American Sociological Review* 76(5):713-36. doi: 10.1177/0003122411420816.

13. Wodtke, Geoffrey T., David J. Harding and Felix Elwert. 2011. "Neighborhood Effects in Temporal Perspective: The Impact of Long-Term Exposure to Concentrated Disadvantage on High School Graduation." *American Sociological Review* 76(5):713-36. doi: 10.1177/0003122411420816.

14. National Center for Education Statistics. 2019. *The Condition of Education 2019*. Washington, DC: National Center for Education Statistics, U.S. Department of Education.

15. Collins, Randall. 1979. *The Credential Society: An Historical Sociology of Education and Stratification*. New York: Academic Press.

16. Buckles, Kasey, Andreas Hagemann, Ofer Malamud, Melinda Morrill and Abigail Wozniak. 2016. "The Effect of College Education on Mortality." *Journal of Health Economics* 50:99-114.

17. OECD. 2018. *Pisa 2015: Results in Focus*. Paris: Organisation for Economic Co-operation and Development.

18. Abrams, Samuel E. 2011. "The Children Must Play: What the United States Could Learn from Finland About Education Reform." *The New Republic* January 28:http://www.tnr.com/article/politics/82329/education-reform-Finland-US; Anderson, Jenny. 2011. "From Finland, an Intriguing School-Reform Model." *The New York Times* December 13:A33; Eggers, Dave and Ninive Clements Calegari. 2011. "The High Cost of Low Teacher Salaries." *The New York Times* May 1(WK12); Hancock, LynNell. 2011. "Why Are Finland's Schools Successful?". *Smithsonian.com* September:http://www.smithsonianmag.com/people-places/Why-Are-Finlands-Schools-Successful.html?c=y&story=fullstory; Sahlberg, Pasi. 2011. *Finnish Lessons: What Can the World Learn from Educational Change in Finland?* New York: Teachers College Press; Strauss, Valerie. 2019. "What Finland Is Really Doing to Improve Its Acclaimed Schools." *The Washington Post* August 30:https://www.washingtonpost.com/education/2019/08/30/what-finland-is-really-doing-improve-its-acclaimed-schools/.

19. Ballantine, Jeanne H., Floyd M. Hammack and Jenny Stuber. 2017. *The Sociology of Education: A Systematic Analysis*. New York: Routledge.

20. Potter, Halley. 2019. Integrating Classrooms and Reducing Academic Tracking: Strategies for School Leaders and Educators. New York: The Century Foundation.

21. Grodsky, Eric, John Robert Warren and Erika Felts. 2008. "Testing and Social Stratification in American Education." *Annual Review of Sociology* 34(1):385-404.

22. Booher-Jennings, Jennifer. 2008. "Learning to Label: Socialisation, Gender, and the Hidden Curriculum of High-Stakes Testing." *British Journal of Sociology of Education* 29:149-60.

23. Cole, Mike. 2008. "Marxism and Educational Theory: Origins and Issues." New York: Routledge.

24. Thorne, Barrie. 1993. Gender Play: Girls and Boys in School. New Brunswick, NJ: Rutgers University Press.

25. Chetty, Raj, John N. Friedman, Nathaniel Hilger, Emmanuel Saez, Diane Whitmore Schanzenbach and Danny Yagan. 2011. "How Does Your Kindergarten Classroom Affect Your Earnings? Evidence from Project Star." *Quarterly Journal of Economics* 126:1593-660; Schanzenbach, Diane Whitmore. 2006. "What Have Researchers Learned from Project Star?" 2012(January 12).

26. Rosenthal, Robert, & Jacobson, Lenore. 1968. *Pygmalion in the Classroom.* New York: Holt.

27. Jones, Susanne M. and Kathryn Dindia. 2004. "A Meta-Analytic Perspective on Sex Equity in the Classroom." *Review of Educational Research* 74:443-71.

28. Kozol, Jonathan. 1991. *Savage Inequalities: Children in America's Schools.* New York, NY: Crown.

29. Kozol, Jonathan. 1967. *Death at an Early Age: The Destruction of the Hearts and Minds of Negro Children in the Boston Public Schools.* Boston: Houghton Mifflin.

30. Kozol, Jonathan. 1991. *Savage Inequalities: Children in America's Schools.* New York: Crown.

31. Kozol, Jonathan. 1991. *Savage Inequalities: Children in America's Schools.* New York: Crown.

32. Tauber, Eugene. 2018. "Map: What It Costs to Educate Children in Pennsylvania, District by District." *The Morning Call* August 28:https://www.mcall.com/news/education/mc-school-district-snapshots-2018-expenditures-20180825-htmlstory.html.

33. García, Emma and Elaine Weiss. 2019. "Low Relative Pay and High Incidence of Moonlighting Play a Role in the Teacher Shortage, Particularly in High-Poverty Schools." *Economic Policy Institute* May 9:https://www.epi.org/publication/low-relative-pay-and-high-incidence-of-moonlighting-play-a-role-in-the-teacher-shortage-particularly-in-high-poverty-schools-the-third-report-in-the-perfect-storm-in-the-teacher-labor-marke/.

34. Torgan, Allie. 2016. "Introducing Kids to the Ocean… and a Career in Science." *CNN* June 10:https://www.cnn.com/2016/04/07/us/cnnheroes-shara-fisler-ocean-discovery-institute/index.html.

35. Kozol, Jonathan. 2005. *The Shame of the Nation: The Restoration of Apartheid Schooling.* New York: Crown.

36. Mervosh, Sarah. 2019. "How Much Wealthier Are White School Districts Than Nonwhite Ones? $23 Billion, Report Says." *The New York Times* February 27:https://www.nytimes.com/2019/02/27/education/school-districts-funding-white-minorities.html?module=inline.

37. Lukas, J. Anthony. 1985. *Common Ground: A Turbulent Decade in the Lives of Three American Families.* New York: Knopf.

38. Rossell, Christine H. 2017. "The Case against Magnet Schools." Pp. 194-214 in *The Wiley Handbook of School Choice*, edited by R. A. Fox and N. K. Buchanan. Malden, MA: John Wiley & Sons.

39. Fox, Robert A. and Nina K. Buchanan, eds. 2017. *The Wiley Handbook of School Choice.* Malden, MA: John Wiley & Sons.

40. Center for Research on Education Outcomes. 2009. *Multiple Choice: Charter School Performance in 16 States.* Stanford, CA: Center for Research on Education Outcomes, Stanford University.

41. Berends, Mark. 2015. "Sociology and School Choice: What We Know after Two Decades of Charter Schools." *Annual Review of Sociology* 41:159-80.

42. Basile, Marco. 2010. *False Impression: How a Widely Cited Study Vastly Overstates the Benefits of Charter Schools.* New York: The Century Foundation.

43. Centers for Disease Control and Prevention. 2016. "Understanding School Violence Fact Sheet."https://www.cdc.gov/violenceprevention/pdf/School_Violence_Fact_Sheet-a.pdf.

44. Moon, Byongook, Hye-Won Hwang and John D. McCluskey. 2011. "Causes of School Bullying: Empirical Test of a General Theory of Crime, Differential Association Theory, and General Strain Theory." *Crime & Delinquency* 57:849-77.

45. St. George, Donna. 2011. "Bullying Linked to Lower School Achievement." *The Washington Post* September 5:http://www.washingtonpost.com/local/education/bullying-linked-to-lower-school-achievement/2011/09/01/gIQArmQw4J_story.html?hpid=z3.

46. U.S. Department of Health & Human Services. 2019. "What Is Bullying."https://www.stopbullying.gov/what-is-bullying/index.html#frequency.

47. Adams, Frank D. and Gloria J. Lawrence. 2011. "Bullying Victims: The Effects Last into College." *American Secondary Education* 40(1):4-13.

48. Boccanfuso, Christopher and Megan Kuhfeld. 2011. *Multiple Responses, Promising Results: Evidence-Based, Nonpunitive Alternatives to Zero Tolerance.* Washington, DC: Child Trends.

49. Skiba, R. J. and M.K. Rausch. 2006. "Zero Tolerance, Suspension, and Expulsion: Questions of Equity and Effectiveness." Pp. 1063-89 in *Handbook of Classroom Management: Research, Practice, and Contemporary Issues*, edited by C. M. Evertson and C. S. Weinstein. Mahwah, NJ: Lawrence Erlbaum Associates.

50. Payne, Allison Ann and Kelly Welch. 2016. "The Centrality of Schools in the Lifecourse: The Case for Focusing on School-Related Influences in Developmental Theory and Research." Deviant Behavior 37(7):748-60.

51. National Center for Education Statistics. 2019. *Digest of Education Statistics: 2017.* Washington, DC: National Center for Education Statistics https://nces.ed.gov/programs/digest/.

52. Hess, Abigail. 2019. "Here's How Much the Average Student Loan Borrower Owes When They Graduate." *CNBC* May 20:https://www.cnbc.com/2019/05/20/how-much-the-average-student-loan-borrower-owes-when-they-graduate.html.

53. Golden, Serena. 2010. "'When College Is Not the Best Time.'" *Inside Higher Ed* September 15:http://www.insidehighered.com/news/2010/09/15/leibow.

54. Wolverton, Brad. 2019. "As Students Struggle with Stress and Depression, Colleges Act as Counselors." *The New York Times* February 21:https://www.nytimes.com/2019/02/21/education/learning/mental-health-counseling-on-campus.html.

55. Center for Collegiate Mental Health. 2016. *2015 Annual Report.* University Park, PA: Center for Collegiate Mental Health, Penn State University.

56. Delisle, Jason D. and Preston Cooper. 2018. *Low-Income Students at Selective Colleges: Disappearing or Holding Steady?* Washington, DC: American Enterprise Institute.

57. Smith, Clint. 2019. "Elite Colleges Constantly Tell Low-Income Students That They Do Not Belong." *The Atlantic* March 18:https://www.theatlantic.com/education/archive/2019/03/privileged-poor-navigating-elite-university-life/585100/.

58. Jack, Anthony Abraham. 2019. The Privileged Poor: How Elite Colleges Are Failing Disadvantaged Students. Cambridge, MA: Harvard University Press; Smith, Clint. 2019. "Elite Colleges Constantly Tell Low-Income Students That They Do Not Belong." *The Atlantic* March 18:https://www.theatlantic.com/education/archive/2019/03/privileged-poor-navigating-elite-university-life/585100/.

59. Kahlenberg, Richard D., ed. 2010. *Affirmative Action for the Rich: Legacy Preferences in College Admissions.* New York: The Century Foundation.

60. Kahlenberg, Richard. 2011. "Do Legacy Preferences Count More Than Race?". *The Chronicle of Higher Education* January 6:http://chronicle.com/blogs/innovations/do-legacy-preferences-count-more-than-race/28294.

61. Medina, Jennifer, Katie Benner and Kate Taylor. 2019. "Actresses, Business Leaders and Other Wealthy Parents Charged in U.S. College Entry Fraud." *The New York Times* March 12:https://www.nytimes.com/2019/03/12/us/college-admissions-cheating-scandal.html?action=click&module=inline&pgtype=Homepage.

62. National Center for Education Statistics. 2019. *The Condition of Education 2019.* Washington, DC: National Center for Education Statistics, U.S. Department of Education.

63. National Center for Education Statistics. 2019. *Digest of Education Statistics: 2017.* Washington, DC: National Center for Education Statistics https://nces.ed.gov/programs/digest/.

64. Luhby, Tami. 2011. "College Graduation Rates: Income Really Matters." *CNN.COM* November 28:http://money.cnn.com/2011/11/21/news/economy/income_college/index.htm.

65. Krugman, Paul. 2012. "America's Unlevel Field." *The New York Times* January 9:A19.

66. Gonzalez, Jennifer. 2010. "Reports Highlight Disparities in Graduation Rates among White and Minority Students." *The Chronicle of Higher Education* August 9:http://chronicle.com/article/Reports-Highlight-Disparities/123857/.

67. Casey, Nicholas. 2020. "For Classmates, Zoom Exposes a Class Divide." *The New York Times* April 5:A1.

68. Kolodner, Meredith. 2020. "Low-Income College Students Already Faced Barriers to Graduating. The Coronavirus Multiplied Them." *The Washington Post* April 8:https://www.washingtonpost.com/education/2020/04/08/low-income-college-students-already-faced-barriers-graduating-coronavirus-multiplied-them/.

69. Chetty, Raj, John N. Friedman, Nathaniel Hilger, Emmanuel Saez, Diane Whitmore Schanzenbach and Danny Yagan. 2011. "How Does Your Kindergarten Classroom Affect Your Earnings? Evidence from Project Star." *Quarterly Journal of Economics* 126:1593-660.

70. Downey, Douglas B. and Benjamin G. Gibbs. 2012. "How Schools Really Matter " Pp. 80-86 in *The Contexts Reader*, edited by D. Hartmann and C. Uggen. New York: W.W. Norton; Ladd, Helen F. and Edward B. Fiske. 2011. "Class Matters. Why Won't We Admit It?". *The New York Times* December 12:A23.

71. Farhi, Paul. 2011. "Five Myths About America's Schools." *The Washington Post* May 20:http://www.washingtonpost.com/opinions/five-myths-about-americas-schools/2011/05/09/AFunW27G_story.html.

72. Hanauer, Nick. 2019. "Better Schools Won't Fix America." The Atlantic July:https://www.theatlantic.com/magazine/archive/2019/07/education-isnt-enough/590611/.

73. Downey, Douglas B. and Benjamin G. Gibbs. 2012. "How Schools Really Matter " Pp. 80-86 in *The Contexts Reader*, edited by D. Hartmann and C. Uggen. New York: W.W. Norton.

74. Rank, Mark Robert. 2004. *One Nation, Underprivileged: Why American Poverty Affects Us All*. New York: Oxford University Press.

75. Lowrey, Annie. 2012. "Big Study Links Good Teachers to Lasting Gain." The New York Times January 6:A1.

76. Addonizio, Michael. 2019. "America's Schools Are Crumbling—What Will It Take to Fix Them?". *The Conversation* March 5:https://theconversation.com/americas-schools-are-crumbling-what-will-it-take-to-fix-them-111720; American University School of Education. 2019, "5 Ways Policy Makers Can Improve the Quality of Education," https://soeonline.american.edu/blog/5-ways-policy-makers-can-improve-the-quality-of-education; King, John B. 2018. "What Will It Take to Fix Public Education?". *Yale Insights* March 26:https://insights.som.yale.edu/insights/what-will-it-take-to-fix-public-education.

77. Roksa, Josipa and Daniel Potter. 2011. "Parenting and Academic Achievement: Intergenerational Transmission of Educational Advantage." *Sociology of Education* 84:299-321.

78. Farrington, David P. and Maria M. Ttofi. 2009. "School-Based Programs to Reduce Bullying and Victimization." *Campbell Systematic Reviews* 2009(6):1-148.

CHAPTER 12
Work and the Economy

Social Problems in the News

"Why GM Workers are Striking," the headline said. In September 2019, the nearly 50,000 members of the United Auto Workers (UAW) employed by General Motors (GM) went on strike to secure higher pay, better job security, and more affordable health care among other goals. As one striker put it, "We're out here to preserve our livelihood and preserve the middle class, allow our child to live a comfortable life like we have." Another striker explained that he was "doing it for the people coming in behind us. To have a better life, better education and things like that." One of the strikers' goals was to improve the situation of temporary workers at GM, who lack full pay and other benefits. Reflecting this concern, one striker said, "The poor temps, those people are treated like dogs in here. They have no recourse."

Source: Cromie 2019[1]

One of the most momentous events of the twentieth century was the Great Depression, which engulfed the United States in 1929 and spread to the rest of the world, lasting almost a decade. Millions were thrown out of work, and bread lines became common. In the United States, a socialist movement gained momentum for a time as many workers blamed U.S. industry and capitalism for their unemployment.

The Great Depression involved the failing of the economy in the 1930s. The economy also failed in the United States beginning in March 2020, when the economy shut down because of the coronavirus pandemic. Tens of millions of people filed for unemployment benefits virtually overnight, and the unemployment rate soared in a matter of days to levels not seen since the Great Depression. Even before this devastating development, the news story that began this chapter reminds us that many workers still needed higher pay, better working conditions, and better health benefits.

This chapter examines the many problems related to work and the economy in the United States today. It also examines the related issues of economic inequality and economic mobility. As we shall see, the United States has a mediocre record in both these areas when compared to other wealthy democracies.

12.1 Overview of the Economy

Learning Objectives

1. Describe the three sectors of the economy.
2. Distinguish the two major economic systems in the world today.
3. Discuss the advantages and disadvantages of capitalism and socialism.

Clerical work and other occupations that provide services rather than products constitute the tertiary sector in the economy.

Source: Prostock-studio/Shutterstock.com

economy

The social institution that organizes the production, distribution, and consumption of a society's goods and services.

primary sector

The part of the economy that takes and uses raw materials directly from the natural environment.

secondary sector

The part of the economy that transforms raw materials into finished products.

tertiary sector

The part of the economy that provides services rather than products.

capitalism

An economic system in which the means of production are privately owned.

When we hear the term *economy*, it is usually in the context of how the economy "is doing": Is inflation soaring or under control? Is the economy growing or shrinking? Is unemployment rising, declining, or remaining stable? Are new college graduates finding jobs easily or not? All these questions concern the economy, but sociologists define **economy** more broadly as the social institution that organizes the production, distribution, and consumption of a society's goods and services. Defined in this way, the economy touches us all. Keep in mind that the economy is not the same as *government*, which is the social institution through which power is distributed and exercised. Economy and government are social institutions that are certainly intertwined, but conceptually they are distinct.

The economy is composed of three sectors. The **primary sector** is the part of the economy that takes and uses raw materials directly from the natural environment. Its activities include agriculture, fishing, forestry, and mining. The **secondary sector** of the economy transforms raw materials into finished products and is essentially the manufacturing industry. Finally, the **tertiary sector** is the part of the economy that provides services rather than products; its activities include clerical work, health care, teaching, and information technology services.

Types of Economic Systems

The two major economic systems in modern societies are capitalism and socialism. In practice, no one society is purely capitalist or socialist, so it is helpful to think of capitalism and socialism as lying on opposite ends of a continuum. Societies' economies mix elements of both capitalism and socialism but do so in varying degrees, so that some societies lean toward the capitalist end of the continuum, while other societies lean toward the socialist end. For example, the United States is a capitalist nation, but the government still regulates many industries to varying degrees. The industries usually would prefer less regulation, while their critics usually prefer more regulation. Let's see how capitalism and socialism differ.

Capitalism

Capitalism is an economic system in which the means of production are privately owned. By *means of production*, we mean everything—land, tools, technology, and so forth—that is needed to produce goods and services. The most important goal of capitalism is the pursuit of personal profit. As individuals seek to maximize their own wealth, society as a whole is said to benefit. Goods get produced, services are rendered, people pay for the goods and services they need and desire, and the economy and society as a whole prosper.

As people pursue personal profit under capitalism, they compete with each other for the greatest profits. Businesses try to attract more demand for their products in many ways, including lowering prices and creating better products. In capitalist theory, such competition helps ensure the best products at the lowest prices, again benefiting society as a whole. In a "pure" capitalist economy, this competition that characterizes capitalism should be left to operate on its own, free of government intervention or control. For this reason, capitalism is often referred to as *laissez-faire* (French for "leave alone") capitalism, and terms to describe capitalism include the *free-enterprise system* and the *free market*.

One important hallmark of capitalism is competition for profit. This competition is thought to help ensure the best products at the lowest prices, as companies will ordinarily try to keep their prices as low as possible to attract buyers and maximize their sales.

Source: © Thinkstock

Socialism

The features of socialism differ greatly from those of capitalism. **Socialism** is an economic system in which the means of production are collectively owned, usually by the government. Whereas the United States has several airlines that are owned by airline corporations, a socialist society might have one government-owned airline.

The most important goal of socialism is not the pursuit of personal profit but rather work for the collective good: The needs of society are considered more important than the needs of the individual. Reflecting this view, individuals do not compete with each other for profit; instead they work together for the good of everyone. If under capitalism the government is supposed to let the economy alone, under socialism the government controls the economy.

Recall that societies can be ranked on a continuum ranging from mostly capitalist to mostly socialist. At one end of the continuum, we have societies characterized by a relatively free market, and at the other end we have those characterized by strict government regulation of the economy. Figure 12.1 depicts the nations of the world along this continuum. Capitalist nations are found primarily in North America and Western Europe but also exist in other parts of the world.

socialism

An economic system in which the means of production are collectively owned, usually by the government.

FIGURE 12.1 Capitalism and Socialism across the Globe

- 80–100
- 70–79.9
- 60–69.9
- 50–59.9
- 0–49.9
- N/A

Source: Adapted from The Heritage Foundation. 2019. 2019 Index of economic freedom. Retrieved from https://www.heritage.org/index/

Comparing Capitalism and Socialism

The relative merits of capitalism and socialism have long been debated (Bowles 2012; Cohen 2009).[2] Compared to socialism, capitalism has several claimed advantages. It produces greater economic growth and productivity, at least in part because it provides more incentives (i.e., profit) for economic innovation. It also is often characterized by greater political freedom in the form of civil rights and liberties. As an economic system, capitalism seems to lend itself to personal freedom: Because its hallmarks include the private ownership of the means of production and the individual pursuit of profit, there is much more emphasis in capitalist societies on the needs and desires of the individual and less emphasis on the need for government intervention in economic and social affairs.

Yet capitalism also has its drawbacks. There is much more economic inequality in capitalism than in socialism. Although capitalism produces economic growth, not all segments of capitalism share this growth equally, and there is a much greater difference between the rich and poor than under socialism. People can become very rich in capitalist nations, but they can also remain quite poor.

Another possible drawback depends on whether you prefer competition or cooperation. It is often said that important values in the United States include competition and individualism, both of which arguably reflect this nation's capitalist system. Children in the United States are raised with more of an individual orientation than children in socialist societies, who learn that the needs of their society are more important than the needs of the individual. Whereas U.S. children learn to compete with each other for good grades, success in sports, and other outcomes, children in socialist societies learn to cooperate to achieve tasks.

More generally, critics say that capitalism encourages selfish and even greedy behavior: If individuals try to maximize their profit, they do so at the expense of others. In competition, someone has to lose. A company's ultimate aim, and one that is generally lauded, is to maximize its profits by driving another company out of the market altogether. If so, that company succeeds even if some other party is hurting. The small mom-and-pop grocery stores, drugstores, and hardware stores are almost a thing of the past, as big-box stores and then online businesses arose and drove their competition out of business. To its critics, then, capitalism encourages harmful behavior, and there are many losers in capitalism. Yet it is precisely this type of behavior that is taught in business schools.

Democratic Socialism

democratic socialism

An economic system in which the government owns several important industries, but much property remains in private hands, and political freedom is widespread.

Some nations combine elements of both capitalism and socialism and are called *social democracies*, while their combination of capitalism and socialism is called **democratic socialism**. In these nations, which include Denmark, Sweden, and several other Western European nations, the government owns several important industries, but much property remains in private hands, and political freedom is widespread. The governments in these nations have extensive programs to help the poor and other people in need. Although these nations have high tax rates to help finance their social programs, their experience indicates it is very possible to combine the best features of capitalism and socialism while avoiding their faults (Russell 2018)[3] (see "Lessons from Other Societies").

Why Democratic Socialism Is Gaining Popularity in the United States

Several European nations feature democratic socialism, which combines capitalism and socialism while retaining political freedoms. Compared to the United States, these nations have extensive programs to help their poor and other people in need.

View the video online at: http://www.youtube.com/embed/BlrDpTGRREA?rel=0

The economies of Denmark, pictured here, and several other Western European nations feature a combination of capitalism and socialism that is called democratic socialism. In these economies, the government owns important industries, but private property and political freedom remain widespread.

Source: © Thinkstock

Lessons from Other Societies

Democratic Socialism in Scandinavia

The five Scandinavian nations, also called the Nordic nations, are Denmark, Finland, Iceland, Norway, and Sweden. These nations differ in many ways, but they also share many similarities. In particular, they are all social democracies, as their governments own important industries while their citizens enjoy much political freedom. Each nation has the three branches of government with which most people are familiar—executive, judicial, and legislative—and each nation has a national parliament to which people are elected by proportional representation.

Social democracies like the Scandinavian nations are often called controlled capitalist market economies. The word *controlled* here conveys the idea that their governments either own industries or heavily regulate industries they do not own. A key feature of these social democracies' economies is that inequality in wealth and income is not generally tolerated. Employers, employees, and political officials are accustomed to working closely to ensure that poverty and its related problems are addressed as much as possible and in as cooperative a manner as possible.

Underlying this so-called *social welfare model* is a commitment to *universalism*. All citizens, regardless of their socioeconomic status or family situation, receive various services, such as child care and universal health care, that are free or heavily subsidized. To support this massive provision of benefits, the Scandinavian nations have very high taxes that their citizens generally accept as normal and necessary.

The Scandinavian nations rank at or near the top in international comparisons of health, education, economic well-being, and other measures of quality of life. The Scandinavian experience of social democracy teaches us that it is very possible to have a political and economic model that combines the best features of capitalism and socialism while retaining the political freedom that citizens expect in a democracy.

Sources: Russell 2018; Sejersted 2011[4]

The U.S. Labor Force

civilian labor force

All noninstitutionalized civilians 16 years old or older who work for pay or are looking for work.

We now turn from a general discussion of economic systems to some basic facts on the labor force in the world's leading capitalist nation, the United States. (All data in this section and the remainder of the chapter are from the period just before the onset of the 2020 coronavirus pandemic.) The **civilian labor force** in the United States consists of all noninstitutionalized civilians 16 years of age or older who work for pay or are looking for work. The civilian labor force (hereafter *labor force*) consists of about 164 million people ages 16 and older, including about 69 percent of men and 57 percent of women in that age range (2018 data) (Bureau of Labor Statistics 2019).[5]

Of those who are currently employed, most work full-time, but some work only part-time. About one-third of this latter group simply cannot find full-time work, but the majority of part-time workers have noneconomic reasons for working only part-time. For example, they may have child-care or other family obligations, or they are in school.

Approximately 95 million Americans ages 16 and older are not in the labor force. Of this number, almost all do not desire a job. Most of these people are retired, disabled, or taking care of children and/or other family members. Of the remainder who would like a job but are still not in the labor force, most have dropped out of the labor force (stopped looking for a job) because they have become discouraged after previously looking for work but not finding a job.

Chapter 4 noted that women's labor force participation climbed since the 1950s. Figure 12.2 depicts this increase: Despite a slight downturn in this century thanks in part to the deep recession that began in 2008; women are significantly more likely now to be in the labor force than they were in 1960.

FIGURE 12.2 Women's Labor Force Participation Rate, 1960–2017

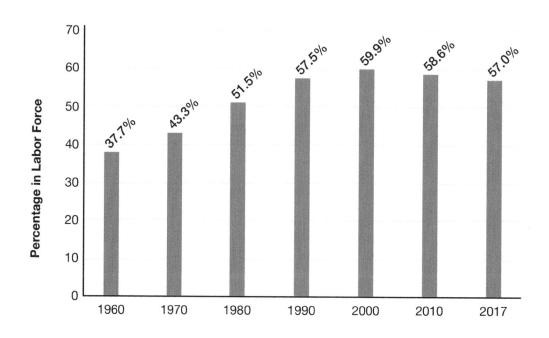

Source: Bureau of Labor Statistics. 2018. Women in the Labor Force: A Databook. https://www.bls.gov/opub/reports/womens-databook/2018/home.htm.

Key Takeaways

- The economy is the social institution that organizes the production, distribution, and consumption of a society's goods and services. It consists of three sectors: the primary sector, the secondary sector, and the tertiary sector.
- The two major economic systems in modern societies are capitalism and socialism. In practice, most societies have economies that mix elements of both systems but that lean toward one end of the capitalism–socialism continuum.
- Social democracies combine elements of both capitalism and socialism. They have achieved high economic growth while maintaining political freedom and personal liberty.

For Your Review

1. In what ways might capitalism be a better economic system than socialism? In what ways might socialism be a better economic system than capitalism?
2. Write a brief essay in which you discuss the values capitalism and socialism seem to develop among the people who live under either type of economic system.

12.2 Sociological Perspectives on Work and the Economy

Learning Objectives

1. List any two functions of work and the economy as emphasized by functionalism.
2. Summarize conflict theory's critique of work and the economy.
3. Explain the overall approach of symbolic interactionism to understanding work and the economy.

The three sociological perspectives examined in earlier chapters continue to offer insights that help us understand the economy, including the nature of work on which any economy rests. Table 12.1 summarizes these insights.

TABLE 12.1 Theory Snapshot

Theoretical perspective	Major assumptions
Functionalism	Work and the economy serve several functions for society. The economy makes society possible by providing the goods and services it needs. Work gives people an income and also provides them some self-fulfillment and part of their identity.
Conflict theory	Control of the economy enables the economic elite to maintain their position at the top of society and to keep those at the bottom in their place. Work is often alienating, and the workplace is often a site for sexual harassment and other problems.
Symbolic interactionism	This perspective focuses on social interaction in the workplace, on how employees respond to problems in their workplaces, and on how they perceive the work they do.

Functionalism

An important function of work is that it provides a context for coworker friendships. Many people have friends whom they met in their workplaces or through their work.

Source: Flamingo Images/Shutterstock.com

Recall that the functionalist perspective highlights the many functions that social institutions serve for society. Accordingly, this perspective paints a positive picture of work and the economy by pointing to their many benefits.

The economy's major function is also an absolutely essential function: the provision of goods and services. Because the economy provides the goods and services that any society needs, the economy makes a society possible. As we saw earlier, capitalist and socialist societies provide goods and services in different ways, and each type of economy has its advantages and disadvantages. Regardless of the relative merits of capitalism and socialism, however, both a capitalist economy and socialist economy make possible the societies in which they are found.

Whether or not they go to college, most people work for pay once they reach adulthood. Some work full-time until they retire, some alternate full-time work and part-time work, and some may start out with a job but drop out of the labor force to raise their children. Regardless of these various work patterns, the most important function that most people derive from working is their paycheck. Simply put, work provides the income that most people need for food, clothing, shelter, and other essential needs in today's society.

But work has important, nonmaterial functions beyond helping us pay the bills. Many people consider their job part of their overall identity, just as the college students reading this book consider being a student as part of their current identity. As we enter adulthood, we are not just a spouse, partner, parent, or child of our parents; we are also an accountant, banker, claims adjuster, day-care worker, elementary school teacher, financial consultant, garage door installer, and so forth. The job we have helps provide us with a sense of who we are or, to put it another way, a sense of our identity.

Especially if we enjoy our jobs, work can also give us a sense of self-fulfillment, self-confidence, and self-esteem. These psychological effects combine to form yet another important function of work.

Another nonmaterial function of work is friendship. Many people have friends and acquaintances whom they met at their workplaces or at least through their work (McGuire 2007).[6] Coworkers discuss all kinds of topics with each other, including personal matters, sports, and political affairs, and they often will invite other coworkers over to their homes or go out with them to a movie or a restaurant. These friendships are yet another benefit that work often provides.

Conflict Theory

Conflict theory's views of work and the economy largely derive from the writings of Karl Marx and Friedrich Engels during the nineteenth century. As Chapter 1 discussed, Marx and Engels sharply criticized capitalism as an economic system that inherently oppresses workers. Although today's conflict theorists are not necessarily Marxists, they nonetheless criticize many aspects of capitalism, and the earlier discussion of the disadvantages of capitalism reflects their views. They also criticize how large companies treat their workers. As just one example, they call attention to the fact that many companies maintain dangerous workplaces that result in injury, illness, and/or death for tens of thousands of workers annually. We return to this particular problem later in this chapter.

Two Killed in Boone County, WV, Coal Mine

Conflict theory emphasizes that many companies have dangerous workplaces. As this video illustrates, the coal industry is hazardous for its workers because companies may violate safety and health standards for coal mining.

View the video online at: http://www.youtube.com/embed/bQMePGMgiwl?rel=0

Conflict theorists also point out that the workplace is a setting for sexual harassment, which was discussed in Chapter 4. Although work can and does bring the many benefits assumed by functionalist theory, work can also be a source of great distress for the hundreds of thousands of women and men who are sexually harassed every year.

Marx also wrote that work in a capitalist society is inherently alienating. This is so, he said, because workers do not design the products they build, because factory work (which was the dominant mode of production in Marx's time) involves boring and repetitive tasks, and because workers are treated by their employers as mere commodities to be hired and fired at will. Reflecting Marx's views, conflict theory today also points to the alienating nature of work.

Symbolic Interactionism

Recall that symbolic interactionism focuses on the interaction of individuals and on how they interpret their interaction. In line with this "micro" focus, many scholars have generated rich descriptions of how certain workplaces' behaviors and understandings are negotiated and of how certain kinds of workers view aspects of their work and interpret the meaning of their work. Numerous studies of this type exist of police officers, prostitutes, attorneys, nurses and physicians, teachers, and a variety of other occupations. Most of these studies are based on intensive interviews of people in these occupations. Taken together, they provide a sensitive portrait of why people enter these various jobs and careers, what they like and dislike about their jobs, how they interact with other people in their workplaces, and a host of other issues.

Studies of police officers' behavior and perceptions provide an excellent example of the symbolic interactionist understanding of work. According to Jonathan Rubinstein, an important goal of officers is to maintain the respect of other officers.

Source: Drop of Light/Shutterstock.com

A classic study of the workplace grounded in the symbolic interactionist tradition was sociologist Joan Emerson's (1970)[7] study of gynecological exams. At the time Emerson wrote her study, most gynecologists were men. Because these men are necessarily viewing and touching their women patients' genitals, they have to ensure their patients do not think their gynecologist is behaving in a sexual manner. For this to happen, Emerson wrote, (male) gynecologists take pains to appear as medical professionals rather than as men interested in having sex or aroused by what they were seeing and feeling. In this way, they "define the situation" as a professional encounter rather than as a sexual encounter.

Male gynecologists use several strategies to appear as professionals, according to Emerson. For example, they have a (female) nurse present during the exam to help the patient feel comfortable. They also certainly avoid saying anything that might suggest they are sexually aroused. More generally, gynecologists and nurses always act in a nonchalant, matter-of-fact manner, which sends the patient an implicit message: "In the medical world the pelvic area is like any other part of the body; its private and sexual connotations are left behind when you enter the hospital" (Emerson 1970:78).[8] In all these ways, gynecological exams are defined only as medical encounters, and patients are helped to feel as comfortable as possible under rather uncomfortable circumstances.

In another classic study grounded in the symbolic interactionist tradition, Jonathan Rubinstein (1993)[9] spent a year riding around and otherwise interacting with police officers in Philadelphia. He later wrote compellingly about police officers' constant fear for their safety, about how they try to control suspects and other threatening people without drawing their guns, about how they interact with each other and with their superiors, and many other matters.

Key Takeaways

- Functionalism emphasizes the importance of the economy for any society, and the income and self-fulfillment that work often provides.
- Conflict theory highlights the control of the economy by the economic elite, the alienation of work, and various problems in the workplace.
- Symbolic interactionism focuses on interaction in the workplace and how workers perceive many aspects of their work and workplace interaction.

For Your Review

1. Which of the three major sociological approaches to understanding work and the economy do you most prefer? Why?
2. Write a brief essay in which you use a symbolic interactionist approach to understand some aspect of a job you have held or hold now.

12.3 Problems in Work and the Economy

Learning Objectives

1. Outline recent trends in jobs and wages.
2. Discuss the effects of unemployment.
3. Summarize the problems associated with increasing economic inequality.

The economy and the quality and quantity of work certainly affect the lives of all Americans. At the same time, work and the economy give rise to many kinds of problems that also affect millions of Americans. This section examines several of these problems.

The Loss of Jobs

The American economy went into a deep recession in 2008, recovered several years later, and then collapsed in 2020 after the COVID-19 pandemic began. Before these momentous developments, certain ominous trends in the American economy were already evident. These trends involved a general loss of jobs in many sectors and stagnating wages. This situation partly reflected the fact that the United States has joined other industrial nations in moving into a postindustrial economy. In a postindustrial economy, information technology and service jobs replace the machines and manufacturing jobs that are hallmarks of an industrial economy. If physical prowess and skill with one's hands were prerequisites for many industrial jobs, mental prowess and communication skills are prerequisites for postindustrial jobs.

This move to a postindustrial economy has been a mixed blessing for many Americans. The information age has obvious benefits too numerous to mention, but there has also been a cost to the many workers whom postindustrialization and the globalization of the economy have left behind. Since the 1980s, many manufacturing companies moved their plants from American cities to sites in the developing world in Asia and elsewhere, a problem called **capital flight**. Along with the faltering economy, these trends have helped fuel a loss of 7.5 million manufacturing jobs from the American economy since 1980 (Hernandez 2018).[10]

A related problem is **outsourcing**, in which U.S. companies hire workers overseas for customer care, billing services, and other jobs that Americans used to do. These workers numbered more than 14 million in 2015 (Amadeo 2019).[11] Because many of these jobs would otherwise have gone to Americans, outsourcing has been very controversial since it became popular in the early 2000s.

capital flight

The moving of manufacturing companies from U.S. cities to sites in the developing world in Asia and elsewhere.

outsourcing

The hiring by U.S. companies of overseas workers for customer care, billing services, and other jobs that Americans used to do.

Many American jobs have been lost because of outsourcing to other countries.

Source: © Thinkstock

The development of capital flight and outsourcing reflects a more general shift in the U.S. economy from goods-producing jobs to service jobs. Although some of these service jobs, such as many in the financial and computer industries, are high paying, many are in low-wage occupations, such as restaurant and clerical work, that pay less than the goods-producing jobs they replaced. Partly as a result, the average hourly wage (adjusting for inflation) in the United States for workers in the bottom tenth of wages rose by only 4.1 percent from 1979 to 2018. In contrast, wages for people in the top 5 percent of wages rose by 56.1 percent during this period, while wages for those in the top 1 percent of wages rose by 157.3 percent (Gould 2019).[12]

As these figures suggest, social class strongly affects wage growth. An additional comparison reinforces this point: From 1978 to 2018, the average compensation (earnings and other monetary benefits, such as stock options) of chief executive officers (CEOs) of large corporations grew by 940 percent, while that for the typical worker grew by only 12 percent (Mishel and Wolfe 2019).[13] Another way of understanding this disparity is perhaps more striking. In 1965, the average compensation of CEOs was 20 times greater than that of the typical worker; in 2018, their compensation was 221 times greater than that of the typical worker (Mishel and Wolfe 2019).[14] These figures reflect growing economic inequality in the United States.

The Decline of Labor Unions

From the 1870s through the 1930s, labor unions fought companies over issues such as low wages and substandard working conditions.

Source: Everett Historical/Shutterstock.com

One of the most important developments accompanying industrialization in the nineteenth century was the rise of labor unions and their conflict with management over low wages and miserable working conditions (Dubofsky and McCartin 2017).[15] The typical employee worked at least ten hours a day for six or seven days a week, with almost no overtime pay and no paid vacations or holidays. After the Civil War, this situation led to the rise of many labor unions, which then encountered determined opposition from companies, the government, and the courts. Companies told each other which workers were suspected of being union members, and these workers were then prevented from getting jobs. Strikers were often arrested for violating laws prohibiting strikes. When juries began finding them not guilty, employers turned to asking judges for injunctions that prohibited strikes. Workers who then went on strike were held in contempt of court by the judge as juries were kept out of the process. Some strikes ignited a violent reaction by police and company guards, who beat, shot, and killed workers in several strikes. Perhaps the most shameful such incident was the Ludlow Massacre, in which the Colorado National Guard and company guards rained bullets into a tent colony of coal miners and their families in Ludlow, Colorado, in April 1914 and also set the encampment on fire. These actions killed more than five dozen men, women, and children (Mauk 2014).[16]

Labor strife also marked the Great Depression, when masses of people blamed business leaders for their economic plight. Huge sit-ins and other labor protests occurred at auto plants in Detroit. In response, the Congress passed several laws that gave workers a minimum wage, the right to join unions, a maximum-hour workweek, and other rights that Americans now take for granted.

Today labor unions have lost some of their influence, especially as postindustrialization has supplanted the industrial economy and as the United States has lost much of its manufacturing base. Five decades ago, about one-fourth of all private-sector nonagricultural workers belonged to labor unions. By 1985 this figure had dropped to 14.6 percent, and today it stands at only 6.4 percent (Hirsch and Macpherson 2019).[17] In response, labor unions have intensified their efforts to increase their membership, only to find that U.S. labor laws are filled with loopholes that allow companies to prevent their workers from forming a union. For example, after a company's workers vote to join a union, companies can appeal the vote, and it can take several years for courts to order the company to recognize the union. In the meantime, the low wages, substandard working conditions, and other factors that motivated workers to want to join a union are allowed to continue.

Just as the growth of unions during the late nineteenth and early twentieth centuries helped to raise workers' wages, the decline of unions has lowered wages. Two reasons explain this decline (Shierholz 2019).[18] First, union workers earn about 13 percent more than nonunion workers (controlling for experience, education, occupation, and other factors), a phenomenon known as the *union wage premium*. Because fewer workers are now in unions than four decades ago, they are less likely to benefit from this premium. Second, as unions have declined, there has been less pressure on nonunion employers to raise their wages to match union wages.

Because the union wage premium is greater for African Americans and Latinxs than for whites, the wage decline caused by the decline of unions has probably been steeper for those two groups than for whites. It is also true that union workers are more likely than nonunion workers to be covered by employer-sponsored health insurance and also to have lower health premiums and deductibles. The decline of unions has thus meant that the average worker today is less likely to have employer-paid health insurance and, if they do, more likely to have higher premiums and deductibles.

Unemployment

Unemployment is a fact of life. There will always be people who voluntarily quit their jobs, or who just graduated school and are still looking for work. But most unemployed people are involuntarily unemployed, and for them the financial and psychological consequences can be devastating.

Unemployment rates rise and fall with the economy, and the national unemployment rate was as high as 10.2 percent in October 2009 amid the deep recession that began more than a year earlier. It had fallen to 3.5 percent by September 2019, amounting to almost 5.8 million unemployed people, before soaring after the onset of the coronavirus pandemic a few months later and amounting to tens of millions of more people. But whether unemployment is high or low, it always varies by race and ethnicity, with African American and Latinx unemployment rates much higher than the white rate. Unemployment is also higher for younger people than for older people. In September 2019, when the unemployment rate for people ages 20 and older, was about 3.2 percent, the corresponding rate just for teenagers (aged 16–19) was 12.5 percent. The unemployment rate for African Americans in this young age group was a very high 18.3 percent, as compared to 11.9 percent figure for whites in this age group. Meanwhile, the Latinx unemployment rate for this age group was also higher at 15.1 percent (Bureau of Labor Statistics, 2019).[19]

Unemployment figures are misleading in an important respect, as they do not include people who are *underemployed*. Underemployment includes the unemployed and also two other types of people: (a) those who are working part-time but who want to work full-time—the so-called *marginally attached*, and (b) those who have stopped looking for work because they have not been able to find a job. Many economists think that underemployment provides a more accurate measure than unemployment of the number of people with employment problems. For example, when the official unemployment rate in early 2015 was 5.7 percent, the underemployment rate then was twice as high at 11.3 percent (McCloskey 2015).[20]

Several kinds of problems make it difficult for people of color to be hired into jobs and thus contribute to the racial/ethnic disparity in unemployment. The "Applying Social Research" box discusses these problems.

Applying Social Research

Race, Ethnicity, and Employment

As the text discusses, people of color are more likely than whites to be unemployed. While a relative lack of education helps explain these higher rates for people of color, other kinds of problems are also apparent.

One problem is racial discrimination on the part of employers, regardless of how conscious employers are of their discriminatory behavior. Chapter 3 recounted a study by sociologist Devah Pager (2003),[21] who had young white and African American men apply independently in person for various jobs in Milwaukee. These men wore the same type of clothing and reported similar levels of education and other qualifications. Some said they had a criminal record, while others said they had not committed any crimes. In striking evidence of racial discrimination in hiring, African American applicants *without* a criminal record were hired at the same low rate as white applicants *with* a criminal record.

Pager and sociologists Bruce Western and Bart Bonikowski also investigated racial discrimination in another field experiment in New York City (Pager et al. 2009).[22] They had white, African American, and Latinx "testers," all of them "well-spoken, clean-cut young men" (p. 781), apply in person to low-level service jobs (e.g., retail sales and delivery drivers) requiring no more than a high school education; all the testers had similar (hypothetical) qualifications. Almost one-third (31 percent) of white testers received a call back or job offer, compared to only 25.2 percent of Latinx testers and 15.2 percent of African American testers. The researchers concluded that their findings "add to a large research program demonstrating the continuing contribution of discrimination to racial inequality in the post-civil rights era" (p. 794).

Other kinds of evidence also reveal racial discrimination in hiring. Two scholars sent job applications in response to help-wanted ads in Boston and Chicago (Bertrand and Mullainathan 2003).[23] They randomly assigned the applications to feature either a "white-sounding" name (e.g., Emily or Greg) or an "African American–sounding" name (e.g., Jamal and Lakisha). White names received 50 percent more callbacks than African American names for job interviews.

Racial differences in access to the informal networks that are often so important in finding a job also contribute to the racial/ethnic disparity in employment. In a study using data from a nationwide survey of a random sample of Americans, sociologist Steve McDonald and colleagues found that people of color and women are less likely than white males to receive informal word of vacant, high-level supervisory positions (McDonald et al. 2009).[24]

As these studies indicate, research by sociologists and other social scientists reveals that race and ethnicity make a difference in employment prospects for Americans. This body of research reveals clear evidence of discrimination, conscious or unconscious, in hiring and also of racial/ethnic differences in access to the informal networks that are often so important for hiring. By uncovering this evidence, these studies underscore the need to address discrimination, access to informal networks, and other factors that contribute to racial and ethnic disparities in employment.

The Impact of Unemployment

Unemployed people may experience psychological and social problems stemming from their unemployment. Evidence of this fact comes from a Pew Research Center report based on a 2010 survey of two groups of adults: (a) 810 adults who were currently unemployed or had been unemployed since the deep recession that began in December 2007, and (b) 1,093 adults who had never been unemployed during the recession (Morin and Kochhar 2010).[25] The report's title, *Lost Income, Lost Friends—and Loss of Self-Respect*, summarized its major findings.

This line of people looking for a job reminds us that unemployment remains a problem for many Americans. Long-term unemployment often causes various social and psychological difficulties.

Source: Andrey_Popov/Shutterstock.com

Of those who had been unemployed for at least six months (*long-term unemployment*), 44 percent said that the recession had caused "major changes" in their lives, versus only 20 percent of those who had never been unemployed. More than half of the long-term unemployed said their family income had declined, and more than 40 percent said that their family relations had been strained and that they had lost contact with close friends. In another finding, 38 percent said they had "lost some self-respect" from being unemployed. One-third said they were finding it difficult to pay their rent or mortgage, compared to only 16 percent of those who had never been unemployed during the recession. Half had borrowed money from family or friends to pay bills, versus only 18 percent of the never unemployed. Of all the people who had been unemployed, almost half had experienced sleep difficulties, and 5 percent had experienced drug or alcohol problems. All these numbers paint a distressing picture of the social and psychological impact of unemployment during that period's deep recession.

 ## Soaring Unemployment after the Coronavirus Pandemic Hit

After the Coronavirus pandemic began in the United States in March 2020, unemployment claims soared into the millions. This video provides useful information about how to file for unemployment benefits.

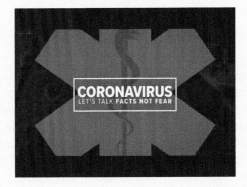

View the video online at: http://www.youtube.com/embed/Ea6r68UOmC4?rel=0

Unemployment also has a significant impact on children whose parent or parents are unemployed. The "Children and Our Future" box discusses this impact.

Children and Our Future

The Hidden Casualties of Unemployment

As unemployment soared in the wake of the deep recession that began in 2007, many more children lived in a household where a parent had become unemployed. By early 2010, 11 percent of American children, or 8.1 million children overall, had an unemployed parent. Just slightly more than two years earlier, this number had been much smaller, 4.8 million. In just over two years, then, the number of children with an unemployed parent grew by two-thirds.

After their parents became unemployed, these children began to suffer various psychological effects. One news report summarized this psychological impact as follows: "For many families across the country, the greatest damage inflicted by this recession has not necessarily been financial, but emotional and psychological. Children, especially, have become hidden casualties, often absorbing more than their parents are fully aware of. Several academic studies have linked parental job loss—especially that of fathers—to adverse impacts in areas like school performance and self-esteem."

The emotional and psychological effects for children of the unemployed occur for at least two reasons. First, unemployed parents tend to experience extra stress and to become withdrawn. Second, married parents and unmarried partners often experience interpersonal conflict when one of them becomes unemployed. Both of these consequences of unemployment in turn affect children in a household where at least one parent is unemployed.

Children suffered in other ways from the rise in unemployment during the deep recession. More children became homeless as their households fell into poverty. In addition, children of an unemployed parent were more likely to repeat a grade or, if they were adolescents, to drop out of school. Child abuse probably also increased in families where a parent became unemployed.

At the time of this writing, unemployment was again beginning to soar because of the coronavirus pandemic. The experience of the deep recession reminds us that the United States needs to do everything possible for the sake of our children to put parents and other adults back to work and to provide income support to the families of the unemployed.

Sources: Lovell and Isaacs 2010; Luo 2009[26]

American Workers amid the COVID-19 Pandemic

The low-wage workforce comprises more than 25 million adults. When the pandemic began in 2020, it affected low-wage workers much more severely than higher-wage workers. This consequence occurred because low-wage workers tend to work in the hospitality, retail, and other service industries. As such, many were laid off when the economy shut down. Because those who were not laid off did not have the kinds of jobs that allowed them to work from home, they had to continue to commute to work and interact with each other and/or with the public. This situation exposed them to the coronavirus. For these reasons, the financial and health effects of the pandemic were much more severe for low-wage workers than for high-wage workers. As the Kaiser Family Foundation observed, "Many low-wage workers were already living in precarious financial situations before the pandemic and may not be able to absorb loss of income or pay health care costs if they become ill" (Garfield et al. 2020).[27]

Corporations

One of the most important but controversial features of modern capitalism is the **corporation**, a formal organization that has a legal existence, including the right to sign contracts, that is separate from that of its members.

Adam Smith (1910/1776),[28] the founder of capitalism, envisioned that individuals would own the means of production and compete for profit, and this is the model the United States followed in its early stage of industrialization. After the Civil War, however, corporations quickly replaced individuals and their families as the owners of the means of production and as the competitors for profit. As corporations grew following the Civil War, they quickly tried to control their markets by, for example, buying up competitors and driving others out of business. To do so, they engaged in bribery, kickbacks, and complex financial schemes of dubious ethics. They also established factories and other workplaces with squalid conditions. Their shady financial practices won their chief executives the name "robber barons" and led the federal government to pass the Sherman Antitrust Act of 1890 designed to prohibit restraint of trade that raised prices (Hillstrom and Hillstrom 2005).[29]

More than a century later, corporations have increased in both number and size. Although several million U.S. corporations exist, most are fairly small. Each of the largest five hundred corporations, however, has annual revenues in the billions of dollars and employs thousands of workers; their combined total assets run into the trillions of dollars (*Fortune* 2019).[30] It is no exaggeration to say they control the nation's economy, as together they produce most of the U.S. private-sector output, employ millions of people, and have revenues equal to most of the U.S. gross domestic product. In many ways, the size and influence of corporations stifle the competition that is one of the hallmarks of capitalism. For example, several markets, including that for breakfast cereals, are controlled by four or fewer corporations. This control reduces competition because it reduces the number of products and competitors, and it thus raises prices to the public (Parenti 2011).[31]

The last few decades have seen the proliferation and rise of the **multinational corporation**, a corporation with headquarters in one nation but with factories and other operations in many other nations. The assets of the largest multinational corporations exceed those of many of the world's nations. Often their foreign operations are in poor nations, whose low wages make them attractive sites for multinational corporation expansion. Many multinational employees in these nations work in sweatshops at very low pay and amid substandard living conditions. Critics of this practice say multinationals not only mistreat workers in poor nations but also exploit these nations' natural resources. In contrast, defenders of the practice say multinationals are bringing jobs to poor nations and helping them achieve economic growth. As this debate illustrates, the dominance of multinational corporations will certainly continue to spark controversy.

As we first discussed in Chapter 8, another controversial aspect of corporations is the white-collar crime in which they engage (Rosoff et al. 2020).[32] Price fixing by corporations costs the U.S. public some $60 billion annually (Simon 2012).[33] Workplace-related illnesses and injuries that could have been prevented if companies had safe workplaces kill about 50,000 workers each year (AFL-CIO 2019).[34] Several thousand Americans die annually from unsafe products, including contaminated food (Barkan 2018).[35] All in all, corporate lawbreaking and neglect probably result in almost 100,000 deaths annually and cost the public nearly $600 billion annually (Barkan 2018).[36]

corporation

An organization that has a legal existence apart from that of its members.

Corporations such as Exxon dominate the U.S. economy. They employ thousands of workers, and their assets total many trillions of dollars.

Source: Image courtesy of David Shankbone, http://commons.wikimedia.org/wiki/File:1251_Avenue_of_the_Americas.JPG.

multinational corporation

A corporation with headquarters in one nation but with factories and other operations in many other nations.

Purdue Pharma Knew How Addictive Opioids Were Twenty Years Ago

Corporations certainly do much good, but they also engage in behavior that eventually kills or injures many Americans. This video discusses how a pharmaceutical company allegedly deceived the public regarding opioids and therefore helped ignite the opioid crisis of the past decade.

View the video online at: http://www.youtube.com/embed/vvaH3MKtoWk?rel=0

In sum, corporations are the dominant actors in today's economy. They provide most of our products and many of our services and employ millions of people. It is impossible to imagine a modern industrial system without corporations. Yet they often stifle competition, break the law, and, according to their critics, exploit people and natural resources in developing nations.

Economic Inequality

In 2011, the Occupy Wall Street movement gave national attention to economic inequality by emphasizing the differences between the "1%" and the "99%." Proclaiming "We are the 99%," they decried the concentration of wealth in the richest of the rich and the growing inequality of the last few decades. (See "People Making a Difference"). The issue of economic inequality merits further attention here.

People Making a Difference

Occupy Wall Street

Before 2011, economic inequality in the United States certainly existed and in fact had increased greatly since the 1970s. However, although economic inequality was a topic of concern to social scientists, it was not a topic of concern to the general news media. Because the news media generally ignored economic inequality, it was also not a topic of concern to the general public.

That all changed beginning on September 17, 2011, when hundreds of people calling themselves "Occupy Wall Street" marched through the financial district in New York City before dozens encamped overnight and for weeks to come. Occupy Wall Street took these actions to protest the role of major banks and corporations in the economic collapse of 2007 and 2008 and to call attention to their dominance over the political process. Within weeks, similar Occupy encampments had spread to more than one hundred cities in the United States and hundreds more across the globe. "We are the 99%," they said again and again, as "occupy" became a verb heard repeatedly throughout the United States.

By winter, almost all Occupy encampments had ended either because of legal crackdowns or because of the weather conditions. By that time, however, the Occupy protesters had won news media attention everywhere. In a December 2011 poll by the Pew Research Center, 44 percent of Americans supported the Occupy Wall Street movement, while 35 percent opposed it. Almost half (48 percent) said they agreed with the concerns raised by the movement, compared to 30 percent who said they disagreed with these concerns. In the same poll, 61 percent said the U.S. economic system "unfairly favors the wealthy," while 36 percent said it was fair to all Americans. In a related area, 77 percent said "there is too much power in the hands of a few rich people and corporations."

As these numbers suggest, Occupy Wall Street succeeded in bringing economic inequality and related issues into the national limelight. In just a few short months in 2011, it made a momentous difference.

Sources: Pew Research Center 2011; vanden Heuvel 2012[37]

Let's start by defining **economic inequality**, which refers to the extent of the economic difference between the rich and the poor. Because most societies are stratified, there will always be some people who are richer or poorer than others, but the key question is *how much* richer or poorer they are. When the gap between them is large, we say that much economic inequality exists; when the gap between them is small, we say that relatively little economic inequality exists.

economic inequality

The extent of the economic difference between the rich and the poor.

FIGURE 12.3 Share of National Income Going to Income Fifths, 2018

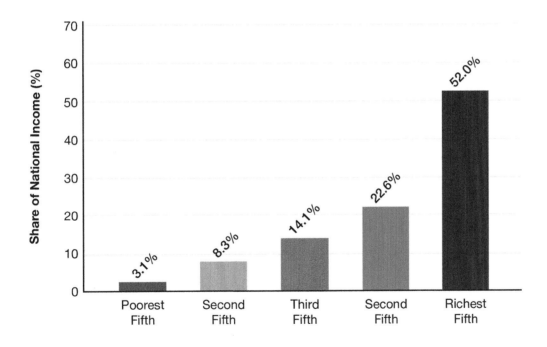

Source: Data from U.S. Census Bureau. 2019. Historical Income Tables: Households.Retrieved from https://www.census.gov/data/tables/time-series/demo/income-poverty/historical-income-households.html.

Considered in this light, the United States has a very large degree of economic inequality. A common way to examine inequality is to rank the nation's families by income from lowest to highest and then to divide this distribution into *fifths*. Thus we have the poorest fifth of the nation's families (or the 20 percent of families with the lowest family incomes), a second fifth with somewhat higher incomes, and so on until we reach the richest fifth of families, or the 20 percent with the highest incomes. We then can see what percentage each fifth has of the nation's *entire* income. Figure 12.3 shows such a calculation for the United States. The poorest fifth enjoys only 3.1 percent of the nation's income, while the richest fifth enjoys 52.0 percent. Another way of saying this is that the richest 20 percent of the population have slightly more income than the remaining 80 percent of the population. The U.S. degree of inequality is the highest among the world's wealthy democracies.

The Role of Tax Policy

As noted earlier for wage data, economic inequality in the United States has increased during the last three decades. The loss of manufacturing jobs and unions accounts for some of this increase. However, a primary reason for the rising inequality has been tax policy. More specifically, the federal government at several junctures has implemented steep cuts in the highest tax rates for income from salaries and wages and especially in tax rates for income from dividends and capital gains. This latter cut is especially important because dividends and capital gains account for a much larger share of the income of wealthy families than the income of ordinary families.

Tax rates for the very wealthy have declined dramatically since the 1970s. This decline has helped fuel a rise in economic inequality.

INTERNAL REVENUE SERVICE

Source: © Thinkstock

Tax policy has so favored the wealthy that in 2017 the 400 richest households paid a lower total tax rate (federal, state, and local taxes) than did any other income group. Several decades ago, these households paid the highest tax rate. To be more specific, the total tax rate for the 400 richest households was 23 percent of total income in 2017, whereas this rate was 70 percent in 1950 (Saez and Zucman 2019).[38]

Critics decry the low tax rates for America's wealthiest. As the director of Citizens for Tax Justice once explained, "The low taxes on capital gains and dividends are why people who make a ton of money, which is largely from investment income, do awfully well. The Warren Buffetts, the hedge fund managers—they pay really low tax rates" (Confessore et al. 2011:A1).[39] This situation prompted Paul Krugman, winner of the Nobel Prize in economics, to ask: "Is there a good reason why the rich should bear a startlingly light tax burden?" His answer: "Such low taxes on the very rich are indefensible" (Krugman 2012:A27).[40]

The Impact of Economic Inequality

Why should we care if economic inequality has increased and if the United States has the highest degree of inequality of all industrial democracies? One answer is that it is a matter of fairness. The United States is not only the wealthiest nation in the world; it is also a nation that historically has stressed that everyone is created equal and that everyone has an equal opportunity to pursue the "American dream" by becoming economically successful. Against this backdrop, a high degree of economic inequality is simply "un-American" and unfair.

Beyond this rather philosophical critique are more practical considerations. First, a high degree of economic inequality is strongly associated with a high degree of poverty and near poverty: If the rich are getting richer, there is normally less wealth to "go around," and the poor get poorer. For the same reason, high economic inequality is also associated with a shrinking of the middle class. In the United States, as both poverty (and near poverty) and wealth have increased, the size of the middle class has reduced, as a former chair of the Council of Economic Advisers has emphasized (Krueger 2012).[41]

Second, a high degree of economic inequality is also associated with low *economic mobility* (the movement of people up or down the socioeconomic ladder) (Krueger 2012).[42] As noted earlier, the United States is the most economically unequal of all industrial democracies. It also has lower economic mobility: Americans born into poverty or near poverty are less likely than their counterparts in other wealthy democracies to be able to move up the socioeconomic ladder (DeParle 2012).[43]

Next, high economic inequality may slow economic growth. This possible effect occurs for at least three reasons (Krueger 2012).[44] First, the wealthy tend to save their money rather than spend it. Second, a shrinking middle class means there is less spending by the middle class to stimulate the economy. Third, workers' morale is likely to be lower in a society with higher economic inequality, and their lower morale decreases their productivity.

Finally, many social scientists consider nations with high degrees of economic inequality to be "unhealthy societies," to quote the title of a book on this issue (Wilkinson 1996).[45] Economic inequality is thought to undermine social cohesion and increase polarization, and also to cause other problems (Fissinger 2017; Stiglitz 2012; Wilkinson and Pickett 2011).[46] Among the world's industrial nations, higher degrees of economic inequality are associated with worse physical and mental health, lower life expectancy, and higher rates of violent crime. High economic inequality, then, is a matter not only of fairness but also of life and death.

Tax Evasion

Another significant problem in the American economy is *tax evasion*. The Internal Revenue Service (IRS) periodically estimates the amount of tax evasion and derives a figure it calls the tax gap: the difference between what Americans owe in federal taxes and what they actually pay. Much of the annual tax gap results from the failure of professionals such as physicians and attorneys to report self-employment income and from the claiming of false deductions by wealthy individuals and families.

In 2019 the IRS released its estimate of the tax gap for the 2008–2010 period (Internal Revenue Service 2019).[47] This estimate averaged $458 billion annually across these three years. After payment of late taxes and certain enforcement efforts, this gap was reduced to $406 billion annually, still an astronomical figure; tax evasion by corporations accounted for $35 billion of this amount. The tax gap is about twenty times greater than the annual economic loss from property crimes such as burglary and motor vehicle theft.

Despite the huge problem of tax evasion, budget cuts during the past decade have greatly weakened the IRS's ability to enforce the tax code. This situation led two critics to wryly observe, "That's good news for corporations and the wealthy" (Kiel and Eisinger 2018).[48]

Crime in the Workplace

An unfortunate fact about work in the United States is crime in the workplace, which is the last problem in work and the economy that we will examine. Two major types of such crime exist: employee theft and workplace violence.

Employee theft costs about $15 billion annually. Workers' dissatisfaction with various aspects of their jobs is a major reason for this form of theft.

Source: © Thinkstock

Employee Theft

employee theft

Theft of objects or money by employees from their workplaces.

pilferage

The stealing of goods by employees from their workplaces.

embezzlement

The stealing of money in its various dimensions (cash, electronic transactions, etc.) by employees from their workplaces.

professional fraud

Stealing by physicians, attorneys, and other professionals from their patients/clients or from the government.

Employee theft takes two forms: pilferage and embezzlement. **Pilferage** involves the stealing of goods, while **embezzlement** involves the stealing of money in its various dimensions (cash, electronic transactions, etc.). Whichever form it takes, employee theft is so common that is has been called a "widespread, pervasive, and costly form of crime" (Langton et al. 2006:539).[49] It is estimated that about 75 percent of employees steal at least once from their employers and that the annual amount of employee theft is $15 billion (National Retail Federation 2015).[50]

Employee theft occurs for many reasons, but a common reason is worker dissatisfaction with various aspects of their job. They may think their wages or salaries are too low, they may feel they have been treated unfairly by their employer, and so forth. As well, many workplaces have informal norms approving of certain forms of theft—for example, it is OK to steal inexpensive objects such as (depending on the workplace) utensils, food, pencils and pens, or toilet paper. Not surprisingly, embezzlement is often more costly to an employer than pilferage; although it can involve just a few dollars from a cash register, it can also involve hundreds of thousands or millions of dollars acquired through more sophisticated means.

When we think of employee theft, we probably usually think of theft by blue-collar or lower white-collar employees. However, physicians, attorneys, and other professionals also steal from their patients/clients or from the government, even if their form of theft is often much more complex and sophisticated than what the term "employee theft" may usually imply. Attorneys may bill their clients for work that was never done, and physicians may bill Medicare or private insurance for patients they never saw or for procedures that were never performed. We call this form of "employee" theft **professional fraud**. Fraud by physicians and other health-care professionals (including nursing homes and medical testing laboratories) is thought to amount to at least $77 billion annually and perhaps as much as $259 billion annually (Insurance Information Institute 2016).[51]

Workplace Violence

About five hundred homicides occur at workplaces every year. The majority of these homicides result from robberies, not from the actions of disgruntled workers.

Many people die or are injured by acts of violence at their workplaces every year in the United States. In 2017, 458 people were slain at their workplaces, according to the National Safety Council (2019),[52] and 18,400 people were injured in assaults. Somewhat older data from the National Crime Victimization Survey suggest that nearly 600,000 acts of violence occur in the workplace annually (Harrell 2011).[53]

In terms of who is involved and the reasons for their involvement, three kinds of workplace homicides are the most common. The first and by far the most common type is homicide as the result of robbery. This category includes the many store clerks, gas station attendants, taxi drivers, and other employees who are slain during a robbery, as well as police who are killed as they try to stop a robbery or apprehend the offender. The second category is homicide committed as an act of domestic violence; in this type, the offender, almost always a man, seeks out his wife or girlfriend (or ex-wife or ex-girlfriend) at her workplace and kills her. The third category involves disgruntled workers who kill one or more people at their workplace whom they blame for problems the killers have been having. Although this type of homicide is the type that the phrase "workplace violence" or "workplace killings" usually brings to mind, it is actually the least common of the three types listed here (Fox 2010).[54]

Source: © Thinkstock

Key Takeaways

- The move to a postindustrial economy has resulted in a loss of jobs and wages in the United States, thanks in part to capital flight and outsourcing.
- Unemployment soared after the Great Recession that began in late 2007. Joblessness has significant consequences for the financial and psychological well-being of the millions of people who are unemployed.
- Economic inequality has greatly increased since the 1970s, thanks in large part to changes in the tax code that favored the wealthy.
- Corporations often engage in white-collar crime that costs hundreds of billions of dollars annually and results in tens of thousands of deaths.

For Your Review

1. Write a brief essay in which you discuss the benefits and disadvantages of corporations in modern society.
2. Write a brief essay in which you summarize the problems associated with increasing economic inequality.
3. Fewer workers belong to labor unions now than just a few decades ago. Do you think this is a good development or a bad development? Explain your answer.
4. Think of a job you now have or your most recent job if you are currently not employed. On a scale of 1 (very dissatisfied) to 10 (very satisfied), how satisfied are you (were you) with your job? Explain why you have (had) this level of satisfaction.

12.4 Improving Work and the Economy

Learning Objective

1. Understand several types of social reform for improving work and the economy.

This chapter has discussed problems related to work and the economy. Critics of capitalism say many of these and other problems arise from the nature of capitalism. According to this way of thinking, capitalism as an economic system emphasizes competition and thus a "winner takes all" mentality. In this kind of system, there are many losers, and there is also unbridled greed for ever greater wealth. Further, because there is relatively little government regulation in the free-market system that is a hallmark of capitalism, large corporations are left relatively free to engage in behavior that advances their profits but that also stifles competition, harms the environment, and causes other social ills. Regardless of the merits of this general critique, capitalism is not about to disappear. Any improvement in work and the economy, then, must stem from social reforms based on sound social research. This chapter's discussion points to several important problems that must be addressed.

One problem is racial and ethnic discrimination in hiring and employment. Several kinds of studies, but especially field experiments involving job applicants who are similar except for their race and ethnicity, provide powerful evidence of continuing discrimination despite federal and state laws banning it. This evidence certainly suggests the need for stronger enforcement of existing laws against racial and ethnic bias in employment and for public education campaigns to alert workers to signs of this type of discrimination.

A second problem concerns worker morale. Economic inequality and a faltering economy continue to threaten to undermine worker morale and hence worker productivity. Individual employers can do little about these two fundamental problems in the larger economy, but they can do something about worker morale. In this regard, this chapter discussed the importance of coworker friendships for workers' satisfaction with their jobs and for their more general individual well-being. In view of this importance, employers and employees alike should make special efforts to promote coworker friendships. Because work is such an important part of most people's lives, these efforts should prove beneficial for many reasons. Employers should also take other measures to improve worker morale, including improvements in wages and working conditions.

A third problem is unemployment. Sociologists, psychologists, and other scholars have documented the social and emotional consequences of unemployment. The effects of unemployment go far beyond the loss of money. Revealed by much research, these consequences sometimes seem forgotten in national debates over whether to extend unemployment insurance benefits. But unemployment does have a human face, and it is essential to provide monetary benefits and other kinds of help for the unemployed.

A fourth problem is corporate misbehavior. As this chapter discussed, corporations are essential to the U.S. economy but also cause great harm. It is not an exaggeration to say that corporate crime is rampant and that it goes largely unpunished. Stricter federal and state oversight of and sanctions against corporate misbehavior are needed.

A fifth problem is economic inequality. The degree of inequality has grown during the past few decades, thanks in large part to changes in the tax codes that greatly favored the wealthy. Restoring tax rates to their standards before the 1980s would help to lessen economic inequality and thus help lessen the problems arising from this type of inequality (Saez and Zucman 2019).[55] In a related area, many corporations pay a much lower tax rate than the official tax rate for them because of various loopholes and shelters in the federal tax code. Curtailing or ending these loopholes and shelters will help greatly to increase federal revenue. As the advocacy group Citizens for Tax Justice once observed, "Closing the loopholes will have real benefits, including a fairer tax system, reduced federal budget deficits and more resources to improve our roads, bridges and schools—things that are really important for economic development here in the United States" (Kocieniewski 2011:B1).[56]

To improve the economy and create many jobs, many observers say the federal government needs to follow the example of Western Europe by expanding its role in the economy.

Source: © Thinkstock

More generally, it is worth noting a recommendation of many observers concerning the federal government's role in the economy. These observers say the government must follow the example of other wealthy democracies by taking a more active role in improving the national infrastructure, job training, and research and development, and in more generally providing incentives for large corporations to invest their resources in job creation (Jacobs 2012).[57]

In this regard, a comprehensive approach involving job-creation funding is essential (Fieldhouse and Thiess 2011).[58] This approach would involve federal funding and/or budgetary policy reform in the following areas: (1) funding for the renovation of schools, improvement in transportation, and improvements in other components of the national infrastructure; (2) funding for the hiring of thousands of teachers, child-care workers, and community service workers; and (3) expansion of unemployment insurance benefits, both to help the families of the unemployed and to give them money that they will spend to help stimulate the economy.

Taken together, these measures promise to create millions of jobs. Because these jobs would stimulate the economy and increase tax revenue, these measures would help to pay for themselves. Additional funding for these measures would come from raising tax rates on the very wealthy, as discussed earlier, and from other types of tax reform, including ending tax loopholes for the oil and gas industry and implementing a "financial speculation tax" (Fieldhouse and Thiess 2011).[59] This last type of tax reform would involve a small tax on all stock transactions, with a 0.5 percent tax raising about $80 billion annually (Bivens 2011).[60]

More generally, recall that the social democracies of Scandinavia have combined democratic freedom and economic prosperity. Although there are certainly no signs that the United States is about to follow their example, our nation also has much to learn from these societies as it considers how best to rebuild its economy and to help the millions of people who are unemployed or underemployed.

Key Takeaways

- Certain social reforms are necessary to improve aspects of work and the economy.
- Returning tax codes to their rates before the 1980s will help lessen economic inequality.
- Stricter federal and state oversight of corporate behavior is needed to help address corporate crime.
- A greater investment of federal funding in job creation and the raising of taxes for the very wealthy is necessary to create jobs while stimulating the economy.

For Your Review

1. Write a brief essay that summarizes any three strategies for improving work and the economy.
2. To what extent, if any, do you think capitalism is to blame for the problems in work and the economy discussed in this chapter? Explain your answer.

12.5 End-of-Chapter Material

Summary

1. Capitalism and socialism are the two primary types of economic systems in the world today. Capitalism involves private ownership, the pursuit of profit, and competition for profit, while socialism involves the collective ownership of goods and resources and efforts for the common good. Several nations practice democratic socialism, which is meant to combine the best of capitalism and socialism.

2. According to functionalism, the economy makes society possible by providing essential goods and services, while work gives people income and self-fulfillment. According to conflict theory, work is alienating, and the economic elite uses its control of the economy to maintain their elite position. Symbolic interactionism focuses on social interaction in the workplace and on how employees perceive the work they do.

3. Problems in work and the economy include the following: (a) the loss of jobs and wages; (b) the decline of labor unions; (c) unemployment; (d) corporate misbehavior; (e) rising economic inequality; (f) tax evasion; and (g) workplace crime. Several of these problems considerably worsened with the onset of the COVID-19 pandemic in early 2020.

4. Social reforms based on sound social science research are needed to improve work and the economy. Two important reforms would involve stricter enforcement of laws against racial discrimination in hiring and employment and of penalties for corporate crime.

Using What You Know

You graduated from college a year ago and have begun working in sales for a "big box" electronics company. You've become good friends with a coworker, with whom you often "hang out" at bars and the occasional party. However, one day you notice this coworker pocketing a smartphone, and you realize that a theft is occurring. What, if anything, do you do? Explain your answer.

What You Can Do

To help deal with the work and economy problems discussed in this chapter, you may wish to do any of the following:

1. Start or join a group that tries to educate the public about economic inequality.
2. Assist a local labor union in its efforts to have safer workplaces.

Endnotes

1. Cromie, Elaine. 2019. "Why Gm Workers Are Striking." *npr.org* September 20:https://www.npr.org/sections/pictureshow/2019/09/20/762347761/why-gm-workers-are-striking.

2. Bowles, Paul. 2012. Capitalism. New York: Longman; Cohen, G. A. (2009). *Why not socialism?* Princeton, NJ: Princeton University Press; Cohen, G.A. 2009. Why Not Socialism? Princeton: Princeton University Press.

3. Russell, James W. 2018. *Double Standard: Social Policy in Europe and the United States*. Lanham, MD: Rowman & Littlefield.

4. Russell, James W. 2018. Double Standard: Social Policy in Europe and the United States. Lanham, MD: Rowman & Littlefield; Sejersted, Francis. 2011. The Age of Social Democracy: Norway and Sweden in the Twentieth Century. Translated by R. Daly. Princeton: Princeton University Press.

5. Bureau of Labor Statistics. 2019. *2019 Employment and Earnings Online*. Washington, DC: Bureau of Labor Statistics, U.S. Department of Labor https://www.bls.gov/opub/ee/home.htm.

6. McGuire, Gail M. 2007. "Intimate Work: A Typology of the Social Support That Workers Provide to Their Network Members." *Work and Occupations* 34:125-47.

7. Emerson, Joan P. 1970. "Behavior in Private Places: Sustaining Definitions of Reality in Gynecological Examinations." Pp. 74-97 in Recent Sociology, Vol. 2, edited by H. P. Dreitzel. New York: Collier.

8. Emerson, Joan P. 1970. "Behavior in Private Places: Sustaining Definitions of Reality in Gynecological Examinations." Pp. 74-97 in *Recent Sociology*, Vol. 2, edited by H. P. Dreitzel. New York: Collier.

9. Rubinstein, Jonathan. 1993. *City Police*. New York: Farrar, Straus and Giroux.

10. Hernandez, Richard. 2018. "The Fall of Employment in the Manufacturing Sector." *Monthly Labor Review* August:https://www.bls.gov/opub/mlr/2018/beyond-bls/the-fall-of-employment-in-the-manufacturing-sector.htm.

11. Amadeo, Kimberly. 2019. "How Outsourcing Jobs Affects the U.S. Economy." *The Balance* July 23:https://www.thebalance.com/how-outsourcing-jobs-affects-the-u-s-economy-3306279.

12. Gould, Elise. 2019. *State of Working America: Wages 2018*. Washington, DC: Economic Policy Institute.

13. Mishel, Lawrence and Julia Wolfe. 2019. *CEO Compensation Has Grown 940% since 1978*. Washington, DC: Economic Policy Institute.

14. Mishel, Lawrence and Julia Wolfe. 2019. *CEO Compensation Has Grown 940% since 1978*. Washington, DC: Economic Policy Institute.

15. Dubofsky, Melvyn and Joseph A. McCartin. 2017. *Labor in America: A History Malden*, MA: Wiley-Blackwell.

16. Mauk, Ben. 2014. "The Ludlow Massacre Still Matters." *The New Yorker* April 18:https://www.newyorker.com/business/currency/the-ludlow-massacre-still-matters.

17. Hirsch, Barry and David Macpherson. 2019. "Union Membership and Coverage Database from the CPS" http://unionstats.com.

18. Shierholz, Heidi. 2019. *Working People Have Been Thwarted in Their Efforts to Bargain for Better Wages by Attacks on Unions*. Washington, DC: Economic Policy Institute.

19. Bureau of Labor Statistics. 2019. *2019 Employment and Earnings Online*. Washington, DC: Bureau of Labor Statistics, U.S. Department of Labor https://www.bls.gov/opub/ee/home.htm.

20. McCloskey, Abby. 2015. "More Than One in 10 American Workers Unemployed or Underemployed." *Forbes* February 18:https://www.forbes.com/sites/abbymccloskey/2015/02/18/more-than-one-in-ten-workers-unemployed-or-underemployed/#2b290762122b.

21. Pager, Devah. 2003. "The Mark of a Criminal Record." *American Journal of Sociology* 108:937-975.

22. Pager, Devah, Bart Bonikowski and Bruce Western. 2009. "Discrimination in a Low-Wage Labor Market: A Field Experiment." *American Sociological Review* 74(5):777-99.

23. Bertrand, Marianne and Sendhil Mullainathan. 2003. "Are Emily and Greg More Employable Than Lakisha and Jamal? A Field Experiment on Labor Market Discrimination." *National Bureau of Economic Research Working Paper* No. 9873 http://papers.nber.org/papers/w9873.pdf.

24. McDonald, Steve, Lin Nan and Dan Ao. 2009. "Networks of Opportunity: Gender, Race, and Job Leads." *Social Problems* 56(3):385-402.

25. Morin, Rich and Rakesh Kochhar. 2010. *Lost Income, Lost Friends—and Loss of Self-Respect: The Impact of Long-Term Unemployment*. Washington, DC: Pew Research Center.

26. Lovell, Phillip and Julia B. Isaacs. 2010. *Families of the Recession: Unemployed Parents & Their Children*. Washington, DC: The Brookings Institution; Luo, Michael. 2009. "Job Woes Exacting a Toll on Family Life." *The New York Times* November 12:A1.

27. Garfield, Rachel, Matthew Rae, Gary Claxton and Kendal Orgera. 2020. *Double Jeopardy: Low Wage Workers at Risk for Health and Financial Implications of Covid-19*. San Francisco: Kaiser Family Foundation.

28. Smith, Adam. 1910 (1776). *The Wealth of Nations*, Edited by London.

29. Hillstrom, Kevin and Laurie Collier Hillstrom, eds. 2005. *The Industrial Revolution in America*. Santa Barbara, CA: ABC-CLIO.

30. Fortune. 2019, "Fortune 500." Retrieved January 14, 2012 (https://fortune.com/fortune500/2019/).

31. Parenti, Michael. 2011. *Democracy for the Few*. Belmont, CA: Wadsworth Publishing.

32. Rosoff, Stephen M., Henry N. Pontell and Robert Tillman. 2020. *Profit without Honor: White Collar Crime and the Looting of America*. Hoboken, NJ: Pearson.

33. Simon, David R. 2012. *Elite Deviance*. Upper Saddle River, NJ: Pearson.

34. AFL-CIO. 2019. *Death on the Job: The Toll of Neglect, 2019*. Washington, DC: AFL-CIO.

35. Barkan, Steven E. 2018. *Criminology: A Sociological Understanding*. Upper Saddle River, NJ: Pearson.

36. Barkan, Steven E. 2018. *Criminology: A Sociological Understanding*. Upper Saddle River, NJ: Pearson.

37. Pew Research Center. 2011, "Frustration with Congress Could Hurt Republican Incumbents." Retrieved January 19, 2012 (http://www.people-press.org/files/legacy-pdf/12-15-11 Congress and Economy release.pdf); vanden Heuvel, Katrina. 2012. "The Occupy Effect." https://www.thenation.com/article/occupy-effect/.

38. Saez, Emmanuel and Gabriel Zucman. 2019. *The Triumph of Injustice: How the Rich Dodge Taxes and How to Make Them Pay*. New York: W.W. Norton.

39. Confessore, Nicholas, David Kocieniewski and Ashley Parker. 2011. "Romney Shares Some Tax Data; Critics Pounce." *The New York Times* January 18:A1.

40. Krugman, Paul. 2012. "Taxes at the Top." *The New York Times* January 20:A27.

41. Krueger, Alan B. 2012, "The Rise and Consequences of Inequality in the United States." Retrieved January 19, 2012 (http://www.american-progress.org/events/2012/01/pdf/krueger.pdf).

42. Krueger, Alan B. 2012, "The Rise and Consequences of Inequality in the United States." Retrieved January 19, 2012 (http://www.american-progress.org/events/2012/01/pdf/krueger.pdf).

43. DeParle, Jason. 2012. "Harder for Americans to Rise from Lower Rungs." *The New York Times* January 5:A1.

44. Krueger, Alan B. 2012, "The Rise and Consequences of Inequality in the United States." Retrieved January 19, 2012 (http://www.american-progress.org/events/2012/01/pdf/krueger.pdf).

45. Wilkinson, Richard G. 1996. *Unhealthy Societies: The Afflications of Inequality.* New York: Routledge.

46. Fissinger, Michael. 2017. "The Social Costs of Income Inequality." *Fordham Political Review* November 7:http://fordhampoliticalreview.org/the-social-costs-of-income-inequality/; Stiglitz, Joseph E. 2012. *The Price of Inequality: How Today's Divided Society Endangers Our Future* New York: W.W. Norton; Wilkinson, Richard and Kate Pickett. 2011. *The Spirit Level: Why Greater Equality Makes Societies Stronger.* New York: Bloomsbury Press.

47. Internal Revenue Service. 2019. *Tax Gap Estimates for Tax Years 2008–2010.* Washington, DC: Internal Revenue Service https://www.irs.gov/pub/newsroom/tax gap estimates for 2008 through 2010.pdf.

48. Kiel, Paul and Jesse Eisinger. 2018. "How the Irs Was Gutted." *ProPublica* December 11:https://www.propublica.org/article/how-the-irs-was-gutted.

49. Langton, Lynn, Nicole Leeper Piquero and Richard C. Hollinger. 2006. "An Empirical Test of the Relationship between Employee Theft and Low Self-Control." *Deviant Behavior* 27:537-65.

50. National Retail Federation. 2015. "National Retail Security Survey 2015."https://nrf.com/resources/retail-library/national-retail-security-survey-2015.

51. Insurance Information Institute. 2016. *Insurance Fraud*: http://www.iii.org/issues_updates/insurance-fraud.html.

52. National Safety Council. 2019. "Assaults Fourth Leading Cause of Workplace Deaths." https://www.nsc.org/work-safety/safety-topics/workplace-violence.

53. Harrell, Erika. 2011. *Workplace Violence, 1993-2009.* Washington, DC: Bureau of Justice Statistics, U.S. Department of Justice.

54. Fox, James Alan. 2010. "Workplace Homicide: What Is the Risk?". http://boston.com/community/blogs/crime_punishment/2010/08/workplace_homicide_the_risks.html.

55. Saez, Emmanuel and Gabriel Zucman. 2019. *The Triumph of Injustice: How the Rich Dodge Taxes and How to Make Them Pay.* New York: W.W. Norton.

56. Kocieniewski, David. 2011. "Biggest Public Firms Paid Little US Tax, Study Says." *The New York Times* November 3:A1.

57. Jacobs, E. (2012). *Growth through innovation: Lessons for the United States from the German labor market miracle.* Washington, DC: Brookings Institution.

58. Fieldhouse, Andrew and Rebecca Thiess. 2011. "The Restore the American Dream for the 99% Act: An Analysis of Job-Creation Provisions." Washington, DC: Economic Policy Institute.

59. Fieldhouse, Andrew and Rebecca Thiess. 2011. "The Restore the American Dream for the 99% Act: An Analysis of Job-Creation Provisions." Washington, DC: Economic Policy Institute.

60. Bivens, Josh. 2011. "Truly Shared Sacrifice Includes Wall Street." (http://www.epi.org/blog/shared-sacrifice-wall-street-financial-specula-tion-tax/).

CHAPTER 13
Health and Health Care

Social Problems in the News

"More Than Half of Cleveland Children Live in Poverty," the headline said. New data from the U.S. Census showed that 50.5 percent of children in Cleveland, Ohio, were living in poverty in 2019. An official with the city's Center for Community Solutions emphasized this troubling statistic's implications: "Children who live in poverty are much more likely to go to school hungry and are then less prepared to learn. Numerous studies link the tensions of growing up poor to different long-term health impacts."

Source: Mosby 2019[1]

This news story reminds us that social class is linked to health and illness, and it illustrates just one of the many ways in which health and health care are urgent problems in our society. Accordingly, this chapter examines these problems. Its discussion is based on the common sociological view that health and illness are not just medical problems but social problems.

Unlike physicians, sociologists and other public health scholars do not try to understand why any one person becomes ill. Instead, they typically examine rates of illness to explain why people from certain social backgrounds are more likely than those from others to become sick. Here, as we will see, our social backgrounds—our social class, race and ethnicity, gender, and other aspects—make a critical difference.

The fact that our social backgrounds affect our health may be difficult for many of us to accept. We all know someone who has died from a serious illness or currently suffers from one. There is always a medical cause of this person's illness, and physicians do their best to try to cure it and prevent it from recurring. Sometimes they succeed; sometimes they fail. Whether someone suffers a serious illness is often simply a matter of bad luck or bad genes: We can do everything right and still become ill. In saying that our social backgrounds affect our health, sociologists do not deny any of these possibilities. They simply remind us that our social backgrounds also play an important role.

With this basic understanding in mind, we now turn to sociological perspectives on health and health care. As you proceed through the chapter, please keep in mind that the 2020 COVID-19 pandemic both manifested and aggravated the many problems of health and health care discussed in this chapter.

A sociological approach emphasizes that our social class, race and ethnicity, and gender, among other aspects of our social backgrounds, influence our levels of health and illness.

Source: Rawpixel.com/Shutterstock.com

13.1 Sociological Perspectives on Health and Health Care

Learning Objective

1. List the assumptions of the functionalist, conflict, and symbolic interactionist perspectives on health and medicine.

health

The extent of a person's physical, mental, and social well-being.

medicine

The social institution that seeks to prevent, diagnose, and treat illness and to promote health in its various dimensions.

health care

The provision of medical services to prevent, diagnose, and treat health problems.

Before discussing these perspectives, we must first define three key concepts—health, medicine, and health care—that lie at the heart of their explanations and of this chapter's discussion. **Health** refers to the extent of a person's physical, mental, and social well-being. As this definition suggests, health is a multidimensional concept. Although the three dimensions of health just listed often affect each other, it is possible for someone to be in good physical health and poor mental health, or vice versa. **Medicine** refers to the social institution that seeks to prevent, diagnose, and treat illness and to promote health in its various dimensions. This social institution in the United States is vast, to put it mildly, and involves millions of people (physicians, nurses, dentists, therapists, medical records technicians, and many other occupations). Finally, **health care** refers to the provision of medical services to prevent, diagnose, and treat health problems.

With these definitions in mind, we now turn to sociological explanations of health and health care. As usual, the major sociological perspectives that we have discussed throughout this book offer different types of explanations, but together they provide us with a more comprehensive understanding than any one approach can do by itself. Table 13.1 summarizes what they say.

TABLE 13.1 Theory Snapshot

Theoretical perspective	Major assumptions
Functionalism	Good health and effective medical care are essential for the smooth functioning of society. Patients must perform the "sick role" in order to be perceived as legitimately ill and to be exempt from their normal obligations. The physician-patient relationship is hierarchical: The physician provides instructions, and the patient needs to follow them.
Conflict theory	Social inequality characterizes the quality of health and the quality of health care. People from disadvantaged social backgrounds are more likely to become ill and to receive inadequate health care. Partly to increase their incomes, physicians have tried to control the practice of medicine and to define social problems as medical problems.
Symbolic interactionism	Health and illness are *social constructions*: Physical and mental conditions have little or no objective reality but instead are considered healthy or ill conditions only if they are defined as such by a society. Physicians "manage the situation" to display their authority and medical knowledge.

The Functionalist Approach

As conceived by Talcott Parsons (1951),[2] the functionalist perspective emphasizes that good health and effective medical care are essential for a society's ability to function. Ill health impairs our ability to perform our roles in society, and if too many people are unhealthy, society's functioning and stability suffer. This is especially true for premature death, said Parsons, because it prevents individuals from fully carrying out all their social roles and thus represents a "poor return" to society for the various costs of pregnancy, birth, child care, and socialization of the individual who ends up dying early. Poor medical care is likewise dysfunctional for society, as people who are ill face greater difficulty in becoming healthy and people who are healthy are more likely to become ill.

For a person to be considered *legitimately* sick, said Parsons, several expectations must be met. He referred to these expectations as the **sick role**. First, sick people should not be perceived as having caused their own health problem. If we eat high-fat food, become obese, and have a heart attack, we evoke less sympathy than if we had practiced good nutrition and maintained a proper weight.

sick role

Expectations of how people are supposed to think and act when they are ill.

Second, sick people must want to get well. If they do not want to get well or, worse yet, are perceived as faking their illness or malingering after becoming healthier, they are no longer considered legitimately ill by the people who know them or, more generally, by society itself.

Third, sick people are expected to have their illness confirmed by a physician or other health-care professional and to follow the professional's instructions in order to become well. If a sick person fails to do so, she or he again loses the right to perform the sick role.

Talcott Parsons wrote that for a person to be perceived as legitimately ill, several expectations, called the sick role, must be met. These expectations include the perception that the person did not cause her or his own health problem.

If all these expectations are met, said Parsons, sick people are treated as sick by their family, their friends, and other people they know, and they become exempt from their normal obligations to all these people. Sometimes they are even told to stay in bed when they want to remain active.

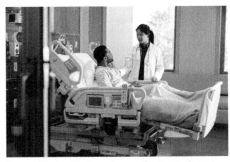

In discussing the sick role, Parsons emphasized the need for patients to follow their physician's instructions. He thus viewed the physician-patient relationship as hierarchical: The physician gives the orders (or, more accurately, provides advice and instructions), and the patient follows them.

Source: Monkey Business Images/Shutterstock.com

Parsons was certainly right in emphasizing the importance of individuals' good health for society's health, but his perspective has been criticized for several reasons. First, his idea of the sick role applied more to acute (short-term) illness than to chronic (long-term) illness. Although his discussion implied a person temporarily enters a sick role and leaves it soon after following adequate medical care, people with chronic illnesses can be locked into a sick role for a very long time or even permanently. Second, Parsons's discussion ignored the fact, mentioned earlier, that our social backgrounds affect the likelihood of becoming ill and the quality of medical care we receive. Third, Parsons wrote approvingly of the hierarchy implicit in the physician-patient relationship. Many experts say today that patients need to reduce this hierarchy by asking more questions of their physicians and by taking a more active role in maintaining their health. To the extent that physicians do not always provide the best medical care, the hierarchy that Parsons favored is at least partly to blame.

The Conflict Approach

The conflict approach emphasizes inequality in the quality of health and health-care delivery. The quality of health and health care differs greatly around the world and within the United States. Society's inequities along social class, race and ethnicity, gender, and other dimensions are reproduced in our health and health care. People from disadvantaged social backgrounds are more likely to become ill, and once they do become ill, inadequate health care makes it more difficult for them to become well. As we will see, the evidence of disparities in health and health care is vast and dramatic.

The conflict approach also critiques efforts by physicians over the decades to control the practice of medicine and to define various social problems as medical ones. Physicians' motivation for doing so has been both good and bad. On the good side, they have believed they are the most qualified professionals to diagnose problems and to treat people who have these problems. On the negative side, they have also recognized that their financial status will improve if they succeed in characterizing social problems as medical problems and in monopolizing the treatment of these problems. Once these problems become "medicalized," their possible social roots and thus potential solutions are neglected.

The history of obstetrical care provides an example of this critique. In most of human history, midwives or their equivalent were the people who helped pregnant women deliver their babies. In the nineteenth century, physicians claimed they were better trained than midwives and won legislation giving them authority to deliver babies. They may have honestly felt that midwives were inadequately trained, but they also fully recognized that obstetrical care would be quite lucrative (Ehrenreich and English 2005).[3]

According to conflict theory, physicians have often sought to define various social problems as medical problems. An example is the development of the diagnosis of ADHD, or attention deficit/hyperactivity disorder.

Source: © Thinkstock

In another example, many hyperactive children are now diagnosed with ADHD, or attention deficit/hyperactivity disorder. A generation or more ago, they would have been considered merely as overly active. After Ritalin, a drug that reduces hyperactivity, was developed, their behavior came to be considered a medical problem, the ADHD diagnosis was increasingly applied, and tens of thousands of children went to physicians' offices and were given Ritalin or similar drugs. The definition of their behavior as a medical problem was very lucrative for physicians and for the company that developed Ritalin, and it also obscured the possible roots of their behavior in inadequate parenting, stultifying schools, or even gender socialization, as most hyperactive kids are boys (Conrad 2008; Macht 2017).[4]

Critics say the conflict approach's assessment of health and medicine is overly harsh and its criticism of physicians' motivation too cynical. Scientific medicine has greatly improved the health of people around the world. Although physicians are certainly motivated, as many people are, by economic considerations, their efforts to extend their scope into previously nonmedical areas also stem from honest beliefs that people's health and lives will improve if these efforts succeed. Certainly there is some truth in this criticism of the conflict approach, but the evidence of inequality in health and medicine and of the negative aspects of the medical establishment's motivation for extending its reach still supports conflict theory.

The Symbolic Interactionist Approach

The symbolic interactionist approach emphasizes that health and illness are *social constructions*. This means that various physical and mental conditions have little or no objective reality but instead are considered healthy or ill conditions only if they are defined as such by a society and its members (Hanson 2018).[5] The ADHD example just discussed also illustrates symbolic interactionist theory's concerns, as a behavior that was not previously considered an illness came to be defined as one after the development of Ritalin. In another example first discussed in Chapter 7, in the late 1800s opium use was quite common in the United States, as opiates were included in numerous over-the-counter products. Their use was considered neither a major health nor legal problem. That changed by the end of the century, as prejudice against Chinese Americans led to the banning of the opium dens (similar to today's bars) they frequented, and calls for the banning of opium led to federal legislation early in the twentieth century that banned most opium products except by prescription (Musto 2002).[6]

In a more current example, an attempt to redefine obesity is now under way in the United States. Obesity is a known health risk, but a "fat pride" or "fat acceptance" movement composed mainly of heavy individuals is arguing that obesity's health risks are exaggerated and calling attention to society's discrimination against overweight people (Saguy 2013).[7] Although such discrimination is certainly unfortunate, critics say the movement is going too far in trying to minimize obesity's risks (Diamond 2011).[8]

Fat Pride and Fat Acceptance

Although obesity is a health risk, a "fat pride" movement is attempting to redefine obesity as something that is not a health problem and is also calling attention to discrimination against obese and overweight people. This effort illustrates the emphasis in the symbolic interactionist approach on health and illness as social constructions.

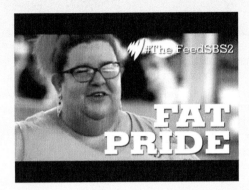

View the video online at: http://www.youtube.com/embed/yP9zIW2TTgc?rel=0

The symbolic interactionist approach has also provided important studies of the interaction between patients and health-care professionals. Consciously or not, physicians "manage the situation" to display their authority and medical knowledge. Patients usually have to wait a long time for the physician to show up, and the physician is often in a white lab coat; the physician is also often addressed as "Doctor," while patients are often called by their first name. Physicians typically use complex medical terms to describe a patient's illness instead of the more simple terms used by laypeople and the patients themselves.

Management of the situation is perhaps especially important during a gynecological exam, as first discussed in Chapter 12. When the physician is a man, this situation is fraught with potential embarrassment and uneasiness because a man is examining and touching a woman's genital area. Under these circumstances, the physician must act in a purely professional manner. He must indicate no personal interest in the woman's body and must instead treat the exam no differently from any other type of exam. To further "desex" the situation and reduce any potential uneasiness, a female nurse is often present during the exam.

Critics fault the symbolic interactionist approach for implying that no illnesses have objective reality. Many serious health conditions do exist and put people at risk for their health regardless of what they or their society think. Critics also say the approach neglects the effects of social inequality for health and illness. Despite these possible faults, the symbolic interactionist approach reminds us that health and illness do have a subjective as well as an objective reality.

Key Takeaways

- A sociological understanding emphasizes the influence of people's social backgrounds on the quality of their health and health care. A society's culture and social structure also affect health and health care.
- The functionalist approach emphasizes that good health and effective health care are essential for a society's ability to function, and it views the physician-patient relationship as hierarchical.

- The conflict approach emphasizes inequality in the quality of health and in the quality of health care.
- The interactionist approach emphasizes that health and illness are social constructions; physical and mental conditions have little or no objective reality but instead are considered healthy or ill conditions only if they are defined as such by a society and its members.

For Your Review

1. Which approach—functionalist, conflict, or symbolic interactionist—do you most favor regarding how you understand health and health care? Explain your answer.
2. Think of the last time you visited a physician or another health-care professional. In what ways did this person come across as an authority figure possessing medical knowledge? In formulating your answer, think about the person's clothing, body position and body language, and other aspects of nonverbal communication.

13.2 Global Aspects of Health and Health Care

Learning Objectives

1. Describe how the nations of the world differ in important indicators of health and illness.
2. Explain the health-care model found in industrial nations other than the United States.

As we have seen in previous chapters, understanding what happens in other societies helps us to understand what happens in our own society. This section's discussion of health and health care across the globe, then, helps shed some light on what is good and bad about U.S. health and medicine.

International Disparities in Health and Illness

The nations of the world differ dramatically in the quality of their health and health care. The poorest nations suffer terribly. Their people suffer from poor nutrition, unsafe water, inadequate sanitation, rampant disease, and inadequate health care. One disease they suffer from is HIV/AIDS, which has killed more than 35 million people worldwide since emerging in the 1980s. Today nearly 37 million people have HIV, while AIDS kills more than 900,000 people, most of them in Africa, annually (World Health Organization 2018).[9] HIV/AIDS and these health problems produce high rates of infant mortality and maternal mortality and high death rates. For all these reasons, people in the poorest nations have shorter life spans than those in the richest nations.

Most of the 37 million people worldwide who have HIV/AIDS live in sub-Saharan Africa. This terrible fact illustrates just one of the many health problems that people in poor nations suffer.

Source: Herb Klein/Shutterstock.com

 ### Saving Mothers, Giving Life Halves Maternal Deaths

Maternal mortality is a serious problem in the low-income nations of Africa and elsewhere. This video describes a comprehensive effort to save pregnant women's lives in sub-Saharan Africa.

View the video online at: http://www.youtube.com/embed/xdfY-r414GY?rel=0

Child mortality (number of deaths before age 5 per 1,000 live births) illustrates the dire situation of the poorest nations. Figure 13.1 compares this outcome for nations grouped into four income categories. The striking contrast across these four groups provides dramatic evidence of the health problems poor nations face. When, as Figure 13.1 indicates, 68 children in the poorest nations die before their fifth birthday for every 1,000 live births (equivalent to almost 7 out of 100), the poor nations have serious health problems indeed.

FIGURE 13.1 Child Mortality for Low-Income, Lower-Middle-Income, Higher-Middle-Income, and High-Income Nations, 2018

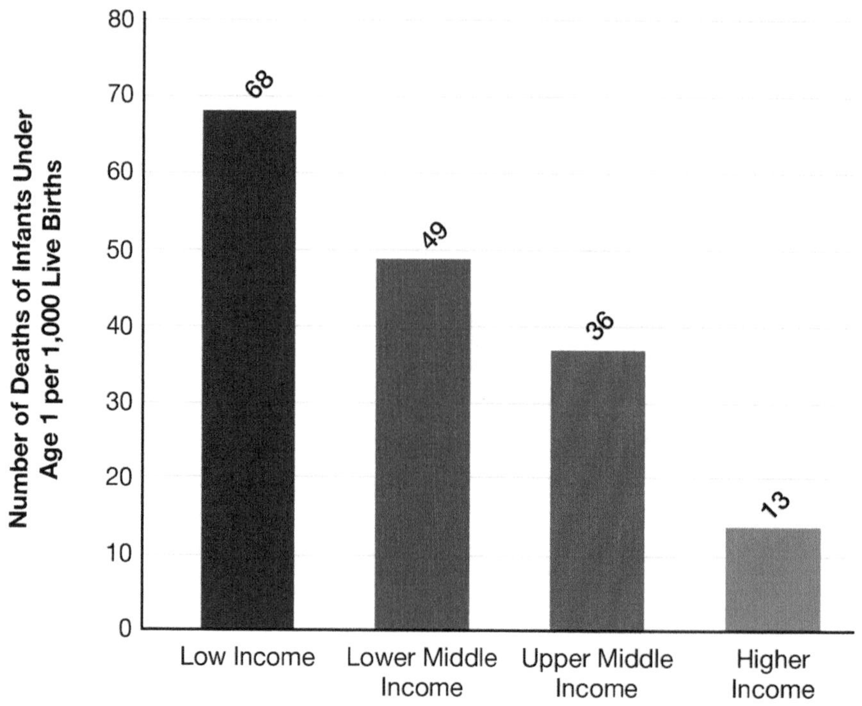

Source: Data from World Bank. 2019. Morality Rate, Under-5 (per 1,000 Live Births). Retrieved from https://data.worldbank.org/indicator/SH.DYN.MORT.

Life expectancy is another important measure of a nation's health and is very relevant for understanding worldwide disparities in health and health care. Once again, the poorest nations are at a considerable disadvantage, as their life expectancy is only 63 years. In contrast, the life expectancy of high-income nations is 81 years (World Bank 2019).[10] People in low-income nations, then, can expect on the average to live 18 fewer years than people in high-income nations.

As discussed in Chapter 2, the global coronavirus pandemic that began in early 2020 disproportionately threatened people who lived in low-income nations. Greater incidences of health problems and substandard living conditions made them that much more vulnerable to contracting the coronavirus and then dying from COVID-19. Their health-care systems are woefully lacking, even in normal times; in the wake of the pandemic, their health-care systems were simply overwhelmed (Shah and Parkinson 2020).[11]

Health Care in Industrial Nations

national health insurance

A system of medicine in which the government pays all or most of the costs of health care, prescriptions, and other items for the entire population.

Industrial nations throughout the world, with the notable exception of the United States, provide their citizens with some form of national health care and **national health insurance**. Although their health-care systems differ in several respects, their governments pay all or most of the costs for health care, drugs, and other health needs. In Denmark, for example, the government provides free medical care and hospitalization for the entire population and pays for some medications and some dental care. In France, the government pays for some of the medical, hospitalization, and medication costs for most people and all these expenses for the poor, unemployed, and children under the age of 10. In Great Britain, the National Health Service pays most medical costs for the population, including medical care, hospitalization, prescriptions, dental care, and eyeglasses. In

Canada, the National Health Insurance system also pays for most medical costs. Patients do not even receive bills from their physicians, who instead are paid by the government.

Although these national health insurance programs are not perfect—for example, people sometimes must wait for elective surgery and some other procedures—they are commonly credited with reducing infant mortality, extending life expectancy, and, more generally, for enabling their citizenries to have relatively good health. Their populations are generally healthier than Americans, even though health-care spending is much higher per capita in the United States than in these other nations. In all these respects, these national health insurance systems offer several advantages over the health-care model found in the United States (Barkan 2020)[12] (see "Lessons from Other Societies").

Lessons from Other Societies

National Health Care in Wealthy Democracies

As the text discusses, industrial nations other than the United States provide free or low-cost health care to their citizens in what is known as national (or universal) health insurance and national health care. Although the United States spends more per capita than these nations on health care, it generally ranks much lower than they do on important health indicators. Of twenty-four wealthy democracies from North America, Western Europe, and certain other parts of the world (Australia, Japan, New Zealand; the exact number of nations varies slightly by indicator), the United States has the lowest life expectancy, the highest infant mortality, and the highest rates of obesity, adult diabetes, and HIV and AIDS. It also ranks low in mortality from heart disease and only tenth in breast cancer mortality rate. According to policy analyst Lawrence Mishel and colleagues, the conclusion from these international comparisons is inescapable: "Although the United States spends more on health care than other countries with similar per capita income and populations, it has worse health outcomes, on average...Compared to the United States, other countries are more committed to the health and well-being of their citizens through more-universal coverage and more-comprehensive health care systems."

A fair conclusion from all the evidence is that U.S. health lags behind that found in other wealthy nations because the latter provide free or low-cost national health care to their citizens and the United States does not. If so, the United States has much to learn from their example. Because the health-care reform ("Obamacare") achieved in the United States in 2009 and 2010 did not include a national health-care model, the United States will likely continue to lag behind other democracies in the quality of health and health care. At the same time, the cost of health care will certainly continue to be much higher in the United States than in other Western nations, in part because the United States uses a *fee-for-service* model in which many physicians are paid for every procedure they do rather than the set salary that some other nations feature.

Sources: Barkan 2020; Mishel et al. 2009[13]

Key Takeaways

- The world's nations differ dramatically in the quality of their health and health care. People in poor nations suffer from many health problems, and poor nations have very high rates of infant mortality and maternal mortality.
- Except for the United States, industrial nations have national health-care systems and national health insurance. Their health-care models help their citizens to have relatively good health at affordable levels.

For Your Review

1. What do you think should be done to help improve the health of poor nations? What role should the United States play in any efforts in this regard?
2. Do you think the United States should move toward the national health insurance model found in other Western nations? Why or why not?

13.3 Problems of Health in the United States

Learning Objectives

1. Describe how and why social class, race and ethnicity, and gender affect physical health and health care in the United States.
2. Summarize the differences that social class, race and ethnicity, and gender make for mental health.

Cigarette smoking in the United States has declined considerably since the 1960s.

Source: © Thinkstock

When we examine health and health care in the United States, there is both good news and bad news. The good news is considerable. Health has improved steadily over the last century, thanks in large part to better public sanitation and the discovery of antibiotics. Illnesses and diseases such as pneumonia and polio that used to kill or debilitate people are either unknown today or treatable by modern drugs. Other medical discoveries and advances have also reduced the extent and seriousness of major illnesses, including many types of cancer, and have prolonged our lives.

Because of these and other factors, the U.S. life expectancy climbed from about 47 years in 1900 to almost 79 years during the past decade. Similarly, infant mortality dropped dramatically in the last half-century from 29.2 infant deaths per 1,000 live births in 1950 to only 5.8 in 2017. Cigarette smoking declined from 51 percent for men and 34 percent for women in 1965 to 18 percent and 14 percent, respectively, in 2016 (National Center for Health Statistics 2018).[14]

The Poor Status of American Health

Unfortunately, the bad news is also considerable. Despite all the gains just mentioned, the United States lags behind most other wealthy democracies in several health indicators, as we have seen, even though it is the wealthiest nation in the world. Moreover, 11.1 percent of U.S. households and more than 37 million Americans, including 6 million children, are "food insecure" (lacking sufficient money for adequate food and nutrition) at least part of the year; almost one-fifth of all children live in food-insecure households (U.S. Department of Agriculture 2019).[15] More than 8 percent of all infants are born at low birth weight (under 5.5 pounds), putting them at risk for long-term health problems; this figure is higher than the 1970 rate (National Center for Health Statistics 2018).[16] These and other health indicators suggest that the United States still has a long way to go in improving the nation's health.

There is also bad news in the *social distribution* of health. Health problems in the United States are more often found among the poor, among people from certain racial and ethnic backgrounds, and, depending on the problem, among women or men. **Social epidemiology** refers to the study of how health and illness vary by sociodemographic characteristics, with such variations called **health disparities**. When we examine social epidemiology in the United States, we see that many health disparities exist. In this way, health and illness both reflect and reinforce society's social inequalities. We now turn to the most important health disparities, starting with physical health and then mental health.

Health Disparities: Physical Health

Social Class

The poor have less money, and they also have worse health, as the news story that began this chapter illustrated. Many types of health indicators illustrate the social class–health link in the United States. In the 2018 General Social Survey, for example, 40.1 percent of respondents with annual household incomes under $30,000 say their health is only fair or poor, compared to just 16.2 percent of respondents with incomes above $75,000. This self-report measure of health is subjective, and it is possible that not everyone interprets "fair" or "poor" health in the same way. But objective indicators of actual health also indicate a strong social class–health link (Barkan 2020).[17]

Children and Our Future

The Poor Health of Poor Children

When we consider health disparities, some of the most unsettling evidence involves children. As a report by the Robert Wood Johnson Foundation concluded, "As family income and levels of education rise, health improves. In almost every state, shortfalls in health are greatest among children in the poorest or least educated households, but even middle-class children are less healthy than children with greater advantages." Reflecting this situation, government data show that children of poor mothers are more likely than those born to wealthier mothers to have asthma, to suffer ear infections, to exhibit serious emotional or behavior difficulties, to experience food insecurity, and to be obese. In addition, low-income parents are more likely than higher-income parents to report that their children's health is only fair for poor.

Many of the health problems low-income children experience last into adolescence and adulthood. Poor children's poor health thus makes a critical difference throughout their lives. As sociologist Steven A. Haas and colleagues have observed, "A growing body of work demonstrates that those who experience poor health early in life go on to complete less schooling, hold less prestigious jobs, and earn less than their healthier childhood peers."

One reason for the poor health of poor children is that their families are more likely to experience many kinds of stress (see Chapter 2). Another reason is that their families are more likely to experience food insecurity and, if they are urban, to live in neighborhoods with higher levels of lead and pollution. Low-income children also tend to watch television more often than wealthier children and for this and other reasons to be less physically active; their relative lack of physical activity is yet another reason for their worse health. Finally, their parents are much more likely than wealthier parents to smoke cigarettes; the secondhand smoke they inhale impairs their health.

The clear evidence of poverty's effects on the health of poor children underscores the need of the United States to do everything possible to minimize these effects. Any money spent to reduce these effects will pay for itself many times over throughout these children's lifetimes: They will have fewer health problems as they grow up, costing the United States much less in health care, and be better able to do well in school and to have higher incomes as adults. In both the short run and long run, then, improving the health of poor children will also improve the economic and social health of the whole nation.

Sources: Haas et al. 2011; Murphey et al. 2018; National Center for Health Statistics 2018; Robert Wood Johnson Foundation 2008[18]

For example, poor adults are also at much greater risk for many health problems, including heart disease, diabetes, arthritis, and some types of cancer. These and other social class differences in health contribute to a striking difference in life expectancy. Among 40-year-olds, for example, women in the bottom 1 percent of household incomes can expect to live to 10 fewer years than those in the top 1 percent of household incomes, while men in the bottom 1 percent can expect to live almost 15 fewer years than those in the top 1 percent (Chetty 2016).[19]

 ### U.S. Child Mortality Rate May Be Linked to Poverty

Poor Americans suffer poor health along many dimensions. One of these dimensions is child mortality, with poor children at a higher risk of dying than wealthier children.

View the video online at: http://www.youtube.com/embed/ywpkfyuYWdk?rel=0

Several reasons account for the social class–health link (Lee et al. 2019; Pampel et al. 2010).[20] One reason is stress, which, as Chapter 2 explained, is higher for people with low incomes because of unemployment, problems in paying for the necessities of life, and a sense of little control over what happens to them. Stress in turn damages health because it impairs the immune system and other bodily processes.

A second reason is that poor people live in conditions, including crowded, dilapidated housing with poor sanitation, that are bad for their health and especially that of their children. Although these conditions have improved markedly in the United States over the last few decades, they continue for many of the poor.

Another reason for the poor's worse health is their lack of access to adequate health care. As is well known, many poor people lack medical insurance and in other respects have inadequate health care. These problems make it more likely they will become ill in the first place and more difficult for them to become well because they cannot afford to visit a physician or to receive other health care.

A fourth reason is a lack of education, which, in ways not yet well understood, leads poor people to be unaware or unconcerned about risk factors for health and to have a fatalistic attitude that promotes unhealthy behaviors and reluctance to heed medical advice (Barr 2019; Ross and Mirowsky 2010).[21] In one study of whether smokers quit smoking after a heart attack, only 10 percent of heart attack patients without a high school diploma quit smoking, compared to almost 90 percent of those with a college degree (Wray et al. 1998).[22]

A final reason for the poor health of poor people is unhealthy lifestyles, as just implied. Although it might sound like a stereotype, poor people are more likely to smoke, to eat high-fat food, to avoid exercise, to be overweight, and more generally not do what they need to do (or do what they should not be doing) to be healthy. Scholars debate whether unhealthy lifestyles are more important in explaining poor people's poor health than the other factors just discussed. Regardless of the proper mix of reasons, the fact remains that the poor have worse health.

Although poor Americans experience worse physical health than wealthier Americans, it is also generally true that Americans are unhealthy compared to their counterparts in other democracies. Thanks in large part to diets filled with processed foods high in sugar, fat, and salt, most Americans have one or more metabolic health problems that weaken their immune systems by causing body-wide inflammation (Brody 2020).[23] To be more specific, nearly 90 percent of Americans have at least one of these conditions: diabetes or pre-diabetes, high blood pressure, or high cholesterol! Americans' poor diets cause an estimated half-million deaths annually and almost certainly contributed greatly to the spread of the coronavirus across the nation after the pandemic began in early 2020 and to the tens of thousands of deaths that resulted.

Many people who are poor or near poor lack medical insurance and in other ways have inadequate health care. These problems make it more likely they will become ill and, once ill, less likely they will become well.

Source: © Thinkstock

Race and Ethnicity

Health differences also exist when we examine the effects of race and ethnicity, and they are literally a matter of life and death. We can see this when we compare life expectancies for non-Latinx whites and African Americans born in 2017 (Table 13.2). When we do not take gender into account, African Americans can expect to live 3.6 fewer years than whites. Among men, they can expect to live 4.6 fewer years, and among women, 2.9 fewer years. Meanwhile, Latinx can actually expect to live a few years longer than whites, thanks partly to the fact that they tend to have healthier diets.

TABLE 13.2 U.S. Life Expectancy at Birth for People Born in 2017

African American	**Both sexes**	**74.9**
	Men	71.5
	Women	78.1
Latinx	**Both Sexes**	**81.8**
	Men	79.1
	Women	84.3
White, non-Latinx	**Both sexes**	**78.5**
	Men	76.1
	Women	81.0

Source: Data from National Center for Health Statistics. 2018. *Health, United States, 2017*. Hyattsville, MD: Centers for Disease Control and Prevention.

At the beginning of the life course, infant mortality also varies by race and ethnicity (Table 13.3), with African American infants more than twice as likely as white infants to die before their first birthday. Infant mortality among Native Americans is almost 1.7 times the white rate, while that for Latinxs is about the same, and Asians a bit lower. In a related indicator, the rate of maternal mortality (death of a mother from complications of pregnancy or childbirth) is about three times higher for African Americans and Native Americans than for non-Latinx whites (Solly 2019).[24]

TABLE 13.3 Mother's Race/Ethnicity and U.S. Infant Mortality, 2015 (Number of Infant Deaths per 1,000 Live Births)

African American	11.0
Asian or Pacific Islander	4.2
Latinx	5.0
Native American	8.3
White	4.9

Source: Data from National Center for Health Statistics. 2018. *Health, United States, 2017*. Hyattsville, MD: Centers for Disease Control and Prevention.

In other indicators, African Americans are more likely than whites to die from heart disease, although the white rate of such deaths is higher than the rates of Asians, Latinxs, and Native Americans. African Americans are also more likely than whites to be overweight and to suffer from asthma, diabetes, high blood pressure, and several types of cancer. Latinxs and Native Americans have higher rates than whites of several illnesses and conditions, including diabetes.

Commenting on all these disparities in health, a former head of the U.S. Department of Health and Human Services said more than two decades ago, "We have been—and remain—two nations: one majority, one minority—separated by the quality of our health" (Penn et al., 2000:102).[25] The examples just discussed certainly indicate that her statement is still true today.

Why do such large racial and ethnic disparities in health exist? To a large degree, they reflect the high poverty rates for African Americans, Latinxs, and Native Americans compared to those for whites. In addition, inadequate medical care is perhaps a special problem for people of color, thanks to unconscious racial bias among health-care professionals that affects the quality of care that people of color receive (see discussion later in this chapter).

An additional reason for racial disparities in health is diet. Many of the foods that have long been part of African American culture are high in fat. Partly as a result, African Americans are much more likely than whites to have heart disease and high blood pressure and to die from these conditions (Parra-Medina et al. 2010).[26] In contrast, first-generation Latinxs tend to have diets consisting of beans, grains, and other low-fat foods, preventing health problems stemming from their poverty from being even worse. But as the years go by and they adopt the typical American's eating habits, their diets tend to worsen, and their health worsens as well (Pérez-Escamilla 2009).[27]

In a significant finding, African Americans tend to have worse health than whites even among those with the same incomes. Several reasons explain this racial gap. One is the extra stress that African Americans of all incomes face because they live in a society that is still racially prejudiced and discriminatory (Williams et al. 2019).[28] In this regard, studies find that African Americans and Latinxs who have experienced the most racial discrimination in their daily lives tend to have worse physical health (Lee and Ferraro 2009).[29] Some middle-class African Americans may also have grown up in poor families and incurred health problems in childhood that continue to affect them. As a former U.S. surgeon general once explained, "You're never dealing with a person just today. You're dealing with everything they've been exposed to throughout their lives. Does it ever end? Our hypothesis is that it never ends" (Meckler 1998:4A).[30]

To some degree, racial differences in health may also have a biological basis. For example, African American men appear to have higher levels of a certain growth protein that may promote prostate cancer; African American smokers may absorb more nicotine than white smokers; differences in the ways African Americans' blood vessels react may render them more susceptible to hypertension and heart disease; and certain biological factors may explain the higher rates of deaths from breast cancer among African American women (Meckler 1998; National Cancer Institute 2015; Ricker and Bird 2005).[31] Because alleged biological differences have been used as the basis for racism, and because race is best thought of as a social construction rather than a biological concept (see Chapter 3), we must be very careful in acknowledging such differences. However, if they do indeed exist, they may help explain at least some of the racial gap in health.

A final factor contributing to racial differences in health is physical location: Poor people of color are more likely to live in urban areas and in other locations that are unhealthy places because of air and water pollution, hazardous waste, and other environmental problems (Williams et al. 2019).[32] This problem is termed *environmental racism*. One example of this problem is found in the so-called Cancer Alley on a long stretch of the Mississippi River in Louisiana populated mostly by African Americans; 80 percent of these residents live within three miles of a polluting industrial facility (Cernansky 2011).[33]

As Chapter 3 explained, the social factors just discussed for racial and ethnic disparities in health contributed mightily to the higher rates of COVID-19 cases and deaths among African Americans, Latinx, and Native Americans in early 2020. These groups have higher rates of chronic health conditions in part because of their higher rates of poverty, because they tend to live in areas with higher levels of air pollution and/or other environmental problems, and because they experience high levels of stress from the racial/ethnic discrimination they encounter. They also encounter unconscious racial bias by health-care professionals for their health conditions, possibly including COVID-19. When the pandemic began, it was thus very likely that these three groups would end up with higher rates of COVID-19 cases and deaths, and that is exactly what happened.

African Americans have worse health than whites, even when people with the same incomes are compared. One reason for this racial gap is the continuing racial discrimination that African Americans experience and the stress that accompanies this experience.

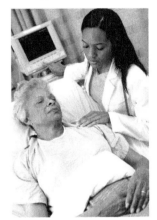

Source: © Thinkstock

Gender

The evidence on gender and health is both complex and fascinating. Although women outlive men by five years, women have worse health than men in many areas. For example, they are more likely to suffer from migraine headaches, osteoporosis, and immune diseases such as lupus and rheumatoid arthritis. Women thus have more health problems than men do even though they outlive men—a situation commonly known as the *gender paradox* (Bastos et al. 2015).[34] Why, then, do women outlive men? Conversely, why do men die earlier than women? The obvious answer is that men have more life-threatening diseases, such as heart disease and emphysema, than women, but that raises the question of why this is so.

Several reasons explain the gender gap in longevity. One might be biological, as women's estrogen and other sex-linked biological differences may make them less susceptible to heart disease and other life-threatening illnesses, even as they render them more vulnerable to some of the health problems already listed. A second reason is that men lead more unhealthy lifestyles than women because of differences in gender socialization. For example, men are more likely than women to smoke, to drink heavily, and to drive recklessly. All such behaviors make men more vulnerable than women to life-threatening illnesses and injuries. Men are also more likely than women to hold jobs in workplaces filled with environmental and safety hazards that kill thousands of people—most of them men—annually.

A final reason is men's reluctance to discuss and seek help for their medical problems, owing to their masculine socialization into being "strong, silent types." Just as men do not like to ask for directions, as the common wisdom goes, so do they not like to ask for medical help. As one physician put it, "I've often said men don't come in for checkups because they have a big *S* tattooed on their chests; they think they're Superman" (Guttman 1999:10).[35]

Studies find that men are less likely than women to tell anyone when they have a health problem and to seek help from a health-care professional (Magaard et al. 2017).[36] When both sexes do visit a physician, men ask fewer questions than women do. In one study, the average man asked no more than two questions, while the average woman asked at least six. Because patients who ask more questions get more information and recover their health more quickly, men's silence in the exam room may contribute to their shorter longevity (Foreman 1999).[37] Interestingly, the development of erectile dysfunction drugs like Viagra may have helped improve men's health, as men have had to see a physician to obtain prescriptions for these drugs when otherwise they would not have seen a physician (Guttman 1999).[38]

We have just discussed why men die sooner than women, which is one of the two gender differences that constitute the morbidity paradox. The other gender difference concerns why women have more nonfatal health problems than men. Several reasons explain this difference (Schone 2018).[39]

One reason arises from the fact that women outlive men. Because women are thus more likely than men to be in their senior years, they are also more likely to develop the many health problems associated with old age.

However, women still tend to have worse health than men even when age is taken into account. Medical sociologists attribute this gender difference to the gender inequality in the larger society (Read and Gorman 2010).[40] For example, women are more likely than men to live in poverty or near poverty, which, as we have seen, is a risk factor for worse health. Women are also more likely than men to experience stressful events in their everyday lives, such as caring for a child or an aging parent. Their increased stress impairs their immune systems and thus worsens their health. It also is an important cause of their greater likelihood of depression and the various physical health problems (weakened immune system, higher blood pressure, lack of exercise) that depression often causes. Finally, women experience discrimination in their everyday lives because of our society's sexism, and (as is also true for people of color) this discrimination is thought to produce stress and thus poorer physical health (Wong 2018).[41]

Women more than men tend to have more health problems that are not life threatening. Two reasons for this gender difference are gender inequality in the larger society and the stress accompanying women's traditional caregiving role in the family.

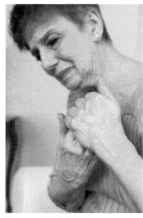

Source: © Thinkstock

Health Disparities: Mental Health

Health consists of mental well-being as well as physical well-being, and people can suffer mental health problems in addition to physical health problems. Scholars disagree over whether mental illness is real or, instead, a social construction. The predominant view in psychiatry, of course, is that people do have actual problems in their mental and emotional functioning and that these problems are best characterized as mental illnesses or mental disorders and should be treated by medical professionals. But other scholars say mental illness is a social construction or a "myth" (Szasz 2010).[42] In their view, all kinds of people sometimes act oddly, but only a few are labeled as mentally ill. If someone says she or he hears the voice of an angel, we ordinarily attribute their perceptions to their religious views and consider them religious, not mentally ill. But if someone instead insists that aliens from Mars have been in touch, we are more apt to think there is something mentally wrong with that person. Mental illness thus is not real but rather is the reaction of others to problems they perceive in someone's behavior.

This intellectual debate notwithstanding, many people do suffer serious mental and emotional problems, such as severe mood swings and depression, that interfere with their everyday functioning and social interaction. Sociologists and other researchers have investigated the social epidemiology of these problems. Several generalizations seem warranted from their research regarding disparities in mental health (Cockerham 2017).[43]

Social Class

First, social class affects the incidence of mental illness. To be more specific, poor people exhibit more mental health problems than richer people: They are more likely to suffer from schizophrenia, serious depression, and other problems. A major reason for this link is the stress of living in poverty and the many living conditions associated with it. One interesting causal question here is whether poverty leads to mental illness or mental illness leads to poverty. Although there is evidence of both causal paths, most scholars believe that poverty contributes to mental illness more than the reverse (Warren 2009).[44]

Race and Ethnicity

Second, there is no clear connection between race/ethnicity and mental illness (American Psychiatric Association 2017).[45] African Americans and Latinxs generally have mental health that is at least as good overall as that of non-Latinx whites. However, Native Americans tend to have worse mental health than whites. When people of color do have mental health problems, their greater poverty and worse health insurance status makes it more difficult for them to receive adequate treatment.

Gender

Third, gender is related to mental illness but in complex ways, as the nature of this relationship depends on the type of mental disorder. Women have higher rates of bipolar disorder than men and are more likely to be seriously depressed, but men have higher rates of antisocial personality disorders that lead them to be a threat to others. Sociologists attribute these differences to differences in gender socialization that lead women to keep problems inside themselves while encouraging men to express their problems outwardly, as through violence. To the extent that women have higher levels of depression and other mental health problems, the factors that account for their poorer physical health, including their higher rates of poverty and stress and rates of everyday discrimination, are thought to also account for their poorer mental health (Read and Gorman 2010).[46]

Women are more likely than men to be seriously depressed. Sociologists attribute this gender difference partly to gender socialization that leads women to keep problems inside themselves while encouraging men to express their problems outwardly.

Source: © Thinkstock

Key Takeaways

- Social class, race and ethnicity, and gender all influence the quality of health in the United States. Health problems are more common among people from low-income backgrounds and among people of color. Women are more likely than men to have health problems that are not life threatening.
- Although debate continues over whether mental illness is a social construction, many people do suffer mental health problems. The social epidemiology for mental health and illness resembles that for physical health and illness, with social class, race/ethnicity, and gender disparities existing.

1. In thinking about the health problems of individuals from low-income backgrounds, some people blame lack of access to adequate health care for these problems, while other people blame unhealthy lifestyles practiced by low-income individuals. Where do you stand on this debate? Explain your answer.

2. Write a brief essay in which you present a sociological explanation of the higher rate of depression found among women than among men.

13.4 Problems of Health Care in the United States

Learning Objectives

1. Summarize the problems associated with the model of private insurance that characterizes the U.S. health system.
2. Explain how and why mistakes and infections occur in hospitals.
3. Describe any two other problems in U.S. health care other than the lack of health insurance.

As the continuing debate over health care in the United States reminds us, the practice of medicine raises many important issues about its cost and quality. We now turn to some of these issues. The 2020 coronavirus pandemic manifested all the problems in this section. For example, Americans without insurance or who were underinsured were less likely to seek health care when they developed symptoms of COVID-19. In particular, 14 percent of American adults reported in a national poll that they would not seek care for these symptoms because it would be too expensive (Witters 2020).[47]

Health Insurance Coverage

Although the United States spends much more per capita on health care than any other wealthy democracy, it lags behind many of its peer nations in several important health indicators, as we have already seen. Why is this so?

direct-fee system

A system of medicine in which patients pay for health care, prescriptions, and other medical costs themselves.

An important reason is the U.S. system of *private health insurance*. As discussed earlier, other Western nations have national systems of health care and health insurance. In stark contrast to these nations, the United States relies largely on a **direct-fee system**, in which patients under 65 (those 65 and older are covered by Medicare) are expected to pay for medical costs themselves, aided by private health insurance, usually through one's employer. Although the Affordable Care Act (Obamacare) enacted in 2010 expanded the ranks of insured Americans, about 10 percent of the under-65 population, or 27 million Americans, still lacked health insurance at the end of 2018 (Kaiser Family Foundation 2018).[48] Many Americans are also *underinsured*, meaning they experience large out-of-pocket health-care costs because of high deductibles, significant co-pays, and, depending on how underinsurance is defined, very large premiums.

Underinsurance or the actual lack of health insurance has deadly consequences because people who are uninsured or underinsured are less likely to receive preventive health care and care for various conditions and illnesses. The "Applying Social Research" box discusses a very informative real-life experiment on the difference that health insurance makes for people's health.

Applying Social Research

Experimental Evidence on the Importance of Health Insurance

As the text discusses, studies show that Americans without health insurance are at greater risk for a variety of illnesses and life-threatening conditions. Although this research evidence is compelling, uninsured Americans may differ from insured Americans in other ways that also put their health at risk. For example, perhaps people who do not buy health insurance may be less concerned about their health and thus less likely to take good care of themselves. Because many studies have not controlled for all such differences, experimental evidence would be more conclusive.

For this reason, the results of a real-life experiment in Oregon were very significant. In 2008, Oregon decided to expand its Medicaid coverage. Because it could not accommodate all the poor Oregonians who were otherwise uninsured, it had them apply for Medicaid by lottery. Researchers then compared the subsequent health of the Oregonians who ended up on Medicaid with that of Oregonians who remained uninsured. Because the two groups resulted from random assignment (the lottery), it is reasonable to conclude that any later differences between them stemmed from the presence or absence of Medicaid coverage.

During the first two years after the randomized Medicaid coverage began, the newly insured Oregonians rated themselves happier and in better health than their uninsured "control group" counterparts, and they also reported fewer sick days from work. They were also more likely to have seen a primary care doctor in the year since they received coverage, and women were 60 percent more likely to have had a mammogram. In another effect, they were much less likely to report having had to borrow money or not pay other bills because of medical expenses. In addition, they were less likely to suffer from depression. However, the two groups of subjects exhibited similar blood pressure and cholesterol levels and similar cardiovascular risks.

Because of this study's experimental design, it "represents the best evidence we've got," according to a news report, of the benefits of health insurance coverage. As researchers continue to study the two groups in the years ahead and begin to collect data on blood pressure, cardiovascular health, and other objective indicators of health, they will add to our knowledge of the effects of health insurance coverage.

Sources: Baicker and Finkelstein 2011; Fisman 2011; James 2015[49]

Americans 65 and older are covered by Medicare. Although Medicare pays some medical costs for the elderly, we saw in Chapter 6 that its coverage is hardly adequate, as many people must pay hundreds or even thousands of dollars in premiums, deductibles, coinsurance, and co-payments. The other government program, Medicaid, pays some health-care costs for the poor, but many low-income families are not poor enough to receive Medicaid. Eligibility standards for Medicaid vary from one state to another, and a family poor enough in one state to receive Medicaid might not be considered poor enough in another state. The State Children's Health Insurance Program (SCHIP), begun in 1997 for children from low-income families, has helped somewhat, but it, too, fails to cover many low-income children. Given this context, it should come as no surprise that low-income families are less likely than wealthier families to have health insurance. In 2018, 14 percent of Americans with annual household incomes under $25,000 were uninsured, compared to less than 5 percent of Americans with annual household incomes at or above $125,000 (Berchick et al. 2019).[50]

Not surprisingly, the uninsured rate varies by race and ethnicity (see Figure 13.2). Almost 18 percent of Latinxs and 10 percent of African Americans were uninsured in 2018, compared to less than 7 percent of Asians and 6 percent of non-Latinx whites. Latinxs were thus more than three times as likely as whites to be uninsured, while African Americans were almost twice as likely as whites to be uninsured. As discussed earlier, the lack of health insurance among the poor and people of color is a significant reason for their poorer health.

FIGURE 13.2 Race, Ethnicity, and Lack of Health Insurance, 2018 (Percentage of People under Age 65 with No Insurance)

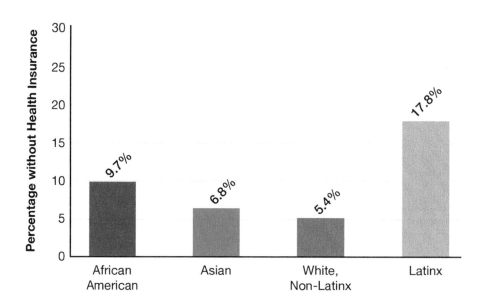

Source: Berchick, Edward R., Jessica C. Barnett and Rachel D. Upton. 2019. *Health Insurance Coverage in the United States: 2018*. Washington, DC: U.S. Census Bureau.

The High Cost of Health Care

As noted earlier, the United States spends much more money per capita on health care than any other wealthy democracy. Its annual expenditure on health care exceeded $3.6 trillion in 2018. This huge expenditure might be justified if the quality of health and of health care in this nation outranked that in its peer nations. As we have seen, however, the United States lags behind many of its peer nations in several indicators of health and health-care quality. If the United States spends far more than its peer nations on health care yet still lags behind them in many indicators, an inescapable conclusion is that the United States is spending much more than it should be spending.

Why Medical Bills in the U.S. Are So Expensive

Health care in the United States is very expensive, and much more expensive than health care in other democracies. Two reasons for this situation involve administrative costs from private insurance and the fee-for-service model.

View the video online at: http://www.youtube.com/embed/3NvnOUcG-ZI?rel=0

Why is U.S. spending on health care so high? Although this is a complex issue, two reasons stand out (Barkan 2021).[51] First, administrative costs for health care in the United States are the highest in the industrial world. Because so much of U.S. health insurance is private, billing and record-keeping tasks are immense.

Second, the United States relies on a *fee for service* model for private insurance, as noted earlier. Under this model, physicians, hospitals, and health-care professionals and businesses are relatively free to charge whatever they want for their services. In the other industrial nations, government regulations keep prices lower. This basic difference between the United States and its peer nations helps explain why the cost of health-care services in the United States is so much higher. Simply put, U.S. physicians and hospitals charge much more for their services than do their counterparts in other industrial nations. And because physicians are paid for every service they perform, they have an incentive to perform more diagnostic tests and other procedures than necessary.

A few examples illustrate the higher cost of medical procedures in the United States compared to other nations. To keep things simple, we will compare the United States with just Spain. The average U.S. appendectomy cost almost $16,000 in 2015, compared to only $2,000 in Spain; the average U.S. bypass surgery cost more than $78,000, compared to less than $15,000 in Spain; and the average U.S. hip replacement cost more than $29,000, compared to less than $7,000 in Spain (International Federation of Health Plans 2016).[52]

Other Problems in the Quality of Care

Other problems in the quality of health care also put patients unnecessarily at risk. We examine several of these here:

1. *Racial and Gender Bias in Health Care.* As Chapter 3 discussed, African Americans are less likely than whites with the same health problems to receive various medical procedures. Gender bias also appears to affect the quality of health care. Research that examines either actual cases or hypothetical cases posed to physicians finds that women are less likely than men with similar health problems to be recommended for various procedures, medications, and diagnostic tests (Borkhoff et al. 2008).[53]

2. *Sleep Deprivation among Health-Care Professionals.* Many physicians get very little sleep. Studies have found that the performance of surgeons and medical residents who go without sleep is seriously impaired (Ulmer et al. 2008).[54] One study found that sleepless surgeons have their performance impaired as much as a drunk driver. Surgeons who stayed awake all night made 20 percent more errors in simulated surgery than those who slept normally, and they also took 14 percent longer to complete the surgery (Wen 1998).[55]

3. *Shortage of Physicians and Nurses.* Another problem is a shortage of physicians and nurses. This is a general problem around the nation, but even more of a problem in poor urban areas and in rural areas. As discussed further in Chapter 14, many rural residents lack convenient access to hospitals, health-care professionals, and ambulances and other emergency care. This lack of access contributes to many health problems in rural areas.

4. *Mistakes by Hospitals.* Partly because of sleep deprivation and the shortage of health-care professionals, many hospital patients suffer from mistakes made by hospital personnel. They receive the wrong diagnosis, are given the wrong medication, have a procedure done on them that was intended for someone else, or incur a serious bacterial infection. Such problems kill many patients every year, with estimates of deaths from hospital errors ranging from a low of 44,000 annually to a high of 440,000 (Institute of Medicine 2000; James 2013).[56]

Key Takeaways

- The U.S. health-care model relies on a direct-fee system and private health insurance. This model has been criticized for contributing to high health-care costs, high rates of uninsured and underinsured people, and high rates of health problems in comparison to other wealthy democracies.
- Other problems in U.S. health care include racial/ethnic and gender bias in health-care delivery, shortages of nurses and physicians, and mistakes by hospitals.

For Your Review

1. Do you know anyone, including yourself or anyone in your family, who lacks health insurance or who has had trouble paying for health insurance or for medical bills? If so, do you think this situation has contributed to any health problems? Write a brief essay in which you discuss the evidence for your conclusion.
2. One of the most controversial features of Obamacare was the requirement to have health insurance. Although this requirement is no longer in effect at the time of this writing, it remains controversial. Do you believe everyone should be insured, or do you think that decision should be left up to the individual? Explain your answer.

13.5 Improving Health and Health Care

The U.S. health-care system, despite the recent health-care reform legislation and medical advances that used to be only a dream, still has a long way to go before affordable and high-quality health care is available to all. With the health of so many people at stake, the United States needs to make every effort to achieve this essential goal. How might we achieve this goal?

We have seen throughout this chapter that social class, race and ethnicity, and gender all play a profound role in the quality of health and health care. People from low-income backgrounds have higher rates of physical and mental illness because of the stress and other factors associated with living with little money and also because of their lack of access to adequate health care. Partly because they tend to be poorer and partly because of the discrimination they experience in their daily lives and in the health-care system, people of color also have higher rates of physical illness. Meanwhile, women have higher rates than men of nonfatal physical illness and of depression and other mental illness, and they experience lower quality of health care for certain conditions.

To improve health and health care in the United States, then, the importance of social class, race and ethnicity, and gender must be addressed. Efforts, as outlined in earlier chapters, that reduce poverty and racial/ethnic and gender inequality should also improve the physical and mental health of those currently at risk because of their low incomes, race or ethnicity, and/or gender, as public health experts recognize. At the same time, special efforts must be made to ensure that these millions of individuals receive the best health care possible within the existing system of social inequality.

In this regard, the national health-care and health insurance systems of Canada, the United Kingdom, and many other Western nations provide models for the United States. As discussed in this chapter, these nations provide better health care to their citizens in many ways and at a lower cost than that incurred under the U.S. model of private insurance. Their models are not perfect, but a government-funded and government-run **single-payer system**—or "Medicare for All," as it has been called—shows great promise for improving the health and health care of all Americans (Barkan 2017).[57]

Many Medicare for All models exist, but they all would enable more Americans to be insured and at a lower cost, as suggested by the health-care systems of the other wealthy democracies. Although some people criticize a Medicare for All model as being socialistic, the very popular Medicare for the nation's elderly was similarly criticized as being socialistic when it was enacted in the 1960s. As one single-payer proponent has observed, "A public role in health care shouldn't be any scarier or more repugnant than a public fire department" (Kristof 2009:A31).[58] (The "People Making a Difference" box highlights a national physicians group that advocates for a single-payer system.)

Canada and other wealthy nations have national health-care systems that provide models for the United States to follow.

Source: © Thinkstock

single-payer system

A program of health insurance for all citizens that is funded and operated by the federal government.

People Making a Difference

Physicians in Favor of National Health Insurance

Physicians for a National Health Program (PNHP) is a national organization of more than 20,000 physicians who support a single-payer system of national health insurance in the United States. They advocate for this goal through the PNHP's website and through a variety of advocacy efforts. These efforts include writing articles for medical and public health journals; writing op-ed columns for newspapers; and making educational materials available to members of the public who wish to contact their members of Congress. PNHP members also appear on local and national television news shows and coordinate and speak at public health forums. PNHP has local chapters and allied groups in more than forty states and the District of Columbia.

According to PNHP, a single-payer system would greatly reduce the billing, paperwork, and other administrative costs of the private insurance model that now dominates the U.S. health-care system. These costs, PNHP says, account for a huge portion of U.S. health expenditures; if the United States were to adopt a national single-payer system, administrative costs would be reduced by more than $500 billion. PNHP also emphasizes that a national single-payer system would greatly reduce the number of Americans who continue to be uninsured even after Obamacare's reforms.

An important reason for the high administrative costs of U.S. health care, PNHP explains, is the fact that private insurance companies are for-profit companies. Because their goal is to make a profit, they advertise and engage in various marketing activities, and their CEOs and other executives receive extremely high salaries and other compensation. A single-payer system would eliminate all these problems.

By calling attention to the many problems in the current U.S. health model and by advocating for a national single-payer system, Physicians for a National Health Program is helping to make a difference. For more information, visit http://www.pnhp.org.

Short of adopting national health insurance, other efforts to improve health and health care are certainly essential. One such effort would include an expansion of measures that fall broadly into what the field of public health calls *preventive care*. This approach recognizes that the best approach to health and health care is to prevent illness and disease before they begin. One facet of this approach focuses on the unhealthy behaviors and lifestyles, including lack of exercise, obesity, and smoking, characteristic of millions of Americans. Although the United States has public education campaigns and other initiatives on these risk factors, more could still be done. Another facet of this approach focuses on early childhood in general but especially on early childhood among low-income families. As this chapter has emphasized beginning with the "Social Problems in the News" story, many health problems begin very early in childhood and even in the womb. Home visitation and nutrition assistance programs must be expanded across the country to address these problems.

Another effort must focus on the high cost of health care. We saw earlier that the U.S. fee-for-service model, in which hospitals and physicians largely set the prices for their services, contributes greatly to the high cost of health care in the United States. Related to this model, physicians are paid for each patient they see, rather than receiving a set salary, as teachers, firefighters, police officers, and most other occupations that service large numbers of people receive. Yet there are some outstanding hospitals, such as the Mayo Clinic in Minnesota and the Cleveland Clinic in Ohio, where physicians do work on salary rather than charging for each patient or for each surgery; costs per patient at these hospitals tend to be lower (Gawande et al. 2009).[59] Moving toward this model would help lower health-care costs.

It is also essential to reduce medical errors in hospitals and to raise the rate of hand washing. Many hospitals have adopted strict protocols, such as frequent washing of hands and the use of checklists before surgeries, to reduce infection and errors, but many hospitals have also failed to adopt these protocols. Their failure to do so is a hidden national scandal that kills thousands of people annually.

What can be done to improve world health? Because the poorest nations have the poorest health, it is essential that the wealthy nations provide them the money, equipment, and other resources they need to improve their health and health care. The residents of these nations also need to be given the resources they need to undertake proper sanitation and other good health practices. In this regard, organizations like the World Health Organization have been instrumental in documenting the dire status of health in the poor nations and in promoting efforts to help them, and groups like Doctors Without Borders have been instrumental in bringing health-care professionals and medical care to poor nations. Ultimately, however, these nations' poor health is just one of the consequences of the global inequality examined in Chapter 2. Until these nations' economic circumstances and high rates of illiteracy improve dramatically, their health status will remain a serious problem.

Key Takeaways

- Effective health-care reform must address social class, racial and ethnic, and gender inequalities in health and health care.
- National health insurance involving a single-payer system would improve many aspects of health and health care in the United States.
- In the absence of national health insurance, several types of changes could still help to reduce health-care costs.

For Your Review

1. Do you favor or oppose national health insurance for the United States? Explain your answer.
2. Why do you think the United States remains the only industrial nation without national health insurance?

13.6 End-of-Chapter Material

Summary

1. A sociological approach emphasizes the relationship between health, medicine, and society. In particular, our social backgrounds influence our health and access to health care.
2. Sociological perspectives on health and illness fall into the functional, conflict, and interactionist approaches encountered in previous chapters. The functional view emphasizes the importance of health for a society's stability and the roles that people play when they are sick. The conflict view stresses inequality in the quality of health and health-care delivery and efforts by physicians to monopolize the practice of medicine to increase their profits. According to the interactionist view, health and illness are social constructions subject to people's and society's interpretations. The interactionist view also studies how medical professionals and patients interact and the way professionals manage understandings of such interaction.
3. Health and the quality of health care differ widely around the world and reflect global inequality. The earth's poorest nations have extremely high rates of infant mortality and life-threatening diseases such as AIDS and very low life expectancy.
4. The United States lags behind most other industrial nations in important health indicators such as infant mortality and life expectancy. Moreover, serious disparities exist within the United States in the social distribution of health, as evidenced by the study of social epidemiology. The general poor health of Americans almost certainly contributed greatly to the spread of the coronavirus in early 2018 and to the many deaths it caused.

5. Social class, race and ethnicity, and gender all affect the quality of health. The health of poor people is worse than that of the nonpoor. African Americans, Hispanics, and Native Americans all fare worse than whites on many health indicators, in large part because of their poverty and history of discrimination. Women fare worse than men on several heath indicators, but men have lower life expectancies because of their higher rates of certain life-threatening illnesses.

6. Health care in the United States today faces several problems. The United States is alone among the world's industrial nations in not offering universal national health insurance; its absence is thought to help account for the country's low ranking in the industrial world on major health indicators. Racial and gender bias in health care is another problem that has adverse effects on the nation's health. Other quality-of-care problems include tired physicians, a lack of physicians, and numerous mistakes made in hospitals.

Using What You Know

You have been working for two months as a volunteer in a hospital in or near your hometown. Your duties include bringing food to patients, talking with them, and otherwise helping them to feel comfortable. However, you have noticed that many of the physicians and nurses you have seen coming into patients' rooms do not wash their hands, and you doubt that they washed their hands immediately before entering the rooms. What, if anything, do you do? Explain your answer.

What You Can Do

To help deal with the health and health-care problems discussed in this chapter, you may wish to do any of the following:

1. Volunteer at a local hospital or health clinic.

2. Start a group on your campus to advocate for national health insurance, or join an existing group in the nearby community.

3. Volunteer for a local agency that tries to address the health-care needs of low-income children and their families.

Endnotes

1. Mosby, Chris. 2019. "More Than Half of Cleveland Children Live in Poverty: Data." *Patch* October 15:https://patch.com/ohio/cleveland/more-half-cleveland-children-live-poverty-data.

2. Parsons, Talcott. 1951. *The Social System*. New York: Free Press.

3. Ehrenreich, Barbara and Deirdre English. 2005. *For Her Own Good: Two Centuries of the Experts' Advice to Women*. New York: Anchor Books.

4. Conrad, Peter. 2008. *The Medicalization of Society: On the Transformation of Human Conditions into Treatable Disorders*. Baltimore: Johns Hopkins University Press; Macht, Joel. 2017. *The Medicalization of America's Schools: Challenging the Concept of Educational Disabilities*. Cham, Switzerland: Palgrave Macmillan.

5. Hanson, Barbara. 2018. "Social Constructions of Fatness: Legal Proceedings in Canada as a Case in Point." *Disability & Society* 33(6):954-73.

6. Musto, David. F. (ed). 2002. *Drugs in America: A Documentary History*. New York: New York University Press.

7. Saguy, Abigail C. 2013. *What's Wrong with Fat?* New York: Oxford University Press.

8. Diamond, Anne. 2011. "Acceptance of Fat as the Norm Is a Cause for Concern." *Nursing Standard* 25(38):28-28.

9. World Health Organization. 2018. "Hiv/Aids." https://www.who.int/news-room/fact-sheets/detail/hiv-aids.

10. World Bank. 2019. *Life Expectancy at Birth, Total (Years)*. Retrieved from https://data.worldbank.org/indicator/sp.dyn.le00.in.

11. Shaw, Saeed and Joe Parkinson. 2020. "Coronavirus Is Advancing on Poor Nations, and the Prognosis Is Troubling." *The Wall Street Journal* March 25:https://www.wsj.com/articles/coronavirus-is-advancing-on-poor-nations-and-the-prognosis-is-troubling-11585149183.

12. Barkan, Steven E. 2020. *Health, Illness, and Society: An Introduction to Medical Sociology*, 2nd ed. Lanham, MD: Rowman and Littlefield.

13. Barkan, Steven E. 2020. *Health, Illness, and Society: An Introduction to Medical Sociology*, 2nd ed. Lanham, MD: Rowman and Littlefield; Mishel, Lawrence, Bernstein, Jared, and Shierholz, Heidi. 2009. *The State of Working America* Ithaca, NY: ILR Press

14. National Center for Health Statistics. 2018. *Health, United States, 2017*. Hyattsville, MD: Centers for Disease Control and Prevention.

15. U.S. Department of Agriculture. 2019. *Food Security in the U.S.* Retrieved from https://www.ers.usda.gov/topics/food-nutrition-assistance/food-security-in-the-us/key-statistics-graphics.aspx.

16. National Center for Health Statistics. 2018. *Health, United States, 2017*. Hyattsville, MD: Centers for Disease Control and Prevention.

17. Barkan, Steven E. 2020. *Health, Illness, and Society: An Introduction to Medical Sociology*, 2nd ed. Lanham, MD: Rowman and Littlefield.

18. Haas, Steven A., Maria Glymour and Lisa F. Berkman. 2011. "Childhood Health and Labor Market Inequality over the Life Course." *Journal of Health and Social Behavior* 52:298-313; Murphey, David, Elizabethk Cook, Samuel Beckwith and Jonathan Belford. 2018. *The Health of Parents and Their Children: A Two-Generation Inquiry*. Washington, DC: Child Trends; National Center for Health Statistics. 2018. *Health, United States, 2017: With Special Feature on Mortality*. Hyattsville, MD: U.S. Department of Health and Human Services; Robert Wood Johnson Foundation. 2008. *America's Health Starts with Healthy Children: How Do States Compare?* Princeton, NJ: Robert Wood Johnson Foundation.

19. Chetty, Raj, Michael Stepner, Sarah Abraham, Shelby Lin, Benjamin Scuderi, Nicholas Turner, Augustin Bergeron and David Cutler. 2016. "The Association between Income and Life Expectancy in the United States, 2001–2014." *JAMA* 315(16):1750-66.

20. Lee, Tae Kyoung, Kandauda A. S. Wickrama and Catherine Walker O'Neal. 2019. "Early Socioeconomic Adversity and Cardiometabolic Risk in Young Adults: Mediating Roles of Risky Health Lifestyle and Depressive Symptoms." *Journal of Behaviorial Medicine* 42(1):150-161; Pampel, Fred C., Patrick M. Krueger and Justin T. Denney. 2010. "Socioeconomic Disparities in Health Behaviors." *Annual Review of Sociology* 36:349-70.

21. Barr, Donald A. 2019. *Health Disparities in the United States: Social Class, Race, Ethniicty, and the Social Determinants of Health*. Baltimore: Johns Hopkins University Press; Ross, Catherine E. and John Mirowsky. 2010. "Why Education Is the Key to Socioeconomic Differentials in Health." *Handbook of Medical Sociology*, edited by C. E. Bird, P. Conrad, A. M. Fremont and S. Timmermans. Nashville: Vanderbilt University Press.

22. Wray, Linda A., A. Regula Herzog, Robert J. Willis and Robert B. Wallace. 1998. "The Impact of Education and Heart Attack on Smoking Cessation among Middle-Aged Adults." Journal of Health and Social Behavior 39:271-94.

23. Brody, Jane E. 2020. "How Poor Diet Contributes to Coronavirus Risk." *The New York Times* April 20:https://www.nytimes.com/2020/04/20/well/eat/coronavirus-diet-metabolic-health.html.

24. Solly, Meilan. 2019. "C.D.C. Says More Than Half of the U.S.' Pregnancy-Related Deaths Are Preventable." *Smithsonian.com* May 9:https://www.smithsonianmag.com/smart-news/cdc-says-more-half-us-pregnancy-related-deaths-are-preventable-180972140/.

25. Penn, N. E., Kramer, J., Skinner, J. F., Velasquez, R. J., Yee, B. W. K., Arellano, L. M., et al. (2000). Health practices and health-care systems among cultural groups. In R. M. Eisler & M. Hersen (Eds.), *Handbook of gender, culture, and health* (pp. 101–132). New York, NY: Routledge.

26. Parra-Medina, Deborah, Sara Wilcox, Dawn K. Wilson, Cheryl L. Addy, Gwen Felton and Mary Beth Poston. 2010. "Heart Healthy and Ethnically Relevant (Hher) Lifestyle Trial for Improving Diet and Physical Activity in Underserved African American Women." *Contemporary Clinical Trials* 31(1):92-104. doi: 10.1016/j.cct.2009.09.006.

27. Pérez-Escamilla, Rafael. 2009. "Dietary Quality among Latinos: Is Acculturation Making Us Sick?". *Journal Of The American Dietetic Association* 109(6):988-91.

28. Williams, David R., Jourdyn A. Lawrence and Brigette A. Davis. 2019. "Racism and Health: Evidence and Needed Research." *Annual Review of Public Health* 40:105-25.

29. Lee, Min-Ah and Kenneth F. Ferraro. 2009. "Perceived Discrimination and Health among Puerto Rican and Mexican Americans: Buffering Effect of the Lazo Matrimonial?". *Social Science & Medicine* 68:1966-74.

30. Meckler, Laura. 1998. "Health Gap between Races Persists." *Ocala Star-Banner* November 27:4A.

31. Meckler, Laura. 1998. "Health Gap between Races Persists." *Ocala Star-Banner* November 27:4A; National Cancer Institute. 2015. "The Biology of Cancer Health Disparities."https://www.cancer.gov/research/progress/discovery/biology-cancer-health-disparities; Ricker, Patricia P. and Choe E. Bird. 2005. "Rethinking Gender Differences in Health: Why We Need to Integrate Social and Biological Perspectives." *Journals of Gerontology Series B* 60:S40-S47.

32. Williams, David R., Jourdyn A. Lawrence and Brigette A. Davis. 2019. "Racism and Health: Evidence and Needed Research." *Annual Review of Public Health* 40:105-25.

33. Cernansky, Rachel. 2011, "Cancer Alley: Big Industry & Bigger Illness Along Mississippi River." Retrieved January 21, 2012 (http://www.treehugger.com/corporate-responsibility/cancer-alley-big-industry-bigger-illness-along-mississippi-river.html).

34. Bastos, Tássia Fraga, Ana Maria Canesqui and Marilisa Berti de Azevedo Barros. 2015. "'Healthy Men' and High Mortality: Contributions from a Population-Based Study for the Gender Paradox Discussion." *PLOS One* 10(12):1-11.

35. Guttman, Monika. 1999. "Why More Men Are Finally Going to the Doctor." *USA Weekend*:10.

36. Magaard, Julia Luise, Tharanya Seeralan, Holger Schulz and Anna Levke Brütt. 2017. "Factors Associated with Help-Seeking Behaviour among Individuals with Major Depression: A Systematic Review." *PLOS* One 12(5):e0176730.

37. Foreman, Judy. 1999. "A Visit Most Men Would Rather Not Make." *The Boston Globe*:C1.

38. Guttman, Monika. 1999. "Why More Men Are Finally Going to the Doctor." *USA Weekend*:10.

39. Schone, Barbara. 2018. "Understanding Differences in Mortality and Morbidity by Sex: The Role of Biological, Social, and Economic Factors." Pp. 673-98 in *The Oxford Handbook of Women and the Economy*, edited by S. L. Averett, L. M. Argys and S. D. Hoffman. New York: Oxford University Press.

40. Read, Jen'nan G. and Bridget M. Gorman. 2010. "Gender and Health Inequality." *Annual Review of Sociology* 36:371-86.

41. Wong, Kristin. 2018. "There's a Stress Gap between Men and Women. Here's Why It's Important." *The New York Times* November 14:https://www.nytimes.com/2018/11/14/smarter-living/stress-gap-women-men.html.

42. Szasz, Thomas S. 2010. *The Myth of Mental Illness: Foundations of a Theory of Personal Conduct*. New York: Harper Perennial.

43. Cockerham, William C. 2017. *Sociology of Mental Disorder*. New York: Routledge.

44. Warren, John Robert. 2009. "Socioeconomic Status and Health across the Life Course: A Test of the Social Causation and Health Selection Hypotheses." *Social Forces* 87(4):2125-53.

45. American Psychiatric Association. 2017. "Mental Health Disparities: Diverse Populations."https://www.psychiatry.org/psychiatrists/cultural-competency/education/mental-health-facts.

46. Read, Jen'nan G. and Bridget M. Gorman. 2010. "Gender and Health Inequality." *Annual Review of Sociology* 36:371-86.

47. Witters, Dan. 2020. "In U.S., 14% with Likely Covid-19 to Avoid Care Due to Cost." *Gallup* News April 28:https://news.gallup.com/poll/309224/avoid-care-likely-covid-due-cost.aspx.

48. Kaiser Family Foundation. 2018. "Key Facts About the Uninsured Population."https://www.kff.org/uninsured/fact-sheet/key-facts-about-the-uninsured-population/.

49. Baicker, Katherine and Amy Finkelstein. 2011. "The Effects of Medicaid Coverage; Learning from the Oregon Experiment." *New England Journal of Medicine* 365(8):683-85; Fisman, Ray. 2011. "Does Health Coverage Make People Healthier?". *slate.com* July 7:http://www.slate.com/articles/business/the_dismal_science/2011/07/does_health_coverage_make_people_healthier.single.html; James, Julia. 2015. "The Oregon Health Insurance Experiment." *Health Affairs* July 16:https://www.healthaffairs.org/do/10.1377/hpb20150716.236899/full/.

50. Berchick, Edward R., Jessica C. Barnett and Rachel D. Upton. 2019. *Health Insurance Coverage in the United States: 2018*. Washington, DC: U.S. Census Bureau.

51. Barkan, Steven E. 2021. *Health, Illness, and Society: An Introduction to Medical Sociology*, 2e. Lanham, MD: Rowman & Littlefield.

52. International Federation of Health Plans. 2016. *2015 Comparative Price Report*. London: International Federation of Health Plans.

53. Borkhoff, Cornelia M., Gillian A. Hawker, Hans J. Kreder, Richard H. Glazier, Nizar N. Mahomed and James G. Wright. 2008. "The Effect of Patients' Sex on Physicians' Recommendations for Total Knee Arthroplasty." *Canadian Medical Association Journal* 178(6):681-87.

54. Ulmer, Cheryl, Diane Miller Wolman and Michael M.E. Johns. 2008. *Resident Duty Hours: Enhancing Sleep, Supervision, and Safety*. Washington, DC: Institute of Medicine.

55. Wen, Patricia. 1998. "Tired Surgeons Perform as If Drunk, Study Says." Pp. A9 in *The Boston Globe*.

56. Institute of Medicine. 2000. To Err Is Human: Building a Safer Health System. Washington, DC: National Academy Press; James, John T. 2013. "A New, Evidence-Based Estimate of Patient Harms Associated with Hospital Care." *Journal of Patient Safety* 9(3):122-28.

57. Barkan, Steven E. 2017. *Health, Illness, and Society: An Introduction to Medical Sociology*. Lanham, MD: Rowman & Littlefield.

58. Kristof, Nicholas D. 2009. "Health Care That Works." *The New York Times* September 3:A31.

59. Gawande, Atul, Donald Berwick, Elliott Fisher and Mark McClellan. 2009. "10 Steps to Better Health Care." *The New York Times* August 13:A27.

PART 5

Global Problems

Source: TTstudio/Shutterstock.com

CHAPTER 14
Urban and Rural Problems

Social Problems in the News

"City's Demolition of Vacant Homes at Heart of Neighborhood Revitalization," the headline said. Evansville, Indiana, a city with almost 120,000 residents, was trying in the fall of 2019 to deal with urban blight in the form of vacant and abandoned homes. With the aid of federal funding, it had bought and razed dozens of homes since 2014, most of them in the city's poorest neighborhoods, and sold other homes and vacant lots to people wanting to renovate them. A city official applauded these results, noting that abandoned homes had driven up homeowners' insurance for families living near them. The official also said that the Evansville program was helping the residents of its poor neighborhoods feel better about their situation. "There is a tension and nervousness in neighborhoods where they have boarded up and abandoned homes," the official said. "There is a social cost that is almost hard to measure but intrinsically, you know there is this pressure homeowners feel."

Source: Wilson 2019[1]

America's cities are centers of culture, innovation, fine dining, world-class medical research, high finance, and so many other hallmarks. Yet, as this news story from Evansville reminds us, our cities also have abandoned housing and many other problems. So do the nation's rural areas. This chapter examines urban and rural problems in the United States.

We will see that many of these problems reflect those that earlier chapters discussed. But we will also see that some problems are worse in cities precisely because they are cities (and therefore are crowded with traffic and many buildings and people). And we'll see that some problems are worse in rural areas precisely because they are rural (and therefore are isolated with long distances to travel). These defining features of cities and rural areas, respectively, should be kept in mind as we examine the problems occurring in these two important settings for American life.

Once again the 2020 COVID-19 pandemic highlights many of these problems. Cities were breeding grounds for infectious disease during the nineteenth century, and that is still true today (Whooley 2013).[2] When the coronavirus pandemic began, it was especially severe in New York City, Detroit, and some other urban areas because of these cities' population density, mass transportation, and air pollution (Rubin and Offit 2020).[3] As the pandemic spread across the nation, it eventually struck more rural areas, whose small, underfunded, and understaffed hospitals were ill-equipped to treat COVID-19 patients (Smith and Garcia 2020).[4] And because rural areas lack the kinds of jobs that enable people to work from home, many rural and small-town workers had to continue to perform their jobs at their workplaces, which potentially exposed them to the coronavirus (McArdle 2020).[5] As well, rural people tend to be older and in poorer health than urban people, yet another risk factor for the severe impacts of the coronavirus (Fehr et al. 2020).[6] In all these ways, the pandemic threw into sharp relief how certain features of both urban and rural life contribute to health problems and other social problems.

14.1 A Brief History of Urbanization

urbanization

The rise and growth of cities.

Muckraker Lincoln Steffens wrote a classic work, *The Shame of the Cities*, that criticized the municipal corruption characterizing many U.S. cities at the turn of the twentieth century.

Source: Everett Historical/Shutterstock.com

One of the most significant changes over the centuries has been **urbanization**, or the shift from rural areas to large cities. Urbanization has had important consequences for many aspects of social, political, and economic life (Kleniewski and Thomas 2019).[7]

The earliest cities developed in ancient times after the rise of horticultural and pastoral societies made it possible for people to stay in one place instead of having to move around to find food. Because ancient cities had no sanitation facilities, people typically left their garbage and human waste in the city streets or just outside the city wall (which most cities had for protection from possible enemies). This poor sanitation led to rampant disease and high death rates. Some cities eventually developed better sanitation procedures, including, in Rome, a sewer system. Still, the world remained largely rural until the industrialization of the nineteenth century.

During the American colonial period, cities along the eastern seaboard were the centers of commerce and politics. Boston, New York, and Philadelphia were the three largest cities in population size. Yet they were tiny in comparison to their size today. In 1790, the year after George Washington became the first president of the new nation, New York's population was only 33,131; Philadelphia's was 28,522; and Boston's was 18,230 (Gibson 1998).[8] Today, of course, cities of this size are called small towns.

U.S. cities became more numerous and much larger during the nineteenth century because of two trends. The first was immigration, as waves of immigrants from Ireland and then Italy and other nations began coming to the United States during the 1820s. The second was industrialization, as people moved to live near factories and other sites of industrial production. These two trends were momentous: People crowded together as never before, and they crowded into living conditions that were often squalid. Lack of sanitation continued to cause rampant disease, and death rates from cholera, typhoid, and other illnesses were high.

Crime also became a significant problem, as did riots and other mob violence beginning in the 1830s. This type of mass violence was so common that the 1830s have been called the "turbulent era" (Feldberg 1980).[9] Most of this mass violence was committed by native-born whites against African Americans, Catholics, and immigrants. Native whites resented these groups' presence and were deeply prejudiced against them. During the three decades beginning in 1830, almost three-fourths of U.S. cities with populations above 20,000 had at least one riot.

American cities grew even more rapidly after the Civil War as both industrialization and immigration continued. By the early years of the twentieth century, cities on the East Coast were almost unimaginably crowded, and their living conditions continued to be wretched for many of their residents. Their city governments, police forces, and business worlds were also notoriously corrupt. In 1904, Lincoln Steffens, a renowned "muckraking" journalist, published his classic work, *The Shame of the Cities* (Steffens 1904).[10] In this book, Steffens used biting prose to attack municipal corruption in Chicago, Philadelphia, St. Louis, and other cities. A decade earlier, another muckraker, Jacob Riis, had published *How the Other Half Lives: Studies among the Tenements of New York* (Riis 1890),[11] a book of searing photographs of poverty in the largest American city. The books by Steffens and Riis remain vivid reminders of what cities were like a century ago, and perhaps are still like today in some respects.

As Americans moved west after the Civil War and during the twentieth century, western cities appeared almost overnight and expanded the pace of urbanization. Continued industrialization, immigration, and general population growth further increased the number and size of cities. Internal migration had a similar impact, as waves of African Americans moved from the South to Chicago and other northern cities.

Since the 1950s, several northern cities have lost population. This trend reflects two other trends affecting cities in the past half-century: (1) the movement of people from cities to suburbs; and (2) the movement of Americans from northern cities to southern and southwestern cities. Reflecting this second trend, and also reflecting increases in immigration from Mexico and Asia, southern and southwestern cities have grown rapidly during the past few decades. For example, during the 1970–2018 period, the populations of Albuquerque, New Mexico, and Phoenix, Arizona, more than doubled, while the populations of Cleveland, Ohio, and Detroit, Michigan, both fell by about half (see Figure 14.1).

FIGURE 14.1 Population Change from 1970 to 2018 for Selected Cities

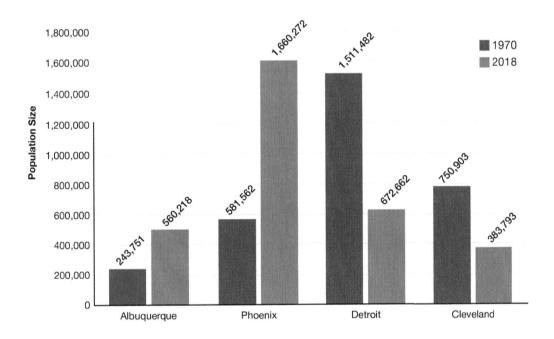

Sources: https://www.census.gov/population/www/documentation/twps0027/tab20.txt; https://factfinder.census.gov/faces/tableservices/jsf/pages/productview.xhtml?src=CF

This trend in urbanization aside, the fact remains that the United States has become much more urbanized since its formation. Today, more than three-fourths of the U.S. population lives in an **urban area** (defined generally as an incorporated territory with a population of at least 2,500), and less than one-fourth lives in a rural area. As Figure 14.2 shows, the degree of urbanization rose steadily through the nineteenth and twentieth centuries before slowing down by the end of the last century.

urban area

Defined generally as an incorporated territory with a population of at least 2,500.

FIGURE 14.2 Urbanization in the United States (Percentage Living in Urban Areas)

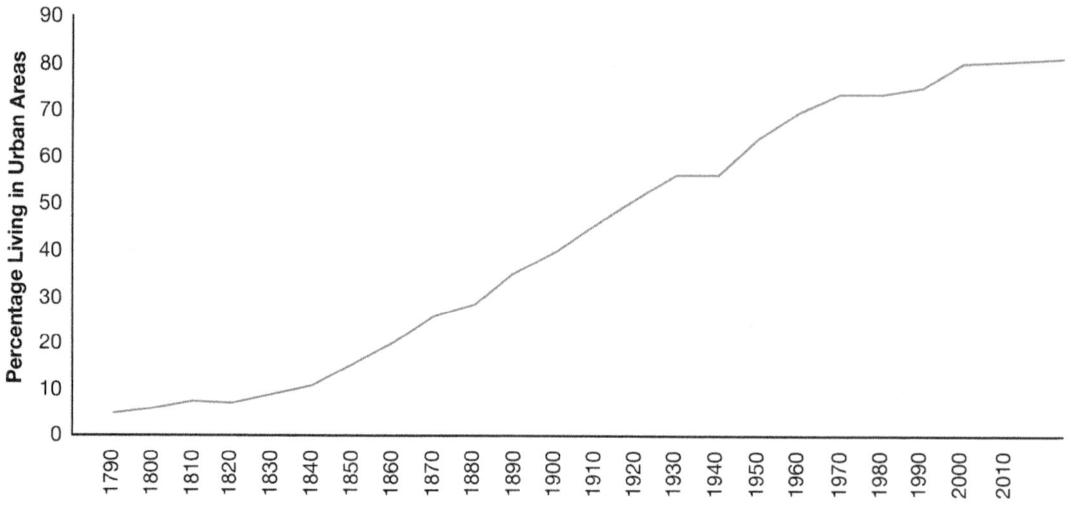

Sources: http://www.census.gov/population/www/censusdata/files/table-4.pdf; http://www.fhwa.dot.gov/planning/census_issues/
archives/metropolitan_planning/cps2k.cfm; https://www.census.gov/newsroom/press-releases/2016/cb16-210.html; https://www.
census.gov/programs-surveys/geography/about/faq/2010-urban-area-faq.html

Global Urbanization

If the United States has urbanized during the last two centuries, so has much of the rest of the world. Only 3 percent of the world's population lived in urban areas in 1800. By a century later in 1900, 14 percent of the world's population lived in urban areas, and twelve cities had populations over 1 million. Just a half-century later in 1950, the world's urban population had doubled to 30 percent, and the number of cities over 1 million grew six times to eighty-three cities.

megacities

Cities with populations over 10 million.

Today, more than half the world's population lives in urban areas, and the number of cities over 1 million stands at more than 400. By 2050, two-thirds of the world's population is projected to live in urban areas. The number of **megacities**—cities with populations over 10 million—rose from three in 1975 to sixteen in 2000, and is expected to reach twenty-seven by 2025 (Kaneda and Bietsch 2016; Population Reference Bureau 2012).[12]

Despite all this growth, the degree of urbanization still varies around the world, with Africa and parts of Asia the least urbanized. In general, wealthy nations are more urban than poor nations, thanks in large part to the latter's rural economies. Still, urbanization in poor nations is proceeding rapidly. Most megacities are now in, and will continue to be in, nations that are relatively poor or desperately poor. The number of urban residents in these nations will increase greatly in the years ahead as people there move to urban areas and as their populations continue to grow through natural fertility. Fertility is a special problem in this regard for two reasons. First, women in poor nations have high fertility rates. Second, poor nations have very high proportions of young people, and these high rates mean that many births occur because of the large number of women in their childbearing years.

Rapid urbanization poses both opportunities and challenges for poor nations. The opportunities are many. Jobs are more plentiful in cities than in rural areas and incomes are higher, and services such as health care and schooling are easier to deliver because people are living more closely together. In another advantage, women in poor nations generally fare better in cities than in rural areas in terms of education and employment possibilities (Population Reference Bureau 2015).[13]

But there are also many challenges. In the large cities of poor nations, homeless children live in the streets as beggars, and many people lack necessities and conveniences that urban dwellers in industrial nations take for granted. The rapid urbanization of poor nations will compound the many problems these nations already have, just as the rapid urbanization in the industrial world more than a century ago led to the disease and other problems discussed earlier. Helping these nations meet the needs of their cities remains a major challenge for the world community in the years ahead.

In large cities in poor nations, as this scene illustrates, many people live in deep poverty and lack clean water and sanitation.

Source: Yavuz Sariyildiz/Shutterstock.com

 ## Providing Hope to Street Children in India

In large cities in low-income nations, many children are homeless. This video depicts an effort to help these children in India.

View the video online at: http://www.youtube.com/embed/wmhQmTTxruk?rel=0

Key Takeaways

- U.S. cities grew rapidly during the nineteenth century because of industrialization and immigration.
- The United States is now a heavily urbanized society, whereas it was largely a rural society just a century ago.
- Urbanization poses special challenges for poor nations, which are ill equipped to address the many problems associated with urbanization.

For Your Review

1. Write an essay in which you discuss the advantages and disadvantages of urbanization.
2. If you had your preference, would you want to live in a large city, small city or town, or rural area? Explain your answer.

14.2 Sociological Perspectives on Urbanization

Learning Objective

1. List the assumptions of the three major sociological perspectives concerning urbanization.

Once again the three major sociological perspectives offer important but varying insights to help us understand urbanization. Table 14.1 summarizes their assumptions.

TABLE 14.1 Theory Snapshot

Theoretical perspective	Major assumptions
Functionalism	Cities serve many important functions for society but also have their dysfunctions. Functionalist theorists differ on the relative merits and disadvantages of urban life, and in particular on the degree to which a sense of community and social bonding exists within cities.
Conflict theory	Cities are run by political and economic elites that use their resources to enrich their positions and to take resources from the poor and people of color. The diversity of social backgrounds found in cities contributes to conflict over norms and values.
Symbolic interactionism	City residents differ in their types of interaction and perceptions of urban life. Cities are not chaotic places but rather locations in which strong norms and values exist.

Functionalism

A basic debate within the functionalist perspective centers on the relative merits of cities and urbanization: In what ways and to what extent are cities useful (functional) for society, and in what ways and to what extent are cities disadvantageous and even harmful (dysfunctional) for society? Put more simply, are cities good or bad?

In essence, there is no one answer to this question, because cities are too complex for a simple answer. Cities are both good and bad. They are sites of creativity, high culture, population diversity, and excitement, but they are also sites of crime, impersonality, and other problems.

Since sociologists began studying urbanization in the early years of the discipline, an important question has been the degree to which cities are impersonal and alienating for their residents. In 1887, German sociologist Ferdinand Tönnies (1887/1963)[14] raised this question when he wrote about the changes that occurred as societies changed from small, rural, and traditional cultures to larger, urban, and industrial settings. He said that a sense of community, or **Gemeinschaft**, characterizes traditional societies. In these societies, family and community ties are quite strong, with people caring for each other and looking out for one another. As societies grew and industrialized and as people moved to cities, he wrote, social ties weakened and became more impersonal. Tönnies called this type of society a **Gesellschaft**, and he was quite critical of this development. He lamented the loss in urban societies of close social bonds and of a strong sense of community, and he feared that a sense of rootlessness in these societies begins to replace the feeling of stability and steadiness characteristic of small, rural societies.

One of the key founders of sociology, French scholar Émile Durkheim, was more positive than Tönnies about the nature of cities and urbanized societies. He certainly appreciated the social bonds and community feeling, which he called **mechanical solidarity**, characteristic of small, rural societies. However, he also thought that these societies stifled individual freedom and that social ties still exist in larger, urban societies. He called these latter ties **organic solidarity**, which he said stems from the division of labor. When there is a division of labor, he wrote, everyone has to depend on everyone else to perform their jobs. This interdependence of roles creases a solidarity that retains much of the bonding and sense of community found in small, rural societies (Durkheim, 1893/1933).[15]

Contemporary research tends to emphasize that strong social bonds do exist in cities (Feldmeyer et al. 2019).[16] Although cities can be anonymous (think of the mass of people walking by each other on a busy street in the downtown area of a large city), many city residents live in neighborhoods where people do know each other, associate with each other, and look out for each other. In these neighborhoods, a sense of community and strong social bonds do, in fact, exist.

In 1938, University of Chicago sociologist Louis Wirth wrote a very influential essay, "Urbanism as a Way of Life," in which he took both a positive and a negative view of cities (Wirth 1938).[17] He agreed with Tönnies that cities have a weaker sense of community and weaker social bonds than do rural areas. But he also agreed with Durkheim that cities generate more creativity and greater tolerance for new ways of thinking. In particular, he said that urban residents are more tolerant than rural residents of nontraditional attitudes, behaviors, and lifestyles, in part because they are much more exposed than rural residents to these nontraditional ways. Supporting Wirth's hypothesis, contemporary research finds that urban residents indeed hold more tolerant views on several kinds of issues (Moore and Ovadia 2006).[18]

Gemeinschaft

According to Ferdinand Tönnies, traditional societies in which family and community ties are quite strong, with people caring for each other and looking out for one another.

Gesellschaft

According to Ferdinand Tönnies, the weakening of social ties and personal relationships as societies grow and become industrialized.

mechanical solidarity

According to Émile Durkheim, the social bonds and community feeling characteristic of small, rural societies.

organic solidarity

According to Émile Durkheim, the social ties that still exist in larger, urban societies, which stem from the division of labor.

In many urban neighborhoods, people are friendly with each other and feel a strong sense of community.

Source: Monkey Business Images/Shuttertock.com

Conflict Theory

We just saw that functionalism has mixed views about the benefits and disadvantages of cities and urban life and thus of urbanization. In contrast to this ambivalence, conflict theory's views are uniformly critical. In this regard, recall from Chapter 1 that conflict theory assumes a basic conflict between society's "haves" and "have-nots," or between the economic and political elites and the poor and people of color. This type of conflict, says conflict theory, manifests itself especially in the nation's cities, in which the "haves" and "have-nots" live very different lives. On the one hand, the rich in American cities live in luxurious apartments and work in high-rise corporate buildings, and they dine at the finest restaurants and shop at the most expensive stores. On the other hand, the poor and people of color live in dilapidated housing and can often barely make ends meet.

Beyond this basic disparity of city life, conflict theorists add that the diverse backgrounds and interests of city residents often lead to conflict because some residents' beliefs and practices clash with those of other residents. In one of the earliest statements of this position, sociologist Thorsten Sellin (1938),[19] who was writing during an era of mass immigration into American cities, said that crime is the result of "culture conflict." In particular, he wrote that crime by immigrants often results from the clash of their traditional ways of thinking and acting with the norms of American society. As one example, he wrote that a father in New Jersey who had emigrated from Sicily killed a teenage boy who had slept with his daughter. The father was surprised when he was arrested by local police, because in the traditional Sicilian culture a man was permitted and even expected to defend his family's honor by acting as the father did!

political economy

The interaction of political and economic institutions and processes.

More recent applications of conflict theory to urbanization emphasize the importance of **political economy**, or the interaction of political and economic institutions and processes. In this way of thinking, political and economic elites in a city (bankers, real estate investors, politicians, and others) collaborate to advance their respective interests. Thus, urban development often takes the form of displacing poor urban residents from their homes so that condominiums, high-rise banks and other corporate buildings, posh shopping malls, or other buildings favoring the rich can be built.

Symbolic Interactionism

Consistent with the overall approach of symbolic interactionism, scholars of the city who take this approach focus on the nature of urban residents' interaction with each other, the reasons for their patterns of interaction, and their perceptions of various aspects of urban life. Their work has yielded many rich, vivid descriptions of the urban life. Many and probably most of these accounts have concerned the lives of the poor and of people of color. The late Elliott Liebow wrote two of the most famous accounts. The first of these two was his majestic *Tally's Corner* (Liebow 1967),[20] which depicted the lives of African American men who "hung around" a particular street corner in a large city. His second account was *Tell Them Who I Am: The Lives of Homeless Women* (Liebow 1993),[21] which, as its title implies, depicted the lives of urban homeless women. Yet another classic account is William Foote Whyte's (1943)[22] *Street Corner Society*, which examined leadership in a street gang in Chicago, Illinois.

These and other accounts all depict cities as places where various norms and values prevail, in contrast to views of cities that depict them as wild, chaotic places. Building on these more positive accounts, sociologist Elijah Anderson emphasizes that most poor urban residents are "decent" (as they call themselves), law-abiding people who strongly disapprove of the crime and drug use in their neighborhoods (Anderson 1999).[23] He also emphasizes that cities are filled with parks and other public settings in which people from different racial and socioeconomic backgrounds gather every day and interact in various ways that help foster interracial understanding. Anderson calls these settings "cosmopolitan canopies," and says they "offer a respite from the lingering tensions of urban life and an opportunity for diverse peoples to come together...Through personal observation, they may come casually to appreciate one another's differences and empathize with the other in a spirit of humanity" (Anderson 2011:xiv–xv).[24] In this manner, writes Anderson, people from different races can at least partly overcome the racial tensions that afflict many American cities.

Types of Urban Residents

Other work in the symbolic interactionist tradition seeks to understand the different lifestyles of city residents. Sociologist Herbert Gans (1982)[25] authored a classic typology of urban residents based on their differing lifestyles and experiences. Gans identified five types of city residents.

The first type is *cosmopolites*. These are people who live in a city because of its cultural attractions, restaurants, and other features of the best that a city has to offer. Cosmopolites include students, writers, musicians, and intellectuals. *Unmarried and childless* individuals and couples are the second type; they live in a city to be near their jobs and to enjoy the various kinds of entertainment found in most cities. If and when they marry or have children, respectively, many migrate to the suburbs to raise their families. The third type is *ethnic villagers*, who are recent immigrants and members of various ethnic groups who live among each other in certain neighborhoods. These neighborhoods tend to have strong social bonds and more generally a strong sense of community. Gans wrote that all these three types generally find the city inviting rather than alienating and have positive experiences far more often than negative ones.

In contrast, two final types of residents find the city alienating and experience a low quality of life. The first of these two types, and the fourth overall, is the *deprived*. These are people with low levels of formal education who live in poverty or near poverty and are unemployed, are underemployed, or work at low wages. They live in neighborhoods filled with trash, broken windows, and other signs of disorder. They commit high rates of crime and also have high rates of victimization by crime. The final type is the *trapped*. These are residents who, as their name implies, might wish to leave their neighborhoods but are unable to do so for several reasons: they may be alcoholics or drug addicts, they may be elderly and disabled, or they may be jobless and cannot afford to move to a better area.

In thinking about this typology, it is important to keep in mind that city residents' social backgrounds—their social class, race/ethnicity, gender, age, and sexual orientation and gender identity—all influence the kind of lifestyle they tend to adopt and thus the type of resident they are according to the typology. As earlier chapters documented, these dimensions of our social backgrounds often yield many kinds of social inequalities, and the quality of life that city residents enjoy depends heavily on these dimensions. For example, residents who are white and wealthy have the money and access to enjoy the best that cities have to offer, while those who are poor and of color typically experience the worst aspects of city life. Because of fear of rape and sexual assault, women often feel more constrained than men from traveling freely throughout a city and being out late at night; older people also often feel more constrained because of physical limitations and fear of muggings; and gays and lesbians are still subject to physical assaults stemming from homophobia. The type of resident we are, then, in terms of our sociodemographic profile affects what we experience in the city and whether that experience is positive or negative.

Herbert Gans identified several types of city residents. One of these types is the cosmopolites, who include students, writers, musicians, and intellectuals, all of whom live in a city because of its cultural attractions and other amenities.

Source: © Thinkstock

Key Takeaways

- Functionalism offers both a positive and a negative view of urbanization. Functionalist sociologists differ on the degree of social solidarity that exists in cities.

- According to conflict theory, economic and political elites use their resources to develop cities in a way that benefits them. The diverse social backgrounds of urban residents also contribute to certain types of conflict.
- According to symbolic interactionism, social inequality based on social class, race/ethnicity, gender, age, and sexual orientation affects the quality of urban experiences. In addition to differences in their sociodemographic profiles, city residents differ in other ways. Herbert Gans identified several types of urban dwellers: cosmopolites, unmarried and childless, ethnic villagers, deprived, and trapped.

For Your Review

1. Write an essay that summarizes the assumptions of any two of the major sociological perspectives on urbanization.
2. Which of the three perspectives makes the most sense to you? Why?

14.3 Problems of Urban Life

Learning Objectives

1. Discuss any three problems of urban life.
2. Provide an example of a problem that specifically arises from the fact that cities consist, by definition, of large numbers of people living in a relatively small space.

Life in U.S. cities today is certainly complex. On the one hand, many U.S. cities are vibrant places, filled with museums and other cultural attractions, nightclubs, theaters, and restaurants and populated by people from many walks of life and from varied racial and ethnic and national backgrounds. Many college graduates flock to cities, not only for their employment opportunities but also for their many activities and the sheer excitement of living in a metropolis.

On the other hand, many U.S. cities are also filled with abject poverty, filthy and dilapidated housing, high crime rates, traffic gridlock, and dirty air. Many Americans would live nowhere but a city, and many would live anywhere but a city. Cities arouse strong opinions, pro and con, because there are many things both to like and to dislike about cities.

By definition, cities consist of very large numbers of people living in a relatively small amount of space. Some of these people have a good deal of money, but many people, and in some cities most people, have very little money. Cities must provide many kinds of services for all their residents, and certain additional services for their poorer residents. These basic facts of city life make for common sets of problems affecting cities throughout the nation, albeit to varying degrees, with some cities less able than others to address these problems. This section examines several of these problems.

Fiscal Problems

One evident problem is *fiscal*: Cities typically have serious difficulties in paying for basic services such as policing, public education, trash removal, street maintenance, and snow removal (at least in cold climates), and in providing certain services for their residents who are poor or disabled or who have other conditions. The fiscal difficulties that cities routinely face become even more serious when the economy lags, as happened during the nation's deep recession that began in late 2007.

Applying Social Research

Urban Neighborhoods and Poor Health

Social scientists have long thought that poor urban neighborhoods pose, in and of themselves, significant health risks for their residents. These neighborhoods lack supermarkets with fresh fruits and vegetables, and they lack safe parks and other settings for exercise. They are also neighborhoods with high crime rates and thus much stress. For all these reasons, they should impair the physical health of their residents. Reflecting this argument, the residents of poor urban neighborhoods do, in fact, exhibit significant health problems compared to the residents of wealthier neighborhoods.

Although this argument might sound compelling, the residents of poor and wealthier neighborhoods might differ in other ways that affect their respective health. For example, people living in wealthier neighborhoods are generally more educated and more conscious of taking care of their health. If their health, then, is better than that of their counterparts in poor neighborhoods, it is difficult to know how much the neighborhood setting itself plays a role in the health of residents.

For this reason, a recent study of a real-life experiment provided compelling evidence of the importance of the quality of a neighborhood for one's health. In the 1990s, the federal government conducted an experiment in which 1,800 poor urban women were randomly selected and, with their permission, assigned to move from their neighborhoods to wealthier neighborhoods. The women were studied a decade after they moved. In particular, they were weighed and had their blood checked for evidence of diabetes. Their results were then compared to women in their original neighborhoods who were not selected to move away. The women who did move away ended up with somewhat lower rates of diabetes and obesity than those who stayed behind.

The experimental design of this study allowed the researchers to conclude that the change in neighborhoods was the reason for their improvement in these two health measures. Reflecting this conclusion, the secretary of the U.S. Department of Housing and Urban Development said, "This study proves that concentrated poverty is not only bad policy, it's bad for your health." A news report observed that the results of this study "offered some of the strongest support yet for the idea that where you live can significantly affect your overall health, especially if your home is in a low-income area."

The results of this experimental study underscore the need to improve the living conditions of poor urban neighborhoods, as these conditions affect many life outcomes of the adults and children who live in them.

Sources: Ludwig et al. 2011; Stobbe 2011[26]

Crowding

Another problem is *crowding*. Cities are crowded in at least two ways. The first involves *residential crowding*: large numbers of people living in a small amount of space. City streets are filled with apartment buildings, condominiums, row houses, and other types of housing, and many people live on any one city block. Residential crowding is perhaps the defining feature of any large city. In this regard, let's compare the Manhattan borough of New York City with the state of Idaho. Slightly more than 1.6 million people live in Manhattan, while a similar number, slightly more than 1.7 million people, live in Idaho. However, Manhattan's residents are packed into only about 24 square miles, while Idaho's residents live within 84,000 square miles. As noted in the beginning of this chapter, New York City's severe crowding contributed to the greater impact it suffered from the coronavirus in 2020.

Cities experience many kinds of problems, and crowding is one of them. People who live amid crowding are more likely to experience stress and depression and to engage in aggressive behavior or be victimized by it.

Source: © Thinkstock

The second type of crowding is *household crowding*: Dwelling units in cities (apartments and houses) are typically small because of lack of space, and much smaller overall than houses in suburbs or rural areas. This forces many people to live in close quarters within a particular dwelling unit, especially if they are low-income individuals or families.

Either type of crowding tends to produce higher levels of stress, depression, aggression and crime (Rollings and Evans 2019).[27] Here an interesting gender difference may exist (Regoeczi 2008):[28] Household crowding may produce depression in women but not men, and aggression in men but not women.

Although crowding of both types is a problem, then, there is probably little that cities can do to reduce crowding. This fact underscores the need to undertake other efforts that might address the various consequences of residential and household crowding. In this regard, Chapter 8 outlined several efforts to help reduce crime and delinquency.

Housing

A third problem involves *housing*. Here there are several related issues. Much urban housing is *substandard* and characterized by such problems as broken windows, malfunctioning heating systems, peeling lead paint, and insect infestation.

At the same time, adequate housing is *not affordable* for many city residents, as housing prices in cities can be very high, and usually higher than in rural areas, and the residents' incomes are typically very low. Cities thus have a great need for adequate, affordable housing, especially because many of their low-income residents may find themselves evicted with no recourse (Desmond 2016).[29]

Another housing issue concerns *racial segregation*. Although federal law prohibits segregated housing, cities across the country are nonetheless highly segregated by race, with many neighborhoods all or mostly African American. In a widely cited book, sociologists Douglas S. Massey and Nancy A. Denton (1993)[30] termed this situation "American apartheid." They said that these segregated neighborhoods result from a combination of several factors, including (a) "white flight" into suburbs, (b) informal—and often illegal—racially discriminatory actions that make it difficult for African Americans to move into white neighborhoods (such as real estate agents falsely telling black couples that no houses are available in a particular neighborhood), and (c) a general lack of income and other resources that makes it very difficult for African Americans to move from segregated neighborhoods.

Massey and Denton argued that residential segregation worsens the general circumstances in which many urban African Americans live. Several reasons account for this effect. As whites flee to the suburbs, the people left behind are much poorer. The tax base of cities suffers accordingly, and along with it the quality of city schools, human services, and other social functions. All these problems help keep the crime rate high and perhaps even raise it further. Because segregated neighborhoods are poor and crime ridden, businesses do not want to invest in them, and employment opportunities are meager. This fact worsens conditions in segregated neighborhoods even further. Consequently, concluded Massey and Denton, racial segregation helps to keep very poor people living in deep poverty and decaying neighborhoods.

To improve the socioeconomic status and living circumstances of African Americans, then, it is critical that residential segregation be reduced. Although Latinxs live in segregated neighborhoods to a smaller degree, reducing segregation would also help their circumstances.

Children and Our Future

The Plight of Homeless Children

One of the most disheartening social problems of urban areas is the plight of homeless children. The number of children who are homeless at least part of the year now reaches more than 1.3 million annually, equal to almost 2 percent of all American children. Because of their circumstances, they are at greater risk than their housed peers for hunger, asthma and other chronic health conditions, and stress and emotional problems. They also are at greater risk for poor school performance.

To help these children, some school districts have sent special buses to homeless shelters, motels, and other settings for homeless children and their parents so that the children could continue attending their regular school. They have also assigned social workers to help homeless families and other personnel to bring them school supplies, to drive them to look at shelters where they could live, and to perform other tasks. Federal legislation in fact requires schools to take extra measures to help homeless children, but school superintendents say that the federal government has not provided them the necessary funds to carry out the intent of the legislation.

The United States Interagency Council on Homelessness has called for additional research to gather needed data on family homelessness. According to this council, "There continues to be a concerted effort to more closely align existing data on families with children to better understand the scope, scale, and characteristics of family homelessness. Federal agencies and states and communities continue to use the data they have to better understand and respond to local needs. There remains a need, however, for a more detailed understanding of which families with children fall into homelessness and precipitating causes. There is also a need for expanded evidence regarding the impact of housing and services interventions on a range of family- and child-level outcomes and on achieving sustained and stable exits from homelessness." To help reduce the shocking sight and plight of homeless children in one of the wealthiest nations in the world, the United States should increase its funding for research to gather this kind of evidence, and it should also increase its funding to help our homeless kids.

Sources: Eckholm 2009; United States Interagency Council on Homelessness 2018[31]

Homelessness

Homelessness is a major problem in many cities. The federal government estimates that 650,000 Americans are homeless on any given night.

Source: Belish/Shutterstock.com

A related problem to housing is *homelessness*. In cities throughout the United States, men, women, and children live in the streets, abandoned vehicles or houses, cheap motels, or trailers, or in someone else's home temporarily. In cities with cold climates, homelessness can be life-threatening during the winter. But regardless of climate, the homeless are in a dire situation. Homeless shelters provide some relief against crime, hunger, and the many other problems arising from homelessness, but too few shelters exist to meet the demand, and those that do exist are underfunded.

As should be clear, the problem of homelessness cannot be understood apart from the problem of poverty (see Chapter 2). Wealthy families that lose their homes, as after a fire, usually can expect to find suitable temporary lodging and have their homeowners' insurance pay for a new home. Meanwhile, poor families who can no longer pay their rent or mortgage payments face eviction and homelessness from which they find it difficult to recover (Desmond 2016).[32]

The homeless population is at much greater risk for a variety of physical and mental health problems and other difficulties (Lee et al. 2010).[33] In particular, they are much more likely than housed Americans to experience hunger and food insecurity, and they are also much more likely to suffer from chronic illnesses such as hepatitis, high blood pressure, tuberculosis, and vascular disease. On the average, homeless adults die by their midfifties, about twenty years shorter than the average life span of housed adults.

Traffic and Transportation

Traffic is a major problem in cities. The great number of motor vehicles in a relatively small space often leads to gridlock and contributes greatly to air pollution.

Source: Nicole Glass Photography/Shutterstock.com

A fifth problem of city life is *traffic and transportation*. For better or worse, a fact of city life that arises from the defining feature of cities—many people living in a relatively small area—is that many people need to travel to get to work or school and to visit stores, museums, and any number of other leisure-time settings. Someone living in a rural area is probably able to drive ten miles to work in no longer than twenty minutes, but someone living in an urban area may easily take an hour or longer to travel the same distance after crawling along in traffic and stopping at light after light, or sitting and crawling along in long miles of traffic on an urban highway.

One manifestation of the traffic problem in cities is traffic *gridlock*, when traffic in all directions is barely moving or not moving at all. Gridlock occurs in urban areas, not rural ones, because of the sheer volume of traffic and the sheer number of intersections controlled by traffic lights or stop signs. Some cities have better public transportation than others, but congested traffic and time-consuming commuting are problems that urban residents experience every day (see "Lessons from Other Societies").

Boston Traffic So Bad It Has Become a 'Public Safety Hazard'

A major problem in many American cities and also cities in many other nations is traffic congestion. This congestion contributes to these cities' pollution and may harm the health of their residents, as this video about Boston's traffic discusses.

View the video online at: http://www.youtube.com/embed/AblmyLiEW58?rel=0

Lessons from Other Societies

Making Drivers Miserable to Reduce Traffic Congestion

One of the costs of urbanization and modern life is traffic. Urban streets and highways are clogged with motor vehicles, and two major consequences of so much traffic are air pollution and tens of thousands of deaths and injuries from vehicular accidents. To reduce city traffic, many European cities are trying to make driving so burdensome that commuters and other drivers will seek other forms of transportation. As a news story summarized this trend, these cities are "creating environments openly hostile to cars. The methods vary, but the mission is clear: to make car use expensive and just plain miserable enough to tilt drivers toward more environmentally friendly modes of transportation."

For example, Copenhagen, Munich, and Vienna have banned cars on many streets. Barcelona and Paris have replaced car lanes with bicycle lanes. London and Stockholm now require drivers entering their downtowns to pay a heavy toll charge. Many German cities restrict parts of their downtowns to cars that meet certain limits on carbon dioxide emission. Other European cities have sharply limited the number of parking spaces at shopping malls and other areas, and they have also eliminated on-street parking.

This European strategy to relieve traffic congestion differs greatly from the strategy the United States uses. As a European environmental official explained this difference, "In the United States, there has been much more of a tendency to adapt cities to accommodate driving. Here there has been more movement to make cities more livable for people, to get cities relatively free of cars."

Zurich, the largest city in Switzerland, has made special efforts to "torment drivers," said the news story, in the hope that drivers will seek other modes of transportation. For example, it added more traffic lights to cause more traffic delays, and it shortened the length of green lights and lengthened red lights. It also banned cars in one of its busiest downtown areas and elsewhere imposed speed limits of just a few miles an hour so that pedestrians are free to cross the street whenever they want. Although store owners in Zurich worried that they would lose business after their streets were closed to traffic, that effect has not happened because pedestrian traffic increased.

Despite some exceptions, most American cities have tried to make it easier for drivers through such measures as synchronizing green lights and developing apps to help drivers find parking. However, these measures do not reduce the number of cars and do little to relieve traffic congestion. Instead, they tend to make it more likely that people will want to drive in the downtown areas. In contrast, Europe has tried to relieve traffic congestion by reducing the number of cars. Its model offers more potential for reducing the pollution and other problems caused by traffic, and it is one that the United States should adopt.

Sources: Puentes 2015; Rosenthal 2011[34]

To help reduce traffic congestion, cities long ago developed various means of public transportation: buses, subways, and light rail. Some cities have better public transportation than other cities; Los Angeles has a notoriously bad reputation for the quality of its public transportation. Yet residents of cities with relatively good public transportation still experience severe traffic congestion, long commutes, and related problems. Public transportation is sometimes faster than commuting by car or SUV, but it can still be very time consuming. People who take a bus or other public transportation can easily spend an hour or more (depending on how far they have to travel and the quality of their city's transportation system) traveling to a bus or train station, waiting for their transportation, making any necessary connections, and then traveling to their workplace.

One consequence of traffic congestion is stress. As one mental health expert observed, "Commuters can experience greater stress than fighter pilots in battle" (Greenfield 2011).[35] Another consequence is huge financial costs, because sitting in traffic wastes both time and fuel. The Texas Transportation Institute (TTI), perhaps the leading scholarly unit for the study of traffic problems, estimates that traffic congestion costs the nation $166 billion annually in wasted time and fuel, or $1,010 for every auto commuter. Traffic congestion wastes 54 hours per commuter annually and 3.3 billion gallons of gasoline annually (Schrank et al. 2019).[36] To relieve traffic congestion, TTI recommends significant investments of public funds in public transportation and more efficient designs in private and public transportation systems, such as the greater use of electronic toll-taking and better timing of traffic lights to increase traffic flow.

Air Pollution

Traffic congestion and the sheer amount of traffic in cities also contribute mightily to *air pollution*, which we consider here as a separate urban problem. Traffic creates pollution from motor vehicles' exhaust systems, and some cities have factories and other enterprises that also pollute. As a result, air quality in cities is substandard. This poor air quality has significant health consequences, as it produces higher rates of respiratory and heart disease and higher mortality rates in cities. Because even fairly low levels of air pollution can have these health effects, cities are unhealthy places and even deadly places for many people. As also noted in the beginning of this chapter, large cities' high levels of air pollution contributed to higher rates of COVID-19 deaths during the 2020 pandemic.

Both to decrease their "carbon footprint" and to get some exercise, many urban residents bicycle in traffic to and from work or bicycle during their leisure time. Ironically, doing so subjects them to air pollution from the traffic surrounding them. This pollution may impair their cardiovascular and respiratory functioning (Giménez-Gaydou et al. 2019).[37]

Because people of color disproportionately live in cities, urban air pollution affects them more than it affects white people. As Chapter 13 noted, this disparity is part of the larger problem of *environmental racism*. Cities are bad in many ways for their residents, and the air pollution of cities is bad for the health of their residents, who are overwhelmingly people of color in many cities.

If urban residents in general suffer health consequences from air pollution, these consequences are particularly serious and more common among children. Air pollution increases their rates of asthma and other respiratory diseases, which in turn may impair their school performance and have other lifelong consequences.

Mental Health Problems

Our earlier discussions of crowding and of traffic congestion indicated that stress is one of the most important consequences of these two urban problems. Stress in turn impairs the mental health of urban residents. Much research finds that urban residents tend to have worse mental health than rural residents (Okkels et al. 2018).[38]

Public Education

Yet another issue for cities is the state of their *public education*. As Chapter 11 emphasized, many city schools are housed in old buildings that, like much city housing, are falling apart. City schools are notoriously underfunded and lack current textbooks, adequate science equipment, and other instructional materials.

People Making a Difference

Working to Achieve Social Justice

Nancy Radner has been a tireless advocate for the homeless and for social justice more generally. From 2006 to 2012, she served as the head of the Chicago Alliance to End Homelessness, which works with eighty-four homeless service agencies and manages more than $50 million in state and federal funding for homeless services. The Alliance also gathers and distributes various kinds of information on homelessness and coordinates political, educational, and public relations events to increase understanding of homelessness.

Before joining the Chicago Alliance, Radner was a program officer at the Corporation for Supportive Housing, a national organization that engages in many kinds of efforts aimed at helping the homeless and other low-income individuals find affordable housing. She also served as a staff attorney at the Legal Assistance Foundation of Chicago, where she specialized in housing law.

In 2012, Radner left the Chicago Alliance for another social justice position when she joined the Ounce of Prevention Fund as director of Illinois policy. The Ounce, as this Illinois organization calls itself, advocates for early childhood education and other programs and policies aimed at helping low-income children. She later became the chief operating officer of the Primo Center for Women and Children, which provides housing and other services for homeless families in Chicago.

Many people who receive a law degree from a top law school, as Radner did, take a job in a large law firm or with a large corporation and spend their careers helping the wealthy. Instead, Radner chose to use her legal knowledge to help achieve social justice for the poor. She once said of her efforts to end homelessness, "People call us starry-eyed dreamers. But I actually say we're steely-eyed realists because ending homelessness is not hard. We know exactly how to do it. And what we're trying to do is create the political will to get it fully done. We can't prevent people from losing their housing. But what we can do is ensure that if that happens that there's a system in place to get them out of homelessness really quickly."

In working her entire career to help the poor and homeless, Nancy Radner has helped make a difference.

Sources: Kapos 2012; Schorsch 2010; Studenkov 2019[39]

Crime

When many people think about the disadvantages of city life, they probably think about crime, a problem mentioned several times already in this chapter. Their fears are well grounded. Simply put, cities have much higher rates of violent and property crime than do small towns or rural areas. For example, the violent crime rate (number of crimes per 100,000 residents) in 2018 was 3.6 times higher in the nation's largest cities than in its rural counties, while the property crime rate was almost three times higher (Federal Bureau of Investigation 2019).[40]

Why are city crime rates much higher? Because crime *rates* take the number of people into account, the answer is not simply that cities have more people than rural areas. Nor is the answer simply that cities have higher poverty than rural areas, because rural areas in fact have higher poverty overall, as we discuss later in this chapter. Rather, an important answer is that cities have higher residential crowding (or higher population density) and also more household crowding, as we saw earlier.

Crime rates are higher in cities in part because the great numbers of urban residents provide many potential targets for criminals.

Source: © Thinkstock

Several reasons explain why higher residential crowding produces higher crime rates. Consider violent crime. For a violent crime to occur, it takes two people to tangle, so to speak. Criminals cannot kill, rob, or assault someone unless there is a "someone" to assault. In a city, there are many potential targets of violence all crowded together into a relatively small space, and thus many potential targets for criminals. In a rural area, potential targets are spread across miles, and a robber can go a long time without ever seeing a potential victim. Many assaults are also committed not by hardened criminals but by people (usually men) who get angry because of some perceived insult. In a city, there is a much greater chance for interaction to occur where someone might feel insulted, simply because there are so many people living within a small space, and bars and other venues for them to congregate. A thousand people living on one city block are more likely to encounter each other than a thousand people living across thirty square miles in a rural area. Because there is more opportunity in a city for insults and other problems to occur that lead to violence, more violence occurs.

Cities also have more crowded households than rural areas, as we saw earlier, and these also make a difference for at least two reasons (Stark 1987).[41] Crowded households are more stressful, and people who experience stress are more likely to be aggressive. Further, people (and perhaps especially young people) who live in crowded households often find they need to "get outside" to be away from the stress of the household and to have some "elbow room" and privacy. But once outside, they are that much more likely to interact with other people. Because, as we just noted, social interaction is a prerequisite for violence, household crowding indirectly contributes to violence for this reason.

deviant places

Sociologist Rodney Stark's term for neighborhoods that have severe crowding and other features that promote high crime rates.

Residential crowding and household crowding thus combine to produce higher crime rates in cities than in rural areas. City neighborhoods differ in their degree of both types of crowding, and those that have higher crowding rates should have higher crime rates, all else equal. In sociologist Rodney Stark's (1987)[42] term, these neighborhoods are **deviant places** because their structural features, such as crowding, almost automatically contribute to higher crime rates regardless of who is living in these neighborhoods.

Another structural feature of cities helps to explain why they have a higher property crime rate than rural areas. Burglars obviously cannot burglarize a home unless there is a nearby home to burglarize. In cities, there are many homes to serve as potential targets for burglars; in rural areas, these homes are few and far between. Similarly, if someone wants to shoplift in a store or break into a store overnight, they can more easily do so in an urban area, where there are many stores, than in a rural area, where the landscape is filled with trees or fields rather than Walmarts or Best Buys.

Although Stark (1987)[43] coined the term *deviant places* to refer to urban neighborhoods that had certain features that contribute to high crime rates, his term can also refer to cities themselves. For the reasons just discussed, cities are inevitably much more likely than rural areas to be deviant places. The defining feature of a city—large numbers of people living in a small area—guarantees that cities will have higher crime rates than rural areas. Cities are deviant places precisely because they are cities.

14.4 Problems of Rural Life

Learning Objectives

1. List three positive aspects of rural life in the United States.
2. Describe two problems of rural life in the United States.

About one-fourth of the U.S. population and more than 40 percent of the world population live in rural areas. As the previous section demonstrated, a dual view of cities exists: They have many advantages, but they also have many disadvantages. This dual view also applies to rural areas, but it does so in a sort of mirror image: The advantages of cities are often disadvantages for rural areas, and the disadvantages of cities are often advantages for rural areas.

On the positive side, and focusing on the United States, rural areas feature much more open space and less crowding. Their violent and property crime rates are much lower than those in large cities, as we have seen. The air is cleaner because there is less traffic and fewer factories and other facilities that emit pollution. Life in rural areas is thought to be slower paced, resulting in lower levels of anxiety and a greater sense of relaxation. For these and other reasons, rural residents exhibit better mental health on the average than do urban residents.

On the negative side, rural areas are often poor and lack the services, employment opportunities, and leisure activities that cities have. Teens often complain of boredom, and drug and alcohol use can be high (Patrick et al. 2019).[44] Public transportation is often lacking, making it difficult for people without motor vehicles, who tend to have low incomes, to get to workplaces, stores, and other venues. Rural residents with motor vehicles often must still travel long distances to shop, visit a doctor, go to work, and do any number of other activities. Many rural areas in the United States lack high-speed broadband, a necessity in today's economy; this situation impairs their economy. All these challenges contribute to special problems in rural areas. We now examine some of these problems.

Rural areas can be beautiful and relaxing, but they also must confront important challenges. These problems include a lack of public transportation, human services, and medical professionals and facilities.

Source: © Thinkstock

Rural Health

As Chapter 13 noted, rural areas often lack sufficient numbers of health-care professionals, hospitals, and medical clinics. Compounding these shortages are other problems. The first is that the small hospitals typical of rural areas generally lack high-quality care and equipment. A patient who needs heart bypass surgery, brain surgery, or other types of complex medical care is likely to have to travel or be taken to an urban hospital far away. As mentioned in the beginning of this chapter, this situation made it very difficult for some rural areas to treat COVID-19 patients during the 2020 pandemic.

The second problem is the long distances that ambulances and patients must travel. Because ambulances and other emergency vehicles must travel so far, rural residents with emergencies receive medical attention more slowly than their urban counterparts. As well, the long distances that people must travel make it more difficult for patients with health problems to receive medical care. For example, a rural cancer patient who needs chemotherapy or radiation might have to travel two to three hours in each direction to receive treatment. Travel distances in rural areas also mean that rural residents are less likely than urban residents to receive preventive services such as physical examinations; screenings for breast cancer, cervical cancer, and colorectal cancer; and vaccinations for various illnesses and diseases.

In yet another problem, rural areas are also much more likely than urban areas to lack mental health care, drug abuse counseling and programs, and other services related to physical and mental health. This problem has been compounded in recent years by the closing of many rural hospitals across the nation due to underfunding and rising operating costs.

 ### Rural Hospitals Across Tennessee at Risk of Closing

Rural residents in the United States face many health care problems because of their rural residence. One of these problems is the closing of rural hospitals during the past decade, as this video illustrates.

View the video online at: http://www.youtube.com/embed/uqql4lq-RJU?rel=0

For all these reasons, rural residents are more at risk than urban residents for certain health problems, including mortality. One study found, for example, that only one-third of all motor vehicle accidents happen in rural areas, but that two-thirds of all deaths from such accidents occur in rural areas. These problems help explain why rural residents are more likely than urban residents to report being in only fair or poor health in government surveys (Bennett et al. 2009).[45]

An additional health problem in rural areas arises from the age profile of their populations. Compared to urban areas, rural areas have an "aging population," or a greater percentage of adults aged 65 and older. This fact adds to the health-care problems that rural areas must address.

Rural Schools and Education

The discussion of education in Chapter 11 focused mostly on urban schools. Many of the problems discussed there also apply to rural schools. However, rural schools often face hurdles that urban and suburban schools are much less likely to encounter (Walker 2017).[46]

First, because rural areas have been losing population, they have been experiencing declining school enrollment and school closings. When a school does close, teachers and other school employees have lost their jobs, and students have to rather suddenly attend a new school that is usually farther from their home than their former school.

Second, rural populations are generally older than urban populations, as mentioned earlier, and have a greater percentage of retired adults. Therefore, rural areas' per-capita income and sales tax revenue are lower than those of urban and suburban areas, and this lower revenue makes the funding of public schools more challenging.

Third, rural families live relatively far from the public schools, and the schools are relatively far from each other. As a result, rural school districts have considerable expenses for transporting children to and from school, after-school athletic events, and other activities.

Finally, it is often difficult to recruit and retain quality teachers in rural areas. This problem has forced some rural school districts to offer hiring bonuses or housing assistance to staff their schools.

Rural Poverty

Although many U.S. cities have high poverty rates, the poverty rate is actually slightly higher in rural areas than in urban areas (Semega et al. 2019).[47] Several factors contribute to this higher rate. These factors include the out-migration of young, highly skilled workers; the lack of industrial jobs that typically have been higher paying than agricultural jobs; and limited opportunities for the high-paying jobs of the information age. Biotech companies, electronics companies, and other symbols of the information age are usually not found in the nation's rural areas. Instead, they are located in or near urban areas, in which are found the universities, masses of people, and other necessary aspects these companies need to succeed.

Compounding the general problem of poverty, rural areas are also more likely than non-rural areas to lack human services programs to help the poor, disabled, elderly, and other people in need of aid. Because rural towns are so small, they often cannot afford services such as soup kitchens, homeless shelters, and Meals on Wheels, and thus must rely on services located in other towns. Yet rural towns are often far from each other, making it difficult and expensive for rural residents to obtain the services they need. For example, a Meals on Wheels program in an urban area may travel just a few miles and serve dozens or hundreds of people, while it may have to travel more than one hundred miles in a rural area and serve only a few people. Adding to this problem is the strong sense in many rural areas that individuals should be strong enough to fend for themselves and not accept government help. Even when services are available, some people who need them decline to take advantage of them because of pride and shame.

Domestic Violence

One of the sad facts of rural life is domestic violence. This form of violence is certainly common in urban areas, but the defining feature of rural areas—a relatively low number of people living in a relatively broad area—creates several problems for victims of domestic violence, most of them women (DeKeseredy 2019).[48]

For example, these women often find it difficult to get help and/or to leave their abusers wherever they live. However, it is often even more difficult for rural women to do so. Rural police may be unenlightened about domestic violence and may even know the abuser; for either reason, they may not consider his violence a crime, and abused women may be that much more reluctant to tell the police about their abuse.

Another problem concerns the availability of battered women's shelters, which provide invaluable services for abused women and any children they might have. These shelters tend to be found in cities, which still do not have nearly enough shelters. Rural areas generally lack shelters, and any shelters that exist are often long distances from the homes of abused women. In rural areas, abused women are also more likely than their urban counterparts to lack neighbors and friends to whom they can turn for support, or at least to live farther from these individuals. For all these reasons, rural women who experience domestic violence face a problem that has been called "dangerous exits" (DeKeseredy and Schwartz 2009).[49]

Key Takeaways

- Like cities, rural areas also have their advantages and disadvantages. They can be beautiful, relaxing places in which to live, but they also lack many of the cultural advantages and other amenities that cities feature.
- Rural areas are characterized by sparse populations and long distances that people must travel. These conditions make it difficult to provide adequate public transportation and various kinds of human services. The poverty of many rural areas aggravates these problems.

For Your Review

1. If you had your choice, would you want to live in a large city, medium-sized city, small town, or rural area? Explain your answer.
2. Because rural residents often live far from health care providers, telemedicine (in which patients and health care providers communicate visually over the Internet) may be a solution. Do you think this is an adequate solution, or should rural areas give health care providers financial and other incentives to move to their locations? Explain your answer.

14.5 Improving Urban and Rural Life

Learning Objective

1. Explain the value of a sociological perspective for addressing urban housing and crowding problems.

Many urban problems are not, strictly speaking, sociological or other social science problems. For example, traffic congestion is arguably more of an engineering issue than a sociological issue, even if traffic congestion has many social consequences. Other urban problems are problems discussed in previous chapters that disproportionately affect urban areas. For example, crime is more common in urban areas than elsewhere, and racial and ethnic inequality is much more of an issue in urban areas than rural areas because of the concentration of people of color in our cities. Previous chapters have discussed such problems in some detail, and the strategies suggested in those chapters need not be discussed again here.

Still other urban issues exist that this chapter was the first to present. Two of these involve crowding and housing. Cities are certainly crowded, and some parts of cities are especially crowded. Housing is expensive, and many urban residents live in dilapidated, substandard housing. Here again a sociological perspective offers some insight, as it reminds us that these problems are intimately related to inequalities of social class, race and ethnicity, and gender. Although it is critical to provide adequate, affordable housing to city residents, it is also important to remember that these various social inequalities affect who is in most need of such housing. Ultimately, strategies aimed at providing affordable housing will not succeed unless they recognize the importance of these social inequalities and unless other efforts reduce or eliminate these inequalities. Racial residential segregation also remains a serious problem in our nation's urban centers, and sociologists have repeatedly shown that residential segregation contributes to many of the problems that urban African Americans experience. Reducing such segregation must be a fundamental goal of any strategy to help American cities.

Although traffic congestion is largely an engineering issue, engineers do not operate in a social vacuum. People will be more likely to drive in a city when it is easier for them to drive, and less likely to drive when it is more difficult for them to drive. As the "Lessons from Other Societies" box illustrated, European cities have done much more than U.S. cities to reduce traffic congestion and thus improve air quality in their cities. Americans may resist the measures the European nations have taken, but the success of these measures suggests that the United States should also use them to deal with the many problems associated with traffic congestion.

Certain problems discussed in previous chapters are also more urgent in rural areas. In particular, the isolation and long distances of rural areas pose special challenges for the provision of adequate health care and for addressing the needs of victims of domestic violence. Ironically, some of the very features that make rural areas so attractive to many people also make them difficult settings for other people. In view of this context, it is essential that public transportation in rural areas be expanded, and that the many types of medical care and social and legal services commonly found in urban areas also be expanded. Although rural residents undoubtedly do not expect to find the range of care and services available to their urban counterparts, they should not have to suffer from a lack of adequate care and services.

Key Takeaways

- Many of the problems of urban and rural life were addressed in earlier chapters. The strategies discussed in those chapters to address these problems thus also apply to the problems examined in this chapter.
- Many urban problems are associated with poverty and racial discrimination. Reducing these problems should help relieve urban problems.
- The characteristics of rural areas that often make them so appealing also lead to certain problems that are especially urgent in rural areas.

For Your Review

1. How do you think American cities should try, if at all, to reduce traffic congestion?
2. Are urban problems worse than rural problems, or are rural problems worse than urban problems? Explain your answer.

14.6 End-of-Chapter Material

Summary

1. Urbanization is a consequence of population growth. Cities first developed in ancient times after the rise of horticultural and pastoral societies and "took off" during the Industrial Revolution as people moved to be near factories. Urbanization led to many social changes then and continues today to affect society.
2. Functionalism, conflict theory, and symbolic interactionism offer varied understandings of urbanization. Functionalists have a mixed view of urbanization, while conflict theorists hold a negative view.
3. Cities face many problems, several of which reflect the fact that cities feature large numbers of people living within a relatively small space. Among the most serious of these problems are residential crowding, substandard and racially segregated housing, heavy traffic and great amounts of air pollution, and high crime rates. Several of these problems resulted in a heavier impact on large cities when the 2020 COVID-19 pandemic began.
4. Rural areas face many challenges that result from their sparse populations and the great distances that people must often travel. Among other problems, rural areas have a lack of economic opportunities in today's information age and a general lack of various kinds of human services. Rural areas faced special challenges during the 2020 COVID-19 pandemic for several reasons, including the fact that rural hospitals tend to be small, underfunded, and understaffed.

Using What You Know

After graduating from college, you are now working as an entry-level assistant to the mayor of a medium-sized city. You are aware that many city residents are unhappy with the quality of housing in their neighborhoods. The mayor thinks the city has little, if any, money to help improve the city's housing, and also thinks that the housing problem is not nearly as bad as the city's residents seem to think. The mayor asks your opinion about this issue. Based on what you have learned in this chapter and perhaps in other coursework and reading, what do you tell the mayor?

What You Can Do

To help deal with the urban and rural problems discussed in this chapter, you may wish to do any of the following:

1. Volunteer at a social service agency in your community.

2. Start or join a Habitat for Humanity or other group that builds homes for low-income families.

3. Attend local city council meetings to learn about budgetary issues so that you will be in a more knowledgeable position to help your community.

Endnotes

1. Wilson, Mark. 2019. "City's Demolition of Vacant Homes at Heart of Neighborhood Revitalization." *Courier & Press* September 30:https://www.courierpress.com/story/news/local/2019/09/30/evansville-blight-program-demolishes-abandoned-homes/3821009002/.

2. Whooley, Owen. 2013. *Knowledge in the Time of Cholera: The Struggle over American Medicine in the Nineteenth Century*. Chicago: University of Chicago Press.

3. Rubin, David and Paul A. Offit. 2020. "Crowding May Mean More Death." *The New York Times* April 28(A23).

4. Smith, Stacey Vanek and Cardiff Garcia. 2020. "Covid-19 Pandemic Puts Rural Hospitals under Even More Pressure." *npr.org* Aoril 23:https://www.npr.org/2020/04/23/842195550/covid-19-pandemic-puts-rural-hospitals-under-even-more-pressure.

5. McArdle, Megan. 2020. "Rural Areas Think They're the Coronavirus Exception. They're Not." *The Washington Post* April 17:https://www.washingtonpost.com/opinions/rural-areas-think-theyre-the-coronavirus-exception-theyre-not/2020/04/16/d488b800-8028-11ea-13-1b6da0e4a2b7_story.html.

6. Fehr, Rachel, Jennifer Kates, Cynthia Cox and Josh Michaud. 2020. *Covid-19 in Rural America—Is There Cause for Concern?* San Francisco: Kaiser Family Foundation.

7. Kleniewski, Nancy and Alexander R. Thomas. 2019. *Cities, Change, and Conflict*. New York: Routledge.

8. Gibson, Campbell. 1998. "Population of the 100 Largest Cities and Other Urban Places in the United States: 1790-1990." Washington, D.C.: U.S. Census Bureau.

9. Feldberg, Michael. 1980. *The Turbulent Era: Riot and Disorder in Jacksonian America*. New York: Oxford University Press.

10. Steffens, Lincoln. 1904. *The Shame of the Cities*. New York: McClure, Phillips.

11. Riis, Jacob. 1890. *How the Other Half Lives: Studies among the Tenements of New York*. New York: Charles Scribner's Sons.

12. Kaneda, Toshiko and Kristin Bietsch. 2016. *2016 World Population Data Sheet*. https://www.prb.org/2016-world-population-data-sheet/. Population Reference Bureau; 2012. *Human Population: Urbanization*. Retrieved from http://www.prb.org/Educators/TeachersGuides/HumanPopulation/Urbanization.aspx.

13. Population Reference Bureau. 2015. *The Urban-Rural Divide in Health and Development*. Washington, DC: Population Reference Bureau.

14. Tönnies, Ferdinand. 1963. *Community and Society*. 1963. New York: Harper and Row. (Original work published 1887)

15. Durkheim, Émile. 1933. *The Division of Labor in Society*. London: Free Press. (Original work published 1893)

16. Feldmeyer, Ben, Madero-Hernandez Arelys, Carlos E Rojas-Gaona and Sabon Lauren Copley. 2019. "Immigration, Collective Efficacy, Social Ties, and Violence: Unpacking the Mediating Mechanisms in Immigration Effects on Neighborhood-Level Violence." *Race and Justice* 9(2):123-50.

17. Wirth, Louis. 1938. "Urbanism as a Way of Life." *American Journal of Sociology* 44:3-24.

18. Moore, Laura M. and Seth Ovadia. 2006. "Accounting for Spatial Variation in Tolerance: The Effects of Education and Religion." *Social Forces* 84(4):2205-22.

19. Sellin, Thorsten. 1938. "Culture Conflict and Crime." *Bulletin* 41. New York: Social Science Research Council.

20. Liebow, Elliott. 1967. *Tally's Corner*. Boston: Little, Brown.

21. Liebow, Elliot. 1993. *Tell Them Who I Am: The Lives of Homeless Women*. New York: Free Press.

22. Whyte, William Foote. 1943. *Street Corner Society: The Social Structure of an Italian Slum*. Chicago: University of Chicago Press.

23. Anderson, Elijah. 1999. *Code of the Street: Decency, Violence, and the Moral Life of the Inner City*. New York: W.W. Norton.

24. Anderson, Elijah. 2011. *The Cosmopolitan Canopy: Race and Civility in Everyday Life*. New York: W.W. Norton.

25. Gans, Herbert J. 1982. *The Urban Villagers: Group and Class in the Life of Italian-Americans*. New York: Free Press.

26. Ludwig, Jens, Lisa Sanbonmatsu, Lisa Gennetian, Emma Adam, Greg J. Duncan, Lawrence F. Katz, Ronald C. Kessler, Jeffrey R. Kling, Stacy Tessler Lindau, Robert C. Whitaker and Thomas W. McDade. 2011. "Neighborhoods, Obesity, and Diabetes: A Randomized Social Experiment." *New England Journal of Medicine* 365(16):1509-1519; Stobbe, Mike. 2011. "Decade-Long Study Links Living in Low-Income Neighborhoods to Poor Health." *The Boston Globe* October 20:A15.

27. Rollings, Kimberly A. and Gary W. Evans. 2019. "Design Moderators of Perceived Residential Crowding and Chronic Physiological Stress among Children." *Environment and Behavior* 51(5):590-621.

28. Regoeczi, Wendy C. 2008. "Crowding in Context: An Examination of the Differential Responses of Men and Women to High-Density Living Environments." *Journal of Health and Social Behavior* 49:254-68.

29. Desmond, Matthew. 2016. *Evicted: Poverty and Profit in the American City*. New York: Crown Publishers.

30. Massey, Douglas S. and Nancy A. Denton. 1993. *American Apartheid: Segregation and the Making of the Underclass*. Cambridge, MA: Harvard University Press.

31. Eckholm, Erik. 2009. "Surge in Homeless Pupils Strains Schools." *The New York Times* September 6:A1; United States Interagency Council on Homelessness. 2018. "Homelessness in America: Focus on Families with Children."https://www.usich.gov/resources/uploads/asset_library/Homelessness_in_America_Families_with_Children.pdf.

32. Desmond, Matthew. 2016. *Evicted: Poverty and Profit in the American City*. New York: Crown Publishers.

33. Lee, Barrett A., Kimberly A. Tyler and James D. Wright. 2010. "The New Homelessness Revisited." *Annual Review of Sociology* 36:501-21.

34. Puentes, Robert. 2015. "Rethinking Urban Traffic Congestion to Put People First." *Brookings.com*:https://www.brookings.edu/blog/the-avenue/2015/08/27/rethinking-traffic-congestion-to-put-people-first/; Rosenthal, Elizabeth. 2011. "Across Europe, Irking Drivers is Urban Policy." *The New York Times* June 27:A1.

35. Greenfield, Beth. 2011. "America's Most Stressful Cities." *Forbes* September 23:http://www.forbes.com/sites/bethgreenfield/2011/09/23/americas-most-stressful-cities/.

36. Schrank, David, Bill Eisele and Tim Lomax. 2019. *2019 Urban Mobility Report*. College Station, TX: Texas Transportation Institute.

37. Giménez-Gaydou, Diego A., Amândio Cupido dos Santos, Gabriel Mendes, Inês Frade and Anabela S.N. Ribeiro. 2019. "Energy Consumption and Pollutant Exposure Estimation for Cyclist Routes in Urban Areas." *Transportation Research Part D: Transport and Environment* 72(July):1-16.

38. Okkels, Niels, Christina Blanner Kristiansen, Povl Munk-Jørgensen and Norman Sartorius. 2018. "Urban Mental Health: Challenges and Perspectives." *Current Opinion in Psychiatry* 31(3):258-64.

39. Kapos, S. (2012, January 31). Nancy Radner leaves poverty group's top job to direct policy at Ounce of Prevention. *Chicago Business*. Retrieved from http://www.chicagobusiness.com/article/20120131/BLOGS03/120139929/nancy-radner-leaves-poverty-groups-top-job-to-direct-policy-at-ounce-of-prevention; Schorsch, K. (2010, October 17). Alliance sees a path to ending homelessness. *Chicago Tribune*. Retrieved from http://articles.chicagotribune.com/2010-10-17/news/ct-met-holiday-giving-chicago-allianc20101017_1_end-homelessness-nancy-radner-homeless-system; Studenkov, Igor. 2019. "Family Tranistional Housing Coming to Austin." *Austin Weekly News* September 30:https://www.austinweeklynews.com/News/Articles/9-30-2019/Family-transitional-housing-facility-coming-to-Austin/.

40. Federal Bureau of Investigation. 2019. *Crime in the United States 2018*. Washington, DC: Federal Bureau of Investigation.

41. Stark, R. (1987). Deviant places: A theory of the ecology of crime. *Criminology, 25*, 893–911.

42. Stark, R. (1987). Deviant places: A theory of the ecology of crime. *Criminology, 25*, 893–911.

43. Stark, R. (1987). Deviant places: A theory of the ecology of crime. *Criminology, 25*, 893–911.

44. Patrick, Stephen W., Melinda B. Buntin, Peter R. Martin, Theresa A. Scott, William Dupont, Michael Richards and William O. Cooper. 2019. "Barriers to Accessing Treatment for Pregnant Women with Opioid Use Disorder in Appalachian States." *Substance Abuse* 40(3):356-62.

45. Bennett, Kevin J., Bankole Olatosi and Janice C. Probst. 2009. *Health Disparities: A Rural-Urban Chartbook*. Columbia, SC: South Carolina Rural Health Research Center.

46. Walker, Tim. 2017. "Who's Looking out for Rural Schools?". *NEA Today* September 12:http://neatoday.org/2017/09/12/whos-looking-out-for-rural-schools/.

47. Semega, Jessica, Melissa Kollar, John Creamer and Abinash Mohanty. 2019. "Income and Poverty in the United States: 2018." *Current Population Reports*, P60-266. Washington, DC: U.S. Government Printing Office.

48. DeKeseredy, Walter S. 2019. "Intimate Violence against Rural Women: The Current State of Sociological Knowledge." *International Journal of Rural Criminology* 4:312-331.

49. DeKeseredy, Walter S. and Martin D. Schwartz. 2009. *Dangerous Exits: Escaping Abusive Relationships in Rural America*. New Brunswick, NJ: Rutgers University Press.

CHAPTER 15

Population and the Environment

This news story reminds us that air pollution is a worldwide problem. The story also reminds us that a major reason for India's air pollution problem is its sheer population size, as India ranks second in the world with more than 1.3 billion people, just behind China. As India's example suggests, population and environmental problems are often intertwined.

This chapter examines problems such as food scarcity and climate change associated with population growth and the environment. We will see that these problems raise complex issues without easy solutions, but we will also see that these are urgent problems that must be addressed. Indeed, it is no exaggeration to say that the fate of the earth depends on adequate solutions to these problems.

15.1 Sociological Perspectives on Population and the Environment

Learning Objective

1. Understand the perspectives that functionalism, conflict theory, and symbolic interactionism offer on population and the environment.

As usual, the major sociological perspectives offer insights that help us understand issues relating to population growth and to the environment. Table 15.1 summarizes their assumptions.

TABLE 15.1 Theory Snapshot

Theoretical perspective	Major assumptions
Functionalism	Population and the environment affect each other. Normal population growth is essential for any society, but population growth that is too great or too little leads to various problems. Environmental problems are to be expected in an industrial society, but severe environmental problems are dysfunctional.
Conflict theory	Population growth is not a serious problem because the world has sufficient food and other resources, all of which must be more equitably distributed. The practices of multinational corporations and weak regulation of these practices account for many environmental problems.
Symbolic interactionism	People have certain perceptions and understandings of population and environmental issues. Their social backgrounds affect these perceptions, which are important to appreciate if population and environmental problems are to be addressed.

Functionalism

Functionalism considers population growth and its various components (birth, death, and migration) as normal and essential processes for any society. A society certainly cannot survive if it loses members, but it can thrive only if it grows so that it can meet future challenges. Functionalism also considers pollution and other environmental problems to be inevitable consequences of today's society, but it assumes that environmental problems that are too severe are certainly dysfunctional for society.

The reasons for the importance of population growth depend on the type of a society's economy. For example, agricultural and other nonindustrial societies need high birth rates to counteract their high death rates. Industrial societies have lower death rates, but they still need to be able to hire younger workers as older workers retire, while new industries need to be able to count on hiring enough young workers with the skills and knowledge these industries require. However, population growth that is too rapid and severe can be dysfunctional for a society. Such growth creates crowding and can use up valuable resources such as food, and it can also harm the environment.

As this discussion suggests, functionalism emphasizes how the population and environment affect each other. Population growth leads to certain environmental problems, as we shall see, while environmental problems have important consequences for the populations for whole nations and even the world. At the same time, several industrial nations today actually do not have enough population growth to provide sufficient numbers of younger workers to replace retiring workers and to maintain their tax bases. While too much population growth causes many problems, then, too little population growth also causes problems.

Conflict Theory

Conflict theory assumes that the earth in fact has enough food and other resources to meet the needs of its growing population. To the extent that food shortages and other problems meeting these needs exist, these problems reflect decisions by economic and political elites in poor nations to deprive their peoples of food and other resources; they also reflect operations by multinational corporations that deprive these nations of their natural resources. If population growth is a problem, then, it is a problem not because there is a lack of food and other resources, but rather because these resources are not distributed fairly. Efforts to satisfy the world's need for food and other resources should thus focus on distributing these resources more equitably rather than on limiting population growth.

At the same time, conflict theory recognizes that many poor nations still have population growth that is more than desirable. The theory blames this growth on the failure of these nations' governments to make contraceptives readily available and to do everything possible to increase women's education and independence (which both reduce their birth rates).

Conflict theory blames many environmental problems on pollution by multinational corporations that occurs because of weak regulations and a failure to enforce the regulations that do exist.

Source: Susan Santa Maria/Shutterstock.com

In regard to a particular population issue we will discuss (immigration), conflict theory emphasizes the role played by racial and ethnic prejudice in popular views on immigration. It generally favors loosening restrictions on immigration into the United States and making it possible for undocumented immigrants to become U.S. citizens if they so desire.

Conflict theory also assumes that the world's environmental problems are not inevitable and instead arise from two related sources. First, multinational corporations engage in practices that pollute the air, water, and ground. Second, the United States and other governments fail to have strong regulations to limit pollution by corporations and other sources, and they fail to adequately enforce the regulations they do have.

 ## Corporate America's Refusal to Limit Pollution Will "Break the Climate System"

Conflict theory emphasizes that multinational corporations pollute the air, water, and ground by the practices in which they engage. This pollution contributes to climate change and endangers the public in other ways.

View the video online at: http://www.youtube.com/embed/epyyftdNRXc?rel=0

Symbolic Interactionism

Symbolic interactionism offers four kinds of understandings of population and environmental problems. First, it seeks to understand why people engage or do not engage in activities related to population growth and other problems (e.g., the use of contraception) and to environmental problems (e.g., recycling). In order to address population growth and environmental problems, it is important to understand why people become involved, or fail to become involved, in various activities related to these problems.

Second, it emphasizes people's perceptions of population and environmental problems. To the extent that public attitudes play a key role in the persistence of these problems, it is important to know the reasons for public views on these problems so that efforts to address the problems may be better focused.

Next, symbolic interactionism assumes that population and environmental problems are to some extent social constructions (see Chapter 1), as these problems do not come to be considered *social problems* unless sufficient numbers of people and/or influential organizations in the public and private sectors recognize them as problems. For example, lead was a serious health problem long before the U.S. government banned it in paint in 1977 and in gasoline in 1990. As early as the first few years of the twentieth century, scientists were calling attention to the toxic properties of lead paint and more generally of lead itself. Still, lead was added to gasoline in 1922 to raise octane levels. Despite growing evidence over the next few decades of lead's toxic qualities, various industries continued to say that lead was safe for the general public (Michaels 2008).[2] The banning of lead was ultimately due to the efforts of environmental groups and to the fact that the growing amount of scientific evidence of lead's dangers became overwhelming.

Finally, symbolic interactionism emphasizes that people from different social backgrounds and cultures may have different understandings of population issues and environmental issues. For example, someone who grows up in a rural area may consider even a small city to be incredibly crowded and polluted, while someone who grows up in a large city may view a small city as almost deserted and having relatively clean air.

Key Takeaways

- Functionalism recognizes the problems arising from population growth that is too rapid, but disagrees on the extent to which overpopulation is a serious problem.
- Conflict theory attributes world hunger to inequalities in the distribution of food rather than to overpopulation.
- Symbolic interactionism considers people's perceptions and activities regarding population (e.g., contraception) and the environment.

For Your Review

1. Which of the three major perspectives—functionalism, conflict theory, or symbolic interactionism—seems to have the best approach in how it understands population and environmental issues? Explain your answer.

15.2 Population

Learning Objectives

1. Describe the central concepts of the study of demography.
2. Understand demographic transition theory and how it compares with the views of Thomas Malthus.
3. Explain why some experts feel that world hunger does not result from overpopulation.
4. Provide examples of how U.S. history is marked by anti-immigrant prejudice.

Population change often has weighty consequences throughout a society. As we think about population change, we usually think about and worry about population growth, but population decline is also a concern. For example, several states, especially those in the Northeast, have lost population during the past few decades (Sullivan 2019),[3] thanks to lower birth rates and the departure of many families, young adults, and aging baby boomers to states in the South and Southwest. This population decline has led to several problems (Ozimek et al. 2019).[4] One of these problems is smaller secondary school populations, with many schools having to close as a result. Moreover, because many of the out-migrants from these states are young, college-educated adults, they take with them hundreds of millions of dollars in paychecks from their state's economy and tax revenue base. They also leave behind empty houses and apartments that help depress their state's real estate market. Because of the loss of younger residents from the declining birth rate and out-migration, the states with declining populations have become older on the average. This shift means that there is now a greater percentage of residents in their older years, who need state services.

Among other consequences, then, these states' population decline has affected their economy, educational system, and services for their older residents. While these states are shrinking, states in the South and Southwest are growing, with their large cities becoming even larger. This population growth also has consequences. For example, schools become more crowded, pressuring communities to hire more teachers and either enlarge existing schools or build new ones. The population growth also strains hospitals, social services, and many other sectors of society, and it drives up real estate prices.

This brief discussion of U.S. cities underscores the various problems arising from population growth and decline. These are not just American problems, as they play out across the world. The remainder of this section introduces the study of population and then examines population problems in greater depth.

The Study of Population

We have commented that population change is an important source of other changes in society. The study of population is so significant that it occupies a special subfield within sociology called **demography**. To be more precise, demography is the study of changes in the size and composition of population. It encompasses several concepts: fertility and birth rates, mortality and death rates, and migration. Let's look at each of these briefly.

demography

The study of population growth and changes in population composition.

Fertility and Birth Rates

Fertility refers to the number of live births. Demographers use several measures of fertility. One measure is the **crude birth rate**, or the number of live births for every 1,000 people in a population in a given year. We call this a "crude" birth rate because the population component consists of the total population, not just the number of women or even the number of women of childbearing age (commonly considered 15–44 years).

A second measure is the **general fertility rate** (also just called the *fertility rate* or *birth rate*), or the number of live births per 1,000 women aged 15–44 (i.e., of childbearing age). The provisional U.S. general fertility rate for 2018 was 59.0 (i.e., 59.0 births per 1,000 women aged 15–44) (Hamilton et al. 2019).[5]

A third measure is the **total fertility rate**, or the number of children an average woman is expected to have in her lifetime (taking into account that some women have more children and some women have fewer or no children). This measure often appears in the news media and is more easily understood by the public than either of the first two measures. In 2018, the provisional U.S. total fertility rate was about 1.728 (or 1,728 births for every 1,000 women). The general and total fertility rates have declined for more than a decade and were at record lows in 2018 (Hamilton et al. 2019).[6]

Fertility rates differ around the world and are especially high in the poor nations of Africa and certain parts of Asia. Demographers identify several reasons for these high rates (Weeks 2016).[7]

First, poor nations are usually agricultural ones. In agricultural societies, children are an important economic resource, as a family will be more productive if it has more children. This means that families will ordinarily try to have as many children as possible. Second, infant and child mortality rates are high in these nations. Because parents realize that one or more of their children may die before adulthood, they have more children to make up for the anticipated deaths.

Demographers use several measures of fertility. The general fertility rate refers to the number of live births per 1,000 women aged 15–44. The U.S. general fertility rate is about 59.0.

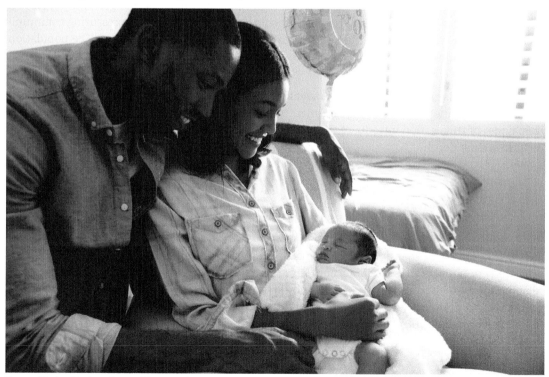

Source: Monkey Business Images/Shutterstock.com

A third reason is that many parents in low-income nations prefer sons to daughters, and if a daughter is born, they try again for a son. Fourth, traditional gender roles are often very strong in poor nations, and these roles include the belief that women should be wives and mothers above all. With this ideology in place, it is not surprising that women will have several children. Finally, contraception is uncommon in poor nations. Without contraception, many more pregnancies and births inevitably occur. For all these reasons, then, fertility is much higher in poor nations than in rich nations.

Poor nations have higher birth rates for several reasons. One reason is the agricultural economies typical of these nations. In these economies, children are an important economic resource, and families will ordinarily try to have as many children as possible.

Source: Travel Stock/Shutterstock.com

Mortality and Death Rates

Mortality is the flip side of fertility and refers to the number of deaths. Demographers measure it with the **crude death rate**, the number of deaths for every 1,000 people in a population in a given year. We call this a "crude" death rate because the population component consists of the total population and does not take its age distribution into account. All things equal, a society with a higher proportion of older people should have a higher crude death rate. Demographers often calculate *age-adjusted* death rates that adjust for a population's age distribution.

mortality

The number of deaths.

crude death rate

The number of deaths for every 1,000 people in a population in a given year.

Migration

Another important demographic concept is **migration**, the movement of people into and out of specific regions. Since the dawn of human history, people have migrated in search of a better life, and many have been forced to migrate by ethnic conflict or the slave trade.

Several classifications of migration exist. When people move into a region, we call it *in-migration*, or *immigration*; when they move out of a region, we call it *out-migration*, or *emigration*. The *in-migration rate* is the number of people moving into a region for every 1,000 people in the region,

migration

The movement of people into or out of specific regions.

while the *out-migration rate* is the number of people moving from the region for every 1,000 people. The difference between the two is the *net migration rate* (in-migration minus out-migration). Recalling our earlier discussion, some Northern states have had a net migration of less than zero, as their out-migration has exceeded their in-migration.

Migration can also be either domestic or international in scope. *Domestic migration* happens within a country's national borders, as when retired people from the Northeastern United States move to Florida or the Southwest. *International migration* happens across national borders. When international immigration is heavy, the effect on population growth and other aspects of national life can be significant, as can increased prejudice against the new immigrants. Domestic migration can also have a large impact. The great migration of African Americans from the South into northern cities during the first half of the twentieth century changed many aspects of those cities' lives (Wilkerson 2011).[8] Meanwhile, the movement during the past few decades of northerners into the South and Southwest also had quite an impact: The housing market initially exploded, for example, and traffic increased.

Population Growth and Decline

natural growth rate

The difference between the crude birth rate and the crude death rate.

Now that you are familiar with some basic demographic concepts, we can discuss population change in more detail. Three of the factors just discussed determine changes in population size: fertility (crude birth rate), mortality (crude death rate), and net migration. The **natural growth rate** is simply the difference between the crude birth rate and the crude death rate. The U.S. natural growth rate is about 0.3 percent (or 3 persons per 1,000 population) per year (Population Reference Bureau 2019).[9] When immigration is also taken into account, the total population growth rate has been almost 0.7 percent per year (or 7 persons per 1,000 population).

Figure 15.1 depicts the annual population growth rate (including both natural growth and net migration) of all the nations in the world. Note that many African nations are growing by at least 3 percent per year or more, while most European nations are growing by much less than 1 percent or are even losing population. Overall, the world population is growing by about 80 million people annually, representing just over a 1.0 percent annual increase (Worldometers 2019).[10]

To determine how long it takes for a nation to double its population size, divide the number 70 by its population growth rate. For example, if a nation has an annual growth rate of 3 percent, it takes about 23.3 years (70 ÷ 3) for that nation's population size to double. As you can see from the map in Figure 15.1, several nations will see their population size double in this time span if their annual growth continues at its present rate. For these nations, population growth will be a serious problem if food and other resources are not adequately distributed.

Demographers use their knowledge of fertility, mortality, and migration trends to make *projections* about population growth and decline several decades into the future. Coupled with our knowledge of past population sizes, these projections allow us to understand population trends over many generations. One clear pattern emerges from the study of population growth. When a society is small, population growth is slow because there are relatively few adults to procreate. But as the number of people grows over time, so does the number of adults. More and more procreation thus occurs every single generation, and population growth then soars in a virtual explosion.

FIGURE 15.1 International Annual Population Growth Rates (%), 2018

< -3.98
-3.98 - -0.09
-0.09 - 0.81
0.81 - 1.73
> 1.73

Source: Adapted from https://data.worldbank.org/indicator/SP.POP.GROW?view=map

For example, when agricultural societies developed some 12,000 years ago, only about 8 million people occupied the planet. This number had reached about 300 million about 2,100 years ago, and by the fifteenth century it was still only about 500 million. It finally reached 1 billion by about 1850; by 1950, only a century later, it had doubled to 2 billion. Just fifty years later, it tripled to more than 6.8 billion, and it is projected to reach more than 9 billion by 2050 and 10 billion by 2100 (Gillis and Dugger 2011).[11]

Eventually, however, population growth begins to level off after exploding, as explained by *demographic transition theory*, discussed later. Although the world's population has been growing rapidly as just stated, the average annual growth rate has in fact declined over the last few decades and is projected to further decline over the next few decades. This means that while the world's population will continue to grow during the foreseeable future, it will grow by a smaller rate as time goes by. The growth that does occur will be concentrated in the poor nations in Africa and some other parts of the world. Still, even in some of these nations the average number of children a woman has in her lifetime dropped from six a generation ago to three or fewer today.

Views of Population Growth

Thomas Malthus, an English economist who lived about 200 years ago, wrote that population increases geometrically while food production increases only arithmetically. These understandings led him to predict mass starvation.

Source: http://commons. wikimedia.org/wiki/File:Thomas_ Robert_Malthus.jpg.

The numbers just discussed show that the size of the United States and world populations has increased tremendously in just a few centuries. Not surprisingly, people during this time have worried about population growth and specifically overpopulation. One of the first to warn about population growth was Thomas Malthus (1766–1834), an English economist, who said that population increases *geometrically* (2, 4, 8, 16, 32, 64, 128, 256, 512, 1024...). If you expand this list of numbers, you will see that they soon become overwhelmingly large in just a few more "generations." Malthus (1798/1926)[12] said that food production increases only *arithmetically* (1, 2, 3, 4, 5, 6...) and thus could not hope to keep up with the population increase, and he predicted that mass starvation would be the dire result.

During the 1970s, population growth became a major issue in the United States and some other nations. *Zero population growth*, or ZPG, was a slogan often heard. There was much concern over the rapidly growing population in the United States and especially around the world, and there was fear that our "small planet" could not support massive increases in the number of people (Ehrlich 1969).[13] Some of the most dire predictions of the time warned of serious food shortages by the end of the century.

Fortunately, Malthus and ZPG advocates were wrong to some degree. Although population levels have certainly soared, the rate of increase is slowing, as we have noted. Among other factors, the development of more effective contraception, especially the birth control pill, has limited population growth in the industrial world and, increasingly, in poorer nations. Food production has also increased by a much greater amount than Malthus and ZPG advocates predicted.

The Debate over Overpopulation

Calls during the 1970s for zero population growth (ZPG) population control stemmed from concern that the planet was becoming overpopulated and that food and other resources would soon be too meager to support the world's population.

Source: © Thinkstock

Many experts continue to be concerned about overpopulation and blame it for the hunger and malnutrition that plague hundreds of millions of people in poor nations (Ehrlich and Harte 2018).[14] However, other experts say the world's resources remain sufficient and minimize the problem of overpopulation. They acknowledge that widespread hunger in Africa and other regions does exist. However, they attribute this problem not to overpopulation and lack of food but rather to problems in distributing the sufficient amount of food that does in fact exist. As an official for Oxfam International once explained, "Today's major problems in the food system are not fundamentally about supply keeping up with demand, but more about how food gets from fields and on to forks" (King 2011).[15] The official added that enough grain (cereal and soy) exists to easily feed the world, but that one-third of cereal and 90 percent of soy feed livestock instead. Moving away from a meat-laden Western diet would thus make much more grain available for the world's hungry poor.

Sociologists Stephen J. Scanlan and colleagues add that food scarcity results from *inequalities in food distribution* rather than from overpopulation: "[Food] scarcity is largely a myth. On a per capita basis, food is more plentiful today than any other time in human history...Even in times of localized production shortfalls or regional famines there has long been a global food surplus...A good deal of thinking and research in sociology...suggests that world hunger has less to do with the shortage of food than with a shortage of *affordable* or *accessible* food. Sociologists have found that social inequalities, distribution systems, and other economic and political factors create barriers to food access" (Scanlan et al. 2010:35).[16]

This sociological view has important implications for how the world should try to reduce global hunger. International organizations such as the World Bank and several United Nations agencies have long believed that hunger is due to food scarcity, and this belief underlies the typical approaches to reducing world hunger that focus on increasing food supplies with new technologies and developing more efficient methods of delivering food. But if food scarcity is not a problem, then other approaches are necessary. According to Scanlan and colleagues, these approaches involve reducing the social inequalities that limit poor nations' access to food.

As an example of one such inequality, Scanlan et al. point out that poor nations lack the funds to import the abundant food that does exist. These nations' poverty, then, is one inequality that leads to world hunger, but gender and ethnic inequalities are also responsible. Nations with higher rates of gender inequality and ethnic inequality have higher rates of hunger. In view of this fact, the authors emphasize that improvements in gender and ethnic equality are necessary to reduce global hunger.[17]

Demographic Transition Theory

As we consider whether overpopulation is the threat that Malthus and contemporary concerned scientists have considered it to be, it is important to appreciate **demographic transition theory**, mentioned earlier. This theory links population growth to the level of technological development across three stages of social evolution and suggests that this growth slows considerably as nations become more industrialized.

> **demographic transition theory**
>
> A theory that links population growth to the level of technological development across three stages of social evolution.

In the first stage, coinciding with preindustrial societies, the birth rate and death rate are both high. The birth rate is high because of the lack of contraception and the several other reasons cited earlier for high fertility rates, and the death rate is high because of disease, poor nutrition, lack of modern medicine, and other problems. These two high rates cancel each other out, and little population growth occurs.

In the second stage, coinciding with the development of industrial societies, the birth rate remains fairly high, owing to the lack of contraception and a continuing belief in the value of large families, but the death rate drops because of several factors, including increased food production, better sanitation, and improved medicine. Because the birth rate remains high but the death rate drops, population growth takes off dramatically.

In the third stage, the death rate remains low, but the birth rate finally drops as families begin to realize that large numbers of children in an industrial economy are more of a burden than an asset. Another reason for the drop is the availability of effective contraception. As a result, population growth slows, and, as we saw earlier, it has become quite low or even gone into a decline in several industrial nations.

Demographic transition theory, then, gives us more reason to be cautiously optimistic regarding the threat of overpopulation: As poor nations continue to modernize—much as industrial nations did 200 years ago—their population growth rates should start to decline.

Still, population growth rates in poor nations continue to be high, and, as already mentioned, gender and ethnic inequality helps allow rampant hunger to persist. Hundreds of thousands of women die in poor nations each year during pregnancy and childbirth. Reduced fertility would save their lives, in part because their bodies would be healthier if their pregnancies were spaced further apart. Although world population growth is slowing, then, it is still growing too rapidly in poor nations. To reduce it further, more extensive family planning programs are needed, as is economic development in general: Women who are better educated and have more money tend to have lower fertility.

Population Decline and Pronatalism

If population growth remains a problem in poor nations, actual population decline is a problem in some industrial nations. For a country to maintain its population via natural growth, the average woman needs to have 2.1 children, the *replacement level* for population stability. But dozens of countries, including Canada and most of Western Europe, are below this level (Chamie 2018).[18] Increased birth control is one reason for their lower fertility rates but so are decisions by women to stay in school longer, to go to work right after their schooling ends, and to postpone having their first child.

Ironically, these nations' population declines have begun to concern demographers and policy-makers (Haartsen and Venhorst 2010).[19] Because people in many industrial nations are living longer while the birth rate drops, these nations are increasingly having a greater proportion of older people and a smaller proportion of younger people. As this trend continues, it will become increasingly difficult to take care of the health and income needs of so many older persons, and there may be too few younger people to fill the many jobs and provide the many services that an industrial society demands. The smaller labor force may also mean that governments will have fewer income tax dollars to provide these services.

pronatalist

Referring to policies that encourage women to have children.

To deal with these problems, several governments have initiated **pronatalist** policies aimed at encouraging women to have more children. In particular, they provide generous child-care subsidies, tax incentives, and flexible work schedules designed to make it easier to bear and raise children, and some even provide couples outright cash payments when they have an additional child. These nations provide the equivalent of $1,000–$2,000 or more per child annually for all these reasons (Matthews 2016).[20]

Spain is one of several European nations that have been experiencing a population decline because of lower birth rates. Like some other nations, Spain has adopted pronatalist policies to encourage people to have more children and provides cash payments to families for the children they have.

Source: leonov.o/Shutterstock.com

Which Countries Have Shrinking Populations?

Many wealthy nations are experiencing population declines, with their number of births lower than their number of deaths. This decline concerns demographers and policymakers as it could mean that there will be too few younger people to care for the elderly and to perform the many jobs these nations require.

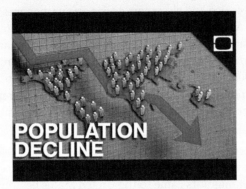

View the video online at: http://www.youtube.com/embed/qn9DDsxfpCA?rel=0

Two Other Problems Related to Population Growth

As we saw, population experts debate the degree to which population growth contributes to global poverty and hunger. But there is little debate that population growth contributes to two other global problems.

Population growth causes many environmental problems, one of which is deforestation.

One of these problems concerns the *environment*. Population growth in both wealthy and poor nations has damaged the environment in many ways. As the news story that opens this chapter illustrated, countries with large numbers of people drive many motor vehicles that pollute the air, and these countries engage in many other practices of the industrial era that pollute the air, water, and ground. Further, as populations have expanded over the centuries, they have cut down many trees and deforested many regions across the globe. This deforestation ruins animal habitats and helps to contribute to global warming because trees help remove carbon dioxide from the atmosphere and release oxygen into the atmosphere.

Source: Marten_House/Shutterstock.com

Another problem is *interpersonal conflict* in general and *armed conflict* in particular. As populations grow, they need more and more food, water, and other resources. When these resources have become too scarce over the centuries, many societies have decided to take resources from other societies "by any means necessary," as the old saying goes, meaning the use of force.

Population growth thus helps to create armed conflict between societies, but it also helps to generate conflict within a single society. As a society grows, people begin to compete for resources. This competition has often led to hostility of many types, including interpersonal violence. As we shall discuss shortly, the history of immigration in the United States illustrates this dynamic. As the number of immigrants grew rapidly in various historical eras, native-born whites perceived threats to their jobs, land, and other resources and responded with mob violence.

Immigration

Recall that migration generally and immigration specifically are central concepts in the study of population. As just indicated, immigration is also a source of great controversy in the United States and in many other countries. In the contemporary United States, this has especially been true since Donald Trump began running for president in June 2015. During his campaign, he often depicted immigrants from Mexico and elsewhere as dangerous menaces, and he continued to do so after he became president. As president, he also issued executive orders and took other actions to restrict immigration, including the detention of thousands of children at detention facilities. Many critics said his warnings and actions reflected shameful prejudice toward immigrants, with one historian declaring that President Trump "has spread more fear, resentment and hatred of immigrants than any American in history" (Anbinder 2019).[21] These critics also emphasized that immigrants have helped American society in many ways in the recent and more distant past (Barkan 2018).[22]

The history of the United States is filled with prejudice and hostility toward immigrants (Osborne 2016).[23] Starting with the Pilgrims, this nation was settled by immigrants who came to these shores seeking political and religious freedom and economic opportunity. Despite these origins, when great waves of immigrants came to the United States beginning in the nineteenth century, they were hardly greeted with open arms. During this time, some 3 million Irish immigrants, most of them Catholic, moved to the United States. Because these immigrants were not Anglo-Saxon Protestants, native-born whites (most of whom were Anglo-Saxon Protestants) detested them and even considered them to be a different race from white. During the 1850s, the so-called Know-Nothing Party, composed of native-born whites, was openly hostile to Irish immigrants and would engage in mob violence against them, with many murders occurring. Later waves of immigrants from Italian, Polish, and Jewish backgrounds were also subject to employment discrimination and other ethnic prejudice and hostility.

Beginning with the California Gold Rush of 1849 and continuing after the Civil War, great numbers of Chinese immigrants came to the United States and helped to build the nation's railroads and performed other important roles. They, too, were greeted with hostility by native-born whites, who feared the Chinese were taking away their jobs (Pfaelzer 2008).[24] As the national economy worsened during the 1870s, riots against the Chinese occurred in western cities. In more than 300 cities and towns, whites went into Chinese neighborhoods, burned them down, and murdered some Chinese residents while forcing the remainder to leave town. Congress finally outlawed Chinese immigration in 1882, with this ban lasting more than sixty years.

During the 1930s, rising numbers of Mexican Americans in the western United States led to similar hostility (Daniels 2002).[25] The fact that this decade was the time of the Great Depression deepened whites' concerns that Mexican immigrants were taking away their jobs. White-owned newspapers falsely claimed that these immigrants posed a violent threat to white Americans, and that their supposed violence was made more likely by their use of marijuana. It is estimated that at least 500,000 Mexicans returned to their native country, either because they were forcibly deported or because they returned there themselves under great pressure.

Immigration Today

Immigration continues to trouble many native-born Americans today, whose concern centers mostly on immigrants from Mexico and other Latin American nations. Amid this concern, some basic facts about these and other immigrants are worth appreciating.

First, roughly 11.6 million Mexican immigrants now live in the United States (2017 data) (Gonzalez-Barrera and Krogstad 2019).[26] This figure includes about 5 million people who are unauthorized immigrants.

Second, the number of unauthorized Mexican immigrants peaked at almost 7 million in 2007 and has declined by 2 million since then. This decline thus began nine years before Mr. Trump became president, and it has continued since he became president.

Third, immigrants add an estimated $2 trillion to the gross domestic product (GDP) annually through their employment and other activities, while unauthorized immigrants pay an estimated $10 billion annually into Social Security and $12 billion annually in state and local taxes (Center for American Progress 2017).[27] In these and other ways, immigrants and immigration are a boon to the national, state, and local economies. If all unauthorized immigrants somehow left the United States, the U.S. economy would suffer an annual decline of 2.6 percent in GDP, amounting to $4.7 trillion over ten years; a loss of federal tax revenue of $900 billion over ten years; and significant annual GDP losses to specific industries amounting to tens of billions of dollars for each industry.

 ## The Economic Benefits of Immigration

Although many Americans dislike immigration, immigration is in fact good for the American economy, as this video explains.

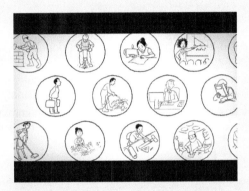

View the video online at: http://www.youtube.com/embed/6nCY2Ncvk-g?rel=0

Fourth, and despite the pronouncements of President Trump, immigrants, both authorized and unauthorized, in fact have lower crime rates than native-born Americans (Ousey and Kubrin 2018).[28] These low rates are thought to stem from immigrants' stable families, strong churches, and high numbers of small businesses that make for stable neighborhoods.

As this evidence on immigrants' economic contributions and low crime rates suggest, the concern of many native-born Americans about immigration, and especially immigration from Mexico and other Latin American nations, is simply unfounded. History is repeating itself with today's concern against immigrants and immigration. Even so, immigrants have helped make America great since this nation began, and they will certainly continue to do so in the years ahead.

Lessons from Other Societies

The Status of Legal Immigrants in Western Democracies

The Migrant Integration Policy Index (MIPEX) is an effort of the Migration Policy Group, an international consortium, and the Barcelona Centre for International Affairs. This index ranks the United States and thirty-seven other nations on the extent to which legal immigrants are integrated into each nation's political and economic life and on the path to full citizenship. It also considers the extent to which each nation has antidiscrimination laws to protect immigrants. MIPEX consists of 167 policy indicators overall.

In the latest (2015) MIPEX report, issued a year before Donald Trump became president and made U.S. immigration policy much harsher, the United States ranked ninth out of the 38 nations on this index. Sweden ranked first, followed by Portugal and New Zealand; Canada ranked sixth. Cyprus, Latvia, Turkey, and some other European nations ranked at the bottom.

The report applauded the United States for having strong antidiscrimination laws, but faulted it for posing obstacles, such as high fees and limited visas, to full citizenship for legal immigrants. The report noted that the nations ranking higher than the United States "outperform [it] on issues such as reuniting families, encouraging workers and students to settle, facilitating the requirements for naturalization and working to recognize immigrants' credentials."

If a new MIPEX ranking becomes available after the time of this writing, it would likely rank the United States lower than it did in 2015 because U.S. immigration policy has become harsher in several respects since 2017. The higher status enjoyed by immigrants in Canada and some other democracies even in 2015 points to directions the United States should follow to improve its ranking and create a better climate for its immigrants.

Source: Migration Policy Group and Barcelona Centre for International Affairs 2015[29]

Key Takeaways

- To understand changes in the size and composition of population, demographers use several concepts, including fertility and birth rates, mortality and death rates, and migration.
- Although overpopulation remains a serious concern, many experts say the world's food supply is sufficient providing that it is distributed efficiently and equitably.
- Although many Americans are concerned about immigration, immigrants in fact contribute significantly to the American economy and have lower crime rates than native-born Americans.

For Your Review

1. How concerned are you about population growth and overpopulation? Explain your answer in a brief essay.
2. Before you began reading this chapter, did you think that food scarcity was a major reason for world hunger today? Why do you think that a belief in food scarcity is probably so common among Americans?
3. Do you think nations with low birth rates should provide incentives for women to have more babies? Why or why not?
4. If immigrants contribute significantly to the American economy and have low crime rates, as the text discusses, why do you think so many Americans have negative views about immigration and immigrants? Explain your answer.

15.3 The Environment

Learning Objectives

1. List two reasons that make the environment an appropriate topic for sociologists to study.

2. Describe two of the environmental problems facing the world today.

3. Describe what is meant by the assertion that environmental problems are human problems.

4. Explain the concepts of environmental inequality and environmental racism.

5. Understand the various environmental problems that exist today.

At first glance, the environment does not seem to be a sociological topic. The natural and physical environment is something that geologists, meteorologists, oceanographers, and other scientists should be studying, not sociologists. Yet we have just discussed how the environment is affected by population growth, and that certainly sounds like a sociological discussion. In fact, the environment is very much a sociological topic for several reasons.

First, climate change and other serious environmental problems are the result of human activity, and this activity, like many human behaviors, is a proper topic for sociological study. This textbook has discussed many behaviors: racist behavior, sexist behavior, criminal behavior, sexual behavior, and others. Just as these behaviors are worthy of sociological study, so are the behaviors that harm (or try to improve) the environment.

Second, environmental problems have a significant impact on people, as do the many other social problems that sociologists study. We see the clearest evidence of this impact when a hurricane, an earthquake, or another natural disaster strikes, but slower changes in the environment can also have a large social impact. As noted earlier, industrialization and population growth have increased the pollution of our air, water, and ground. Climate change has also been relatively slow in arriving but threatens the whole planet in ways that climate change researchers have documented and will no doubt be examining for the rest of our lifetimes and beyond. We return to these two environmental problems shortly.

As is evident in this photo taken in the aftermath of a 2010 earthquake that devastated Haiti, changes in the natural environment can lead to profound changes in a society. Environmental changes are one of the many sources of social change.

Source: Image courtesy of United Nations, http://www.flickr.com/photos/37913760@N03/4274632760.

A third reason the environment is a sociological topic is a bit more complex: Solutions to our environmental problems require changes in economic and environmental policies, and the potential implementation and impact of these changes depends heavily on social and political factors. In the United States, for example, the two major political parties, corporate lobbyists, and environmental organizations regularly battle over attempts to strengthen environmental regulations.

A fourth reason is that many environmental problems reflect and illustrate social inequality based on social class and on race and ethnicity. To say this another away, and in line with many problems in our society, the poor and people of color often fare worse when it comes to the environment. We return to this theme later in our discussion of environmental racism.

Fifth, efforts to improve the environment, often called the *environmental movement*, constitute a social movement and, as such, are again worthy of sociological study. Sociologists and other social scientists have conducted many studies of why people join the environmental movement and of the impact of this movement.

Environmental Sociology

All these reasons suggest that the environment is quite fittingly a sociological topic, and one on which sociologists should have important insights. In fact, so many sociologists study the environment that their collective study makes up a subfield in sociology called **environmental sociology**, which refers simply to the sociological study of the environment. More specifically, environmental sociology is the study of the interaction between human behavior and the natural and physical environment. According to a report by the American Sociological Association, environmental sociology "has provided important insights" (Nagel et al. 2010:13)[30] into such areas as public opinion about the environment, the influence of values on people's environmental behavior, and inequality in the impact of environmental problems on communities and individuals.

Environmental sociologists emphasize two important dimensions of the relationship between society and the environment: (a) the impact of human activity and decision making and (b) the existence and consequences of environmental inequality and environmental racism. We now turn to these two dimensions.

Human Activity and Decision Making

The April 2010 BP oil spill occurred after BP made several decisions that may have increased the possibility of a catastrophic explosion of the well.

Source: Cheryl Casey/Shutterstock.com

Perhaps more than anything else, environmental sociologists emphasize that *environmental problems are the result of human decisions and activities that harm the environment*. Masses of individuals acting independently of each other make decisions and engage in activities that harm the environment, as when we leave lights on, keep our homes too warm in the winter or too cool in the summer, drive motor vehicles that get low gas mileage, and discard plastic that makes its way into our oceans. Corporations, government agencies, and other organizations also make decisions and engage in practices that greatly harm the environment. Sometimes individuals and organizations know full well that their activities are harming the environment, and sometimes they just act carelessly without much thought about the possible environmental harm of their actions. Still, the environment is harmed whether or not individuals, corporations, and governments intend to harm it.

Sociologists Leslie King and Deborah McCarthy Auriffeille (2019)[31] cite several environmental accidents that stemmed from reckless decision making and natural disasters in which human decisions accelerated the harm that occurred. One accident was the British Petroleum (BP) oil spill that began in April 2010 when an oil rig exploded in the Gulf of Mexico and eventually released more than 200 million gallons of oil into the ocean. It was later revealed that BP had tried to save money by using an inferior casing for the oil well, which helped lead to the explosion. A similar accident occurred in Bhopal, India, in 1984, when a Union Carbide pesticide plant leaked forty tons of deadly gas. Between 3,000 and 16,000 people died immediately and another half million suffered permanent illnesses or injuries. A contributing factor for the leak was Union Carbide's decision to save money by violating safety standards in the construction and management of the plant.

Yet another preventable accident was the 1989 *Exxon Valdez* oil tanker disaster, in which the tanker hit ground off the coast of Alaska and released 11 million gallons of oil into Prince William Sound. Among other consequences, the spill killed hundreds of thousands of birds and marine animals and almost destroyed the local fishing and seafood industries. The immediate cause of the accident was that the ship's captain was an alcoholic and left the bridge in the hands of an unlicensed third mate after drinking five double vodkas in the hours before the crash occurred. Exxon officials knew of his alcoholism but let him command the ship anyway. Also, if the ship had had a double hull (one hull inside the other), it might not have cracked on impact or at least would have released less oil, but Exxon and the rest of the oil industry had successfully lobbied Congress not to require stronger hulls.

Hurricane Katrina in 2005 was still another environmental disaster in which human decision making resulted in a great deal of *preventable* damage. After Katrina hit the Gulf Coast and especially New Orleans, the resulting wind and flooding killed more than 1,800 people and left more than 700,000 homeless. Long before Katrina hit, it was well known that a major flood could easily breach New Orleans levees and have a devastating impact. Despite this knowledge, federal, state, and local officials did nothing over the years to strengthen or rebuild the levees. In addition, coastal land that would have protected New Orleans had been lost over time to commercial and residential development. In short, the flooding after Katrina was a human disaster, not a natural disaster.

 ### BP Oil Spill Five Years Later: Wildlife Still Suffering

The 2010 British Petroleum oil spill in the Gulf of Mexico was preventable, as BP reportedly used an inferior casing for the oil well that helped to cause the explosion that created the spill.

View the video online at: http://www.youtube.com/embed/zcZ9MLDull0?rel=0

Environmental Inequality and Environmental Racism

environmental inequality

The disproportionate exposure of low-income people and people of color to various environmental problems.

environmental racism

The disproportionate exposure of people of color to various environmental problems.

environmental justice

Scholarship on environmental inequality and racism, and public policy efforts and activism aimed at reducing these forms of inequality and racism.

A second emphasis of environmental sociology is *environmental inequality* and the related concept of *environmental racism*. **Environmental inequality** (also called *environmental injustice*) refers to the fact that low-income people and people of color are disproportionately likely to experience various environmental problems, while **environmental racism** refers just to the greater likelihood of people of color to experience these problems. The term **environmental justice** refers to scholarship on environmental inequality and racism and to public policy efforts and activism aimed at reducing these forms of inequality and racism (Holifield et al. 2018).[32] The "Applying Social Research" box discusses some very significant scholarship on environmental racism.

Applying Social Research

Environmental Racism in the Land of Cotton

During the 1970s, people began to voice concern about the environment in the United States and across the planet. As research on the environment grew by leaps and bounds, some scholars and activists began to focus on environmental inequality in general and on environmental racism in particular. During the 1980s and 1990s, their research and activism spawned the environmental justice movement that has since shed important light on environmental inequality and racism and helped reduce these problems.

Research by sociologists played a key role in the beginning of the environmental justice movement and continues to play a key role today. Robert D. Bullard of Clark Atlanta University stands out among these sociologists for the impact of his early work in the 1980s on environmental racism in the South and for his continuing scholarship since then. He has been called "the father of environmental justice" and was named by *Newsweek* as one of the thirteen most influential environmental leaders of the twentieth century, along with environmental writer Rachel Carson, former vice president Al Gore, and ten others.

Bullard's first research project on environmental racism began in the late 1970s after his wife, an attorney, filed a lawsuit on behalf of black residents in Atlanta who were fighting the placement of a landfill in their neighborhood. To collect data for the lawsuit, Bullard studied the placement of landfills in other areas. He found that every city-owned landfill in Houston was in a black neighborhood, even though African Americans amounted to only one-fourth of Houston residents at the time. He also found that three out of four privately owned landfills were in black neighborhoods, as were six of the eight city-owned incinerators. He extended his research to other locations and later recalled what he discovered: "Without a doubt, it was a form of apartheid where whites were making decisions and black people and brown people and people of color, including Native Americans on reservations, had no seat at the table."

In 1990, Bullard published his findings in his book *Dumping in Dixie: Race, Class, and Environmental Quality*. This book described the systematic placement in several Southern states of toxic waste sites, landfills, and chemical plants in communities largely populated by low-income residents and/or African Americans. *Dumping in Dixie* was the first book to examine environmental racism and is widely credited with helping advance the environmental justice movement. It received some notable awards, including the Conservation Achievement Award from the National Wildlife Federation.

More recently, Bullard, along with other sociologists and scholars from other disciplines, documented the impact of race and poverty on the experience of New Orleans residents affected by the flooding after Hurricane Katrina. As in many other cities, African Americans and other low-income people largely resided in the lower elevations in New Orleans, and whites and higher-income people largely resided in the higher elevations. The flooding naturally had a much greater impact on the lower elevations and thus on African Americans and the poor. After the flood, African Americans seeking new housing in various real estate markets were more likely than whites to be told that no housing was available.

Bullard's early work alerted the nation to environmental racism and helped motivate the Environmental Protection Agency in the 1990s to begin paying attention to it. His various research efforts are an outstanding example of how social research can increase understanding of a significant social problem.

Sources: Bullard 1990; Bullard and Wright 2009; Dicum 2006[33]

Examples of environmental racism and inequality abound. Almost all the hazardous waste sites we discuss later in this chapter are located in or near neighborhoods and communities that are largely populated by low-income people and people of color. When factories dump dangerous chemicals into rivers and lakes, the people living nearby are very likely to be low-income and of color. Around the world, the people most affected by climate change and other environmental problems are those in poor nations and, even within those nations, those who are poorer rather than those who are wealthier.

Oil, Gas, and the Effects of Environmental Racism

The poor and people of color tend to suffer more than other people from environmental problems. This situation is called environmental inequality and environmental racism, respectively.

View the video online at: http://www.youtube.com/embed/vWfRbKY9gJM?rel=0

Some evidence shows that although low-income people are especially likely to be exposed to environmental problems, this exposure is even more likely if they are people of color than if they are white. As a review of this evidence concluded, "It would be fair to summarize this body of work as showing that the poor and especially the nonwhite poor bear a disproportionate burden of exposure to suboptimal, unhealthy environmental conditions in the United States. Moreover, the more researchers scrutinize environmental exposure and health data for racial and income inequalities, the stronger the evidence becomes that grave and widespread environmental injustices have occurred throughout the United States" (Evans and Kantrowitz 2002:323).[34]

As should be apparent from the discussion in this section, the existence of environmental inequality and environmental racism shows that social inequality in the larger society exposes some people much more than others to environmental dangers. This insight is one of the most important contributions of environmental sociology.

Global climate change is very likely to have its greatest impact on people in the poorest nations, even though these nations are the least responsible for greenhouse gases.

Source: Salvacampillo/Shutterstock.com

Environmental Problems

To say that the world is in peril environmentally might sound extreme, but the world is in fact in peril. An overview of environmental problems will indicate the extent and seriousness of this problem.

Air Pollution

According to the World Health Organization (2019),[35] 4.2 million people die annually from exposure to outdoor air pollution. These deaths stem from the health conditions that air pollution causes, including heart disease, lung cancer, and respiratory disease such as asthma. Most air pollution stems from the burning of fossil fuels such as oil, gas, and coal. This problem occurs not only in the wealthy industrial nations but also in the nations of the developing world; countries such as China and India have some of the worst air pollution. Reflecting the unequal impact of air pollution, an estimated 90 percent of air pollution deaths occur in low-income and middle-income nations.

Air pollution's health effects were exposed during the 2020 coronavirus pandemic. Cities in the United States and across the globe had higher rates COVID-19 deaths for many reasons, but a likely major reason was higher levels of air pollution. Because the chronic health conditions that air pollution causes may weaken urban residents' immune systems, their impaired immune systems may have made them more vulnerable to death from COVID-19. Accordingly, an important study found that U.S. counties with higher levels of air pollution had higher rates of COVID-19 deaths (Friedman 2020).[36]

Air pollution probably kills thousands of Americans every year and 2 million people across the planet.

Source: Andrius Kaziliunas/Shutterstock.com

Pollution of many types especially harms children's health. The "Children and Our Future" box discusses this harm in greater detail.

Children and Our Future

Children and Environmental Health Hazards

As we consider environmental problems, we must not forget the world's children, who are at special risk for environmental health problems precisely because they are children. Their bodies and brains grow rapidly, and they breathe in more air per pound of body weight than adults do. They also absorb substances, including toxic substances from their gastrointestinal tract, faster than adults do.

These and other physiological differences all put children at greater risk than adults for harm from environmental health hazards. Children's behavior also puts them at greater risk. For example, no adult of normal intelligence would eat paint chips found on the floor, but a young child can easily do so. Children also play on lawns, playgrounds, and other areas in which pesticides are often used, and this type of activity again gives them greater exposure. Young children also put their hands in their mouths regularly, and any toxins on their hands are thereby ingested.

Poverty compounds all these problems. Poor children are more likely to live in houses with lead paint, in neighborhoods with higher levels of air pollution, and in neighborhoods near to hazardous waste sites. Poor children of color are especially at risk for these environmental problems.

Three of the greatest environmental health hazards for children are lead, pesticides, and air pollution. Lead can cause brain and nervous system damage, hearing problems, and delayed growth, among other effects; pesticides can cause various problems in the immune, neurological, and respiratory systems; and air pollution can cause asthma and other respiratory illnesses. All these health problems can have lifelong consequences.

Unfortunately, certain environmentally induced health problems for children are becoming more common. For example, U.S. children's asthma cases have increased significantly over the past several decades thanks partly to air pollution, and 6.1 million American children now have asthma. Certain types of childhood cancers thought to stem at least partly from pollution and other environmental hazards have also increased during the past few decades.

It should be evident from this overview that environmental health hazards pose a serious danger for children in the United States and the rest of the world. Because children are our future, this danger underscores the need to do everything possible to improve the environment.

Sources: American Lung Association 2019; Children's Environmental Health Network 2019[37]

Global Climate Change

Climate change is causing many problems, including weather disasters such as the one depicted here.

Source: © Thinkstock

The burning of fossil fuels also contributes to *global climate change*, often called *global warming*, thanks to the oft-discussed *greenhouse effect* caused by the trapping of gases in the atmosphere that is turning the earth warmer. In addition to affecting the ecology of the earth's polar regions and ocean levels throughout the planet, climate change is producing many problems that threaten the planet. These problems include coastal flooding, increased disease transmitted via food and water, malnutrition resulting from decreased agricultural production and drought, a higher incidence of hurricanes and other weather disasters, and extinction of several species. As a recent news report put it, "The warming climate is killing coral reefs, supercharging monster storms, and fueling deadly marine heat waves and record losses of sea ice... [These] effects foreshadow a more catastrophic future as long as greenhouse gas emissions remain unchecked" (Mooney and Brady 2019).[38]

All these problems have been producing, and will continue to produce, higher mortality rates across the planet. The World Health Organization (2018)[39] estimates that climate change will cause 250,000 annual deaths worldwide by 2030 just from increased diarrhea, extreme heat, malaria, and malnutrition. Hundreds of thousands of additional annual deaths are also expected to occur from additional effects of climate change (Haines and Ebi 2019).[40] Climate change is also making people sicker in many other ways, including increased rates of allergies, pregnancy complications, heart and lung disease, dehydration and kidney problems, and infectious diseases in addition to malaria (Holden 2019).[41]

Another problem caused by climate change may be interpersonal violence and armed conflict (Mach et al. 2109),[42] already discussed as a consequence of population growth. Historically, when unusual weather events have caused drought, flooding, or other problems, violence and armed conflict have resulted. For example, witch-burnings in medieval Europe accelerated when extremely cold weather ruined crops and witches were blamed for the problem. Economic problems from declining farm values are thought to have increased the lynchings of African Americans in the U.S. South. As crops fail from global warming and reduced rainfall in the years ahead, African populations may plunge into civil war: According to an Oxford University economist, having a drought increases by 50 percent the chance that an African nation will have a civil war a year later (Kristof 2008).[43]

As we consider climate change, it is important to keep in mind certain inequalities mentioned earlier (Dunlap and Brulle 2015).[44] First, the world's richest nations contribute more than their fair share to climate change. The United States, Canada, France, Germany, and the United Kingdom compose about 15 percent of the world's population but are responsible for at least half of the planet's carbon dioxide emissions. Second, the effects of climate change are more severe for poor nations than for rich nations. Africans, for example, are much less able than Americans to deal with the effects of drought, weather disasters, and the other problems caused by climate change.

Water Pollution and Inadequate Sanitation

Water quality is another serious problem. Drinking water is often unsafe because of poor sanitation procedures for human waste in poor nations and because of industrial discharge into lakes, rivers, and streams in wealthy nations and less wealthy nations. Inadequate sanitation and unsafe drinking water cause parasitic infections and diseases such as diarrhea, malaria, cholera, intestinal worms, typhoid, and hepatitis A. The World Health Organization and other international agencies estimate that unsafe drinking water and inadequate sanitation cause 829,000 deaths annually from diarrhea, including nearly 300,000 child deaths from diarrhea. These problems also contribute to the more than 400,000 annual deaths from malaria and the 5 million annual deaths from malnutrition of children under age 5 (UNIGME 2019).[45]

The United States is not immune from tainted water, as lead and other contaminants sometimes make their way into Americans' water supply. In a recent example, the city of Flint, Michigan, switched its water supply in 2014 from Detroit's system to the Flint River in order to save money (Denchak 2018).[46] But its failure to adequately treat and test the water that Flint residents were now drinking led to many health problems, including elevated blood lead levels in Flint's children. By the time this problem was discovered, these children had been drinking lead-laden water for eighteen months. The water was also discovered to be contaminated with deadly bacteria and certain cancer-causing chemicals.

Nuclear Power

Nuclear power has been an environmental controversy at least since the 1970s. Proponents of nuclear power say it is a cleaner energy than fossil fuels such as oil and coal and does not contribute to global warming. Opponents of nuclear power counter that nuclear waste is highly dangerous no matter how it is disposed of, and they fear meltdowns that can result if nuclear power plant cores overheat and release large amounts of radioactive gases into the atmosphere.

The most serious nuclear plant disaster involved the Chernobyl plant in Ukraine in 1986. Chernobyl's core exploded and released radioactive gases into the atmosphere that eventually spread throughout Europe. The amount of radiation released was 400 times greater than the amount released by the atomic bomb that devastated Hiroshima at the end of World War II. About five dozen people (Chernobyl workers or nearby residents) soon died because of the disaster. According to the United Nations Scientific Committee of the Effects of Atomic Radiation (UNSCEAR), an estimated 27,000 additional cancer deaths worldwide will eventually result from the Chernobyl disaster (Gronlund 2011).[47]

Seven years earlier in March 1979, a nuclear disaster almost occurred in the United States at the Three Mile Island plant in central Pennsylvania. A series of technological and human failures allowed the plant's core to overheat to almost disastrous levels. The nation held its breath for several days while officials sought to bring the problem under control. During this time, some 140,000 people living within twenty miles of the plant were evacuated. The near disaster severely weakened enthusiasm for nuclear power in the United States, and the number of new nuclear plants dropped sharply in the ensuing two decades (Fischer 1997).[48]

Japan was the site of the worst nuclear disaster since Chernobyl in March 2011, when an earthquake and tsunami seriously damaged a nuclear plant in the Fukushima region, 155 miles north of Tokyo. More than 80,000 residents had to be evacuated because of the massive release of radioactive gases and water, and they remained far from their homes a year later as high levels of radiation continued to be found in the evacuated area (Fujita 2012).[49] Several U.S. nuclear reactors are of the same design as the Fukushima reactors and thus potentially at risk for a similar outcome if damaged bye an earthquake (Union of Concerned Scientists 2011).[50]

Critics say that oversight by the Nuclear Regulatory Commission (NRC) of the nuclear industry is too lax. A 2011 investigation by the Associated Press (AP) supported this criticism (Donn 2011).[51] The AP found that the NRC has been "working closely with the nuclear power industry to keep the nation's aging reactors operating within safety standards by repeatedly weakening those standards or simply failing to enforce them." For example, when certain valves at nuclear plants leaked, the NRC revised its regulations to permit more leakage. Also, when cracking of steam generator tubes allowed radiation to leak, standards on tubing strength were weakened. And when reactors began to violate temperature standards, the NRC almost doubled the permitted temperatures. The investigation found "thousands" of problems in aging reactors that it said the NRC has simply ignored, and it concluded that a "cozy relationship" exists between the NRC and the nuclear industry.

Critics say many U.S. nuclear plants lack adequate protection against several kinds of dangers.

Source: © Thinkstock

Ground Pollution and Hazardous Waste

Pollution of the air and water is an environmental danger, as we saw earlier, but so is pollution of the ground from hazardous waste. *Hazardous wastes* are unwanted materials or by-products that are potentially toxic. If discarded improperly, they enter the ground and/or bodies of water and eventually make their way into the bodies of humans and other animals and/or harm natural vegetation.

Two major sources of hazardous waste exist: (1) commercial products such as pesticides, cleaning fluids, and certain paints, batteries, and electronics and (2) by-products of industrial operations such as solvents and wastewater. Hazardous waste enters the environment through the careless actions of homeowners and other consumers, and also through the careless actions of major manufacturing corporations. It can cause birth defects, various chronic illnesses and conditions, and eventual death.

Sometimes companies have dumped so much hazardous waste into a specific location that they create *hazardous waste sites*. These sites are defined as parcels of land and water that have been contaminated by the dumping of dangerous chemicals into the ground by factories and other industrial operations. The most famous (or rather, infamous) hazardous waste site in the United States is undoubtedly Love Canal, an area in a corner of Niagara Falls, New York. During the 1940s and 1950s, a chemical company dumped 20,000 tons of toxic chemicals into the canal and then filled it in with dirt and sold it for development to the local school board. A school and more than 800 homes, many of them low income, were later built just near the site. The chemicals eventually leached into the groundwater, yards, and basements of the homes, reportedly causing birth defects and other health problems. (See "People Making a Difference")

Love Canal, an area in Niagara Falls, New York, was the site of chemical dumping that led to many birth defects and other health problems.

Source: Image courtesy of U.S. Environmental Protection Agency, http://commons. wikimedia.org/wiki/File:Love_ Canal_protest.jpg.

People Making a Difference

In Praise of Two Heroic Women

In the annals of activism against hazardous waste dumping, two women stand out for their contributions.

One was Lois Gibbs, who led a movement of residents of Love Canal to call attention to the dumping of hazardous waste in their neighborhood, as just discussed in the text. Gibbs had never been politically active before 1978, when evidence of the dumping first came to light. After reading a newspaper article about the dumping, she began a petition to shut down a local school that was next to the dump site. Her efforts generated a good deal of publicity and prompted state officials to perform environmental tests in the homes near the site. Two years later the federal government authorized funding to relocate 660 families from the dangerous area.

The second woman was Erin Brockovich, the subject of a 2000 film of that name starring Julia Roberts. Brockovich also was not politically active before she discovered hazardous waste dumping while she was working as a legal assistant for a small California law firm. As part of her work on a real estate case, she uncovered evidence that Pacific Gas & Electric had been dumping a toxic industrial solvent for thirty years into the water supply of the small town of Hinkley. Her investigation led to a lawsuit that ended in 1996 with the awarding of $333 million in damages to several hundred Hinkley residents.

Both Lois Gibbs and Erin Brockovich have remained active on behalf of environmental safety in the years since their celebrated initial efforts. They are two heroic women who have made a very significant difference.

Sources: Biography.com Editors 2019; Gibbs 2011[52]

The Superfund program of the U.S. Environmental Protection Agency (EPA), begun about four decades ago, monitors and cleans up extremely dangerous hazardous waste sites throughout the country. Since its inception, the Superfund program has identified and taken steps to address more than 1,300 of these so-called "Superfund sites" (Johnson 2017).[53] About 11 million people live within one mile of one of these sites.

Oceans

The world's oceans are at peril for several reasons. A major reason is that overfishing of fish and mammals has dramatically reduced the supply of certain ocean animals. This reduction certainly makes it difficult for people to eat certain fishes at restaurants or buy them at supermarkets, but a far more important problem concerns the ocean food chain (Cirino 2018).[54] As the supply of various ocean animals has dwindled, the food supply for the larger ocean animals that eat these smaller animals has declined, putting the larger animals at risk. And as the number of these larger animals has declined, other animals that prey on these larger animals have had to turn to other food sources or not have enough to eat. This chain reaction in the ocean food chain has serious consequences for the ocean's ecosystem.

One example of this chain reaction involves killer whales and sea otters in the ocean off of western Alaska (Weise 2011).[55] Killer whales eat many things, but sea lions and harbor seals form a key part of their diet. However, the supply of these ocean mammals in western Alaska and elsewhere has decreased because of human overfishing of their prey fish species. In response, killer whales have been eating more sea otters, causing a 90 percent decline in the number of sea otters in western Alaska. Because sea otters eat sea urchins, the loss of sea otters in turn has increased the number of sea urchins there. And because sea urchins consume kelp beds, kelp beds there are disappearing, removing a significant source of food for other ocean life (Estes et al. 2011).[56]

Another example of the ocean chain reaction concerns whales themselves. The whaling industry that began about 1,000 years ago and then intensified during the eighteenth century severely reduced the number of whales and made right whales almost extinct. In southern oceans, whale feces are an important source of nutrients for very small animals and plankton. As the whale population in these oceans has declined over the centuries, these animals and plankton that are essential for the ocean's ecosystem have suffered immeasurable losses (Weise 2011).[57]

Bycatch. In addition to overfishing, *bycatch*, or the unintentional catching and killing of fish, marine mammals, sea turtles, and seabirds while other fish are being caught, also endangers hundreds of ocean species and further contributes to the chain reaction we have described. The U.S. National Oceanic and Atmospheric Administration (2019)[58] says that bycatch is a complex, global issue that threatens the sustainability and resiliency of our fishing communities, economies, and ocean ecosystems. Bycatch of protected species, such as sea turtles and marine mammals, remains a significant threat to recovering dwindling populations."

The decline of the whale population due to the whaling industry threatens the world's supply of plankton and other very small marine animals.

Source: Image courtesy of Joel T. Barkan.

A familiar bycatch example to many Americans is the accidental catching and killing of dolphins when tuna are being caught by large fishing nets. A less familiar example involves sea turtles. These animals' numbers have declined so steeply in recent decades that six of the seven species of sea turtles are in danger of extinction. The major reason for this danger is bycatch from shrimp trawl nets and other types of fishing. This bycatch has killed millions of sea turtles since 1990 (World Wildlife Fund 2019).[59]

Climate change. Other ocean problems stem from climate change. The oceans' coral reefs are among the most colorful and beautiful sights in the world. More important, they are an essential source of nutrients for the oceans' ecosystem and a major source of protein for more than 500 million people. They help protect shorelines from natural disasters such as tsunamis, and they attract tens of billions of dollars in tourism.

Despite all these benefits, coral reefs have long been endangered by overfishing, tourism, and coastal development, among other factors. Scientists have now found that climate change is also harming coral reefs (Warren 2019).[60] The global warming arising from climate change is overheating coral reefs throughout the world. This overheating in turn causes the reefs to expel the algae they consume for food; the algae are also responsible for the reefs' bright colors. The reefs then turn pale and die, and their deaths add to the ocean's food chain problem already discussed. Scientists estimate that three-fourths of the earth's reefs are at risk from global warming, and that half of all reefs have already been destroyed.

Global warming will continue to be a main culprit in this regard, but so will increasing acidity, yet another problem arising from climate change. As carbon dioxide is released into the atmosphere, much of it falls into the ocean. This lowers the oceans' pH level and turns the oceans more acidic. This increasing acidity destroys coral reefs and also poses a risk to commercial species such as clams, lobsters, and mussels.

An additional ocean problem stemming from climate change is rising sea levels. Global warming has caused polar ice caps to melt and the seas to rise. This problem means that storm surges during severe weather are becoming an ever-greater problem. Even without storm surges, much coastal land has already been lost to rising ocean levels. Despite these problems, many coastal communities have failed to build adequate barriers that would minimize damage from ocean flooding, and climate scientists expect major continuous flooding in coastal cities across the world if climate change continues (Mooney and Dennis 2019).[61]

Food

This chapter discussed food shortages earlier as a population problem, but food can also be an environmental hazard. Simply put, food is often unsafe to eat because of deadly bacteria that emerge from improper handling and processing and other factors. According to the U.S. Centers for Disease Control and Prevention (CDC), 16 percent of Americans are sickened every year by contaminated food and beverages, with 3,000 Americans dying annually from these illnesses (CDC 2018).[62]

Key Takeaways

- Environmental problems are largely the result of human behavior and human decision making. Changes in human activity and decision making are thus necessary to improve the environment.
- Environmental inequality and environmental racism are significant issues. Within the United States and around the world, environmental problems are more often found where poor people and people of color reside.
- Air pollution, global climate change, water pollution and inadequate sanitation, and hazardous waste are major environmental problems that threaten the planet, with air pollution contributing mightily to higher COVID-19 death rates during the 2020 pandemic.

For Your Review

1. Pretend you are on a debate team and that your team is asked to argue in favor of the following resolution: *Be it resolved, that air and water pollution is primarily the result of reckless human behavior rather than natural environmental changes.* Using evidence from the text, write a two-minute speech (about 300 words) in favor of the resolution.
2. How much of the environmental racism that exists do you think is intentional? Explain your answer.
3. List one thing you did yesterday that was good for the environment and one thing that was bad for the environment.

15.4 Addressing Population Problems and Improving the Environment

Learning Objectives

1. Outline sociological-based strategies that should help address population issues.
2. List sociological-based strategies and other efforts that should help improve environmental problems.

The topics of population and the environment raise many issues within the United States and across the globe for which a sociological perspective is very relevant. We address a few of these issues here.

Population

We saw earlier that experts disagree over how concerned we should be generally about global population growth, and especially about the degree to which overpopulation is responsible for world hunger. Still, almost everyone would agree that world hunger is a matter of the most serious concern, even if they do not agree on why world hunger is so serious and so persistent. Both across the globe and within the United States, children and adults go hungry every day, and millions starve in the poorest nations in Africa and Asia.

As our earlier discussion indicated, many experts believe it is a mistake to blame world hunger on a scarcity of food. Instead, they attribute world hunger to various inequalities in access to, and in the distribution of, what is actually a sufficient amount of food to feed the world's people. To effectively reduce world hunger, inequalities across the globe and within the United States based on income, ethnicity, and gender must be addressed; some ways of doing so have been offered in previous chapters.

Population growth in poor nations has slowed but remains a significant problem. Their poverty, low educational levels, and rural settings all contribute to high birth rates. More effective contraception is needed to reduce their population growth, and the United Nations and other international bodies must bolster their efforts, with the aid of increased funding from rich nations, to provide contraception to poor nations. But contraceptive efforts will not be sufficient by themselves. Rather, it is also necessary to raise these nations' economic circumstances and educational levels, as birth rates are lower in nations that are wealthier and more educated. In particular, efforts that raise women's educational levels are especially important if contraceptive use is to increase. In all these respects, we once again see the importance of a sociological perspective centering on the significance of socioeconomic inequality.

The Environment

Environmental problems cannot be fully understood without appreciating their social context. In this regard, we discussed two major emphases of environmental sociology. First, environmental problems are largely the result of human decision making and activity and thus preventable. Second, environmental problems disproportionately affect the poor and people of color.

These two insights have important implications for how to improve our environment. Simply put, we must change the behaviors and decisions of individuals, businesses, and other organizations that harm the environment, and we must do everything possible to lessen the extra environmental harm that the poor and people of color experience. Many environmental scholars and activists believe that these efforts need to focus on the corporations whose industrial activities are often so damaging to the air, water, and land.

Beyond these general approaches to improving the environment, there are many strategies and policies that the United States and other nations could and should undertake to help the environment. Although a full discussion of these lies beyond the scope of this chapter, environmental experts recommend a number of actions for the United States to undertake (Dunnivant 2017; Erickson and Brase 2019; Harris 2019).[63] These include the following:

1. Establish mandatory electricity and natural gas reduction targets for utilities.
2. Expand renewable energy (wind and sun) by setting a national standard of 25 percent of energy (or some higher percentage) to come from renewable sources by a specified year.
3. Reduce deforestation by increasing the use of sustainable building materials and passing legislation to protect forests.
4. Reduce the use of fossil fuels by several measures, including higher fuel economy standards for motor vehicles, closing down older coal-fired power plants, and establishing a *cap-and-trade* system involving large payments by companies for carbon emissions to encourage them to reduce these emissions.
5. In cities, increase mass transit and develop more bicycle lanes and develop more efficient ways of using electricity and water.

If the rooftops of houses were painted white or covered with light-colored shingles, atmospheric temperatures would reduce.

Source: © Thinkstock

Another strategy is perhaps delightfully simple: turn rooftops and paved surfaces white! In many U.S. cities, roofs of houses, high-rises, and other buildings are covered with dark asphalt shingles. Dark surfaces trap heat from the sun and promote higher air temperatures. Painting roofs white or using white shingles to reflect the sun's heat would reduce these temperatures and help offset the effects of global warming (Pearce 2018).[64] A similar offset would occur from changing the color of our streets. Many roads in cities and other areas are composed of dark asphalt; using a lighter material would also help reduce air temperature and counter global warming. If these measures reduced air temperature in warm cities, less air conditioning would be needed. In turn, electricity use and carbon dioxide emissions would also decline.

To repeat what was said at the outset of this chapter, it is no exaggeration to say that the fate of our planet depends on the successful implementation of these and other strategies and policies. Because, as sociology emphasizes, the environmental problems that confront the world are the result of human activity, changes in human activity are necessary to save the environment.

Key Takeaways

- Efforts to address population issues should focus on the various inequalities that lead to both overpopulation and food scarcity.
- Efforts to improve the environment should keep in mind the greater environmental harm that the poor and people of color suffer.

For Your Review

1. If you had a million dollars to spend to address one population problem, would you use it to provide contraception, or would you use it to improve the distribution of food? Explain your answer.

2. Which one of the environmental problems discussed in the text concerns you the most? Why?

15.5 End-of-Chapter Material

Summary

1. Functionalism stresses the value of normal changes in population growth and the environment, but recognizes that certain population and environmental problems are dysfunctional. Conflict theory stresses that world hunger stems from lack of access to food, not from overpopulation, and it blames multinational corporations for environmental problems. Symbolic interactionism emphasizes people's activities and perceptions in regard to population and the environment.

2. Demography is the study of population. It encompasses three central concepts—fertility, mortality, and migration—which together determine population growth.

3. The world's population is growing by about 80 million people annually. Population growth is greatest in the low-income nations of Africa and other regions, while in several industrial nations it is declining.

4. Thomas Malthus predicted that the earth's population would greatly exceed the world's food supply. Although his prediction did not come true, hunger remains a serious problem around the world. Food supply is generally ample thanks to improved technology, but the distribution of food is inadequate in low-income nations.

5. Demographic transition theory helps explain why population growth did not continue to rise as much as Malthus predicted. As societies become more technologically advanced, first death rates and then birth rates decline, leading eventually to little population growth.

6. U.S. history is filled with prejudice against immigrants. Immigrants today contribute in many ways to the American economy and have relatively low crime rates. Despite these facts, many people are opposed to immigration, and many states have passed laws to restrict benefits and movement for immigrants.

7. Environmental sociology is the sociological study of the environment. One major emphasis of environmental sociology is that environmental problems are largely the result of human activity and human decision making. A second major emphasis is that environmental problems disproportionately affect low-income people and people of color. These effects are called environmental inequality and environmental racism, respectively.

8. Environmental problems include climate change, air and water pollution, and hazardous waste. Children are particularly vulnerable to the health effects of environmental problems. During the 2020 coronavirus pandemic, air pollution may have increased rates of COVID-19 deaths across the United States.

Using What You Know

You are in your second year in the accounting division of a large company that operates a factory on the main river in a small town. One day you notice some financial documents. These documents suggest to you that your company has been dumping a toxic solvent into the river rather than having it collected and taken to a safe site. Having had an environmental sociology course in college, you are very concerned about this possible problem, but you are not certain that the dumping is in fact occurring, and you also do not want to lose your job. Do you take any action related to your new suspicion of the possible dumping, or do you remain silent? Explain your answer.

What You Can Do

To help deal with the population and environmental problems discussed in this chapter, you may wish to do any of the following:

1. Contribute money to a national environmental organization or join a local environmental group in your activity.
2. Start an organization on your campus to deal with world hunger.
3. Organize a speaker series on your campus to address various environmental topics.

Endnotes

1. Mansoor, Sanya. 2019. "Air Pollution Turned India's Capital into a 'Climate Emergency.'" *Time* November 6:https://time.com/5718012/new-delhi-pollution-2019/.

2. Michaels, David. 2008. *Doubt Is Their Product: How Industry's Assault on Science Threatens Your Health*. New York: Oxford University Press.

3. Sullivan, Riley. 2019. "Aging and Declining Populations in Northern New England: Is There a Role for Immigration?" *Bostonfed.org* July 17:https://www.bostonfed.org/publications/new-england-public-policy-center-regional-briefs/2019/aging-and-declining-populations-in-northern-new-england.aspx.

4. Ozimek, Adam, Kenan Fikri and John Lettieri. 2019. *From Managing Decline to Building the Future: Could a Heartland Visa Help Struggling Regions*. Washington, DC: Economic Innovation Group.

5. Hamilton, Brady E., Joyce A. Martin, Michelle J.K. Osterman and Lauren M. Rossen. 2019. "Births: Provisional Data for 2018." *National Center for Health Statistics Vital Statistics Rapid Release: Report No. 007*(July):1-25.

6. Hamilton, Brady E., Joyce A. Martin, Michelle J.K. Osterman and Lauren M. Rossen. 2019. "Births: Provisional Data for 2018." *National Center for Health Statistics Vital Statistics Rapid Release: Report No. 007*(July):1-25.

7. Weeks, John R. 2016. *Population: An Introduction to Concepts and Issues*, 12th ed. Belmont, CA: Wadsworth.

8. Wilkerson, Isabel. 2011. *The Warmth of Other Suns: The Epic Story of America's Great Migration* New York: Vintage Books.

9. Population Reference Bureau. 2019. *World Population Data Sheet*. Retrieved from https://www.prb.org/worldpopdata/

10. Worldometers. 2019. *Current World Population*. Retrieved from https://www.worldometers.info/world-population/.

11. Gillis, Justin and Celia W. Dugger. 2011. "U.N. Forecasts 10.1 Million by Century's End." *The New York Times* May 4:A1.

12. Malthus, Thomas Robert. 1926(1798). *First Essay on Population*. London: Macmillan.

13. Ehrlich, Paul R. 1969. *The Population Bomb*. San Francisco: Sierra Club.

14. Ehrlich, Paul R. and John Harte. 2018. "Analysis: Pessimism on the Food Front." *Environmental Health News* April 25:https://www.ehn.org/what-are-the-threats-to-future-food-security-2562981347.html.

15. King, Richard. 2011. "Global Food Crisis: The Challenge of Changing Diets." *The Guardian* June 1:http://www.guardian.co.uk/global-development/poverty-matters/2011/jun/01/global-food-crisis-changing-diets.

16. Scanlan, Stephen J., J. Craig Jenkins and Lindsey Peterson. 2010. "The Scarcity Fallacy." *Contexts* 9(1):34-39.

17. Scanlan, Stephen J., J. Craig Jenkins and Lindsey Peterson. 2010. "The Scarcity Fallacy." *Contexts* 9(1):34-39.

18. Chamie, Joseph. 2018. "Replacement Fertility Declines Worldwide." *YaleGlobal Online* July 12:https://yaleglobal.yale.edu/content/replacement-fertility-declines-worldwide.

19. Haartsen, T., & Venhorst, V. (2010). Planning for decline: Anticipating on population decline in the Netherlands. *Tijdschrift voor Economische en Sociale Geografie (Journal of Economic & Social Geography)*, 101(2), 218–227.

20. Matthews, Dylan. 2016. "Sweden Pays Parents Benefits for Having Kids—and It Reaps Huge Rewards. Why Doesn't the Us?". *Vox.com* May 23:https://www.vox.com/2016/5/23/11440638/child-benefit-child-allowance.

21. Anbinder, Tyler. 2019. "Trump Has Spread More Hatred of Immigrants Than Any American in History." *The Washington Post* November 7:https://www.washingtonpost.com/outlook/trump-has-spread-more-hatred-of-immigrants-than-any-american-in-history/2019/11/07/7e253236-ff54-11e9-8bab-0fc209e065a8_story.html.

22. Barkan, Steven E. 2018. "Immigrants Help Make America Great." *Bangor Daily News* September 25:https://bangordailynews.com/2018/09/25/opinion/contributors/immigrants-help-make-america-great/.

23. Osborne, Linda Barret. 2016. *This Land Is Our Land: A History of American Immigration*. New York: Harry N. Abrams.

24. Pfaelzer, Jean. 2008. *Driven Out: The Forgotten War against Chinese Americans*. Berkeley: University of California Press.

25. Daniels, Roger. 2002. *Coming to America: A History of Immigration and Ethnicity in American Life*. New York: Harper Perennial.

26. Gonzalez-Barrera, Ana and Jens Manuel Krogstad. 2019. "What We Know About Illegal Immigration from Mexico." *Pew Research Center* June 28:https://www.pewresearch.org/fact-tank/2019/06/28/what-we-know-about-illegal-immigration-from-mexico/.

27. Center for American Progress. 2017. "The Facts on Immigration Today: 2017 Edition."https://www.americanprogress.org/issues/immigration/reports/2017/04/20/430736/facts-immigration-today-2017-edition/.

28. Ousey, Graham C. and Chris E. Kubrin. 2018. "Immigration and Crime: Assessing a Contentious Issue." *Annual Review of Criminology* 1:63-84.

29. Migration Policy Group and Barcelona Centre for International Affairs. 2015. *Migrant Integration Policy Index 2015*. Retrieved from http://www.mipex.eu/.

30. Nagel, Joane, Thomas Dietz and Jeffrey Broadbent, eds. 2010. *Workshop on Sociological Perspectives on Global Climate Change*. Washington, DC: National Science Foundation and American Sociological Association.

31. King, Leslie and Deborah McCarthy Auriffeille, eds. 2019. *Environmental Sociology: From Analysis to Action*. Lanham, MD: Rowman & Littlefield

32. Holifield, Ryan, Jayajit Chakraborty, Gordon Walker, ed. 2018. *The Routledge Handbook of Environmental Justice*. New York: Routledge.

33. Bullard, Robert D. 1990. *Dumping in Dixie: Race, Class, and Environmental Quality*. Boulder, CO: Westview Press. Bullard, Robert D. and Beverly Wright. 2009. "Race, Place, and the Environment in Post-Katrina New Orleans." Pp. 19-48 in *Race, Place, and Environmental Justice after Hurricane Katrina: Struggles to Reclaim, Rebuild, and Revitalize New Orleans and the Gulf Coast*, edited by R. D. Bullard and B. Wright. Boulder, CO: Westview Press; Dicum, Gregory. 2006. "Meet Robert Bullard, the Father of Environmental Justice." *Grist Magazine* March 14:http://www.grist.org/article/dicum/.

34. Evans, Gary W. and Elyse Kantrowitz. 2002. "Socioeconomic Status and Health: The Potential Role of Environmental Risk Exposure." *Annual Review of Public Health* 23(1):303.

35. World Health Organization. 2019. "Ambient Air Pollution: Health Impacts."https://www.who.int/airpollution/ambient/health-impacts/en/.

36. Friedman, Lisa. 2020. "Study Finds a Link between Air Pollution and Virus Deaths." *The New York Times* April 8:A16.

37. American Lung Association. 2019. "Children and Air Pollution."https://www.lung.org/our-initiatives/healthy-air/outdoor/air-pollution/children-and-air-pollution.html; Children's Environmental Health Network. 2019. "Cancer and Children's Environmental Health." Retrieved from https://cehn.org/our-work/childhood-cancer/.

38. Mooney, Chris and Brady Dennis. 2019. "New U.N. Climate Report: Monumental Change Already Here for World's Oceans and Frozen Regions." *The Washington Post* September 25:https://www.washingtonpost.com/climate-environment/2019/09/25/new-un-climate-report-massive-change-already-here-worlds-oceans-frozen-regions/.

39. World Health Organization. 2018. "Climate Change and Health." Retrieved from https://www.who.int/news-room/fact-sheets/detail/climate-change-and-health.

40. Haines, Andy and Kristie Ebi. 2019. "The Imperative for Climate Action to Protect Health." *New England Journal of Medicine* 380:263-73.

41. Holden, Emily. 2019. "Climate Change Is Having Widespread Health Impacts." *Scientific American* September 16:https://www.scientificamerican.com/article/climate-change-is-having-widespread-health-impacts/.

42. Mach, Katharine J., Caroline M. Kraan, W. Neil Adger, Halvard Buhaug, Marshall Burke, James D. Fearon, Christopher B. Field, Cullen S. Hendrix, Jean-Francois Maystadt, John O'Loughlin, Philip Roessler, Jürgen Scheffran, Kenneth A. Schultz and Nina von Uexkull. 2019. "Climate as a Risk Factor for Armed Conflict." *Nature* 571:193-97.

43. Kristof, Nicholas D. 2008. "Extended Forecast: Bloodshed." *The New York Times* April 13:http://www.nytimes.com/2008/04/13/opinion/13kristof.html.

44. Dunlap, Riley E. and Robert J. Brulle, eds. 2015. *Climate Change and Society: Sociological Perspectives*. New York: Oxford University Press.

45. United Nations Inter-agency Group for Child Mortality Estimation. 2019. *Levels & Trends in Child Mortality: Report 2019*. New York: United Nations Children's Fund.

46. Denchak, Melissa. 2018. "Flint Water Crisis: Everything You Need to Know." *National Resources Defense Council*:https://www.nrdc.org/stories/flint-water-crisis-everything-you-need-know.

47. Gronlund, Lisbeth. 2011. "How Many Cancers Did Chernobyl Really Cause?—Updated Version." Cambridge, MA: Union of Concerned Scientists.

48. Fischer, David. 1997. *History of the International Atomic Energy Agency: The First Forty Years*. Vienna: International Atomic Energy Agency.

49. Fujita, Akiko. 2012. "Japan's Nuclear Exclusion Zone Shows Few Signs of Life." *abcnews.com* February 6:http://abcnews.go.com/International/fukushimas-nuclear-exclusion-zone-shows-signs-life/story?id=15521091#.TzFSXONSRyc.

50. Union of Concerned Scientists. 2011, "Nuclear Reactor Crisis in Japan Faqs." Retrieved from http://www.ucsusa.org/nuclear_power/nuclear_power_risk/safety/nuclear-reactor-crisis-faq.html#us-plant-risk.

51. Donn, Jeff. 2011. "As Nuclear Plants Age, Nrc Loosens Safety Regulations." *The Boston Globe* June 20:A2.

52. Biography.com Editors. 2019. "Erin Brockovich Biography." Retrieved from https://www.biography.com/activist/erin-brockovich; Gibbs, Lois Marie. 2011. *Love Canal and the Birth of the Environmental Movement*. Washington, DC: Island Press.

53. Johnson, David. 2017. "Do You Live near Toxic Waste? See 1,317 of the Most Polluted Spots in the U.S." *Time* March 22, 2017.

54. Cirino, Erica. 2018. "Overfishing of Krill Is Disrupting Antarctic Food Chains." *Pacific Standard* March 30, 2018.

55. Weise, Elizabeth. 2011. "Predator Loss Can Start Food-Chain Reaction." *USA Today* July 15:9A.

56. Estes, James A., John Terborgh, Justin S. Brashares, Mary E. Power, Joel Berger, William J. Bond, Stephen R. Carpenter, Timothy E. Essington, Robert D. Holt, Jeremy B. C. Jackson, Robert J. Marquis, Lauri Oksanen, Tarja Oksanen, Robert T. Paine, Ellen K. Pikitch, William J. Ripple, Stuart A. Sandin, Marten Scheffer, Thomas W. Schoener and Jonathan B. Shurin. 2011. "Trophic Downgrading of Planet Earth." *Science* 333(6040):301-06. doi: 10.1126/science.1205106.

57. Weise, Elizabeth. 2011. "Predator Loss Can Start Food-Chain Reaction." *USA Today* July 15:9A.

58. National Oceanic and Atmospheric Administration. 2019. "Bycatch." Retrieved from https://www.fisheries.noaa.gov/topic/bycatch.

59. World Wildlife Fund. 2019. "Protecting Turtles from the Threat of Bycatch." Retrieved from https://www.worldwildlife.org/initiatives/protecting-turtles-from-the-threat-of-bycatch.

60. Warren, Hayley. 2019. "Half the World's Coral Reefs Already Have Been Killed by Climate Change." *Bloomberg Business* October 11:https://www.bloomberg.com/graphics/2019-coral-reefs-at-risk/.

61. Mooney, Chris and Brady Dennis. 2019. "New U.N. Climate Report: Monumental Change Already Here for World's Oceans and Frozen Regions." *The Washington Post* September 25:https://www.washingtonpost.com/climate-environment/2019/09/25/new-un-climate-report-massive-change-already-here-worlds-oceans-frozen-regions/.

62. Centers for Disease Control and Prevention. 2018. "CDC and Food Safety." Retrieved from https://www.cdc.gov/foodsafety/cdc-and-food-safety.html.

63. Dunnivant, Frank. 2017. Environmental Success Stories: Solving Major Ecological Problems and Confronting Climate Change. New York: Columbia University Press; Erickson, Larry C. and Gary Brase. 2019. *Reducing Greenhouse Gas Emissions and Improving Air Quality: Two Interrelated Global Challenges* New York: CRC Press; Mark Anglin Harris. 2019. *Confronting Global Climate Change: Experiments & Applications in the Tropics*. New York: CRC Press.

64. Pearce, Fred. 2018. "Urban Heat: Can White Roofs Help Cool World's Warming Cities?". *Yale Environment 360* March 7:https://e360.yale.edu/features/urban-heat-can-white-roofs-help-cool-the-worlds-warming-cities.

CHAPTER 16
War and Terrorism

Social Problems in the News

"U.S. Drone Killed Afghan Civilians, Officials Say," the headline said. In late November 2019, an American drone strike on a car in Afghanistan killed the five people inside the car, according to Afghan officials. One of these victims was a woman who had just given birth at home to her second child. When her health soon deteriorated, relatives took her to a clinic. The group was returning home when the drone strike hit the car. In addition to the woman, her three relatives died, as did the driver. Her newborn, still at home, was now motherless.

Source: Mangal and Abed 2019[1]

Great war novels like *The Red Badge of Courage* and *War and Peace* highlight the heroism and horror that both occur on the battlefield. This news story likewise reminds us that war, however heroic, is also horrible. Atrocities happen; soldiers are killed or wounded, physically and/or mentally; and civilians suffer and die. As Sydney H. Schanberg (2005:1),[2] a former *New York Times* reporter who covered the U.S. wars in Vietnam and Cambodia, once bluntly observed, "'History,' Hegel said, 'is a slaughterhouse.' And war is how the slaughter is carried out."

For much of human history, people considered war a necessary evil that was often waged for noble reasons. World War II, for example, was what we now call "the good war," fought to end Hitler's attempt to conquer much of the world. Tens of millions died on the battlefield, in cities bombed by planes, and in concentration camps before Hitler and his allies were finally defeated.

About two decades after World War II ended, the United States began fighting another war meant to save the world for democracy, but this war was very different from the one against Hitler. This war was fought in Vietnam, and however a noble effort World War II might have been, the Vietnam War was just as ignoble to its critics. It was a war, some said, not to save the world for democracy but to help extend America's power where it did not belong. The war's severest critics called it an act of genocide against Asians. If the World War II generation grew up with a patriotic love for their nation, the Vietnam War generation grew up with much more cynicism about their government and the military.

Ironically, that generation's concern about the military was shared by none other than President Dwight D. Eisenhower, who warned about the dangers of what he called the **military-industrial complex**—the friendly interplay of the military, the defense industry, and political leaders—in his farewell presidential address (Ledbetter 2011).[3] Eisenhower himself had been a member of the military-industrial complex, having served as a five-star general and supreme commander of the Allied forces in Europe during World War II before becoming president. His military experience made him no fan of warfare; as he once observed, "I hate war as only a soldier who has lived it can, only as one who has seen its brutality, its futility, its stupidity." He also feared that the military-industrial complex was becoming too powerful and gaining "unwarranted influence" over American life as it acted for its own interests and not necessarily for those of the nation as a whole. He warned that the "potential for the disastrous rise of misplaced power exists and will persist" (Eisenhower 1961).[4]

President Dwight D. Eisenhower warned about what he called the "unwarranted influence" of the military-industrial complex.

Source: Department of Defense. Department of the Army. Office of the Deputy Chief of Staff for Operations. U.S. Army Audiovisual Center. ca. 1974-5/15/1984. Dwight D. Eisenhower. National Archives Identifier: 531434. Retrieved from: https://catalog.archives.gov/id/531434.

military-industrial complex

The close relationships among military leaders, government officials, and defense contractors.

Eisenhower's "Military-Industrial Complex" Speech Origins and Significance

In his farewell address, President Dwight D. Eisenhower warned about the effects of the military-industrial complex, saying that its huge expenditure was taking needed dollars away from America's social needs.

View the video online at: http://www.youtube.com/embed/Gg-jvHynP9Y?rel=0

militarism

An overemphasis on military policy and spending.

Eisenhower's fears about the military-industrial complex reflected his more general concern about **militarism**, or an overemphasis on military policy and spending, which he thought was costing the nation far too much money. In a remarkable and now famous statement made early in his presidency, Eisenhower (1953)[5] declared, "Every gun that is made, every warship launched, every rocket fired, signifies in the final sense, a theft from those who hunger and are not fed, those who are cold and are not clothed. This world in arms is not spending money alone. It is spending the sweat of its laborers, the genius of its scientists, the hopes of its children. This is not a way of life at all in any true sense. Under the clouds of war, it is humanity hanging on a cross of iron."

Eisenhower's concerns are even more valid today. As the United States and other governments spend hundreds of billions of dollars annually on their militaries, mass death and destruction from war beyond what Eisenhower could have ever imagined are a major concern, and serious social needs go unmet. It is probably trite to say that war profoundly affects societies, but that is precisely why war and the threat of war are considered one the most pressing social problems of our times and a threat to the entire planet.

Terrorism also profoundly affects societies. Yet most Americans probably did not consider terrorism a social problem before September 11, 2001, when, as has often been said, the world changed. On that terrible day, terrorists drove two passenger jets into the World Trade Center in New York and another into the Pentagon; a fourth plane apparently headed for a Washington, DC, target crashed in central Pennsylvania when brave passengers fought back. The shock of the 3,000 deaths that resulted continues to haunt us even as we have become accustomed to homeland security measures in our airports and elsewhere that would have seemed inconceivable a generation ago.

Against this horrific backdrop of the modern era, this chapter examines war and terrorism as the final social problems discussed in this book. As forms of armed conflict that aim to defeat an opponent, war and terrorism have been part of the human experience for thousands of years. However, their manifestation in the contemporary era is particularly frightening, thanks to ever more powerful weapons, such as nuclear arms, that threaten human existence. We consider their causes, dynamics, and consequences before discussing certain actions and policies that might conceivably reduce these threats to peaceful societies and human existence.

16.1 Sociological Perspectives on War and Terrorism

1. Summarize the key assumptions and emphases of the functionalist, conflict, and symbolic interactionist perspectives on war and terrorism.

The three major sociological perspectives offer some very different understandings of war and terrorism. You might agree with some of their assumptions and disagree with other assumptions, but together they capture the major dimensions of these two forms of armed conflict. Table 16.1 summarizes these assumptions.

TABLE 16.1 Theory Snapshot

Theoretical perspective	Major assumptions
Functionalism	War and terrorism serve several important functions. For example, they increase social solidarity as a society unites to defeat a perceived enemy. Some wars have also helped preserve freedom and democracy.
Conflict theory	War and militarism primarily advance the interests of the military-industrial complex and take billions of dollars from unmet social needs.
Symbolic interactionism	Symbols such as the flag play an important role in marshaling support for war. Definitions of several concepts also play an important role in public opinion regarding war and terrorism.

Functionalism

Recall that functionalism emphasizes the usefulness of certain behaviors and social institutions for many aspects of society. One of functionalism's most important insights is that social problems might actually be useful in this way, however many difficulties they might otherwise cause. To use an example from Chapter 1, crime certainly causes many problems, but it also creates hundreds of thousands of jobs in law enforcement, courts and corrections, home security, and other sectors of the economy that deal with crime.

In this spirit, functionalism similarly emphasizes the ways in which war and terrorism are useful for society, however horrible they are in so many other ways. Perhaps the first sociologist to make this point for war was Robert E. Park, the 1925 president of the American Sociological Association (which was then called the American Sociological Society—a name that was later changed because of its acronym!). In January 1941, less than a year before the bombing of Pearl Harbor, Park published an influential essay called "The Social Function of War: Observations and Notes," in a leading sociology journal (Park 1941).[6]

Park's essay outlined several functions of war. First, war *helps resolve international disputes* over matters such as territorial boundaries and religious and other ideologies. No matter what one might think of war, historically it has resolved disputes between nations, with the winner of the war winning the dispute. Even though very few people would say that war is a preferred method for resolving a dispute, it still has performed this function.

War generates a sense of social cohesion among the people in a society that is at war.

Source: © Thinkstock

Second, war *generates a stronger sense of social bonding and solidarity* within the societies that are at war. Having a common enemy, people within a society at war "come together" with a shared purpose and feel more united and patriotic than before. This dynamic is called the *external conflict/internal cohesion* process (Markides and Cohn 1982).[7] Although Park did not discuss terrorism, this form of armed conflict can also create social solidarity. In the days and weeks after 9/11, Americans came together as one people, and the president of France famously said, "We are all Americans."

Third, wars many centuries ago, such as those in which ancient Rome in essence formed and grew from conquering various tribes, *led to the development of the nation-state* as a political institution. As these tribes came under the rule of nation-states, their separate tribal identities weakened as they gradually identified themselves as one people belonging to their nation-state; Park (p. 569) referred to this process as "the coming-together and integration of races and peoples." Moreover, the size and resources of these nation-states allowed them to generate scientific, cultural, and political advances that played an important role in world history. War, then, indirectly contributed to these advances. Although nation-states still might have eventually developed even without war, their development was accelerated by war.

Other functions of war can also be cited. Some wars, including the American colonists' war against England and the Allies' war against Hitler and Japan, have helped *maintain and establish freedom and democracy*. In the past and also today, war and military service have also *provided important opportunities for jobs and career advancement for people of color and women*. Related to this, the U.S. military provides hundreds of thousands of jobs annually and is a ready form of employment for people who only have a high school education. More generally, the military and the defense industry are certainly important components of the U.S. economy, and military spending in some eras *has helped stimulate the U.S. economy*. In perhaps the most notable example of this effect, spending for World War II is commonly credited with helping to lift the United States out of the Great Depression (Shiller 2012).[8]

In a final function, weapons research and other types of military research *have contributed to scientific and technological development* in general. For example, military research played a key role in the early development of the internet.

Conflict Theory

Conflict theory's perspective on war and the military is decidedly more negative than that of functionalism. There are actually many different views within conflict theory about war and the military, but three related views stand out. The first view echoes President Eisenhower's concern over the power and influence of the military-industrial complex. According to conflict theory, the United States spends so much on the military and even goes to war because military officials, defense contractors, and political leaders work hand-in-hand in a rather cozy relationship. Although they may profess that their actions are meant to keep the nation safe, their ultimate goal is to enhance their political power and financial well-being.

power elite

C. Wright Mills's term for the government, big business, and the military, which he said collaborate to advance their own interests.

The most famous critique of the military-industrial complex from a conflict theorist is undoubtedly that of sociologist C. Wright Mills in his book *The Power Elite* (1956).[9] According to Mills, the **power elite** is composed of government, big business, and the military, which together constitute a *ruling class* that controls society and works for its own interests, not for the interests of the citizenry. Members of the power elite, Mills said, see each other socially and serve together on the boards of directors of corporations, charitable organizations, and other bodies. When cabinet members, senators, and top generals and other military officials retire, they often become corporate executives; military officials in particular join defense contractors. Conversely, corporate executives often become cabinet members and other key political appointees, and defense industry executives often end up in the Pentagon. This *circulation of the elites* creates a rather cozy relationship that helps ensure their dominance over American life and in particular ensures that the military-industrial complex has an untold influence over economic and foreign policy.

A more recent critique of the military-industrial complex and foreign policy by sociologist Mark P. Worrell (2011:51)[10] bluntly stresses the role played by the desire for corporate profits: "War is business and it is profitable…What we learned in the aftermath of World War II is that mass destruction is great for corporate profits…War is driven by corporate profits and corporations drive politics." According to Worrell and other contemporary critics of what they call the *warfare state*, the United States now has a *permanent war economy*. In their view, the war on terrorism after 9/11 and the wars in Iraq and Afghanistan "have only deepened the trend toward ever more concentrated state, corporate, and military power in a society that ostensibly embraces democratic values" (Boggs 2011:ix).[11]

The second view of conflict theory concerns **imperialism**, or the use of military power and other means to extend a nation's influence and control over other nations. This view, held by the more radical proponents of conflict theory, argues that war and other military ventures by the United States are done for the sake of imperialism rather than for noble goals such as the preservation and extension of democracy. In this view, the United States wages war and engages in other military actions to gain access to oil and other resources of other societies, with the ultimate aim of enriching multinational corporations and other parties. The characterization does not hold true for World War II, conflict theorists concede, but they argue it holds true for many and perhaps most other U.S. wars and military actions, historically and today. In their view, this century's wars in Iraq and Afghanistan in particular were initiated under false pretenses to maintain adequate oil supply and more generally to extend America's military and economic influence around the world (Worrell 2011).[12]

A third view of conflict theory criticizes the size of the military budget and emphasizes the billions of dollars it takes from social needs such as poverty and climate change. As sociologist Carl Boggs (2011:17)[13] argues, "The war economy, for its part, devours roughly one trillion dollars in material, technological, and human resources yearly…, ensuring a pattern of waste, destruction, uneven development, eroded public infrastructures, and decimated social programs. Decaying American cities have become a supreme legacy of the warfare system." We return to this issue later in this chapter.

> **imperialism**
>
> The use of military power and other means to extend a nation's influence and control over other nations.

Symbolic Interactionism

Symbolic interactionist writing on war features several emphases. One theme concerns the perceptions and experiences of people involved in war: soldiers, civilians, and others. There are many moving accounts, for example, both real and fictitious, of soldiers' life on the battlefield and after they come home from war.

A second emphasis concerns the use of symbols to marshal support for war or protest against war. Symbols such as the flag evoke feelings of patriotism, perhaps especially when a nation is at war. The president and other politicians typically display a flag when they give major speeches, and it would be unthinkable for a flag not to be showing when the speech is about war or the threat of war. During the Vietnam War, protesters sometimes flew the U.S. flag upside-down (the international symbol of distress) to show their hatred of the war, and some protesters also burned the flag—an act that is almost guaranteed to provoke outrage and hostility from onlookers.

Other symbols can also be important. When the United States invaded Iraq in March 2003, millions of Americans put magnetic yellow ribbons on their cars, SUVs, and pickup trucks to show their support for the troops. Another ubiquitous symbol during the Vietnam War was the so-called international peace symbol (see [Unsupported Reference Type: informalfigure]), originally designed in the late 1950s to symbolize concern over nuclear weapons. Vietnam War protesters wore this

The international peace symbol can be seen here.

Source: Clip art: http://www. homemade-preschool.com/ image-files/peace-sign-black.png.

symbol on their clothing, and many put peace symbol decals on their motor vehicles, book bags, and other possessions.

A third emphasis of symbolic interactionism concerns how concepts related to war and terrorism come to be defined in ways that advance the goals of various parties. For example, a key goal of the military in basic training is to convince trainees that people they may face on the battlefield are *the enemy* and, as such, an appropriate target for killing. Related to this goal is the need to convince trainees that when they kill an enemy soldier, the killing is a justified killing and not murder. Similarly, the military often refers to civilian deaths or wounding as *collateral damage* in a conscious or unconscious attempt to minimize public horror at civilian casualties.

Another definitional issue concerns *terrorism*. As we shall discuss later, the definition of *terrorism* is very subjective, as actions that some people might regard as terrorism might be regarded by other people as freedom fighting or some other much more positive term than terrorism.

With this theoretical background in mind, we now turn to several issues and problems of war and terrorism.

Key Takeaways

- War and terrorism serve several functions, including the creation of social solidarity.
- According to conflict theory, war advances the interests of the military-industrial complex, while militarism takes money away from unmet social needs.
- Symbolic interactionism emphasizes the importance of symbols in support for war and terrorism and the experience of civilians and veterans as victims of war.

For Your Review

1. Which one of the three perspectives on war and terrorism do you most favor? Why?
2. Why do you think the flag has so much symbolic importance in American society?

16.2 War

Learning Objectives

1. Explain why war is best understood as a social phenomenon and why nations go to war.
2. Outline both sides to the debate over the size of the U.S. military budget.
3. List the types of problems that military veterans often face.

War is "sustained armed conflict" that causes "large-scale loss of life or extreme material destruction" (Worrell, 2011, p. 1).[14] Wars occur both between nations and within nations, when two or more factions engage in armed conflict. War between nations is called **international war**, while war within nations is called **civil war**.

war
Sustained armed conflict resulting in large-scale loss of life or extreme material destruction.

international war
War between nations.

civil war
War within nations.

The World at War

More than 100 million soldiers and civilians are estimated to have died during the international and civil wars of the twentieth century (Leitenberg 2006).[15] Although this is almost an unimaginable number, there is cause for some hope, even as there is also cause for despair.

The hope arises from historical evidence that the number of international wars, civil wars, and other types of armed conflict has in fact declined over the centuries, with the number in the past half-century much smaller than in centuries past (Pinker 2012).[16] Reflecting this decline, a smaller percentage of the world's population died in armed conflict during the past century than in earlier eras.

To illustrate this trend, compare two periods of history (Pinker 2012).[17] The first is the thirteenth century, when the Mongol Empire under the initial leadership of Genghis Khan became an empire in Asia and Eastern Europe through wars and conquest in which it killed 40 million people. The second period is 1939–1945, when World War II killed an estimated 75–85 million people. Although 75–85 million is more than 40 million, the world's population in the thirteenth century was only one-seventh its population during the World War II period. A quick calculation shows that about 11 percent of the world's population died from the Mongolian wars, while 3 percent died from World War II. In terms of the risk of dying in war, then, the Mongolian wars were five times more deadly than World War II. Although wars, other armed conflicts, terrorism, and genocide certainly continue, the world overall is in fact more peaceful now than in the past.

That is the good news and the cause for hope. The cause for despair is twofold. First, war, terrorism, genocide, and other armed conflicts *do* continue. Even if they are less frequent and less deadly than in the past, that is of little comfort to the tens of millions of people around the world during the past century who died or otherwise suffered in war and other armed conflict and who live in fear today of becoming a victim of armed conflict.

Second, the world today is a much more dangerous place than in the past because of the existence of nuclear weapons. In the thirteenth century, the Mongol Empire under the initial leadership of Genhis Khan killed 40 million people with battle-axes and other crude weapons. During World War II, the millions of deaths on battlefields resulted from gunfire and conventional bombs. At the end of that war, however, the nuclear age began when the United States dropped two atomic weapons on Japan that killed tens of thousands instantly and tens of thousands more from radiation exposure.

Those two weapons were tiny in both number and size compared to nuclear weapons today. Nearly 14,000 nuclear weapons now exist, 3,600 of these are operational, and 1,800 (most of them held by the United States and Russia) are on high alert, ready to be used at any time (Federation of American Scientists 2019).[18] Each of these warheads is an average of at least twenty times more powerful than each of the atomic bombs that decimated Japan.

Although World War II killed an estimated 55 million people, a smaller percentage of the world's population died in armed conflict during the twentieth century than in earlier eras.

Source: © Thinkstock

Nuclear Weapons: Last Week Tonight with John Oliver

Some 1,800 nuclear weapons, most held by the United States and Russia, are on high alert. These weapons are much more powerful than the atomic bombs that fell on Japan and pose a great danger to the planet.

View the video online at: http://www.youtube.com/embed/1Y1ya-yF35g?rel=0

The United States at War

If we say the history of the United States has been written in war, that is not too much of an exaggeration. The United States, of course, began with the colonial war against England. The American Civil War, also called the War Between the States, then tore it apart less than a century later. Between 1861 and 1865, more than 498,000 soldiers in both the Union and the Confederacy died on the battlefield or from disease. The minimum estimate almost matches the number of American deaths in all the other wars the United States has fought, and the maximum estimate greatly exceeds this number (see Table 16.2).

TABLE 16.2 U.S. Participation in Major Wars

War	Number of troops	Troop deaths	Troops wounded
Revolutionary War	184,000–250,000	4,435	6,188
War of 1812	286,730	2,260	4,505
Mexican War	78,218	13,283	4,152
Civil War	2,813,363-3,713,363	498,332+	307,881-312,881
Spanish-American War	306,760	2,446	1,662
World War I	4,734,991	116,516	204,002
World War II	16,112,566	405,399	671,846
Korean War	5,720,000	36,574	103,284
Vietnam War	8,744,000	58,220	303,644
Persian Gulf War	2,225,000	383	467
Iraq and Afghanistan Wars	2,778,000	6,768	52,138
Note: Deaths are from combat, disease, and other causes.			

Sources: Congressional Research Service. 2019. "American War and Military Operations Casualties: Lists and Statistics.Retrieved from https://fas.org/sgp/crs/natsec/RL32492.pdf; McCarthy, Niall. 2018. "2.77 Million Service Members Have Served on 5.4 Million

Deployments since 9/11." *Forbes* March 20. Retrieved from https://www.forbes.com/sites/niallmccarthy/2018/03/20/2-77-million-service-members-have-served-on-5-4-million-deployments-since-911-infographic/#2fbdf37250db.

The United States has been at war in more than one-fifth of the years it has existed (Bumiller 2010).[19] Between the end of the colonial period and 1993, the U.S. military was involved in at least 234 declared wars, undeclared wars, or other situations abroad involving actual or potential armed conflict (Collier 1993).[20] Since 1993, U.S. armed forces have waged war in Iraq and in Afghanistan and also joined international military operations in such countries as Bosnia, Herzegovina, and Libya. By any measure, then, the U.S. military has played a fundamental role, for better or worse, in the nation's foreign affairs historically and also today. Supporters of this role say the military has both protected and advanced the political and economic interests of the United States, while critics, as we have seen, charge that the military has been an instrument of imperialism.

Explaining War

The enormity of war has long stimulated scholarly interest in why humans wage war (Levy and Thompson 2010).[21] A popular explanation for war derives from evolutionary biology. According to this argument, war is part of our genetic heritage because the humans who survived tens of thousands of years ago were those who were most able, by virtue of their temperament and physicality, to take needed resources from other humans they attacked and to defend themselves from attackers. In this manner, a genetic tendency for physical aggression and warfare developed and thus still exists today.

Scholars have attempted to explain why human beings wage war. A popular explanation comes from the field of evolutionary biology and claims that a tendency toward warfare is hardwired into our genetic heritage because it conferred certain evolutionary advantages.

Source: Gorodenkoff/Shutterstock.com

However, other scientists dispute the evolutionary explanation for several reasons (Begley 2009).[22] First, the human brain is far more advanced than the brains of other primates, and genetic instincts that might drive these primates' behavior do not necessarily drive human behavior. Second, many societies studied by anthropologists have been very peaceful, suggesting that a tendency to warfare is more cultural than biological. Third, most people are not violent, and most soldiers have to be resocialized (in boot camp or its equivalent) to overcome their deep moral convictions against killing. If warlike tendencies were part of human genetic heritage, these convictions would not exist.

War as a Social Phenomenon

If warfare is not biological in origin, then it is best understood as a social phenomenon, one that has its roots in the decisions of political and military officials. Sometimes, as with the U.S. entrance into World War II after Pearl Harbor, these decisions are sincere and based on a perceived necessity to defend a nation's people and resources, and sometimes these decisions are based on cynicism and deceit (Solomon 2006).[23]

A prime example of this latter dynamic is the Vietnam War. The 1964 Gulf of Tonkin Resolution, in which Congress authorized President Lyndon Johnson to wage an undeclared war in Vietnam, was passed after North Vietnamese torpedo boats allegedly attacked U.S. ships. However, later investigation revealed that the attack never occurred and that the White House lied to Congress and the American people (Hastings 2018).[24] Four decades later, questions of deceit were again raised after the United States began the war against Iraq because of its alleged possession of weapons of mass destruction. These weapons were never found, and critics charged that the White House had fabricated and exaggerated evidence of the weapons in order to win public and congressional support for the war (Danner 2006).[25]

Population Change and Environmental Change

Although war is a social phenomenon arising from decisions of political and military officials, other phenomena can make it more likely that these officials will decide to go to war. These more basic causes of war include population change and environmental change. As Chapter 15 discussed, population growth may lead to armed conflict of various types, including war, because growing populations need more food, water, and other resources. History shows that when these resources become too scarce within a society, that society is more likely to go to war to wrest these resources from another society (Gleditsch and Theisen 2010).[26]

Chapter 15 also discussed environmental change as a source of armed conflict, including war. Recall that when weather disasters and other environmental changes cause drought and other problems, crops and other resources become scarcer. Historically, this scarcity has again motivated societies to go to war.

A severe type of population change is a pandemic that kills or even just infects tens or hundreds of millions of people. After the 2020 COVID-19 pandemic began, foreign affairs experts worried that it could heighten military conflict in the Middle East and elsewhere because of the devastation and desperation it was causing. They also worried that terrorist groups and other extremist groups would take advantage of the situation to strike at various governments, and that the pandemic would interfere with efforts of the United Nations and other international organizations to prevent or resolve armed conflict (Rater 2020).[27]

Ideology and Prejudice

Nations also go to war for ideological reasons: They have certain belief systems that lead them to hold prejudice and other hostile feelings toward nations with different belief systems. Religion is a very important ideology in this regard. Historically and also today, nations in the Middle East and elsewhere have gone to war or are otherwise in conflict because of religious differences. Although the causes of World War II are complex, Hitler's effort to conquer much of Europe stemmed at least partly from his belief that Aryans (Germans and other Europeans with blond hair and blue eyes) were a superior species and that Jews and other non-Aryans were an inferior species (Rees 2018).[28]

Civilians: The Casualties of War

Table 16.2 listed the hundreds of thousands of troop deaths in American wars. The nation rightly grieved these deaths when they occurred and built monuments, such as the Korean and Vietnam veterans memorials in Washington, DC, that list the names of the dead.

In an essay a decade ago that is still relevant today, John Tirman, director of the Center for International Studies at the Massachusetts Institute of Technology, worried that Americans have neglected the civilian victims of war. He applauded the Korean and Vietnam memorials in Washington, but he lamented that "neither mentions the people of those countries who perished in the conflicts" (Tirman 2012:B01).[29] "When it comes to our wars overseas," he added, "concern for the victims is limited to U.S. troops."

Tirman noted that approximately 6 million civilians and soldiers died in the Korean, Vietnam/ Indochina, Iraq, and Afghanistan wars. Most of these victims were civilians, and most of these civilian deaths were the result of actions by the United States and its allies. These deaths stemmed from bombs and other weapons that went astray, from orders by military and political leaders to drop millions upon millions of bombs on civilian areas, and sometimes from atrocities committed by U.S. personnel. In World War II, Tirman added, the United States dropped two atomic bombs that killed tens of thousands of civilians, and it joined its allies in the *carpet bombing* of German and Japanese cities that also killed hundreds of thousands.

Tirman (2012)[30] acknowledged that the carpet bombing, atomic bombing, and other actions in World War II that killed hundreds of thousands of civilians may have had strategic purposes. But he also noted that the Korean and Vietnam wars included many atrocities committed by American troops against civilians. To be blunt, American troops simply shot untold hundreds of Korean and Vietnamese civilians in cold blood.

Tirman described one Korean incident in which machine gun fire from U.S. warplanes killed about one hundred civilian refugees who were resting on a road. The remaining several hundred refugees hid and were shot at for three days by U.S. ground soldiers. Tirman (2012:107)[31] wrote, "Surviving Koreans from the onslaught described in detail the chaotic panic they experienced; having believed the Americans were protecting them, they then saw the U.S. troops fire indiscriminately at men, women, and children at the scene." At the end of the three days, about 400 civilians lay dead.

In Vietnam, Tirman wrote, American troops and planes routinely razed villages to the ground, killing villagers indiscriminately, and then evacuated any survivors. Once they were evacuated, their villages were designated "free fire zones," and then often bombed indiscriminately once again, killing any villagers who managed to remain in these zones despite the evacuations. All these killings were outright slaughter.

In one example of what Tirman (2011:153)[32] called a typical massacre, U.S. soldiers arrived at a village that had just been bombed and ordered survivors to gather at the center of the town. After they did so, U.S. ground troops shot them and left a pile of dead bodies that included twenty-one children. As this brief discussion indicates, although the massacre of 347 Vietnamese at the hamlet of My Lai is undoubtedly the Vietnam massacre that is best known (and perhaps the only known) to the American public, massacres were far from rare and in fact were rather common.

A central aspect of U.S. military strategy in Vietnam involved destroying rice fields and the rest of the countryside to make it difficult for the Vietcong forces to engage in guerrilla warfare. To do so, it routinely deployed chemical weapons such as Agent Orange (dioxin, a known carcinogen), napalm, and white phosphorous. Planes sprayed and bombed these chemicals. These actions did destroy the countryside, but they also destroyed humans. The "Children and Our Future" box discusses this problem in greater detail.

The two atomic bombs dropped by the United States over Japan during World War II killed tens of thousands of civilians. Scholar John Tirman worries that Americans have generally ignored the civilian victims of U.S. wars.

Source: "Victim of Atomic Bomb of Hiroshima," Wikipedia, Last modified on October 10, 2011, http://commons.wikimedia.org/wiki/File:Victim_of_Atomic_Bomb_001.jpg.

Children and Our Future

"Napalm Sticks to Kids"

This book has emphasized that children are often the innocent victims of various social problems from the time they are born, with important consequences for their futures. There are also many innocent victims in wartime, but when children are victims, our hearts especially go out to them. The Vietnam War marked a time when many Americans became concerned about children's suffering during wartime. A key focus of their concern was the use of napalm.

Napalm is a very flammable jelly-like substance made out of gasoline, soap, and white phosphorous. Napalm bombs were used in World War II to set fire to cities, military bunkers, and other targets. When napalm ends up on human skin, it causes incredibly severe pain and burns down to the bone, with death often resulting. Because napalm is very sticky, it is almost impossible to wipe off or remove with water once it does end up on skin.

Bombs containing napalm made by Dow Chemical were routinely used by the U.S. military and its South Vietnamese allies during the Vietnam War to defoliate the countryside and to attack various targets. Some 400,000 tons of napalm were used altogether. When a napalm bomb explodes, it ignites an enormous fireball that burns everything in its path. Inevitably, Vietnamese civilians were in the path of the fireballs generated by the U.S. and South Vietnamese militaries. An unknown number of civilians were burned severely or, if they were lucky, died. Many antiwar protests in the United States focused on the civilian suffering from napalm. Protesters at Dow Chemical's New York office carried signs that said, "Napalm Burns Babies, Dow Makes Money."

One of these civilians was a 9-year-old girl named Phan Thi Kim Phuc. An Associated Press photo of her running naked and screaming with burns after her village was napalmed was one of the most memorable photos of that war. Although she survived, it took seventeen surgeries to turn her whole again.

A poem about napalm, reportedly written by members of the U.S. First Air Cavalry, surfaced during the war. Some verses follow.

We shoot the sick, the young, the lame,
We do our best to kill and maim,
Because the kills all count the same,
Napalm sticks to kids.

Ox cart rolling down the road,
Peasants with a heavy load,
They're all V.C. when the bombs explode,
Napalm sticks to kids.

A baby sucking on his mother's t*t,
Children cowering in a pit,
Dow Chemical doesn't give a s!#t,
Napalm sticks to kids.

Blues out on a road recon,
See some children with their mom,
What the hell, let's drop the bomb,
Napalm sticks to kids.

Flying low across the trees,
Pilots doing what they please,
Dropping frags on refugees,
Napalm sticks to kids.

They're in good shape for the shape they're in,
But, God I wonder how they can win,
With Napalm running down their skin,
Napalm sticks to kids.

Drop some napalm on the barn,
It won't do too much harm,
Just burn off a leg or arm,
Napalm sticks to kids.

Sources: Hastings 2018; Vietnam Veterans Against the War 1971[33]

Veterans: The Casualties of War

The attention just given to civilians should in no way obscure or minimize the fact that veterans are also casualties of war. The Korean and Vietnam veterans' memorials in the nation's capital and so many other memorials across the nation remind us of the hundreds of thousands of brave men and women who have died serving their country. But veterans are casualties in other ways, as they may suffer terrible physical and mental wounds that can maim them for life.

Veterans of the Vietnam War came back to a nation that often did not greet them as heroes. Many came back addicted to heroin and other drugs, many were unemployed, and many became homeless. Many veterans of the wars in Iraq and Afghanistan have also come back home with these problems. Many veterans, more often those who served in Iraq than those who served in Afghanistan, are experiencing posttraumatic stress disorder (PTSD), marked by nightmares, panic attacks, and other symptoms (Badger 2014).[34] Veterans with PTSD often end up with problems in their marriages or other relationships and are more likely to commit violence against their spouses or partners. When these problems occur, they may worsen the psychological state of these veterans. Suicide is sometimes the result (Durkin 2018).[35]

Spouses and other family members who have to help or live with veterans with the problems are also casualties of war. So, too, are the families of deployed troops. There is the natural fear that loved ones will never return from their overseas involvement in armed conflict. This fear can take a psychological toll on all members of these families, but perhaps especially on children. One teenager recalled the tensions that arose when his father was in Iraq: "I was in eighth grade when my dad deployed to Iraq. A kid walked up to me and said, 'Your dad's a baby killer.' I didn't handle that well. We both wound up suspended for that one" (Ashton 2011).[36]

One study found that adolescents with a deployed parent are more likely than those with civilian parents to feel depressed and suicidal. They are also more likely to engage in drug use and binge drinking. Reflecting on these findings, an author of the study said, "It's really time to focus on the children that are left behind" (Ashton 2011).[37]

Many veterans of the Iraq and Afghanistan wars have ended up with PTSD and other psychological problems, including suicidal tendencies.

Source: © Thinkstock

Rape and Sexual Assault

Women veterans face a special problem that most male veterans do not have to fear. That problem is rape, as at least one-fifth and perhaps as many as 84 percent of all military service women are raped or sexually assaulted (including sexual harassment) by other military personnel (Turchik and Wilson, 2010).[38] More than 20,000 U.S. military personnel, most of them women, said in a survey that they had been raped or sexually assaulted in the 2018 fiscal year (Kime 2019; Philipps 2019).[39] Of the women surveyed, 6 percent said they had been sexually assaulted within the past year; 1 percent of the men surveyed said they had been assaulted. In 90 percent of the assaults revealed in the survey, the assailant was another member of the military, and two-thirds were also acquaintances. Less than one-third of these survivors reported their rapes and sexual assaults to military officials. Of the roughly 6,000 cases that were reported, only about 300 cases, or 5 percent, resulted in prosecution.

Applying Social Research

Determining the Prevalence of Rape and Sexual Assault in the Military

As the text discusses, most military women who are raped or sexually assaulted do not report these crimes to military authorities. As a result, reported rapes and sexual assaults compose only a very small percentage of all military rapes and sexual assaults. To get a more accurate estimate of how many such crimes occur, sound social research is necessary.

Despite this need, research on sexual assault in the military was scant before the early 2000s. This type of research accelerated, however, after several scandals involving sexual assault and harassment occurred during the 1990s on military bases and at military academies. Although the military now conducts a biennial survey to determine the number of sexual assaults in the previous year, other researchers have conducted their own surveys of service members. The samples are almost always of women, given their higher risk of being sexually assaulted.

In these surveys, between 10 percent and 33 percent of women report ever being raped (including attempts) while they were serving in the military. When sexual assaults and sexual harassment are added to the crimes mentioned to respondents, between 22 percent and 84 percent of women report being raped, sexually assaulted, and/or sexually harassed while serving. Very few studies include men in their surveys, but one study reported a 3 percent rate of sexual assault victimization for men while they were in the military.

One major problem in this research literature is that different studies use different definitions and measures of sexual assault. Regardless of these problems, this growing body of research documents how often rape and sexual assault in the military occur. It also documents the psychological and health effects of military sexual assault (MSA). These effects are similar to those for civilians, and include anxiety, depression, PTSD, poorer physical health, and poorer job performance (in this case, their military duties).

In shedding light on the prevalence of military rape and sexual assault and on the many negative effects of these crimes, social science research has performed an important service. Future research will no doubt build on existing studies to further illuminate this significant problem.

Sources: Stander and Thomsen 2016; Turchik and Wilson 2010[40]

Women veterans who are raped or sexually assaulted often suffer PTSD. In fact, rape and sexual assault are the leading cause of PTSD among women veterans, while combat trauma is the leading cause of PTSD among male veterans. Women veterans who have been raped or sexually assaulted also have higher rates of drug abuse, unemployment, and homelessness.

Women veterans say that when they do report rape and sexual assault, military commanders typically either blame them for what happened, ignore the crime altogether, or give the offender a very mild punishment such as not being allowed to leave a military base for a short period (Protect Our Defenders 2018).[41] When one woman who was raped by two soldiers in Iraq told her commander, he threatened her with a charge of adultery because she was married (Speier 2012).[42]

Helping American Veterans

After World War II, the GI Bill helped millions of veterans to go to college and otherwise readjust to civilian life. But many observers say that the United States has neglected the veterans of later wars. Although education benefits and many other services for veterans exist, the nation needs to do much more to help veterans, these observers say (Gade 2019; Shane III 2018).[43]

The PTSD and other problems experienced by Iraq and Afghanistan veterans have made this need even more urgent. Advocates for veterans with severe physical or cognitive problems also urge the government to greatly expand its very small program of monthly cash payments to these veterans' families to help replace their lost incomes (Einhorn 2011).[44]

As this brief discussion suggests, U.S. veterans have many unmet needs. Our nation's failure to meet their needs is shameful.

Other Impacts of War

When we think of the impact of war, the consequences for civilians and veterans as just discussed come most readily to mind. But not all civilians are affected equally. One of the many sad truisms of war is that its impact on a society is greatest when the war takes place within the society's boundaries. For example, the Iraq war that began in 2003 involved two countries more than any others, the United States and Iraq. Because it took place in Iraq, many more Iraqis than Americans died or were wounded, and the war certainly affected Iraqi society—its infrastructure, economy, natural resources, and so forth—far more than it affected American society. Most Americans continued to live their normal lives, whereas most Iraqis had to struggle to survive the many ravages of war.

War also has impact beyond the consequences for civilians and veterans. As historians and political scientists have often described, wars have a significant economic and political impact. Many examples of this impact exist, but one well-known example involves the defeat of Germany in World War I, which led to a worsening economy during the next decade that in turn helped fuel the rise of Hitler.

War can also change a nation's political structure in obvious ways, as when the winning nation forces a new political system and leadership on the losing nation. Other political and economic changes brought by war are less obvious. World War I again provides an interesting example of such changes. Before the war, violent labor strikes were common in Britain and other European nations. When the war began, a sort of truce developed between management and labor, as workers wanted to appear patriotic by supporting the war effort and hoped that they would win important labor rights for doing so. Although the truce later dissolved and labor-management conflict resumed, labor eventually won some limited rights thanks partly to its support for the war (Halperin 2004).[45]

Other types of less obvious social changes have also resulted from various wars. For example, the deaths of so many soldiers during the American Civil War left many wives and mothers without their family's major breadwinner. Their poverty forced many of these women to turn to prostitution to earn an income, resulting in a rise in prostitution after the war (Rafter 1990).[46] Some eighty years later, the involvement of African Americans in the U.S. armed forces during World War II helped begin the racial desegregation of the military. This change is widely credited with helping spur the hopes of Southern African Americans that racial desegregation would someday occur in their hometowns (McKeeby 2008).[47]

Militarism and the U.S. Military Budget

As discussed earlier, President Eisenhower eloquently warned about the influence of the U.S. military and the size of the military budget. The defense industry remains a powerful force in the U.S. economy seven decades after Eisenhower issued his warning, and U.S. military spending continues unabated. Current base military spending (fiscal 2019; defense outlays by the Department of Defense, including costs for Iraq and Afghanistan operations) is approximately $726 billion. Additional military and protection costs from the Department of Veterans Affairs, Homeland Security, the Departments of Energy, Justice, and State equal $241 billion. Adding these two figures together, the United States is spending almost $1 trillion annually on military and protection costs (Amadeo 2019).[48] This figure exceeds the combined military budget of the next nine nations. Critics say that the U.S. military budget should be reduced, with the savings spent on domestic needs (Amadeo 2019).[49]

Critics say that U.S. military spending is too high and takes needed dollars from domestic essentials like schooling and health care.

Source: © Thinkstock

Beyond this huge figure, the nation also spends approximately $216 billion annually on veterans' benefits and $544 billion annually in interest on the national debt from past military spending (War Resisters League 2019).[50] When these costs are taken into account, the total annual military/protection budget amounts to about $1.7 trillion annually. This sum equals 48 percent of total federal discretionary spending funded by federal income tax dollars. To say this another way, 48 percent of every income tax dollar pays for current and past military expenses (War Resisters League 2019).[51]

Lessons from Other Societies

Guns or Butter?

"Guns versus butter" is a macroeconomics phrase that illustrates the dilemma that nations face in deciding their spending priorities. The more they spend on their military (guns), the less they can spend on food for their poor and other domestic needs (butter).

In making this very important decision, European nations have chosen butter over guns. The nations that compose the European Union spend 1.5 percent of their gross domestic product (GDP) on their militaries. In contrast, the United States spends 3.2 percent of its GDP on its base military budget, which, as the text notes, does not include costs for veterans benefits, for the Iraq and Afghanistan military operations, and certain other costs. The European nations' decisions to limit their military spending allows more spending for social needs. Partly as a result, many Europeans enjoy universal health care, subsidized or free child care, subsidized or free college tuition, and good mass transit, features that the United States lacks.

Compared to Europe, then, the United States has chosen guns over butter, leaving far less money for its social needs. In making this classic macroeconomics decision, the United States has much to learn from the wealthy nations of Europe.

Sources: Russell 2018; The World Bank 2019[52]

"A Theft from Those Who Hunger and Are Not Fed"

Oscar Arias, a former president of Costa Rica and a winner of the Nobel Peace Prize, echoed these famous words from President Eisenhower when he wrote two decades ago that U.S. military spending took money away from important domestic needs. "Americans are hurt," he warned, "when the defense budget squanders money that could be used to repair schools or to guarantee universal health care" (Arias 1999:A19).[53]

The $423 million cost of each F-35 fighter aircraft could pay for the salaries of 10,575 new teachers.

Source: "First F-35C Flight," Wikipedia, Last modified on November 20, 2011, http://commons.wikimedia.org/wiki/File:First_F-35C_Flight.ogv.

Since Arias wrote these words, the United States has spent approximately $13 trillion on defense outlays and other military and protection costs, including nearly $2 trillion on the wars in Iraq and Afghanistan (Amadeo 2019).[54] Cost equivalencies illustrate what is lost when so much money is spent on the military, especially on weapons systems that do not work and are not needed.

For example, the F-35 fighter aircraft was plagued a decade ago with "management problems, huge cost-overruns, [and] substantial performance shortfalls" (Kaplan 2012).[55] These performance problems still exist (Insinna 2019).[56] Even so, the Defense Department agreed in 2019 to purchase an additional 478 F-35 aircraft for $34 billion, or $71 million per plane. Each such plane will cost an additional $352 million in operating costs over its 8,000-hour lifespan (Mizokami 2019).[57] Adding these figures, each of these F-35 planes will ultimately cost at least $423 million. This same sum could be used to pay the salaries of 10,575 new teachers earning the national average of $40,000 per year, or to build 25 elementary schools at a cost of $17 million each. This amount per plane could also be used to pay the 2019 national average of $10,230 in tuition and fees at public universities for 41,349 students. Any one of these equivalencies demonstrates the huge social cost of each F-35, but if we multiply any of the equivalencies by 478 for all the purchased aircraft, this social cost becomes absolutely staggering.

All these figures demonstrate that war and preparation for war indeed have a heavy human cost, not only in the numbers of dead and wounded, but also in the diversion of funds from important social functions and needs.

The Debate over the Size of the Military Budget

This diversion of funds to military spending is unfortunate, but it might still be necessary if the high level of military spending is needed to ensure the nation's security. Experts disagree over this issue. Some think the United States needs to maintain and in fact increase its level of military spending, even with the Cold War long ended, to replace aging weapons systems, to meet the threat posed by terrorists and by "rogue" nations such as Iran, and to respond to various other trouble spots around the world. Military spending is good for workers, they add, because it creates jobs, and it also contributes to technological development (Perdue 2019; Spoehr 2019).[58]

Other experts echo President Eisenhower's concern over the size of the military budget (Given 2019; Koshgarian 2019).[59] Noting that the military budget today exceeds the average budget during the Cold War, they think military spending is far higher than it needs to be to ensure the nation's defense with the Soviet Union no longer a threat. They say the United States could safely decrease its nuclear and conventional weapons arsenals without at all endangering national security. They also say that the stationing of nearly 250,000 American troops on some 800 military bases abroad at an annual cost of $156 billion is hardly needed to ensure the nation's defense (Vine 2015).[60] As one critic said a decade ago of the military bases, "It makes as much sense for the Pentagon to hold onto 227 military bases in Germany as it would for the post office to maintain a fleet of horses and buggies" (vanden Heuvel 2011).[61]

These experts say the military budget is bloated for at least four reasons. First, the defense industry is very effective at lobbying Congress for increased military spending, with the cozy relationship among members of the military-industrial complex helping to ensure the effectiveness of this lobbying. Second, members of Congress fear being labeled "weak on defense" if they try to reduce the military budget or do not agree to new weapons systems requested by the Pentagon. Regarding this fear, the late U.S. senator and presidential candidate George McGovern (2011:47),[62] a decorated World War II hero, once wrote, "We need to end the false choice between a bloated budget and a weak spine."

Third, and helping to explain the success of this lobbying, military spending provides jobs and income to the home districts of members of Congress. Fourth, *military waste* in the form of cost overruns from poor accounting and other management failures is rampant.

Critics also argue that military spending actually produces fewer jobs than spending in other sectors (Ledbetter 2011).[63] According to a recent estimate, $1 billion spent by the Pentagon creates 11,200 jobs, but the same $1 billion spent in other sectors would create 16,800 clean energy jobs, 17,200 health-care jobs, and 26,700 education jobs (Watson Institute 2019).[64]

As this overview of the debate over military spending indicates, the military remains a hot topic more than three decades after the Cold War ended following the demise of the Soviet Union. As we move further into the twenty-first century, the issue of military spending will present a major challenge for U.S. political and economic institutions to address in a way that meets America's international and domestic interests.

Key Takeaways

- War is a social phenomenon in which a mixture of motives underlies decisions to go to war.
- Civilians and veterans are often casualties of war.
- U.S. military spending amounts to more than $1 trillion annually.
- Critics of the military budget say that the billions of dollars spent on weapons and other military needs would be better spent on domestic needs such as schools and day care.

For Your Review

1. Do you think the U.S. military budget should be increased, be reduced, or stay about the same? Explain your answer.
2. What do you think is the worst problem that veterans have faced in returning from the wars in Iraq and Afghanistan? Why?

16.3 Terrorism

Learning Objectives

1. Explain why terrorism is difficult to define.
2. List the major types of terrorism.
3. Evaluate the law enforcement and structural-reform approaches for dealing with terrorism.

The 9/11 attacks spawned an immense national security network and prompted the expenditure of at least $5 trillion on the war against terrorism.

Source: Dan Howell/Shutterstock.com

Terrorism is hardly a new phenomenon, but Americans became horrifyingly familiar with it on September 11, 2001. The 9/11 attacks remain in the nation's consciousness, and many readers may know someone who died on that terrible day. The attacks also spawned a vast national security network that now reaches into almost every aspect of American life. The United States has spent at least $5 trillion dollars since 9/11 on the war on terrorism, including the cost of the wars in Iraq and Afghanistan, whose relevance for terrorism has been sharply questioned (Thrall and Goepner 2017).[65] Questions of how best to deal with terrorism continue to be debated, and there are few, if any, easy answers to these questions. Some experts even go so far as to say that "the staggering costs of the War on Terror have far outweighed the benefits" (Thrall and Goepner 2017).[66]

Compounding the problem, the war on terrorism has largely been aimed at preventing violent attacks by people with Middle Eastern backgrounds. However, terrorism within the United States by white supremacists, anti-Semites, and other far-right extremists has become a much more serious problem during the past decade. Such "home grown" or domestic terrorism has killed and maimed about as many and perhaps even more Americans since 9/11 than terrorism by individuals with Middle Eastern backgrounds (Byman 2019).[67]

Not surprisingly, sociologists and other scholars have written many articles and books about terrorism. This section draws on their work to discuss the definition of terrorism, the major types of terrorism, explanations for terrorism, and strategies for dealing with terrorism. An understanding of all these issues is essential to make sense of the concern and controversy about terrorism that exists throughout the world today.

Defining Terrorism

There is an old saying that "one person's freedom fighter is another person's terrorist." This saying indicates some of the problems in defining terrorism precisely. Some years ago, the Irish Republican Army (IRA) waged a campaign of terrorism against the British government and its people as part of its effort to drive the British out of Northern Ireland. Many people in Northern Ireland and elsewhere hailed IRA members as freedom fighters, while many other people condemned them as cowardly terrorists. Although most of the world labeled the 9/11 attacks as terrorism, some people applauded them as acts of heroism. These examples indicate that there is only a thin line, if any, between terrorism on the one hand and freedom fighting and heroism on the other hand. Just as beauty is in the eye of the beholder, so is terrorism. The same type of action is either terrorism or freedom fighting, depending on who is characterizing the action.

Although dozens of definitions of **terrorism** exist, most take into account what are widely regarded as the three defining features of terrorism: (a) the use of violence; (b) the goal of making people afraid; and (c) the desire for political, social, economic, and/or cultural change. A definition by political scientist Ted Robert Gurr (1989:201)[68] captures some of these features: "The use of unexpected violence to intimidate or coerce people in the pursuit of political or social objectives."

terrorism

The use of unexpected violence to intimidate or coerce people in the pursuit of political, social, economic, and/or cultural change.

As the attacks on 9/11 remind us, terrorism involves the use of indiscriminate violence to instill fear in a population and thereby win certain political, economic, or social objectives.

Source: Anthony Correia/Shutterstock.com

Types of Terrorism

When we think about this definition, 9/11 certainly comes to mind, but there are, in fact, several kinds of terrorism—based on the identity of the actors and targets of terrorism—to which this definition applies. A typology of terrorism, again by Gurr (1989),[69] is popular: (a) vigilante terrorism, (b) insurgent terrorism, (c) transnational (or international) terrorism, and (d) state terrorism. Table 16.3 summarizes these four types.

TABLE 16.3 Types of Terrorism

Vigilante terrorism	Violence committed by private citizens against other private citizens.
Insurgent terrorism	Violence committed by private citizens against their own government or against businesses and institutions seen as representing the "establishment."
Transnational terrorism	Violence committed by citizens of one nation against targets in another nation.
State terrorism	Violence committed by a government against its own citizens.

vigilante terrorism

Terrorism committed by private citizens against other private citizens.

Vigilante terrorism is committed by private citizens against other private citizens. Sometimes the motivation is racial, ethnic, religious, or other hatred, and sometimes the motivation is to resist social change. The violence of racist groups like the Ku Klux Klan was vigilante terrorism, as was the violence used by white Europeans against Native Americans from the 1600s through the 1800s. What we now call "hate crime" is a contemporary example of vigilante terrorism, as is the right-wing extremist violence mentioned earlier.

🎥 How the Tree of Life Shooting Reflects American Anti-Semitism

The several mass shootings in recent years in the United States by racists and anti-Semites are examples of vigilante terrorism. This video discusses one such example, the mass shooting in October 2018 at a Pittsburgh, Pennsylvania, synagogue that killed 11 people and wounded 6 others.

View the video online at: http://www.youtube.com/embed/_PHZf_N5Lgs?rel=0

insurgent terrorism

Terrorism committed by private citizens against their own government or against businesses and institutions seen as representing the "establishment."

Insurgent terrorism is committed by private citizens against their own government or against businesses and institutions seen as representing the "establishment." Insurgent terrorism is committed by both left-wing groups and right-wing groups and thus has no partisan connotation. U.S. history is filled with insurgent terrorism, starting with some of the actions the colonists waged against British forces before and during the American Revolution, when "the meanest and most squalid sort of violence was put to the service of revolutionary ideals and objectives" (Brown 1989:25).[70] An example here is tarring and feathering, which involves hot tar and then feathers smeared over the naked bodies of Tories. Some of the labor violence committed after the Civil War also falls under the category of insurgent terrorism, as does some of the violence committed by left-wing groups during the 1960s and 1970s. One of the many examples of right-wing insurgent terrorism in recent years was also the deadliest: the infamous 1995 bombing of the federal building in Oklahoma City by Timothy McVeigh and Terry Nichols that killed 168 people.

transnational terrorism

Terrorism committed by the citizens of one nation against targets in another nation.

Transnational terrorism is committed by the citizens of one nation against targets in another nation. This is the type that has most concerned Americans at least since 9/11, yet 9/11 was not the first time Americans had been killed by transnational terrorism (also called international terrorism). A decade earlier, a truck bombing at the World Trade Center killed six people and injured more than 1,000 others. In 1988, 189 Americans were among the 259 passengers and crew who died when a plane bound for New York exploded over Lockerbie, Scotland; agents from Libya were widely thought to have planted the bomb. Despite all these American deaths, transnational terrorism has actually been much more common in several other nations: London, Madrid, and various cities in the Middle East have often been the targets of international terrorists.

State terrorism involves violence by a government that is meant to frighten its own citizens and thereby stifle their dissent. State terrorism may involve mass murder, assassinations, and torture. Whatever its form, state terrorism has killed and injured more people than all the other kinds of terrorism combined (Wilson 2019).[71] Genocide, of course, is the most deadly type of state terrorism, but state terrorism also occurs on a smaller scale. As just one example, the violent response of Southern white law enforcement officers to the civil rights protests of the 1960s amounted to state terrorism, as officers murdered or beat hundreds of activists during this period. Although state terrorism is usually linked to authoritarian regimes, many observers say the U.S. government also engaged in state terror during the nineteenth century, when U.S. troops killed thousands of Native Americans (Brown 2009).[72]

Genocide is the most deadly type of state terrorism. The Nazi Holocaust killed some 6 million Jews and 6 million other people.

Source: National Archives. These are slave laborers in the Buchenwald concentration camp near Jena; many had died from malnutrition when U.S. troops of the 80th Division entered the camp. Germany, April 16, 1945. National Archives Identifier: 535561. Retrieved from: https://catalog.archives.gov/id/535561.

Explaining Terrorism

Why does terrorism occur? It is easy to assume that terrorists must have psychological problems that lead them to have sadistic personalities, and that they are simply acting irrationally and impulsively. However, most researchers agree that terrorists are psychologically normal despite their murderous violence and, in fact, are little different from other types of individuals who use violence for political ends. As one scholar observed, "Most terrorists are no more or less fanatical than the young men who charged into Union cannon fire at Gettysburg or those who parachuted behind German lines into France. They are no more or less cruel and coldblooded than the Resistance fighters who executed Nazi officials and collaborators in Europe, or the American GI's ordered to 'pacify' Vietnamese villages" (Rubenstein 1987:5).[73]

state terrorism

Violence by a government that is meant to frighten its own citizens and thereby stifle their dissent.

If terrorism cannot be said to stem from individuals' psychological problems, then what are its roots? In answering this question, many scholars say that terrorism has structural roots. In this view, terrorism is a rational response, no matter how horrible it may be, to perceived grievances regarding economic, social, and/or political conditions (White 2017).[74] The heads of the U.S. 9/11 Commission, which examined the terrorist attacks of that day, reflected this view in the following assessment: "We face a rising tide of radicalization and rage in the Muslim world—a trend to which our own actions have contributed. The enduring threat is not Osama bin Laden but young Muslims with no jobs and no hope, who are angry with their own governments and increasingly see the United States as an enemy of Islam" (Kean and Hamilton 2007:B1).[75] As this assessment indicates, structural conditions do not justify terrorism, of course, but they do help explain why some individuals decide to commit it.

The Impact of Terrorism

The major impact of terrorism is apparent from its definition, which emphasizes public fear and intimidation. Terrorism can work, or so terrorists believe, precisely because it instills fear and intimidation. The people who happened to be in or near New York City on 9/11 will always remember how terrified the local populace was to hear of the attacks and the fears that remained with them for the days and weeks that followed.

Hardly anyone likes standing in the long airport security lines that are a result of the 9/11 attacks. Some experts say that certain airport security measures are an unneeded response to these attacks.

Source: James R. Martin/Shutterstock.com

Another significant impact of terrorism is the response to it. As mentioned earlier, the 9/11 attacks led the United States to develop an immense national security network, as well as the Patriot Act and other measures that some say threaten civil liberties; to start the wars in Iraq and Afghanistan; and to spend several trillion dollars on homeland security and the war against terrorism. Airport security increased, and Americans have grown accustomed to having to take off their shoes, display their liquids and gels in containers limited to three ounces, and stand in long security lines as they try to catch their planes.

People critical of these effects say that the "terrorists won." For better or worse, they may be correct. As one columnist wrote on the tenth anniversary of 9/11, "And yet, 10 years after 9/11, it's clear that the 'war on terror' was far too narrow a prism through which to see the planet. And the price we paid to fight it was far too high" (Applebaum 2011:A17).[76] In this columnist's opinion, the war on terror imposed huge domestic costs on the United States; it diverted U.S. attention away from important issues regarding China, Latin America, and Africa; it aligned the United States with authoritarian regimes in the Middle East even though their authoritarianism helps inspire Islamic terrorism; and it diverted attention away from the need to invest in the American infrastructure: schools, roads, bridges, and medical and other research. In short, the columnist concluded, "in making Islamic terrorism our central priority—at times our only priority—we ignored the economic, environmental and political concerns of the rest of the globe. Worse, we pushed aside our economic, environmental and political problems until they became too great to be ignored" (Applebaum 2011:A17).[77]

Critics like this columnist acknowledge the 9/11 tragedy and the real fears of Americans, but they also point out that in the years since 9/11, the number of Americans killed in car accidents, by air pollution, by homicide, or even by choking or lightning strikes has greatly exceeded the number of Americans killed by terrorism (Saliba 2017).[78] They add that the threat is overhyped because defense industry lobbyists profit from overhyping it and because politicians do not wish to be seen as "weak on terror" (Mueller 2017).[79] And they also worry that the war on terror has been motivated by and also contributed to prejudice against Muslims (Khan 2018).[80]

Key Takeaways

- Terrorism involves the use of intimidating violence to achieve political ends. Whether a given act of violence is perceived as terrorism or as freedom fighting often depends on whether someone approves of the goal of the violence.
- Several types of terrorism exist. The 9/11 attacks fall into the transnational terrorism category.

For Your Review

1. Do you think the U.S. response to the 9/11 attacks has been appropriate, or do you think it has been overdone? Explain your answer.
2. Do you agree with the view that structural problems help explain Middle Eastern terrorism? Why or why not?

16.4 Preventing War and Stopping Terrorism

Learning Objectives

1. Outline approaches that show promise for preventing war.
2. Understand the differences between the law enforcement and structural-reform approaches to preventing terrorism.

War has existed since prehistoric times, and terrorism goes back at least to the days of the Old Testament (e.g., when Samson brought down the temple of the Philistines in an act of suicide that also killed scores of Philistines). Given their long histories, war and terrorism are not easy to prevent. However, theory and research by sociologists and other social scientists point to several avenues that may ultimately help make the world more peaceful.

Preventing War

The usual strategies suggested by political scientists and international relations experts to prevent war include arms control and diplomacy. Approaches to arms control and diplomacy vary in their actual and potential effectiveness. The historical and research literatures on these approaches are vast and beyond the scope of this chapter. Regardless of the specific approaches taken, suffice it here to say that arms control and diplomacy will always remain essential strategies to prevent war, especially in the nuclear age when humanity is only minutes away from possible destruction.

Beyond these two essential strategies, the roots of war must also be addressed. As discussed earlier, war is a social, not biological, phenomenon and arises from decisions by political and military leaders to go to war. There is ample evidence that deceit accompanies many of these decisions, as leaders go to many wars for less than noble purposes. To the extent this is true, citizens must always be ready to question any rationales given for war, and a free press in a democracy must exercise eternal vigilance in reporting on these rationales. According to critics, the press and the public were far too acquiescent in the decision to go to war in Iraq in 2003, just as they had been acquiescent a generation earlier when the Vietnam War began being waged (Bacevich 2018).[81] To prevent war, then, the press and the public must always be ready to question assumptions about the necessity of war. The same readiness should occur in regard to militarism and the size of the military budget.

In this regard, history shows that social movements can help prevent or end armament and war and limit the unchecked use of military power once war has begun (Almeida 2019; Snow et al. 2019).[82] While activism is no guarantee of success, responsible nonviolent protest against war and militarism provides an important vehicle for preventing war or for more quickly ending a war once it has begun.

People Making a Difference

Speaking Truth to Power

The American Friends Service Committee (AFSC) is a Quaker organization that has long worked for peace and social justice. Its national office is in Philadelphia, Pennsylvania, and it has local offices in more than thirty other U.S. cities and also in more than a dozen other nations.

AFSC was established in 1917 to help conscientious objectors serve their country in nonmilitary ways during World War I. After that war ended with the defeat of Germany and Austria, AFSC provided food to thousands of German and Austrian children. It helped Jewish refugees after Hitler came to power, and sent various forms of aid to Japan after World War II ended. During the 1960s, it provided nonviolence training for civil rights activists and took a leading role in the movement to end the Vietnam War. Since the 1960s, AFSC has provided various types of help to immigrants, migrant workers, prisoners, and other "have-not" groups in need of social justice. It also works to achieve nonviolent conflict resolution in urban communities and spoke out against plans to begin war in Iraq in 2003.

In 1947, AFSC and its British counterpart won the Nobel Peace Prize for their aid to hungry children and other Europeans during and after World Wars I and II. The Nobel Committee proclaimed in part, "The Quakers have shown us that it is possible to carry into action something which is deeply rooted in the minds of many: sympathy with others; the desire to help others...without regard to nationality or race; feelings which, when carried into deeds, must provide the foundations of a lasting peace."[83]

For more than a century, the American Friends Service Committee has been active in many ways to achieve a more just, peaceable world. It deserves the world's thanks for helping to make a difference. For further information, visit http://www.afsc.org.

As we think about how to prevent war, we must not forget two important types of changes that create pressures for war: population change and environmental change. Effective efforts to reduce population growth in the areas of the world where it is too rapid will yield many benefits, but one of these is a lower likelihood that certain societies will go to war. Effective efforts to address climate change will also yield many benefits, and one of these is also a lower likelihood of war and ethnic conflict in certain parts of the world.

Finally, efforts to prevent war must keep in mind the fact that ideological differences and prejudice sometimes motivate decisions to go to war. It might sound rather idealistic to say that governments and their citizenries should respect ideological differences and not be prejudiced toward people who hold different religious or other ideologies or have different ethnic backgrounds. However, any efforts by international bodies, such as the United Nations, to achieve greater understanding along these lines will limit the potential for war and other armed conflict. The same potential holds true for efforts to increase educational attainment within the United States and other industrial nations but especially within poor nations. Because prejudice generally declines as education increases, measures that raise educational attainment promise to reduce the potential for armed conflict in addition to the other benefits of increased education.

In addition to these various strategies to prevent war, it is also vital to reduce the size of the U.S. military budget. Defense analysts who think this budget is too high have proposed specific cuts in weapons systems that are not needed and in military personnel at home and abroad who are not needed (Center for International Policy 2019).[84] Making these cuts would save the nation at least $120 billion annually without at all endangering national security. This large sum could then be spent to help meet the nation's many unmet domestic needs.

Stopping Terrorism

Because of 9/11 and other transnational terrorism, most analyses of "stopping terrorism" focus on this specific type. Traditional efforts to stop transnational terrorism take two forms (White 2017).[85] The first strategy involves attempts to capture known terrorists and to destroy their camps and facilities and is commonly called a *law enforcement* or *military* approach. The second strategy stems from the recognition of the structural roots of terrorism just described and is often called a *structural-reform* approach. Each approach has many advocates among terrorism experts, and each approach has many critics.

Law enforcement and military efforts have been known to weaken terrorist forces, but terrorist groups have persisted despite these measures. Worse yet, these measures may ironically inspire terrorists to commit further terrorism and increase public support for their cause. Critics also worry that the military approach endangers civil liberties, as the debate over the U.S. response to terrorism since 9/11 so vividly illustrates (Friedersdorf 2016).[86]

In view of all these problems, many terrorism experts instead favor the structural-reform approach, which they say can reduce terrorism by improving or eliminating the conditions that give rise to the discontent that leads individuals to commit terrorism. Here again the assessment of the heads of the 9/11 Commission illustrates this view: "We must use all the tools of U.S. power—including foreign aid, educational assistance and vigorous public diplomacy that emphasizes scholarship, libraries and exchange programs—to shape a Middle East and a Muslim world that are less hostile to our interests and values. America's long-term security relies on being viewed not as a threat but as a source of opportunity and hope" (Kean and Hamilton 2007:B1).[87]

Although there are no easy solutions to transnational terrorism, then, efforts to stop this form of terrorism must not neglect its structural roots. As long as these roots persist, new terrorists will come along to replace any terrorists who are captured or killed. Such recognition of the ultimate causes of transnational terrorism is thus essential for the creation of a more peaceable world.

Key Takeaways

- Arms control and diplomacy remain essential strategies for stopping war, but the roots of war must also be addressed.
- The law enforcement/military approach to countering terrorism may weaken terrorist groups, but it also may increase their will to fight and popular support for their cause, and endanger civil liberties.

For Your Review

1. Do you think deceit was involved in the decision of the United States to go to war against Iraq in 2003? Why or why not?
2. Which means of countering terrorism do you prefer more, the law enforcement/military approach or the structural-reform approach? Explain your answer.

16.5 End-of-Chapter Material

Summary

1. President Eisenhower warned of the dangers of a high military budget and the militarism of the United States.
2. War actually serves several functions according to functional theory, but conflict theory emphasizes the many problems war causes and the role played in militarism by the military-

industrial complex. Symbolic interactionism focuses on the experiences of soldiers and civilians in the military and in wartime and on their perceptions of war and the military.

3. War is best regarded as a social phenomenon rather than a biological phenomenon. Decisions to go to war are sometimes based on noble reasons, but they also involve deceit and prejudice.

4. Civilians and veterans are both victims of war. Civilian deaths in war are almost inevitable, and atrocities are far from rare. American veterans are at greater risk for PTSD, unemployment, and several other problems that also affect their families.

5. The United States has the highest military budget by far in the world. Debate continues over the size of this budget; critics say that the United States would have a higher quality of life if the military budget were reduced and the saved dollars spent on unmet social needs.

6. Terrorism is best regarded as rational behavior committed for political reasons rather than as psychologically abnormal behavior. The U.S. response to the 9/11 attacks has cost hundreds of billions of dollars, and critics say that the war on terrorism has both exaggerated the threat of terrorism and diverted attention and funds from unmet social needs.

Using What You Know

You are a key aide to a U.S. senator who has been asked to participate in a university forum on the size of the U.S. military budget. The senator asks you to write a memo for her that summarizes the arguments on both sides of debate on the military budget and that also indicates your own view of what position the senator should take on this debate. What position will you recommend to the senator? Explain your answer in detail.

What You Can Do

To help deal with the problems of war and terrorism discussed in this chapter, you may wish to do any of the following:

1. Educate yourself about the military budget and publish a pamphlet on the web and/or in print that critically examines the size of this budget.

2. Form or join a peace group on your campus or in the surrounding community that calls attention to the various problems related to the military that were discussed in this chapter.

3. Because prejudice against Muslims increased after 9/11, form or join a group in your campus or surrounding community that seeks to improve relations between Muslims and non-Muslims.

Endnotes

1. Mangal, Farooq Jan and Fahim Abed. 2019. "U.S. Drone Killed Afghan Civilians, Officials Say." *The New York Times* December 1:https://www.nytimes.com/2019/12/01/world/asia/drone-civilians-afghanistan.html.

2. Schanberg, Sydney H. 2005. "Not a Pretty Picture." *The Village Voice* May 10:1.

3. Ledbetter, James. 2011. *Unwarranted Influence: Dwight D. Eisenhower and the Military-Industrial Complex*. New Haven: Yale University Press.

4. Eisenhower, Dwight David. (1961, January 17). *Farewell Speech*. DDE's Papers as President, Speech Series, Box 38, Final TV Talk (1); NAID #16972219. Dwight D. Eisenhower Presidential Library, National Archives. Retrieved from: https://www.eisenhowerlibrary.gov/research/online-documents/farewell-address.

5. U.S. Department of State. (1953, April 16). *The Chance for Peach: Address by Dwight D. Eisenhower, President of the United States*. Department of State publication No. 5042.

6. Park, Robert E. 1941. "The Social Function of War: Observations and Notes." *American Journal of Sociology* 46:551-70.

7. Markides, Kyriacos C. and Steven F. Cohn. 1982. "External Conflict/Internal Cohesion: A Reevaluation of an Old Theory." *American Sociological Review* 47:88-98.

8. Shiller, Robert J. 2012. "Spend, Spend, Spend. It's the American Way." *The New York Times* January 15:BU3.

9. Mills, C. W. (1956). *The power elite*. New York, NY: Oxford University Press.

10. Worrell, Mark P. 2011. *Why Nations Go to War: A Sociology of Military Conflict*. New York: Routledge.

11. Boggs, Carl. 2011. *Empire Versus Democracy: The Triumph of Corporate and Military Power*. New York: Routledge.

12. Worrell, M. P. (2011). *Why nations go to war: A sociology of military conflict*. New York, NY: Routledge.

13. Boggs, Carl. 2011. *Empire Versus Democracy: The Triumph of Corporate and Military Power*. New York: Routledge.

14. Worrell, M. P. (2011). *Why nations go to war: A sociology of military conflict*. New York, NY: Routledge.

15. Leitenberg, Milton. 2006. *Deaths in Wars and Conflicts in the 20th Century*. Ithaca, NY: Cornell University Peace Studies Program.

16. Pinker, Steven. 2012. *The Better Angels of Our Nature: Why Violence Has Declined*. New York: Penguin.

17. Pinker, S. (2012). *The better angels of our nature: Why violence has declined*. New York, NY: Penguin.

18. Federation of American Scientists. 2019. "Status of World Nuclear Forces." Retrieved from https://fas.org/issues/nuclear-weapons/status-world-nuclear-forces/.

19. Bumiller, Elisabeth. 2010. "The War: A Trillion Can Be Cheap." *The New York Times* July 25:WK3.

20. Collier, Ellen C. 1993. "Instances of Use of United States Forces Abroad, 1798–1993," Washington, DC: United States Navy. (http://www.history.navy.mil/wars/foabroad.htm).

21. Levy, Jack S. and William R. Thompson. 2010. *Causes of War*. Malden, MA: Wiley-Blackwell.

22. Begley, Sharon. 2009. "Don't Blame the Caveman." *Newsweek* June 29:52-62.

23. Solomon, Norman. 2006. *War Made Easy: How Presidents and Pundits Keep Spinning Us to Death* Hoboken, NJ: Wiley.

24. Hastings, Max. 2018. *Vietnam: An Epic Tragedy, 1945-1975*. New York: Harper.

25. Danner, M. (2006). *The secret way to war: The Downing Street memo and the Iraq War's buried history*. New York, NY: New York Review of Books.

26. Gleditsch, N. P., & Theisen, O. M. (2010). Resources, the environment, and conflict. In M. D. Cavelty & V. Mauer (Eds.), *The Routledge handbook of security studies* (pp. 221–232). New York, NY: Routledge.

27. Rater, Philippe. 2020. "Will Coronavirus Slow the World's Conflicts—or Intensify Them?". *Miltiary.com* March 22: https://www.military.com/daily-news/2020/03/22/will-coronavirus-slow-worlds-conflicts-or-intensify-them.html.

28. Rees, Laurence. 2018. *The Holocaust: A New History*. New York: PublicAffairs.

29. Tirman, John. 2012. "Do We Care When Civilians Die in War?". *The Washington Post* January 8:B01.

30. Tirman, John. 2012. "Do We Care When Civilians Die in War?". *The Washington Post* January 8:B01.

31. Tirman, John. 2012. *The Deaths of Others: The Fate of Civilians in America's Wars*. New York: Oxford University Press.

32. Tirman, John. 2011. *The Deaths of Others: The Fate of Civilians in America's Wars*. New York: Oxford University Press.

33. Hastings, Max. 2018. *Vietnam: An Epic Tragedy, 1945-1975*. New York: Harper; Vietnam Veterans Against the War. 1971, "Napalm Sticks to Kids." Retrieved from http://www.vvaw.org/veteran/article/?id=823).

34. Badger, Emily. 2014. "Why the Iraq War Has Produced More Ptsd Than the Conflict in Afghanistan." *The Washington Post* April 3:https://www.washingtonpost.com/news/wonk/wp/2014/04/03/why-the-iraq-war-has-produced-more-ptsd-than-the-conflict-in-afghanistan/.

35. Durkin, Erin. 2018. "'A National Emergency': Suicide Rate Spikes among Young Us Veterans." *The Guardian* September 26:https://www.theguardian.com/us-news/2018/sep/26/suicide-rate-young-us-veterans-jumps.

36. Ashton, Adam. 2011. "Children of Deployed Troops Struggle, Study Finds." *Bangor Daily News* July 22: http://bangordailynews.com/2011/07/22/health/children-of-deployed-troops-struggle-researchers-find.

37. Ashton, Adam. 2011. "Children of Deployed Troops Struggle, Study Finds." *Bangor Daily News* July 22: http://bangordailynews.com/2011/07/22/health/children-of-deployed-troops-struggle-researchers-find.

38. Turchik, J. A., & Wilson, S. M. (2010). Sexual assault in the US military: A review of the literature and recommendations for the future. *Aggression and Violent Behavior*, 15, 267–277.

39. Kime, Patricia. 2019. "Despite Efforts, Sexual Assaults up Nearly 40% in Us Military." Military.com:https://www.military.com/daily-news/2019/05/02/despite-efforts-sexual-assaults-nearly-40-us-military.html; Philipps, Dave. 2019. "'This Is Unacceptable.' Military Reports a Surge of Sexual Assaults in the Ranks." *The New York Times* May 2:https://www.nytimes.com/2019/05/02/us/military-sexual-assault.html.

40. Stander, Valerie A. and Cynthia J. Thomsen. 2016. "Sexual Harassment and Assault in the U.S. Military: A Review of Policy and Research Trends." *Military Medicine* 181:20-27; Turchik, Jessica A. and Susan M. Wilson. 2010. "Sexual Assault in the U.S. Military: A Review of the Literature and Recommendations for the Future." *Aggression and Violent Behavior* 15:267-77.

41. Protect Our Defenders. 2018. *2018 Annual Report*. Alexandria, VA: Protect Our Defenders.

42. Speier, J. (2012, February 8). Victims of military rape deserve justice. *CNN.com*. Retrieved http://www.cnn.com/.Speier, Jackie. 2012. "Victims of Military Rape Deserve Justice." CNN.COM February 8:http://www.cnn.com/2012/02/07/opinion/speier-military-rape/index.html.

43. Gade, Daniel M. 2019. "A Better Way to Help Veterans." *National Affairs* 41(Fall):https://www.nationalaffairs.com/publications/detail/a-better-way-to-help-veterans; Shane III, Leo. 2018. "Studies Show Shortfalls in Veterans' Mental Health Care Needs." *Military Times* February 1:https://www.militarytimes.com/veterans/2018/02/01/studies-show-shortfalls-in-veterans-mental-health-care-needs/.

44. Einhorn, Catrin. 2011. "Looking after the Soldier, Back Home and Damaged." *The New York Times* September 28:A12.

45. Halperin, Sandra. 2004. *War and Social Change in Modern Europe: The Great Transformation Revisited*. Cambridge: Cambridge University Press.

46. Rafter, Nicole Hahn. 1990. *Partial Justice: Women, Prisons, and Social Control*. New Brunswick, NJ: Transaction Publishers.

47. McKeeby, David. 2008. "End of U.S. Military Segregation Set Stage for Rights Movement." *America.gov* February 25:http://www.america.gov/st/peopleplace-english/2008/February/20080225120859liameruoy0.9820215.html.

48. Amadeo, Kimberly. 2019. "US Military Budget, Its Components, Challenges, and Growth." *The Balance* December 7:https://www.thebalance.com/u-s-military-budget-components-challenges-growth-3306320.

49. Amadeo, Kimberly. 2019. "US Military Budget, Its Components, Challenges, and Growth." *The Balance* December 7:https://www.thebalance.com/u-s-military-budget-components-challenges-growth-3306320.

50. War Resisters League. 2019. "Where Your Income Tax Money Really Goes." Retrieved from https://www.warresisters.org/resources/pie-chart-flyers-where-your-income-tax-money-really-goes.

51. War Resisters League. 2019. "Where Your Income Tax Money Really Goes." Retrieved from https://www.warresisters.org/resources/pie-chart-flyers-where-your-income-tax-money-really-goes.

52. Russell, James W. 2018. *Double Standard: Social Policy in Europe and the United States*. Lanham, MD: Rowman & Littlefield; The World Bank. 2019. "Military Expenditure (% of GDP)." Retrieved from https://data.worldbank.org/indicator/MS.MIL.XPND.GD.ZS.

53. Arias, Oscar. 1999. "Stopping America's Most Lethal Export." *The New York Times*:A19.

54. Amadeo, Kimberly. 2019. "Us Military Budget, Its Components, Challenges, and Growth." *The Balance* December 7:https://www.thebalance.com/u-s-military-budget-components-challenges-growth-3306320.

55. Kaplan, Fred. 2012. "What Happened to a Leaner, Meaner Military." *slate.com* February 13:http://www.slate.com/articles/news_and_politics/war_stories/2012/02/_13_pentagon_budget_why_so_much_spending_on_big_war_weapons_.single.html.

56. Insinna, Valerie. 2019. "The Pentagon Is Battling the Clock to Fix Serious, Unreported F-35 Problems." *Defense News* June 12:https://www.defensenews.com/air/2019/06/12/the-pentagon-is-battling-the-clock-to-fix-serious-unreported-f-35-problems/.

57. Mizokami, Kyle. 2019. "The F-35 Is Cheap to Buy (but Not to Fly)." *Popular Mechanics* October 30:https://www.popularmechanics.com/military/aviation/a29626363/f-35-cheap/.

58. Perdue, David. 2019. "The US Military Will Pay the Price If No Budget Deal Is Reached." *Defense News* July 15:https://www.defensenews.com/opinion/commentary/2019/07/15/the-us-military-will-pay-the-price-if-no-budget-deal-is-reached/; Spoehr, Thomas. 2019. "The 5 Deadly Myths of Defense Spending." *York Dispatch* January 3:https://www.yorkdispatch.com/story/opinion/contributors/2019/01/03/oped-deadly-myths-defense-spending/38837055/.

59. Given, Casey. 2019. "Time to Get Serious About Military Spending." *Washington Examiner* May 30:https://www.washingtonexaminer.com/opinion/time-to-get-serious-about-military-spending; Koshgarian, Lindsay. 2019. "We Don't Need to Raise Taxes to Have 'Medicare for All'." New York Times October 17.

60. Vine, David. 2015. "The United States Probably Has More Foreign Military Bases Than Any Other People, Nation, or Empire in History." *The Nation* September 14:https://www.thenation.com/article/the-united-states-probably-has-more-foreign-military-bases-than-any-other-people-nation-or-empire-in-history/.

61. vanden Heuvel, Katrina. 2011. "Around the Globe, Us Military Bases Generate Resentment, Not Security." *The Nation* June 13:http://www.thenation.com/blog/161378/around-globe-us-military-bases-generate-resentment-not-security.

62. McGovern, George. 2011. *What It Means to Be a Democrat*. New Yorik: Penguin.

63. Ledbetter, James. 2011. *Unwarranted Influence: Dwight D. Eisenhower and the Military-Industrial Complex*. New Haven: Yale University Press.

64. Watson Institute. 2019. "Costs of War: Employment Impact." Retrieved from https://watson.brown.edu/costsofwar/costs/economic/economy/employment.

65. Thrall, A. Trevor and Erik Goepner. 2017. "Step Back: Lessons for U.S. Foreign Policy from the Failed War on Terror." *Cato Institute*:https://www.cato.org/publications/policy-analysis/step-back-lessons-us-foreign-policy-failed-war-terror.

66. Thrall, A. Trevor and Erik Goepner. 2017. "Step Back: Lessons for U.S. Foreign Policy from the Failed War on Terror." *Cato Institute*:https://www.cato.org/publications/policy-analysis/step-back-lessons-us-foreign-policy-failed-war-terror.

67. Byman, Daniel. 2019. "Right-Wingers Are America's Deadliest Terroristss." *Slate* August 5:Right-Wingers Are America's Deadliest Terrorists.

68. Gurr, Ted Robert. 1989. "Political Terrorism: Historical Antecedents and Contemporary Trends." Pp. 201-30 in *Violence in America: Protest, Rebellion, Reform, Vol. 2*, edited by T. R. Gurr. Newbury Park, CA: Sage Publications.

69. Gurr, Ted Robert. 1989. "Political Terrorism: Historical Antecedents and Contemporary Trends." Pp. 201-30 in *Violence in America: Protest, Rebellion, Reform, Vol. 2*, edited by T. R. Gurr. Newbury Park, CA: Sage Publications.

70. Brown, Richard Maxwell. 1989. "Historical Patterns of Violence." Pp. 23-61 in *Violence in America: Protest, Rebellion, Reform, Vol. 2*, edited by T. R. Gurr. Newbury Park, CA: Sage Publications.

71. Wilson, Tim. 2019. "State Terrorism." Pp. 331-47, edited by E. Chenoweth, R. English, A. Gofas and S. N. Kalyvas. New York: Oxford University Press.

72. Brown, Dee Alexander. 2009. *Bury My Heart at Wounded Knee: An Indian History of the American West*. New York: Sterling Innovation.

73. Rubenstein, Richard E. 1987. *Alchemists of Revolution: Terrorism in the Modern World*. New York: Basic Books.

74. White, Jonathan R. 2017. *Terrorism and Homeland Security*. Boston: Cengage.

75. Kean, Thomas H. and Lee H. Hamilton. 2007. "Are We Safer Today?" *The Washington Post* September 9:B1.

76. Applebaum, Anne. 2011. "The Price We Paid for the War on Terror." *The Washington Post* September 2:A17.

77. Applebaum, Anne. 2011. "The Price We Paid for the War on Terror." *The Washington Post* September 2:A17.

78. Saliba, Emmanuelle. 2017. "You're More Likely to Die Choking Than Be Killed by Foreign Terrorists, Data Show." *NBC News* February 1:https://www.nbcnews.com/news/us-news/you-re-more-likely-die-choking-be-killed-foreign-terrorists-n715141.

79. Mueller, John. 2017. "Why We Shouldn't Exaggerate the Scale of Terrorism." *Time* November 1:https://time.com/5006353/why-we-shouldnt-exaggerate-the-scale-of-terrorism/.

80. Khan, Aysha. 2018. "Seventeen Years after 9/11, Muslims Are Still 'Presumed Guilty.'" *Religion News* September 10:https://religionnews.com/2018/09/10/seventeen-years-after-9-11-muslims-are-still-presumed-guilty/.

81. Bacevich, Andrew J. 2018. *Twilight of the American Century*. Notre Dame, IN: University of Notre Dame Press.

82. Almeida, Paul. 2019. *Social Movements: The Structure of Collective Mobilization*. Berkeley: University of California Press; Snow, David A., Sarah A. Soule, Hanspeter Kriesi and Holly J. McCammon, eds. 2019. *The Wiley Blackwell Companion to Social Movements*. Hoboken, NJ: Wiley.

83. Award Ceremony Speech (1947). *Presentation Speech by Gunnar Jahn, Chairman of the Nobel Committee*. Retrieved from: https://www.nobel-prize.org/prizes/peace/1947/ceremony-speech/.

84. Center for International Policy. 2019. *Sustainable Defense: More Security, Less Spending*. Washington, DC: Center for International Policy.

85. White, Jonathan R. 2017. *Terrorism and Homeland Security*. Boston: Cengage.

86. Friedersdorf, Conor. 2016. "Civil Liberties Keep Americans Safe." *The Atlantic* June 15:https://www.theatlantic.com/politics/archive/2016/06/terror-civil-liberties/487115/.

87. Kean, Thomas H. and Lee H. Hamilton. 2007. "Are We Safer Today?". *The Washington Post* September 9:B1.

Index